The Question of
Palestine, 1914-1918

The Question of Palestine, 1914–1918

British-Jewish-Arab Relations

Isaiah Friedman

Schocken Books · New York

Published in U.S.A. in 1973
by Schocken Books Inc.
200 Madison Avenue, New York, N.Y. 10016
Copyright © 1973 by Isaiah Friedman
Library of Congress Catalog Card No. 73-80510
Printed in Great Britain

To my father, Jonah Friedman,
who died somewhere in Soviet Russia
during the Second World War and
whose burial place is not known

Contents

vii

Preface

This work developed from what originally was intended as an article to supplement Mr Leonard Stein's book *The Balfour Declaration*, published by Vallentine & Mitchell in 1961. His is a monumental study, a model of scholarship and objectivity, written in a superb style that could hardly be bettered. It will certainly remain a classic in this particular field. Yet the more I delved into the newly available records at the Public Record Office in London, to which Mr Stein had no access, the more convinced I became that there was room for a more ambitious undertaking.

Nor could I subscribe to the view, dominant among British historians, that the Balfour Declaration was the result of miscalculation, a product of sentiment rather than of considered interests of state. The Foreign Office files, the War Cabinet papers, and other previously untapped sources gave me a coveted opportunity to find more satisfactory answers to heretofore unanswered questions, primarily on the motivations of British policy towards the Zionist movement. These were manifold; the most important was to counter the possibility of a Turco-German protectorate of a Jewish Palestine emerging in the aftermath of the war. In 1917 an Allied victory was by no means certain, and it was generally believed that, at best, the conflict would end in a negotiated peace. With the belligerents proclaiming themselves strongly in favour of the principle of self-determination, as opposed to annexation, the nature of Jewish representations at the future Peace Conference (so it was reasoned) could have made all the difference. This was the Zionists' strength, of which they were not fully aware.

Nor do the records confirm the assumption that, when the formula for a declaration was considered at the Foreign Office, the key-words were 'asylum' or 'refuge'. In fact, all the evidence points the other way. In my last chapter I have tried to show how the term Jewish National Home was understood by contemporary public men and statesmen, and what were the expectations of those who shaped the Declaration. I found that it was also necessary to reassess the relations between the Zionists and the anti-Zionists, as the issue could no longer be approached in entirely black-and-white terms.

Other matters also called for revision. The Sykes-Picot Agreement has acquired a bad name, and been depicted as a 'product of greed' and a 'startling piece of double dealing'. This opinion is no longer tenable. The official records show that the policy of the Asquith-Grey administration was essentially non-annexationist in character, and it was not before the revelation of Germany's ambitions in the East that, during Lloyd George's premiership, dismemberment of the Ottoman Empire came to be regarded as indispensable. It was not the Constantinople Agreement, as is generally presumed, that was the progenitor of the Sykes-Picot Agreement, but the negotiations with Sharif Hussein. It was in order to make the Arab revolt against the Turks possible that an inter-Allied Agreement was concluded in 1916. There was no material incompatibility between that agreement and the pledges made to Hussein.

I was also privileged to be the first scholar to examine heretofore inaccessible documents relating to the intricate question of whether or not Palestine was the 'twice promised land'. This controversial issue bedevilled Middle Eastern politics for over half a century, and it still has, as Professor Arnold Toynbee pointed out (Comment, *Journal of Contemporary History*, October 1970), a political bearing. I have no axe to grind, but I am convinced, from my close reading of the available documentary evidence, that the hands of the British Government were clean. The understanding with Sharif Hussein was not of a unilateral nature, and it was not the British who remained in debt.

I intended to bring my story up to the eve of the Peace Conference in Paris; to deal with the Arab reaction to the Balfour Declaration, and with Arab relations with the British and the Zionists in 1918, but this would have made the book too long. For this omission I apologise; I hope to treat the issue elsewhere. References to German-Zionist relations were also reduced to an absolute minimum, since this is fully covered in my forthcoming *Germany and Zionism, 1897–1918*. In writing, I took it for granted that the reader was acquainted with Mr Stein's book and therefore tried to avoid unnecessary repetition.

In addition to the official records at the Public Record Office, I have drawn extensively on the unpublished private papers of British officers, as well as on Zionist archival material, as listed in the bibliography.

Acknowledgments

It is with pleasure that I thank many distinguished people and institutions for their help.

I have benefited greatly from many discussions, both oral and written, with Mr Stein. Professor W. N. Medlicott, Professor Emeritus of International History at the London School of Economics and Political Science, and his successor Professor James Joll, gave me generously of their time and knowledge in reading and criticising the first draft of my work. For this, and for their interest and encouragement during and after my post-graduate studies at the School, I am greatly indebted.

I had also the immense advantage of gaining the goodwill of Professor Sir Isaiah Berlin, O.M., President of Wolfson College, Oxford, whose faith in my work helped me over many a bad patch. Had it not been for his unflagging support, the book would never have been completed. I had many useful and inspiring conversations with Dr Robert Weltsch, Director of the Leo Baeck Institute, London; Professor Walter Laqueur, Director of the Institute of Contemporary History; Dr S. Levenberg, Representative of the Jewish Agency for Israel, and the late Samuel Landman. I felt honoured when Professor Arnold Toynbee invited me to join him in a discussion on the McMahon-Hussein Correspondence, published in the *Journal of Contemporary History*.

I should like to acknowledge my debt to the staff of the Public Record Office, the British Museum, London University Library and the library of the London School of Economics, the Institute of Historical Research, and the Wiener Library, for their invaluable and willing help.

I am very grateful to Lady Clayton and Mr S. W. Clayton for placing at my disposal the papers of Sir Gilbert Clayton; to Mr Richard Hill, formerly Lecturer at the School of Oriental Studies of Durham University, and to Mr I. J. C. Foster, Keeper of Oriental Books, for permitting me to consult the Wingate Papers, and to Miss Elizabeth Monroe, Senior Fellow at St Antony's College, Oxford, for allowing me to use the Sledmere Papers, the Yale Reports (in microfilm), the Allenby Papers and Samuel Papers (xeroxed).

I should also like to thank Mr Mark Bonham-Carter for his kind permission to quote from the Asquith Papers at the Bodleian Library, MSS Department, Oxford; Mrs Judith Gendel, for permitting me to cite from a memorandum of her late father, Edwin S. Montagu; Professor A. J. P. Taylor, Director of the Beaverbrook Library, for permission to quote from Lloyd George's letters; and the President of the Anglo-Jewish Association for his kind consent to the use of the records of the Conjoint Foreign Committee.

Transcripts and quotations of Crown Copyright material appear by permission of the Controller of H.M. Stationery Office.

The late Lavy Bakstansky, formerly General Secretary of the Zionist Federation of the United Kingdom, and I. J. Miller, currently its Executive Secretary, gave me permission to use Zionist archival material without restriction. Dr Michael Heymann, Director of the Central Zionist Archives in Jerusalem, and Dr Alex Bein, his predecessor, accorded me a similar privilege. I owe them a great debt for their courtesy and invaluable help. Nor can I omit to mention the Trustees of the Weizmann Archives, and its Director, Mr Julian Meltzer, who kindly allowed me to quote from the Weizmann Papers. I should also like to thank Mr Yoram Ephrati, the Curator of the Aaron Aaronsohn Archives, for permission to quote from the Aaronsohn Diaries, when still unpublished. These have recently appeared in print in Hebrew.

I gratefully acknowledge the permission granted me by the following copyright holders and publishers to quote from their books: The Rt Hon. Julian Amery, M.P., from Leopold Amery: *My Political Life*; First Beaverbrook Foundation and its Hon. Director, Professor A. J. P. Taylor, from Lloyd George: *The Truth about the Peace Treaties*; Chatto & Windus, from Charles K. Webster, *The Art and Practice of Diplomacy*; The Clarendon Press, from Arnold Toynbee, *Acquaintances*; Curtis Brown, from Viscount Samuel, *Memoirs*; Victor Gollancz, from *Chaim Weizmann*, edited by Paul Goodman; A. P. Watt, from A. J. Balfour, *Opinions and Arguments*.

Several persons have suffered from my attachment to this subject, but none more than my wife and son, who showed sympathetic understanding during the long hours I remained locked in my study; my wife's contribution in encouragement and criticism was more than can be adequately acknowledged here.

It gives me great pleasure to thank the Hebrew University's Institute of Contemporary Jewry and its Head, Professor Moshe Davis, for the generous grant which enabled me to undertake the preliminary research connected with this book. I am grateful to Dr Israel Kolath, and particularly to Dr Yehuda Bauer, members of the Institute, for their unflagging interest and many stimulating conversations.

A grant from the Miriam and Harry Sacher Foundation was important at a critical time. A Fellowship Grant from the Memorial Foundation for Jewish Culture enabled me to write the last two chapters of my book. To its President, Dr Nahum Goldmann, I owe more than I can possibly convey. A grant from the Lucius Littauer Foundation (New York) made the publication of this book possible. To the Foundation's Chairman, Mr Harry Starr, and the Members of the Board I owe a debt of gratitude.

1 Palestine—a Strategic Bulwark of Egypt?

Colonel Charles H. Churchill, the grandson of the fifth Duke of Marlborough and from 1842 to 1852 a staff officer in the British Expedition to Syria, was one of the first Englishmen to realise the strategic importance of Palestine to British interests. He insisted that when Palestine ceased to be Turkish 'it must either become English, or else form part of a new independent State, which without the incentives to territorial aggrandizement, or to means of military aggression, shall yet be able . . . to promote the great object for which it will be called into existence'.[1] He envisaged that the Jews would play a conspicuous rôle in its revival. But the essential prerequisite was that they should resume their 'existence as a people'. The European Powers obviously would have to aid them but it was up to the Jews themselves to make a start. Should they mobilise their resources to promote the regeneration of this part of the world, they would doubtless 'end by obtaining the sovereignty of at least Palestine'. The attempt to prop up the Turkish Empire had failed miserably.[2]

Churchill's views were not representative of the official attitude. When Lord Palmerston, the Foreign Secretary, was seized by the idea of promoting Jewish settlement in Palestine, he had in mind the interests of the Ottoman State and thus indirectly the British. A Palestine inhabited by loyal and productive settlers could help to improve the Sultan's finances and serve as a bulwark against 'any future evil designs of Mehemet Ali or his successor'.[3]

Neither Churchill's nor Palmerston's scheme got off the ground, but subsequent events were to bear out Churchill's words. During the latter part of the First World War and afterwards, when the British Government found it advantageous to establish good relations with the Zionists, it supported their aspirations not in order to bolster up the Ottoman Empire but to justify its dismemberment and legitimise its own presence in Palestine. This concept did not mature before 1917 but its origins go much further back. The more firmly entrenched the British position in Egypt (since its occupation in 1882), the deeper grew the estrangement from Turkey in the pre-war period, the more compelling became the need to change British policy. In contrast to the nineteenth century, it was now Egypt, not the Ottoman Empire, that required British protection. Henceforth, the urge to widen the *cordon sanitaire* off the Suez Canal zone became almost irresistible. Such an expansion, to encompass subsequently the whole of Palestine and Mesopotamia, was dictated by the logic of geopolitical realities.

It was in order to secure the Suez Canal, the 'jugular vein' of the British Empire, that Lord Cromer, the British Agent in Cairo, had managed in 1892 against considerable odds to establish a new delineation of the frontier running from Rafah to the Gulf of Aqaba. Under this arrangement, the whole of the Sinai Peninsula, though it remained under the formal suzerainty of the Sultan, was to be administered by the Anglo-Egyptian authorities. The importance that the British attached to this achievement was clearly demonstrated in 1906 when the Porte went back on the original understanding and staged an incident in Tabah in the neighbourhood of the boundary-line to test the British reaction. Both Whitehall and Cairo firmly resisted the Turkish encroachment and the Porte had finally to reaffirm the arrangement made in 1892.[4]

This incident, combined with the construction of the Hedjaz railway, re-emphasised the strategic importance of the Sinai Peninsula and opened British eyes to the possibility of a serious invasion of Egypt from the east by Turkey. On 11 May 1906 the Committee of Imperial Defence decided that 'for the security and tranquillity of Egypt, it is essential to preserve intact the strip of desert country, about 130 miles broad, which separates that frontier from the Canal'.[5] But could the 'strip of desert' provide the required security? Both ancient and modern military history belied the belief that the Sinai Peninsula presented an insuperable obstacle to the passage of large armies. It was General Sir John French[6] who first challenged the findings of the Defence Committee. He foresaw that within the following ten years a situation might arise necessitating the employment of an army of 150,000 men to meet enemies, both from within and without, who might seek in unison to drive the British out of Egypt. 'The hand will be of Turkey [but] the voice will be the voice of Germany.' With the latter's connivance the Turks might easily concentrate within striking distance of Suez a force of at least 100,000 men and, drawing on his own personal experience and other evidence, Sir John gave warning that 'the Sinai desert should not be regarded as impassable'.[7]

By 1912 the General Staff fully subscribed to this assessment[8] but in 1906 it was still regarded as too pessimistic. Lord Cromer was sceptical of the Turks' capability to undertake so complicated an operation,[9] and Richard Haldane, the Secretary of State for War, thought that the Canal itself, when properly equipped and fortified, constituted 'the strongest defensive position'.[10] However, Cromer underestimated the extent of the encouragement that Germany might give to Turkey, whereas Haldane seemed to have completely overlooked the legal stipulations which precluded the use of the Canal for belligerent purposes. The Convention of 29 October 1888 guaranteed unimpeded freedom of navigation through the Canal in times of peace and war.[11] It is true that the Convention was never brought into practical operation, but the British Government none the less considered its provisos as 'valid and binding'[12] and never violated the Canal's neutrality. Any doubts on this score were finally dispelled when the principle of freedom of navigation was endorsed by Article VI of the Anglo-French Treaty of 8 April 1904.[13] Hence the Canal could not be an instrument of war even for Egypt's defence.

This was not the only legal disability. International agreements imposed serious restrictions on the size and deployment of the British army of occupation. It could be used solely for the purpose of maintaining order, and any increase in its strength could be justified only on grounds of some 'transitory and exceptional' circumstances.[14] As a result, Britain's military position was so weak that the standing garrison would be unable to defend Egypt against an external attack of even 5,000 men.[15] The garrison, in any case, could not be deployed freely. Article VIII of the 1888 Convention provided that in case of external aggression the signatory Powers were bound to turn first to the Khedivian Government and (according to the second paragraph of Article IX) should the latter be unable to protect the Canal, the Powers could then appeal to the Ottoman Government to take the necessary steps. Any unilateral action by Britain or any other Power was tantamount to usurpation of the prerogatives of the Sultan who still held suzerainty over Egypt. However, what would be the legal position should Turkey herself be involved in a military operation against the Canal? Such a possibility was obviously not envisaged in the 1888 Convention, but in the year before 1914 it placed the British in an additional predicament. Moreover, even supposing that these stipulations could be ignored, as in fact they were when Britain proclaimed her protectorate over Egypt on 18 December 1914, a purely defensive stance, however effective, was not satisfactory. 'Great Britain in dealing with a Power like Turkey', reads the recommendation of Major-General J. C. Ewart, Director of Military Intelligence, 'could not afford merely to stand on the defensive. If we assumed such an attitude, our prestige in the East would be gone. We must adopt a more active policy and find a theatre of operations outside the Canal zone. Such a theatre the General Staff consider can be found in Syria'[16] and Palestine.

This was by no means wishful thinking. As early as 1906, after the Tabah incident, plans were elaborated for a landing at Haifa.[17] By 1909 a fully-fledged plan of invasion had been developed: the Haifa-Acre coast was designated as the most suitable landing area, Nazareth and Lower Galilee as intermediate objectives, and Damascus as the target. The threat of a raid on Egypt by Turkey or the massacre of Christians in the Lebanon would constitute a valid pretext.[18] Both the scope of the operation and the depth of the strike suggested that this would not be merely a tactical skirmish to disrupt Turkish communications but a considered design, should political circumstances permit, to occupy parts of Palestine and Syria.

In March 1909 a special sub-committee under the chairmanship of Lord Morley, Secretary of State for India, was appointed to examine the question. The Committee was struck by disquieting evidence that a successful crossing of the Suez Canal even by 'a few Turks would have a serious effect not only on the inhabitants of Egypt, but on the *fellaheen* portion of the Egyptian Army'. A seriously intended invasion of Egypt was considered unlikely unless preceded by a good deal of preparation and the construction of an adequate railway network; nevertheless, should it be attempted, the Committee thought it imperative to put into operation the plan for an attack on Haifa as prescribed by the General Staff. A force of at least four divisions was to be committed to such an undertaking. These recommendations were approved three months later by the Committee of Imperial Defence and subsequently (on 2 June 1910) an alternative proposal to defend Egypt by a naval force based on Suez was rejected.[19]

For a while it was thought that garrisons at the oases of El-Arish, Nahal, and Katia in the Sinai would provide the answer. But it was soon realised that such outposts could at best delay but not stop an invasion of Egypt.[20] By 1912 the General Staff had to reckon seriously with the possibility of Turkey joining the Triple Alliance, in which case the figure of 100,000 Turkish troops to be used against Egypt, an estimate made by General French in 1906, was not exaggerated. British military reconnaissance disproved the theory that the inhospitable nature of the Sinai Peninsula and the lack of water supplies might preclude military movement of any magnitude. It would take only one month for the enemy to reach Egypt both by land and sea from a base somewhere in Syria.[21] To forestall the danger a better base was needed than Sinai. Nor could Egypt, for reasons mentioned earlier, be employed by Britain as a reliable *place d'armes*. An effective barrier against an invasion could be established only in Palestine.

Yet despite the weight of military argument pointing to Palestine as an ideal bulwark for Egypt, there were wider considerations pointing to restraint. The Haifa project was no more than a contingency plan in response to a possible Turkish attack; but it would be wrong to see in it a deliberate intention to carve out some additional territory for British interests. Such a move would inevitably have invited other Powers to follow suit, with fatal consequences for Turkey-in-Asia. The risks involved in its dissolution outweighed by far the danger that might threaten Egypt on its north-eastern border. As a neighbour, a weak Turkey was preferable to a European Power, such as France or Germany. Hence the rationale of the *status quo*. The only policy to which the British Government could subscribe was, as Sir Edward Grey, the Foreign Secretary, informed Sir George Buchanan, the Ambassador at St. Petersburg, 'one directed to avoid collapse and partition of Asiatic Turkey'.[22]

This message followed closely on Grey's conversation with Raymond Poincaré, the French President, and Stéphen Pichon, his Foreign Minister, during their visit to London early in July 1913. Grey emphasised that he regarded the preservation of Turkey-in-Asia as 'one of the most important aims of his policy'.[23] It was all the more important for Grey to make his position clear as the French, following his professed disinterestedness in Syria,[24] tended to interpret their rights there too liberally. On 21 December 1912[25] Poincaré, addressing both Houses of the French Parliament, had pointedly referred to the 'faulty' administration of the Sublime Porte, and noted that in the Lebanon and Syria the French had 'special and long-seated interests which . . . must [be] respected. The British Government', he went on, 'declared that . . . it has no political aspirations and no wish or intention to do anything'[26] to stand in the way of the French.

That this differed substantially from what Grey had in mind transpires from his despatch to Sir William Goschen, the British Ambassador in Berlin. 'I observed to Cambon that what I said about Syria did not imply a disturbance of the *status quo* which it was our object to preserve.'[27] Curiously, in order to balance the French, Grey found common ground with the Germans, who had nothing to gain from Turkey's partial or complete disappearance, though as *Realpolitiker* they were ready to take full advantage of partition should it take place.[28] Grey was no less a realist than his German counterpart and had to consider the possibility that partition might be unavoidable, but there was little doubt where his priority lay. Pragmatic and cautious as he was, his diplomacy finally triumphed. The French, faced with a solid Anglo-German front, had to fall into line. Poincaré and Pichon finally assured Grey (during their meeting in London) that France too would do everything in her power to support his policy.[29] Henceforth the Quai d'Orsay consistently adhered to the *status quo* principle.[30]

Against this background it is clear why, despite its sympathy, the British

Government was in no position to give positive support to Zionist aspirations. A proposal like that made by Colonel Claude Conder in 1903 for a Jewish settlement in Palestine that could serve as an ideal outpost in the neighbourhood of Egypt[31] was rare. If Theodor Herzl's cause made so powerful an appeal to some British statesmen, it was out of humanitarian rather than political considerations. 'The motives which had actuated the Government', Earl Percy, the Under-Secretary of State for Foreign Affairs, told the House of Commons on 20 June 1904, 'had been inspired by those feelings of sympathy . . . which had always been felt by the British race, for that persecuted and oppressed people.' In the same debate Sir Edward Grey spoke of an attempt to provide 'a refuge and a home', and six months later Joseph Chamberlain, the Colonial Secretary, recalled the need to find 'some country [not necessarily Palestine] if possible under the ægis of the British flag, or under the protection . . . of a Concert of nations . . . in which these poor exiles could dwell in safety'. If Chamberlain had in addition some imperial purpose in mind, when encouraging the El-Arish proposal, as his biographer is inclined to think, it soon came up against the political realities. Herzl was finally told that 'the establishment of a large cosmopolitan society in the Sinai Peninsula [which *de jure* was still part of the Sultan's dominions] would entail a material increase of the difficulties which the [Anglo-]Egyptian Administration has already to encounter.'[32]

Arthur Balfour, writing to Israel Zangwill, the celebrated novelist and a leader of the Jewish Territorial Organization (ITO),[33] recalled that, when Prime Minister, he had had several opportunities to discuss Jewish settlement in East Africa, 'and', he added, 'I have not altered my view that, if such a scheme be desired by the Jewish community generally, an effort should be made to carry it out. . . . My anxiety is simply to find some means by which the present dreadful state of [sic] so large a proportion of the Jewish race finds themselves may be brought to an end.'[34] This letter, dated 21 February 1906, was written only four to five weeks after Balfour had reassured Weizmann that 'if a home was to be found for the Jewish people. . . it was in vain to seek it anywhere but in Palestine';[35] not too glaring a contradiction considering that Balfour was at that time electioneering and wished to satisfy all shades of Jewish opinion. Winston Churchill, the Liberal M.P. for North-west Manchester (a constituency near Balfour's) also acknowledged the need for a 'safe and settled home [for these] scattered and persecuted people'. Early in January 1906, during his election campaign, he publicly declared his support for the idea of creating an autonomous Jewish colony in East Africa, only to realise its impracticability six months later when Colonial Under-Secretary. The territory in question was not an unoccupied land and the violent opposition of the white settlers posed a serious obstacle. Moreover, division within the Jewish ranks put a question mark over the whole venture.[36] By 1908 Churchill had come to the conclusion that:[37]

> Jerusalem must be the only ultimate goal. When it will be achieved, it is vain to prophesy: but that it will some day be achieved is one of the few certainties of the future. The establishment of a strong, free Jewish State astride the bridge between Europe and Africa, flanking the land roads to the East, would not only be an immense advantage to the British Empire, but a notable step towards a harmonious disposition of the world among its peoples.

This sounded like a powerful echo of the plea made about five decades earlier by Colonel Charles Churchill, his remote kinsman.[38] Like him, Churchill was far ahead of his time. Not before 1917–18 did the British Government feel able to embrace this concept, though phrased in more moderate terms. But early in the war, when Herbert Samuel, President of the Local Government Board, ventured to propound it officially, it was still premature.

2 The Samuel Proposal and British Policy in Turkey-in-Asia

At the beginning of the First World War only a handful of British statesmen envisaged that with the probable disintegration of the Ottoman
Empire, the foundations of a Jewish state in Palestine could be laid. Herbert Samuel was among the few. That a person of his standing and up-
bringing should take such a vivid interest in the renaissance of his people
in their historic homeland, is rather remarkable. Yet the Zionist idea was
far from alien to him. Some twenty years earlier, his imagination had been
fired by Herzl's ideal, but with Herzl's failure, he felt it prudent to leave
the pursuit of such a 'distant ideal' to others. Contact with Rabbi Dr
Gaster kept his interest in Zionism alive, but it was Turkey's entry into the
war, on 5 November 1914 that opened Samuel's eyes to the future possibilities of Palestine. The speech by Herbert Asquith, the Prime Minister,
at the Lord Mayor's Banquet on 9 November, confirmed his belief that
the British Government aimed at the dismemberment of the Ottoman
Empire.[1] Though, as we shall see later, he was mistaken, since Asquith's
statement was more a rhetorical warning to the Ottoman Government
than a declaration of policy, Samuel, like most of his contemporaries, read
it to mean literally what it said.

He confided his views first to Sir Edward Grey. Given the jealousies of
the European Powers in that area which made it unlikely that they would
agree to any one of them assuming a dominant position there, 'perhaps
the opportunity might arise for the fulfilment of the ancient aspiration of
the Jewish people and the restoration there of a Jewish State'. Such an
entity, were it to be established, might become 'the centre of a new culture . . . a fountain of enlightenment and a source of a great literature and
art and development of science'. Samuel hoped that Russia would co-
operate, but it was primarily to Britain that his eyes were turned. Britain
'ought to play a considerable part in the formation of such a state, because
the geographical situation of Palestine, and especially its proximity to
Egypt, would render its goodwill to England a matter of importance to
the British Empire'. Here was the germ of the strategic concept which
Samuel was to develop fully in his memoranda of January and March
8

1915. But in November 1914 he still did not think in terms of a British protectorate.

Grey was favourably disposed towards Samuel's proposal and was ready to work for it should the opportunity arise. The idea had always a 'strong sentimental attraction to him'. Grey agreed with Samuel that the proposed state should be neutral and that it would be advantageous to have a European Power, such as France, as a neighbour on its northern borders, rather than Turkey. Should however France, or any other Power, advance claims to Syria in its entirety, it would be important, Grey emphasised, 'not to acquiesce in any plan which would be inconsistent with the creation of a Jewish State in Palestine'. Lloyd George, with whom Samuel spoke on the same day, was also 'very keen' to see the establishment of a Jewish state;[2] his interest predated Grey's. Questions which Lloyd George put to Chaim Weizmann, in the presence of Samuel and C. P. Scott on 15 December 1914 about the relative proportions of Jews and Arabs in Palestine, and his remark that Judea when mature might constitute 'a possible link between East and West',[3] show how seriously the question had preoccupied him. The localities in Palestine mentioned by Weizmann sounded to him, versed in the Bible and Jewish history, 'more familiar . . . than those on the Western Front'.[4] The idea of restoring Palestine to the Jews obviously appealed to him but, as we shall see later, it played only a subsidiary part in the formulation of his policy when Prime Minister.

About six weeks later Samuel circulated a memorandum under the title *The Future of Palestine*.[5] It started on an almost messianic note:

> there is a stirring among the twelve million Jews scattered throughout
> the countries of the world. A feeling is spreading with great
> rapidity that now, at last, some advance may be made, in some way,
> towards the fulfilment of the hope and desire, held with unshakeable
> tenacity for eighteen hundred years, for the restoration of the Jews
> to the land to which they are attached by ties almost as ancient as
> history itself.

However, Samuel thought the time was not ripe for the establishment of an independent, autonomous Jewish State. In Jerusalem proper, two-thirds of the inhabitants were Jews, but in the country as a whole their number did not exceed one-sixth. Hence,

> if the attempt were made to place the 400,000 or 500,000
> Mahommedans of Arab race under a Government which rested upon
> the support of 90,000 or 100,000 Jewish inhabitants, there can be no

assurance that such a Government, even if established by the authority of the Powers would be able to command obedience. The dream of a Jewish State, prosperous, progressive and the home of a brilliant civilisation, might vanish in a series of squalid conflicts with the Arab population. And even if a State so constituted did not succeed in avoiding or repressing internal disorder, it is doubtful whether it would be strong enough to protect itself from external aggression from the turbulent elements around it. To attempt to realise the aspiration of a Jewish State a century too soon might throw back its actual realisation for many centuries more.

The most desirable solution therefore would be to annex Palestine to the British Empire. Under British rule Jewish colonisation and institutions would prosper and immigration be encouraged, 'so that in course of time, the Jewish people, grown into a majority and settled in the land, may be conceded such a degree of self-government as the conditions of that day may justify'. England, true to her traditions, would bring civilisation to a backward country, and this would have strategic advantages, since Palestine was ideally suited to serve as an outpost for Egypt. All other options were inadmissible. To leave Palestine to Turkey would condemn it to permanent stagnation. Annexation by France was unjustifiable; even less desirable was an international administration. Palestine would become a theatre of intrigue, and German influence, which predated the war, might easily be exerted again to the detriment of the French position in Syria and that of the British in Egypt.

Samuel was not so unrealistic as to suggest that the development of a sizeable Jewish community would solve the Jewish problem in Europe. It would not. A country equal in size to Wales, much of which was barren mountain and partly waterless, could not hold more than three or four million people, but it would relieve the pressure in Russia and elsewhere. Of greater importance would be the educational effect. It would re-establish an authentic image of the Jew and give him status and dignity.

The Jewish brain [Samuel wound up] is a physiological product not to be despised. For fifteen centuries the race produced in Palestine a constant succession of great men—statesmen and prophets, judges and soldiers. If a body be again given in which its soul can lodge, it may again enrich the world. Till full scope is granted, as Macaulay said in the House of Commons, 'let us not presume to say that there is no genius among the countrymen of Isaiah, nor heroism among the descendants of Maccabees'.

It was an extremely able memorandum appealing both to imagination and to self-interest. Visionary as his conclusion was, Samuel was not blind to the limitations. Palestine was a small country and, though predominantly derelict, was not completely uninhabited. The stark fact that it contained over half a million Arabic-speaking people forced him to the conclusion that the time was not ripe for the establishment of a Jewish state. But was he not aware of the numerical preponderance of the Arabs when unfolding his ideas to Grey on 9 November? It was one of the reasons, he told Grey, which made the task of building up a new state so 'formidable', and it was, apparently in order to enable the Jews to reach majority status in a shorter time that he explicitly excluded from the boundaries of the projected state Beirut and Damascus, 'since they contained a large non-Jewish population which could not be assimilated'.[6] What then made Samuel modify his approach?

We can only conjecture. It would not be too far-fetched to assume that the telegram of 7 January from the British Agent in Egypt, mentioned in Samuel's memorandum, gave him a sense of urgency. The Agent in question was Sir Milne Cheetham, acting High Commissioner.[7] On the basis of information indicating that a large proportion of the population of Syria and Palestine would welcome the advent of the British, Cheetham urged a military offensive with a landing in Alexandretta, north of Syria, as the key to the operation.[8] The political implication of this scheme was that the area, when liberated from the Turks, could at best result in an Arab state or semi-state, under British protection. Such a prospect was sufficiently alarming to prompt Samuel to put the Jewish case before the Cabinet. In November, when he had sounded out Grey, the question of the future of Palestine was still academic, and he felt at liberty to put his desideratum as he did. But after Cheetham's cable, insistence on the establishment of a Jewish state would obviously have been premature, if not self-defeating. Hence the proposal for colonisation under British protection. However, the change was only tactical. The ultimate objective remained the same.

Samuel was not moving in a vacuum. On 10 December 1914 he had met Weizmann. Weizmann was convinced that England would win the war[9] and that only under her wing would Zionism prosper. When asked by Samuel what he expected from the British Government, Weizmann replied: 'encouragement . . . in our work . . . a wide measure of local government and freedom for the development of our own culture'.[10] This was a much more modest formula[11] than that put by Samuel to Grey a month earlier and this too may have persuaded Samuel to shelve the proposal for a Jewish state to some indefinite future. But Weizmann's desideratum was much more ambitious: 'England would have an effective barrier and we would have a country', he had told Zangwill on 10 October 1914.[12] A month later he wrote to Scott that, should Palestine fall within the British sphere of influence and Jewish settlement be encouraged there 'we could have in twenty or thirty years a million Jews out there, perhaps more; they would develop the country . . . and form a very effective guard for the Suez Canal.' And in March 1915 he wrote to Scott in still bolder terms: if, eventually, the Jews took over the country, the entire burden of administration would fall on them, but for the next ten or fifteen years they would work under a British protectorate.[13] The resemblance between this train of thought and that running through Samuel's January memorandum is striking. British protection was not only an end in itself but also a means to an end. The essential defect however in their thinking was the assumption that during the transitional period the Arabs would remain passive onlookers. What the effect on the British attitude would be should the Arabs resist was not considered. In fact Arab opposition was to emerge as the key problem, but at that time the difficulty was not foreseen.

This was not the only flaw. Samuel and Weizmann gave insufficient weight to the fact that Britain was disinclined to undertake new imperial responsibilities and that the wishes of the French in that region were to be respected. The idea of British protection might have found a ready ear among annexationists such as Scott and Lloyd George, but it tended to alienate Asquith, Grey and the Foreign Office. Samuel's proposal appealed to Lloyd George's 'poetic and imaginative as well as to the romantic and religious qualities of his mind'.[14] Lloyd George indeed did not miss an opportunity during Cabinet meetings to advocate the annexation of Palestine,[15] and to him British and Jewish Palestine were almost identical in meaning, but in 1915, as Chancellor of the Exchequer, his influence on foreign policy was marginal; it was Grey's opinion that counted.

On 5 February 1915, when Samuel met the Foreign Secretary again, he found him still anxious to promote Jewish settlement in Palestine 'in a way favourable to Zionist ideas' but 'very doubtful of the possibility or desirability of the establishment of a British Protectorate'. He did not know what views the French Government held in this matter and was willing to sound them out, but Samuel demurred. Grey was opposed to Britain's assuming any fresh military and diplomatic responsibilities. Asked by Samuel what alternative solution he had in mind, Grey said that

it might be possible to neutralize the country under international guarantee; to place the control of the Holy Places in the hands of a

Commission in which the European Powers, the Pope, and perhaps the United States, would be represented; and to vest the government of the country in some kind of Council to be established by the Jews.

This resembled Samuel's original proposal of November 1914, but Samuel who had in the meantime modified it, doubted whether in the prevailing circumstances a Jewish administration would be acceptable to the Arabic-speaking population. Grey thereupon saw no other course than to establish in Palestine a similar régime to that in the Lebanon, that is to leave the country under Ottoman suzerainty but with a governor appointed by the Powers to safeguard the interests of the Jewish population. Samuel was not content. He pointed to the danger of any power other than England holding Palestine and to the risk that under the cloak of an international government, some European state such as Germany might gain a foothold. Grey 'agreed that that was so'.[16]

The conclusion of Samuel's note suggests that he might have been under the impression that Grey had come round to his point of view concerning a British Protectorate. This was not the case. The same considerations that precluded unilateral British operations in Alexandretta, proposed by Cheetham, applied also in this case. Grey's advice to Samuel during their conversation on 5 February, that the Zionists should interest the French, American and other Governments as well in their programme,[17] reflects his rooted objection to earmarking Palestine as a solely British concern. A year later Grey recalled in a cable to Sir Mark Sykes: 'I told Mr. Samuel at the time that a British Protectorate was quite out of the question.'[18]

But Samuel remained unshaken. Prominent members of the Anglo-Jewish community like Lord Rothschild, his cousin Leopold de Rothschild, and Claude Montefiore, reinforced his belief that a British Protectorate was the best course. Moreover, learning from Weizmann that a memorandum presented to the Russian Government by Tschlenow,[19] recommending 'a Jewish Palestine under [the protectorate of] a great Power' had been well received,[20] Samuel may have believed that at least Russia would not oppose a British Protectorate, in which case France could perhaps be persuaded to agree. The more he explored the situation in Palestine, the clearer it became to him that the idea of a Jewish State was 'impracticable. At some future time, perhaps, it might come about ... but so long as the great majority of the inhabitants were Arabs it was out of the question.'

To impose a Jewish minority government would be in flat contradiction to one of the main purposes for which the Allies were fighting. At the same time it was not necessary to accept the position that the existing population, sparse as it was, should have the right to bar the door to the return of a people whose connection with the country long antedated their own, especially as it had resulted in events of spiritual and cultural value to mankind in striking contrast with the barren record of the last thousand years.[21]

This remained Samuel's credo from which he was not deflected. Lucien Wolf may have been under the impression, when he met him, that Samuel agreed with him;[22] but he was mistaken for in contrast to Wolf, who viewed the Palestine question through a purely Jewish prism, Samuel was also concerned with its compatibility with British imperial interests. Wolf saw in the 'cultural' plan, freedom of immigration, facilities for colonisation, and equality of rights with the native population, the sole objectives to which Jews should limit their ambitions, but Samuel was equally committed to 'free opportunity for political development', a phrase which was merely a euphemism for an unimpeded development towards a Jewish majority in Palestine. The right of Jews to Palestine in his opinion was inviolable and their return could not be dependent on the consent of the indigenous Arabic-speaking population. In his second memorandum of March 1915[23] the significant paragraph

> under British rule . . . Jewish immigration . . . would be given preference, so that in course of time the Jewish inhabitants, grown into a majority . . . may be conceded such degree of self-government as the conditions of that day might justify

remained virtually unaltered. Though not formally a member of the Zionist Organization, Samuel was essentially a political Zionist, or to be more precise, he blended the 'political' and the 'cultural' schools of thought into a harmonious whole. This provided a splendid basis for a complete rapport between him and Weizmann.[24] Both held strong views on the advantages of a British Protectorate in Palestine; and just as Weizmann endeavoured to argue away the reservations of some British statesmen,[25] so Samuel completely ignored Grey's advice on this subject.[26]

Samuel's move was ill-timed. It coincided with Russia's claim to Constantinople and the Straits. Although her Allies had no choice but to accept it, Grey was wary of drifting into the unpredictable currents leading to Turkey's vivisection. It is a fallacy to believe that the idea of dismemberment of the Ottoman Empire was a predetermined line of British policy. Had this been so, Samuel's proposal would have been received favourably and would, perhaps, have become part of the British desiderata. The fact is that it did not. It was no accident that Samuel's March memorandum (as presumably also the January one) was not discussed by the Cabinet or War Council at all.[27] Contrary to what is generally presumed by historians,[28] acceptance of the Russian demands did not make partition of Turkey inevitable, whereas the inclusion of Palestine amongst the British desiderata would have made all the difference. Not only would it have played into Russia's hands, it would have also provoked France into demanding her share of the spoils, a course which would have put an end to Turkey-in-Asia. This in fact did happen, but not in consequence of the Constantinople Agreement.

Grey did his best to preserve the status quo. This was his policy before the war as it was in 1915. But in 1915 his task was far more difficult. Turkey was at war with the Allies and, following the British proclamation of a Protectorate in Egypt (on 18 December 1914) and with the Dardanelles Expedition unfolding,[29] Russia's claims to Constantinople and the Straits were coming to the fore. However, Grey was reluctant to give ground. On 3 March 1915 he told Count Benckendorff, the Russian Ambassador, that 'a territorial expansion of Russia would raise . . . the question of partitioning of the whole of Turkey, thus whetting the appetites of many Powers'. He assured them that England had 'no designs whatever on any part of Asia Minor or Syria, except for some points in the area of the Persian Gulf'.[30] He was therefore all the more shocked to receive the next day Sazonow's telegram demanding the Allies' consent to the annexation of Constantinople, the Straits, and a sizeable hinterland.[31] It involved, as Grey put it, 'a complete reversal of the traditional policy of [the British] Government'. But, if the Foreign Secretary had to concede this 'richest prize of the entire war', it was not merely as a 'proof of friendship' to Russia[32] but in fear of losing her to Germany. Berlin, as the War Council was told by Grey on 10 March 1915, was anxious to conclude a separate peace with Russia and France to isolate England and thereafter to deal her a death-blow. France's loyalty was beyond doubt, but this could not be said of Russia. Russia believed that in the early days of the war she had saved the Allies from defeat and it was therefore 'essential' for the successful prosecution of the war that she should be reassured about Constantinople.[33]

Nevertheless, Grey refrained from following Sazonow's example, and made no claim to Turkish territory to balance Russia's. Such a move would have sealed the fate of Turkey-in-Asia. It would have revived the spectre of Nicholas I's prescription for the 'Sick Man of Europe'. Grey, therefore, formulated his desiderata as modestly as possible, limiting them to a request for a revision of the Anglo-Russian Agreement of 1907 regarding spheres of influence in Persia and to a stipulation that 'the Mussulman Holy Places and Arabia shall . . . remain under independent Mussulman dominion'.[34] Neither of these counter-claims would have jeopardised the viability of the Turkish state.

Grey's position was all the more difficult since only a few of his colleagues supported him. 'I believe that Grey and I are the only two men', Asquith noted in March 1915, 'who doubt and distrust any such settlement'[35] as Turkey's partition. Balfour[36] had his eyes fixed on Alexandretta, while Lloyd George thought that Palestine was more rewarding 'owing to prestige involved in its occupation'. Lord Kitchener, Secretary for War, dismissed Palestine as of 'no value' and claimed Alexandretta.[37] Kitchener's basic premise was that if the war was brought to a successful conclusion and if Russia secured Constantinople and control of the Straits, partition of the Turkish dominions was unavoidable. With Russia emerging as a Mediterranean Power and France in possession of Syria, the whole balance of power in the Levant would be profoundly changed; and this inevitably would affect the position of Egypt. Should Britain decide to incorporate Mesopotamia in its Empire, occupation of Alexandretta was indispensable. 'If we do not take Mesopotamia, the Russians undoubtedly will sooner or later. This would give them an outlet into the Persian Gulf, and enable them eventually to control the military situation and the greater part of its commerce.' The potential agricultural and mineral resources of Mesopotamia, notably oil, were assets not to be brushed aside, and if irrigated the country could become again 'one of the most fertile and highly productive areas in the world'. With Alexandretta, Mesopotamia and the Bagdad Railway, Egypt, the Suez Canal, and India would have greater security.[38]

The Admiralty supported Kitchener.[39] So did Sir Arthur Hirtzel, Secretary of the Political and Secret Department of the India Office.[40] But General Edmund Barrow, its Military Secretary, thought differently. He dismissed Alexandretta as both politically and militarily untenable. Its acquisition was bound to set Britain on a collision course with her Allies and involve her in 'enormous and unprofitable expenditure . . . Mesopotamia and Egypt, with Palestine as the connecting link between the two, are British interests, the rest are not.' The 'ideal' border for the British sphere of interests in the north, General Barrow concluded, stretched from the Mediterranean at Cape Nakurah, between Tyre and Acre, to the Euphrates at Deir, thence down the right bank of the Arah and across El Jezirah to the Persian frontier.

Such a line would include all Palestine from Dan to Beersheba, the Upper Jordan and Mount Hermon, as well as the oases of Damascus and Palmyra, and thus enable us to construct an all-British railway from Acre or Haifa through Damascus to Bagdad and the Gulf . . . to connect with the Egyptian [railway] system . . . consolidating our oriental empire.

Should however this programme prove too ambitious and beyond Britain's military capacity, or likely to involve her in a clash with France, Britain should abandon all idea of expansion. She had much more to gain by supporting Turkey as an Asiatic state and championing Islam, than by giving rein to annexationist appetites. In practical terms, Turkey-in-Asia ought to be maintained as a buffer state, though shorn of certain provinces: Armenia under Russian, the Lebanon under French, and Basra vilayet under British influence respectively, whilst Palestine should be 'neutralised and administered as an autonomous province of the Turkish Empire by an International Commission . . . under the protection of the allied Powers'. General Barrow concluded:[41]

The abolition of direct Turkish rule in Palestine is . . . a political consummation which will appeal to many, both Christian and Jew, but which would inevitably create dissension among the Powers unless they were all equally interested in the new dispensation. Any attempt to acquire a special privileged position by one would be resented by the rest of the Powers and would speedily lead to that Armageddon in the valley of Esdraelon which has terrified the imagination of the world for ages past.

It was Barrow's impeccable logic that killed the Alexandretta scheme in favour of Haifa as a British interest. His influence on the de Bunsen Committee[42] was profound. When circumstances changed, his concept of Palestine's importance as an indispensable geopolitical link between Mesopotamia and Egypt became a constant in British strategic doctrine. It survived the inter-war period and was dropped only after Britain's final withdrawal from India and the Middle East.

Closely reasoned as Barrow's memorandum was, it does not seem to have made any immediate impact on the War Council. British Ministers remained as divided as ever. During the meeting on 19 March 1915 Balfour reiterated his belief that Mesopotamia and Alexandretta were inseparable components of one scheme, whereas Lord Kitchener advanced the view that without Alexandretta, they had better not take Mesopotamia at all. On the other hand Lord Haldane, the Lord Chancellor, concluded that the total destruction of Germany and Turkey was not 'in the interest of a lasting peace . . . a permanent peace could not be obtained except by general consent'. This provoked the fury of Winston Churchill, First Lord of the Admiralty: 'surely, we do not intend to leave this . . . inefficient and out-of-date [Turkish] nation, which has long misruled one of the most fertile countries in the world, still in possession? . . . it is time for us to make a clean sweep.'[43]

The tenor of the discussion was disconcerting to Grey. 'I was not very anxious to carve up Asia Minor in advance', he wrote in his memoirs; 'if we won the war, spheres of interest would have to be defined; but the thing seemed rather premature.'[44] The cardinal question which he put to his colleagues was whether the acquisition of new territories would make Britain stronger or weaker. Moreover, would it be wise to ignore the intense feeling of loyalty of the Moslem world towards Turkey, their political and religious centre? Grey was fortunate in enjoying the support of the Prime Minister, but at this meeting it was not given without qualification. Asquith was fully aware that, should the Russians take a good slice of Turkey and other Powers followed suit, the British could no longer remain 'free agents'. If for one reason or another they left other nations to scramble for Turkey without taking anything themselves, they would not be doing their duty. This delphic statement suggested that Asquith, as Prime Minister, had to consider also the opinions of those members of the War Council who opposed Grey. Yet it was the policy of the Foreign Minister, though outnumbered, which finally won the day. It was decided *inter alia* that 'it would be premature to discuss the partition of Turkey.'[45] This explains why Samuel's memorandum was bypassed altogether, even though such staunch supporters as Lloyd George, Lord Haldane, and Lord Crewe were present at the meeting.

Ambivalent as Asquith's statement at the War Council on 19 March sounded, at heart he was, like Grey, deeply anti-annexationist. 'It is very difficult to convince the ignorant or the foolish that swollen boundaries mean, or may mean, anything else than greater wealth [and] . . . authority', he wrote on 22 April 1915 to Admiral Fisher,[46]

It must be remembered that there may be territories which we must take because we do not want other countries to take them. Further, there may be territories which we must take because there is nobody else to give them to. The Turks may have disappeared. You cannot hand important pieces of land to savages and Great Britain may be forced to new responsibilities as reluctantly as she has on occasions been forced in the past . . . But new territories require the expenditure of more money, and even more important, the expenditure of more men. We shall be short of both at the end of this war. . . . New territories will require new armies, new navies, new civil servants, new expenses, teachers, doctors. Where are these to come from? . . .

I believe that we have not the men or the money to make new countries out of barren and savage deserts; and if we try . . . we shall arrest progress at home and in the other countries for which we are responsible, and we shall saddle the British taxpayer with huge liabilities for defence.

Asquith's comment on Lord Kitchener's Mesopotamian project is as revealing:

He is a man of great imagination. . . . He thinks a new country in Asia can be made as quickly as a new army in England . . . It has taken many years to make the Punjab, [but] it is yet not self-supporting . . . How long will it be before Mesopotamia can give to the subjects of King George's great grandson some part of the expenditure which we to-day will have to bear for the fortifications on Alexandretta and the vast army necessary to defend it and the railway from there to Basra.

Given this attitude, it is most unlikely that, in his Guildhall speech of 9 November 1914, Asquith had in mind the dismemberment of the Turkish Empire as one of British war aims.[47] But with the opinions among ministers divided, he appointed early in April 1915 a special interdepartmental Committee to 'consider the nature of British desiderata in Turkey-in-Asia in the event of a successful conclusion of the War'. The Committee, better known by the name of its chairman, Sir Maurice de Bunsen, Assistant Under-Secretary of State at the Foreign Office, submitted its report on 30 June 1915.[48] It was a document of acute political thinking, analytical, detached, and far-sighted, though circumstances gave it no more than temporary value. The Committee were realistic enough to admit that British desiderata in Asiatic Turkey were circumscribed by those of other Powers who, although Allies today, might tomorrow become competitors. Having carefully weighed the advantages to the British Empire of annexation against the risks involved in the increased responsibilities, the Committee examined four courses, of which the first (A) and the last (D) were the most important:

(A) Limitation of Turkish sovereignty to Anatolia and the partition of the non-Turkish portions of the Ottoman Empire among the European Powers.

(D) Maintenance of the Ottoman Empire[49] as an independent but decentralised and federal State.

Should (A) be decided upon among the Powers, it was imperative for Britain to stake her claim to the territory which lay south of the line running from Acre north-eastwards to Tadmor-Sinjar-Amadia and to the Persian border; a stretch of land which included in the east the *vilayets* of Mosul, Bagdad, and Basra, and in the west central and southern Palestine and the whole of the Sinai Peninsula. There could be no half-measures. Britain could not afford a situation in which 'the real master of Bagdad and owner of Mesopotamia will be France or Russia'. If Britain were established in Mesopotamia, an outlet to the Mediterranean was essential for both strategic and commercial reasons. Here the Committee took a leaf from General Barrow's memorandum[50] ruling out Alexandretta and substituting Haifa which, though not as good a natural harbour, was capable of development into a satisfactory port easily connected by rail with Mesopotamia and Egypt. Should Alexandretta be annexed, France could not be refused Palestine, an outcome 'scarcely tolerable', since it would bring her frontier close to the Suez Canal and Arabia. Haifa was therefore preferable.

Yet despite the alluring prospect of Mesopotamia developing into a British granary and of the exploitation of inexhaustible oil deposits, the disadvantages of partitioning the Ottoman Empire outweighed, in the Committee's opinion, the advantages. It would both prolong and alter the character of the war;[51] it would deeply offend the Moslems and entail extensive military liabilities. The French would be prompted to establish a naval base at Alexandretta and perhaps a submarine and torpedo-boat station at Beirut. This would pose a permanent threat to Haifa and, in the event of war, would materially add to the difficulties of keeping British communications in the Eastern Mediterranean open. The Haifa-Mosul-Bagdad railway would be in constant jeopardy either from a French or a Russian thrust or a combination of the two. This would require large land forces and a basic re-examination of the traditional postulates of British imperial strategy. 'Our Empire is wide enough already, and our task is to consolidate the possessions we already have.' As for Palestine, an unwanted responsibility would be thrown on British shoulders which, in the Committee's opinion, was an international concern rather than that of a single power.

The Committee therefore favoured Course (D): that is maintenance of an independent Ottoman Empire but with a decentralised system of administration. Accordingly, Turkey was to be divided into five great provinces: Anatolia, Armenia, Syria, Palestine, and Irak.[52] Such a division corresponded to the ethnic composition of its inhabitants and was more likely to meet their hopes for autonomy, a goal which was fully in line with the declared aims of the Allies. Moreover, a federal Ottoman Empire would have a better chance of survival, and rivalry among the Powers would be greatly reduced. The Committee thus hit on a well-balanced solution; whilst securing vital British interests, it opened up prospects for Turkey's reform.

This remarkable document bore testimony to the essentially non-annexationist character of British policy. By curbing Britain's appetites, the Committee hoped to restrain those of her Allies. The report showed that, despite the intended amputation of Constantinople and the Straits by Russia, partition of the remainder of the Empire, as seen from the British angle, was not inevitable. But if with regard to Turkey's future the Committee showed restraint, in the matter of Palestine their attitude appeared deliberately disinterested. The position of Palestine was unique, transcending the usual pattern of power politics. Internationally significant, Palestine could not be the exclusive preserve of a single power. The Committee therefore was convinced that just as 'the French claim will be rejected, since . . . the forces opposed are too great . . . to make [it] good', so also for similar reasons 'it will be idle for His Majesty's Government to claim the retention of Palestine in their sphere. Palestine must be recognized as a country whose destiny must be the subject of special negotiations, in which both belligerents and neutrals are alike interested.'[53] The desirability of Palestine's neutralisation and internationalisation, expressed earlier by Grey and Barrow,[54] was now endorsed, and indeed extended by bringing in the neutrals and the Central Powers. This was diametrically opposed to the Samuel-Weizmann thesis.

At the end of November 1915, when Weizmann and Samuel, accompanied by Scott, met Lloyd George, they received little comfort. However cogently they may have argued the case for a British-protected Palestine, Lloyd George could say no more than that 'France would probably object' and that there would be objections in England as well to such an extension of responsibilities. 'George thought', Scott recorded, 'a condominium of the three [Allied] Powers might be proposed, but Samuel and Weizmann agreed that from their point of view this would be the worst solution.'[55]

It was not until early in 1917 that the Samuel-Weizmann-Scott doctrine began to appear relevant to British strategic interests. But during 1915-16 it was still condemned to the sidelines. Samuel obviously took Asquith's Guildhall speech at its face value. Nor was he aware, when preparing his memoranda, of the factors determining British policy. Notes from Lord Bryce[56] and Lord Fisher,[57] both annexationists, were encouraging, as was the news conveyed by Weizmann on 21 March 1915 that in Scott's view events were shaping in favour of a British Palestine.[58] This assessment, as we are able now to surmise, was misleading. Eric Drummond's[59] marginal comment on Samuel's March memorandum[60] reflects official reactions more faithfully. On the section advocating a British protectorate over Palestine, Drummond noted:

> I do not know whether the possibility of a United States protectorate has well been considered. I believe public opinion [there] would be much flattered at the idea, and I do not see any insuperable objections, though it might conflict with French claims.

Asquith was much less charitable to Samuel than his Secretary. His contemptuous remarks about Samuel's 'dithyrambic memorandum' are too familiar to the readers of his diary[61] to be quoted in full. They are in the same tone as those he made on Kitchener and his Mesopotamian scheme. It is not unlikely that in Samuel's case Asquith was influenced by his friend Edwin Montagu, Chancellor of the Duchy of Lancaster,[62] whose opposition to Zionism was a matter of common knowledge,[63] as was his close association with Asquith.[64] On 16 March 1915, in response to Samuel's memorandum, he wrote to Asquith:[65]

> I think it is quite clear that the position of Palestine in itself offers little or no attraction to Great Britain from a strategical or material point of view. The defence of Egypt must obviously be easier when it is bounded by desert almost unpassable in its nature than if we had territorial interests on each side of the Asiatic Saharas. Commercially and strategically Palestine is incomparably a poorer possession than, let us say, Mesopotamia, and therefore it seems to me that the interest in the question is on the whole confined to the possibility of founding ultimately . . . a Jewish State under British Protectorate.

He went on:

> I find myself very strongly convinced that this would be a disastrous policy. I believe that the Jewish hopes of once again finding themselves in Palestine are based on their interpretation of divine prophecy in the Old Testament, but the return of the Jews to the

Promised Land was predicted in that book by divine agency and by miracle, and I think it would require nothing short of a miracle to produce a Jewish State in Palestine.

Montagu rejected the idea that the Jews constituted a race. Those in Great Britain were as remote from those in Morocco as the Christian Englishman was from the Moor or the Hindu. Nor could he believe that a Jewish State could ever become a viable entity. Jews tending olive trees or herding sheep could not be imagined. As to commerce, it would be a pity to give anti-Semites an opportunity to discriminate against Jewish imports, and for their literary talents greater opportunities could be found in their countries of domicile. It would therefore be hardly worth while to transplant 'one-third of the Jewish peoples of the world for the sake of Zangwill!' In Palestine, Montagu was convinced, the Jewish community would have no common tongue. Hebrew was of little use in practice, and could no more serve as a means of communication than Latin could for Roman Catholics. Should a state be formed out of 'a polyglot, many-coloured, heterogeneous collection of people of different civilisations', it would create the confusion that followed the erection of the Tower of Babel.

The consequences of the establishment of a Jewish State for the Jews outside Palestine, nine million strong, would be even more disastrous. Unable to absorb more than three million at the most, it could not be 'a very promising Jewish State', yet it would be weighty enough to unleash a virulent anti-Semitism and undermine the civic status of those in the West. The alleged sympathy of the Protestant world for the idea of restoring the Jews to the Holy Land was, in Montagu's opinion, 'a thinly cloaked desire to get rid' of them; if it came about, 'the President of the Local Government Board would be asked to look after the Borough Council of Jerusalem rather than the West Riding of Yorkshire; the Lord Chief Justice [Lord Reading] would be told to preside at the Beth Din and not at the Court of Appeal; while I should be asked to fit myself for appointing Rabbis in the Duchy of Lebanon rather than Anglican Parsons in the Duchy of Lancaster.'

But the misfortune of highly-placed individuals would be slight compared to the catastrophe which might befall millions of Jews, those in Eastern Europe in particular. Montagu predicted that should it be made known that the Jews had or were about to have a country of their own, they would inevitably 'be invited to clear out'. With their eyes turned to a state of their own, they would no longer be considered patriotic citizens of their respective countries and this would invalidate their claim to hospitality. Montagu concluded that Samuel's proposal, though 'trimmed with . . . arguments of strategy and foreign policy', was in fact a 'presumptuous and almost blasphemous attempt to forestall Divine agency in the collection [sic] of Jews, which would be punished, if not by a new captivity in Babylon, by a new and unrivalled persecution of the Jews left behind.' He wound up:

> If only our peoples would cease to ask for special favours and cease to cry out together at the special disadvantages . . . if only they would take their place as non-conformists, Zionism would obviously die and Jews might find their way to esteem.

3 The Zionists and the Assimilationists

Montagu and Samuel were cousins but in temperament and outlook they were poles apart. The principal bone of contention between them was the one that polarised Anglo-Jewry. It centred on the problem of Jewish identity: whether the Jews were a nation or a religious community. The dispute was more than academic. At stake was the question whether recognition of Jews as a nation would impair their civic status in their countries of domicile. As events showed, apprehension on this count was unfounded,[1] but in order to understand its deeper causes it is necessary to trace the evolution of the controversy between Zionists and assimilationists.

In the pre-Emancipation period no distinction was made between 'nation' and 'religious community'. The concept of Jewish identity was synthetic. From Biblical times they had regarded themselves as an *am*, *umma*, *goy*, *leom* (nation, people), though not in its exclusively secular connotation. They considered themselves also to be an *am kadosh* (a holy people) chosen by the Lord and bearing a particular religious message. They were pioneers of monotheism, yet their religion had all the national attributes acquired in specific historical conditions. Their God was a universal God, and also a Jewish God. The national and religious elements in the concept of their identity were inextricably interwoven. As Sir Isaiah Berlin put it, 'The Jews were a unique combination of religion, race and people that . . . could not be classified in normal terms.'[2]

The absence of a state of their own had no appreciable effect on their self-identification. In defiance of all precedent they went on living as a distinct entity, building on the foundations of their historical legacy and faith in their eventual redemption. Dispersed over all countries and without a territory, they existed as a corporate body, as *Klal Israel*, bound by common tradition, mutual responsibility, and the hope of Return. The secular elements in their communal life were too many to qualify them merely as a religious sect. The ghetto, in the Middle Ages, formed an extra-territorial entity, almost a state within a state. The Jews had their juridical and taxation system and even their own police. Wherever they were, they carried with them the values and characteristics which distinguish one people from another. Thus the community itself became for its members a spiritual home, a substitute for the real homeland which they had lost—a unique phenomenon in human history. But despite their extraordinary gift for adaptation, they never accepted the abnormal conditions of a national-religious existence in the Diaspora as final. The *Galuth* (exile) was suffered as a penance. The ultimate goal of their aspirations remained immutably the Land of Israel. It dominated their minds and hearts, exerting the most comprehensive, potent, and formative influence in their life. It abounded in Jewish liturgy and kept the Messianic idea alive. Even a cool-headed philosopher like Maimonides treated the laws regulating the Jewish state to be re-established in Palestine (*Hilhoth Malhuth*) as an integral part of his great legal code.

Emancipation brought in its wake a radical departure from traditional concepts and aspirations. The primary object was to gain acceptance in Western society. Since it was implicitly stipulated that equality of rights could be conferred upon Jews only after they had discarded their peculiarities and renounced their identity, the consequences were soon to become manifest. What centuries of deprivation and persecution had failed to do, the dazzling light of emancipation achieved. Yet the choice was limited. The words of Clermont-Tonnère, a liberal Deputy in the French National Assembly: '*Aux Juifs comme nation nous ne donnons rien; aux Juifs comme individuels nous donnons tout*' [reiterated by Abbé Grégoire, an ardent advocate of Emancipation] reveal how restricted was the application of Liberty. Only Frenchmen were entitled to enjoy the fruits of the Revolution, not aliens.

The slogan was consistent with the new doctrine of nationality. The nation became omnipotent, all-embracing, the supreme entity through which an individual could obtain satisfaction, and to which, conversely, he owed his undivided loyalty and allegiance. The old maxim *cuius regio eius religio* was now superseded by the principle of *cuius regio eius natio*. Ethnic minorities and alien elements had to be integrated and fused with the main body or weeded out to prevent disunity. In France, not only Jews but also the Bretons, the Basques, the Flemish and the German-speaking Alsatians had to fall into line and become French. Since the trend towards nationalism went hand in hand with political loyalty, it is clear how little choice was left to dissenters. The Jews, in any case, were in no position to opt out. Since the collapse of the Shabbetai Zevi movement, Messianic Redemption seemed a remote prospect; the spiritual diet of rabbinical learning could hardly counter the irresistible attraction of the

Enlightenment, and there was no possibility of going back to the ghetto. Jewish autonomy could be maintained in the framework of the feudal system but had no place in a centralised nation-state. On the other hand, the slogans of the French Revolution were closely akin to the humanist principles of Judaism and, having a direct relevance to their civic status, evoked an enthusiastic response among French Jewry.

When an assembly of Jewish notables was convened by Napoleon on 30 May 1806 and asked bluntly, among twelve specific questions, whether French Jews, who according to law enjoyed equality of rights with other citizens, considered themselves to be Frenchmen and regarded France as their country, the answer was in the affirmative. The notables were naturally sensitive lest doubt be cast on the patriotism of their community. They were, however, on solid ground when assuring him that it had always been a cardinal principle of Judaism to abide by the laws of the State. Notwithstanding this reassurance, ten months later (on 8 February 1807) Napoleon summoned the Great Sanhedrin, the first since the destruction of the Temple by the Romans, eighteen hundred years before, to confirm the notables' answer and make it binding upon Jewry. The Sanhedrin made the momentous decision to differentiate between the religious and political provisions of Mosaic law: whilst the former were absolute and immutable, the latter, which had been established for the Land of Israel, were no longer applicable. Since the destruction of their state by the Romans, Jews had ceased to be a polity and no longer constituted a national entity. They were henceforth 'neither a nation within a nation, nor cosmopolitan'; they were an integral part of the nations among whom they lived and entitled to claim the same rights and discharge the same duties as their fellow-citizens, from whom they differed only in religion.[3]

It would be incorrect to conclude that the Sanhedrin's affirmations were given under duress[4] or that their performance could be simply dismissed as opéra bouffe. On the other hand, it is legitimate to ask whether the participants grasped what was at stake. 'The ultimate aim of the Napoleonic system was the destruction of the nationality of the subject peoples', the Spaniards, the Germans, and others,[5] and in his drive for denationalisation Napoleon did not overlook the Jews; it is ironic that only in their case could the French Emperor congratulate himself on a notable success. The resolutions adopted by the Great Sanhedrin, though meant primarily for local consumption and the territories occupied by the French troops, became the cornerstone on which the battle for Jewish emancipation in the Western world was fought. They were confirmed by the conferences of Reform Rabbis in Germany in 1845 and in the United States in 1869, and furnished Lord Macaulay with a powerful argument against the opponents of the political enfranchisement of Jews in Britain.[6] The new doctrine produced a radical re-definition of Jewish identity in the West and threatened the maintenance of the historical continuity so jealously guarded through the generations. It deepened the gulf between West and East European Jewry. It cut a great divide between those who saw in social integration with Gentile society the only salvation for their co-religionists, and those who believed that the individual's gain was the community's loss, that the process of assimilation was bound to loosen the bonds and destroy the internal coherence of Judaism and lead to its gradual extinction.

The concept that the Jews are a religious community struck root also in England. This is surprising, for in England political conditions and the intellectual milieu were completely different from those in France or Germany, and the formula of 'British citizen of Jewish persuasion' served no practical purpose. There was no such identification between state and nation as preached on the other side of the Channel; diversity rather than homogeneity was the natural pattern of British society. British nationality was of a composite character and proved elastic enough to accommodate not only the loyal Scots and Welsh but even the defiant Irish. British nationalism was less assertive, more humane and tolerant of differences. It sprang from a totally different system of political thought and was based upon individual liberties and self-government. Its early growth was stimulated by the seventeenth-century Puritan revolution and was deeply influenced by the Old Testament. Hence the identification of the English people with ancient Israel and the appeal of the idea of the Restoration of Israel to the Holy Land.[7]

In Britain civil disabilities were not dependent, as they were in France, on the implied or expressed undertaking that the Jews renounce their specific identity. That the struggle for emancipation was so protracted[8] was due rather to the fact that the English were a conservative people and sought to retain the old concept of a Christian polity, than to anti-Jewish prejudice. It was the formula 'on the true faith of a Christian' in the Oath of Abjuration which kept Jews out of Parliament, not their identity. Once the new philosophy of a secular state triumphed, all previous reservations, regardless of denomination, were swept away. Although it was suggested in Parliament that because they were a nation, with the idea of a return to Palestine commanding their supreme loyalty, the Jews were *ipso facto* disqualified from enfranchisement, such voices were few and by no means representative. Lord Palmerston's recognition of the

Jews as a nation (bound by a world-wide unity like a 'Free Mason fraternity')[9] complemented his staunch support of their emancipation in England. Moses Montefiore's dedicated service on behalf of his people in various countries earned him a knighthood from Queen Victoria, whilst Disraeli's romantic pride in his Jewish race in no way hampered his advance to the highest office. Nor did Herbert Samuel's Zionist convictions prejudice his career. The British Government did not interfere with the internal affairs of the Jewish community and it was more in imitation of the pattern evolving among their co-religionists on the Continent, rather than under the pressure of British public opinion, that British Jews embraced the concept of 'religious community'. This was strange because they were under no obligation to abide by the resolutions of the Great Sanhedrin, and it is equally strange that the historian Lucien Wolf should have held the contrary belief[10] since when at war with Great Britain, one of Napoleon's reasons for convening the Sanhedrin was to drive a wedge between French and British Jewry.

It was the Chief Rabbi, Dr Herman Adler, who more than any of his predecessors or successors was responsible for propagating the message that 'the great bond which unites Israel is not one of race, but the bond of a common religion'. In 1878 he wrote:[11]

When we dwelt in the Holy Land we had a political organisation of our own; we had judges and kings to rule over us. But ever since the conquest of Palestine by the Romans, we have ceased to be a body politic: we are citizens of the country in which we dwell. We are simply Englishmen, or Frenchmen, or Germans, as the case may be, certainly holding particular theological tenets and practising special religious ordinances; but we stand in the same relation to our countrymen as any other religious sect, having the same stake in the national welfare and the same claim on the privileges and duties of citizens. To [the] question, What is the political bearing of Judaism? I would reply that Judaism has no political bearing whatever . . . religion is the main bond.

This was the classic doctrine of the French Sanhedrin. Its transplantation to English soil seems all the more astonishing when we consider that twenty years had elapsed since Baron de Rothschild took his seat in Parliament and that there was no danger of the Act for the removal of Jewish disabilities being repealed. Rabbi Adler carried his message much further than Anglo-Jewry had ventured even at the height of their struggle for equality of rights. Thus in 1847 the Jewish Association for the Removal of Civil and Religious Disabilities proclaimed amongst other things:[12]

> Far be it from us . . . to renounce our faith in prophecy . . . for a
> return to Palestine . . . or to resign our hope in the eventual
> restoration of Israel. . . . The revelation which bids us cherish that
> hope, also commands us to promote the welfare of the land we
> live in . . . and to love the land of our birth . . . No one could
> charge us with lukewarm or divided allegiance. And we now say to
> you, give us the right to serve our country . . . and you will see
> whether our religious aspirations clash with our civil duties; whether
> our love of Zion will interfere with our love of England.

And yet Rabbi Adler's statement came to be regarded by Anglo-Jewry
during succeeding decades as the most authoritative interpretation of
Jewish history. It became an article of faith, a dogma in which, it was
believed, the whole edifice of emancipation rested. In the autumn of 1917,
when the Balfour Declaration was still hanging fire, it was quoted, much
to the discomfiture of the British Government, by Edwin Montagu and
Sir Philip Magnus, M.P., in their respective memoranda[13] as a peremptory
mandamus. The Zionists were fortunate in enjoying the unreserved support of both Rabbi Moses Gaster, the Haham of the Spanish and Portu-
guese Congregation and Dr Joseph Herman Hertz, Chief Rabbi of Great
Britain and the British Empire; both repudiated the doctrine enunciated
by Rabbi Adler.

Gaster's views were made known in 1916 in his essay 'Judaism—a
National Religion'.[14] Judaism was primarily a national religion.

> The concept of a mere religious confraternity . . . the claim to be
> Englishmen of the Jewish persuasion—that is, English by nationality
> and Jewish by faith—is an absolute self-delusion. . . . For the Jew
> faith is not a mere profession of spiritual truths or of dogmatic
> principles detached entirely from the historical evolution of the
> Jewish people as a nation; [it] is a profession of national and religious
> unity.

Such a definition, Gaster asserted, by no means cast doubt on the essential
loyalty of the Jews to the country of their adoption. Nor was it incompatible with the accepted concept of British nationality. Confusion reigned
only in the minds of those 'who did not know how to reconcile their
religious nationality with the duties and obligations of British citizenship'.

Gaster was following in distinguished footsteps. In modern times Moses
Hess was the first to protest in his *Rom und Jerusalem*[15] against the fallacy

that the Jews were a religious group. At the other end of the spectrum the Serbian Rabbi and Cabalist, Yehuda Alkalai, and the German-Polish Rabbi Zvi Hirsch Kalischer advanced the concept, revolutionary by the standards of their time, that the redemption of Israel should not be imagined as a sudden miracle of Divine grace. It would begin with the efforts of the Jews themselves. The resettlement of Palestine and cultivation of its soil fully accorded with Biblical law and the Jews were obliged to initiate the preparatory stages in anticipation of the Messianic times.[16]

Alkalai and Kalischer produced hardly a ripple among their contemporaries, whilst Moses Hess remained a prophet without much honour in his own generation. It was not before the appearance of Herzl's *Der Judenstaat* (1896), in which he proclaimed boldly: 'We are a people, one people'[17] that the leading circles in Western Jewry were thrown off balance. By endeavouring to identify Zionist ambitions with the interests of the European Powers, Herzl made nonsense of the charge that Zionism was unpatriotic. But in fact a confrontation with the assimilated was no part of his policy. The Jewish state was meant for those who could not or would not assimilate. Ironically, a Jewish state could even be an advantage to the assimilationists, for a sizeable reduction in the number of Jews in the Diaspora would create more favourable conditions for assimilation for those who preferred to stay.[18]

It was the East European Jews who were hostile to assimilation. Cooped up in their Pale of Settlement, they formed a compact and homogeneous community. Degraded politically and economically, exposed to harsh governmental oppression and the prejudice of an ignorant populace, they developed a strong instinct of self-preservation and a vigorous inner life. Conscious of their separate ethnic individuality, they had a sense of moral superiority over their neighbourhood which made them impervious to external assimilating influences. It was here that revulsion against the ill effects of the trends in the West was at its strongest. Enlightened individuals and writers of the *Haskalah* movement[19] pointed untiringly to the corrosive influence of assimilation upon Jewish life. Yet it needed the shock of the pogroms of the 1880s to make Leo Pinsker, a deeply assimilated Jewish physician, despair of Russification and to write his well-known pamphlet *Auto-Emanzipation* (1882), a classic in Zionist literature.[20] It was, however, in Ahad Ha'am[21] that anti-assimilationism found its most eloquent exponent. Of a broad humanitarian outlook, he was intolerant of what he considered a gross distortion of a historical heritage. Reform Judaism[22] was an artificial response to environmental pressures. Trimmed to suit the expectations and codes of a non-Jewish milieu, it cut itself off from the sources of Jewish tradition and common purpose. The cloak of their political freedom concealed moral and intellectual slavery; the privileges were not worth the price.

> I may not be emancipated [he protested]. I at least can remember Jerusalem . . . without being asked what Zion is to me, or I to Zion . . . I at least know 'why I remain a Jew' . . . I have no reason for concealing . . . beliefs and opinions which I have inherited from my ancestors . . . or denying them, for deceiving others or myself. And this spiritual freedom . . . I would not exchange or barter for all the emancipation in the world.[23]

Nineteen years later Ahad Ha'am returned to the attack: with assimilation 'there is no room . . . for compromise'.[24] He felt that the only chance for Jewry to survive in the modern world was by means of a liberal nationalism based on the ideals of the Hebrew prophets. Unlike that of Herzl and Pinsker, Ahad Ha'am's Zionism was a response not to anti-Semitism but to assimilation in the West and to ossified rabbinism in the East. Herzl and Pinsker saw the solution in a voluntary mass exodus of Jews from European countries. Ahad Ha'am, by contrast, doubted whether Palestine could absorb more than a fraction of the Jewish people. And since the Diaspora was to remain a permanent feature of Jewish life and was to contain the majority of Jewish people all over the world, the problem was not *Judennot*, as Herzl believed, but the 'plight of Judaism'. Hence the need for a 'national spiritual centre in Palestine', which would serve as a cultural power-house to restore the cohesion and sense of purpose of the Jewish people, and to counter assimilation. 'The influence of the centre', Ahad Ha'am wrote, 'will strengthen the national consciousness in the Diaspora . . . and will fill our spiritual life with a national content which will be true and natural'.[25]

Ahad Ha'am's concept presupposed that the Diaspora Jews would willingly submit to the cultural hegemony of the Palestinian centre and respond to its rejuvenating and cleansing influence. Whatever the practicability of this idea, it was inherently incompatible with the assimilationist point of view. Yet so long as it remained theoretical, few if any pundits cared to cross swords with Ahad Ha'am. Reserved and socially isolated in his fourteen years in London (1908–22), he had hardly left a mark on the public life of the Anglo-Jewish community.[26] But the moment the concept of nationality entered the realm of practical politics it became an explosive issue. We shall see how much the ideological theme propagated by his disciples affected the relationship between the Zionists and the Conjoint Foreign Committee[27] and, rather than cementing the bond, served as a disruptive factor within the Anglo-Jewish community.

One of the Zionist leaders on whom Ahad Ha'am made a particular mark was Weizmann. Ahad Ha'am was Weizmann's mentor and friend. Weizmann venerated him and consulted him at every turn of his political career.[28] Eclectic in his approach, Weizmann could accommodate both Herzl's vision of Jewish statehood and Ahad Ha'am's spiritual Zionism. But it was from the latter that he inherited his aversion to assimilation. It was not until he encountered personally the phenomenon of 'Germans of Jewish persuasion' during his student days in Germany, that Weizmann was able to appreciate the full meaning of Ahad Ha'am's essay 'Slavery in the Midst of Freedom'.[29] So traumatic was the experience that he came to detest the assimilationists, whether socialist,[30] or bourgeois as in Britain. His contempt for the wealthy assimilated English Jews stood in inverse ratio to his deep admiration for England. He preferred, as Richard Crossman noted, 'the company of British Gentiles to that of assimilated Jews'. 'Every Jew' was to Weizmann 'a potential Zionist, and those whose Jewish patriotism was qualified by any other national loyalty were to be pitied or despised.'[31] They were simply 'the wrong kind of Jews'.[32] Some of his British friends were astonished at the vehemence of his feelings. 'No one admires Weizmann more than I do,' Ormsby-Gore wrote to Hankey when accompanying the Zionist Commission in Palestine in 1918, 'but he is at times too fanatical and too partisan and uncompromising. He wants all Jews to be 100% Zionist and few even here can stand quite so strong a dose.'[33] Peculiar as Weizmann's thorough-going nationalism seemed to a non-Jew, it was not at all out of tune with his mental predisposition; his Jewishness and his Zionism were interwoven. 'You cannot destroy the second without destroying the first.'[34] That the Jews constituted a nationality was to him 'strictly a question of fact . . . attested by the conviction of the overwhelming majority of Jews throughout all ages . . . shared by non-Jews in all countries'.[35] 'To deny this fact—to believe, as some highly intelligent Western Jews were inclined to do, that the Jews were or could collectively become entirely and utterly German, French, English, different from their fellow-citizens only in religious belief . . . was a profound and fatal illusion which the rest of the world did not entertain.'[36] To define the Jews simply as a 'religious group' was to disregard the very nature of the Jewish religion.[37]

Weizmann's premonition that the representatives of assimilated English Jewry would stand in his way[38] was fortified by Ahad Ha'am. Early in the war he strongly advised the Zionists against co-operation with assimilated circles on the Palestine programme. The Anglo-Jewish leadership, he wrote Weizmann in November 1914, 'would protest against any semblance of the national character of our enterprise and would endeavour to degrade it to a level of philanthropy and assistance to destitute Jews.'[39] Six days later, in a combative mood, Weizmann frankly advised some of his closest friends: 'The gentlemen of the type of L.W. have to be told that we and not they are the masters of the situation; that if we come to them, it is only and solely because we desire to show the world a *united* Jewry, and we don't want to expose them as self-appointed leaders . . . I am going to fight openly *sans trève* but before opening the fight we will attempt everything to rope these Jews in and work with them harmoniously. If they don't come they will be removed from their pedestal.'[40]

The gentleman foremost in Weizmann's mind was Lucien Wolf, a journalist and historian of distinction, then Secretary of the Conjoint Foreign Committee.[41] Equally at home in Jewish and international affairs, Wolf was more than the Committee's spokesman. He was its mainspring and theoretician, but his intellectual abilities were outweighed by some serious shortcomings in public life. Conceited and suspicious, he failed to inspire confidence. Search for a compromise was not his habit, and wielding a sharp pen he could at times be a formidable controversialist. However, his dogmatism told against him. Equally self-defeating was his opposition to Zionism.

Zionism was his *bête noire*, but not during its early stages. In 1896 he reviewed Herzl's *Der Judenstaat* favourably.[42] Herzl's personality left upon him an indelible impression. 'I shall not soon forget how strongly I was impressed when I first met Herzl . . . four years ago', he wrote in the *Daily Graphic* of 16 August 1900. 'Would the creation of a Jewish State prove an adequate solution?' he asked, to which he unhesitatingly replied: 'We could not but assent.' The proceedings of the Fourth Zionist Congress in London in 1900 commanded his sympathetic attention. He described Herzl as 'the Modern Moses', 'a new Prophet' and 'the leader of the chosen People who is . . . to restore the glories of the Kingdom of Judea'. The Zionist Organization was 'a sort of Jewish revolt', and should the European Powers one day ponder more seriously the solution of the Jewish problem, 'Herzl will lead his Zionists to the Promised Land'.[43]

Three years later, in a letter to *The Times* (8 September 1903), he was still of the opinion that, should the scheme for a Jewish State under the protection of the Powers become real, 'the whole Jewish people should strain their utmost . . . to make such a State a social and political success'. Yet one year later he turned his back on Zionism, delivering a wholesale attack on its very foundations. Zionism, he said, was trying to 're-nationalise' Judaism; it was based on a 'misconception of the religious mission of Israel', it was 'an ally of anti-Semitism', 'a negation of the policy of emancipation'. The Jews, he concluded, formed 'merely a religious community'.[44]

Whatever the explanation of Wolf's *volte face*, the similarity between his views as expressed in the *Jewish Quarterly Review* and those of its editors, Israel Abrahams and Claude G. Montefiore,[45] is striking. The more involved Wolf became in public life, the more noticeable became his identification with the orthodox position of Anglo-Jewry. This is not to say that he or other Anglo-Jewish leaders were totally insensitive to the fate of Palestine. 'It is a question in which our co-religionists take the profoundest interest', Alexander and Montefiore, the co-Presidents of the Conjoint Foreign Committee, told Sir Edward Grey in 1916.[46] The Anglo-Jewish Association indeed, like its counterparts in France and Germany, the *Alliance Israélite Universelle* and the *Hilfsverein der deutschen Juden*, had done excellent work in setting up schools in Palestine before the War and in initiating other fruitful ventures which commended themselves to the Zionists. They were not unmindful of the historical association with Palestine, but their activities bore a strictly philanthropic character. Nationalism was anathema. It was in their eyes retrogressive, a gratuitous gift to anti-Semites and prejudicial to emancipation.

Early in the War differences with the Zionists seemed not at all unbridgeable. Counting on the resolution of the Tenth Zionist Congress in 1911[47] (which suppressed the political aspect of Zionism in favour of cultural and economic policy), Wolf concluded that friendly relations between the Conjoint Committee and the Zionists could be established.[48] Preliminary conversations, with Harry Sacher on 17 November 1914 and a month later with Sacher and Weizmann, passed in a friendly atmosphere. However, both parties were under a misapprehension: Weizmann in assuming that 'an entente between the nationalist sections of Jewry and their former opponents . . . might be possible',[49] and Wolf, in taking the meaning of the term 'cultural' literally. For 'cultural' was only a euphemism for national indoctrination,[50] and this was the last thing Wolf desired.

The differences became apparent during a conference on 14 April 1915. The Zionists were represented by Dr Tschlenow and Sokolow, as delegates of the Inner Actions Committee, Rabbi Gaster, Vice-President of the Zionist Congress, Joseph Cowen, President of the English Zionist Federation, and Herbert Bentwich, President of the Order of Ancient Maccabeans. D. L. Alexander, C. G. Montefiore, H. S. Q. Henriques and Lucien Wolf represented the Conjoint Foreign Committee. Neither Leopold de Rothschild nor Dr Weizmann was able to attend.

Dr Tschlenow's opening speech reflected deep anxiety for the millions of his Jewish countrymen made homeless in the Russian war zone. An ominous upsurge of nationalism in Eastern Europe and the problem of refugees (which was bound to follow the termination of hostilities) weighed heavily on his mind. On the other hand, he believed that the future Peace Conference might give the Jews a unique opportunity to press their claims, and it was up to them to make themselves heard in unison. Rumania's persistent defiance of Article XLIV of the 1878 Treaty of Berlin was a reminder of the folly of relying solely on formal civic emancipation. Current events had fully vindicated the Zionist programme. The Russian Government and public opinion, Tschlenow asserted, approved of the Zionist aspirations; given the positive results of colonisation and the small size of the native Arab population, Palestine could absorb millions of immigrants, and should the country fall within the British sphere of influence, the Jews might be able to develop a viable Jewish Commonwealth.[51] Fears that such an outcome would diminish the prospects for emancipation in East European countries were unfounded. Tschlenow admitted that there would always be Jews living outside Palestine, but a centre was necessary, 'a metropolis in which the cultural, religious and national traditions could be developed'.

The representatives of the Conjoint Committee were not impressed. They dismissed the Zionists' prognostication as too pessimistic and thought that it was none of their business 'to promote the establishment of a Jewish commonwealth, merely in fulfilment of Jewish Nationalist aspirations'. Their aim was to obtain for their co-religionists full rights of citizenship in the lands in which they were still oppressed, and to protect them in the enjoyment of such rights where they were already in possession of them. The Zionist plan was 'reactionary'. The idea of a Jewish nationality, the talk of a Jew 'going home' to Palestine, raised the vexed question of dual nationality and highlighted the 'perpetual alienage of Jews everywhere outside Palestine'. Nor did Zionism offer a comprehensive solution. Emigration to Palestine, even if a million Jews were to settle there within a decade, would hardly diminish the Jewish population in the Pale or relieve their economic distress. The hearts of the Russians and the Poles were unlikely to be softened by Jewish emigration, whilst the probability of giving an opening to the advocates of wholesale deportation to Palestine was quite real.

The Conjoint Committee disliked the Zionist scheme for a Chartered Company. It would in their opinion invest the Jewish colonists in Palestine with exclusive privileges not extended to the rest of the population. Such differential treatment was incompatible with democracy and detrimental to the struggle for Jewish liberties all over the world. 'How could we ask for equal rights for the Jews in Russia and Rumania if we claimed special rights for the Jews in Palestine?' The Zionists' invitation to co-operate was therefore rejected, but the door was left open for a rapprochement should the Zionists modify their views and eliminate the doctrine of nationalism and 'exclusive rights' from their programme.[52]

Although the Zionists were reluctant to precipitate an internal controversy, they had to make their position clear. Jewish nationality, they maintained, was a fact that could not be denied or suppressed, and at a time when the rights of small nationalities were being vigorously championed it was inconceivable to expect them to abandon Jewish national claims. The contention of the Conjoint Committee that recognition of Jews as a nation would stimulate anti-Semitism was not borne out by conclusive evidence and there were numerous historical instances to indicate that antagonism towards Jews was provoked by assimilation. 'The only way to satisfy anti-Semitism is to cease to exist.' Zionism and emancipation were not incompatible. However commendable the fight for equality of rights, they could not rest content with that objective alone. The object of Zionism was to remove the stigma of homelessness from the Jewish people. As for the Chartered Company, it was merely an instrument of colonisation, and all the inhabitants of Palestine were to benefit from its activities. Any talk of 'exclusiveness' or intention to impose restrictions or prohibitive measures against Arab Mohammedans or Christians was sheer nonsense.[53] If Sokolow, the author of this letter, hoped to narrow the differences he was to be disappointed. The Conjoint Foreign Committee remained adamant in their belief that their course was the right one.[54] With diagnoses so divergent, an entente between the two parties seemed far off.

4   The Jews and the War

With the inter-Jewish controversy unresolved, each of the parties felt at liberty to make independent overtures to the British Government. Weizmann deliberately bypassed Wolf. Encouraged by his meetings with Lloyd George and Balfour,[1] he called on 18 August 1915 on Lord Robert Cecil, the Under-Secretary of State for Foreign Affairs. Cecil was quick to detect Weizmann's desire to win him over to the idea of the restoration of Jews to Palestine under a British Protectorate. It was however the sufferings of his co-religionists in Russia that prompted Weizmann to press his views so urgently. Their position as a minority who were discriminated against and exposed to persecution was an anomaly which, he claimed, could be rectified only by allowing them to live in a country of their own. 'I am not romantic except that Jews must always be romantic [since] for them the reality is too terrible.' The enthusiasm with which Weizmann spoke made an impact on Cecil.[2] The Zionist idea was not new to him[3] and judging from later remarks, it commanded his sympathy, but in practical terms the interview did not yield immediate results. Weizmann left with the impression that Cecil 'was disposed to agree',[4] but this was not so. In 1915–16 the protection of Palestine formed no part of British desiderata and there was little or nothing that the British could do to alleviate the situation of the Jews in Russia.

It was with good reason that Weizmann expressed anxiety. Since the outbreak of the war the position of Russian Jews had been deteriorating steeply. In August of the previous year Grand Duke Nicholas, the Russian Commander-in-Chief, ordered wholesale evacuation of the western war zone[5] and by spring 1915 hundreds of Jewish communities were ruined. Fourteen Russian and Polish provinces and a large part of Galicia lost their Jewish inhabitants. The number of refugees exceeded 500,000. During the great Austrian and German offensive in May–September 1915 an additional half-million or more were driven out at short notice from their homes, bringing the total of refugees to a million and a half.[6] Expulsions *en masse* assumed such proportions that they were said to overshadow the

Spanish exodus.[7] By December 1915 the figures reached 2,700,000 and five months later 3,300,000.[8] The Jews were not the only ones in the war zone to suffer, but they were far more severely affected than their Christian fellow-citizens. However, it was not their distress, though growing in intensity and volume, that pained them so much as the humiliating attitude of the Russian authorities who accused them *in toto* of being spies, at a time when about 400,000 Jewish soldiers were fighting in the Russian army.

Enlightened individuals such as Baron Rosen, a former Russian Ambassador in Washington, warned his countrymen that the inconsiderate treatment of various minorities had done immense harm to Russia's cause; and it was with an eye to American public opinion that a reform was soon introduced in the Duma. The formation of the moderate block was followed by an announcement on the 'complete and decisive cessation of all religious persecution', abolition of the Jewish Pale, freedom of choice of professions and other privileges.[9] However, the execution of this liberal legislation was disappointing. The reform remained on paper.[10] The British Vice-Consul in Moscow, Bruce Lockhart, was of the opinion that the Russian Government had been 'assiduously fostering anti-Semitic sentiments among the people, probably with a view to providing a safety valve for . . . some of the discontent which would otherwise fall on itself.'[11]

Such an attitude turned every Jew in the world into Russia's enemy, whilst the Allies felt the backwash. Balfour was astonished when meeting Weizmann on 12 December 1914 that such 'a friend of England could be so anti-Russian when Russia was doing so much to help England win the war.' Weizmann thereupon pointed to 'the pogroms, and the expulsions which made every Russian victory a horror for the Jews—this while hundreds of thousands of Jews were fighting in the Russian Army'.[12] One reason why the Jews in Rumania sympathised with Germany was that she 'was fighting Russia, [whom] they hated'.[13] Even in Egypt the Anglo-Russian Alliance was 'distasteful to Muslims and to the powerful Austro-Jewish families of Alexandria',[14] though to each of them for different reasons. In London, David Alexander, President of the Board of Deputies of British Jews, and Claude Montefiore, President of the Anglo-Jewish Association, warned the British Government that Russia was playing into the enemy's hands. In sharp contrast, the German army, in their zone of occupation, freed the Jews from all disabilities, brought them relief and promised 'ultimate political liberation'; a policy that had paid them substantial dividends. 'A glance at any batch of American newspapers showed that the Germans have found among American Jewry [a] not unimportant ally.'[15]

This statement was not far from the truth. So overwhelming was the pro-German predisposition among American Jews that Richard Gottheil, a Professor at Columbia University and a leading Zionist, was seriously reprimanded in public for having taken up the defence of the Allies.[16] He wrote to Lucien Wolf:[17]

> We have to proceed very carefully, because the ramifications of the German-Jewish bankers here are very wide and they have a splendid lever in the Russian happenings which they use to the greatest extent possible . . . Mr. Schiff . . . is secretly working in the cause of Germany. . . . Even the German Zionists had sent men over here to gain the support of their fellow Zionists for the German cause.

Gottheil, British-born and a member of the American Rights Committee, a movement which aimed to bring the United States in on the side of the Allies, was anxious to counter the ill effects of the German propaganda. He had reason to think that, should Russia modify her attitude towards her Jewish subjects, much of the ill-feeling stirred up by American Jews against the Allies would evaporate. But Sir Cecil Spring-Rice, the British Ambassador, to whom Gottheil aired his suggestion, doubted whether the British Government could act as Russia's adviser in this matter.[18]

No more successful in this respect was Oscar Straus, a former American Ambassador in Constantinople and a member of Theodore Roosevelt's administration. Should Russia liberalise her policy and grant her Jewish citizens equality of rights, 'the Jewish communities in the United States would be absolutely swept away', he told Sir Robert Borden, the Canadian Prime Minister.[19] Sir Robert agreed and Sir George Perley, Governor-General of Canada, also thought that Straus's suggestion pinpointed 'a very weighty matter', but in London Bonar Law, the Colonial Secretary, doubted whether Whitehall could convey such a suggestion to their Ally.[20]

The British regretted Russia's conduct but felt completely powerless to influence her. 'All this oppression, unscrupulous and stupid injustice', Sir Gilbert Parker, head of the Information Department, noted, 'has an unfavourable effect upon opinion in the United States,'[21] Lord Percy had pointed out earlier that two-thirds of Jewish papers in America published a manifesto against the export of arms to the Entente countries.[22] Reports about the ill-treatment of Jews in Russia filled Lord Robert Cecil with horror: 'The story is deplorable. Of course, the Russians are savages but they are also incredibly foolish. We can do nothing.' To which he added later: 'It might be pointed out to the Russian Minister of Finance that anti-

Semitism makes Jewish financial assistance to the allies very difficult to obtain, and this war may well turn on finance.' However, Sir Arthur Nicolson, Permanent Under-Secretary of State for Foreign Affairs, remained pessimistic: 'we can do nothing'.[23]

As a last resort, on 3 February 1916 Sir George Buchanan, the British Ambassador at St Petersburg, ventured to take the question up with the Tsar. Buchanan pointed out that the Jews were 'a very important factor in Great Britain, in the United States, and in other countries, and exercised a very powerful influence in the money markets of the world'. He thought it advisable for the Russian Government to conciliate Jewish public opinion: 'What Russia would require after the war was money and expert advice to develop her immense resources and to enlarge her industries.' But the Tsar was not responsive. 'It was rather a monologue, not a conversation.'[24]

If the British Ambassador ventured, against all diplomatic custom, to raise a subject relating to the internal situation of the host country, it was because, unlike the Sovereign himself, he must have been concerned about its ominous undercurrents. The heavier the toll of the war, the more reactionary the attitude of the ruling circles in Russia, the more widespread became political and economic discontent among the population. The most active agitation emanated from the Socialist party and the oppressed minority groups, amongst whom were the Jews. The Jews *qua* Jews could hardly pose a threat to the security of the State, but they were in a position to cause the Government considerable harm indirectly. The dissatisfaction of Jewish youth drove them into the Socialist movement, supplying it with leaders and agitators, and it was their pacifist propaganda which undermined morale and destroyed the will to fight on the side of the Entente against the Germans. This was Lockhart's prognostication,[25] gloomy enough to prompt Buchanan to convey his concern to Nicholas II but insufficient to cause the latter to reflect on the rights and wrongs of his policy. The situation seemed hopeless, but the need to placate the Jews, particularly in the United States, and win them over to the Entente, did not diminish.

That the British Government should have been so sensitive to American Jewish opinion is not surprising. The initial advantage that the Entente enjoyed in propaganda warfare was soon spent. The shock produced in America by the violation of Belgian neutrality was gradually giving way to irritation at British interference with American commerce. British 'navalism' became equated with German militarism. Particularly offensive to the Americans was the embargo imposed on American trade and export of munitions to Germany. By January 1916 the situation had worsened. 'The spirit of the Congress', Sir Cecil Spring-Rice told Grey, 'is somewhat menacing. . . . The general tone of debate in the Senate and in the House of Representatives was not favourable to us . . . violent attacks were made upon our commercial policy.' James Mann, Republican leader in the House of Representatives, went so far as to declare that he had 'much more fear . . . of war with England than . . . with Germany'. 'A most active propaganda is going on', Spring-Rice noted, 'and all the enemies of England have been marshalled against us . . . the Irish have lent their . . . power of political organization to Jews, Catholics and Germans'[26] and it was particularly important that the first of these groups should not be hostile to England. The influence of American Jews was known to be considerable. They were prominent in the press, in finance and in politics, and it was imprudent to disregard them, for, in contrast to the Germans and the Irish who were implacably anti-British, opinion among Jews was divided. That Jacob Schiff, their recognised leader and a prominent banker, was 'openly pro-German' was deplorable, but it was no less significant that the principal Jewish journalists in New York, the editors of the *Sun* and the *Times*, strongly favoured the Allies and did them 'a very great deal of good'. On the other hand, Jewish bankers acted on the whole for German interests:

> The German Embassy [Spring-Rice complained] . . . does most of its work through them. The most powerful German agent in Washington is Herr Warburg, of the great Hamburg house, who is the most influential member of the Federal Reserve Board and has immense influence in the Treasury. The German Ambassador is constantly with him and through him is supposed to exert a great deal of influence over the head of the Treasury . . . The Democratic party owing to its quarrel with the principal Christian bankers was thrown upon the Jewish . . . for financial support and advice. This gives the Jewish community a great influence in Washington, and in addition . . . as they control the majority of the advertisements, their influence is very great. It would be untrue to say that they are altogether on the German side but a very large number of them are and I am assured that some of the principal reasons for this is their dislike and fear of Russia.[27]

Here lay the crux of the matter. The anti-Russian sentiment among American Jews was of long standing. For the most part composed of immigrants from Russia or their descendants, they could not ignore the oppression of their co-religionists. So powerful was its effect that in January 1913 the United States Government was forced to terminate their

Commercial Treaty of 1832 with the Russian Government.[28] Even at the beginning of the war, when a movement was afoot to take advantage of Germany's withdrawal from Russian markets, the opposition of Jews proved an insurmountable obstacle to its renewal.[29] The alarming news of the treatment of their kin in the Russian war zone in 1914–16 exacerbated their feelings. But what could the British Government do?

It was Dr Horace Kallen, a Professor at Wisconsin University and an ardent Zionist, who first put to the Foreign Office an alternative method of winning over the American Jews to the Entente: should the Allies issue a statement 'analogous to the Teutonic announcements . . . favouring Jewish rights in every country, and a very veiled suggestion concerning nationalization in Palestine',[30] it would, he was convinced, 'more than counterbalance German promises . . . and would give a natural outlet for the spontaneous pro-English, French, and Italian sympathies of the Jewish masses.' He urged the British to despatch suitable emissaries to New York to outbid German propaganda.[31] The Foreign Office was favourably disposed, but no suitable candidate for the job could be named; Lucien Wolf seemed unsuitable.[32]

That Palestine was close to the heart of American Jewry, the Foreign Office was well aware. It was in deference to their sentiments that, in conjunction with the French, the British Government made considerable concessions, granting freedom of passage to United States warships carrying supplies for Palestine. Impressed by America's persistent efforts to assist Jewish settlement, Whitehall consented also to the remittance of funds collected by British Jews; and when Grey was reminded that among the beneficiaries of the charity there might also be some of Ottoman nationality, he dismissed it lightly as a 'technical difficulty . . . counterbalanced by the favourable impression which would be produced in influential Jewish circles in the United States . . . and elsewhere'.[33] The British displayed goodwill also towards Russian Jews expelled by the Turkish authorities in Palestine in December 1914; the refugees were allowed to stay in Alexandria[34] throughout the war. But these gestures were mainly of a humanitarian nature. The idea of recognising Jewish national rights in Palestine, as broached by Horace Kallen, went much further. It required a major decision of policy. This the Foreign Office was not in a position to make immediately.

While Kallen's proposal was still under consideration, a scheme of an entirely different nature was expounded by Vladimir Jabotinsky.[35] Jabotinsky was a brilliant Russian journalist, a gifted writer, an impressive orator, and deeply assimilated to Russian culture. It was not until the pogroms of 1903 that he became an ardent Zionist. They kindled his zeal for Jewish self-defence, an idea that persisted throughout his political career. It found its first concrete expression during the First World War in the scheme for a Jewish Legion. With Turkey's entry into the war—he was then serving as a roving correspondent of the liberal daily *Russkie Vedomosti*—he became convinced that the only hope for the restoration of Palestine lay in the dismemberment of the Ottoman Empire.

Following the arrival of the first refugees in Alexandria in December 1914 (after they had been expelled by Djemal Pasha, the Commander of the Ottoman IV Army), Jabotinsky suggested the formation of a Jewish military unit to fight for the liberation of Palestine. Over six hundred and fifty men volunteered but the scheme foundered when General Sir John Maxwell, the Officer Commanding in Egypt, made it clear that no offensive on the Palestinian front was contemplated. Moreover, the Army Act prohibited the enlistment of foreign nationals for active service. Instead Maxwell proposed the formation of a non-combatant transport unit for the Turkish Mediterranean front. Jabotinsky rejected the alternative and left for Europe 'to try to find other generals willing to support him'.

Twelve years later he confessed that he had been mistaken.[36] The unit, which became known as the Zion Mule Corps, was noted for its excellent work which gained the approbation of its commanding officers. General Sir Ian Hamilton, shortly after relinquishing his post as Commander-in-Chief of the Mediterranean Expeditionary Force, wrote to Jabotinsky:[37]

> From the outset I have been much interested in the Zion Mule
> Corps. I liked the look of the men and have always taken special
> trouble to keep the unit on its legs . . . The men have done extremely
> well, working their mules calmly under heavy shell[fire] . . . and
> thus showing a more difficult type of bravery than the men in the
> front line, who had the excitement of the combat to keep them
> going.

But the greatest admirer of the Mule Corps was Colonel John Henry Patterson, its Commander.[38] It was Patterson who put the idea of the Legion to General Birdwood, the Officer Commanding at Cape Helles in Gallipoli. Realising how useful such a unit would be, Birdwood sent Patterson to London to assist Jabotinsky in his efforts,[39] but the difficulties proved far greater than one might have expected. Kitchener was opposed to any kind of 'fancy regiments'[40] and Jabotinsky was told that his proposal could not be entertained. Yet opinion at the War Ministry was by no means unanimous. Leopold Amery, at that time serving on the General

Staff, was attracted by the project. 'In view of the fact that anti-Russian feeling has rather lobbed Jewry, at large, to the Boches,' he wrote to Lord Robert Cecil, 'this might be a very useful demonstration in the opposite sense, and I think it would be worthwhile for you to see Patterson and see how far the F.O. could support him.'[41] But the Foreign Office considered that the matter fell within the purview of the War Office, which was not at all favourably disposed. 'There are some military objections to and distinct administrative difficulties in the formation of a Jewish Foreign Legion,' H. J. Creedy, Kitchener's Private Secretary, observed, 'but we feel there is a wider question of policy which influences us against the scheme. Is it not likely that this Corps may, in some way, be brought into connection with the Zionist movement?'[42] The consideration at the War Office, it appears, was not military but political.

Patterson was not discouraged. The Zion Mule Corps, the first Jewish unit to go into battle since the days of the Maccabees, had fired the imagination of Jews and non-Jews, and he had received many encouraging letters, notably from Theodore Roosevelt, the American ex-President. The raising of a Jewish force, Patterson was convinced, 'would resound throughout the world and the moral and material benefit would be enormous'. Moreover, the landing of such a force on Palestinian shores, 'would be a signal for an uprising of 40,000 Jews, who would, at once, destroy railways, bridges, roads . . . and do all the damage possible to the Turkish lines of communication'. But even if the Jewish Division never left Britain, the very fact that England 'recognized Jewish nationality, would in itself be a great asset. I hear,' he added caustically, 'that the War Office will be opposed to the scheme, but then the War Office is always opposed to any and every innovation. In a question of policy, I consider that the hands of the War Office should be forced if necessary.'[43]

Whatever the rights or wrongs of Patterson's charge, he was surely over-optimistic, if he believed that the Foreign Office would force the issue. 'From the F.O. point of view,' Cecil noted, 'there is a good deal to be said for Patterson's proposal. But after knowing what he has to say, I feel it is really a matter for W.O.'[44]

The Information Department of the Foreign Office took greater interest. Both E. A. Gowers, its Director, and Charles Masterman, his assistant, were impressed by Jabotinsky;[45] Jabotinsky suggested that as the British Government was unable to influence the situation in Russia, the only means to counter German propaganda among the Jews was through Zionism. It could form a *point d'appui* for the Allies, and the formation of a Jewish Legion could serve as an interim measure. Thus, without binding themselves officially with regard to the future of Palestine, the British would strengthen the belief that with an Allied victory Zionist aspirations would have a fair chance of realisation. He hoped that the Legion, enrolled from British-born as well as foreign Jews resident in England and France, would reach the size of a brigade.[46]

But the decision did not rest with any of the Foreign Office departments. Jabotinsky enjoyed the support of distinguished British generals, as well as of Ambassador Benckendorff, and as a journalist he was doing his best to enlighten Russian public opinion about Britain's war effort. He therefore felt that his proposal had not been fairly considered. Although his letter was not calculated to suit British tastes, it prompted Cecil to make jointly with Amery yet another attempt to breach the barrier. They had little success. Jabotinsky was told that unless the military could be induced to change their mind, it was useless to proceed further.[47] But Amery did not give in. Two weeks later he advised Cecil to approach the War Office officially, keeping well in mind the specific character of the Unit. In the absence of any reference to Palestine, it would lose its attraction for the Jews. Their ambition, as he understood it, was to cross the Sinai Peninsula, 'marching in triumph into Jerusalem. And who would grudge them the sentiment?'[48]

Amery's appeal met with a ready response from Hugh J. O'Beirne, formerly Counsellor and Chargé d'Affaires at the British Embassy in St Petersburg and Sofia, and since November 1915 a senior member of the Foreign Office in London. He advised Cecil that the Foreign Office had no political objection to the raising of a Jewish corps. 'We are not at all irrevocably opposed to Zionism. It is mainly a question for the W.O.'[49] Cecil hardly needed any prodding. The issue coincided with top-level discussions about a pro-Zionist declaration[50] and the announcement of the formation of a Jewish regiment could not have come at a more auspicious moment. As a result of Cecil's probings the War Ministry waived their earlier objections. The only qualification was that the Legion had to be limited to British or Allied subjects, as recruitment of Jews from neutral countries, such as the United States, could lead to complications.[51]

At Wellington House, Charles Masterman was elated. He urged Lord Newton[52] to follow up the matter energetically. A volunteer Jewish Legion would be 'an enormous asset for our propaganda work in America' and would counter the perennial stories of persecution and outrages committed against the Jews by the Russians, so widely publicised in the pro-German press.[53] Lord Newton went fully into the matter but only to reach a dead end. He discussed the question with various authorities but could find no unanimity of opinion. The War Office reverted to its discouraging attitude and nothing could be done. This made Lord

Hardinge, the newly-appointed Permanent Under-Secretary of State for Foreign Affairs, finally decide to drop the matter.[54]

This was by no means the only difficulty. Jabotinsky also failed to rally his own people. Lucien Wolf was disdainful when Hubert Montgomery, the Deputy Director of the Department of Information, sounded him out about the Jewish Legion. The idea, Wolf noted, had never been brought before any official Jewish body and he thought that even among the Zionists it was regarded 'with a good deal of disfavour'. Anglo-Jewish leaders would do anything to help the Government to recruit foreign Jews of military age, but to segregate them in a specifically Jewish force was unthinkable. They feared that it could lead to 'all sorts of . . . complications'.[55] The Anglo-Jewish establishment deplored any manifestation of Jewish nationalism, and in July 1917 when the War Office was about to give its approval to the formation of a Jewish regiment, with its own badge representing King David's shield, so incensed were the anti-Zionists that the emblem had to be dropped and the name of the regiment altered to the Royal Fusiliers.[56]

As for the Zionists, their attitude was governed by the principle of strict neutrality adopted at the meeting of the Zionist Executive (Inner Actions Committee) in Copenhagen in December 1914. When the Zionist Council met there six months later, the idea of a Jewish Legion was condemned in unequivocal terms. Any overt pro-Entente demonstration by Zionists in any part of the world, let alone military action against Turkey, could it was feared, gravely jeopardise the position of the Palestinian Jews. Jabotinsky's campaign was denounced as an unforgivable breach of neutrality as a stab in the back. In England, too, with notable exceptions such as Chaim Weizmann, Joseph Cowen, and Dr M. D. Eder,[57] the Zionists dissociated themselves from the scheme. In the East End of London, where Jabotinsky hoped to obtain the bulk of volunteers, the atmosphere was hostile. Composed of fugitives from Russian oppression, they had little taste for fighting as comrades-in-arms of Tsarist troops. None the less, by the end of August 1917 a Jewish fighting unit did become a reality. But during 1916 it still looked as if the project was to be allowed to die. Yet Jabotinsky's arguments did not go by default. They helped to persuade the Foreign Office that support of Jewish national aspirations presented a sound card in propaganda warfare.

5 Jewish Palestine—A Propaganda Card

During the early part of the war Wolf had a built-in advantage over the Zionists. His role as the spokesman for the Conjoint Foreign Committee entitled him to some measure of formal authority. The Committee's relations with the British Government were of long standing and Wolf expected that his would be the commanding voice in all dealings between Anglo-Jewry and the Foreign Office. However, the odds were against him. His pleadings on behalf of the Russian Jews proved to be fruitless, and his subsequent probings into the Palestine question, ironically, proved ultimately to be to the Zionists' advantage rather than to his own.

Late in 1915 Wolf was reliably informed by his friends in Paris that the French Government had begun to interest itself in the Jewish question; Victor Basch, a Professor at the Sorbonne, had been dispatched in November of that year on a reconnaissance mission to the United States. His objective was to win over American Jewry, but soon after his arrival it became evident that ill-feeling towards Russia presented an insuperable obstacle. This was as true of Catholics and Protestants as it was of Jews. The result of this hostility was that France and England had to bear the odium. They were reproached for tolerating the persecutions of the Jews and labelled as Russia's indirect accomplices. To his relief, however, Basch discovered that among Jews there was still a considerable store of good-will towards France and England which could be cultivated. If the Allies pledged themselves to champion Jewish emancipation at the end of the war (in countries where they heretofore had been discriminated against) and guarantee freedom of immigration to Palestine with cultural and religious autonomy there, he was convinced that the pro-German trend would be effectively checked and the scales tipped in the Allies' favour.[1]

The French meant business. Soon after Basch's departure a *Comité de Propagande français auprés des Juifs neutres* was set up. Its name explains its purpose. It included Jewish and non-Jewish personalities prominent in politics, literature and science. Its president was Georges Lèygnes, Chairman of the Foreign Affairs Commission in the Chamber of Deputies, and one of its secretaries was Jacques Bigart, secretary of the Alliance Israélite

48

Universelle. The latter thought it advisable that a parallel Committee be formed in London.[2] Wolf was responsive although, as transpires from his letter to Lord Robert Cecil dated 16 December 1915, not without ulterior motives. To let the French monopolise the field was to him unthinkable. Having little to add to the ideas taking shape in Paris, he endeavoured now to outbid them in a sphere in which they were known to be lukewarm: Zionism.

Wolf was not a Zionist. He deplored the Jewish national movement. 'To bottle them up in a single national life would be tantamount to a renunciation of all their most sacred ideals, and would retard their political assimilation in the lands of their present dispersion.' But he was too much of a realist to ignore the shift in the balance of power which had taken place since the outbreak of the war. In America, he conceded, Zionism had captured Jewish opinion, and in view of the forthcoming American Jewish Congress, he thought it important that 'in any bid for Jewish sympathies . . . very serious account must be taken of the Zionist movement . . . This is the moment for the Allies to declare their policy in regard to Palestine.' In contrast to the Central Powers who, on account of their attachment to Turkey, were unable to take any initiative in this matter, the hands of the Allies were free. This did not mean that in order to steal the limelight they could 'promise to make a Jewish State of a land in which only a minority of the inhabitants are Jews', but there was still a great deal for them to say which he hoped would conciliate Zionist opinion:

If, for example, they would say that they thoroughly understand and sympathise with Jewish aspirations in regard to Palestine, and that when the destiny of the country comes to be considered, those aspirations will be taken into account, and that, in addition to equal rights with the remainder of the population, they would be guaranteed reasonable facilities for immigration and colonization, for a liberal scheme of local self-government for the existing colonies, for the establishment of a Jewish University, and for the recognition of the Hebrew language as one of the vernaculars of the land . . . they would sweep the whole American Jewry into enthusiastic allegiance to their cause.

He went on: 'What the [British] Zionists would especially like to know is that Great Britain will become mistress of Palestine.' In view of the French claims and of assurances said to have been given to France about Syria, the French understood to include Palestine as well, he doubted whether it would be possible to say this. But apart from the question of sovereignty he was confident that all other guarantees would suffice. What the Zionist feared above all was 'an increase of Russian influence, . . . or an International Commission, which would be soulless, if . . . not a hot-bed of demoralising intrigue'.[3]

The Foreign Office approved of Wolf's memorandum in principle but had reservations about his eligibility for the prescribed task. 'I agree about sending Jews [to the United States] . . . if they are the *right sort* and are carefully and selectively chosen', Sir Gilbert Parker wrote to Lord Robert Cecil.[4] In official circles there was an underlying feeling that if Zionism was the best bet to influence American Jews, then it would sound infinitely more convincing if the message was conveyed by a genuine Zionist than by one who appropriated their clothes out of expediency. But the Zionist Federation in Great Britain had at that time no *locus standi* at the Foreign Office and Weizmann and Sokolow were still unknown quantities.

Sir Cecil Spring-Rice discouraged the Foreign Office from pursuing Wolf's ideas. He feared that any relations with him or his Committee would involve the British Government in great difficulties with Russia. 'Better course is for Lord Reading and other prominent [British Jews] to explain . . . danger to Jews in Europe . . . [resulting from] active pro-German propaganda of American Jews.' It was only two weeks later, on receipt of his letter of 29 January, that Spring-Rice's intention became clearer. The majority of American Jews, he reiterated, were friendly to the Allies; some of the most powerful financiers, such as Otto Kahn, and most prominent journalists sided with them and against the Germans; the *New York Times* had done tremendous service, but hatred for Russia overrode all considerations. Thus, the net result was that Jewish influence was predominantly pro-German. What however seemed to him unforgivable was that some of the Jews had become involved not only in anti-Russian but also in anti-British propaganda. 'France and England cannot fail to draw their own conclusions', and their Jewish communities should be warned of the danger threatening them on account of anti-Ally feelings among some American Jews.'[5]

This was a most surprising conclusion. Whilst dismissing Wolf's scheme for propaganda, Spring-Rice's alternative proposal to hold the British and French Jews to ransom and make them responsible for the opinions of their co-religionists overseas, in a neutral country, smacked of an attitude which was alien to the British mind. Had it been made public, it would have had the opposite effect to that desired. Bewildered, Cecil turned for advice to Lord Eustace Percy, formerly on the staff of the British Embassy in Washington. Percy was aware of the preparations taking place at that time for the meeting of the American Jewish Congress and that its moving spirit was Louis D. Brandeis. Percy knew and admired Brandeis and regarded him as one of the leading Jews in the United States 'with the outlook of a statesman'. He therefore advised Sir Cecil to seek his counsel on suitable means of propaganda.[6] Whether Brandeis, despite his marked leaning towards the Allies, would have departed from his official policy of neutrality is doubtful, but no document has come to light so far to show that Spring-Rice made any attempt to follow Percy's advice. It was not until January 1918, following the Balfour Declaration, that he first met him. Even then he did not accord Brandeis a cordial reception. 'I reminded him', Rice wrote to Balfour, 'of the attitude of the Jews and crypto-Jews in Turkey at the time of the Young Turk Revolution and of a similar attitude of the Jews now in control of the Russian revolution.'[7] If the reference to the first was groundless[8] and by 1918 obsolete, the implication that American Jews were responsible for the anti-war attitude of the Bolshevik leaders of Jewish extraction was ludicrous. When Balfour visited the United States in April–May 1917 he appears to have come to the conclusion that Spring-Rice was not up to the job and advised Lloyd George, then Prime Minister, that 'some person of the highest prestige and political position should be selected as a special and permanent British representative in the United States'. Grey, the most suitable candidate, declined the offer,[9] and Spring-Rice remained in Washington till January 1918, when Lord Reading replaced him.

Unaware of the adverse undercurrents, on 18 February 1916 Wolf made yet another *démarche*. He drew attention to the desperate position of Jews in Russia and pressed for a public statement on the Palestine question, only to be told by Lord Robert Cecil that it would be a great mistake for the British and French Governments to intervene directly or indirectly in Russian internal questions. Nor did Cecil think that such an intervention would be in the interests of Russian Jews themselves.[10] This coolness puzzled Wolf, particularly when compared to the warmth shown by the Foreign Affairs Commission of the French Chamber of Deputies. Moreover, Briand, the Prime Minister, though formerly reluctant to raise the Jewish question at Petrograd, was now prepared to make representations in case of need, with the evident motive of securing the support of the American public. The question was also freely aired in the French press. Such a divergence between Paris and London put Wolf at a disadvantage; but rather than press the British to revise their attitude, he preferred to bring his French colleagues nearer to the British line. To reach some show of uniformity he advised Lèygnes (after his draft letter had been approved by the Foreign Office) to shelve his preoccupation with Russia and Rumania for the time being and to concentrate on Palestine. He suggested the following formula as a basis for a public pronouncement:[11]

> In the event of Palestine coming within the spheres of influence of Great Britain or France, at the close of the war, the Governments of those Powers will not fail to take account of the historic interest that country possesses for the Jewish community. The Jewish population will be secured in the enjoyment of civil and religious liberty, equal political rights with the rest of the population, reasonable facilities for immigration and colonization, and such municipal privileges in the towns and colonies inhabited by them as may be shown to be necessary.

This formula was in fact an elaboration of the points made in Wolf's memoranda of 16 December 1915 and 18 February 1916. To Harold Nicolson, Lancelot Oliphant, and Hugh O'Beirne it appeared to be 'moderate and acceptable'. Nor did Sir Arthur Nicolson raise any objections, although he thought that, before giving their *imprimatur*, the British ought to consult the French Government or at least to sound out the views of Ambassador Cambon.[12]

But Wolf was impatient. Only three days after submitting his formula on 3 March 1916, he pressed the Foreign Office for permission to make it public at a mass meeting to be held under his presidency in the East End of London on the following Sunday. Oliphant assured him that the matter was being considered carefully but, as it was necessary for the British Government to consult their Allies, some time might elapse before a final decision could be taken. Why did Wolf display such undue urgency? Was it because he wished both to forestall the Franco-Jewish Propaganda Committee and to steal a march on the Zionists, with whom he was at that time at loggerheads? Lord Robert Cecil sensed some hidden motive and forewarned his colleagues: 'May I add that if and when we are allowed by our allies to say anything worth saying to the Jews, it should not be left to Mr. Lucien Wolf to say it?'[13] The Foreign Office had additional reasons for caution. Although at first Wolf's formula seemed acceptable, doubts later developed as to whether a declaration along these lines would make a strong enough appeal to the Jewish communities all over the world. These considerations weighed heavily since a rival suggestion was being examined at the Foreign Office at the same time. This proposition came from an unexpected quarter. Its author was Edgar Suarès,[14] a prominent businessman and head of the Jewish community in Alexandria. Suarès thought that by disregarding the interests of the Jewish people England was making a great mistake. Should the British Government give concrete assurances on the Palestine question, it would 'almost . . . with a stroke of the pen', convert the indifference, if not hostility of American and other Jews into enthusiastic support. The pro-German Jews favoured a German protectorate of Palestine whilst he, like many of his co-religionists, greatly preferred British sovereignty. Though a self-confessed anti-Zionist, Suarès was anxious to see Palestine open to Jewish immigration and that 'the management of its internal affairs should be in the hands of Jews . . . under British Protection'. Sir Henry McMahon, the High Commissioner in Egypt, considered the proposal interesting enough to forward it to London.[15]

Suarès scheme followed the familiar Zionist pattern but the fact that it came from an anti-Zionist made it all the more attractive. But what made an impact on the Foreign Office, and particularly on Grey, was the allusion to the prospect of a German protectorate in Palestine. Curiously, the Nicolsons, both father and son, were slow to grasp the importance of the Suarès message. On 23 February, the day of its arrival, Harold Nicolson noted: 'I fear that for H.M.G. to announce publicly their determination to support Zionist aspirations in Palestine would be a course of more difficulty than Mr. Suarès appears to imagine, and that it is doubtful whether the favour which this move would find with *some* (but by no means *all*) Jews, would be worth it.'[16] Hugh O'Beirne disagreed with Nicolson sharply. His minute is worth reproducing in full.[17]

It has been suggested to me that if we could offer the Jews an arrangement as to Palestine which would strongly appeal to them we might conceivably be able to strike a bargain with them as to withdrawing their support from the Young Turk Government which would then automatically collapse.

The tremendous political consequences of such a deal are quite obvious. I am told that notwithstanding the indifference or hostility of a great many Jews to the Zionist idea an arrangement completely satisfactory to Jewish aspirations in regard to Palestine might nevertheless have immense attractions for the great body of Jews. The Zionists are opposed to an international protectorate and would wish for a British protectorate, which seems impracticable. But I understand that the idea has been put forward that there might be an American protectorate which would probably appeal intensely to the very influential body of American Jews. While there would necessarily be an international administration of some kind in Jerusalem itself it is conceivable that in the rest of Palestine the Jews could be given special colonising facilities which in time would make them strong enough to cope with the Arab element, when the management of internal affairs might be placed in their hands under America's protection. Meanwhile Palestine outside Jerusalem might possibly be left under the administration of some neutral nationality if the United States would not agree to undertake the administration themselves.

I do not feel competent to express any opinion as to the feasibility of these schemes. The difficulty of Jewish colonists displacing any large proportion of the 6–700,000 Arabs in Palestine, or growing strong enough to administer them, seems to me almost insurmountable. I would suggest that we might consult Mr. Fitzmaurice.

No document has come to light so far among the Foreign Office files to show what Fitzmaurice's opinion was. If he was consulted, his opinion would presumably have been no different from that expressed on 18 September 1917, when interviewed by William Yale, an American Intelligence Officer. According to Yale, Fitzmaurice favoured 'giving the Jews a chance in Palestine, even at the expense of the Arab'. He did not anticipate much friction with them and thought that the matter 'could be arranged',[18] and as it was he who was principally responsible for stirring up the Arab members of the Ottoman Parliament against the Young Turk Government, using Zionism as a stick with which to beat them,[19] he apparently felt qualified enough to discount any serious trouble.

O'Beirne's assumption that a bargain on the question of Palestine might cause the Jews to withdraw 'their support from the Young Turk Government, which would then automatically collapse', is much more puzzling. O'Beirne could not have reached this extreme conclusion from Suarès's statement. Perhaps it came from Fitzmaurice, although there is no evidence to prove this. In the British Embassy before the war it became an *idée fixe* that the Committee of Union and Progress represented

a Judeao-Turkish dual alliance, the Turks supplying a splendid military material and the Jews the brain, enterprise, money . . . and a strong press influence in Europe . . . The Jews, in order to maintain their position of influence in Young Turkey circles, have to play up to, if not encourage, Turkish 'nationalistic' tendencies, and the two elements make a distinctive strong combination;[20]

a combination, which was believed to be closely linked with Germany.

How firmly entrenched this opinion was is evident from a remark made by George Kidston on 25 October 1916:[21]

It is notorious that the Committee of Union and Progress and indeed the whole Young Turkish movement originated with the Jews of Salonica and that Jewish influence has always predominated in it; it was the Jewish element which shaped its development, alienated genuine reformers and transformed an admirable movement for freedom into the unscrupulous reign of terror which the Committee now exercise with German assistance.

In his book *The Rise of Nationality in the Balkans* (published early in 1917), Professor R. W. Seton-Watson made the same point. 'The real brains of the movement were Jewish or Judeo-Moslem [Jews] . . . Financial aid came from wealthy Dunmehs and Jews of Salonica, and from the capitalists, international and semi-international of Vienna, Budapest, Berlin and perhaps also of Paris and London.'[22] If this was the prevailing belief, was it not natural for the idea to arrive of using Zionism to entice Ottoman Jewry and so undermine the stability of the Young Turk Government? Such a line of reasoning is characteristic of British pragmatism and tends to explain O'Beirne's bizarre assumption. However, the premise on which it was based was shaky, since Jewish influence in Young Turk counsels was nowhere near as great as the idea implied; although it is worth pointing out that the underlying assumption that assurances on the question of Palestine would win over not only the Jews in neutral but also in enemy countries proved right and was confirmed by events following the Balfour Declaration.

Sir Arthur Nicolson was not convinced:[23]

I am not clear as to the strength of the Zionist movement among the Jews. I was under the impression that Zionists are in a considerable minority. As we are proposing to Russia, in conjunction with the French, the placing of Palestine under an international administration we cannot advocate another scheme.

Sir Arthur was overruled by Grey. Whatever the numerical strength of the Zionists, Palestine appealed to all sections of Jewry, though to each of them for different motives. The proposal to place it under international administration, one of the items being discussed at that time in Petrograd by Sykes, Picot, and Sazonow, did not necessarily exclude the possibility of Jewish immigration and colonisation.[24] The risk of Palestine falling under a German protectorate outweighed all other considerations. 'Tell M. Cambon', Grey instructed Nicolson, 'that it has been suggested that

Jewish feeling which is now hostile and favours a German Protectorate over Palestine might be entirely changed if an American Protectorate was formed with the object of restoring Jews to Palestine. There would have to be international control of Christian Holy Places.' But Cambon doubted whether his own or the Russian Government would entertain the proposal, and Nicolson thereupon suggested that the matter be left in abeyance. At this point Lord Crewe stepped in. 'It is a vexed question', he noted, 'because even Jewish opinion is by no means unanimous . . . but no doubt it embraces remarkable possibilities.'[25]

Crewe had just relinquished his post as Secretary of State for India and, before accepting that of Lord President of the Council, was deputising for Grey at the Foreign Office. Grey had complete confidence in Crewe's judgment[26] and the latter could therefore speak with full authority on the Foreign Minister's behalf. Crewe was known to have expressed some sympathy with Zionism. His brilliant brother-in-law, Neil Primrose, was also deeply interested in the Jewish national movement and Lady Crewe was overheard at a dinner party to have declared to Lord Robert Cecil that in her house all were 'Weizmannites'.[27]

Cecil followed Crewe's lead readily. Unlike Sir Arthur Nicolson, Cecil cared about propaganda and was quick to point to the 'international power of the Jews'.[28] But the most outspoken advocate was O'Beirne. After Cambon's rebuff to Nicolson, O'Beirne suggested that the French Government be approached directly, hoping that, in view of the interest shown by the French Foreign Affairs Commission, Paris would be more responsive than its Ambassador in London.

As this minute was being drafted there arrived Wolf's note pressing for authorisation to make his formula public but O'Beirne was nursing a much more ambitious text. He noted:[29]

> The one ruling consideration, as it seems to me, by which we should be guided in the present stage of this matter is to be found in the answer to the question whether any of the suggestions [i.e. Wolf's and Suarès's, modified by the Foreign Office to an American Pro-tectorate of Palestine, excepting the Holy Places] . . . would appeal powerfully to a large and influential section of Jews throughout the world. If that question is answered in the affirmative, and I believe it is so answered by good authorities, then it is clear that the Palestine scheme has in it the most far-reaching political possibilities and we should be losing a great opportunity if we did not do our utmost to overcome any difficulties that may be raised by France and Russia . . .

Another point . . . is that in any communications which we may address to Mr. Wolf or any other representative Jew we should be careful to make it clear that we do not propose to give the Jews a privileged position in Palestine for nothing but that we should expect whole-hearted support from them in return.

Most of Sir Arthur Nicolson's earlier objections had now evaporated, and this encouraged Crewe to press the point.

I am quite clear that this matter ought not to be put aside and I think Sir E.[Grey] is of the same opinion. It is a difficult question because Jewish opinion is considerably divided about it, and Mr. L. Wolf cannot be taken as the spokesman of the whole community . . . But we ought to pursue the subject, since the advantage of securing Jewish goodwill in the Levant and in America can hardly be overestimated, both of present and at the conclusion of the war. And we ought to help Russia to realise this.

Cecil entirely agreed and it devolved now upon Crewe to draft a cable to the British Ambassadors in Paris and Petrograd. It was dated 11 March 1916 and ran as follows:

It has been suggested to us that if we could offer to the Jews an arrangement in regard to Palestine completely satisfactory to Jewish aspirations, such an offer might appeal strongly to a large and powerful section of the Jewish community throughout the world, although it is true that a considerable number of Jews are known to be indifferent to the idea of Zionism. If the above view is correct, it is clear that the Zionist idea has in it the most far reaching political possibilities, for we might hope to use it in such a way as to bring over to our side the Jewish forces in America, the East and elsewhere which are now largely, if not preponderantly hostile to us.

Then followed a definition of Jewish aspirations in regard to Palestine as formulated by Lucien Wolf, with a comment that this formula was 'unobjectionable' and was receiving sympathetic consideration at the Foreign Office. The cable went on:

We consider, however, that the scheme might be made far more attractive to the majority of Jews if it held out to them the prospect that when in course of time the Jewish colonists in Palestine grow strong enough to cope with the Arab population they may be allowed to take the management of the internal affairs of Palestine (with the exception of Jerusalem and the Holy Places) into their own hands.

We have been given to understand that some influential Jewish opinion would be opposed to an international protectorate but we do not desire to state our preference in favour of any particular solution of the problem. Our sole object is to find an arrangement which would be so attractive to the majority of Jews as to enable us to strike a bargain for Jewish support.

Lord Bertie and Sir George Buchanan were requested to sound out the views of the respective Governments to which they were accredited.[30]

Like O'Beirne, Crewe was fully aware of the numerical inferiority of Palestinian Jews, from which followed that if the Allies wished to capture the sympathy of world Jewry, they would have to create such conditions as to make the colonists 'grow strong enough to cope with the Arab population'.[31] Such an outcome, as O'Beirne noted in his subsequent minute, conjured up the prospect of eventual Jewish self-government.[32] The native Arabic-speaking population would then become a minority. To Grey and his advisers, aware of Samuel's arguments,[33] this could not be regarded as violating the principles of democracy. Nor did recognition of Jewish rights conflict with the correspondence with the Sharif Hussein.[34]

The question of the protection of Palestine presented greater difficulty since the Zionists were opposed to the idea of an international regime and the British Government was reluctant to extend its responsibilities. The only way out of the dilemma was an American protectorate, a solution suggested earlier by Sir Eric Drummond, to which both O'Beirne and Grey readily subscribed.[35] When drafting the cable, Crewe hinted at an American protectorate (excepting Jerusalem and the Holy Places) in the hope that this would have a strong appeal for American Jews, but Sir Arthur Nicolson objected and the passage was deleted.

Nicolson's cryptic remark caused Drummond to reconsider tactics. He agreed with the deletion on the ground that it was inappropriate to suggest an American protectorate over part of the territory of a belligerent power before sounding out the United States Government. Whilst the latter might resent the proposal, the Germans (should they learn of it) would be sure to make capital of it, accusing the Allies of an intrigue to involve the United States in the war. Drummond thought it wiser, therefore, to solicit Allied approval first for whatever formula might be agreed upon, and thereafter to suggest 'quite privately and unofficially to some influential Zionist that an American protectorate might be what would suit their movement best and leave it to them to make the necessary propaganda and deal with the U.S. Govt.'[36] Crewe agreed with this, but the ambiguity created by the omission was bound to give rise to some searching questions, particularly in Paris, about the motives for the British move. Even more surprising is that no mention was made in the cable of the possibility of Germany assuming a protectorate over Palestine, since this was what prompted Grey's move. This oversight blunted its edge and detracted from its usefulness.

Against all expectations, Sazonow was favourably disposed towards Grey's *aide-mémoire*, although he doubted whether a considerable number of Jews would migrate. However, on the following day, he authorised Buchanan to inform London that the Russian Government viewed the 'proposed settlement of Jews in Palestine with sympathy, but that Holy Places must be excluded from any such scheme and placed under an International Régime ensuring equality of rights for all Christian Churches'.[37] This tallies with what Yechiel Tschlenow learned from the Near Eastern Department of the Russian Foreign Office. Gulkievich, its head, told Tschlenow on Sazonow's behalf that Russia would support Zionist aspirations as soon as other Allied Powers took the initiative and that, save for interest in the Holy Places, Russia entertained no territorial ambitions in Palestine.[38] This line was expounded as early as April 1915, in a leading article in the influential *Novoe Vremya*,[39] and reiterated in a private conversation between Sazonow and Professor James Simpson;[40] the latter heard the Foreign Minister remark confidentially that when the final disposition of Palestine was discussed, Russia would prefer to see there a British rather than a French protectorate.[41] Hence, with no conflict of interests, there was no reason for Sazonow to block Grey's proposal. England's commitment in Palestine could only ease Russia's establishment in Constantinople and the Straits, while extensive colonisation in Palestine held out some tangible prospects of reducing the number of Jews in Russia.

Paris reactions were different. Bertie forwarded Grey's memorandum to the French Prime Minister, but the wisdom of the whole move seemed to him questionable. 'The German and German-American Jews', he cabled Grey, 'will remain Germanophil' and Schiff and his like wished merely to extract promises for proper treatment of their co-religionists in Russia. But even should St Petersburg give assurances, could England and France guarantee them? An even more onerous task would await the Allies in Palestine. 'The Jews are not a combative race. How could they fare against the warlike Arabs unless physically supported by England and France?' Any promises made to the Jews with regard to Palestine 'would become known at once to the Arabs with disastrous results as far as Arab aid to the cause of the Entente . . . is concerned'.[42]

Bertie was no friend of the Jews[43] and considered Zionism 'an absurd scheme'.[44] Given this frame of mind, he could hardly have been expected to make Grey's proposal plausible to the Quai d'Orsay. He was however experienced enough a diplomat to read the French mind correctly. Several days later Briand echoed his misgivings. The French Premier doubted whether support of the Zionist scheme would influence Jewish communities, since their aversion to the Allies, he believed, sprang from entirely different motives. Moreover there was the risk of offending Arab susceptibilities. On this particular point he reminded the British Government that Grey's scheme 'could not be usefully taken up until after question of creation of Arab Empire has been solved'.[45]

It is worth recalling that the French Government had been the first to discover through Professor Basch that Zionism was the most promising card with which to influence United States Jewry. Its stand therefore seems surprising. Nor does the argument that support of the Palestinian scheme might have a discouraging effect on Sharif Hussein carry much conviction. Examination of British Foreign Office records shows that the Quai d'Orsay showed little enthusiasm for the Sharifian revolt. Not only did the French give it little credit; they feared that the British might eventually use the Arabs as a stalking horse to dislodge them from their projected sphere of influence in Greater Syria. So apprehensive were they lest the British steal a march on them that, given a choice between British predominance in the area, and Turkey-in-Asia, they would have opted for the second choice. With the ghost of the scheme for a landing in Alexandretta still hovering over their heads, they were bound to suspect in Grey's proposal another manoeuvre, with Jewish connivance, to undermine their claim to Palestine. The very fact that Grey did not indicate which power would exercise the protectorate over Palestine served to reinforce their suspicion that this was the thin end of a British wedge. Only when the French official archives are fully explored,[46] shall we be able to know the truth about the French reasons for rejecting the proposal. But one cannot escape the impression that official arguments merely cloaked a much deeper concern.

At the Foreign Office O'Beirne, the chief architect of the proposal, gave the French arguments little credence.[47]

The first paragraph of the French reply seems to me rather to beg the main question at stake. If it is the case that the Zionist scheme does not appeal to any large and influential section of the Jews throughout the world, who are now antagonistic to our cause, then I agree that the whole scheme had better be dropped. But our information so far as I know is not to that effect.

The Arab objection appears to have more force in it. It must be admitted that if the Arabs knew that we were contemplating an extensive Jewish colonisation scheme in Palestine (with the possible prospect of eventual Jewish self government) this might have a very chilling effect on the Arab leaders. The difficulty ought not, however, to be regarded as insoluble, and a good deal depends on the value which we attach to the military cooperation which the Arabs are likely to give us in the war. I had always assumed that this value must be placed very low.

I hope we shall be able to talk over the whole Palestine question with the French when in Paris.

This hope did not materialise. The issue was not discussed.[48] Presumably the same reason that made the British delete the Alexandretta scheme from the agenda impelled them to keep silent on Palestine. At a time when mutual trust was of supreme importance it was not worth while to irritate France by insisting on projects for which she seemed to have little taste. It was characteristic of Grey to have remarked on the eve of the conference in Paris: 'My conclusion is not that we must efface ourselves in the councils of Allies . . . But if we cannot make our views prevail by argument and influence we must be very careful not to proceed to threats or pressure that might alienate our Allies.'[49] A tripartite agreement, negotiated at St Petersburg by Sykes, Picot, and Sazonow, had just been concluded, and any scheme tending to tip the scales in Britain's favour could not be entertained. It is therefore not surprising that early in April 1916, when Sokolow presented his memorandum on a Jewish Commonwealth in Palestine under British protection, the Foreign Office denied him a hearing. Henry Cumberbatch, who wished to introduce Sokolow to Sir Arthur Nicolson, was told that it was inadvisable to pursue the matter.[50] This rebuff did not necessarily mean that *finis* had to be written to Jewish aspirations in Palestine. Reaction to a petition presented by a certain Vendell Coster[51] indicates as much. On 25 June Coster suggested that Britain, jointly with Russia, assume control of Palestine until such time as 'the Jews are able to take over the management of their restored national life' there, to which Sir Maurice de Bunsen replied that 'the interests of Jews to Palestine will not be overlooked' but that at present it was 'not possible to make any statement on the subject'.[52]

In all probability Wolf was unaware of Coster's petition. Impatiently he pressed the Foreign Office for a reply, but Lord Robert Cecil, dubious from the outset about his standing as representative of Jewish opinion, wished to consult Herbert Samuel. Lord Hardinge, who nine days earlier had re-entered the Foreign Office to replace Sir Arthur Nicolson, agreed but in principle was opposed to the publication of all formulas, 'as they invariably create embarrassment'. Wolf was thereupon told that the moment was inopportune for making an announcement. Apparently, Grey was not informed of this message and instructed Oliphant to tell Wolf privately and verbally that, according to the French Government, the main difficulty was that the Jews themselves were not agreed about the scheme.[53] That Jewish opinion was divided is true, but it is strange that Grey should have ascribed to the French Government a reason it had not in fact advanced.

Wolf now suspected that the Zionists had put a spoke in his wheel. He dashed to Paris to find out what had really happened, and on 12 July was received by the Prime Minister. He had heard, he told Briand, that the French Government had rejected his formula on the ground that it would be unsatisfactory to the Zionists. On the authority of Baron Edmond de Rothschild he assured Briand that the Zionists were not opposed to it. Briand thereupon replied that 'no formula on the Palestine question had ever come before him'. Moutet and Bigart of the Franco-Jewish Propaganda Committee, who accompanied Wolf, told him later that the formula had been dealt with by the Ministry but 'without the knowledge of Briand'. Baron Edmond de Rothschild, whom Wolf also saw, was inclined to think that either the British[54]

> had misunderstood the French Government, or that if the French Government had made the excuse attributed to them, it was really because they did not want to make a public declaration on the Palestine question which would either tie their hands in any future negotiations with Turkey, or would have the effect of admitting that the destiny of Palestine was not exclusively a French concern.

Rothschild's guess was probably accurate. The fact that Briand's statement to Wolf, as we may now safely assert, was untrue, reinforces the suspicion that the French had objections other than those disclosed officially to the British, to the scheme. Secrecy was imperative, and by denying any knowledge of the 'formula' Briand apparently intended to silence in advance any discussion on the subject. Whether it was wise for Wolf from the outset to urge London to proceed unilaterally, instead of coordinating the initiative with the Franco-Jewish Propaganda Committee, is open to question. Deprived of his last propaganda weapon, his policy was now in ruins.

The field was now open to the Zionists, and the factors working in their favour were gathering momentum. German propaganda in the United States was gaining the upper hand. 'A vast number of papers . . . and nearly all evening papers' sided with the cause of the Central Powers. Berlin was also said to be spending large sums of money on the Jewish press there, and although Jewish opinion in America was divided, prominent Jewish leaders like Jacob Schiff, the Warburgs and Untermeyer, who were closely connected with the United States administration, were said to be pro-German. 'The Germans, the Jews, and the Irish will never forget nor forgive', Spring-Rice commented. With the Presidential election impending, neither of the candidates could afford to ignore the combined German and Irish vote, especially if supported by the Poles and Jews. The situation was all the more critical since growing estrangement from England stood in a direct ratio to her increasing financial dependence on the United States. It was envisaged that by the spring of 1917 England would have to rely entirely on American loans and credit. Hence the 'importance of maintaining good relations with the United States of America'. It is not clear what Spring-Rice's remedy was. With regard to Jews he reiterated his stereotype prescription to warn the English Jews of the danger to their well-being arising from the attitude of some of their co-religionists in America who played an important part in German propaganda, although he admitted that many of them sympathised strongly with France and England. He added a significant observation:[55]

> The Zionist movement is growing in importance: it is laudable, and we can well sympathise with it. Perhaps here would be a basis of common action.

Thus Spring-Rice had finally reached the conclusion to which Lord Eustace Percy had alluded five months earlier.[56]

Since the outbreak of the war the Zionist movement in the United States had gone from strength to strength. On 30 August 1914 an extraordinary conference held in New York created the Provisional Executive Committee for General Zionist Affairs, with Brandeis as chairman and Stephen Wise as vice-chairman. Brandeis's leadership turned the movement from a parochial organisation into a force to be counted with in Jewish communal life. From an organisation with fewer than 5,000 enrolled members in 1914, it reached the figure of 150,000 by 1918. The modest budget of $15,000 in 1914 had increased to $3,000,000 in 1918. The membership figures by no means reflected its influence. One of its greatest assets was 'the known fact that the President of the United States had come to believe in the Zionist programme as the solution of the

Jewish question and had promised his best efforts in helping to carry it out.'[57] In March 1916 Brandeis was able to assure Boris Goldberg that the American Government, or at least President Wilson, 'would support Zionist aspirations seriously and actively'.[58]

It was, however, not Spring-Rice who had built the bridges to the Zionists but Sir Mark Sykes. His meeting with the Zionist leaders on 7 February 1917, in Rabbi Dr Gaster's home,[59] started the chain of events leading up to the Balfour Declaration. By then the motives of the British Government were far more complex than those entertained early in 1916. But before discussing Sir Mark Sykes's conversion to Zionism, the background of the Agreement bearing his name and that of his French opposite number Georges Picot must be filled in. This Agreement (officially termed the Asia Minor Agreement) was interrelated with the McMahon-Hussein Correspondence. It is therefore essential to examine whether there was any contradiction between the encouragement given to the Zionists and the commitment to the Arabs; more precisely it is our purpose, in the following chapter, to examine whether Palestine was included in or excluded from McMahon's pledge to Sharif Hussein.

6 The McMahon-Hussein Correspondence and the Question of Palestine

The controversy over this question is half a century old. Today it has no more than an academic value, but in the past the keenest brains in Middle East politics were pitted against each other to prove their respective cases, only to demonstrate the gulf that separated them. Despite statements made by the high-ranking British officers directly involved in negotiations with the Arab leaders, passions did not subside. To those who could see only duplicity in the conduct of the British Government of the time, the slogan of the 'twice promised land' became almost an article of faith. It infected some well-meaning and sincere, albeit misguided, British intellectuals.

Publication of the relevant records could have dispelled much of the misunderstanding but, though this was urged in both Houses of Parliament since 1921, successive British Governments objected on the ground that publication would be 'detrimental to the public interest'.[1] The refusal to allow publication was due not to the weakness of the British Government's case, as its critics suspected, but to considerations entirely unconnected with Palestine. The chief reason for official secrecy, as we are now able to learn, was that the Correspondence contained encouragement to the Sharif of Mecca (given both by Lord Kitchener and his successor as High Commissioner in Egypt, Sir Henry McMahon) to rebel against the Sultan-Caliph in Constantinople and seek the Caliphate for himself with British assistance. Publication of this fact, it was feared, would have precipitated a storm of indignation in the Moslem world, particularly in India, with most embarrassing consequences. The Foreign Office held the view that it would not be possible to publish part of the Correspondence, omitting the allusions to the Caliphate and that partial publication would almost certainly lead to complete publication, and, still worse, would have involved raking up the detailed history of serious disagreements between the British and French Governments respecting the Near East in the latter part of the First World War and the earlier armistice period.[2]

Whatever the merits of these considerations, official records now available for research provide us with a long-awaited opportunity to re-examine this complex problem.[3] But, before venturing to investigate whether or not Palestine was included in McMahon's pledge to Sharif Hussein, it is pertinent first to appraise the nature of the British commitments to the Arabs; whether they bore a *unilateral* character—heretofore the accepted criterion by which Anglo-Sharifian relations were judged—or whether the other party, the Arabs, were equally under certain obligations, the discharge of which conditioned the validity of the understanding. Textual examination of the Correspondence alone will not lead us far. The task of interpretation requires a reconstruction of what went on behind the official façade and a scrutiny of the motives and expectations of the chief *dramatis personae*.

The dominant theme in the Correspondence is 'Arab independence'. This loosely-used phrase caused much misunderstanding. What did it mean? A note written by Sir Edward Grey to Sir James Rodd, the British Ambassador in Rome, on 21 September 1916 is illuminating:[4]

> . . . The Shereef of Mecca had communicated to the [Anglo-] Egyptian authorities his desire to make himself independent but had insisted upon knowing whether we were prepared to recognize an independent Arab State. We were, of course, prepared to do that if he succeeded in establishing his independence; for all we were pledged to was that the Moslem holy places should remain in independent Moslem hands . . .

This tallies with Grey's earlier communication. On 14 April he had authorised Sir Reginald Wingate, the Sirdar of the Sudan, to inform the Sharif of Mecca that the British Government 'will make it an essential condition, in any terms of peace, that the Arabian Peninsula and its Mohammedan Holy Places should remain in the hands of an independent Sovereign Moslem State'. The message was apparently passed on to Hussein by Seyyid Sir Ali Morghani, Grand Kadi of the Sudan, who was in close contact with Wingate. By the end of June its substance was embodied in a proclamation which was distributed in the form of a leaflet in Arabia and on 29 July 1916, following the Sharifian revolt against Turkey, an official communiqué to the same effect was made public.[5]

Hence it would be fair to deduce that apart from the Holy Places, Great Britain (as well as the Allied Governments) were not pledged to the establishment of an independent Arab State or Confederation of States. It was up to the Arabs themselves to make good their aspirations to independence. But as there was no likelihood of their being able to stand on their own feet, it was quite natural for the British and French Governments to fill the vacuum and assume the role of 'protectors'.[6] Absence of a protective shield would have inevitably invited 'foreign [i.e. Turkish] aggression', nipping the scheme of an Arab State or Confederation of States in the bud. It was to make the creation of an Arab entity possible, as well as to harmonise it with their own legitimate interests in that region that the British and French Governments concluded the Sykes-Picot Agreement. Although this document became notorious in ensuing years, there was nothing in it that was inconsistent with McMahon's pledge.

It is evident that at that time neither the Arabs nor the British took the meaning of 'independence' in its literal sense. The Arabs, Sir Mark Sykes disclosed to the War Committee after his return from the East '*must* ask for theoretical independence, otherwise, if they ask for an obvious European tutelage, the Committee of Union and Progress will take the reactionary party over on their side'.[7] Despite his grandiose claim, Hussein was well aware of his own limitations. Hence his request for 'assistance' in order to ensure 'the stability of Arab independence'. Not only was he apprehensive of 'constant provocations . . . and utmost vengeance' from the Turks during the war should Great Britain leave him alone, but even after its termination.[8] McMahon indeed reassured the Sharif that Great Britain would not conclude 'any peace . . . of which the freedom of the Arab peoples and their liberation from the German and Turkish domination do not form an essential condition';[9] and it is only in this context that the meaning of Arab 'independence' should be understood: liberation from their supposed adversaries, not necessarily independence. David G. Hogarth, a scholar of repute, soon after joining the Arab Bureau in Cairo as its Director, attested that what the British were asked was simply to promote 'independence of the Arabs from their present over-Lord, the Turk'.[10] Nine years later he reiterated that neither to the Sharif nor to any other Arab did the British 'ever explicitly guarantee or even promise anything beyond liberation from the Turk'.[11]

Least of all did the sponsors of the Arab movement themselves take the word 'independence' at its face value. What McMahon had in mind was, as he told Grey, recognition of 'the principle of Arab independence', but no more. When read together with the text of a subsequent cable, we may well deduce that the term was merely a convenient substitute for autonomy. 'I have endeavoured in my statement to Sherif Hussein [of October 24, 1915] to make any such future Arab state (within the British sphere) subject to our creation, direction and control.' The term 'independent Sovereign State', Grey had been told six months earlier, 'has been interpreted in a generic sense because idea of an Arabian unity under one ruler, recognised as supreme by other Arab chiefs, is as yet inconceivable

to Arab mind'.[12] Lieutenant-Colonel, later General Sir Gilbert F. Clayton, the Director of Military Intelligence in Cairo and one of McMahon's
chief advisers, denied that it was his intention to promote 'the establishment of a powerful Arab Kingdom . . . all we want is to keep the friendship and, if possible, the active assistance of the various Arab chiefs . . .
while at the same time, working towards maintenance of the *status quo
ante bellum*, and merely eliminating Turkish domination from Arabia.'
Five weeks later he confided to another friend:[13]

> to set up a great Arab State . . . was never my idea . . . The con-
> ditions throughout Arabia, Syria and Mesopotamia did not allow of
> such a scheme being practical, even if anyone were so foolish as to
> attempt it . . .
>
> The object we have to aim at is, I consider, to work to preserve
> all the various elements in the Arab territories very much in the
> same position as they were before the war, but minus the Turks. In
> this way we shall have an open field to work in.

The underlying assumption was that the Arabs for some time to come
were bound to need European assistance and protection. This situation, as
Clayton saw it, offered an opportunity for the British to step in. The term
'independence' was merely a euphemism for supersession of Turkish rule
by British and French in their respective spheres of interests. Looked at
from this point of view, the concessions made to Sharif Hussein were not
so far-reaching as they appeared and it explains why McMahon, in his
celebrated letter of 24 October 1915 to the Sharif of Mecca, granted them
so lightly, though this is not the whole explanation.

When in mid-August Hussein's note of 14 July 1915 arrived in Cairo,
to open the long drawn-out correspondence, it was received at the British
Residency with astonishment. 'It was at the time and still is my opinion',
commented Ronald Storrs, its Oriental Secretary, 'that the Sharif opened
his mouth and the British Government their purse a good deal too wide
. . . We could not conceal from ourselves (and with difficulty from him)
that his pretensions bordered upon the tragi-comic.'[14] These related to the
comprehensive demand for recognition of the independence of the Arab
countries bounded on the north by the line Mersin–Adana to parallel
37°N, to include the whole of the Arabian Peninsula (except Aden),
Mesopotamia, Syria, what was later Transjordan and Palestine. Hussein's
messenger, Muhammad Ibn Arif, who brought this letter to Cairo,
assured Storrs on his master's behalf that the Arabs were 'ready and well
prepared'; 'our word', Abdullah, Hussein's son, asked him to tell Storrs,
'is a word of honour and we will carry it out even at the cost of our lives;

we are not under the order of the Turks but the Turks are under our orders.' Arab officers in the Ottoman army, Ibn Arif went on, had sworn allegiance to the Sharif and were prepared to fight under his banner. Many had deserted already and consequently Hussein's prestige had become so paramount that even the Sultan had proclaimed him Chief Governor and Administrator of Hedjaz, with the Wali 'under his orders'. But Storrs was not deceived. 'It may be regarded as certain,' he noted, 'that . . . [Hussein] has received no sort of mandate from other [Arab] potentates.' As to the territorial desideratum, 'he knows he is demanding, possibly as a basis for negotiations, far more than he has the right, the hope, or the power to expect. Like his co-religionists, elsewhere, he will modify his tone later.'[15] To McMahon, Hussein's profession of 'sincere friendship' was welcome, as was the idea of 'reversion of the caliphate to a true Arab'; but as to the question of frontiers and boundaries, so long as the war was in progress and the Turks in effective occupation of their Asiatic provinces, negotiations were 'premature and waste of time'.[16]

McMahon's negative response was fully in line with the attitude adopted by Grey, who was reluctant to commit himself to delimitation of territory of the projected Arab state, particularly in the north.[17] The predicament confronting him emerges clearly from his note quoted earlier:[18]

We had no difficulty in agreeing to any boundaries which the Shereef wanted on the south [i.e. in the Arabian Peninsula] but on the north the Shereef came up against Syria, where we had always admitted French interest and the French would not make concessions to the Shereef of places like Damascus without knowing what the limits of their sphere were to be.

But McMahon had additional grounds for pouring cold water on to Arab territorial desiderata: Syrian Arabs, instead of aiding the British, 'have lent their assistance to the Germans and the Turks' he reminded the Sharif on 30 August 1915. What then made McMahon change his mind two months later and concede so generously to Hussein's demands, as is apparent from his letter of 24 October 1915?

It was the arrival of Muhammad Sharif al-Faruqi in Cairo that constituted the decisive turning-point. Al-Faruqi[19] was an Arab Staff officer in the Ottoman army and a prominent member of a Young Arab secret society called al'-Ahd, an off-shoot of the civilian al-Fatat. On some pretext he managed to desert to the English lines in Gallipoli, whence he was taken to Cairo. Under interrogation he revealed to Colonel Clayton that Young Arab secret societies in Syria and Mesopotamia had decided to co-operate with England in return for British support for Arab independence. Learning of Sharif Hussein's communication with the British High Commissioner in Cairo and realising how far-reaching the consequences might be, they hastened to stake their claim to the northern boundary of the Arab Empire. This would follow the Mersin-Diarbekir line. Direct contact was established thereafter with Jedda. Al-Faruqi claimed that the Young Arab party wielded great influence in Syria and Mesopotamia and that Turkey and Germany, alive to this fact, had approached their leaders and promised to meet their demands 'in full'. The Young Arabs, however, trusted England and preferred a deal with her, but unless they received a favourable reply within a few weeks, al-Faruqi warned, the Young Arabs would throw in their lot with Turkey and Germany in order to secure the best terms they could.[20]

We learn from Antonius that early in the war the *al-Fatat* committee passed a resolution 'to work on the side of Turkey in order to resist foreign penetration of whatever kind or form', but shortly after Emir Feisal's arrival in Damascus on 26 March 1915 they switched their allegiance abruptly and decided on co-operation with Great Britain against Turkey; their so-called 'Damascus Protocol'[21] served later as a blueprint for Hussein, in his letter to McMahon of 14 July 1915, to outline the boundaries for Arab independence. But al-Faruqi's statement on a rival proposition made by Turkey and Germany is puzzling. Antonius is silent about it. Moreover, no evidence of such an offer can be traced in the German Foreign Ministry files. If anything it is rather to the contrary. The Young Turk Government, with its strong centralistic disposition, was in no mood to grant the Arabs autonomy, let alone independence, and with Djemal Pasha's autocratic rule in Syria and Palestine, this was a practical impossibility. As for the Germans, though not slow to criticise Turkish short-sightedness, any negotiation with an Arab secret society behind the back of their ally was out of the question.

German records belie al-Faruqi's testimony on the Young Arabs' influence and the revolutionary fervour among the population. 'The anti-Turk movement . . . aiming at Arab autonomy,' Dr Prüffer, the Consul-General in Damascus, reported early in December 1915,

> appears much to be weakened. Among the wealthier middle classes reformism has scarcely any supporters and among the small land-owners, merchants and workers, who constitute the bulk of the population, the cause of the Ottoman Government is quite popular . . . The brilliant successes of the Ottoman army strengthened the confidence of the people in the future of the Empire.

The anti-Turkish elements enjoyed little support and, with the population riven by dissent, an uprising had little chance of success. Prüffer's successor, Dr Loytved-Hardegg, by no means an anti-Arab, assured Berlin five months later that 'no rebellion need be feared in Syria. The Syrians are shopkeepers but no warriors. They are little gifted for the profession of revolutionaries.'[22] Djemal Pasha had only praise for the loyalty of the Arab regiments in his army. He could find no better proof of his conviction that 'the Arab would not revolt and turn traitor'.[23]

In view of our evidence, al-Faruqi's report about the Turco-German overtures to the al'-Ahd and al-Fatat societies, and the latter's ability to foment a revolt against the Ottoman Government, gains little credence. Moreover, it would be reasonable to assume that this tale was deliberately fabricated in order to strengthen the Arabs' bargaining position vis-à-vis the British, as in fact it did. How successful al-Faruqi was can be gauged from the impression he made on his interrogator, Colonel Clayton, who thought his proposals 'very grave and of urgent importance' and that the rebellious position adopted by the Sharif reflected that 'of the majority of the Arab peoples'. Should the British prove accommodating the Young Arab Committee would embark 'at once' on their operations in Syria, Palestine, Bagdad and Mosul, where their influence was great. On the other hand, rejection, or even evasion of the proposals, Clayton feared,[24] would

> throw the Young Arab party definitely into the arms of the enemy. Their machinery will at once be employed against us throughout the Arab countries, and the various Arab chiefs, who are almost to a man members of, or connected with, the Young Arab party, will be undoubtedly won over . . . the Jehad, so far a failure, may become a very grim reality, the effect of which . . . might well be disastrous.

Clayton was a shrewd and down-to-earth man. Few could rival his experience with the native Arabic-speaking people; and his 'balanced advice', as Storrs put it, could not be hustled by a sudden crisis.[25] His acceptance of al-Faruqi's account is, therefore, difficult to comprehend. Was it because of faulty intelligence and inadequate information on the true state of affairs behind the Turkish lines[26] or because, following the setback at the Dardanelles, the fear of a jehad was so all-pervading that British officers in Egypt were apt to grasp at every floating straw to relieve them of their growing feeling of isolation? Whatever the reason, it was on the basis of these findings that General Sir John Maxwell, Officer Commanding in Egypt, urged Lord Kitchener, then Secretary of State for War, that it was imperative to meet Hussein's wishes:[27]

A powerful organisation . . . of the Young Arab Committee . . . with considerable influence in the [Ottoman] army and among Arab chiefs . . . appears to have made up its mind that the moment for action has arrived. The Turks and Germans are already in negotiations with them and spending money to win their support. The Arab Party is, however, strongly inclined towards England.

. . . If their overtures are rejected, or a reply is delayed . . . the Arab party will go over to the enemy and work with them . . . On the other hand, their active assistance . . . in return for our support, would be of the greatest value in Arabia, Mesopotamia, Syria and Palestine.

Kitchener replied promptly: 'The [British] Government is most desirous of dealing with the Arab question in a manner satisfactory to the Arabs. You must do your best to prevent any alienation of the Arabs' traditional loyalty to England.'[28] McMahon too pressed the Foreign Office to win over the Arabs through a speedy settlement of the boundaries but only 'in so far as England is free to act without detriment to the interests of her present Allies'. This was urgent because the Arab party in Syria was 'ready to revolt . . . they are on the point of parting of their ways'. The Sharif of Mecca was in communication with Imam Yehhia of Yemen and endeavoured to dissuade him from aiding the Turks. It was therefore, imperative, McMahon urged, to deal 'without delay'.[29]

Grey, no less than Kitchener, appreciated the urgency of the matter and was favourably disposed. But suspecting (as it turned out quite correctly) some ulterior motives for the undue haste, he warned the High Commissioner to avoid giving the impression that the British supported Arab interests in Syria merely in order to establish their own at the expense of the French. However, McMahon, without further consultation, dispatched his crucial letter of 24 October 1915, to Sharif Hussein. Two days later he cabled that the matter brooked 'no delay' and he had, therefore, to act 'without further reference'.[30] The Rubicon was crossed. The Arabs won their Magna Carta and Great Britain a standing embarrassment. The responsibility was solely that of McMahon.[31]

The India Office was aghast. Since Britain's declaration of war against Turkey, Moslem loyalty in India had been strained. The position was still more complicated because Hussein was highly unpopular among the pilgrims to Mecca for his extortions and high-handed methods. His rebellion against the Sultan, openly encouraged by the British, might have had an incalculable effect on Moslem opinion. Lord Hardinge, the Viceroy, bitterly complained that he had not been consulted before 'a pledge of such vital importance was given to the Arabs'. He thought that the British Government should not have committed itself to such a policy at all. 'We have always regarded with much [? diffidence] creation of strong Arab state lying astride our interests in the East and in the [Persian] Gulf as not unlikely source of ultimate trouble, and we doubt either military or political advantage likely to accrue from it.'[32] Austen Chamberlain, Secretary of State for India, was also disturbed by McMahon's letter. According to his information, the Grand Sharif of Mecca was 'a nonentity without power to carry out his proposals', the Arabs were 'without unity and with no possibility of uniting' their followers. Chamberlain doubted the reality and certainly the efficacy of the suggested Arab revolt in the Ottoman army and elsewhere. He pointed out that al-Idrissi, the Imam of Asir and Ibn Saud, the Amir of Najd, friends of the British, were hostile to the Sharif, whereas the latter's friends, Imam Yehhia of Yemen, and Ibn Rashid, ruler of Hayil, were pro-Turk. Until therefore both the Sharif and Faruqi proved themselves able to carry out their promises, it was imprudent for the British Government to undertake any commitment.

> The next step should be to make clear to them that promises made by McMahon are dependent on immediate action by them in sense of their offers and will not be binding on us unless they do their part at once.[33]

Lord Crewe, Chamberlain's immediate predecessor, now deputising for Grey, also criticised McMahon for negotiating, as he put it, 'without great wisdom'.[34] Sir Arthur Hirtzel, head of the Political Department of the India Office, subscribed to the Chamberlain–Crewe appraisal. However, should it be considered expedient to pursue the negotiations with the Sharif, he noted, any commitments in future should be 'as vague as possible' and made subject to the extent and success of Arab co-operation.[35]

McMahon disagreed with the India Office. He regarded the Sharif as a leader of importance, both by descent and personality, and the only rallying-point for the Arab cause.[36] Yet, as his policy had been so much censured and Hussein remained elusive about the proposed revolt,[37] McMahon adopted a tougher line. He urged Hussein in no unequivocal terms:[38]

> . . . It is most essential that you spare no effort to attach all the Arab peoples to our united cause and urge them to afford no assistance to our enemies.
> It is on the success of these efforts and on the more active

measures which the Arabs may thereafter take in support of our cause, when the time for action comes, that the permanence and strength of our agreement must depend.

Hussein thereupon assured McMahon that he fully 'understood the contents' of his note.[39]

There was thus no unilateral commitment. The Arabs were equally under definite obligations to fulfil their part towards the common cause, and it was on the nature and quality of their performance that the 'permanence and strength' of the agreement depended.[40] This criterion applied with equal strength to Mesopotamia and Syria.[41] That recognition of the 'independence of the Arabs', in specified areas 'south of latitude 37° was conditional on an Arab revolt', was testified also by T. E. Lawrence in a letter to *The Times*, 11 September 1919, and confirmed by Lloyd George.[42]

Correspondence with the Sharif remained inconclusive. Following his letter of 1 January 1916, questions about boundaries and the constitution of the independent Arab area had been left in abeyance, and subsequent communications referred only to the supply of arms, food and money to make the Arab revolt possible. The Sharif seemed to have been satisfied with assurances he had so far obtained from the British 'without asking for more'.[43] He confided to his friend Sayyid Ali Morghani that he had no reason to discuss the question of the frontiers, other than as a 'preliminary measure'. This admission stood in stark contrast to the position taken up by Hussein in his letter dated 14 July 1915 to McMahon, in which he hoped to conclude a definite treaty with the British Government with regard to the boundaries of Arab independence. However, aware of his weakness and in fear lest a European peace might leave him at the mercy of the Turks, Hussein trod warily and refrained from making extreme claims. 'From the military point of view,' he revealed to Morghani, 'none of us [can] ignore the certainty that we shall stand in great need of the power of Great Britain to extinguish any trouble that is liable to break out in the interior of the country . . . particularly because our [Moslem] friends will not hesitate by all possible means to incite their own partisans against us for their own ends.'[44]

With such self-confessed evidence of dependence, the British officers could not envisage any trouble in their relations with the Arabs in the foreseeable future. McMahon regarded Hussein's letter of 1 January 1916 to be of a 'satisfactory nature', which called for no definite reply except for a reminder of the permanence of Franco-British alliance.[45] Clayton too was satisfied with Hussein's pliancy,[46] while Hogarth could hardly conceal his gratification at Hussein's failure to press the British to define their policy more precisely.[47]

Particularly reassuring was Hussein's letter dated 18 February 1916 in which he expressed his 'utmost pleasure and satisfaction at the attainment of the required understanding'.[48] This letter is significant because it was written in response to McMahon's of 30 January in which the latter rejected Hussein's claim (on 1 January 1916) to 'Beirut and its coastal regions'.[49] Hussein's request had been limited only to the supply of arms, ammunition, gold and food and the subsequent correspondence had no bearing on the question of boundaries. Cairo was confident, as Hogarth's note of 3 May 1916 suggests, that settlement of the political issues had been left in abeyance. However, as events showed, the British had misread Hussein's mind. In 1915–16 it suited him to give the impression of a moderate negotiator, ready to make concessions, but after the Turks had been defeated, he put his claims at their highest. He referred to his understanding with McMahon as an 'agreement', though the Correspondence had no contractual validity. Moreover, he substituted 'independence of Arab [i.e. Sharifian] Kingdom', extending over Syria and Mesopotamia (a phrase not used by McMahon) for 'independence of the Arabs', and took the meaning of 'independence' in its literal sense. He completely ignored the reservations imposed by the British Government in their replies.

Hussein's first challenge, on 28 August 1918, was rebuffed. Both Wingate and the Arab Bureau regarded such a misinterpretation as 'unacceptable',[50] but Hussein bided his time. On 28 April 1920 Emir Abdullah, much to the British Government's surprise, quoted McMahon's letter of 10 March 1916 as proof of the latter granting his father all his territorial demands and Arab independence. In this letter McMahon had assured Hussein that the British Government had approved his requests for the supply of gold, arms, food and munitions, but Abdullah misapplied it to political claims on which no agreement in 1915–16 had been reached. He also misquoted McMahon by prefixing the word 'all' and altered 'requests' to 'claims'.[51]

During the winter and early spring of 1916, there seemed no reason for McMahon to question his trust in the Arabs. According to Brigadier-General W. M. Walton, British Political Resident in Aden, the Sharif of Mecca undertook to organise a 'general rising' of Arabs against the Turks both in the Hedjaz and Syria. Simultaneously Idrissi and Imam Yehhia were to raise the standard of revolt in Asir and the Yemen.[52] The Sharif estimated that he could raise a force of 250,000 men and measure up to the Turks.[53] Some of these good tidings McMahon learned directly from

Hussein, who revealed in his letter of 18 February 1916 that his son Emir Feisal, at that time in Syria, was planning to attack the Turkish troops from the rear, should the latter advance on the Suez Canal. Feisal was awaiting the arrival of troops from Aleppo and Mosul, 100,000 strong, the majority of whom were Arab. Thereafter Abdullah would deploy sufficient forces to buttress Feisal's rebellion and, should circumstances permit, would occupy the Hedjaz railway. This would mark 'the beginning of the principal movement', entirely different from what the Turks expected.[54]

The news that Feisal would enlist the support of the native Arab element in the Ottoman army was very encouraging. However, as the Turco-German advance towards Egypt did not seem to be imminent McMahon suggested that the Sharif employ the Arab tribes in the north to demolish the Bagdad railway instead. To prepare the ground al-Faruqi and al-Masri were to infiltrate the Turkish lines.[55] So elated was Sir Mark Sykes (at that time in Petrograd) that, assuming that the Arab movement would lead to a successful rebellion in Syria and Hedjaz and that Arab troops would defect, he hoped that an 'avenue [would be] open to liquidating Mesopotamian expedition and doing away with [this] theatre of war'.[56]

However, these expectations proved misplaced. The British military authorities in Basra were sceptical as to the advisability of the al-Faruqi/al-Masri mission to Mesopotamia. Experience with Arab officers who had defected from the Ottoman army had been discouraging, and Turkish vigilance remained unabated. As time wore on and the much-vaunted rising did not materialise, London became impatient. Grey warned McMahon not to go beyond assurances already given to the Sharif: 'We are giving arms and money and the sole question is whether the Arabs will do their part.' A week later McMahon received the bad news from Hussein that 'owing to dispersal of chiefs', the Syrians could neither engineer a revolution nor seize the Hedjaz railway. Instead, he asked the British to help the Anaizah tribes (on the eastern side of the river Jordan) financially and blockade the coast of Yemen.[57] Its Imam remained loyal to Turkey and was reluctant to join forces with Hussein.[58] Colonel Clayton had now to admit that 'a certain rapprochement' between the Arab decentralisation party and the Turks, had evidently taken place.[59] A general Arab uprising seemed to be a mirage and Arab unity practically non-existent. Hogarth arrived at the inescapable conclusion that the British had been misled. The Sharif had always posed as spokesman of the Arab Nation, but in fact no such entity or organisation existed; 'nor, given the history, economic environment and character of the Arabs, can it be expected to exist'.[60]

But the most crippling blow for McMahon was the revelation contained in Feisal's confidential message to his father. From its contents McMahon learned, much to his surprise, that Feisal wrote 'as an upholder of Islam against Christian encroachment' and seemed to imply that had the Turks been 'strong enough to keep Moslem frontiers intact . . . he would have backed' them rather than the British. McMahon had to concede the bitter truth that the Hedjaz Arabs were 'unlikely to act efficiently in Syria . . . or to cut the Bagdad Railway'. He advised the Sharif to confine his action to Arabia proper and to recall Feisal. 'We can . . . safely trust Sherif but we have no guarantee of Feisal's attitude.'[61]

Such a contraction of the original plan of the Arab revolt undermined much of the validity of the McMahon understanding with Hussein, but it did not make the High Commissioner draw the logical conclusions. Was it because he attached so little importance to his pledge[62] that he thought modification of the agreement with the Sharif to be superfluous? Or because such a suggestion would have *ipso facto* implied an admission of error of his policy and it was better to gloss over the issue altogether? Whatever the reason, McMahon continued the pretence that it was safe to back the Hedjaz revolt. At any rate, a public demonstration to the Moslem world that the Sharif was against the Turks was still a creditable achievement.[63] Yet, however commendable, this was not why McMahon had agreed to meet such extravagant claims to recognise Arab independence in regions lying north of the Arabian Peninsula.

Sir Arthur Nicolson was indignant. 'As regards . . . the Sherif, I think we have gone far enough . . . we should wait for some action on his part. Hitherto, we had plenty of promises from him—but nothing more— while we have given him, beyond assurances, arms and money.'[64] 'The Arabs', as General Walton commented, 'are waiting for our victories in other fields.'[65] But it was not before the autumn of that year that the bubble exploded. Soon after Hussein had rebelled against the Turks on 6 June 1916, his forces were on the point of collapse. Wingate, much perturbed, cabled from Sudan: 'unless supposed Syrian revolt interferes with . . . Turkish reinforcements . . . Sherif is faced with possible recapture of Medina and an advance on Mecca . . . He will have to choose then between accepting offer by us to dispatch a military expedition and almost certain defeat.' McMahon, who had been responsible for inflating the Arabs' military importance, now claimed that the revolt had been undertaken with 'inadequate preparations in ignorance of modern warfare', whereas four months later Wingate reported that the Arabs, even if adequately equipped and organised, were incapable of acting on the defensive.[66] Both Wingate and McMahon bombarded London with requests for military assistance to cut off the Turks and 'prevent early collapse of Sherif's movement'.[67] This movement not only did not snowball but was widely condemned by Mohammedan opinion, in India and elsewhere, and produced a bad effect in Syria. Hussein was blamed for ingratitude towards the Turks and his revolt commanded little or no sympathy.[68] McMahon and his entourage in Cairo were alarmed. 'We are morally committed to support the Sherif and shall certainly be held in a large measure responsible for his failure.' So hopeless seemed the position that in contravention of Moslem custom, prohibiting the presence of non-Moslems in the Hedjaz, Hussein himself requested British military assistance in troops which, he claimed, 'is a condition of our alliance'.[69] It soon became apparent that the whole Sharifian army consisted of three to four thousand tribesmen as the only reliable force, and that the movement did not command the support of the townsmen of the Hedjaz.[70]

The General Staff was indignant. The Sharif had undertaken to expel the Turks from the Arab area and asked in return for British assistance in the shape of arms and money, which had been given. Before the revolt Hussein had estimated that he could raise a force of 250,000 men and gave the impression of commanding sufficient resources to overcome the Turks. His predicament was as unexpected as it was embarrassing. It was he who had pledged military assistance to the British and not vice versa. Technically, the military argument went on, the British Government was under no obligation to come to his rescue. Yet, as prestige was involved, the General Staff was prepared to overlook that it had not been consulted during the Correspondence with Hussein, and suggested a speed-up of the operations in Sinai in order to capture El-Arish and Aqaba, a move that would simultaneously relieve Turkish pressure on the Sharif and encourage the Syrian Arabs to revolt.[71] The War Council doubted whether an offensive in Sinai would rescue Hussein in time. On the other hand, a landing of Christian troops in the Hedjaz posed a serious problem. Not only would they run a grave risk of offending Mohammedan opinion but various reports indicated that the native troops would disperse rather than be supported by Europeans. In addition, the General Staff strongly objected to mounting another expedition with unforeseen consequences. Overtaxed on the Western front and short of transport and manpower, the Staff feared that the deployment of 15,000 men to save Rabeqh would impair the El-Arish operation.[72] For nearly six months an awkward dilemma confronted the British Government. The difficulty was eventually resolved because the much feared Turkish assault on Rabeqh and Mecca did not materialise.

During this episode the British drew some comfort from the prospect that should succour be brought in time to the Sharif, and when the British army invaded Palestine, the Arabs in the north 'discontented with the Turkish rule', would rise.[73] 'A very favourable turn might [then] be given to events in the whole of Syria and Palestine besides putting the Sherif out of all danger.'[74] Sir Mark Sykes placed so much hope in such a development that he expected Turkish authority to crumble and their military operations to be hindered.[75] This, however, proved to be an illusion. At the turn of 1916 an Arab Legion was organised by the British to prop up the Sharifian forces and to serve as a rallying-point for discontented elements in Syria and Mesopotamia, but this came to nothing. 'I must honestly confess', Clayton told Sykes, 'that, viewed as a symbol of Arab nationalism, the Legion has been a failure. It has not been received with any enthusiasm by the local Arabs, in spite of much propaganda . . . I cannot say that it is worth either the money or the time of skilled officers which has to be expended upon it.'[76] Had it not been for the steady flow of gold from the British Treasury and guidance provided by the British officers,[77] the Northern Arab Army (composed of the Legion, as a regular force, and the Sharifian tribesmen) would have been crushed by the Turks or have disintegrated from within. The conquest of Aqaba on 6 July 1917 was a bold military manoeuvre, but it failed to become the rallying-point for a movement on which the British Residency in Cairo pinned their hopes. Philip Graves had some words of praise for the Arabs of the Hedjaz and their Bedouin allies, but those of Syria and Palestine 'remained passive or aided the Turks'.[78] C. S. Jarvis, formerly Governor of Sinai, expressed himself in even less complimentary terms: 'The Syrians as a people did nothing whatsoever towards assisting the Arab cause . . . beyond hold secret meetings and talk. The inhabitants of Palestine did rather less.'[79] Lloyd George recalled ironically that 'the Arabs of Palestine, who might have been helpful in many ways, were quiescent and cowering. Right through the war and up to the end, there were masses of Arab soldiers from Mesopotamia, Syria and Palestine in the Turkish Armies fighting against the liberation of their own rule'; '. . . the Palestinian Arabs were fighting against us.'[80] Despite much encouragement, when the British troops were already firmly entrenched in Jerusalem, the results of recruiting for the Sharifian forces were disappointing; no more than 150 Arabs were recruited.[81] The verdict of the Palestine Royal Commission was clear: 'It was the Sherif's own people . . . who bore the brunt of the actual fighting. The Arabs of Palestine did not rise against the Turks.'[82]

But in this context Palestine was of marginal importance. The big plum was Damascus, and it was primarily with an eye on the Syrian hinterland that the Declaration to the Seven was issued in June 1918. It pledged that those territories conquered by the Arabs would remain Arab.[83] Yet the response was negligible. With no substantial rising in sight, when Allenby's forces were converging on Damascus towards the end of September 1918, the only way out, for those who engineered it, was to stage a conquest by the Sharifian troops, to give the impression that the Arabs had taken the city from the Turk.[84] Even so, the Sharifians found the city in a state of turmoil,[85]—not of rejoicing, thus giving the lie to the belief that the Syrians craved for nothing better than liberation from Turkish rule. Testifying before the Palestine Royal Commission in 1937, Amin al-Husseini, the Mufti of Jerusalem, denied that the Arabs were ever 'under the yoke of the Turks' or that they expected to be relieved from such a yoke. For centuries they had been fully integrated within the Ottoman Empire and enjoyed equality of rights.[86] During the Committee of Union and Progress regime they might have nourished some grievances against Constantinople, but fundamentally they 'would prefer to remain under Turkish domination, with all its mis-government, tyranny and oppression . . . rather than . . . fall under the Christian yoke.'[87] Arab troops in the Ottoman army remained essentially loyal[88] and would not aid the destruction of a Moslem Power. Throughout the war, the Sharifian rebellion remained an isolated phenomenon. As Wingate, one of its chief protagonists, admitted in September 1918: 'The Moslems in general have hitherto regarded the Hedjaz revolt, and our share in it, with suspicion and dislike.'[89] A distinguished British historian and a close observer of Middle East politics, at that time, attested that 'a *general* Arab insurrection was planned [but] it never took place . . . [It was] mainly the soldiers of Britain, the Commonwealth and India—who played a part in the overthrow of Ottoman rule.'[90] Ronald Storrs, judging retrospectively, doubted whether the deal with the Sharif was after all worth while. It 'imposed upon us the real obligation of raising and maintaining his prestige to the limit of the possible, so that for this and other reasons we were in the end committed far more deeply in bullion, in munitions of war and in promises very hard to fulfil, than most of us dreamed of in September 1914.'[91]

This did not mean that Hussein's revolt, though limited in scope, was devoid of advantages. Politically, it set one Moslem against another,[92] and militarily, it harassed Ottoman troops and occasionally disrupted communications along the Hedjaz railway. But between the original expectations, on which the deal between the British and Hussein was based, and the actual performance, there was a considerable gap. There was no general uprising against the Turk. The Arab revolt, as Lawrence succinctly concluded, bore a distinctly '*local* nature'.[93] If any party remained in debt towards the other, it was rather the Arab to the British than vice versa.

It remains now for us to examine the question whether Palestine was, in fact, included or excluded from the promises made to Hussein, and if so, why McMahon's wording was so vague as to give rise in subsequent years to such an acrimonious controversy.

The point of view advanced during the twenties and thirties by the Arabs was that since Palestine was not specifically mentioned in the reservations made by McMahon in his letter of 24 October 1915, it followed that it was *ipso facto* included in the territory in which Great Britain was to recognise Arab independence.[94] In contrast, the British Government maintained that McMahon's reservation applied to 'those portions of Syria lying to the west of the district of Damascus', reading the term 'district' as equivalent to vilayet; and since the vilayet of Damascus comprised *inter alia* also the sanjaks of Hauran and Maan, which became known as Transjordan, it followed that the vilayet of Beirut and the independent sanjak of Jerusalem were covered by the reservations, to the effect that 'the whole of Palestine, west of the Jordan, was thus excluded from Sir H. McMahon's pledge'.[95] The Arabs rejected the equation of 'district' with vilayet and remained adamant in their position. Yet a succession of British officials, notably McMahon, Clayton and William Ormsby-Gore, then Colonial Secretary, testified that it was never their intention that Palestine 'should be included in the general pledge given to the Sherif'.[96] Clayton according to his own testimony, was 'in daily touch with Sir Henry McMahon throughout the negotiations with King Hussein, and made the preliminary drafts of all the letters', whilst Ormsby-Gore served in 1916 in the Arab Bureau in Cairo and on Sir Henry McMahon's Staff. In Spring 1939, in connection with the Palestine Round Table Conferences held in London, a Joint Committee of British and Arab representatives was set up to examine the McMahon Correspondence but failed to reach agreement on matter of interpretation. The British representatives agreed that the language used to indicate the exclusion of Palestine was 'not so specific and unmistakeable as it was thought to be at the time' and that 'Arab contentions regarding the meaning of the disputed phrase [district] have greater force than has appeared hitherto', but maintained that 'on proper construction of the Correspondence Palestine was in fact excluded'. Lord Maugham, Lord Chancellor and spokesman for the British representatives, confidently reiterated: 'The Correspondence as a whole, and particularly the reservation in respect of French interests in Sir Henry McMahon's letter of the 24th

October, 1915, not only did exclude Palestine but should have been understood to do so.'[97] Official Foreign Office records, now available at the Public Record Office, London, fully confirm this conclusion. It is however a matter of surprise that the Committee, though said to have examined microscopically the wording of the actual Correspondence, did overlook much other material related to its background which tends to support the British case.

It may be recalled that Hussein, in his letter of 14 July 1915, when outlining the boundaries of territory to fall within the sphere of Arab independence, was acting under the inspiration of the Arab secret societies in Syria.[98] Hussein himself declared that these boundaries represented not the suggestion of one individual but the 'demands of our people'[99] in the regions concerned. Although excessive, they were not taken at the British Residency in Cairo at their face value but regarded merely as a basis for negotiations,[100] an assumption which statements made by al-Faruqi in October-November of that year fully endorsed. Al-Faruqi conveyed the impression that the aims of the *al'-Ahd* and *al-Fatat* societies were moderate. They fully realised that the establishment of an Arab Empire, as they visualised it, was entirely outside the realm of practical politics: in al-Faruqi's own words: 'our scheme embraces all the Arab countries, including Syria and Mesopotamia, but if we cannot have all, we want as much as we can get'. They appreciated that in the regions in question England was bound by obligations to her Allies and they would recognise the French position in Syria. The point on which the Young Arabs would not budge was the inclusion of Damascus, Aleppo, Hama and Homs in the Arab Confederation. Otherwise, Clayton noted, the leaders of the Arab societies were 'open to reason and ready to accept a considerably less ambitious scheme than that which they formulated' earlier.[101]

That the inclusion of Aleppo, Homs, Hama and Damascus within the Arab state was the Syrian nationalist leaders' primary concern, is evident also from General Maxwell's cable to Lord Kitchener[102] as well as from McMahon's private communication to Sir Edward Grey of 18 October:[103]

> The occupation by France of the purely Arab districts of Aleppo, Hama, Homs and Damascus, would be opposed by the Arabs by force of arms, but with this exception, they would accept some modifications of the north-western boundaries proposed by the Sherif of Mecca. . . .

On the same day McMahon assured the Foreign Office that the Arabs 'have not included the places inhabited by a foreign race in the territories which they demand'. The message was unmistakably clear and Grey suggested that his main object would be to persuade the French Government to agree to include within the boundaries of the Arab state the cities of Aleppo, Homs, Hama and Damascus.[104] What then was the nature of the modifications of the north-western boundaries and conversely the extent of the territories excluded from the sphere of Arab independence? The answer can be gauged from al-Faruqi's statement made to Sir Mark Sykes on 20 November 1915, during the latter's stay in Cairo. Sykes, anticipating difficulties with France, pressed Faruqi to be specific. The latter responded: 'Arabs would agree to convention with France, granting her monopoly of all concessionary enterprise in Syria and Palestine'; the area to be bounded by the Euphrates in the north running south to Deir Zor, and from there to Deraa and along the Hedjaz Railway to Maan. Furthermore, 'the Arabs would . . . agree to employment of none but Frenchmen as advisers and European employees in this area . . . [and] to all French educational establishments having special recognition in this area.' An identical convention would be concluded with Great Britain with regard to Irak, Jazirah and Northern Mesopotamia, Basra and its enclave to the south to be recognised as British territory.[105]

If Sykes's cryptic language conveyed al-Faruqi's thoughts faithfully and if the terms 'monopoly of all concessionary enterprise' and 'employment of advisers' were substitutes for sphere of influence, which in the given context was most likely, then we can visualise two lines demarcating the French sphere from that designated for an independent Arab state. One was to run in the form of a crescent from Adana to the Euphrates, and from there down, along the river, as far as Der-ez-Zor, taking in the district of Aleppo. The second line was to run from the centre of the crescent southwards towards Deraa and along the Hedjaz railway to Maan, leaving out the four towns of the Syrian hinterland. Thus the Arab state or confederation of states was to cover the districts of Aleppo, Hama, Homs, and Damascus, then southwards the territory which later became known as Transjordan and the Arabian Peninsula, except Aden and the sheikdoms adjacent to the Persian Gulf. The bulk of Mesopotamia eastwards of the Euphrates was to fall within the British sphere of interests whereas the districts of Mersin and Alexandretta, the Lebanon and the whole of Palestine extending eastwards as far as the Hedjaz railway and southwards to the Egyptian border—under the French sphere of influence. The desiderata of al'-Ahd and al-Fatat covered only Aleppo, Hama, Homs and Damascus. Inclusion of these districts was regarded as *conditio sine qua non* for initiating a revolt against Turkey. Palestine and the Syrian littoral were left out. Both because of the long-standing French interests there and because these regions could hardly be termed as 'purely Arab districts', the two Societies did not see fit to claim them. As Lloyd George put it: 'The Arabs special concern was for Irak and Syria . . . Palestine did not seem to give them much anxiety. For reasons which were obvious to them they realised that there were genuine international interests in Palestine, which placed it in a totally different category.[106]

Al Faruqi was operating at a high level. His statements, McMahon understood, conveyed 'the purpose' of Sharif's letter of 14 July, 1915[107] which outlined the boundaries of Arab independence. But Faruqi was more than an interpreter or even a representative of Hussein in Cairo. 'Your honour will have realised', Hussein briefed McMahon on 1 January 1916, 'that after arrival of Mohammad [Faruki] Sharif . . . all our procedure up to the present, was of no personal inclination or the like . . . but that everything was the result of the decisions and desires of our peoples . . . we are but transmitters and executants.'[108] McMahon had therefore justifiable reason to take al-Faruqi's word as reflecting, if not be binding upon his fellow Arabs. Being under the firm impression that Palestine was excluded from Arab desiderata, he was under no compelling necessity to specify its exclusion, all the more as he understood that the Arabs 'have not included the places inhabited by a foreign race in the territories which they demand'.[109] This limitation applied with particular force to Palestine where, according to British Consular reports, there were before the war about 100,000 Jews.[110]

This, however, does not dispose of the enigma of McMahon's ambiguous wording in his fatal letter of 24 October 1915, which left a loophole for future contentions that the British pledge extended also to Palestine. Was the failure a mere accident caused by undue haste in despatching the note which admitted 'no delay' or a deliberately calculated risk? Philip Graves was the first, in a book published in 1923,[111] to throw some light on this question. We are now in a position to confirm that Graves's statement was, in fact, a repetition of McMahon's confidential letter to Sir John Shuckburgh at the Colonial Office dated 12 March 1922. With the controversy unfolding, McMahon wished it to be put on record that in his letter of 24 October 1915 it was his intention to exclude Palestine from the Arab state. He thought that he had so worded his letter as to make this 'sufficiently clear for all purposes'. He elucidated:[112]

My reasons for restricting myself to specific mention of Damascus,

Homs, Hama and Aleppo in that connexion in my letter were:
(1) that these were places to which the Arabs attached vital importance and (2) that there was no place I could think of at the time
of sufficient importance for purposes of definition further south of
the above.

It was as fully my intention to exclude Palestine as it was to
exclude the more northern coastal tracts of Syria.

I did not make use of the [river] Jordan to define the limits of the
southern area, because I thought it might be considered desirable at
some later stage of negotiations to endeavour to find some more
suitable frontier line east of the Jordan and between that river and
the Hejaz Railway. At that moment, moreover, very detailed
definitions did not seem called for.

I may mention that I have no recollection of ever having anything
from the Sherif of Mecca, by letter or message, to make me suppose
that he did not also understand Palestine to be excluded from
independent Arabia . . .

McMahon's predicament is understandable. Neither the river Jordan
nor the eastern limit of the French sphere, as sketched out by al-Faruqi,
namely running from Der-ez-Zor to Deraa and along the Hedjaz railway
to Maan, seemed to him to offer a practical border between Palestine and
the projected Arab State, and since the matter at that time was only of
academic import, McMahon did not think it necessary to spell out a
precise delimitation.

But Palestine's exclusion was embodied also in the phrase 'the regions
. . . in which Great Britain is [not] free to act without detriment to the
interests of her ally France'. In this case we are fortunate to have
McMahon's contemporary explanation. On 26 October 1915 he told
Grey:[113]

The composition of a reply which would be acceptable to the Arab
party and which would at the same time leave as free a hand as
possible to H.M. Government in the future has been a difficult task.

I have been definite in stating that Great Britain will recognise the
principle of Arab independence in purely Arab territory, this being
the main point on which agreement depends, but have been equally
definite in excluding Mersina, Alexandretta and those districts on
the northern coast of Syria, which cannot be said to be Arab and
where I understand that French interests have been recognised.

However, with regard to the portions lying south of the vilayet of
Beirut, he had no option but to be vague:

I am not aware of the extent of French claims in Syria, nor of how far His Majesty's Government have agreed to recognise them. Hence . . . I have endeavoured to provide for possible French pretensions to those places by a general modification to the effect that His Majesty's Government can only give assurances in regard to those territories 'in which she can act without detriment to the interests of her ally France'.

The territory about which McMahon was dubious as to the extent of French claims being recognised by the British Government, was Palestine, or more precisely the sanjak of Jerusalem. It is worth recalling that the de Bunsen Committee, after rejecting French claims to Palestine, considered that for similar reasons it was futile for the British Government to demand it.[114] Such an imprecise formulation of policy could provide no guidance for McMahon in phrasing the relevant passage of his letter. But as France's standing in the Holy Land was a matter of common knowledge in the Levant, it seemed cogent to resort to the ambiguous but also elastic phrase of not being 'free to act without detriment to the interests of her ally France' in order to meet all possible contingencies. This was particularly the case since Grey had specifically forewarned McMahon to take heed of French susceptibilities in that area; and agreed that the general reservation, especially with regard to the north-west boundaries [i.e. Syrian littoral and Palestine], was 'most necessary'.[115]

The recommendations of the de Bunsen Committee, it should be noted, pointed to the internationalisation of Palestine and not to placing it under a single power. Although aware of this, McMahon thought it inadvisable to warn Hussein about it. 'It will be observed', he wrote to Grey on 26 October, 'that I have definitely specified France as the only Ally concerned. The use of the term "Allies" would, I understand, inevitably have aroused the suspicion of the Arabs, who would have conjured up visions of all our Allies putting forward claims in various parts of the Arab territories.' The reference to France was yet no indication that McMahon and his aides in Cairo unreservedly accepted the French claim to Palestine. He was well aware of its strategic importance both as an eastern outpost for Egypt and a link with Mesopotamia. This may explain his interest in Edgar Suarès's scheme for a Jewish settlement in Palestine under British protection,[116] which could have usefully tipped the scales in Britain's favour. That McMahon detected no contradiction between Suarès's scheme and the promises made to Hussein, only reinforces the case that Palestine was not meant to be given to the Arabs. Neither Grey nor his Staff at the Foreign Office discerned any such inconsistency. A marginal annotation on a translated copy of Hussein's letter of 14 July 1915 indicates how London understood the limits of Arab independence. 'It includes vilayets of Basra, Bagdad, Mosul, Aleppo and Damascus.'[117] In other words, in the opinion of the Foreign Office officials, Hussein's desiderata did not include the Syrian littoral and Palestine. If O'Beirne feared that the scheme of Jewish colonisation in Palestine 'with the possible prospect of eventual Jewish self-government . . . might have a very chilling effect on the Arab leaders', it was not because he thought it conflicted with the McMahon-Hussein correspondence, but because it might entail displacement of a 'large proportion of the 6–700,000 [native] Arabs', although he believed the difficulty was not insoluble.[118]

In 1922 Sir Vivian Gabriel testified that Lord Kitchener, when Secretary of State for War, 'would certainly not have admitted the exclusion of Palestine' from the Arab State.[119] Careful examination of both Foreign Office files and the *Kitchener Papers*[120] shows that there is no foundation for such a contention. Kitchener was, indeed 'most desirous', as he told General Maxwell, 'of dealing with the Arab question in a manner satisfactory to the Arabs'[121] but apart from this general statement he made no specific reference to the territory of Arab independence. This was a political matter which lay within the province of the Foreign Office on which he, as Secretary of State for War, would not encroach. As far as Palestine was concerned, Kitchener adhered always to the view that it lay predominantly within the French sphere. 'The French', he told the War Committee on 16 December 1915, 'would leave the [Jerusalem] *enclave* [to be internationalised] but beyond that they would take everything up to the Egyptian boundary.'[122] Kitchener's favourite scheme was the acquisition of Alexandretta linked territorially with Mesopotamia under a British protectorate. Palestine, curiously enough, he dismissed as of 'no value'.[123] Should Turkey be partitioned, he reasoned, an Arab kingdom in Arabia, under British auspices, should be established 'bounded on the north by the . . . Tigris and Euphrates, and containing within it the chief Mohammedan Holy Places; Mecca, Medina and Kerbala'.[124] The omission of Jerusalem, and even of Damascus, was not accidental; it was meant to fall within the French sphere of interest as a recompense for their concession of Alexandretta. It is therefore highly improbable that Kitchener would have had the slightest intention of awarding Palestine to the Arabs. Such an idea never originated with any British Minister or official in London or in Cairo.

Least of all would Lloyd George have entertained it. On 3 April 1917 at a conference held at 10 Downing Street at which Lord Curzon was present, Lloyd George warned Sykes before his departure on a mission to the East, not to commit the British Government to 'any agreement with the [Arab] tribes which would be prejudicial to British interests'. He impressed on Sir Mark also 'the importance of not prejudicing the Zionist movement and the possibility of its development under British auspices'.[125] It would have been inconceivable for the Prime Minister to issue an instruction of such fundamental importance in the knowledge that it was incompatible with earlier promises made to Arab leaders.

'I was a party to the Balfour Declaration', Lord Milner declared in the House of Lords on 29 June 1923. 'I do not believe that the Balfour Declaration is inconsistent with any pledges which have been given to King Hussein or to anybody else . . . When all the documents are published it will be clearly established that in the promises which we made to King Hussein a distinct reservation was made of [Palestine].'

This was the consensus of opinion within the British Government both before the Balfour Declaration was made public and after. A notable exception was Dr Arnold J .Toynbee, at that time attached to the Political Intelligence Department of the Foreign Office. In a 'Memorandum on British Commitments to King Hussein',[126] he stated: 'With regard to Palestine, His Majesty's Government are committed by Sir H. McMahon's letter to the Sherif on the 24th October 1915, to its inclusion in the boundaries of Arab independence.' And in the same breath he added: 'But they have stated their policy regarding the Palestinian Holy Places and Zionist colonisation in their message to him of the 4th January 1918'—the well-known Hogarth Message. In a second memorandum, dated 21 November 1918,[127] in the item dealing with Palestine he wrote: 'We are pledged to King Hussein that this territory [i.e. west of Jordan] shall be "Arab" and "independent".'

This is rather a matter for surprise. Had Toynbee consulted McMahon's letter of 26 October 1915 to Grey,[128] in which the High Commissioner explained why he had phrased his reservation covering the territory of Palestine as he did, Toynbee would have presumably arrived at a different conclusion. But even more puzzling is Toynbee's failure to detect the relation between al-Faruqi's desiderata, which he gives in full, and McMahon's letter to Hussein of 24 October 1915. It was, it may be remembered, al-Faruqi's exclusion of the Syrian littoral, running from Alexandretta down to the Egyptian border near Rafah, from the projected Arab State, which was the corner-stone of McMahon's crucial letter to Hussein.[129] Nor was Toynbee struck by the inconsistency between Hussein's acceptance of the formula conveyed to him by Hogarth and his own conclusion that the British Government had pledged that Palestine should be 'Arab' and 'independent'. Had this been the case

Hussein would not have been slow to protest against such an unwarranted intrusion.

What grounds did Professor Toynbee have for reaching his conclusion? He has been good enough to tell us that in the autumn of 1918, when considering the question, much depended on the meaning of the word '*vilayet* of Damascus'. In Ottoman administrative usage it was applicable in a wider sense covering Cis-Jordanian Palestine, whereas in Arabic *wilayah* it meant 'environs', 'banlieux'. Professor Toynbee thinks that McMahon could not have used the Ottoman terminology in his letter of 24 October 1915, in which case, Palestine was meant to be included.[130] This is, however, a hypothesis, which though cogently argued,[131] cannot hold good when juxtaposed to McMahon's contemporary testimony.[132] The Arab Bureau staff was of course well versed in the administrative division of Syria and Palestine. Thus, Ormsby-Gore specifically referred to the region East of the river Jordan as 'part of the Vilayet of Damascus'.[133] Moreover, in correspondence on political matters, it is most unlikely that a High Commissioner would have resorted to ambiguous wording in the Arab vernacular in preference to accepted terminology in which both Hussein and his son Abdullah were well versed.

Nearer the mark would be the explanation offered by W. J. Childs of the Foreign Office in a paper dated 24 October 1930.[134] Childs pointed out, quite correctly, that Dr Toynbee, when preparing his memorandum, used a copy of the Arab Bureau's *History of the Hedjaz Rising*,[135] as his various references showed. The *History*, in Childs' view, perverted McMahon's pledge. It was 'in no way authoritative and should not be taken at face value'. It read the phrase 'districts of Damascus' as meaning its immediate neighbourhood, thus gratuitously including Palestine in the Arab area; a most peculiar interpretation, since subsequent statements, private and public, made by prominent members of the Arab Bureau contradicted it.[136] At any rate, Childs goes on to explain, when Toynbee was preparing his memorandum, he felt that he was on 'safe grounds, being conclusively supported by the views of the Arab Bureau', a fact which accounted for his fault in making no serious attempt 'to examine the pledge critically'. Toynbee did not trace the connection between al-Faruqi's declaration and McMahon's wording which was 'construed in the wide sense intended by El-Faroki' (sic); that the 'district of Damascus' 'extended to the Gulf of Aqaba', thus, by implication, excluding Palestine from the Arab area.[137]

Lord Curzon, Lord President of the Council, was the only Minister who thought that the British Government had made conflicting promises to Arabs and Jews. On 5 December 1918, at a meeting of the Eastern

Committee, of which he was Chairman, he made a statement which practically amounted to a verbal repetition of that produced by Toynbee.[138] Curzon did not however persist in his mistake for long. On 15 October 1919, in his letter to Emir Feisal, he made no mention of Jerusalem (or of any other city in Palestine) to be included in the area where the British Government was bound to recognise the establishment of 'an independent Arab State'.[139] Several weeks later the whole question was re-examined by Major Hubert Young. Major Young, an Arabist who had participated in Arab military operations east of the Jordan under Emir Feisal and Colonel T. E. Lawrence, served in the Eastern Department of the Foreign Office. In 1920 he read the Arabic text of McMahon's letter of 24 October 1915 and found that the meaning in Arabic of the words 'district of Damascus' was equivalent to the Ottoman *vilayet*, which extended southwards to the Gulf of Aqaba, with Damascus as its capital. It therefore followed that the area of Palestine to the west of the vilayet's boundary (running along the river Jordan and the medial line of the Dead Sea) was excluded.[140] The British Government adopted Young's interpretations and, in the ensuing years, followed it consistently.[141] It was not without good reason that Lloyd George, in his memoirs,[142] when reproducing Lord Curzon's statement in the Eastern Committee almost in its entirety, pointedly omitted Curzon's passage that 'the British Government pledged itself that [Palestine] should be Arab and independent in the future'.

McMahon's statement that the fact that Palestine was not included in his pledge 'was well understood . . . at the time . . . by King Hussein'[143] is fully borne out by contemporary evidence. On 7 November 1915 he reassured London that the Arab representatives 'admitted and fully understood' that in certain territories the British could not act freely and without prejudice to their French allies.[144] Although Hussein must have been aware that Sir Henry's letter of 24 October 1915 was nearly a replica of al-Faruqi's scheme,[145] Wingate was not satisfied and, through Sayyid Ali Morghani, hastened to reiterate the 'reservations which we [the British] have made in Syria, Palestine and Mesopotamia'.[146] On receipt of McMahon's letter of 24 October, Hussein argued that Mesopotamia and the vilayets of Beirut and Aleppo 'are Arab and should therefore be under Muslim Government',[147] though significantly he refrained from placing Palestine in the same category. Again on 1 January 1916 he reminded the High Commissioner that after the conclusion of the war he would claim 'Beirut and its coastal regions' but made no mention of the sanjak of Jerusalem. The following year Fuad Khetib, King Hussein's Under-Secretary for Foreign Affairs, was reported to have said that he anticipated 'no difficulty with the Jews . . . now we understand each other'.[148] Even more indicative of Hussein's attitude was his deliberate silence following the publication of the Balfour Declaration. He categorically refused to add his voice to protest against this document though urged to do so by Syrian notables in Cairo.[149] On the contrary, we learn from Antonius that Hussein 'ordered his sons . . . to allay the apprehensions caused by the Balfour Declaration among their followers [and] dispatched an emissary to Feisal at Aqaba with similar instructions'.[150] When D. G. Hogarth called on the King, on 4 January 1918, the latter seemed quite prepared to accept the formula that 'no obstacle should be put in the way of the realization of [the Zionist] ideal . . . and agreed enthusiastically, saying that he welcomed Jews to all Arab lands'.[151] About three months later, Antonius tells us, Hussein caused an article to be published in *al-Qibla* (23 March 1918), his official mouthpiece. Palestine, the article attested, was 'a sacred and beloved homeland . . . [of] its original sons (*abna'ihil-l-asliyim*)'—the Jews. 'The resources of the country are still virgin soil' which could not provide a livelihood for the Palestinian native. But the Jewish immigrants would develop the country. 'Experience has proved their capacity to succeed in their energies and their labours . . . The return of these exiles (*jaliya*) to their homeland will prove materially and spiritually an experimental school for their [Arab] brethren . . . in the fields, factories and trades.'[152]

In 1920 Colonel C. E. Vickery, an accomplished Arabist, was sent on an official mission from Cairo to Jedda to examine the original Arabic text of the Correspondence and found that Palestine was not included in the proposals to Hussein. But it was not before 1939 that Vickery published his impressions:[153]

> I can say most definitely that the whole of the King's demands were centred around Syria, and only around Syria. Time after time he referred to that vineyard, to the exclusion of any other claim or interest. He stated most emphatically that he did not concern himself at all with Palestine and had no desire to have suzerainty over it for himself or his successors.

As for Feisal, he seemed first to have fallen under the spell of the Syrians in Cairo and was 'inclined the other way', but Clayton endeavoured to persuade him, through Lawrence, that his sphere stretched east of river Jordan and not in Palestine which lay 'outside the real Arab policy'. But it was only following Feisal's meeting with Weizmann in Aqaba on 4 June 1918 that Clayton was able to tell Miss Gertrude Bell:[154]

There is little doubt that the main ambition of the Sherifian Arab lies (at any rate of Sherif Feisal) in Syria. His eyes are fixed on Damascus and Aleppo and nothing else seems to matter to him . . . It is this that leads him to welcome Jewish co-operation, as he is quite prepared to leave Palestine alone provided he can secure what he wants in Syria.

Guided by his mentor T. E. Lawrence, Feisal proved so zealous in forcing his way into Syria, that he soon overplayed his hand. He was urgently summoned by General Allenby who, reminding him of the terms of the Sykes-Picot Agreement, told him that he would 'have the Administration of Syria (less Palestine and the Lebanon Province) [but] under French guidance and financial backing, [and] that the Arab sphere would include the hinterland of Syria only'. Feisal, according to General Chauvel's note, 'objected very strongly' and pretended to have no knowledge about arrangements with France on the matter; he understood from Lawrence that the Arabs were to have 'the whole of Syria including the Lebanon but excluding Palestine'.[155]

Four months later, when asking the Supreme Council at the Versailles Conference for recognition of Arab independence, he specifically excluded the Lebanon and Palestine. 'Palestine, for its universal character,' according to David Hunter Miller, 'be left on one side for the mutual consideration of all parties concerned.'[156] Feisal's Agreement with Weizmann on 3 January 1919[157] shows that in principle he was prepared to give the Zionists a free hand in Palestine and renounce any claims to it provided, as the inserted postscript in Arabic indicates, the Arabs achieved independence in Syria. This was also implicit in Feisal's positive response to William Yale's solution setting Palestine apart under British Mandate and permitting the Zionists to carry out their plan.[158] Not before 1921 were accusations of betrayal and double dealing hurled against Britain. This is understandable. With Feisal's eviction from Damascus, Palestine provided a convenient outlet for the Arabs' mounting frustration, but the charges were unfounded. As Professor Temperley put it: 'Had . . . the Emir not been ejected from Syria by the French, much less might have been heard of his father's claim to Palestine.'[159]

British official records provide us with an interesting insight into the working of the Sharifians' mind and the circumstances that caused their *volte face*. On 12 May 1920 Feisal was officially advised that the Allied Powers, in the Conference at San Remo, had decided to recognise Syria and Mesopotamia as 'independent States, subject to the assistance of a Mandatory Power, until such time as both states can stand alone'. He was also reminded that the British Government was pledged to create a national home for the Jews in Palestine, 'an intention in which you have acquiesced', and was assured that the interests of the indigenous inhabitants would be safeguarded.[160] In his reply, King Hussein did not deny that he and Feisal had acquiesced to the British Jewish National Home policy, but complained that the British Government had not shown itself as conscientious in discharging its obligations to the Arabs with regard to Syria and Mesopotamia as it had towards the Jews. He claimed that the British were bound by a 'covenant',[161] and on 23 and 30 May 1920 made a direct plea to the Prime Minister, only to be reminded that the Peace Conference had recognised 'the principle of independence of Arab countries freed from the domination of the Turk' and that the Hedjaz alone would be 'entirely independent'. Lloyd George's assertion was entirely consistent with the original understanding made in 1915–16, but Hussein would not accept this. The war was over and he no longer required the protection of the Allied Powers; he was not bound by the Peace Conference but to Great Britain which, through its High Commissioner in Egypt (in his letter of 24 October 1915), had pledged itself to Arab independence, thereafter conceding (on 10 March 1916) all his claims. He therefore appealed to Britain to 'give up Mesopotamia, el-Ghezira, Syria and Palestine . . . because the Arabs deserve Britain's sympathy and pity'. This was the first time that Hussein had made a claim to Palestine.[162]

With the French troops poised against Damascus, Abdelmalek el Khatib, Hussein's Foreign Minister, endeavoured to impress Allenby that 'it was the Arab army who had entered the capital of Syria [on 1 October 1918] first and drove out the mutual enemy', and Hussein, raising his grievance to a melodramatic pitch, contended that it was only for Britain's sake that the Arabs had risked the dangers of revolt. For this they had gained 'nothing but hardships and troubles, the anger of the Moslem world in general and the Arabs in particular'. He repeated that Palestine had definitely been covered by McMahon's pledge in his letter of 24 October 1915, and unless the British Government acceded to his former claims, he would not sign the Peace Treaty. The Acting British Agent in Jedda, much taken aback, warned the Residency in Cairo that the King was getting 'more unreasonable and out of hand every day. Is there any prospect of him being invited to abdicate?'[163]

Nor did Hussein refrain from criticising his son. Feisal was blamed for the Arab setback in Syria. His 'comic opera' of self-coronation and setting up a separate kingdom of Syria had provoked the French to attack him, a mishap that could have been averted had Feisal remained the representative of his father. Feisal put the blame on the Syrian extremists who, he maintained, had forced his hand. He made it known that should Britain so desire, he would be ready to rule Mesopotamia instead. But Khetib, who delivered Hussein's message to Feisal, evinced little relish for such unscrupulous 'crown hunting' and considered Abdullah a more suitable candidate.[164]

Censured by his father, dethroned from Syria and with the prospects of becoming King of Mesopotamia remote, Feisal made a determined bid for Palestine. He objected to Herbert Samuel's appointment as High Commissioner on the grounds that he was universally known as a Zionist whose aim was 'to build up a new Jewish State upon the ruins of Palestine, a considerable and integral part of Syria',[165] and on 20 January 1921, in an interview at the Foreign Office with R. C. Lindsay, representing Lord Curzon, the State Secretary for Foreign Affairs, he claimed that 'nothing in the original correspondence stated that Palestine should be excluded from the Arab boundaries. . . . The Arabs had always regarded both Palestine and the hinterland of Syria as being covered by the pledges given by Sir H. McMahon.' To this Lindsay pointed out that Palestine had been 'expressly excluded' from these boundaries and the relevant passage from McMahon's letter of 24 October 1915 was read aloud to the Emir in Arabic. After an exchange of views Feisal conceded that it had been the original intention of the British Government to exclude Palestine. This concession, however, he qualified by the contention that, 'as the Arabic stood, it would clearly be interpreted by any Arab, and had been so interpreted by King Hussein, to refer to the four towns and their immediate surroundings [and as] Palestine did not lie to the west of the four towns [it] was therefore . . . included in the area for which His Majesty's Government had given pledges to his father.'[166]

Childs, who cited Feisal's statement in his memorandum,[167] commented wryly that in 1915 it suited Sharif Hussein and his advisers to give the word 'district' the widest possible interpretation, whereas in 1920, 'the narrowest interpretation promised them the greater advantage'. He found Feisal's arguments 'deliberately disingenuous'. That Feisal persistently substituted the word 'town' (not prefixed in McMahon's letter) for 'districts' suggested that he was fully alive to the weakness of his case. The native Arab populace might have had a local usage of the word *vilayet*, as meaning 'vicinity' or 'immediate surroundings' but this argument, Childs remarked, was 'beside the point'. Childs was convinced that the British Government's interpretation of the contested passage had been adopted on 'adequate grounds, and in good faith'.

Lord Curzon thought that the conversation with Feisal was fruitless because it proceeded on entirely wrong lines. It was 'absurd' for Hussein to pretend that he had a right to be consulted as to the terms of the Mandate for Mesopotamia or that of Palestine.

> He did not conquer either country; we did . . . The idea of a great unified Arab Kingdom—never contemplated or promised by the Powers—though it may have existed in the brain of Hussein, has failed to materialise. Britain has taken the Mandate for Palestine . . . and it has been ratified at San Remo. It is not open to Hussein or Feisal to dispute it.[168]

The dispute which bedevilled Middle East politics during the twenties and thirties can now be comfortably resolved; the exclusion of Palestine from promises made by McMahon to Hussein was covered both in the phrase 'the regions . . . in which Great Britain is [not] free to act without detriment to the interests of her ally France' and in that 'portion of Syria lying to the west of the districts of Damascus'. That advantage would be taken of its ambiguity to interpret 'districts' in the narrower sense of 'neighbourhood' could not be foreseen. Moreover, examination of the Foreign Office records shows how shaky, on all counts, was the basis of the McMahon-Hussein understanding. It was extracted from the British by the unwarranted assertion that a German-Turkish recognition of Arab independence was imminent. McMahon thereupon made a hasty decision, misjudging its far-reaching implications. He made a pledge on behalf of the British Government, yet did little to consult London. The Correspondence, although protracted, remained inconclusive.[169] However, the deal was not a unilateral one. Its permanence and strength depended on how the Arabs fulfilled their part; and as our evidence suggests, it was they who remained in debt, not the British. Hussein contributed his share and for this he was amply rewarded in the Hedjaz.[170] But when the general Arab uprising in the regions of the Fertile Crescent failed to materialise, the corresponding part of the understanding, pledging the recognition of Arab independence east of the Jordan and in the Syrian hinterland, lapsed. All in all, the Correspondence was not a foundation on which sound Anglo-Arab relations could be built; its imperfections were pinpointed by Dr Toynbee:[171]

> Our commitments to King Hussein are not embodied in any agreement or treaty signed or even acknowledged by both parties. In this way they differ from those to Russia, France, Italy [the 1916 Asia Minor Agreement] and certain independent Arab rulers such as the Idrisi and Bin Saud. They can only be analysed by summarizing the

history of our dealings with the King during the War, under different heads. And the position is complicated by the King's habit of ignoring or refusing to take note of conditions laid down by us to which he objects and then carrying on as if the particular question had been settled between us according to his own desires.

Significantly, Emir Feisal made no reference to his father's Correspondence when presenting the Arab case to the Peace Conference in Paris. Neither Britain's Allies, signatories to the Asia Minor Agreement, nor the League of Nations, endorsed it. From the point of view of international law, the McMahon-Hussein Correspondence had no validity.

7 The Sykes-Picot Agreement, the Arab Question, and Zionism

If the myth of the Arab revolt was kept alive, it was not for its intrinsic value to the Allied cause but because the British in Cairo saw it as an instrument by which the French could be dislodged from Syria.

The idea of excluding the French and placing the Arab Middle East under exclusive British control originated with the Syrian émigrés in Cairo, notably the Christians. They maintained that in order to protect the Suez Canal and Egypt after Turkey's defeat, it was essential that England should not allow any other European Power to gain control over Palestine. Haifa was the key to the country and, if linked by rail to Cairo on the one hand, and to the Hedjaz railway and Basra on the other, it could become a terminal of great strategic importance. Alexandretta in northern Syria was also extremely valuable. It had the finest natural port in the Mediterranean, which could be made impregnable; 'whoever holds it, commands the entrance to the Suez Canal'. It could become the outlet for merchandise and products from the Euphrates valley and Bagdad. In contrast to the British, the Syrians argued, the French were generally unpopular. Their merchants exploited Syria, and the Catholic educational and missionary establishments alienated the population. Partition of Syria and Palestine among the powers would engender bitter rivalry and would be detrimental to Arab unity. The Syrian population would welcome a British administration on the Egyptian model, with its Sultan as the nominal suzerain. A British protectorate over the Arab world was 'quite compatible with the integrity of the Holy Cities ... and in full agreement with Arab feeling'. Perhaps France could be compensated elsewhere.[1]

The proposal suggested nothing less than a complete hegemony of the Middle East, an alluring enough prospect to prompt British officers in Cairo to devise a scheme which could simultaneously wrest Syria from the Turks and eliminate any rival claimants. Its centre-piece was a landing at Alexandretta, whence the invading force was to cut Turkish communications to Aleppo and foment a local uprising. As Clayton, the chief architect of Arabian policy, noted, it could be fully justified on military grounds, and at the same time serve as a 'good political card' in British hands for future bargaining.[2]

The Foreign Office was soon advised that, according to intelligence data, a large proportion of the population of Syria and Palestine would welcome the arrival of British forces and might even give active assistance, provided the occupation was permanent. No similar feelings were entertained with regard to the possible advent of the French or the Russians. A landing at Alexandretta was the key to the whole operation.[3] Following McMahon's appointment as High Commissioner in Egypt, the case was re-argued more forcefully: it was 'to England and to England alone' that both Christian and Muslim Pan-Arabs turned; any intervention by France, and still more by Russia, would meet with the 'utmost disfavour and even hostility from the majority of the inhabitants'. McMahon advocated the extension of the dominion of the Sultan of Egypt to Syria, under a British protectorate, a solution that would preclude annexation by any power. 'Penetration of French forces into the country will accentuate the existing rivalry between French and British interests, and foster intrigue.'[4]

To prove his case McMahon appended two notes, one from Syrian Christians in Cairo, mentioned already, and the second from Sheikh Sayed Mohammed Rashid Rida, a leading Moslem theologian and Pan-Arab thinker.[5] That the Christians, Protestants in particular, should have desired Syria's annexation to Egypt under a British protectorate was natural. Apart from the economic advantages, it allowed them to pose as Arab nationalists without risking the hazards of dependence on the Moslem majority. But the same could not be said of Rashid Rida. For even a cursory examination of his note shows that he strongly objected to Britain 'taking possession of the country, or part of it [for] herself, or allowing another Power to do so, either by conquest or in the name of "protection" or "occupation", or any other title known to modern colonisation.' The precepts of the Koran and the sanctity of the Holy Places forbade foreign interference. All that the Moslems, and Arabs in particular, wanted from the British was to bring about 'complete independence' in the Arabian Peninsula and the bordering Arab countries, bounded by Persia and the Persian Gulf in the East, the Indian Ocean, the Red Sea and Egypt in the South, the Mediterranean in the West and Asia Minor in the North. Should Turkey be defeated, the Arabs of Syria and Mesopotamia would be 'ready to take charge of an independent Government on the principles of decentralization or confederation'.

McMahon's assertion is not borne out by contemporary evidence.

Three days before he had written to Grey, Rida had made it plain that he did not share the views of those who sought to make Syria a British Protectorate, or to annex it to Egypt. Should Britain assist the Arabs, defend them from aggression, and provide technical advisers and engineers to develop their dominions and assert their independence, she would earn their friendship, but annexation would deal a death blow to Islam. The Moslems of El-Irak, Syria, India and Persia would not tolerate it. The presence of Europeans in the East would revive the scourge of Christian Crusaders. 'We have already lost Egypt, but we ought not to lose Syria!' Rida admitted that the Arab movement was not actuated by a feeling of enmity towards the Turks. 'Destruction of the Ottoman Empire would involve destruction of Mohammedan principles', and neither Syrian Moslems nor Druzes wished to break away from the Ottoman fold. Rida obviously wanted the best of all worlds: to enjoy the fruits of an Allied victory without undermining Turkish integrity; to attain complete Arab independence without conceding much in return to those who could bring it about; England to become the Arabs' 'instructor . . . guider and defender [but] not their guardian or tutelary' power, since any encroachment on their independence would put the Moslems on the 'same level with the Jews'.[6]

In Palestine before the war there was a desire, particularly among the Christian elements, for foreign occupation, but the Moslems, both in the villages and the urban centres, were bitterly opposed to it, and were said to be ready to join the Ottoman troops in resisting any foreign intrusion. Their opposition was motivated primarily by religious sentiments,[7] which became even more intense after Turkey entered the war and proclaimed the *jehad*. Sheikh Abdel Aziz Shawish, a Jerusalemite Seminar teacher, Suleiman el Barouni of the Abadia sect, and Shekib Arslam, a Druze notable from the Lebanon, played a conspicuous role in the Pan-Islamic propaganda, and after June 1916 attacked Sharif Hussein with unusual vehemence.[8]

Nor was France as universally disliked as McMahon wished London to believe. A great number of Christians, notably the Catholics, looked to Paris for both inspiration and protection. They maintained that the heterogeneous population of Syria was unfit for self-government and discounted the slogan of 'complete and unconditional independence', used by the Moslems, as unrealistic.[9] Even more revealing about the desires of the different parties in Syria is a confidential intelligence report of March 1916:[10]

Generally speaking the following is roughly the truth:

Moslems plump for an Arab independent Kingdom and Khalifate; Christians for Allied assistance to get rid of the Turk, followed by a guarantee of their liberties for the future. Realising that Great Britain does not intend to go to Syria they are prepared to accept French protection . . . but with a guarantee by Gt. Britain that France will not abuse her position . . . The Maronites are whole-heartedly for the French without any conditions.

From this it would appear that it is not the case that, were the French to land there to-day, even without ourselves, the population would go with the Turks, rather than with the French, which is what is claimed by certain [anti-French] Moslems from Syria.

The Foreign Office disapproved of the Alexandretta scheme. It was loaded with political dynamite. 'To act . . . independently of our Allies is out of the question,' Oliphant minuted, a statement in which Sir Arthur Nicolson fully concurred. Besides, as Sir Arthur's son Harold pointed out, the British had nothing to offer the French as a *quid pro quo*.[11] Since Crusader times the French had regarded Syria as their sphere of influence and the *Matin* of 30 December 1914 went so far as to propose to merge it with Palestine under one name, *La France du Levant*.[12] On 23 January 1915, Augagner, the French Minister of Marine, conveyed to Churchill his Government's objection to the Alexandretta scheme.[13] Paul Cambon also reminded Grey that this was a matter on which the French Government should be consulted. Grey, loyal to the *status quo* principle and to the *entente cordiale*, assured Cambon, that should military operations take place, French forces would be associated with them. On 17 February he instructed McMahon unequivocally:[14]

French Ambassador has spoken to me about agitation in Egypt for annexation of Syria. It is a point on which French opinion is most sensitive and you should do all you can to discourage any movement of the kind, even as regards Alexandretta or places near Syria [like Haifa or Gaza]. We have promised to associate the French with us if we undertake any serious military operations in that region.

By mid-December Clayton arrived at the conclusion that the favourable moment for his 'forward policy' had passed and that it would be extremely difficult, if not dangerous, to pursue it. Despondently he divulged to a friend: 'Had the authorities [in London] decided to hold the gate to Syria and Mesopotamia in the neighbourhood of Alexandretta, I am sure it would have been the best solution to the problem, and would have enabled us to utilize the Arab movement to its utmost . . . it would have assured Arab support and enabled us to promise them very much less.'[15]

With the prospects of the 'forward policy' vanishing, McMahon became all the more eager to accommodate Hussein, expecting from him a double advantage: of detaching the Arabs from the Turk and using them to lay the foundation for British predominance in the area. This was implicit in McMahon's crucial letter of 24 October 1915 in which he reminded the Sharif that the Arabs would have 'to seek the advice of Great Britain only, and that such European advisers and officials as may be required for the formation of a sound form of administration will be British.' This, together with the suggestion made to Grey two days later that France should forego any territorial claims to the strip of land from Damascus to Aleppo,[16] pointed clearly to Cairo's objective.

The Foreign Office rejected this policy. Sir George Clerk pinpointed the dilemma from the start: 'We cannot win the Arabs unless we recon-cile French and Arab claims and the position must be clearly understood from both the French and Arab side from the outset, or we shall be head-ing straight for serious trouble.' With the British contemplating a pro-tectorate in Mesopotamia, Clerk had grave doubts about the possibility of persuading the French to abandon their aspirations in Syria, even in return for compensation in Africa; that the Arabs recognised the im-possibility of totally excluding France was a good omen.[17]

Sir Edward Grey too was concerned lest the advocated support of Arab demands in Syria would give rise to an impression in France that the British were merely intending to establish their own interests at the expense of the French. He made it unmistakably clear that if the British were to secure a French concession for the inclusion of Damascus, Homs, Hama and Aleppo in a future Arab State, they must forego the provision that the Arabs were 'to seek the advice and guidance of Great Britain only. Our primary and vital object', he emphasised, 'is not to secure a new sphere of British influence, but to get the Arabs on our side,' a ruling which suggested that Grey was not at all anxious to expand British influence, let alone acquire new territories. Austen Chamberlain was of the same opinion: 'the clause placing whole of Greater Arabia under British protection would saddle us with embarrassing and useless liability and destroy possibility of agreement with France.'[18]

An agreement with France was indispensable, not only to avoid the impression that Britain had acted in bad faith since McMahon's dealings with the Arabs could not remain secret, but simply because it was im-possible to by-pass her counsel. On 10 November 1915 Cambon com-plained to Grey that there had been 'too much talk in Cairo' and pointedly reminded him of France's long-standing connection with Syria. 'France really regarded Syria as a dependency,' he said. Susceptible as the French were on this point, a separate arrangement with the Sharif without France's participation could have had a most chilling effect on the cordiality of the *entente*. Grey thereupon suggested that Paris send a competent representative to discuss the matter.[19]

Not all departments at Whitehall were as appreciative of the French position as the Foreign Office was. At the War Office, those who were in close touch with the Residency in Cairo wished to play the Arab card for all it was worth and buy the French out of Syria. Major Vivian Gabriel, Lieutenant-Colonel A. C. Parker, and Major-General C. E. Calwell, Director of Military Operations, pressed this point hard. But the Foreign Office could not entertain it for a moment. In Sir Arthur Nicolson's opinion the Arab movement was too unreal and incoherent to be of any use, while France had a rightful claim to Syria. To attempt to outbargain her was impracticable.

How inflexible and determined the French were became evident during the first round of discussions which took place in London on 23 November 1915. The French Government was represented by François Georges-Picot, a professional diplomat with extensive experience in the Levant, at the outbreak of the war Consul-General in Beirut, a tough and shrewd negotiator. The British delegation was led by Sir Arthur Nicolson.[20] Picot's attitude was uncompromising; he insisted that Syria was a purely French possession and by Syria he meant the region bounded by the Taurus ridges on the north, Diarbekir—Mosul—Kerkuk—Deir-Zor, on the Euphrates, on the east, and the Egyptian frontier on the south. No French Government that surrendered this claim, he maintained, would survive a day. Picot thought that the British authorities in Cairo had exaggerated the strength of the Arab-Syrian movement, and he doubted its reliability. Whatever was promised, the Arabs would find it difficult to resist the appeal to religious solidarity on which Turkey and Germany were playing so skilfully, and even if some Arab tribes went over to the Entente, they would immediately quarrel among themselves. He recounted with amusement that in Cairo recently he had been told by the same Syrian officers who were soliciting the British authorities to protect them from French domination, how much they were longing for the arrival of French troops and the establishment of French supremacy in the Levant.

Nicolson replied that the Allies were not taking undue risks, since any promises made to the Arabs were conditional upon their assisting the Allies. He insisted that it was imperative to counter the *jehad*; that there was a real possibility that the Syrian troops, 100,000 strong, would defect from the Turkish army, and endeavoured to impress that, with Arab rule, France had better prospects of establishing her influence than under a Turkish régime. Though the Arabs claimed considerable portions of Syria, they were willing to concede to the French a monopoly of concessions, grant security to their educational and other establishments, and admit French advisers. In these circumstances, in a short time, Syria would become in fact a French protectorate. Picot was not impressed. He maintained that with the exception of Jerusalem and Bethlehem, which might be formed into a separate enclave under an international régime, the whole of Syria and Palestine must be treated as French.[21] Thus the proceedings reached an impasse and Picot returned to Paris to submit the matter to his Government.

Before Picot entered the second round of discussions in London, Sir Mark Sykes returned from his six-month mission to the East, ebullient and armed with first-hand information about the Arab movement and the views current among British officials on the spot. But before dealing with his personal contribution to the negotiations with Picot, a few words should be said about Sir Mark's qualities and experience. He had already established a reputation as a specialist in Oriental affairs and had influenced the thinking at the War Office, where he served as a Lieutenant-Colonel. A Kitchener man, he had strong and original views of his own. He was noted for his quick grasp of complicated situations, power to assimilate detail and faculty for improvisation without losing sight of the long-term objectives. Impressionable and intuitive, he possessed the rare gift of transmitting his enthusiasm and winning over his superiors. Of a romantic predisposition, he remained essentially a realist. Although humane, he was bent on war to the end against the Allies' adversaries. A patron of the nascent nationalities in the East, he was too mindful of Britain's own interests to be swayed by sentiment. He was an enlightened imperialist *par excellence*.

In April–May 1915, jointly with Major General Calwell, his chief, Sykes represented the War Office on the de Bunsen Committee. He was known to have favoured the (A) course, a concept which crystallised during his stay in the East. On learning soon after his arrival in Cairo that the French would be prepared to give up the coastal strip to the south of Acre, essential to the British position in Mesopotamia, he proposed certain amendments should course (D) be decided upon, namely Britain to be granted the status of a titular power over Palestine, the territory east of the river Jordan and Mesopotamia, and France a similar status in Syria. However, in principle, 'it would meet with the aspirations of many, and solve future difficulties if France were willing to forego her rights in Syria and would allow us to control [it] in return for compensation elsewhere ... The Ayalets could then be under the government of the Sultan of Egypt and the spiritual dominion of the Sherif of Mecca.'[22]

This view faithfully mirrored that of the British Residency in Cairo; in the East, in contrast to Whitehall, expansionism was the order of the day. H. F. Jacob, Assistant Resident in Aden, propagated the idea of 'the white man's burden', of the mission of gradual penetration, 'the maintenance of law and the *pax Britannica*. If we do not, other white men ... will'—a position which General William Walton, his chief, fully shared. Wingate, Sirdar of the Sudan, saw the Middle East evolving into 'a federation of semi-independent Arab states ... owing spiritual allegiance to a single Arab Primate, and looking to Great Britain as its Patron and Protector'. And in Basra, both Sir Percy Cox, Chief Political Officer, and the Army Commander of a section of the Indian Expeditionary Force, thought that maintenance of Turkey-in-Asia would jeopardise British interests; only its partition, as outlined in course (A), would guarantee the security of the Persian Gulf—a view which made Sir George Clerk note with resignation: 'I fear that events have made much of the Asiatic Turkey Committee Report wasted labour.'[23]

General Sir John Maxwell, Officer Commanding in Egypt, was the lone exception; he supported course (D). The devolutionary scheme, in his opinion, was in harmony with the traditional British policy of identification with the Sunni Moslem world and was less likely to precipitate friction with India and Egypt. It had also the added advantage of deferring the establishment of a French naval base at Alexandretta. But Sykes ignored Maxwell's advice, as he did the decision taken by the de Bunsen Committee. Returning to Cairo from a flying visit to Basra and Simla, he recommended a 'declaration of a British internal and external protectorate over an area in Southern Syria [i.e. Palestine] and Mesopotamia, to be agreed upon with France and Russia', and a similar declaration with regard to France northwards of the British area. He was anxious lest arrangements with the Arabs might offend French susceptibilities, but al-Faruqi, whom he met on 20 November, reassured him. On the following day Sykes cabled: 'Our task is to get Arabs to concede as much as possible to French and to get our Haifa outlet and Palestine included in our sphere of enterprise in the form of French concession to us. Thus we smooth the way for France with Syrians and in the matter where France has a traditional interest'; to which he added in a footnote: 'Arabs will always welcome any extension of our sphere of enterprise.' With such high stakes defence of the Canal would have to be radically overhauled.

He warned the War Office that unless a military offensive was launched on the Eastern front, the Allies ran grave risks. The Christian population in the Lebanon would be exposed to massacre, the Turks would establish themselves in the Holy Cities and install a puppet Sharif, and Britain's prestige would suffer an irreparable blow.[24]

Sykes's primary concern on his return to London was to transmit his sense of urgency to the War Committee, before which he appeared on 16 December 1915. This he did with consummate skill: if Britain remained passive, the Young Arabs would side with the Central Powers, the Sharif would be assassinated by the Turks, and Mecca would fall under Turco-German control; if the Ottoman Empire remained intact after the war, the British position in Egypt and India would be imperilled. Yet, in contrast to the Cairo officials, Sykes did not overrate the Arabs. When Asquith asked him what he thought about their military value, he admitted: 'They have a negative value, they are bad if they are against us, because they add to the enemy's forces . . . but I do not count upon them as a positive force . . . [even when] they are armed . . . they do not fight to win.' Moreover under no circumstances, should encouragement of the Arabs be at the expense of good relations with France. Until diplomatic questions were settled with Paris, no further negotiations with Hussein could be pursued. When asked by Balfour what sort of arrangement with France he had in mind, Sykes tersely summed up: (a) French sphere extending from Acre in the south to Alexandretta in the north; (b) British control over the strip of land stretching from the sea coast of Haifa-Acre bay to Kirkuk in Mesopotamia; (c) an international enclave of Jerusalem.[25] This was in fact a variation of General Barrow's scheme, outlined nine months earlier, and of course (A) considered by the de Bunsen Committee.[26]

Like his colleagues in Cairo, Sykes was under the erroneous impression that the Young Arabs had received a rival offer from Turkey and Germany. None the less, the impact he made on the War Committee was considerable. On the following day, writing to Ambassador Bertie, Lord Crewe described Sykes as 'a very capable fellow, with plenty of ideas, but at the same time painstaking and careful.'[27] The invitation to join the delegation negotiating with Picot was a further reflection of the high regard in which Sykes was held.

Picot met his opposite numbers on 21 December, this time in a more accommodating mood. After considerable difficulties, he said, he had managed to persuade his superiors at the Quai d'Orsay to include the four Arab towns of the Syrian hinterland in the Arab zone to be self-administered, but under French influence. His Government realised the importance of detaching the Arabs from the Turks and was prepared to make the utmost sacrifices towards this end. Hence, as a corollary, the French Government proposed to divide the Arab State into British and French commercial and administrative spheres of influence, the former based on Mesopotamia and the latter in Syria. Paris reserved its right to appoint a French Governor-General in the Lebanon, whilst for Jerusalem a special enclave would be formed, with boundaries still to be defined. The allocation of the Mosul vilayet and the position of Haifa and Acre as a Mediterranean outlet for the British in Mesopotamia were left open.[28]

If the French had become more amenable it was partly because they were subjected to considerable British pressure,[29] and partly because it seemed useless to swim against the tide of events. But in fact they conceded little and gained much. The scheme hatched in Paris naturally suited their interests. Delimitation of respective spheres of influence was an up-to-date version of the old plan of partition of Asia-in-Turkey, for which France had laboured in vain before the outbreak of the war.[30] The French seemed to have grasped the golden opportunity to nail the British down and obtain at no cost *de jure* recognition of their hold in Syria and northern Palestine. Arab autonomy in the Syrian interior, an extraneous enclave around Jerusalem, and a British trans-Asian railway with a terminus at Haifa-Acre were only minor concessions, compared to such an outstanding gain. But as the primary objective of British policy in Grey's definition was to win the Arabs over, not necessarily to acquire new spheres of interests,[31] the French conditions seemed to present no difficulty. Moreover, Nicolson saw no incompatibility between Picot's proposals and the British understanding with Hussein, and readily accepted them.[32] With the principles agreed, elaboration of details was delegated to Sykes. There could have been no better choice. For Sykes, alliance with France was of permanent value and he was predisposed to negotiate in a spirit of moderation and candour.

No minutes of the discussions between Sykes and Picot have come to light, but their joint memorandum[33] enables us to trace their outline. When the desiderata of all parties concerned were juxtaposed, they were seen to overlap. The French Government staked its claim over an area bounded by the Taurus and the anti-Taurus ridges on the north and a line drawn from El-Arish to Kasr-i-Shirin on the south, thus covering the whole area termed in Paris as Syria *intégrale*. This was by no means the caprice of some extremists. The French had a *locus standi* in the East. For centuries they had been regarded as the champions and protectors of the Catholics in the Ottoman Empire; they played a prominent rôle in the intellectual development of the native population in the Levant, their financial investments exceeded those of any other European country, and as a result a strong public opinion had grown up in France advocating French expansion in Syria and Palestine. But this clashed with British interests. The British 'ideal solution' prescribed administrative control and priority of enterprise in the region bounded on the north by a line running from Acre to Lake Tiberias—Tadmor (Palmyra)—Ras-ul-Ain—Jeziriret-ibn-Omar towards the Persian border. However, they were prepared to limit their desiderata to the Persian Gulf and Lower Mesopotamia and connect it with Haifa by a land route for an outlet on the Mediterranean.

But Sykes and Picot had not only to reconcile British and French interests, but to adjust them to Arab aspirations as well. This did not seem to present insuperable difficulties. Arab leaders had recognised that a coherent Arab State[34] was 'neither in harmony with the national genius of the Arabs nor feasible from the point of view of finance and administration'; they hoped that, with protection against Turkish and German domination assured, some kind of confederation of Arabic-speaking States could be formed. Sykes and Picot had therefore reason to believe that, from the Arab point of view, British and French protection was a desirable if not an indispensable expedient, that French and British administrative advisers would be welcome, and that special facilities in matters of business and industrial development would be readily accorded to both protecting Powers. On this assumption they marked out the respective French and British spheres of interests in areas (A) and (B) of the Arab State, and designating the French sphere as the 'Blue Area', and the British as the 'Red Area'.[35]

There was still a fourth item on the agenda which had to be integrated into the general scheme. It concerned the international religious interests in Palestine of Moslems, Christians, and Jews. Regarding the last, note was taken that 'the members of the Jewish community, throughout the world, have a conscientious and sentimental interest in the future of the country'. Hence, with so many parties concerned with the Holy Land, and with French and British claims overlapping, the only feasible solution seemed to be the establishment of an international administration in the so-called 'Brown Area'. Its form would have to be decided after consultation with Russia and later with Italy and the representatives of Islam. The international régime was, in a way, a modified version of that proposed several months earlier by the de Bunsen Committee,[36] but territorially it was narrower in scope and administratively limited to the Entente Powers exclusively.

In the years that followed, the Sykes-Picot Agreement became the target of bitter criticism, both in France[37] and in England. Lloyd George referred to it as an 'egregious' and 'a foolish document'. He was particularly indignant that Palestine was inconsiderately mutilated; 'the carving knife of the Sykes-Picot Agreement was a crude hacking of a Holy Land'. Curzon thought that it was 'a sort of fancy sketch to suit a situation that had not then arisen, and which it was thought extremely unlikely would ever arise',[38] while General Smuts condemned it as 'a hopeless blunder of policy'.[39] As seen through the glasses of 1917 this was, perhaps, true, but in the winter of 1915–16, when negotiations with the French were in full swing, the strategic importance of Palestine had not yet been fully appreciated in official circles. Save for securing an outlet in the Mediterranean for Mesopotamia, Palestine was not considered essential to British interests. The principal concern was to smooth the way for the Arabs and make their revolt against Turkey possible. It was characteristic of the atmosphere prevalent at the Foreign Office that with the conclusion of the discussions between Sykes and Picot, Sir Arthur Nicolson noted triumphantly that 'the four towns of Homs, Hama, Aleppo and Damascus will be included in the Arab State or Confederation of States',[40] which, considering former French opposition, seemed to be no mean success.

Nor was it fair of Lord Bertie to allege that Sykes had been outwitted by Picot.[41] The primary responsibility for the agreement lay with the inter-departmental delegation led by Sir Arthur Nicolson. Sykes merely worked out the details and, as contemporary evidence shows, he did his best to retain Palestine within the British sphere. On 28 December, just before his discussions with Picot began, he wired Clayton that he was 'eager to put sufficient force in Egypt to start an offensive . . . and to obtain from them [the French] recognition of our political and economic interests south of the line Haifa–Rowandus'.[42] Picot's report to Paris confirms this: 'Sir Mark Sykes reclamait pour l'Angleterre la Palestine, moins les Lieux Saints qui devaient être internationalisés.'[43] Picot was equally adamant on Palestine but eventually both representatives realised that they had to compromise. Sykes's position was not easy. His overriding aim was to make the Arab rising possible and this hinged on French concessions in the Syrian hinterland. Nor could military operations on the eastern front take place without French concurrence, a consideration which weakened Sykes's bargaining position with regard to Palestine. Three years later Hirtzel summed up the problem: 'French consent was therefore doubly necessary before the [Arab uprising and Allied military] offensive could be begun, and the *Sykes-Picot Agreement was the price we had to pay for it*. Without the British offensive there could have been no

Arab revolt; and without the Sykes-Picot Agreement there would have been no British offensive.'[44]

From this point of view Arab criticism is even less justified. Antonius painted the Sykes-Picot Agreement in the darkest colours and labelled it 'a shocking document', a 'product of greed' and 'a startling piece of double dealing'.[45] The joint memorandum of the two negotiators is sufficient testimony to the contrary. They showed meticulous consideration for Arab interests and blended it with healthy realism. The power vacuum created by the destruction of the Ottoman Empire had to be filled by new authority; the alternative was chaos. Absolute independence of the Arabs would have invited anarchy or an invasion from outside. There was no material incompatibility between the Agreement and the pledges made to Sharif Hussein. Whilst attempting to satisfy what seemed to them the legitimate ambitions of their respective countries, Sykes and Picot undertook to ensure the success of the Arab movement and to provide the protective umbrella under which the Arab State or Confederation of States could freely develop. However distasteful the document was to Lloyd George, he did acknowledge that 'the first promise of national liberation given by the Allies was the Sykes-Picot Agreement of May 1916. It guaranteed freedom to the Arabs from the shores of the Red Sea to Damascus.'[46]

The party that stood most to lose from the Agreement was Britain. Pro-Arab policy hardly paid its dividends, for the Arab revolt proved an illusion. Had the British not insisted so firmly on the inclusion of the four towns of the Syrian hinterland in the Arab 'zone', they could in all likelihood have secured better terms for themselves in Palestine and Mosul. This was apparently what Sir Edward Grey had in mind when writing to the French Ambassador that 'the acceptance of the whole project [of the Asia Minor Agreement] . . . will involve the abdication of considerable British interests'.[47] Grey was no convert to the idea of annexation and greater imperial responsibilities. Yet if the partition of Asia-in-Turkey was unavoidable, Britain had to take her rightful share, along the lines sketched out earlier by General Barrow, examined by the de Bunsen Committee, and supported by the British officers in the East and Sir Mark Sykes. 'Provided that the co-operation of the Arabs is secured, and that the Arabs fulfil the conditions and obtain the towns of Homs, Hama, Damascus, and Aleppo,' Grey told Cambon in the above-mentioned note, 'His Majesty's Government . . . are ready to accept the arrangement' arrived at in London and Petrograd. Later Lloyd George was to brace himself to rectify the deficiencies of this arrangement; at the end of 1918 he was able to extract an assurance from Clemenceau, the French Prime

Minister, that France would assent to a British, instead of an international administration for Palestine, as well as to the transfer of Mosul from the French to the British sphere in Mesopotamia, presumably in return for British recognition of unqualified French control of the Damascus-Aleppo districts in addition to the Syrian littoral.[48] But early in 1916, when it was taking shape, only a few competent observers were able to detect the blunder.

That the draft Agreement attracted no comment at the Foreign Office, where the whole scheme had been nurtured, is not surprising. Sir Arthur Hirtzel, on behalf of the India Office, objected to the inclusion of Mosul in the French sphere. At the War Office, Brigadier-General Macdonogh, Director of Military Intelligence, took a rather academic view. He regarded discussion of the division of the Ottoman Empire as premature: 'We are rather in the position of the hunters who divided the skin of the bear before they had killed it.' The situation at the end of the war could not be foreseen and the delimitation of spheres of interest could only be of a provisional nature. The only aspect that commanded his attention was the military one.[49] But if to Macdonogh the proposed Agreement was chiefly of academic interest, to William Reginald Hall, head of the Intelligence Department at the Admiralty, it was defective, if not superfluous. The military value of the Arabs had, in his opinion, been inflated; and the advantage was merely the negative one of denying them to the enemy. In principle, Hall thought, successful military operations would have a far more stimulating effect than paper assurances. 'Force is the best Arab propaganda.' It was erroneous to assume that the Arabs desired unity under Franco-British ægis. 'They will never be united . . . What they aim at is independence,' and this ambition might one day turn against their protectors.

Nor did the second motive of the Agreement commend itself to Hall. It was hoped that it would materially galvanise the Franco-British alliance in the East, but there was no evidence that the pro-German elements in France, whose eyes were fixed on Syria, would split the Entente if there was no such agreement. In any case, France was to obtain the best part of the loaf. She would receive all the large towns and practically all the cultivatable area in Syria and Northern Mesopotamia and a self-supporting line of railway; while Great Britain secures only a naval base at Haifa and a right of user or construction of a railway, through waterless desert, with no right to maintain a force to defend it. This is a high price to pay. The theoretical elaboration of spheres of influence was 'valueless except as a means to the end.' However, should conclusion of the Agreement be unavoidable, France's claim to Palestine should be rejected, whilst for Britain it was necessary to include the assurance of the right to occupy part of Palestine and Moab, with exclusive control of all railways there, and the right to have and to fortify a naval base on the Syrian coast.

> It is a strategical necessity that there should be railway communication between the Mediterranean and Mesopotamia through territory which is either British or under British influence. This is essential now for the safety of Mesopotamia, and in the future will be imperative to safeguard British interests in a sphere of influence which will run without a break from Egypt through [Palestine], Mesopotamia and Southern Persia to Baluchistan and India.

Another point which Hall disputed concerned the Jews. In contrast to Sykes and Picot, who assumed them to have only a sentimental attachment to Palestine, Hall pointed out that 'the Jews have a strong *material*, and a very strong *political*, interest in the future of the country'. He envisaged opposition on their part 'throughout the world, to any scheme recognizing Arab independence and foreshadowing Arab predominance in the southern Near East', but hoped that they 'may be partly placated by the status proposed for the "*Brown Area*" '. He added:[50]

> In the *Brown area* the question of Zionism, and also of British control of all Palestinian railways . . . [will] have to be considered. It would be more satisfactory if the line of demarcation between French and British spheres of influence was drawn *straight* from [Tyre to] the Sea of Galilee [and] to Tadmor (Palmyra). As the line curves at present, our area of influence is almost entirely sheer desert.

This was a remarkable memorandum. Hall's assessment of the prospects of the Arab contribution to the war was more realistic than that of McMahon, and subsequent events proved him right. The concept of a continuous territory from Egypt to Mesopotamia, with Palestine as a link, under British control, was well ingrained among British military circles, and Hall was not the first to propound it. What is striking is the relation between advocacy of a British presence in Palestine and consideration for Zionist interests; not perhaps too surprising a thesis if we recollect that Lord Fisher lent Samuel his unqualified support and told him that his memorandum had been studied at the Admiralty.[51]

Curzon was also dissatisfied with the draft Agreement, but Grey assured him that it would become effective only if and when the Arabs threw in their lot with the Allies, a condition that had been expressly stipulated in the arrangement.[52] Grey's statement, as well as his subsequent note to Cambon of 16 May 1916, already quoted, was fully in line with the decision adopted by an inter-departmental Committee on 4 February 1916 in which, in addition to Grey, Crewe, and Nicolson (Foreign Office), Kitchener, Bonar Law (Leader of the House of Commons), Holderness and Hirtzel (India Office) also participated. An Admiralty representative was also present but abstained from giving an opinion. Their decision reads as follows:[53]

> M. Picot may inform his Government that the acceptance of the whole project would entail the abdication of considerable British interests, but provided that the co-operation of the Arabs is secured, and that the Arabs fulfil the conditions and obtain the towns of Homs, Hama, Damascus and Aleppo, the British Government would not object to the arrangement. But . . . it would be absolutely essential that, before anything was concluded, the consent of Russia was obtained.

The Agreement, even after it had been endorsed by Russia, bore a strictly provisional character and was conditional upon action taken by the Arabs.[54] Failing such action, the Agreement would become null and void. Its underlying motive was to detach the Arabs from the Turks. There was no double-dealing on the part of the Allies. Delimitation of their respective spheres of interest in Turkey-in-Asia was the direct consequence of negotiations with the Arab leaders. The true progenitor of the Sykes-Picot Agreement was not the Constantinople Agreement,[55] as has been generally assumed, but the McMahon-Hussein Correspondence.

There is no evidence to show whether Sykes read Hall's paper, but it is most unlikely that a matter which concerned him so closely would not have been brought to his attention. If he did examine it, it signalled the beginning of his interest in Zionism. Thereafter he read Samuel's memorandum, but, in his letter to Samuel of 26 February 1916,[56] shortly before his departure for Petrograd, he made no comment on the merits or demerits of Zionism, except to note that its 'principal object' was, as he understood it, 'the realisation of the ideal of an existing centre of nationality rather than boundaries or extent of territory'. This observation mirrored Sykes's own ideas rather than Samuel's. The principal theme of the memorandum was the development of Jewish settlement under British protection into a Jewish State, but Sykes completely ignored this. With his mind fixed on the establishment of an international régime in the 'Brown area' and with the northern part of Palestine allotted to France, Samuel's scheme seemed to be out of place. There was in any case no prospect of France approving it. France was not too sanguine about the idea of an international régime for the Brown area, let alone of a British Protectorate. This became unmistakably clear when Picot suggested that Belgium should administer Palestine as a trustee of the Entente Powers.[57] When Sykes told Samuel in his letter of 26 February 1916 that a Belgian rather than an international administration of Palestine 'was more acceptable to France', he meant to point out how remote was the prospect of a British Protectorate. Sykes was yet honest enough to disclose to Picot the Zionist desire for Britain's protection.[58]

Sykes and Picot seemed to have worked in commendable harmony.[59] Nor did the discussions in Petrograd with Sazonov undermine it. Initial misunderstandings with the Russian Foreign Minister were quickly cleared up and on 15 March Sazonov, with the Emperor's approval, gave the British and French Governments 'a free hand to deal with the question of Arab Confederation'. Two days later the Russian Government declared itself 'completely disinterested' in the region stretching southwards of the line Amadie—Diarbekir—Adana, and was prepared to accept any Anglo-French arrangements, provided that Russian desiderata in Constantinople and the Straits were met. As for Palestine, the Russians hoped that all Orthodox establishments would enjoy religious freedom and their privileges respected. Otherwise, they had 'no objection, in principle, to the admission of Jewish Colonists to the country'.[60] It was at this time that Grey's telegram of 11 March, containing the proposals of Wolf and O'Beirne for a Jewish settlement in Palestine,[61] reached Petrograd. Buchanan communicated its contents to Sykes and the latter discussed it with Picot. Both of them were startled. 'M. Picot made loud exclamations and spoke of pogroms in Paris. He grew calmer but maintained France would grow excited.' The French, Picot told Sykes, 'would never consent to England having temporary or provisional charge of Palestine', not even if Britain offered them Cyprus as a gift and appointed French Governors for Jerusalem, Bethlehem, Nazareth and Jaffa. 'They seem hardly normal on this subject,' Sykes commented, 'and any reference seems to excite memories of all grievances from Joan of Arc to Fashoda.' Sykes too was deeply disturbed. During his recent visit to Cairo he had been told, by Dr Nimir and al-Faruqi, poles apart on political questions, that 'Arabs, Christians and Moslems alike, would fight . . . to the last man against Jewish Dominion in Palestine'. With the Arab revolt uppermost in his mind, Sykes feared lest the Sharif would be in a position to accuse the British of 'introducing idolatrous Indians into Mesopotamia to oust

Moslem Arabs;[62] impose French rule in Syria to Frenchify Arab Christians, and now . . . to flood Palestine with Jews to drive out Arabs, whether Moslems or Christians,' in which case he would say: 'Turks and Germans are preferable.' However, after reflection, Sykes thought the problem 'soluble'; there was 'room for compromise'. He urged upon Picot the advantage to the Allied cause of the active friendship of Jews all over the world, and with the latter's concurrence elaborated a scheme, the essentials of which were the following:

(a) Appointment of one of Abdul Kader or of Sharif Hussein's sons as Sultan of Palestine; Britain and France, with Russia's consent, acting as guarantors of the independent Sultanate.

(b) Incorporation of a privileged Zionist Chartered Company in the constitution of the new State. The Company would be entitled to purchase land for colonization and settlement, it being understood that the Jewish colonists would become citizens of a Palestinian State. Britain would act as arbitrator in any dispute arising between the Zionist Land Company and the Palestinian Government.

(c) An agreement, satisfactory to Russia and France, with regard to the administration and status of the Holy Places; France acting as arbitrator between the administration of the Holy Places and the Palestinian Government.

This was a complex solution which only Sykes, with his unequalled gift for compromise, could have invented. He hoped to reconcile the wishes of all parties concerned: 'France gets a position in Palestine, Russian demands are satisfied, Arabs have a Prince, Zionists get constitutional position and . . . British protection,' which he understood was what they wanted. But before making the Zionists such an offer, Sykes insisted that they should 'give some demonstration of their power', such as an 'accentuation of German financial straits and glow of pro-allied sentiment in certain hitherto anti-Ally neutral papers'.[63]

The scheme found no acceptance at the Foreign Office.

It is clear that the Chartered Jewish Company, suggested by Sir M. Sykes, would very soon gain complete administrative, financial and executive authority in the new State, but our real object in raising the question is to find something with which to dazzle Jewish opinion—and I much doubt whether an Arab Sultanate would have that effect.

This was Harold Nicolson's reaction. Oliphant was also of the opinion that the Arab Sultanate 'would certainly wreck' the bid for Jewish support, and O'Beirne, who had fathered the scheme of Jewish statehood in Palestine, thought that Sir Mark should not have discussed it with Picot at all. The matter was fraught with difficulties:

> It is evident that Jewish colonization of Palestine must conflict, to some extent, with Arab interests. All we can do, if and when the time comes to discuss details, is to try to devise a settlement which will involve as little hardship as possible to the Arab population. We shall then, of course, have to consult experts, but meanwhile, we cannot enter into a discussion with Sir M. Sykes at Petrograd on the subject.

Grey regretted that Sykes had exceeded his brief and advised Nicolson:

> Ask Sir G. Buchanan to tell Sir M. Sykes to obliterate from his memory that Mr. Samuel's Cabinet Memo. made any mention of a British Protectorate . . . I told Mr. Samuel at the time that a British Protectorate was quite out of the question and Sir M. Sykes should never mention the subject without making this point clear.[64]

Nicolson transmitted Grey's note verbatim, prefacing it with a reminder that 'the matter should not have been discussed by Sir M. Sykes with M. Picot'. O'Beirne hoped that this rebuke would have a sobering effect, but Sykes could easily justify his conduct. His informal discussion on Zionism with Picot was 'unavoidable', since Sazonov had shown Grey's telegram of 11 March to the French Ambassador and Picot. To the latter the matter had not come entirely as a surprise, as before their departure for Petrograd Sykes had warned him to expect the Zionists to make a move. Moreover, Sykes argued,

> I have never mentioned Palestine to Picot without making it clear that His Majesty's Government have not idea [sic] to protect Palestine, but I could not [avoid] discussing difficulty arising out of Zionists' known desire for British protection clashing with French susceptibilities. With this in view, Picot and I, jointly and informally, sketched solution suggested in my telegram of March 14th.[65]

A few days later, when Sykes discussed the question with Picot again, he found him quite satisfied with the plan for the Zionist Chartered Company though lukewarm about its being protected by Britain. Picot conceded however that the French Government 'might . . . fall in with it, on the ground that it might materially help in the war'. To Sykes, the Zionists were a factor worthy of consideration. Should they dislike his Palestinian project, he feared they could wreck it. He suggested that the Foreign Office sound out the Zionists carefully and keep them in hopes of a sympathetic hearing. 'I believe we can get them full colonizing facilities coupled with their rights in an enlarged Palestine. We cannot get them either political control of Jerusalem within the walls of the [old] city, nor any scheme tending thereto. I am confident that French, Russians and Arabs would never agree.'

At the Foreign Office end, O'Beirne, irritated by Sykes's action, noted: 'nobody proposes to give the Jews "political control" of Jerusalem, and to speak of the Zionists "making a move" of any kind seems quite premature'. Flexible in mind and highly intuitive as Sykes was, his information about the Zionists at this stage was fragmentary. Another piece of advice to London, that the British must not allow themselves 'to get into an anti-French frame of mind', was equally superfluous, but his suggestion that Arab representatives, such as al-Masri and al-Faruqi, should be invited to London for formal discussions, was sound. In his usual optimism he did not anticipate any serious difficulty. When the Arab representatives reached London on 7 April 1916, 'I believe', he noted, 'by May 8, ground would be clear of Arab–French question and Zionist claims agreed upon.' 'Picot anxious to deal with the problem.'[66] A dialogue, however imperfect, was always preferable in Sykes's eyes to complete lack of contact. It testified to his essential honesty.

The proposal for a round table discussion foundered against Cairo's objections. Clayton maintained that none of the Arab groups was in a position 'to speak representatively' and the presence of Arab officers in London was of little use. Yet six months earlier both he and McMahon had thought the same Arab officers representative enough to negotiate with them, and to conclude thereafter an agreement with Sharif Hussein. An alternative suggestion that Picot pay a visit to Cairo was also rejected.[67] McMahon considered Picot 'a notorious fanatic . . . quite incapable of assisting any mutual settlement on reasonable commonsense grounds', while Clayton labelled him 'an enthusiast in the cause of French expansion in the Eastern Mediterranean and . . . one of the Anglophobe school of 1898'. Clayton was critical of the French methods of direct rule, though, he admitted, that the British were in 'a similar position as regards Bagdad and Basra, and possibly the southern portions of Palestine'.[68] But it was primarily the prospect of a Franco-Arab rapprochement under a British *imprimatur* that prompted McMahon and his like-minded colleagues to reject the conference *à quatre* in London.

Their hostility to the Asia Minor Agreement should be seen in a similar light. That those who had indirectly contributed to its birth should have become its fiercest opponents seems rather ironic, though considering the consistency of objective, that of ultimately dislodging the French, not paradoxical at all. As soon as the document reached Cairo,[69] it came under heavy fire. Hogarth dismissed it as a 'purely opportunistic measure' which could offer no long-term solution. It put the British at a grave disadvantage and did not help their Arabian policy. He doubted whether the French or the Russians possessed the necessary vigour to establish effective control in the areas allotted to them, and criticised the exclusion of Beirut, an important centre of Arab nationalism, from the Arab State. In contrast, Palestine under international control was 'the best solution, especially in view of the aspirations of the Jews to the area in which they may enjoy some sort of proprietorship',[70] a statement which is particularly interesting since only three weeks earlier Hogarth had aired the view that Palestine had been covered by McMahon's pledge to Hussein.[71]

McMahon too disliked the Asia Minor Agreement. Although he admitted that nothing in it conflicted with any assurances given to the Sharif, he considered it inadvisable to divulge it to the Arabs. 'Moment has not yet arrived when we can safely do so without some risk of possible misinterpretation by Arabs. It might be prejudicial to our present good relations.' An identical view was expressed by Captain (later Brigadier-General) Wyndham Deedes, then an Intelligence officer at Cairo Headquarters who feared that premature disclosure might prejudice the hoped-for Arab rebellion, though he too saw no inconsistency between the Agreement and British engagements with the Sharif. There were additional reasons for secrecy. 'Its publication', Clayton said two months later, 'would inevitably produce among the peoples concerned the impression that the Ottoman Empire was to be divided up amongst the Allies and that they were only exchanging a Turkish (and a *Mohammedan*) master for a European (and *Christian*) one. This impression would be fostered sedulously by Turkish and German propagandists to their own great advantage.' Moreover, conditions were changing so swiftly that 'there can be no certainty that an agreement made today will suit the conditions of six months hence'.[72] This latter point goes far to explain Cairo's concern: disclosure, let alone its acceptance by Sharif Hussein, would have legitimised the Agreement, while secrecy held out the prospect that time would render it obsolete.

Grey agreed that 'details' of the Agreement should not be divulged to the Arab leaders,[73] though apparently for different reasons. The Agreement presupposed a total victory over Germany and Turkey, and in 1916 this seemed remote.[74] Partition of Asiatic Turkey was merely a settlement in principle; its application was directly related to Hussein's action, but with the latter remaining elusive, Grey did not feel obliged to accommodate him. 'We have gone far enough with promises to the Sherif and he has as yet done nothing.' Grey insisted that until Hussein restored his credibility, negotiations should not be continued. Sir Arthur Nicolson also objected to any further discussions with the Sharif: 'We should wait for some action on his part. Hitherto we have had plenty of promises from him—but nothing more—while we have given him beyond assurances, arms and money.'[75] However, the decisive factor influencing the British and French Governments to maintain secrecy over the Agreement[76] was apparently Russia's request. In the long run this decision proved a major blunder of policy. The Arabs were directly concerned with the arrangement and by failing to notify them of its terms the Allies, and Britain in particular, laid themselves open to charges of breach of faith. Lloyd George found this conduct 'incomprehensible'.[77] In any case, secrecy could not be maintained indefinitely, and nothing so quickly breeds suspicion as intrigue.

Whether disclosure would have put the Sharifian revolt off altogether is a matter for conjecture. Bearing in mind that delimitation of spheres of interest between Britain and France followed, in general terms, the lines set out by al-Faruqi during his interview with Sykes, and that Hussein (following McMahon's letter of 30 January 1916) did not dispute the need to respect the Anglo-French entente, it is reasonable to suppose that at that time the Arabs would have had little reason to object. Moreover, despite the impression to the contrary created by McMahon, Hussein needed the British more than they needed him, and with the Turks plotting to assassinate him, his choice lay inevitably with the Allies. Yet, ignorance of the Agreement could do him no harm for, officially unaware of its existence, he was in no way bound by its terms, and when Sykes and Picot, during their mission to the East in the spring of 1917, did inform him, he was in a stronger position to extract an important concession.[78]

8   The Breakthrough

We have seen that it was only when in Petrograd that Sykes began seriously to consider how the Jews could be fitted into his arrangement with Picot and Sazonow. Contrary to the accepted view, it was not the Samuel memorandum that converted him to Zionism, at least at this stage. Had this been the case he would not have reacted to Grey's telegram of 11 March 1916 as he did.

Sykes was an unusually perceptive man and, realising the advantages of capturing the allegiance of the Jews, he devised a compromise scheme of an Arab Sultanate in Palestine and a Chartered Zionist Company under British protection. While the first was designed to allay Arab fears, the second was intended to compensate the Jews for becoming subjects of an Arab Sultan and give them a powerful economic lever in the country. Since the Zionists shied away from the idea of sovereignty, at least in the immediate future, and had submitted to the jurisdiction of an Ottoman Sultan in the past, a *modus vivendi* with an Arab ruler did not appear too unrealistic to him, particularly if their interests were now to be safeguarded by Britain. However, such a complex scheme would be workable only if all the parties concerned agreed. Hence the rationale of the conference *à quatre*. The proposal was rejected. Nor did the Foreign Office approve of Sykes's ideas.[1] But Sykes was an unconventional diplomat who had little regard for Foreign Office bureaucracy or its advice. So enamoured did he become of his scheme, and so irresistible was his zest for free-lance diplomacy, that even official censure could not restrain him.

Soon after returning from Petrograd, in April 1916, he set about convincing the Zionists of the merits of his plan. He communicated it to Samuel, who passed it on without specifying the source to Rabbi Gaster, Weizmann and Sokolow. An extract from Gaster's diary, dated 16 April, correctly represents its substance. 'We are offered French–English condominium in Palest[ine]. Arab Prince to conciliate Arab sentiment and as part of the Constitution a Charter to Zionists for which England would stand guarantee and which would stand by us in every case of friction.' Gaster was overjoyed. It sounded like a diluted version of Herzl's abortive scheme propounded to Abdul Hamid fourteen years earlier. 'It practically comes to a complete realisation of our Zionist programme. However, we insisted on: national character of Charter, freedom of immigration and internal autonomy, and at the same time full rights of citizenship to [illegible—?Arabs] and Jews in Palestine.'

Gaster grasped with alacrity the opportunity of dealing with a man of Sykes's calibre. He made no secret of his distaste for any form of combination with France, but Sykes was committed by an agreement to the French, and refused to budge on this. A few days later, when introduced by Sykes to Georges Picot, Gaster was faced with an indivisible entente and changed his tune. He recalled Napoleon's idea of a Jewish Kingdom in Palestine, how the Jews cherished his memory, and dropped a broad hint that 'against positive assurances' for their aspirations in Palestine, the Jews would do their best to create a public opinion favourable to France as well. He told his visitors of 'S[chiff?]'s resignation and . . . [consequently] elimination of German preponderring influence in the U.S.'[2] Gaster thus created the impression that the moment was ripe for launching a successful pro-Entente propaganda campaign, but failed to live up to Sykes's and Picot's expectations. As Sykes intimated later privately to Aaron Aaronsohn, 'Dr. Gaster had assumed pontifical airs and assured him that he could run the whole Zionist work.' Sykes trusted him at first but finally realised that he had been mistaken. 'Gaster's egotism was ruining him'[3] and the cause he espoused.

Though a dignified and impressive personality, Gaster was not a political leader. One of Herzl's earliest followers and a Vice-President of the 1913 Zionist Congress, he had no official status in the British Zionist Federation entitling him to speak in its name, nor did he have the necessary social and organisational connections with American Jews. His secretive nature and egotistic predisposition disqualified him for work of this kind. His contact with Sykes and Picot may have deepened their knowledge of Zionism but on the practical plane it led nowhere.

It was when Gaster's usefulness seemed to be exhausted that Sykes met Aaron Aaronsohn. Aaronsohn was cast in a different mould. He personified the new generation in the pre-war Jewish community of Palestine. His outstanding talents became evident from early childhood in Zichron-Yaakov, and Baron Edmond de Rothschild, the colony's patron, sponsored his education at universities in France, Germany and the United States. The Experimental Station at Athlit, near Haifa, which Aaronsohn founded on returning from his studies, was a pioneering venture; it was here that his discovery of the ancestry of the wheat grain established his international reputation as an agricultural scientist. However, Aaronsohn's range of interests far transcended his daily research. The social and political problems of his people always competed for his attention, but his greatest passion was for Palestine. His knowledge of the country, of the habits of life of Jew and Arab, was unparalleled and he was equally at home in Europe and America. During the war and afterwards, when he threw himself into the mainstream of Zionist political activity, it stood him in good stead. But Aaronsohn was not a popular leader. Though he was endowed with remarkable qualities, which put him head and shoulders above his contemporaries, his individualism worked against him. Temperamental and militant by nature, he was not easy to work with. He found it more congenial to pursue his ideas alone than to seek a compromise with those who disagreed with him. He made friends and foes with equal ease, but his sound judgement of complicated political situations, coupled with his vast knowledge of the East, made him indispensable to those who sought his advice.

Aaronsohn's conviction that the Zionist enterprise could flourish best under British protection had matured as early as 1912–13, when in New York, but he refrained from making his views public lest they embarrass the Berlin-based Zionist leadership and appear disloyal to the Ottoman Government. However, the brutal expulsion of Russian Jews from Jaffa in December 1914 finally shattered his hope that a *modus vivendi* with the Turk was possible. Aaronsohn's forthright manner and his success in fighting a plague of locusts which descended on the Middle East in 1915–16, won the confidence of Djemal Pasha, Commander of the Ottoman Fourth Army. But the more closely he became acquainted with the nature of this despotic ruler, the more concerned Aaronsohn grew about the future of his people. With the tragedy that had befallen the Armenians at the back of his mind, he feared that on the slightest provocation Djemal, with Germany's connivance, would not hesitate to put an end to Zionist colonisation. Though he was wrong about Germany, it was this premise that led him to the radical conclusion that unless Palestine was speedily conquered by the British forces, the prospects of the *Yishuv* surviving the war were gloomy indeed.[4]

It was with this aim in mind that he made his way by a devious route to England, leaving behind a well-organised espionage network. During his stay in London, from 24 October 1916 till the end of November of that year, Aaronsohn gave British Military Intelligence valuable information on internal conditions in Turkey, as well as on troop movements, coastal fortifications, man-power and general war potential. His interrogators at the War Office gathered immediately that 'the inhabitant of Athlit' (Aaronsohn's temporary code name) could give them considerable help; his statements, when checked, were found to be 'very correct', but the object of his visit seemed obscure: 'he might be just as observant of things here as he has been in Turkey and a purveyor of information of the conditions in England if he could get back to Turkey'.[5] But the War Office eventually satisfied themselves of his bona fides; and of the genuinely idealistic character of his motives. What Aaronsohn asked in return was the liberation of Palestine from Turkish rule and some assurance of British sympathy for Zionist aspirations. On neither count was he reassured before leaving London for Cairo to undertake intelligence work, but unwittingly he was successful in converting his interrogators to his cause. Amongst them were: Major Walter Gribbon, the officer in charge of Turkish affairs at General Headquarters, his assistant, Captain Charles K. Webster, and Sir Mark Sykes. In his Weizmann Memorial Lecture, the late Professor Webster spoke of his admiration for Aaronsohn and how it had deepened his sympathy for the Zionist ideal:[6]

> It was he who gave me my first real contact with one of the Yishuv and I cannot forbear to mention how deep that impression was. It was made not only by the story of his great adventure during the war, but his unexampled knowledge of Palestine and his complete faith that the land could be made to blossom like the rose by Jewish skill and industry. Such assurances were all the more important at that time because one of the arguments most frequently used was that it was quite impossible for Palestine to accommodate more than a fraction of the numbers which Zionists claimed could be settled there.

How deeply Sir Mark Sykes was impressed by Aaronsohn can be gathered from the confident and close relations which later developed between them.[7] From the fact that such hard-headed British officers as Ormsby-Gore, Philip Graves, Wyndham Deedes and Richard Meinertzhagen[8] were won over to Aaronsohn's ideas, it would be reasonable to suppose that it was he who was the decisive influence in Sykes's conversion to Zionism. They met in London three times: on 27 and 30 October and on 6 November. The first interview took place in Major Gribbon's presence and the second in that of Fitzmaurice. The conversations centred on Zionism and on conditions in Turkey. Aaronsohn was gratified to note that Sykes's earlier predilection for Turkey[9] had faded and that he listened attentively to the arguments for an early British invasion of Palestine.[10] However, it was not before Lloyd George's accession to power that Aaronsohn's dream came true.

Major Gribbon, with whom Aaronsohn had at least a dozen working sessions, was also impressed, as was Sir Basil Thomson, in charge of counter-espionage at Scotland Yard. Aaronsohn's diagnosis of Turkey's ills was echoed in Sykes's memorandum of 22 November 1916, and sections of his reports were cited subsequently in the *Arab Bulletin*,[11] the organ of the Arab Bureau in Cairo, an unusual privilege since this publication was strictly confidential and of a very limited circulation. The practical achievements of Jewish colonists were henceforth given greater prominence and their aspirations treated with greater respect. Commenting on Italian claims to share in the international administration of Palestine, Sykes noted that they could be met provided the Italians in return acknowledged British railway rights between Haifa and Area 'B', and respected Moslem privileges in their Holy Places and the rights of the Jews to colonisation in Palestine. Lord Drogheda, who summed up the British position *vis-à-vis* the Italian claims, accepted Sykes's brief without reservations. 'Italy must be made to recognise British railway rights . . . and generally respect the civic and colonising rights of the Jews in Palestine.'[12] Jewish colonisation was thus acknowledged officially as part of British interests in Palestine within the framework of the Asia Minor Agreement.

When Sykes met Weizmann and Sokolow at the end of January 1917[13] he was fully convinced of the merits of Zionism. The idea of Jewish national regeneration in their ancient home touched his imagination, whilst his Catholic background made him particularly sensitive to the anomalous position of the Jews among the nations.[14] The impending invasion of Palestine convinced him of the urgent need to reach an accommodation with the Zionists. But this does not fully account for his intense preoccupation with the Zionist question, nor does it resolve the enigma of his sudden reversal to his original idea of a British Palestine. In May–July, when in touch with Gaster, Sykes still adhered strictly to the principle of an Anglo-French condominium, and in his memorandum of 22 November 1916, 'The Italians and the Franco-British Agreement', the underlying assumption was that Palestine would be placed under international administration. Yet from January–February 1917 his overriding aim in dealing with the Zionists was to secure a British trusteeship.

The decisive factor prompting him to revert to his original concept of a British-controlled Palestine was the growing awareness of Germany's ambition to dominate the Middle East. He feared that a Teutonised Turkey would give Germany military bases that would threaten Egypt and India, whilst control of Palestine would give Berlin a lever for exerting pressure on the Papacy, the Orthodox Church, and Zionism. In this context the agreement signed with Picot no longer suited British interests. Despite his earnest desire to maintain the *entente cordiale*, Sykes could not disregard certain risks. He strongly suspected French financiers of playing a double game. If the Entente won they would stake their claim to Syria, Palestine and north Mesopotamia, but if the war ended inconclusively they would be able to take credit for their pre-war Turcophile sentiments and make a deal with their former German partners, with whom, despite the war, they had kept in close touch through Swiss intermediaries. Sykes feared that in the latter case the French concessionaires would become the 'pawn of international financiers of Teutonic bias'.[15] Given the unpredictable nature of French politics, a Franco-German combination in the Near East could not be ruled out.

Not until October 1916 did these gloomy prognostications seem to be partly substantiated. Intelligence reports suggested that French financial circles were moving towards some accommodation with the Ottoman state, whilst the Committee of Union and Progress was planning to drive a wedge between England and Russia on the one side, and France on the other. To forestall these dangers Sykes pondered the advisability of making the 1915 Constantinople Agreement public,[16] presumably to kill pre-emptively any attempts towards a Turco-Russian *rapprochement*. He did not go so far as to suggest the revision of the Asia-Minor Agreement, but this might well have been in his mind. In the circumstances a condominium with France in Palestine was fraught with danger, since the very principle of an international régime left the door open to Germany. Herbert Samuel's advice, given in his January 1915 memorandum, now demonstrated its relevance. But so long as the Asquith-Grey Government remained in power, revision of the Asia Minor Agreement could not be entertained.

This was implicit in the absence of any positive response to a memorandum, circulated to the Cabinet at Grey's suggestion, by Lord Bryce, which advanced the familiar argument that occupation of Mesopotamia necessitated a British protectorate of Palestine, and by Palestine he meant the land stretching north as far as the ladder of Tyre (north of Acre), the Anti-Lebanon and Mount Hermon. He had been told that both the native Moslems and the Jews desired British protection; the country could support a larger number of inhabitants, and under a liberal régime the Jewish population would increase at a still faster rate than the present one. Their immigration would stimulate an inflow of capital from Europe and the United States, where the Zionist movement had gained many sympathisers.[17]

The failure to take up Bryce's suggestion did not indicate indifference to Jewish interests in Palestine. For even if the British Government had resolved to encourage Jewish colonisation more actively, this could not have been done within the framework of a British protectorate such as the Zionists and their sympathisers desired, since this would have conflicted with the inter-Allied Agreement. This goes far to explain why Weizmann and Sokolow's pleas to the Foreign Office during 1915–16 fell on sterile ground.[18]

Lloyd George's accession to the Premiership in December 1916 altered the picture radically. Both his style of government and his thinking were completely different.[19] One of his primary objectives was Palestine. He had advocated its annexation since the outbreak of the war, and to him British and Jewish Palestine were almost synonymous in meaning. He had a long-standing interest in Zionism and Samuel's memorandum appealed to the 'poetic and imaginative qualities of his mind'.[20] It also fitted in well with his strategic and political concepts. The idea of a 'Jewish buffer state' interested him, though he feared that France 'would have strong objections'.[21] But the longer the war lasted the stronger became his determination that 'Palestine, if recaptured, must be one and indivisible'. Lloyd George had had no hand in the making of the Sykes-Picot Agreement and regarded it as an inconvenient legacy. It was a 'fatuous document'[22] based on erroneous calculations. The Arabian policy, which brought this Agreement to life had not paid off. The Sharifian revolt was verging on total collapse and in consequence the Sykes-Picot Agreement was losing its rationale. Britain had paid too great a price for the bargain and the inter-Allied arrangement had to be amended. However, Lloyd George was as anxious as his predecessor not to disrupt the Entente. Hence, as Sir Charles Webster put it, 'a situation had to be created in which the worst features of the Sykes-Picot Agreement could be got rid of without breaking faith, and Britain regarded as the obvious protector . . . In these circumstances Dr Weizmann's offer was an attractive one.'[23] It was ironic that the ill-effects of the Arabian policy had to be undone by the Zionists.

Sykes now enjoyed greater liberty of action. Lloyd George promoted him to a key position as an Assistant Secretary to the War Cabinet and delegated authority in Middle Eastern affairs to him. His status was further enhanced by the remarkable trust which developed between the two men.[24] To Sykes, too, the Agreement became an anachronism.[25] He felt 'ashamed of it . . . resented the constant and indelible reminder that his name was and always would be associated with a pact for which he had only a nominal responsibility'.[26] But it would be a mistake to assume that he desired to undo it altogether. Like Lloyd George, Sykes wanted only to amend it to give Britain sole control of Palestine in return for British support for French claims in Syria. However, the broader aim of his policy was to forestall the possibility of Turco-German predominance in Palestine. Herein lay the *raison d'être* of the alliance with British Zionism. It provided a way to outmanoeuvre the French without breaking faith, and a useful card at the future peace conference to play against any move by Germany to rally the German-oriented and Turcophile Jews to buttress her claim.

Sykes soon found himself in full accord with his colleagues at the War Secretariat, Leopold Amery and Ormsby-Gore. Amery's interest in Zionism could be traced to 1916, when he warmly supported Colonel Patterson and Jabotinsky in the matter of the Jewish Legion, but it may well have been Sykes who opened his eyes to the relevance of Zionism for British strategic requirements. With his concept of Palestine as an 'eastern Belgium' Amery proved a receptive audience. In 1945 Amery recalled[27] that

> Sykes soon persuaded me that, from the purely British point of
> view, a prosperous Jewish population in Palestine, owing its
> inception and its opportunity of development to British policy,
> might be an invaluable asset as a defence of the Suez Canal against
> attack from the North and as a station on the future air-routes to
> the East. Both of us, too, as old travellers in the Middle East,
> believed that nothing could bring so regenerating an influence to
> those ancient centres of the world's civilisation . . . as a fresh
> contact with Western life through a people who yet regarded the
> East as their true home.

Amery may also have detected ominous undercurrents in Egyptian opinion against the British Protectorate. He therefore recommended that Britain should restrict its control to the Suez Canal proper and the Sinai Peninsula. In sparsely populated Sinai Britain could stay indefinitely and secure her sea and air communications with the East, whereas a Jewish settlement in Palestine could exert indirect influence and make Britain's presence in this vital area appear innocuous.

> It was not long before I realized [he wrote[28]] what Jewish energy
> in every field of thought and action might mean for the regenera-
> tion of the whole Middle Eastern region . . . That regeneration
> would be far more effective and, one hoped, more acceptable, if

carried out by people who, bringing the knowledge and energy of the West to bear, still regarded the Middle East as their home, than by capitalists, technicians or administrators from outside. Most of us younger men, who shared this hope were, like Mark Sykes, pro-Arab as well as pro-Zionist, and saw no essential incompatibility between the two ideals.

The Amery-Sykes strategic concept was shared by Ormsby-Gore. Syria and Palestine were his special province. Early in March, when he joined the War Secretariat, his knowledge of Jewish colonisation in Palestine, gathered whilst on the staff of the Arab Bureau in Cairo,[29] provided the necessary data on which long-term calculations could be built. His memorandum of 5 February 1917 was an exhaustive review of the Zionist movement, its practical achievements and standing in the Jewish world. He believed that its potential force was stronger than it appeared to be and, though formally uncommitted, there were signs that 'the whole influence of Judaism outside Germany will be directed in accordance with the attitude of respective powers regarding the Palestine question . . .'

> The slightest hint from the Entente Powers that this peaceful penetration would not be opposed, and Zionism, as a whole will veer to the Entente side. On the other hand, any suggestion that . . . Jewish colonization would be resisted . . . would serve to throw the whole weight of International Zionism against us, without bringing any support from those Jews who are anti-Zionist.[30]

Ormsby-Gore's knowledge was greatly enriched by Aaronsohn, whom, during their constant intercourse in Cairo, he learned to like and admire. There is hardly any memorandum by Gore which does not bear the stamp of Aaronsohn's ideas. It is particularly clear in the one dated 1 April 1917, in which Ormsby-Gore described in meticulous detail avenues suitable for the invasion of Palestine, landing places, climatic conditions, position of food supplies and water resources, morale of Turkish troops and the attitude of the population. 'British Palestine, with possibly Christian shrines international, is undoubtedly what is hoped for by the great mass of the inhabitants of Palestine proper. The delivery of Jerusalem from the Turk would be hailed by every Christian, Jew and Arab . . . would have world wide moral and political effect.' So fascinated was Sir Maurice Hankey, the Secretary to the War Cabinet by Gore's description of Palestine, the best he had ever read, that he commended it strongly to Sir William Robertson, the chief of the Imperial General Staff, and showed it to the Prime Minister.[31]

The Amery, Ormsby-Gore, Sykes trio formed a remarkable combination. They were more than a brains trust feeding the government with ideas and information. They were, in fact, the moving force behind Lloyd George's Eastern policy and, enjoying his unqualified confidence, could either collectively or individually shape its course. Ormsby-Gore acted simultaneously as Private Secretary to Lord Milner, one of the most influential members of the War Cabinet. Before joining the Cabinet Milner had no clear conception of Zionism. The suggestions made in Samuel's memorandum, which the latter sent him in January 1917, were 'new' to him and appeared 'most attractive'.[32] Milner played a significant part in formulating the Government's Zionist policy, but it was Ormsby-Gore to whom he turned constantly for advice. It proved particularly useful in the autumn of 1917 when the War Cabinet was considering the publication of the Balfour Declaration.

Outside government circles the man who exerted the greatest influence on Lloyd George was C. P. Scott, editor of the *Manchester Guardian*. He was 'probably Lloyd George's closest political confidant',[33] though in matters of Zionism, Scott was preaching to the convinced. On 27 November 1914, tentatively reviewing British war aims, he raised the question of Palestine and Zionism, but found that the subject was not new to Lloyd George, who told him that he had had a 'heart to heart' talk with Herbert Samuel, that he sympathised with the aspirations of a small nation and was interested in a 'partly Jewish buffer state'. Scott continued diligently to press the Zionists' case and at the end of January 1917 he urged the British Government to issue a definite statement in favour of making Palestine a national home for the Jews.[34] The timing was not accidental. On 18 December 1916 President Wilson had launched a new peace initiative and on 22 January 1917, in an address to the Senate, he had made a passionate appeal to the belligerent powers for 'a peace without victory'.[35] With Britain's growing dependence on American goodwill, it would have been difficult to explain away the military campaign in Palestine, let alone its occupation. Hence, as Scott recorded, it was 'very important to obtain American Jews' support. It would be unanimous if they could be assured that in the event of a British occupation of Palestine, the Zionist scheme would be considered favourably. Now was the moment for pressing the matter when British troops were actually on Palestine soil.'[36]

Scott was a leading exponent of the strategic school of thought. 'Palestine', he told Lord Milner, was 'a small thing . . . but it was the thing that mattered.' It was with Scott's approval, if not encouragement, that Herbert Sidebotham, the *Manchester Guardian*'s military correspondent aired his view (in the issue of 26 November 1915) that Palestine should become a 'buffer state between Egypt and the North, inhabited ... by an intensely patriotic race ... On the realisation of that condition depends the whole future of the British Empire as a Sea Empire.' Sidebotham was the first journalist to propound publicly the identity of British and Jewish interests. At the end of 1916, jointly with his Jewish friends in Manchester, Harry Sacher, Simon Marks, and Israel Sieff, he founded the British Palestine Committee which advocated support for Zionism from a strictly British point of view. Its weekly journal, *Palestine*, which started to appear on 26 January 1917, was an admirable propaganda organ.[37] Sidebotham expressed his views most forcefully in a letter to *The Nation* (24 February 1917). In it he rejected the editor's advocacy of a neutral Palestine under international guarantee, and pointed to the hazards should Judea become the base of a hostile power. If Palestine remained within the German sphere of influence, Egypt would become the most vulnerable spot in the whole system of Imperial defence. Only an industrious and loyal nation, protected by the British Crown, could forestall such a potential menace.

These ideas were still novel to the British press and *The Nation*'s editor refused to give ground. In his rejoinder he maintained that the desire to annex Palestine would prolong the war, turn it into one of 'pure conquest' and quite unnecessarily provoke French hostility. An internationalised Jewish state, agreed upon by the powers, was a more prudent course to follow. Nor did Sidebotham's ideas receive a warmer welcome at the Foreign Office. At the War Office, the War Secretariat and the British Residency in Cairo, *Palestine* was read regularly, but at the Foreign Office Sidebotham's doctrine made no impression.[38]

Despite the change of Government the Foreign Office remained firmly committed to the Asia Minor Agreement. French susceptibilities were, respected and the idea of a British Palestine could not be countenanced. Thus, with the Prime Minister and the Foreign Office pulling in different directions, there emerged a curious, though not unusual, dichotomy in the machinery of policy-making. If the divergence did not precipitate a more serious inter-departmental clash, it was because Arthur James Balfour, the new Foreign Minister, was not of a combative nature and, though reluctant for Britain to undertake sole responsibility in Palestine, he showed no particular enthusiasm for the idea of an international régime either. 'Personally, I should like to get in the Americans,' he noted on 15 January 1917,[39] a theme which he was to repeat again and again. Under the pressure of circumstances, the Foreign Office had gradually to give way. But early in 1917 Sykes, aware of the divergence in opinion had to proceed with caution. His relations with the Zionists were conducted in his private capacity and, as he confided later to Aaronsohn, the Foreign Office was not briefed at all.[40] It is however quite inconceivable that Sykes, independent-minded as he was, would not have consulted any of his superiors before embarking on the Zionist policy in earnest. According to the late Samuel Landman, the decision was taken with the full knowledge and consent of Sir Maurice Hankey, Secretary to the War Cabinet.[41]

It can safely be assumed that the Prime Minister was also acquainted with Sykes's task. On 5 February 1917, Scott wrote to Lloyd George:[42]

> I dread the matter being handled in the spirit of compromise by the
> F.O. I gather that the whole drift of the F.O. policy is towards
> some sort of dual control . . . with France . . . I don't believe that is
> your view personally, it would be fatal to our interest, but there is
> evidently a strong drift in that direction.

The Zionists too felt uneasy. From Tschlenow's letter, which they had received the previous year, they were vaguely aware of the existence of a tripartite Agreement,[43] and they were under the strong (though it now transpires as quite erroneous) impression that the Foreign Office was antagonistic to their cause.[44] Though contact with Sykes was encouraging, in a broader sense the situation still seemed uncertain. As Weizmann told Israel Sieff, the matter was entirely in Sykes's hands, and only when he was ready would he submit it to the Foreign Office.[45] Two days later Sieff urged Weizmann to 'fight out the condominium idea with Sir Mark'. He should be made aware of 'the evil and dangerous results which would follow a joint administration of Palestine'. But the real test was to persuade the Foreign Office that 'a purely British Palestine is the right solution'.[46]

When Sykes met the Zionist leaders at Gaster's home on 7 February 1917,[47] he heard from them what he had expected. The common denominator in the spectrum of views, ranging from Gaster's recognition of Jews in Palestine 'as a nation, a "millet",' Sokolow's 'a Jewish society', to Lord Rothschild's and Harry Sacher's 'Jewish State in Palestine under the British Crown', was their desire for a British protectorate. All were strongly opposed to the idea of a condominium, not only because such a system of government had never proved workable but, as Sacher pointed out, because of the risk of undermining Jewish unity by setting French and English Jews against each other. It militated against the task of building up a homogeneous Jewish nation in Palestine and its development into a self-governing dominion.

Sykes assured his audience that the idea of a Jewish Palestine commanded his full sympathy. He touched upon his conversations with Sazonow when in Petrograd, but remained silent about the Agreement reached with Picot and the Russian Foreign Minister. Save for guarantees for the Holy Places, he said, no serious obstacles were expected from Petrograd or from Italy. Arab reactions might present some difficulty; they had already begun attacking the Zionists and demanded that the language of the inhabitants should be the decisive criterion in the future disposition of Syria and Palestine. He hoped however that 'the Arabs could be managed, particularly if they received Jewish support in other matters'. The chief hindrance sprang from the attitude adopted by France. 'He could not understand French policy. The French wanted all Syria and a great say in Palestine.' The matter ought to be discussed with them, and it would be useful if the Zionists appointed a representative for this purpose.

Up to this point Sykes's statements reflected more or less the true state of affairs, but his denial of Lord Rothschild's pointed question as to whether any pledges had already been given to the French concerning Palestine, and his assurance that 'the French have no particular position in Palestine and are not entitled to anything there', were contrary to fact. Nor was it quite straight to allow Gaster to believe that the Foreign Office would have no objection to the Zionists negotiating with the French, failing British support for a Jewish Palestine. Herbert Samuel who, as a former Cabinet Minister, was aware of the Inter-Allied Agreement but would not mention it, was unwilling to come to Sykes's rescue; he suggested that it was not the Zionists' business but that of the British Government 'to deal with the French and dispose of their pretensions. The French had no [justified] claims whatsoever in Palestine.' He reiterated his view that it was of 'enormous importance that the territory should not fall into the hands of another Power which might be enabled to threaten the security of the Suez Canal and Egypt'. The problem should be settled at the future peace conference, where the French were likely to get 'one third of Africa, Alsace-Lorraine and Syria. They had no right to anything in Palestine.'

However, from Sykes's veiled allusions it was possible to surmise that Britain was not a free agent. The Zionists expected that the whole of historic Palestine, from the Hauran in the north to the Egyptian border in the south, would come under British protection, but Sykes indicated that British protection would cover only the Zionist Chartered Company and only in specified areas. These corresponded roughly to the British zone of influence in Palestine, namely in the north, along the line running from Acre eastwards to the river Jordan, and in the whole southern territory beyond the 'Brown' area. Galilee and the Hauran, as well as the Jerusalem enclave, connected with Jaffa by a corridor along the railway line, were to be excluded from the sphere where the Company could operate under British protection.

The Zionists were disappointed. Galilee, dotted with Jewish colonies, and the Hauran, the natural granary of the country with its rich sources of water, could not be surrendered, whilst Jerusalem, they maintained, was 'a Jewish city';[48] internationalisation should be limited to the actual sites of the Holy Places. Moreover, most of the Jewish colonies in Judea lay along the Jerusalem-Jaffa railway track, and a truncated Palestine as delineated by Sykes made nonsense of the prospects of efficient administration. Yet this was the limit beyond which Sykes could not go. The Asia Minor Agreement placed Galilee and the Hauran in the French sphere, the former in the 'Blue' and the latter in the 'A' area, whilst the Jerusalem-Jaffa enclave had to be internationalised. The meeting ended inconclusively. It was none the less a promising start. The Zionists were no longer working in a vacuum. An identity of interests, at least as far as Sykes was concerned, was in the making. Both parties needed each other.

The representative chosen to put the Jewish view to Picot, and continue negotiations with Sykes, was Sokolow. Not only did his senior status, as a member of the Executive of the Zionist World Organization, make his nomination natural but his continental background and knowledge of languages made him better qualified than his colleagues in London to appreciate points of view other than British.

On 8 February, when Sokolow met Picot in Sykes's presence, he made it absolutely clear that the Zionists were opposed to the internationalisation of Palestine: such a régime would engender inter-power rivalry and hinder the progress of Zionist colonisation. As protecting power, Britain was preferred. Picot replied that control by a single power was contrary to the inter-Allied arrangement and the antagonism it would provoke in France would wreck the whole scheme. Joint sponsorship was likely to yield more positive results. At this juncture Sykes intervened, hinting that only the Chartered Zionist Company might be taken under the British aegis, but Picot remained unmoved. Sokolow thereupon emphasised the great importance which the Zionists attached to the Chartered Company. From the inception of the movement it had been embodied in their programme and considered an indispensable instrument of colonisation. This too left Picot unmoved; he questioned the Jewish attitude towards the native Moslems and Christians as well as towards the Holy Places. Sokolow replied that 'Palestine was not the national centre of the Arabs', and he understood that they would be given opportunities to develop a national centre of their own elsewhere. As for the Holy Places, the Jews were determined not to interfere with them. He hoped that 'a real religious peace' would prevail and there was no reason to fear that Christians or Moslems in Palestine would be disturbed by Jewish colonisation.

A day later, when Sokolow met Picot again, this time à deux, the conversation was conducted in a lower key. Sokolow was assured that France took a sympathetic interest in Jewish national aspirations, which could however be sanctioned only if France had a rightful share in Palestine's administration. That Picot did not reject Zionism altogether was in itself an achievement on which Sokolow could justly congratulate himself. But when he and Weizmann met Sykes they raised strong objections to any suggestion that the Chartered Company should be in any way circumscribed either in its scope or its powers. An emasculated colonisation scheme would not appeal to the Jewish masses. For his part, Sykes was not dissatisfied with the results of Sokolow's exchanges with Picot, but thought it was necessary 'to keep the idea of British suzerainty in the background for the time being, as it was likely to intensify French opposition'.[49]

Picot's firmness reflected his country's position. Some time in February Briand told the Italian Ambassador in Paris that Syria 'had always been regarded by French public opinion as French,'[50] and by Syria the French meant sizeable sections of Palestine as well. Sykes had, therefore, to proceed warily; he limited himself to discrediting the idea of internationalisation. This was the burden of his letter to Picot, dated 28 February 1917.[51] The Zionists, he argued, were averse to an international régime in Palestine and objected strongly to any form of dual control or condominium. Their ambition was to colonise the whole of historic Palestine with the exception of the Holy Places, under a single protecting power. A mutilated Palestine would have little appeal to them. This was an important point, since it was no use trying to satisfy Jewish aspirations unless their fundamental traditions, sentiment and hereditary longings were given outward prominence.

From this premise Sykes proceeded to search for an eligible suzerain. Since Britain and France were mutually exclusive, Sykes hit finally on the United States as prospective protector. America was unbiased and neutral, and the mere suggestion 'would give a very strong impetus to the Entente cause' there. Should the American Government accept responsibility for Palestine's administration, Anglo-French differences would be bridged. Specific guarantees to the native population would have to be provided but the overriding concern was to allow Zionist colonisation to develop freely.

If the great force of Judaism feels that its aspirations are not only considered but in a fair way towards realisation, then there is hope of an ordered and developed Arabia and Middle East. On the other hand, if that force feels that its aspirations will be thwarted . . . then I see little or no prospect for our own future hopes.

Two features stand out from Sykes's arguments. First, the future Arab principality, agreed upon with Picot whilst in Petrograd, had vanished. Moslem Holy shrines in Jerusalem and elsewhere were to be safeguarded and the existing population in Palestine protected 'against fiscal and political oppression', but apart from this the Jews were to be given a free hand in the colonisation of Palestine, and by Palestine Sykes had in mind the territory between the river Jordan and the Mediterranean. There was no material incompatibility in his mind between pro-Zionism and pro-Arabism. The Zionists were to act as a lever in the regeneration of the Middle East, which could develop in an orderly way if Jew and Arab co-operated. Second, the international régime had to be replaced by one single suzerain. Did Sykes seriously contemplate America in this rôle, as at the same time the London Zionists were permitted to popularise among their colleagues in Russia and the United States the idea of British suzerainty? It was on Sykes's recommendation that Military Intelligence had placed its machinery at their disposal to enable them to communicate with their sister organisations and supporters in other countries. During 1917 alone nearly two hundred letters and telegrams were dispatched to all parts of the world.[52] Sykes was undoubtedly aware of the military plans for the occupation of the 'whole of Palestine', and fully shared Sidebotham's concept of its strategic importance to British interests.[53]

Before leaving for the East, Sykes met Jabotinsky. Despite the over-whelming odds against the project of the Jewish Legion, Jabotinsky refused to accept defeat. No obstacle was too great and no slight from his fellow-Jews could damp his enthusiasm. Having failed to convince the War Office, he now succeeded in winning such important converts as Wickham Steed, editor of *The Times*, and in strengthening his links with C. P. Scott. Both *The Times* and the *Manchester Guardian* advocated the formation of the Legion. The idea also secured the blessing of Herbert Samuel. Both as Jew and as Home Secretary, Samuel found himself in an embarrassing position when his co-religionists from Russia in the East

End of London showed not the slightest inclination to volunteer for the British Army and contribute their part to the war effort. Young men of military age, 20,000 strong, were escaping conscription; an anomaly which prompted Samuel to say in the House of Commons that 'Russians of military age . . . were expected either to offer their services to the British Army or to return to Russia to fulfil their military obligations there'. Since this suggestion had no legal force, and tended only to antagonise the men concerned, Samuel was open to Jabotinsky's arguments. An appeal to national feelings could have a greater impact on Jewish youth than the scourge of deportation to Russia. Weizmann, at Jabotinsky's elbow, was always helpful, but in his own characteristic way elected to use his skill and persuasion discreetly rather than to join Jabotinsky in a public propaganda campaign.[54]

By the end of 1916 a group of some hundred and fifty ex-members of the Zion Mule Corps, disbanded in March 1916, arrived in England and voluntarily enlisted in the Army. Through the intercession of Colonel Patterson and with Amery's assistance, they were assigned to the same battalion, known as the 20th London Regiment and stationed in Winchester. Jabotinsky joined the unit as a private and from there continued his campaign for the Legion. His day came when Amery moved to the War Secretariat. Amery's position became still more influential when he was appointed Assistant Military Secretary to Lord Derby, Secretary of State for War, and it was on Amery's advice that Jabotinsky, jointly with Trumpeldor, submitted on 24 January 1917 a memorandum to the Prime Minister.[55]

In their opinion, the impending British advance in Palestine made the project of a Jewish Regiment for Palestine timely, but its importance transcended its military value. Domestically, it would help to solve the irksome question of aliens of military age; on the propaganda plane it would answer the German charge that the Entente was indifferent to 'the tragedy of the Jewish Nation'. As the Entente was unable to intervene in Russia's internal affairs, the only course open to it to meet Jewish grievances was 'to give a certain official recognition to the Zionist ideal of the Jewish people and to call the Jewish youth to fight on the side of the Allies for the liberation of Palestine'. Should the British Government endorse the scheme, they went on, a Jewish unit, destined to fight for a Jewish future in Palestine, would commend itself strongly to the East End Russian Jews and shake them out of their apathy. There was a good prospect that a number of Russian Jews from France, Switzerland and the Scandinavian countries would also be attracted. In Russia proper there was still a huge untapped reservoir of Jewish youth and, judging from the favourable attitude of the Russian authorities, there was reason to believe that volunteers would be permitted to leave the country to join the unit. In the United States, owing to strict neutrality regulations, joining up was impracticable, but the very formation of the regiment would sweep the American Jewish community off their feet and promote pro-Entente feeling.[56]

Three weeks later Sykes informed Jabotinsky that the military authorities were opposed to the idea, and 'it would probably be necessary to obtain the concurrence of other powers in the employment of special troops ... in areas in which political considerations were of importance'.[57] The reason behind this attitude is not difficult to surmise. At the time, the British Government was strenuously resisting the demands of the French and Italian Governments to increase the number of their troops on the Palestinian front;[58] to agree to the formation of another national unit for the same front would have weakened its hand *vis-à-vis* its allies. Jabotinsky's proposal therefore had to be temporarily shelved. However, at the end of March, on learning that the 20th London Regiment might be posted to France, Sykes changed his mind. If this tiny nucleus were swamped among the vast armies in Flanders it would make nonsense of his own suggestion to keep the idea of a Jewish force 'alive'. After consulting the Director of Military Operations, he suggested to the Foreign Office the desirability in principle of designating about seven hundred men for operations on the Eastern front: 'we should thus be giving encouragement to the Jews and the Zionists and smooth over the difficulties which may arise as regards East End recruiting'; the battalion might later be used for garrisoning and administrative duties in the occupied territories in Palestine. The reaction in the Foreign Office was mixed. Sir George Clerk commented:[59]

A solution of the East End Jew problem would be very welcome— especially to the Home Office. But the difficulty I see in this suggestion is that it raises the whole Zionist question. This is a matter upon which the most representative Jews are utterly divided and it seems to me that H.M. Government may be laying up stores of trouble, if they encourage a scheme which commits them to Zionism.

Lord Hardinge agreed with Clerk and thought that the Government 'ought to be careful not to identify themselves with either Jewish faction'.

The term 'the most representative Jews' referred to Montagu and Samuel.[60] How deeply Montagu opposed Zionism has been pointed out already. He reiterated his stand in a letter of 3 August 1916 to Eric Drummond. In summer 1916, when the Foreign Office was considering ways of gaining Jewish sympathy in the United States, Drummond solicited the assistance of Montagu (then Minister of Munitions), only to receive a lecture that the Jews ought to regard themselves as members of a religion and not as a race. Had he accepted Jewish nationalist doctrine, he would as a patriotic Englishman have resigned his position in the Cabinet. 'Nobody is entitled to occupy the position that I do unless he is free and determined to consider the interests of the British Empire. I regard with perfect equanimity whatever treatment the Jews receive in Russia.' He was confident that in due course Russia would become 'a more habitable country' for the Jews as well, but Zionism on all counts should be discouraged. Jewish nationalism was 'horrible and unpatriotic', if not detrimental to the Allied cause. The British Government should steer clear of this 'pro-German' and uncivilised movement.[61]

Extreme as Montagu's views were, they had some impact on the Foreign Office, at least to the point of deterring it from entering into closer association with the Zionists, who, moreover, had no official standing. This point was made by Lucien Wolf when he met Balfour on 30 January 1917. Wolf told the Foreign Secretary that the only body authorised to speak for the Jewish communities, not only of the United Kingdom but of the British Empire, was the Conjoint Committee. It represented a hundred and thirty congregations, including all the chief synagogues, the Anglo-Jewish Association, and other societies. It did not however represent those of East European origin who, he implied, had imported Zionism into England. The idea that Jews throughout the world were 'members of a Jewish Nationality, distinct from other nationalities', was alien to Jews in Britain. It had developed only in those countries where the struggle for emancipation had failed. 'The native Jews of Western Europe know of no nationality except that of the countries in which they had been born.' Zionism, in Wolf's opinion, offered no solution to the main Jewish problem in Eastern Europe and formed no part of the Conjoint Committee's programme. This, however, did not mean that the Committee was hostile to Zionist aims. For historical reasons it felt a deep sentimental attachment to Palestine, and was interested in its welfare.

> We should rejoice if the Zionists made Palestine the seat of a flourishing and reputable Jewish community. We should have no objection if that Jewish community developed into the local Jewish nation and a Jewish state. But we stipulated that, in its political work, it should not claim the allegiance of the Jews of Western

Europe, who are satisfied with their local nationalities, and further that, in promoting their schemes, they should not adopt methods which might be calculated to compromise the position and aims of Jews in other countries. Thus, for example, we should resist any proposal to give to the Jews of Palestine, privileges not shared by the rest of the population of that country . . . Outside these reservations, we left a perfectly free hand to the Zionists, and we were even disposed within certain limits to cooperate with them in promoting their schemes.

Balfour showed interest in Wolf's exposition and agreed (if the latter noted correctly) that Zionism could offer no radical solution to the Jewish question in Eastern Europe. However, he made it equally clear that the British Government could not interfere in Russia's internal affairs,[62] the implication being that the Zionist programme offered at least a partial solution of the problem.

Balfour was a convinced Zionist, and required no further education on its merits. But whatever his personal inclination, it does not seem that he ever attempted to impose his views on his subordinates when they differed markedly from his own. During the winter of 1916–17 interest in Zionism at the Foreign Office was at its lowest ebb. After the fiasco, following Grey's proposal in March 1916, the idea of using Zionism was shelved, while the death of Hugh O'Beirne in H.M.S. *Hampshire* on 5 June 1916 deprived it of its staunchest supporter. The appointment of Sir Ronald Graham as Assistant Under-Secretary for Foreign Affairs balanced the loss. Sir Ronald was known to have interested himself closely in the Zion Mule Corps when serving as Chief Staff Officer, G.O.C. Egypt, but it was not before the summer of 1917 that he became a leading advocate at the Foreign Office of a British commitment to Zionism.

Amery, aware of the chilly atmosphere at the Foreign Office, but still eager to see the Jewish Legion established, steered his course adroitly. He wrote to Balfour on 23 March 1917:

I do not think it necessary that we should commit ourselves to any scheme of Zionism. But from a purely military point of view, I consider that the utilising of our Russian Jews in a special corps for service in the East will secure us much better fighting value than putting them into ordinary units (where they would not be too welcome) for service in France.

He calculated that it would be possible to raise 'more than one battalion'

in England, and that additional recruits might be found in South Africa
and other Dominions, in Egypt, and possibly also in the United States.
By ostensibly stripping the project of its political implications, and presenting it purely in its military aspect, Amery hoped to facilitate its
acceptance. It was obvious however, that the very fact of a sizeable Jewish
unit being posted to the Palestinian front was bound to make an impression on the political scene.

A few days later, noting that Balfour had expressed himself 'freely in
favour of Zionism at the War Cabinet the other day', Amery suggested
that Balfour should raise the question of the Jewish Legion in the War
Cabinet. He was confident that between twenty to thirty thousand Russian
Jews in England of military age, otherwise not very welcome in an
ordinary British regiment, would join the Legion, and stimulated by the
idea that they were 're-conquering their ancient heritage . . . might prove
to be quite respectable fighters'; alternatively they might be used to
garrison the long lines of communications from Beersheba to Dan. The
effect upon Jews in America and elsewhere 'might be very good. Even in
Austria-Hungary, where the Jews are a big factor, the formation of such a
unit and its military successes in Palestine . . . might cause a great revulsion
of feeling.' General Smuts thought that quite a large contingent could
come from South Africa and 'if the French have any touchiness about our
Palestine scheme, we might always encourage them to raise a battalion of
French Jews, or Morocco Jews'. Amery was sure that the General Staff
was quite favourably disposed, but that the Adjutant-General's Department had always shelved the question because it disliked being bothered
by 'special units'. With the prospect of raising nearly a division of infantry
this consideration was no longer relevant; the idea of 'Jerusalem Highlanders' was as valid as the Gordon Highlanders. Amery considered that it
might be more effective if the scheme was recommended on political
grounds by the Foreign Secretary rather than left exclusively to the War
Office.[63]

Eric Drummond, Balfour's Private Secretary, confirmed that the War
Office had no objection to the scheme, but preferred the Foreign Office to
make the first move. Sykes too thought the moment opportune though,
apparently with an eye on the French, he added the caution that when the
unit was endorsed its ultimate destination should not be mentioned.
Balfour thereupon passed the matter on to Lord Milner to present to the
War Cabinet, but as he was slow to act, Graham approached the Army
Council directly. He made however an important reservation:[64]

it will be important for H.M. Government not to identify themselves too closely with the political objects of a Zionist nature which underlie this proposal, since by so doing they would be committing themselves to a definite course in a matter upon which the most representative Jews of the world are utterly divided.

Amery did not stay idle, and arranged for Jabotinsky and Trumpeldor to meet Lord Derby, Secretary of State for War.[65] That their case was seriously considered is evident from Derby's letter to the Prime Minister requesting sanction, on the War Cabinet's behalf, for the formation of the proposed unit 'at the earliest possible moment'. He went on:[66]

> I am told that many of the men have served in the Russian Army and that they are very well disciplined and extremely intelligent. What their value will be as a fighting machine it is impossible to say, but I think for political reasons it would be most advisable to form these Battalions, because in the first place, it will remove some of the irritation now existing in the East End of London on the part of Christians who are compelled to serve, and, further, it might be a good example which might have a most beneficial effect in Russia itself.

Ormsby-Gore also supported the scheme. While in Cairo he had heard a great deal about it from Aaronsohn, who thought that he would be able to raise at least one thousand 'really good' Palestinian Jews, at that time in Egypt. He expected a number of volunteers from America, Morocco, and the East End of London, and hoped that 'the morale of a Jewish Brigade entering Palestine would be wonderful'.[67] General Smuts also expressed his fullest sympathy with the Jewish Legion scheme and promised his support. The Army Council then consented to the formation of a Russian Jewish battalion, specifying however that 'this decision has been taken on the distinct understanding that it is not to be regarded as in any way connected with, or in promotion of, the Zionist movement'.[68]

Amery's diplomacy had triumphed,[69] but his victory was not unqualified. The battalion was to be manned by Russian conscripts only; British Jews were excluded. No mention was made of its destination, and dissociation from Zionism was stated in unequivocal terms. It is therefore a matter of surprise that on 22 March, when Weizmann met Balfour, he gained a distinct impression that the Foreign Secretary was 'in full sympathy with our aspirations, and I am sure', Weizmann wrote to Brandeis on 8 April, 'that we may reckon on his support'. Balfour's sympathy was beyond doubt, and his support for the Zionists during the forthcoming months proved invaluable, but at this stage it would be going too far to see his statement as a positive commitment. Nor did Balfour develop any views on the strategic importance of Palestine for British interests. Weizmann was dismayed to note that this aspect was apparently 'new to him'; fear of complications with France and Italy made Balfour opt for an American, or for a joint Anglo-American protectorate. Weizmann felt more at home during an interview with the Prime Minister which took place on 3 April. Lloyd George strongly opposed a condominium with France and 'was very emphatic on the point of British Palestine'.[70]

As events showed, it was Lloyd George who was to shape Middle East policy. A few hours after receiving Weizmann he saw Sir Mark Sykes in the presence of Lord Curzon and Sir Maurice Hankey. Sykes explained the purpose of his mission to the East and stated that as soon as parts of Palestine were occupied, he hoped to instigate an Arab rebellion in the region of Jebel Druze (in the Hauran) to disrupt the Turkish lines of communication. The Prime Minister thereupon warned Sykes not to commit the British Government to 'any agreement with the [Arab] tribes which would be prejudicial to British interests'. He also underlined 'the importance of not prejudicing the Zionist movement and the possibility of its development under British auspices'; the Jews might be able to render the British 'more assistance than the Arabs'. There was a considerable number of them in England who were intimately acquainted with Palestine and ought to be employed there rather than at home.

Sykes agreed but thought it imperative 'not to stir up any movement in the rear of the British lines which might lead to a Turkish massacre of the Jews'. He added that 'the Arabs probably realised that there was no prospect of their being allowed any control over Palestine'. Here Curzon interjected that the Jews constituted a minority but Sykes pointed to their qualitative superiority and their higher educational level. Lloyd George finally redirected the discussion to its original theme by emphasising once again the importance of 'securing the addition of Palestine to the British area'; no political pledges ought to be made to the Arabs, 'particularly none in regard to Palestine'.[71]

Three distinct features of this meeting stand out. First, it is clear that among senior ministers and officials there was no doubt that Palestine was excluded from the understanding with Hussein; second that the relationship with the Arabic-speaking population in the occupied territories should not prejudice British or Zionist interests; and third that, in the Prime Minister's judgement, Jewish services to British interests would outweigh those of the Arabs. Weizmann's fear, voiced two weeks earlier, that the Zionist question might be treated as 'an appendix' to the Arab scheme,[72] was without foundation.

Sykes hoped that, through the instrumentality of the Zionists, Palestine could be removed from the grip of the unfortunate Anglo-French Agreement. As Lloyd George said during the meeting, 'the French wished to have a considerable voice in the disposal of the conquered territories', and it is in this light that Sykes's suggestion, made the next day to Weizmann to join him in Egypt, should be seen. Once Palestine was conquered, a climate of opinion among the Jews conducive to a British administration would strengthen Sykes's hand without risking a head-on collision with the French. Thus at an appropriate moment Sykes was to make a pro-Zionist declaration. Its contents are not known, but this is what transpires from Weizmann's letter to Sokolow, dated 4 April:[73]

> I have had a talk with Sir Mark with regard to a declaration to be issued in Palestine when the time arrives. He is fully agreeable . . . and he wishes you to talk the matter over with him . . . Please don't forget to talk the question of declaration over with Sir Mark and try to come to some definite conclusion.

In the same letter Weizmann also told Sokolow (at that time in Paris) that 'practically every paper wrote about Jewish Palestine under British Protectorate. The Daily Chronicle, Evening News, Manchester Guardian, the Liverpool papers and even the Morning Post and The Times. There can be no doubt that the feeling here is very strong.' Whether inspired by the Prime Minister's office or not, the papers continued to dwell on this theme during the following weeks. The *New Europe* (19 April 1917) wrote that 'a British Palestine must be a Jewish Palestine' and on the 26th of April added: 'we cannot allow any great military Power other than ourselves in Palestine . . . the Jews are to be encouraged to establish a self-governing [entity there] under the British flag.' *The Liverpool Courier*, of 24 April made the same point, but the reasons for this public campaign can be gauged from the *Sunday Chronicle* (15 April): 'There is no other race who can do these services for us . . . but the Jews themselves. In the Zionist Movement . . . we have the motive force which will make the extension of the British Empire into Palestine, otherwise a disagreeable necessity, a source of pride and a pillar of strength.'

Lloyd George was conducting his own foreign policy. Though it contrasted sharply with that of the Foreign Office, there is no evidence to show that he consulted it before his meeting on 3 April 1917. In all probability he did not. At the Foreign Office the Anglo-French Agreement remained valid. Wingate's suggestion that the mission of Sykes and Picot to the East would provide an opportunity to consider the future of Syria '*de novo*' was rejected out of hand, and Sykes himself was prompted

to dispel any doubts, warning Wingate that the 'mission is a joint one . . .
cordial co-operation on the strict lines of the Agreement is the basis on
which I and my French colleague intend to work.'[74] This was in accordance with the instructions of February 1917 with regard to the status and
functions of the Chief Political Officer in the occupied territories. They
read in part: 'The terms of the Franco-British agreement are to be
regarded as governing the policy of H.M. Government towards both the
French Commissioner and the native elements in the theatre of operations of the Egyptian force beyond the Egyptian-Syrian frontier.'[75] Yet,
the instructions Sykes received from Lloyd George on 3 April pointed, as
far as Palestine was concerned, in the opposite direction. Shortly before
leaving for Paris, he briefed Graham about them in general terms,[76] but
no official intimation from the Prime Minister's office to this effect could
be traced. There was therefore some uneasiness and annoyance at the
Foreign Office. But it was not until Bertie aired his misgivings that the
Foreign Office sensed the danger of Sykes's free-lance diplomacy. 'I am a
little afraid', Hardinge confided to Wingate, 'of what Sykes may do when
in Palestine. There are so few people who realize the importance attached
by the French to their position on Syria which they conceive to be based
upon claims dating from Napoleonic times, but for which there is really
no serious justification.'[77]

Those who suspected Sykes of adventurous methods in diplomacy were
unaware that he enjoyed the full confidence of the Prime Minister; those
who resented his disregard of French susceptibilities did not know how
much in fact he did care for the durability of the Entente. He believed that
a British presence in Palestine and Mesopotamia and a French establishment in Syria, was the basis on which to build the Anglo-French position
in the Middle East. It made sense and gave more security than a mutilated
Palestine and international administration in the 'Brown' area.

9　Achievements in Paris and Rome

The day before Sykes saw Lloyd George, Picot received meticulous instructions from Alexandre Ribot, the new French Premier and Foreign Minister. Picot's task as High Commissioner, and the task of the French military detachment, was to share with the British the mantle of liberator, and administer the occupied territories in conformity with the May 1916 Agreement. They were to demonstrate the solidarity of the Entente. With regard to Palestine the text reads:

> On your arrival in Palestine you will find numerous Jewish colonies. Right from the outset, it is necessary to display towards the Jewish settlers great benevolence and entrust them with a measure of administration of their own communities and with a share in the government of the country. For you are, undoubtedly, aware that the policy pursued towards them is destined to create a profound impression not only among their co-religionists residing in Allied and neutral countries, but even among those who live in enemy countries. It would, therefore, be to our interest to inspire them with the greatest expectations concerning what the Allies intend to do for them on the soil to which they are tied by a past of a thousand years and to which some of their people wish to return.

Picot was instructed to show a friendly attitude towards the Christian and Moslem Arab population also and spur them on to rebel against the Turks.[1]

A comparison between the British and French instructions is illuminating. Whilst Lloyd George aimed at undermining the condominium in Palestine, Ribot's objective was to put it into effect. 'You will have to organize the occupied territories so as to ensure France an equal footing to that of England,' he told Picot. Being at a grave disadvantage as against the English, the French had to make an extra effort to gain the acceptance of the local population, particularly the Jewish. Given French indifference towards, if not suspicion of the Zionists in the past, Ribot's brief signalled a radical change. Not only was the Jewish historical connection to Palestine acknowledged, and rights of colonisation assured, but, significantly, the Jewish population was to be given 'a share in the government of the country'. The objections raised by Briand in 1916 had evaporated; the new French Government began to consider Zionism as a factor worth taking into account.

This *volte face* was not accidental; nor was it the result of improvisation. Both Professor Basch and Picot, after the latter's return from London, had done their best to influence the French Government. The imminent occupation of Palestine, coupled with the triumphant march of the cause of small nationalities, made Zionism, hitherto regarded as utopian, a topical issue.[2] One of the arguments successfully deployed by Picot to persuade his superiors at the Quai d'Orsay, was that it would be undesirable to let the British monopolise the Zionists; nor was it prudent for the French to antagonise the Jews at the gates of Syria.[3] But perhaps the most weighty consideration calling for a drastic revision was the news that the German Government was about to make the Zionist cause its own and to create 'a Jewish Republic in Palestine'. The German move was designed to win the sympathy of world Jewry, especially in the United States, in the hope of influencing President Wilson, who at that time relied heavily on the Jewish as well as the Irish vote.[4]

Babst, the French envoy at Copenhagen, had received this news from Dr Dernburg (himself a half-Jew), who was in charge of German propaganda in the United States. Dernburg was doing his utmost to popularise his country's cause, but his allusion to the foundation of a Jewish republic (if quoted correctly) was grossly exaggerated. Dernburg's remarks were not without foundation however. Arthur Zimmermann, the German Foreign Minister, was in sympathy with the Zionist cause. Since the beginning of the war he had exerted himself to protect the Palestinian Jews whenever they were threatened by the Turkish authorities, and in March 1917, when the moment seemed auspicious, had mooted the idea of a joint Turco-German declaration in favour of Jewish colonisation. Nothing eventually came of Zimmermann's initiative,[5] but Babst's report made a palpable impact on Cambon, who feared that should the Germans prove successful, French influence in the United States might suffer a setback, and the French position in Palestine be undermined, particularly since the Zionists were known to be averse to an international régime, favouring instead a single protector,[6] other than France.

When Sokolow arrived in Paris the ground was already well prepared. At the first round of conversations Picot put the French claims at their highest, claiming Palestine exclusively for France, and denying it to Great Britain.[7] It was intended to shake Sokolow's confidence in a British trusteeship and make the condominium more palatable. Sokolow, as Mrs Weizmann recorded in her diary, was at first 'most pessimistic'. The tenor of his telegram to his colleagues in London was that 'the French will not hear of a British protectorate; they want Palestine for themselves. They will give Jews "rights" but not autonomy or a charter.'[8] Depressed, Sokolow had to steer his course warily. Mindful of Sykes's warning, he kept the idea of British protection in the background, and throughout his stay in Paris avoided discussing the question of the future suzerainty of Palestine. With no controversial issues to cloud the horizon, the negotiations entered into smoother waters and Picot finally suggested that on the following day, or the day after (7 or 8 April), Sokolow should submit the Zionist desiderata to the French Government. They consisted of facilities for colonisation, communal autonomy, rights of the Hebrew language, and establishment of a Jewish Chartered Company.[9]

The inclusion of the last item, though previously contested by Picot, was apparently made possible after Sokolow agreed to drop the condition that the Company be British. Apologetically, Sokolow later told Sir Mark Sykes, who in the meantime had arrived in Paris, that in his opinion the 'admission by France of [the] principle of recognition of Jewish nationality in Palestine will be a step in advance', with which Sykes agreed. Should the French accept the Zionist desiderata, Sykes wrote to Hankey the next day, 'a great step' would be gained. Recognition of Jewish national aspirations would automatically give the Zionists a say in the future of Palestine; given their preference for British trusteeship, coupled with British military occupation, an irrevocable *fait accompli* would be created.[10]

But Sykes was impatient. Although keeping all his telegrams strictly confidential ('except Hankey . . . I want to keep this dynamite outside the Garden City . . . It is real explosive, not a sham'[11]), he showed his hand prematurely in suggesting that Picot should 'prepare French mind for idea of British suzerainty in Palestine by international consent'; British 'preponderant military effort, rights of trans-Palestine railway construction, rights of annexation at Haifa, coupled with general bias of Zionists in favour of British suzerainty, tended to make such a solution the only stable one.' In return, Sykes offered British support for French claims in Armenia, Syria and area 'A'. Picot gave the impression of being less hostile to such a *quid pro quo* than Sykes had anticipated. However, the average politician in France, Picot pointed out, regarded Palestine as an integral part of Syria, and that before Syria proper and area 'A' came under French control, it would be presumptuous to expect public opinion in France to give ground on Palestine.[12]

The Foreign Office was agreeably surprised to find Picot conciliatory, but their pleasure was premature. A few days later, when Picot broached the idea of a joint Anglo-French post office in Gaza, following the French Government's suggestion to appoint a high-ranking officer to command the French contingent attached to the Egyptian Expeditionary Force, it became clear that Paris had not the slightest intention of abandoning its share in the administration of the 'Brown' area. Sykes's meeting with Ribot passed off smoothly, as the question of Palestine's future was not raised, but Ambassador Bertie, in a better position to gauge French public opinion, remained sceptical. 'In dealing with the question of Syria and Palestine,' he told Graham, 'it must be remembered that the French uninformed general Public imagine that France has special prescriptive rights in Syria and Palestine'. The Roman Catholic Church exerted great influence in this matter, and Ribot (who was a Protestant) would be reluctant to face the combined opposition of the chauvinists, the general public, and the Roman Catholic priesthood.[13]

Sykes was subsequently able to judge the depth of French feeling for himself. Senator Flandin, the great 'vox' of the Syrian party, 'rose like a young trout on a dull day' when approached by Sykes. Picot had foolishly betrayed French interests. 'France required the whole of the Mediterranean littoral down to Arish, and the Hedjaz railway as far as Ma'an.' A small international enclave of Jaffa, Jerusalem and Bethlehem, in which France would be predominant, could be conceded, but the rest of the country should be 'absolute French territory as far East as the Euphrates. England might, if she insisted, be granted the Port of Gaza, but Haifa, never.' Sykes went away with the impression that Flandin's 'gang' would work all out against the Anglo-French Agreement, and that Picot would, willy-nilly, be forced to follow suit. The Christian-Socialist party, headed by Cailloux and Bouillon, and the Nationalists, did not spare much love for the British either. The Nationalists were linked with the schemes of the *Vitali Chemins de fer Orientaux*, who were reputed to be the leading concession-hunters in Turkey, and all these groups, allied with the French priesthood, constituted a formidable phalanx directed against England.[14]

Sykes was quick to realise that in these circumstances it would be premature to press the idea of a British Palestine. However, he told Graham,[15]

if the French agree to recognise Jewish Nationalism and all that carries with it as a Palestinian political factor, I think that it will

prove a step in the right direction and will tend to pave the way to
Great Britain being appointed Patron of Palestine, that is, of the
Brown Zone minus Jerusalem and Bethlehem and a small enclave,
by the whole of the Entente Powers.

Graham did not share Sykes's optimism. He was aware that encouragement of the Zionist movement was in accordance with the instructions
Sykes had received from the Prime Minister.[16] None the less, grave doubts
lingered in his mind: 'I fear the idea that the French will ever be disposed
to hand over the whole administration of Palestine to us is utopian and
yet the Zionist hopes are based on this hypothesis. We should not go too
far in the encouragement of these hopes, for if they are disappointed the
blame will inevitably fall upon us.' But it was not until the arrival of Lord
Bertie's letter of 12 April and Sykes's own account that Graham decided
to consult Lord Hardinge. He wrote:

> His Majesty's Government are now committed to support Zionist
> aspirations. Sir Mark Sykes has received instructions on the subject
> from the Prime Minister and Mr. Balfour and has been taking action
> both in Paris and Rome. He has been assisting to the best of his
> ability M. Sokoloff, the well-known Zionist leader. At the present
> moment I am obtaining leave from the Admiralty for Mr. Weiz-
> mann, another prominent Zionist, to relinquish his official work
> . . . and to proceed to Egypt to join Sir Mark Sykes who has
> urgently asked for his help.
>
> However admirable the Zionist idea may be, and however rightly
> anxious His Majesty's Government are to encourage it, there is one
> aspect of the situation to which attention should be drawn. Every
> Zionist with whom I have discussed the question, Baron James de
> Rothschild, Dr. Weizmann, Mr. Sidebotham of the *Manchester
> Guardian*, etc. etc. . . . . insists that the Zionist idea is based entirely
> on a British Palestine. They are unanimous in the opinion that their
> project would break down were Palestine to be internationalized.

This, Graham pointed out, was inconsistent with article III of the Asia
Minor Agreement which provided that 'in the Brown area shall be
established an international administration'; the Agreement was secret
and could not be divulged to the Zionists. He went on:

> are we justified in encouraging them in so great a measure when the
> prospect of Palestine being internationalised is distinctly stronger
> than the prospect of the country coming under our protection? I
> know the Prime Minister insists that we must obtain Palestine and

that Sir Mark Sykes proceeded on his mission with these instructions. But those who are best qualified to gauge French opinion, including Lord Bertie, are convinced that the French will never abandon their sentimental claims to Palestine.

Graham felt extremely uneasy at being involved in a risky manoeuvre which smacked of double-dealing. Both Dr Weizmann and Baron James de Rothschild were allowed to cable Brandeis and urge him to get American Jews to adopt a resolution in favour of a British administration of Palestine. 'This line of propaganda', Graham remarked, 'may strengthen our position in the matter or it may provoke and solidify French opposition to our pretensions.' But what disturbed him particularly was whether the British were justified by encouraging the Zionists without giving them some intimation of the existing Agreement.

I feel [he concluded] that if in the end the French refuse to give way, and the attitude of Italy and Russia on the subject is also uncertain, the odium of the failure of the Zionists project to which we shall have given so much encouragement will fall entirely upon us.[17]

Graham revealed his disquiet also to Sykes,[18] from whom he apparently learned that the British Government, or at least the Prime Minister, was 'committed'. But if Graham questioned this policy, it was not because he nourished any ill-will towards Zionism. On the contrary; on this count he was already a convert. It was its use in power politics that disconcerted him. Realisation of the Zionist project within the framework of an internationalised Palestine seemed to him a safer course to follow. Lord Hardinge shared Graham's misgivings:

I cannot help feeling that this Zionist movement and its consequences have not so far been sufficiently considered. It appears that it is inseparable from a British Palestine, and this seems at present unrealisable. Are we wise in giving encouragement to a movement based on a condition which we cannot enforce? Failure, when it comes, will be laid at the door of the F.O., and not without reason.

Lord Robert Cecil, deputising for Balfour at the Foreign Office, thought differently. He agreed that there was great difficulty in carrying out the Zionist policy which involved the strong preference for a British protectorate, but thought that it was 'desirable to get France to join [Britain] in an expression of sympathy for Jewish Nationalist aspirations'.[19] Cecil knew what he was saying. Preoccupied with the position in Russia, he was at that time contemplating publication of a joint Entente pro-Zionist declaration in order to counteract Jewish pacifist and socialist propaganda in Russia.[20] French agreement was essential, and Sokolow, under Sykes's guidance, was therefore doing the job that was needed.

As it turned out, the French, though hostile to the idea of a British Palestine, showed a marked sympathy to Zionism, if sheltered under a joint Franco-British ægis. On 9 April Sokolow was received by Jules Cambon, the Secretary-General of the French Foreign Ministry, in the presence of his brother Paul, the Ambassador in London, Georges Picot, and de Margerie, Ribot's Chef de Cabinet. Sokolow was asked point-blank by Picot whether he preferred England or France as sovereign in Palestine. Aware that he was skating on thin ice, Sokolow replied that the Jews were in the position of an infant who could not choose between his mother and father. The question of suzerainty was thus avoided, and, Sokolow was authorised to cable to Brandeis in the United States and Tschlenow in Moscow that 'after favourable results in London and Paris I was received by the French Ministry for Foreign Affairs with goodwill. . . . I have full confidence', he added that 'Allied victory will realise our Palestine Zionist aspirations.' The words 'and Paris' were inserted in the draft cable at the suggestion of his hosts.[21] The Quai d'Orsay was anxious to give American and Russian Zionists the impression that France was not lagging behind in sponsoring their cause. Zionism was to be an Entente and not exclusively a British concern.

A few days later Jules Cambon told Baron Edmund de Rothschild how favourably impressed he was by Sokolow. It was the first time that the Quai d'Orsay had been able to obtain a clear idea of Zionist desiderata; and consequently the French Government had decided to support the plan jointly with Britain.[22] Sykes was elated. His forecast, made on 8 April, that the French were beginning to realise that they were 'up against a big thing', and could therefore not 'close their eyes to it', had proved right. Triumphantly he cabled to Graham that Zionist aspirations had been recognised by the French Government as 'legitimate'; Sokolow had assured him (though the moment was not ripe to make it public) that 'the bulk of the Zionists desire British suzerainty'. Hence, Sykes deduced, 'with a recognized Jewish voice in favour of it', the prospects for British preponderance in Palestine were much brighter.[23]

Two points were impressed on Sokolow by Jules Cambon during their meeting on 9 April: first, that Jewish influence in Russia should be thrown into the scales against pacifists; second, that in Italy it should work to consolidate the Entente.[24]

Whilst the first is self-explanatory, the second can only be interpreted as a roundabout way of urging support for an international régime in Palestine, as opposed to a single protectorate. To neutralise the British, the French had to find common ground with the Italians, their erstwhile competitors in the Middle East. This was an attempt to use Sokolow's good offices to reverse the process started in London. If this interpretation is correct, Sykes had even more cogent reasons to welcome Sokolow's arrival in Italy. Drummond's suggestion that it was in the British 'interest to see Italy in the Mediterranean sufficiently strong to act as a real counterpoise to France and Russia'[25] must have still been fresh in his mind, and he was quick to apply it to the Palestinian context. Sykes, it might be recalled, had his own motives for wanting the Italians to respect Jewish rights of colonisation in Palestine,[26] and Sokolow's efforts could therefore spare the British the inconvenience of direct bargaining. But the primary reason that made Sokolow's arrival in Rome so welcome was that it offered a unique opportunity of bringing together the Zionists and the Vatican. Here was the most sensitive area. With the strongly built-in prejudice against the idea of the Jews' return to the Holy Land, the Vatican provided fertile soil for the French clerics to stir up intrigues. Zionism might inadvertently become a stick with which to beat the British; to forestall such an embarrassment it was imperative to make it acceptable to the Holy See.

On 11 April Sykes saw Monsignor Pacelli, the Vatican's Assistant Under-Secretary for Foreign Affairs. After acquainting him with the nature of his mission to the East, Sykes pointed to the immense difficulties to be expected after the liberation of Jerusalem. Pacelli's response was soothing; he paid tribute to the British spirit of toleration; the French did not seem to impress him as an ideal candidate for patronage of the Holy Places. Sykes thereupon steered the conversation to the delicate subject of Zionism. Its main object, he said, was 'to evolve a self-supporting Jewish community which should raise, not only the racial self-respect of the Jewish people, but should also be a proof to the [world] of the capacity of Jews to produce a virtuous and simple agrarian population'. The realisation of this ideal, he hoped, would strike at the roots of the difficulties which had been 'productive of so much unhappiness in the past'. Zionists' aims 'in no way clashed with Christian desiderata, in general, and Catholic desiderata in particular'. Pacelli was interested and was willing to see Sokolow when in Rome. Two days later Sykes was received by Pope Benedict XV and felt equally gratified by the Pontiff's sympathy. Although the Pope did not say much, Sykes went away with the impression that in the event of Jerusalem being captured, the audience with His

Holiness would strengthen the British position *vis-à-vis* the Latin Patriarch, as well as against German or other enemy clerics.[27]

Sykes's tact in dealing with the Vatican was matched by Picot's shrewdness. On 14 April, during a meeting with Pacelli and Cardinal Gasquet, in Sykes's presence, Picot unexpectedly suggested that the moment might be opportune to consolidate the Catholic institutions in the Orient. With the Provisional Government in Russia disclaiming annexationist ambitions in Asia Minor, a favourable opportunity had arisen to undo the Constantinople Agreement. Sykes suspected that Picot, while harping on the Vatican's fears of the Orthodox Church, in fact was hoping, with the Holy See's backing, to re-establish the French monopoly of protection for Roman Catholics in the Orient. If this was the case, he was even more inclined than before to welcome an Italian contingent in Jerusalem and Bethlehem, in order to counterbalance the French.[28] The Italians had always resisted the traditional French claim to be sole protector of the Catholics in the East. So had the Spaniards who regarded themselves 'independent of French protection', and insisted that no settlement on the question of Palestine be concluded before providing complete freedom of access to the Holy Places in Jerusalem to the Spanish Catholics.[29] With the Latin countries in disarray, and with the Pope's blessing to Sykes, which in the circumstances were bound to have a political connotation, Britain had a good chance of winning the race. But Sykes's greatest triumph was in breaking the ice over Zionism.

Sokolow was taken by surprise when he learned that an appointment with the Vatican had been arranged for him. Aware of Theodor Herzl's ordeal thirteen years earlier, he braced himself for this delicate task. The audiences granted to him by Monsignor Pacelli on 29 April and by Cardinal Gasparri, the Papal Secretary of State, two days later, went off far more successfully than he could have expected. Gasparri reassured him that the Zionists need fear no opposition from the Church. 'On the contrary, you may count on our sympathy.' The Pope, whom Sokolow saw on 4 May, expressed himself in even warmer terms. 'The return of the Jews to Palestine was a miraculous event. It is providential; God has willed it . . . yes, yes—I believe that we shall be good neighbours.' The Pope, like Cardinal Gasparri, alluded to the Holy See's sympathy to the sufferings of the Jews in Tsarist Russia and mentioned the appeal made to him by the American Jewish Committee the previous year.[30]

Sokolow's account tallies with that of Count de Salis, the British envoy to the Holy See. It was he who on Sykes's recommendation had arranged for Sokolow to meet Monsignor Pacelli. When de Salis later met Cardinal Gasparri, the latter expressed his satisfaction with Sokolow's exposition of Zionist aims, as well as assurances that they entertained 'no feelings of hostility . . . towards the Church. I think', de Salis wrote:[31]

> there can be no doubt that the interview left a good impression as Monsieur Sokolof was subsequently received by the Pope and wrote to me that he was exceedingly happy and felt deeply satisfied with the results of the benevolent and gracious manner in which His Holiness received him, as well as with the instructive and edifying conversation.

These manifestations of friendship, so far not confirmed by any available Vatican sources, are surprising. On Scriptural grounds the Church had no reason to subscribe to the Jews' return to Zion.[32] It believed that the destruction of their Temple, the loss of their sovereignty, and their dispersion were the penalty for their crime of deicide. So long as Jews remained incalcitrant towards the Christian faith, they were condemned to perpetual wandering and unrest.[33] For the Jews to return to the Holy Land would contradict this doctrine, and the Church would therefore discourage it. Herzl had felt the backwash of the animus of the Catholic clergy against his movement but it was not before his interview at the Vatican in January 1904 that he became fully aware of the doctrinal gulf that separated the Church from Judaism. The question of the Holy Places, for which Herzl was willing to admit extraterritoriality, was not at the heart of the difficulty. 'As long as the Jews deny the divinity of Christ,' Cardinal Merry del Sal, the Papal Secretary, told him, 'we certainly cannot make a declaration in their favour.' Even less comfort could be drawn from Pius X. All Herzl's arguments fell flat against the Pope's frank avowal of *non possumus*. 'We cannot prevent the Jews from going to Jerusalem,' the Pontiff stated, 'but we could never sanction it . . . The Jews have not recognised our Lord, therefore we cannot recognise the Jewish people . . . *Gerusallemme* must not get into the hands of the Jews.'[34]

Vatican opinion is by nature conservative. Save for the short interlude during 1917–18, the attitude towards Zionism remained unchanged. In the winter of 1918, when Sykes revisited Rome, he found Cardinal Gasparri unsympathetic, and early in 1919 *The Tablet* denied the story that the Holy Father was 'a supporter of Zionism'.[35] A few years later Benedict XV affirmed that the establishment of a Jewish National Home 'would deprive Christianity of the place it occupied in the Holy Land', and his successor, Pius XI, demanded that the rights of the Catholic Church in Palestine be protected from Jews and infidels, as well as from non-Catholic Christians.[36] In 1922 *La Civilta Cattolica*, the official Jesuit organ, denied that the Jews had any special rights to Palestine and accused the

Zionists of introducing an 'immoral' code of conduct into the Holy Land; the combined Protestant-Judean-Bolshevik influence was gravely jeopardising Catholic interests. On 28 June 1922 an official memorandum to this effect was presented to the League of Nations by the Holy See.[37] On 14 May 1948 the *Osservatore Romano*, the semi-official organ of the Vatican, asserted that modern Zionism was 'not the true heir of Biblical Israel but a secular state . . . therefore, the Holy Land and its sacred sites belong to Christianity, the True Israel.'[38] The attitude reflected in the interview with Sokolow must therefore have been based not on a sudden doctrinal transformation but on more mundane considerations.

In 1915–16 the Vatican was looking for an understanding with the Jews. The idea sprang from the fertile mind of François Deloncle, a member of the French Chamber of Deputies and a former editor of *Le Siècle*. A Catholic with an admixture of Jewish blood and an Orientalist, he had a foot in both worlds. Before the outbreak of the war he suddenly discovered an identity of interests between the Church and the Jews, especially in relation to Russia. Both abhorred her expansion in general, and in Palestine in particular. On 23 May 1915, and again on 18 June 1915, Deloncle was received by the Pope. His Holiness seemed to be touched by the plight of the Jews in Russia and professed himself ready to support them if in return the Jews, in America especially, 'would co-operate with him'. He offered to issue an Encyclical on this matter, but to make his intervention effective he thought it essential for his diplomatic position at the future peace conference to be strengthened. Deloncle thereupon proceeded to London with a message that, if given a say in the future conference, the Holy See would champion 'the cause of Religious Liberty, especially the emancipation of the Jews . . . in the Russian Empire'. The proposal held little appeal for the leaders of British Jewry. Sensing an ulterior motive, they were reluctant to make any deal with the Vatican. The American Jewish Committee seemed more interested in Deloncle's proposal, and the Pope made it known that the Vatican would take practical steps to alleviate the sufferings of the Jews in Poland. Deloncle produced a document called 'the Pact of Lugano', the object of which was to rally the support of world Jewry for the independence of Poland. However, it had such strong anti-Russian overtones that the London Conjoint Foreign Committee, fearing lest it might embarrass the Allies, strongly advised their colleagues in the United States against any involvement in this matter. The American Jewish Committee had decided independently to steer clear of the 'Pact' and the whole affair fizzled out.[39]

By the spring of 1917 the matter had lost its relevance and Jewish assistance was no longer essential. Poland's future was no longer in doubt, whilst in Russia persecution of the Jews seemed to be a thing of the past. With the fall of Tsardom, the Vatican's nightmare of the Orthodox Church dominating Constantinople and Jerusalem receded. Why then did both Gasparri and Benedict XV think fit to recall the episode? There was no need at the time to revive Deloncle's defunct scheme, nor did they expect Sokolow's assistance in this matter. Their object was apparently different. The reference to the common fate of Jews and Catholics under the Tsar and to the *pourparlers* with the American Jewish Committee was meant as a broad hint to Sokolow that, despite differences in faith, on the political plane, in the given circumstances, some common ground between the Catholic Church and the Jews did exist. The eyes of the Vatican were now fixed on Palestine. With its liberation imminent, the realisation of the old dream to wrest the Holy Places from the custody of a Moslem overlord seemed to be in sight, and for the Vatican the Holy Places meant a sizeable territory extending well beyond the actual area of the holy shrines. What was glossed over during the conversation with Sir Mark Sykes, was driven home unequivocally to Sokolow. 'The Church', he was told by Gasparri, 'would claim . . . not only Jerusalem and Bethlehem, but Nazareth and its surroundings, Tiberias and even Jericho.'[40] The Pope's assurances of good neighbourliness to Sokolow must therefore be read not in the spiritual but in the geographical context.

Given these territorial ambitions, the Holy See was naturally anxious to secure Zionist goodwill. The Jews living in the countries of the Central Powers, as well as in the United States, were known to have favoured the maintenance of the Ottoman Empire. The Church leaders had therefore cogent reasons for seeking an accommodation with Sokolow. By putting spokes in the wheels of British Zionism, the Vatican would only do itself a disservice; it was only with British support that the Vatican could assume the protectorate of the Holy Places. Sokolow had good reason to congratulate himself on his achievement. The credit for preparing the ground must indisputably go to Sir Mark Sykes, but it is worth noting that Sokolow's success would not have been possible had the Vatican not desired it.

The episode did not remain unnoticed by the Italian Government. 'I understand that M. Sokolow has received encouraging assurances . . . from the Pope,' Baron Sonnino, the Italian Foreign Minister told Sir Rennell Rodd, the British Ambassador in Rome on 10 May. According to Rodd, Sonnino was sympathetic to the idea of Jewish colonisation of Palestine and saw some 'practical advantages' in stimulating the emigration of Jews from East European countries. However, despite Rodd's suggestion, he declined to grant Sokolow an interview.[41] Perhaps he felt that it would be more valuable for the Zionists if an official declaration came from Di Martino, the Secretary-General of the Foreign Ministry, or the Prime Minister, Boselli, who unlike himself was not of Jewish extraction. The question is, however, of secondary importance, since the assurances given to Sokolow by Di Martino on 8 May, and by Boselli four days later, had in fact originated with Sonnino. Sokolow was told of Italy's sympathy with Zionist aspirations; Italy could give moral support but could not take the initiative in the matter.[42]

Italy had no Jewish problem, nor could Zionism further her aims in Asia Minor. Her recognition of Jewish rights of colonisation in Palestine, as implied in the declaration to Sokolow, was all the more useful. Sykes could have hoped for no better outcome. On 27 May Sokolow informed him: 'My work in France and Italy has had great success. Government Committee and Jew[ish] leaders formerly opposed, now accord to our programme full support. I succeeded in inducing even Luzzatti [the Minister of Finance] to join our Committee.' Charles Webster, who quoted this cable in his *Notes*, eighteen months later, commented: 'In view of Italy's interest in Asia Minor and her susceptibilities on the question of Palestine, this sympathetic attitude towards the Zionists is not without importance.'[43]

While Sykes was conducting his diplomatic chess-game in Rome, Lloyd George was conferring with his opposite numbers at St Jean de Maurienne. Time was too short for Sykes, before his departure for Egypt, to report to the Prime Minister, but there is no reason to presume that the latter would have been displeased with Sykes's accomplishments. For, despite the verbal agreement on the international administration of Palestine at the St Jean de Maurienne conference, Lloyd George's goal remained unaltered. Questioned on his Palestine policy by Lord Bertie in Paris (during his return journey), Lloyd George replied: 'We shall be there by conquest and shall remain.' He was totally impervious to Bertie's arguments. That the Jews were meek and not a combative race, that Britain was running the risk of unpopularity among the Arabs, that Ribot was likely to reject the idea of a British Protectorate, made not the slightest impression on him. 'We, being of no particular faith, [are] the only Power fit to rule Mohammedans, Jews, Roman Catholics and keep peace between the[m].'[44] Lloyd George may have treated the sceptical Ambassador too cavalierly, and the latter may have recorded the Prime Minister's statement too one-sidedly, for Lloyd George was not only a determined imperialist but possessed also a streak of genuine idealism, which in the matter of Palestine blended with political and strategic considerations.

Nor did Lloyd George make any attempt to convince his doubting host of the merits of Zionism and its instrumentality for British interests.

Lloyd George conducted his own foreign policy, by-passing the Foreign Office, for whom the Asia Minor Agreement remained obligatory. Weizmann was ignorant of this divergence and erroneously projected the policy of Lloyd George and Sykes on to that of the Foreign Office. He was therefore all the more shocked to learn, through an indiscretion of C. P. Scott, of the existence of the Sykes-Picot Agreement. Much perturbed, he called on Sir Ronald Graham on 24 April and told him that 'unless he has a definite mandate to rouse public Jewish opinion for British Palestine . . . he couldn't go to Egypt . . . That it will carry tremendous weight if he starts his agitation from Jerusalem,' and that annexation, or much worse, division of Palestine, was inadmissible. 'Democratic Russia and America will never allow' it, nor would 'the whole of Jewry'. According to a note in Mrs Weizmann's diary, 'Sir Ronald Graham was most sympathetic . . . he didn't think the situation was satisfactory and . . . a few days ago . . . he presented a memorandum . . . to that effect. He made Chaim understand that though some pledges exist, there is nothing definite.'[45]

The assertion that there was 'nothing definite' in the Anglo-French agreement (based obviously on Weizmann's impression), completely contradicts what Graham had stated in his memorandum of 21 April, already quoted. Even more curious is the discrepancy between the accounts of Weizmann and Robert Cecil about their meeting on the following day.

Cecil's memorandum[46] was written on the very day of the meeting, and is comparatively short, whereas that of Weizmann[47] is more elaborate and presumably some editorial touches were added. The argument against the division of Palestine into a French Galilee and an international Judea runs in both reports, with certain nuances, on almost parallel lines: from the Jewish point of view the partition was 'a Solomon's judgement of the worst character'. The versions differ in recording Weizmann's comparison between the British and French administrative systems. Cecil omitted Weizmann's complimentary remarks to the effect that Jews all over the world trusted Britain and looked on her as 'liberator of Palestine'; England was a 'biblical nation'; under British aegis 'justice would be meted out to the various races', and the Palestinian Jews, when strong enough, would be given a measure of self-government. In contrast, Cecil gave prominence to Weizmann's comments on the French, whom he regarded as incapable of understanding the aspirations of small nations, particularly the Jewish; 'the Zionists throughout the world would regard a French administration in Palestine as a great disaster: "a third destruction of the Temple".'

Weizmann's statements about the strategic importance of Palestine for Britain are mentioned only in his own note. He strongly objected to an international régime, let alone the division of Palestine between the powers. It smacked of annexationism, a principle which since the March Revolution in Russia and the proclamation of American war aims had fallen into disrepute. In contrast, 'a Jewish Palestine under a British Protectorate' could not be seen as annexation. It would be generally understood that Britain was 'keeping the country in trust for the Jews'. What is even more surprising is the conspicuous discrepancy in reporting between these two records of Weizmann's statement concerning the purpose of his impending trip to Egypt. Since this is not a matter of a difference in phrasing or degree of emphasis but a cardinal tenet on which Weizmann built his policy, it is worth reproducing both versions in full.

Cecil's Memorandum
He informed me that . . . he was going to Egypt in order to get into communication with the Jews of Palestine, who also, he said, unanimously desired a British protectorate. From Palestine, indeed from Jerusalem, he contemplated rousing the feelings of Zionist Jews, throughout the world, in favour of the solution which he desired.

I was much impressed, as indeed I have been on previous occasions, by the enthusiasm and idealism of Mr. Weizmann; but of course, I am not in a position to express any opinion as to how far he represents Jewish feeling in this matter.

Weizmann's Note
With regard to Dr. Weizmann's going out to Egypt and Syria, he remarked that he would go on the clear understanding that he is to work for a Jewish Palestine under a British Protectorate. Lord Robert agreed to this view; he mentioned that of course there are considerable difficulties in the way but that it would strengthen the position very considerably if the Jews of the world would express themselves in favour of a British Protectorate. Dr. Weizmann replied that this is exactly the task which he would like to undertake, to bring about such an expression of opinion, and it is for that purpose that he would go to Palestine.

Weizmann's note gives the distinct impression that Cecil not only subscribed to but even encouraged him in the matter of a British Protectorate. Cecil's version does not confirm this. Though impressed by Weizmann, he remained uncommitted. While it would be too cynical to suggest that Weizmann deliberately misquoted Cecil, it would be proper to question his reading of Cecil's mind. The formula of 'a Jewish Palestine under a British Protectorate' was consistent with the Lloyd George-Sykes line of thinking, but it could not sit well with Cecil. Like that of Balfour, his cousin, Cecil's attitude to Zionism was coloured by humanitarian and propaganda motives, not necessarily by strategic considerations.

Cecil's imagination had been captured by the Zionist idea as early as 1906. Later he was convinced that its implementation was 'of vital importance to the world. A nation without a country of its own is an anomaly, and anomalies bring trouble.'[48] Its recognition, he was reported to have stated, was 'one of the greatest steps taken in carrying out the principle . . . of the supremacy of Law and Liberty'.[49] Following the capture of Jerusalem he declared that 'the Jewish Palestine is the first constructive effort in the new settlement of the world after the War'.[50] In his famous London Opera House speech on 2 December 1917, he expressed himself in such blunt terms as 'Judaea for the Jews'.[51] Whatever the meaning of this statement, for Cecil it did not necessarily imply British trusteeship. In December 1918, when Palestine was completely in British hands, Cecil was still no convert to the strategic concept. 'I am not much impressed by the argument', he told the War Cabinet Eastern Committee, 'that in order to defend Egypt we had to go to Palestine, because in order to defend Palestine we should have to go to Aleppo or some such place. You always have to go forward.'[52] This assessment was even more valid in April 1917, and Cecil would not have propounded a view contrary to that held at the Foreign Office. To commit it to a British Palestine whilst Balfour was away in the United States would have been most unlike Cecil. Weizmann was right in detecting a broad streak of idealism in Cecil[53] but was in all likelihood incorrect in assuming that the argument for a British protectorate kindled his enthusiasm.

Three days later Graham cabled to Sykes in an entirely different vein:[54]

Dr. Weizmann is finishing his business with Admiralty and hopes to start for Egypt on May 11th. He has been rather upset at hearing account, which was approximately accurate, given by [a] French journalist of Asia Minor Agreement in regard to Palestine, but is going out with full permission to work for a British Palestine. He and James Rothschild are instigating American and Russian Jews to agitate for this consummation.

Whether this sudden change in Graham's policy had something to do with Lloyd George's return to London is difficult to ascertain. But, as we shall see later, Graham had been steadily moving closer to the 'Garden Suburb' school of thought, bridging thereby the divergence between the Prime Minister and Balfour. He requested the Admiralty to release Weizmann; his mission was 'invaluable'. But Weizmann in the meantime had second thoughts and enquired whether, in view of the adverse military situation on the Palestinian front, 'it would not be better for him to postpone his departure for Egypt for a month or six weeks'. Sykes insisted that 'Weizmann should come as soon as possible' but it was Cecil who eventually overruled both Graham and Sykes. Did Cecil object to Weizmann's trip to Egypt because he believed Weizmann could be more usefully employed in the propaganda campaign, or because he feared lest he himself would be called on to foot the bill?—a most embarrassing predicament since, unlike Graham, Cecil continued to regard the inter-Allied engagement as binding. This transpires from his reaction to a question raised in Parliament by Josiah Wedgwood on 9 May 1917. Wedgwood asked the Secretary of State 'whether any pledges have been given to France or Italy which might impede the establishment of an independent and integral Jewish Palestine under American or British protection'. Cecil gave no clear answer, but the minute on the Foreign Office sheet is suggestive: 'This is not an easy question to answer, as, of course, we are at present pledged to an international administration of Palestine.'[55]

The atmosphere of uncertainty made Weizmann and his colleagues in London view Sokolow's mission with misgivings. These were reinforced by the report of James Malcolm, who had returned from Paris, where he had accompanied Sokolow. Their satisfaction with the newly-found French sympathy was destroyed by the news about the Anglo-French Agreement, and their concern still further enhanced by Sokolow's telegram to Brandeis and Tschlenow of 9 April,[56] which could have been interpreted as an endorsement of a future Franco-British condominium in Palestine. Mrs Weizmann conveys the feeling that pervaded the British Zionist leadership: 'all unanimously agree that Sokolow's presence in Paris any longer is dangerous and all connection with the French ought to be severed'.[57] A telegram to that effect was sent to Sokolow, at that time in Rome.

> Your work in France may be interpreted as negotiations in behalf of our movement in favour of a French alternative. Such an impression is not admissible. You only went on suggestion of Sir M.

Sykes to explain Zionist programme '*à titre d'information*'. I shall only go to Egypt with distinct programme to support Jewish Palestine under British Protectorate. Brandeis and Tschlenow informed accordingly. Your presence here absolutely necessary.

Sokolow replied promptly:

Astonished [at] fallacious commentaries. Acted [in] France strictly '*à titre d'information*'. Closest relations with Sykes. My programme were 'our demands' for which [I] enlisted official sympathy without slightest allusions to French alternative or any engagement. Must protest emphatically against misleading interpretations. My ideal solution is, naturally, British Palestine, for this I am working here also successfully . . . with necessary carefulness. Shall return as soon as possible.

When Weizmann pressed for Sokolow's return, he was still intending to go to Egypt but, though the trip was postponed, another reason emerged that necessitated Sokolow's immediate return. 'Tschlenow wires all Russian-Zionist Conference in Petrograd, 6 June (new style). Consider your presence there absolutely essential and British authorities here share this opinion and will facilitate voyage. Cancel your appointments and leave straight for here. Matter most urgent.' Although exhausted, Sokolow promised Weizmann to do his best; he had to call en route on members of the French Government but hoped to arrive in London in time.[58]

The French Government also regarded Sokolow's mission to Russia as a most useful move in the Allied cause, 'pour peser sur les juifs de russie dans le sens de la continuation de la guerre'.[59] On 25 May Sokolow was received by Ribot, and then by Jules Cambon. Sensing that the moment was propitious to pin the French down to some concrete commitment, Sokolow wired Weizmann that it was necessary for him to stay in Paris for a few days longer, and urged him to ask the Russian Zionists to adjourn their conference for one week. As he explained later to Rosoff, his Russian colleague, he was not content with the verbal, though warm assurances, and pressed the French Government for a statement. He hoped that such a document would not only prevent any adverse moves by the anti-Zionist circles at the Alliance Israélite, heretofore successfully neutralised by himself and Baron Rothschild, but would prove a tangible asset at the future peace conference. Sokolow's perseverance was rewarded. 'I made enormous efforts,' he told Rosoff, 'and happily succeeded in obtaining desired official document today . . . [It] surpassed [my] imagination . . . I consider this was the greatest moral victory our idea ever attained.'[60] The document, dated 4 June which Sokolow received from Jules Cambon, reads as follows:[61]

> You were good enough to present the project to which you are devoting your efforts which has for its object the development of Jewish colonisation in Palestine. You consider that, circumstances permitting, and the independence of the Holy Places being safeguarded on the other hand, it would be a deed of justice and of reparation to assist, by the protection of the Allied Powers, in the renaissance of the Jewish nationality in that land from which the people of Israel were exiled so many centuries ago.
>
> The French Government, which entered this present war to defend a people wrongly attacked, and which continues the struggle to assure the victory of right over might, can but feel sympathy for your cause, the triumph of which is bound up with that of the Allies.
>
> I am happy to give you, herewith, such assurances.

This was an extraordinary document. For the Zionists it was a political victory of the highest order, the French Government being the first among the European Powers to recognise the legitimacy of Zionist aspirations, not merely as a concession to temporary expediency but as a matter of principle. Zionism now became linked with the general Entente war aims to defend the rights of small nationalities. It was formulated, as Sir Ronald Graham rightly observed four months later, in 'more definite terms' than its British counterpart of 2 November 1917.[62]

'To assist by the protection of' is indeed a much stronger expression than 'to facilitate the achievement of this object', which was the central phrase in the Balfour Declaration. Again, apart from safeguards for the Holy Places, there is no other reservation in Cambon's letter as compared to those in Balfour's. The French skilfully bypassed the use of the explosive term 'a national home for the Jewish people', which implied recognition of Jews as a separate nation with a home in Palestine, preferring the less provocative wording: 'the renaissance of the Jewish nationality in that Land' which could have no repercussions on the identity and the status of the Jews in their countries of domicile. Neither did the question of safeguarding 'the civil and religious rights of existing non-Jewish communities in Palestine' disturb the French as it did the British.

The French declaration bestowed political respectability on the Zionist programme. Eighteen years later Sokolow, writing to Ribot, recalled that Cambon's letter, while confirming the historic right of the Jewish people to Palestine, enabled also the British Government to follow suit:[63]

Lord Balfour himself admitted several times that without the Cambon Declaration, his own (of 2 November 1917) would not have been possible. On different occasions he underlined the international character of the Palestine problem . . . It was the French declaration which was . . . the basis of the Balfour Declaration.

We shall see, in the course of our narrative, how correct Sokolow's statement was.

10   British War Aims Reassessed

It may be recalled that during April Lord Bertie's forebodings about Sykes's mission were fully shared by the Foreign Office. Graham in particular was full of doubts, for, as he told Lord Bertie, the British Government was 'more or less committed to encourage Zionism', and all the hopes of the Zionists were based on a British or, failing that, an American Palestine. Moreover, Sykes had received his instructions direct from the Prime Minister, and 'I am not sure what they were, or how far he was to go'.[1] However, by the end of May Graham's dilemma had almost been resolved. Not only had Bertie's dark prophecies proved unfounded, but the way in which the French were courting Sokolow amazed him. 'This is rather an odd intimation,' he minuted on Cambon's letter of 23 May to the Foreign Office. 'Is it to show that the French are watching with interest our dealings with the Zionists?'; to which he added two days later: 'It looks as if the French are trying to get hold of Sokolow. In the meantime, Goldberg is proceeding to Russia and will attend the Zionist Conference in any case.'[2] By that time Graham had become convinced that the British needed the Zionists and their services, especially in Russia; nor did he raise any objections to the idea of a British Palestine.

Graham's change of mind was in line with the conclusions to which the Government was moving. On 28 April the Imperial Sub-Committee on Territorial Desiderata on the terms of Peace submitted its report pointing to the 'great importance that both Palestine and Mesopotamia should be under British control'. The Imperial War Cabinet agreed in principle,[3] thus making a final break with the no-annexations policy of Asquith's administration.[4] The Sykes-Picot Agreement, contrary to what is generally assumed, was provisional in nature; it could come into operation only if and when Turkey was defeated. It did not oblige its signatories to defeat Turkey. Only after German ambitions in the East had become known did destruction of the Ottoman Empire become an unavoidable necessity, and British war aims had to be redefined. Curzon's memorandum, dated 5 December 1917, is most illuminating on this point:[5]

164

When the War began, there was no idea in the minds of the British public, or of the British Government, of acquiring foreign territory in any part of the globe . . . and as soon as Turkey had entered the war [save for securing] the British position at the head of the Persian Gulf . . . any thought of territorial expansion was absent . . .

However as the war has proceeded . . . different views have been forced upon the Allied belligerents . . . German Ministers of State, professors and newspapers, have . . . openly proclaimed to the world in what manner and with what ambitions they propose to reorganise and drill the recovered German colonial dominion of the future . . . Simultaneously we have seen the Turkish Empire infected with the virus of German militarism . . . [and] the almost incredible brutality with which she has sought to extirpate the subject races of Armenians, Syrians and Jews.

As for Palestine's future there was only one answer:

From the strategical point of view it is equally important not to allow the Turks to resume possession and control of a country which is the military gate to Egypt and the Suez Canal. Palestine, armed and fortified, might not merely become a powerful wall of defence to the Turkish armies on the south, but it would provide a rally port from which an attack might be made at any time upon the Sinai Peninsula and the valley of the Nile. Knowing as we do the view of the German strategists about the supreme importance of the Suez Canal as the nerve-centre of the British Empire, any British statesman would indeed be blind who ever allowed the Turks to reappear in the Holy Land.

Curzon was obviously referring to certain German writers and academicians, whose publications were studied in Whitehall. Thus Dr Paul Rohrbach, a popular propagandist working at the Zentralstelle für den Auslandsdienst, claimed that, unlike her adversaries, Germany was not a self-sufficient economic entity. Deficient in raw materials and agricultural products, she was at a grave disadvantage which only expansion in Asia Minor, Syria, Mesopotamia and Palestine could correct. Similarly, Germany could not match England as a maritime power, but she could apply pressure at selected sensitive spots such as the Suez Canal. Should Turkey extend the Syrian railway to the immediate neighbourhood of Egypt and establish military outposts there, Germany would be in a position to compel England 'to yield at any time'.[6] Professor Hans Delbrück, a German historian of note, elaborated this point:

The ganglion of the [British] Empire is Egypt with the Suez Canal. If . . . Turkey emerges from this world-crisis a consolidated State . . . [and] provides itself with railways connecting the remote provinces and making possible the rapid concentration of all its military resources in Palestine and the Sinai peninsula, England's rule over Egypt, which she has hitherto been able to maintain with 6,000 European troops, will no longer be an impregnable fortress in the eyes of the fellaheen and of the whole Moslem world. If the Suez Canal is once lost, all the bonds that bind together the constituent parts of the Empire will be loosed.

'Germany', Delbrück maintained, 'cannot and must not allow the world to be divided between the Russians and Anglo-Saxons.' With Russia in possession of Constantinople, and England in control of an empire from Cairo to Calcutta, no other state would be able to pursue an independent policy. 'It is the special mission of Germany to step in . . . and protect the future not only of its own race, but also of the individualities [sic] of all other small nationalities.' For this reason she should embark on a vigorous colonial policy in Central Africa and revitalise Turkey. The Straits, Asia Minor, Mesopotamia, Syria and Palestine must remain in the orbit of 'European [i.e. German] civilisation'.[7]

The vast output of literature designed to convince the German public that the country's future lay in the East was carefully studied in London and taken to mirror official German policy. Nor was this interpretation far off the mark.[8] Events lent support to the suspicion that Germany was bent on an aggressive course in the East. The crushing defeat of Serbia by the German army, Bulgaria's adherence to the Central Powers, the reverses that the British had sustained at Kut-el-Amara, combined with the earlier débâcle of the Dardanelles expedition, virtually opened the road from Hamburg to Baghdad. The *Mitteleuropa* dream was becoming a reality. A German foothold on the eastern bank of the Canal would have placed British imperial communications in grave jeopardy.

Sir Arthur Hirtzel was the first to give warning of the 'real and permanent' danger arising from German-inspired Pan-Islamism. The British position would not be secure until Turkey was decisively defeated and her Empire reduced to a 'political non-entity'. Sir Mark Sykes went even further. In his opinion it was not enough to weaken Turkey. Exhausted, she would fall an even easier prey to Teutonic colonial ambitions; and a post-war Germanised Turkey would not only give Berlin a military bridgehead from which to attack Egypt and India, but also enable her to stir up trouble among Britain's Moslem subjects and, in Palestine, to tighten her grip on the Zionists, the Catholics and the Orthodox. With the risk of a revived Franco-German partnership in the Baghdad railway, and with Germany in command of Turkey's natural resources, Britain's position in the East would be at first on sufferance and subsequently 'untenable'.[9]

With the stakes so high, it was essential that Palestine come under sole British control. When the de Bunsen Committee was deliberating on the future of Turkey, Germany had not entered the picture. Nor had account to be taken of her early in 1916, when the Allies were hammering out their agreement on Asia Minor. An international régime in Palestine did not then seem to endanger British strategic interests. But several months later, when the nature of German ambitions in this part of the world was grasped, earlier calculations lost their validity. Sykes had to re-think his position. An international and mutilated Palestine could not arrest German expansion. Samuel's thesis, aired in his memoranda of January and March 1915, was now fully vindicated. Sykes did not lament the prospect of the 'sick man's' death. This was in any case inevitable. Since the beginning of the war Turkey had gone steadily downhill. Epidemics, war losses, stagnation in trade and agriculture had sapped her vitality and accelerated the process of internal decomposition. 'The unspeakable atrocities the Turks have committed on subject races . . . made it plain that there can be no peace as long as [they] remain masters of any race other than their own nation.'[10] Here was a ready excuse for Britain to step in. By assuming the role of protector of oppressed nationalities, she could don the mantle of a liberator and justify her campaign.

In the autumn of 1916 there were signs that the military authorities had begun to recognise that the time had come to go over to the offensive on the Eastern front. Until then, military thinking had been dominated by the doctrine that the main theatre of war was in Western Europe. If the Dardanelles expedition was an exception, it was because it was hoped that a successful operation there would facilitate communications with Russia, draw Greece and perhaps also Bulgaria and Rumania into the Allied camp, and ultimately open the way for an attack on Austria from the rear, thereby outflanking Germany. Ill-prepared and badly executed, the expedition came to naught, and the 'Westerners' gained the upper hand. Advocates of the Eastern school of thought, such as Balfour and Lloyd George, were swimming against the tide, for the General Staff had good reason to claim that the ultimate security of Egypt depended on the outcome of the confrontation on the Western front, and that England could not risk seeing France overrun. So much so that on 12 February 1916

Lieutenant-General Robertson, the newly appointed Chief of the Imperial General Staff, mooted the idea of a separate peace with Turkey, which would release seventeen British divisions stationed in Egypt and Mesopotamia, and 150,000 Russian soldiers in the Caucasus for operations against Germany. That the War Council took Robertson's advice seriously is evident from their decision taken on 22 February 1916 not to lose sight of a separate peace with Turkey or Bulgaria, 'should circumstances . . . become more favourable'.[11]

However, with the fighting on the Western front bogged down, and with Germany's drive to the East unfolding, a radical revision of strategy was necessary. On 2 September, Sir Maurice Hankey distributed to some members of the Cabinet a memorandum stressing that from a political point of view, a victory was badly needed—'occupation of . . . Jerusalem or Damascus, would not be a bad reply to Bucharest, and would at any rate be of great assistance to our Russian Allies'. He urged that operations from Egypt be intensified and given a more ambitious scope. Russia at that time was developing a successful offensive on the Caucasus front and a simultaneous onslaught by the British from Mesopotamia and Egypt could both help Russia and offer a fair prospect of crushing Turkey in a gigantic pincer movement. General Robertson also came to realise that a passive defence of the Canal was 'both extravagant in men and encouraging to the enemy'. He hoped that once the railway was constructed in the Sinai desert, General Murray would be able to make a further advance towards El-Arish and give 'encouragement to the Sherif and to all various elements in Syria . . . discontented with Turkish rule'.[12]

The deeper the British became involved in the Palestine campaign, the stronger their conviction that the concept of an international régime was outdated. This became evident on 14 December 1916 when Robertson revealed that the General Staff was contemplating the capture of Rafah and crossing the border into Palestine. He thought that, should the advance continue into the 'Brown' zone, French political co-operation should be invited, but Paris ought to be informed that Britain's sole objective was to defeat the Turks. Moreover, he added, 'we should do our utmost to avoid the association of any French troops with our own, as a mixed force . . . is for many reasons, political and military, always objectionable.' A full-scale offensive with the object of capturing Jerusalem was planned for the following autumn, and Robertson, it seems, was keen to reserve credit for the victory for the British forces alone. The War Cabinet, in its meetings on 15 December 1916 and 2 January 1917, discussed Robertson's recommendations and approved them in principle.[13] Opinion among the military and civilian members of the Government was unanimous. Lloyd George's leaning towards Palestine was a matter of common knowledge, and under his premiership (since 8 December 1916) the Eastern campaign acquired both vigour and a sense of purpose. Yet the British were fully aware that they were skating on thin ice. The inter-Allied agreement, at least outwardly, had to be respected. During the Anglo-French conference in London on 26–28 December 1916, the British representatives agreed that a French Moslem detachment should be associated in the operations, and a French political officer attached to the British Commander-in-Chief, Egypt.[14]

The French were justifiably suspicious, and did their utmost to pin the British down, claiming parity status. Soon after receiving notification of the British intention to launch military operations in the El-Arish and Rafah area, Paris made known its desire 'to participate in the administration of any zone which might be occupied in Palestine . . . and to dispatch M. Picot for this purpose'. The French Minister in Cairo took it for granted that there would be a joint administration of Palestine. The French were however at a disadvantage. Heavily committed on the Western front, they could spare no more than two battalions, and to compensate for this they appointed an officer of the rank of General to command the French detachment and to act simultaneously as Governor-designate of Gaza. Lloyd George was quick to detect some 'ulterior political designs' and replied that this was too lowly a post for so distinguished a General. He also promptly rejected a subsequent suggestion to send a larger French force to Palestine. Robertson too regarded French military co-operation as undesirable and insisted on unity of command and a homogeneous expeditionary force, while Balfour feared that concessions to France would encourage the Italians to make similar demands. The latter, jealous of their rights, insisted that 'whatever was conceded to France ought to be conceded to Italy'. The British finally agreed that both the French and the Italians should dispatch token forces of three hundred men each; the French enjoyed the additional privilege of having Georges Picot assigned, jointly with Sykes, to assist General Murray in dealing with the native population of the occupied territories.[15] The French and Italians were finally warded off and, save for symbolic French and Italian detachments, the Egyptian Expeditionary Force remained British in character. Lloyd George thus gained an advantage which he used skilfully during the peace conference.[16]

Early in 1917, British suzerainty in Palestine was still a long-term objective; the immediate one was to educate public opinion, both at home and abroad, to the idea that Turkish rule over subject nationalities could no longer be tolerated. On 16 January 1917 President Wilson received a despatch from Balfour advising him of the complete reversal of traditional British policy towards Turkey, that circumstances had completely changed, and that the creation of a reformed Turkey was impossible. The Young Turks, under German influence, were 'at least as barbarous and far more aggressive than was Abdul Hamid'. They were 'guilty of massacres in Armenia and Syria more horrible than any recorded in the history even of those unhappy countries ... The interests of peace and the claims of nationality alike require that Turkish rule over alien races shall if possible, be brought to an end.'[17]

Such an argument did not travel well. America was not at war with Turkey and public opinion there was predominantly Turcophile. Moreover, Germany exercised a strong enough influence over the American press to counter British accusations. Aware of these shortcomings, on 1 February 1917 Lloyd George instructed Captain John Buchan, the newly-appointed Director of the Propaganda Bureau:

> When you take in hand the question of Allied and Neutral propaganda, I am anxious you should pay special attention to the futility and iniquity of the Turk ... How the Turk, by his rule, made all the arts of industry and husbandry impossible, and how once rich lands have become a wilderness ... Emphasize his incapacity for good Government, his misrule, and above all, his massacres of all the industrious populations; his brutality ... in Armenia and Syria.
>
> Attention should be drawn to the fact that the Turkish Empire is by no means populated by Turks ... I am anxious gradually to concentrate the minds of the Allied and Neutral Nations on the Turkish problem, and the importance of solving it once and for all in the interests of civilisation.

Buchan was advised to drive this *leitmotiv* home and see to it that articles in the British press were 'spread over a considerable period of time, so as not to make it too obvious what we are driving at'. Until world public opinion grew accustomed to the idea of the dismemberment of the Ottoman Empire, the Turk had to be discredited and the rights of the small nationalities asserted. The impediment to social and economic progress, the ill-treatment of Jews, Armenians, Syrians, and the Balkan races, and the failure to reform the Turkish state—these were among the principal points to be emphasised. The motto, Buchan briefed his Department, was that 'the Turk must go. If Turkey ... disappears, the German *drang nach Osten* fails and with it the major purpose with which Germany entered the War.'[18]

In line with this offensive Sir Mark Sykes recalled how the Armenians had been massacred, Moslem Arabs of Syria 'robbed of their noblest families', and the Jewish colonists 'impoverished, conscripted and subject to vile indignities'. This was the essence of his article published anonymously in *The Times* of 20 February 1917 under the heading 'The clean-fighting Turk'. Ten thousand copies of the article, in the form of a leaflet, were distributed in the United States, the Dominions, and in the neutral countries of Europe and Asia.[19] Intuitively, Jabotinsky caught up the theme: 'The destruction of . . . Ottoman Empire will be a blessing for both Turks and non-Turks.' It would be a shattering blow to Germany's ambitions and would undermine one of the driving motives which made the war, for her, worth while. 'Turkey is . . . the *ultima spes* of the German business man . . . the notorious scheme of . . . *Mitteleuropa*, which represents to German minds the only alternative to oversea expansion. . . . If you strike at it, the whole system collapses,' in which case Palestine, as far north as the Lebanon should 'fall . . . only within the British sphere of influence.'[20]

On 16 March, when Scott met Lloyd George, he gathered that the destruction of the Turkish Empire had become 'one of the great objects of the war'.[21] Four days later, addressing the first meeting of the Imperial War Cabinet, Lloyd George poured scorn on Turkey. Her Asiatic provinces, once the most fertile and richest in the world, were now a blighted desert. This applied particularly to Armenia, Syria, and Palestine. 'The Turk must never be allowed to misgovern these lands in future.' Although Turkey was a constant source of friction, the war was largely the result of Germany's ambitions in the East. The destruction of the Turkish Empire would frustrate Berlin's plans and liberate the Middle Eastern nations. Balfour endorsed the Prime Minister's thesis: the Turk was incorrigible, but the war was waged primarily against the world domination of Germany; her aim was to expand to the Persian Gulf, and ultimately to India and the Far East.[22]

At the meeting held on 30 March 1917, the War Cabinet pressed for further intensification of the educational drive with regard to countries such as Mesopotamia and Palestine, 'where victories have been, or were likely to be achieved'. General Murray was instructed to launch a full-scale offensive with the object of seizing Gaza by a *coup de main*. At the following meeting, on 2 April, great stress was laid on the moral and political advantages to be expected from an advance in Palestine, and particularly from the occupation of Jerusalem which, it was pointed out, would be hailed with great satisfaction throughout the country. To counteract the depressing effects of the strains and economic difficulties at home, military successes were of the utmost importance; and 'nowhere did success appear easier to realise than against Turkey'.[23]

This optimistic view was taken in the light of Robertson's memorandum of 22 February 1917, in which he claimed that the morale of the Turkish troops, 600,000 strong, was low, and that invasion of Syria might lead to a widespread insurrection of the native Arabic-speaking population, of the Anazeh and Beni Sakhr tribesmen east of the Jordan, and of the Druzes in the Deraa district and the Lebanon.[24] A rising of these disaffected elements would render the Hedjaz railway unworkable and deal a severe blow to the Turks. Their evacuation of Syria would have a great moral effect throughout their Empire, and consequently even if sea transport was limited, 'it would be possible to establish ourselves on the line Acre-Lake Tiberias-Deraa within three months. We should thus effectively occupy the whole of Palestine.' However, the Turk proved more resilient than expected and a rising in Syria and Mesopotamia never materialised. The British assault on Gaza on 26 March had ended in failure. Of this the War Cabinet, during its meeting on 2 April, was unaware. But even when the news reached London, compounded by the subsequent setback in Gaza on 17–19 April,[25] the objective which the British set for themselves remained essentially unaltered. General Murray was instructed to take every favourable opportunity to drive the Turkish forces out of Palestine.[26] A few days later, General Smuts expressed very decided views at a War Cabinet meeting (which reflected also those of the Prime Minister) as to the strategic importance of Palestine to the future of the British Empire. Despite the defeats on the Gaza front, he wished to pursue the campaign there 'with great determination'.[27]

This was by no means a matter of prestige or insistence on a victory which the public needed so badly. It concerned the vital interests of imperial security. A memorandum by Leopold Amery, dated 11 April 1917, gives a useful insight into the thinking now asserting itself in Whitehall. Weighing what was the 'irreducible *minimum*' for Britain on possible terms of peace with Germany he wrote:

> We cannot afford to let [Germany] succeed to the point of dominating Europe and becoming the starting point of a second attempt to strike at the British Empire from a larger base. Still less can we afford to let it succeed to the point of dominating the Middle East—and threatening our whole position in Egypt, India and the Eastern Seas.

Moreover, evidence suggested that Germany was aiming to fortify her position in East Africa, in which case:

installed at the gates of Egypt, on one side, and in East Africa on the other, the Prussian instinct would never rest till the two linked up together, and the great Railway Empire became continuous from Hamburg to Lake Nyasa. German control of Palestine, combined with German reacquisition of East Africa is, indeed, the greatest of all dangers which can confront the British Empire in the future.

Only when the British were entrenched in Palestine and Mesopotamia, the French in Syria, and the Russians in occupation of Greater Armenia, Constantinople and the Straits, would 'an effective buffer against the Central Powers . . . be provided.' So long as the Germans remained on French and Belgian soil, and Turkey-in-Asia remained intact, Britain could not entertain the idea of a peace conference.[28] In Amery's eyes, the Eastern theatre of war had acquired a status of parity with that in Western Europe.

Amery's memorandum was distributed among the Cabinet with the Prime Minister's permission, if not encouragement. It coincided with Amery's appointment as one of the principal secretaries to the Sub-Committee on Territorial Desiderata on the Terms of Peace, presided over by Curzon. Other members were Lord Robert Cecil, acting Foreign Secretary, Austen Chamberlain, Secretary of State for India, W. Long, Colonial Secretary, General Smuts, representing South Africa, J. D. Hazen, representing Canada, W. F. Massey, Prime Minister of New Zealand, Sir E. P. Morris, Prime Minister of Newfoundland, and Sir S. P. Sinha, representing the Executive Council of Bengal. This Committee replaced that headed by Louis Mallet, which had failed to outline a coherent policy. Curzon's lead, by contrast, was both determined and ambitious. At the first meeting on 17 April, and again on the 19th, he pointed out that the establishment of German naval and submarine bases in East Africa would constitute a 'very serious menace' to British sea routes round the Cape and through the Suez Canal. In this context he drew special attention to Palestine, which had been left 'undetermined in the agreement'. In his opinion, the only safe solution was for it to be included in a British Protectorate. He understood that the Zionists in particular 'would be very much opposed to Palestine being under any other flag or under a condominium'. Curzon was supported by Smuts, who considered this question from both the military and the political point of view, 'the most important' of all questions under discussion.

We ought to secure the command of Palestine . . . Any other Power [there] would be a very serious menace to our communications. Our control of Palestine and Mesopotamia, which would, no doubt, eventually be connected by railway with each other, would cover the whole approach to the East protecting both Egypt and the Persian Gulf.

Smuts thought that Palestine's frontier should be extended farther north to its natural boundary at the Leontes, and in particular bring in the Hauran region. Otherwise the French presence in Syria and the Russian in Armenia was welcome. It could provide an additional barrier to contain Germany's expansion to the East.

The ideas advanced by Curzon and Smuts won the unanimous approval of the Sub-Committee. Although pleased by this, Amery reminded the Sub-Committee that Curzon's interpretation was incompatible with the Asia Minor Agreement, and that the French parliamentary committee on foreign affairs had recently adopted a secret resolution stating that, with the exception of a small enclave, Palestine should belong to France. This hardly affected Curzon and his colleagues, as is evident from their report. Their desiderata were restated unequivocally, but to ensure that Palestine fell under Britain's 'definite and exclusive' control, they recommended modification of the May 1916 Agreement and an extension of the British sphere as far as the river Leontes and northern Hauran.[29]

This was all the more remarkable as, three days earlier, on 25 April, the War Cabinet had taken the view that although sooner or later the Sykes-Picot Agreement would have to be reconsidered, in view of French susceptibilities, 'no action should at present be taken in this matter'. Lloyd George recalled that at the recent inter-Allied Conference at Saint-Jean de Maurienne his hint that Palestine should come under British control had been 'very coldly received'.[30] This was not the only reason that impelled him to accept Curzon's report with some reservations, however close it came to his own convictions. The report pointed to an ideal at which the British should aim, but it was highly questionable whether it was practicable should the war end in stalemate. If Germany were left in possession of a great deal of Allied territory, Britain would have to barter away, at the peace conference, any territories that she might have conquered. 'Russia would come after having suffered more than seven million casualties, and France with nearly two million dead; could we under such conditions claim that they should get nothing and we should have practically everything?' He suggested that the question might arise 'even within a few weeks'. The telegrams from Russia showed that the party of non-annexation seemed to be getting the upper hand, and 'it would be very difficult if our only response was a demand for all territories mentioned in the Report'. Curzon thereupon agreed that the idea of non-annexation raised very great difficulties.[31]

In Russia, since the March Revolution, non-annexationism had become the slogan of the day, while in the United States it found its most eloquent exponent in President Wilson. It constituted the most serious threat to British war aims. Henceforth, one of the gravest dilemmas of British diplomacy was how to achieve their desiderata without giving offence to the Allies. This could be done only by a marriage with the principle of self-determination. It was here that the importance of Zionism, as far as Palestine was concerned, came in. It provided a cloak under which Britain could appear free from any annexationist taint. The anti-Turkish crusade was essentially negative in nature, and as such could hardly commend itself to American and Russian opinion; but, when clothed in the ideological garb of struggle for the liberation of small nationalities, it acquired a different aspect. The device was not a British monopoly. Germany, too, disguised her imperial ambitions as protection of small nationalities, though in other parts of the world.[32] This was why publications about German-Jewish relations regarding Palestine were studied in London with particular interest. Arnold Toynbee, in charge of Turkish affairs at the Intelligence Bureau of the Department of Information, took note of David Trietsch, a German Zionist publicist, who argued that 'in a certain sense the Jews are a Near Eastern element in Germany and a German element in Turkey', and that 'there are possibilities in a German protectorate over the Jews as well as over Islam'. But Toynbee felt certain that

> Other Powers than Germany may take these possibilities to heart . . . There are Zionists who would like to see Palestine a British Protectorate, with the prospect of growing into a British Dominion. Certainly, if Jewish Colonies are to make progress it can be secured only by better public administration than under Ottoman Government.[33]

The wishes of the Zionists in Britain were well known, as were those of the majority of Palestinian Jews, whose attitude, formerly pro-Turk, had been transformed by the contrast between their ill-treatment by Djemal Pasha and the correct behaviour of the British to the refugees in Alexandria. What they wanted, Ormsby-Gore noted, was 'either British Palestine or . . . under the United States, preferably the former'. For France they had little inclination. In the Levant the French had the reputation of forcing their own culture on subject peoples, and the Jews feared that under the French they would be unable to rebuild their nation and bring about a renaissance of Hebrew culture. Ormsby-Gore concluded:

The important point is that the Zionist leaders regard the success of our arms as the only hope for Zionism and at the same time do not want to have the responsibility of political control of Palestine . . . All that Zionism seeks now is to give the Jewish people freedom to settle, acquire land and build up industries and schools.

But if the British and Palestinian Jews could be relied upon, the position of Jewry elsewhere on the question of British trusteeship was less certain. From the beginning of the war, their attitude to the Allies had been determined on the one hand by the treatment meted out to their co-religionists in Russia, and on the other by the exemplary behaviour of the Germans in the occupied territories of Eastern Europe and the protection they afforded to the Palestinian Jews. Deliberate leaks (not necessarily accurate) that, following the success of German arms, Palestine would be given as a gift to the Jews, also made their mark. The fall of Tsardom in Russia and America's entry into the war in April 1917, had some effect on their attitude to the Allied cause in general, but did not necessarily make them more enthusiastic about the idea of British suzerainty in Palestine. Nor did the world Zionist movement give any indication of which power it preferred as trustee. There was however no longer any doubt as to its weight and influence in the Jewish world. In the United States the Zionists had gained considerable strength. In Justice Brandeis, Ormsby-Gore noted, 'they acquired a leader of note, ability and character', and since their reconciliation with the American Jewish Committee in March 1916, they effectively controlled the policy of organised Jewry. Even more spectacular was the advance of the movement in Russia. Jewish nationalism made itself felt in South Africa, Rumania, Galicia, and to a lesser degree in Italy and Holland.[34] The main problem was how to draw it closer to the Allied camp, Britain in particular, in order to neutralise the anti-annexationist trend in Russia and America and pre-empt Germany's initiative. On this point Ormsby-Gore gave an answer as early as February 1917.[35] Toynbee took a similar view. Fifty years later he recalled:[36]

Zionism was the key. The Western powers must make themselves agents for the fulfilment of the Zionists' aspirations. Here was something that might swing Jewish sympathies over to the Allies' side—at any rate in the United States, and perhaps also in Central Europe.
When H.M.G. noticed this trump card in their hand, they were of course, eager to play it . . .

11   A Missed Opportunity

Among those who benefited most from the Revolution in Russia in February–March 1917, were the 5,000,000 Russian Jews. The abolition of the disabilities to which they had been hitherto subjected was greeted by their co-religionists all over the world with rejoicing; it released tremendous sources of vitality within the Jewish community, which became manifest in all fields of cultural and political activity. Though they comprised only four per cent of the total population, their influence far exceeded their numerical strength. They were active in the Socialist parties, but carried greater weight within the Constitutional Democratic Party, the Cadets. The fact that a number of individuals played a prominent rôle among the extreme Left misled some foreign correspondents, notably that of the London *Times*, into believing that the Jews as a whole were a disruptive and anti-war element. Contemporary investigations disproved it; those conducted on behalf of the Conjoint Foreign Committee show that the bulk of Russian Jewry stood on the moderate side, and even the Socialists among them were predominantly associated with the Menshevik wing. The *Bund* repeatedly affirmed its loyalty to the Provisional Government and rejected the idea of a separate peace with the Central Powers. The middle classes identified themselves fully with the Constitutional Democratic Party, while the Union of Jewish Soldiers pledged themselves to fulfil their patriotic duty. Jews *qua* Jews felt instinctively that their real interests lay in a stable government and the maintenance of liberty. The Provisional Government had brought their enfranchisement, Prime Minister Lwow had distinguished himself during the Tsarist régime by a courageous protest against anti-Semitic circulars of the General Staff, and Alexander Kerensky, his successor, was one of the prime movers behind the Edict of Emancipation. Russian Jews had therefore no reason to feel ungrateful; with the exception of a minority of extremists, who cut their links with their own people, Russian Jews in fact constituted one of the main props of the Provisional Government.[1] This did not necessarily mean that they were *ipso facto* prepared to subscribe blindly to Entente war aims. In this respect they were, as Charles Webster rightly said, 'very lukewarm'.[2]

The most influential party in post-revolutionary Russia was the Zionist. Its rise was spectacular. The number of enrolled members, which before the war amounted to 25,000, rose steeply in the spring of 1917 to 140,000.[3] By the turn of 1918 there were 1,200 registered local Zionist societies all over the country with 300,000 active members.[4] This figure did not include the former Russian territories of Poland, Lithuania, and Bessarabia, then under German and Austrian occupation, where Zionist influence was considerable. The elections to an All-Jewish Congress held in Southern Russia showed that out of the total of 187,485 votes, the Zionists (including the Labour Zionists) secured 59 per cent, the Socialist parties 28 per cent, and the conservative Religious Party (Achduth) 13 per cent. Since the Achduth majority entertained strong pro-Zionist leanings,[5] it is clear that the Zionist movement enjoyed overwhelming support within the Russian Jewish community. These statistics say nothing of those outside the movement, who by tradition and by sentiment were attached to Palestine. British Military Intelligence estimated that 'the great mass of the 6,000,000 Jews in Russia have been more or less in sympathy with the Zionist cause'.[6] Yechiel Tschlenow was not exaggerating when in his inaugural address to the Zionist Conference in Petrograd on 6 June 1917, he said that Zionism had become a mass movement and as such, in a free country, a formidable political factor.[7]

Spontaneous public gatherings and demonstrations illustrated this; the one held in Odessa in spring 1917 was the most impressive. A hundred and fifty thousand men marched in the streets on the heels of several battalions of Jewish soldiers displaying blue and white banners and posters with slogans like: 'Liberty in Russia', 'Liberty in Palestine', while the local military Governor took the salute. In Kiev, where a procession on a similar scale took place, the Town Hall was bedecked with Zionist flags and the municipal orchestra greeted the crowd with the Jewish national anthem. The spectacle was repeated in other cities. In Turkestan and Bokhara the Ashkenazi and Sephardi communities joined hands in pledging their support for a Jewish Palestine. 'In the whole of Turkestan', a delegate from Samarkand told the conference of 6 June, 'there are no Jews who are not Zionists,' and the delegation of Jewish soldiers declared that *practically all Jewish soldiers in the front are Zionists*'; as soon as the war was over they would be ready to go to Palestine.[8]

These facts were mentioned in an appendix to Colonel Hankey's memorandum to the War Cabinet in October 1917, when the Balfour Declaration was hanging fire, but during the spring of that year the strength of the Zionist movement in Russia and its usefulness to Britain were not recognised in official circles in London. Reports suggested that

Russian Jews as a whole were pacifists and anti-British in sentiment. Lockhart was particularly disquieted by the conspicuous rôle the Jews were playing in the leadership of the Social Revolutionary party and in its press, which was 'almost entirely in Jewish hands'. Major-General Alfred Knox, Military Attaché at the British Embassy in Petrograd, referred to the Jews as an 'extreme element' with whom even the Council of Workers' and Soldiers' Deputies was powerless to contend. The Social Revolutionary and the Bolshevik parties had become the source of increasingly anti-Entente propaganda and the General was worried by the demoralising effect it was having on the Russian army and by the disastrous decline in production, which fell to 30 to 60 per cent of normal output.[9]

The British Labour Delegation which visited Russia in April-May 1917 also gained the impression that the influence of the Jewish Socialists, which they said was 'very strong', had nearly always been anti-British. It was they who at delegate meetings invariably brought up questions relating to English rule in Ireland, Egypt, or India, equating it with German imperialism. They urged 'immediate peace at almost any price'. This report, taken together with that of the Vice-Consul in Nikolaev alleging that the Jews were working against England and were strongly in favour of Germany, made bitter reading. England was labelled Russia's 'worst enemy' and the dominating theme of the speeches and reports in the local press was peace.[10]

This Anglophobia was not surprising. It merely reflected the prevailing mood in the country. From the beginning of hostilities the Russian people were convinced that they had been bearing more than their fair share of the burdens of war. Russian losses were counted in millions, those of England only in thousands, and Germanophile circles (amongst whom were members of the Russian Court) were diverting public discontent against the Western Allies, especially England. The March Revolution contributed little to the improvement of relations. The press accused England of waging a capitalist and imperialist war, and Buchanan's complaint on this score was matched by Kerensky's about the absence of cordiality towards the new régime. Expressions of sympathy for the fate of the Tsarist family, comments in some British papers on Russia's internal affairs, and the deeply ingrained suspicion that the continuation of the war was largely London's doing, did not endear Britain to the Russian public.[11]

But the Jews had particular reason for grievance. Were not the hands of the British Government contaminated by an unholy alliance with the Tsar? Did not some British papers, notably The Times, the Morning Post, the Pall Mall Gazette and the Daily Mail project an anti-Semitic image?[12]

Particularly notorious was the Petrograd correspondent of *The Times* whose report on student unrest at the University of Dorpat outraged both Jews and non-Jews. The University authorities saw in it 'nothing but insinuation', whilst the much respected Petrograd paper *Birzheviye Vedomosti* 'showed that the *Times*' version was completely untrue'.[13] The ill-effects of the incident had hardly died down when an English news agency reported that a secret conclave of Russian Jews living in Copenhagen were conspiring to launch pacifist and pro-German propaganda in Russia. The *Birzheviye Vedomosti* (10 May), protested against such an imputation as 'inadmissible and likely to sow discord and rancour between Jews and Russians. . . . We are all equal and free citizens of a democratic Russian State.' On which the British Intelligence Bureau noted: 'It is unfortunate that the English Agency should be mixed up with it. It will do us great harm if we are thought by the Russians to be making any distinction between Jews and Russians . . . It is the very thing which has made the Petrograd Correspondent of *The Times* so unpopular.'[14] Even less fortunate was the wording of Cecil's reply to a Parliamentary question on the Government's attitude to the position of Jews in Rumania. Cecil said that, as the matter was under review by the King and Government of Rumania, it was inappropriate for him to make any statement. This colourless formula caused a misunderstanding and the *Odessa Novosti* (a paper of wide circulation in Southern Russia) accused London of applying a double standard, contrasting its indifference with the sympathy shown by the Russian Foreign Minister, Tereshchenko. Enraged, the British Consul-General in Odessa reported: 'Newspapers, entirely in Jewish hands, make . . . violent anti-English . . . attacks [on] our so-called Imperialistic policy.'[15]

Ormsby-Gore, who in Sykes's absence was evaluating Eastern Intelligence reports for the War Cabinet, was much concerned. However, he always clung to the belief that in Zionism the British Government had the best card to play.[16] It was at this point that Jabotinsky submitted a memorandum pointing out that pacifism was not confined to the Jews, and suggested that a British commitment on the Palestine question and the Jewish Regiment might make a difference.

> Give me and my friends the powerful pro-war argument . . . a
> Jewish force fighting for Zionist ideals on the Entente's side [and]
> we undertake to develop . . . a strong propaganda . . . for winning
> the united Jewish influence . . . in favour of a war to the end.

However tendentious Jabotinsky's arguments, when well presented and supported by first-hand information, they could not fail to impress, as

Harold Nicolson's comment shows. The Intelligence Department was also impressed and suggested that Jabotinsky should go to Russia on a propaganda mission, but he preferred to stay in England. Zionism, he insisted, had become identified with the idea of a British Palestine, and, should the Legion be established in Britain, it would snowball by recruitment from abroad. The fact that thousands of young Jews in Russia would declare themselves in favour of war, that a pro-British propaganda campaign would be launched at mass meetings and in influential Russian papers, would set in motion the very movement that Whitehall desired. 'There is in Russia plenty of inflammable material for a great pro-war movement, and . . . setting it ablaze is only a question of a strong concentrated will and of a good battle-cry. The battle-cry, so far as Jews are concerned, is Palestine.'[17]

Independently of Jabotinsky the Intelligence Department made some discreet enquiries through Leopold Greenberg, editor of the *Jewish Chronicle*. Greenberg's connections with the Foreign Office were of long standing. In 1903–4 he had assisted Theodor Herzl in his negotiations with the British Government on a scheme for Jewish colonisation in the El-Arish area and in East Africa.[18] Soon after the outbreak of war, when the Palestine settlement was cut off, he intervened with Neil Primrose, Parliamentary Under-Secretary of State for Foreign Affairs, to permit shipment of essential supplies from Egypt.[19] The plight of the Jewish fugitives in the Russian war zone in 1915–16 concerned him also. It was 'a terrible story', he wrote to Lucien Wolf on 29 November 1915. 'If the nations have not been moved by what has been published up till now, I am sure that nothing else will move them.'[20] The March Revolution was naturally given an enthusiastic welcome by the *Jewish Chronicle*, but the upsurge of national sentiment among Russian Jewry took even a well-informed journalist like Greenberg by surprise; his conversation with Jabotinsky confirmed his own findings that Palestine was the best propaganda card. 'There can be no doubt', he wrote to the Intelligence Department, 'that if the *Entente* were prepared to make some sort of advance upon Jewish Nationalistic lines . . . in regard to Palestine, it would have an enormous effect in bringing Jews—not only in the *Entente* but also in neutral and even in enemy countries—largely into sympathy with the Allies.' This applied particularly to the Jews in Russia. Though an avowed anti-militarist, Greenberg supported the idea of the Jewish legion.[21]

Cecil suggested that Buchanan should be consulted. This coincided with advice from a Mr G. Hamilton, who thought that a high-powered Zionist mission, composed of personalities like Israel Zangwill, Israel Cohen, Dr Weizmann and Vladimir Jabotinsky, sponsored by the British

Government, should go to Russia to persuade the Jews there that only with Germany's defeat could their ambitions in Palestine be realised. On the same day, a cable drafted by Harold Nicolson, revised by Graham and approved by Cecil and Hardinge, was sent to Buchanan.

> We are advised that one of the best methods of counteracting Jewish pacifist and socialist propaganda in Russia would be to offer a definite encouragement to Jewish nationalist aspirations in Palestine.
>   The question of Zionism is full of difficulties, but I should be glad, in the first place to learn your views as to whether a declaration by the Entente of sympathy for Jewish Nationalist aspirations would help or not in so far as concerns internal and external situation of Russia.

The most notable omission from Nicolson's original draft was the following passage:

> I am aware that to identify ourselves with Zionist programme would be to open up extensive difficulties both as regards Jewish opinion itself and as regards French opinion since full realisation of Zionist aspirations would certainly entail British Protectorate over Palestine.

Buchanan poured cold water on the suggestion. In his opinion there was no great enthusiasm for Zionism among Jews in Russia, and he doubted whether an expression of sympathy for Jewish national aspirations would be of any help; he was told by a leading but unnamed Jew that pacifism was confined solely to the extreme Left. 'Jewish question here is always a delicate one and one has to be so careful as to what one says at present moment that the less said about Jews the better.'[22]

In Cairo Sir Mark Sykes dissented strongly from Buchanan's view. He told Sir Ronald Graham:

> I am of the opinion that it would be quite impossible for British Embassy in Petrograd to ascertain either what were the feelings of Russian Jews or what would be the effect on Pacifists acting under Jewish influence. Any enquiries emanating from the Embassy on such a question would only provoke fear and suspicion and answers quite contrary to facts. Zionist enquiries could only be safely made through . . . M. Sokolow, Dr. Weizmann, V. Jabotinsky . . . The only channel possible would be from a Jew to a Jew and even then the question must be put with the greatest delicacy and care.

1900 years of oppression had made them secretive and distrustful of Christians. Zionists did not necessarily desire 'the proclamation of *a* policy' but only private assurances of sympathy; in return the Government should expect not 'direct action and open propaganda on the side of the Entente in Russia or elsewhere but powerful and impalpable benevolence deflecting hostile forces . . . and transmuting various Pacifist tendencies . . . into friendly political elements.' He warned the Foreign Office to beware of the activities of Lucien Wolf and those of like mind. 'He is an anti-Zionist who desires to focus Jewish power at some point outside Palestine though he has on more than one occasion masqueraded as a Zionist; he has done this in order to stave off Zionist aims.'[23]

Oliphant was taken aback by these remarks but Sykes, aware of Wolf's membership of the Jewish Territorial Organisation,[24] suspected an attempt to divert Foreign Office attention to some territory other than Palestine. More astonishing in Sykes's cable is the assertion that the Zionists did not desire a public declaration, since this was exactly what Weizmann and Sokolow did expect as soon as Jerusalem fell into British hands. The most likely explanation for Sykes's change of mind is that, having learned of the policy of evacuation initiated by the Ottoman authorities against the civilian population in Palestine, he feared that open encouragement of Zionist aspirations by the British might jeopardise the Jews behind the Turkish lines; an argument which held equally good with regard to the Arabs. If the Egyptian Expeditionary Force was bogged down, he told Sir Ronald Graham on 24 April:

> it will be necessary to drop all Zionist projects, all schemes involving negotiations with . . . Arab elements in Syria, whether Christian or Moslem. Any other policy will expose our adherents to greater rigour of oppression than heretofore, and will make us morally responsible for increase of their misery. Zionists in London and United States of America should be warned of this through M. Sokolow; and Jabotinsky scheme should not be proceeded with. The Press should be warned that Zionist newspaper articles can only endanger lives and property of Palestine Jews.

And on 8 May he again argued that if the military advance was halted Weizmann should be told to drop propaganda as this could only add to the suffering of his people.[25]

Discouraged by Buchanan and faced with uncertainties in Palestine, the Foreign Office had to shelve Cecil's idea of a pro-Zionist tripartite Entente declaration. The response to the Balfour Declaration among Russian Jews at the turn of the year made Cecil and his colleagues regret that it had not been published earlier, but in the spring of 1917 the question was still strewn with difficulties and, with inadequate information about the strength of Jewish national movement in Russia, the Foreign Office hesitated to overrule the Ambassador in Petrograd.[26]

Sykes's warning against any overt anti-Turkish manifestation by the Zionists applied with greater strength to Jabotinsky's scheme. The formation of a Jewish unit destined for the Palestinian front, let alone its participation in the fighting, would have given Djemal Pasha an excuse to carry out his designs against the Yishuv. This tallies with what Aaronsohn was told by Clayton and Murray. The former advised Aaronsohn that in view of the uncertainty of a British offensive, a unit such as he desired was bound to put his compatriots in Palestine at a grave risk. Two months later General Murray, though sympathetic, dismissed the idea of a Jewish division as impractical. At least a year would be required to train it,[27] and in the meantime, he implied, the Turks would have an excuse for their conduct.

This line of reasoning had little effect on Jabotinsky. Attacked on this score by his fellow-Zionists he had a ready answer: the fear of provoking massacres in Palestine was groundless because Djemal Pasha did not require any provocation. In December 1914 ten thousand Jews were expelled from Jaffa without reason, whilst the formation of the Zion Mule Corps by those same refugees in Alexandria had confounded the darkest prophecies at that time. A fighting unit commanded the respect of an enemy, and no one could guarantee that Djemal Pasha would refrain from molesting the Palestinian Jews in the absence of a Jewish Legion. In his characteristic style he wrote to the Foreign Office: would the English agree to modify their policy because of the threat against some of their countrymen? They would not, and neither would the Jews. Jabotinsky was obviously unaware that it was mainly due to the intervention of the German and American Embassies in Constantinople that Djemal Pasha's attempts to destroy the Zionist enterprise in Palestine had been foiled. Whatever the rights and wrongs of his arguments, they found a ready ear in Philip Kerr, the Prime Minister's Private Secretary. Should the formation of the unit be coupled with assurances of support for Jewish immigration and colonisation in Palestine, he told Graham, 'it might produce a very beneficial effect in making the Jews in America and Russia much keener on helping to see the war through. I think the British Government can affirm their sympathy for Zionist ideals without committing themselves to the full Zionist programme.'[28]

Fortified by Weizmann's assurances that atrocities in Palestine removed 'all Jewish opposition to the Jabotinsky scheme'[29] and supported by

Amery and Ormsby-Gore, Kerr recommended it wholeheartedly to the Foreign Office. Graham was a convert and did not need much prodding. The Army Council too offered no opposition.[30] However, before the scheme could be put into operation, agreement had to be reached on the conscription of Russian subjects in Britain.[31] A further delay followed, due to a new controversy with anti-Zionist British Jews which weakened the national character of the unit. On both counts its propaganda value was obviously weakened.[32] This was particularly regrettable in view of the deteriorating position in Russia.

Since April there had been growing indications that Russia was drifting out of the war. The new régime rested on a tenuous constitutional basis, weakened still further by a peculiar dualism in administration: the Provisional Government on the one hand, and the Council of Workers' and Soldiers' Deputies on the other. It was the latter which demanded the early conclusion of peace. To the appallingly high casualty rate and the general war-weariness[33] were added industrial anarchy and a steep rise in food prices, all creating a favourable milieu for pacifist propaganda. For the ordinary Russian the war was losing its *raison d'être*.

For the Western Allies this development was serious. Russia alone had enough manpower to wear down the armies of the Central Powers. It was the Russian invasion of Prussia early in the war that was decisive for the fate of the battle of the Marne, and saved the Allies in the autumn of that year.[34] In 1917, when the war was not going too well for the Allies, Russia's massive support was needed still more. It was recognised that a Russian collapse would set free about eighty German and forty Austrian divisions for transfer to the Western theatre of war; the fronts in the Balkans would crumble, and the Turks, freed from the Russian menace in the Caucasus, would be able to divert their forces against Mesopotamia and Palestine. The economic consequences would be no less damaging, neutralising the blockade against Germany and making available to the Central Powers Russia's resources of food-stuff and minerals, essential for the prosecution of the war. The whole strategic situation would be transformed and the moral effect would be devastating. This was the picture presented by Lloyd George to the War Cabinet at a meeting on 9 May. He left no doubt that should Russia back out of the war the only chance left for the Allies was to make a separate peace with Austria. Failing that he saw no hope for the sort of victory the Entente desired, in which case, he admitted, 'it would be a mistaken policy to sacrifice hundreds of thousands of lives in attacks on the Western front'. He proposed concentrating on the Eastern campaign instead. But here his assessment clashed with that of the General Staff. When the latter had advised a forward military policy in Palestine and Mesopotamia, it was on the assumption that Russia would continue to exert pressure in the Caucasus. This no longer being the case, the General Staff had to reconsider its stand. So depressed was General Smuts by Russia's military paralysis and her possible defection that he turned down the offer to take over the command of the Egyptian Expeditionary Force. The whole situation seemed to him 'very uncertain' and he had grave doubts whether a thrust into Palestine and Syria would be successful.[35]

Eventually Lloyd George had his way and on 10 August the War Cabinet finally approved the instructions to General Allenby to launch an all-out offensive against the Turk in the coming autumn and winter, 'since the good success achieved against him will tend to strengthen the *moral* and staying power of this country during the season when important successes may not be feasible in Europe'.[36] The *raison d'être* of this campaign was expounded by Curzon:[37]

> It is clear that unless Palestine can be secured, the position of Great Britain in the Near East will become one of extreme danger. A Teutonised Turkey, left in possession of Asia Minor . . . Syria and Palestine . . . would involve a perpetual menace to Egypt, the disappearance of the Arab Kingdom of the Hedjaz, and the grave peril to the British position at Bagdad. If Russia went out of the war, the danger in Palestine would become one of immediate urgency, since but little time would be left to defeat the Turkish army, now in Palestine, before it was powerfully reinforced, and the last chance of coming to terms with Turkey on conditions favourable to ourselves, would have disappeared.

The problem which confronted the British Government was however not merely a military one. In 1915, to pin Russia down Grey could still dangle 'the richest prize of the entire war'—Constantinople, but in 1917 the Russians no longer cared about the fulfilment of their 'historic mission'; the 'Byzantine mirage' faded away in the prevailing mood of war-weariness and apathy. Prince Lwow declared on 10 April that Russia's aim was 'not dominion over other nations . . . not seizure by force of foreign territory, but confirmation of a lasting peace on the basis of desires of peoples'. The principle of self-determination was the only basis on which the Provisional Government was prepared to continue the war: 'defence at all costs' but not annexation of other peoples' territory.[38]

In these circumstances the invasion of Palestine might have given rise to a suspicion that the British were bent on acquisition of territory with-

out any regard to the harm it was bound to cause Russia by undue prolongation of the war. It could have provided additional ammunition to
the extremists, who accused Britain of territorial expansion, and kill what
was left of Russian loyalty to the common Allied cause. A new campaign
in Palestine could have boomeranged on wider British strategic interests
and made the Eastern offensive not worth while. To make the occupation
of Palestine more palatable it was therefore imperative for the Expeditionary Force to present the image of a liberating army, since, as Ormsby-
Gore reasoned, the principle of non-annexation did not 'necessarily
exclude liberation . . . of Armenia, Arabia and Palestine'.[39] The plight of
their inhabitants and particularly the Jaffa–Tel-Aviv evacuation provided
a heaven-sent opportunity for the British propaganda machine to discredit the Turks on the one hand, and counter the non-annexation cry,
most vociferously aired by the Jewish Socialists in Russia, on the other.
'I think we ought to use pogroms in Palestine as propaganda,' Ormsby-
Gore advised Sykes. 'Any spicy tales of atrocity would be eagerly welcomed by the propaganda people here—and Aaron Aaronsohn could send
some lurid stories for the Jewish papers.'[40]

There was no need for Sykes to encourage Aaronsohn on this score.
Independently, through Reuter, he had given the world the news about
the fate of his people in Tel-Aviv and the Judean colonies. Sykes found
Aaronsohn a ready party to the argument that the Jews should endeavour
to convince Kerensky and the Menshevik Party in Russia that the British
Army was intent on liberating the oppressed Armenians, Jews, and Arabs,
who otherwise would remain under Turkish domination.[41] Two months
later Aaronsohn inspired the *Poale Zion* refugees in Egypt to associate
themselves publicly with the Allied aim to liberate Palestine. The Poale
Zionists appealed to Jewish socialists in the United States and Russia to
defend the cause of the Jewish proletariat in Palestine 'oppressed . . . by
the Turkish régime', and oppose any resolution at the forthcoming
International Socialist Conference in Stockholm that might condemn the
capture of Palestine by the Allied forces. Widest publicity was given
thereafter to this item.[42]

Lord Robert Cecil too embraced the principle of liberation and assured
Petrograd that the British Government was not embarking upon 'a war of
conquest'; their objective was merely 'the liberation of peoples oppressed
by alien tyranny'.[43] The moment seemed to be well chosen, since it
coincided with Russia's diplomatic move for a joint Entente *démarche*
(through the Governments of neutral Spain and the Netherlands) to curb
the Turkish excesses against the Jewish population in Palestine.[44] Tereshchenko, the new Foreign Minister, who initiated this move, expressed

satisfaction with the British note, but Tseretelli, a prominent Menshevik leader and Minister, pressed Buchanan to persuade Britain to abjure all annexationist designs.[45] However shrewd Cecil's formula, the Socialists were not deceived. As the Intelligence Bureau of the Information Department had forewarned:[46]

> The Moderate Socialists refuse to accept the right of possession as the result of military conquest . . . They will not admit that the ill-treatment of peoples by the Germans and Turks gives us . . . the right to annex the territories concerned . . . They regard our explanations as excuses or cloaks for Imperialism. It would appear that we can only meet them on the principle . . . 'the self-determination of nationalities', until or unless that principle can be accepted by England, France and Italy, they will probably continue to denounce the Allied Governments as Imperialists.

There was no way out for the Western Allies but to come to terms with the principle of self-determination, not only because it could improve their own image in the eyes of the Russian people but in all probability it would also strengthen Kerensky who, unlike the extreme Socialists, favoured the prosecution of the war. Such a readjustment of their war aims was all the more necessary since Russia was not alone in voicing the new creed. On 22 May President Wilson addressed a message to the Provisional Government stating that the United States sought 'no material profit or aggrandisement of any kind' and that 'no people must be forced under a sovereignty under which it does not wish to live. No territory must change hands except for the purpose of securing those who inhabit it.'[47] Faced with a united Russo-American front, London sent a revised note to Kerensky from which reference to the liberation of the subject peoples of the Ottoman Empire was omitted, and approval of the principles laid down by President Wilson and Russia inserted.[48]

Self-determination thus became the hallowed principle by which the war was to be given a new lease of life. It was to animate the idealists and serve as a tonic to those infected by the war-weariness. It wrought a momentous change in political thinking. But the strategic requirements of the Western Allies remained unaltered. For Britain one of the most imperative was to secure control of Palestine. With the right of annexation out of date, military conquest alone could not justify its occupation. This was where the Zionists could be useful. They alone could effect the marriage between the wishes of the people concerned and British interests, and make Britain's presence in Palestine more acceptable to Russian and American public opinion. As Weizmann put it: annexation was inadmissible, 'democratic Russia and America will never allow it . . . [but] a Jewish Palestine under a British Protection could not be interpreted in terms of annexation. It would be easily understood that Great Britain is [intent on] keeping the country in trust for the Jews.' Weizmann was hammering this point to Brandeis and Tschlenow. The latter was told at the end of April that, following discussions with leading English Zionists and with friends like Ahad Ha'am, the Rothschilds, and Herbert Samuel, a unanimous decision had been reached in favour of a Jewish Palestine under British protection, and it was most important that the Russian Jews and their organisations should approach their Government to support this programme.

> England is not yearning to annex Palestine, and were it not for the combination with us, she would hardly oppose the international-isation of that country . . . On the contrary, one fears here that, in view of the present feelings in Russia and in America, it is difficult to work in favour of a British protectorate save on the condition that the Jews themselves wish it, in other words, Great Britain is ready to take Palestine under her protection in order to give the Jews the possibility of getting on their feet and living independently. It is, therefore, extremely important that Russian Jewry proclaim the importance of this question and brings it home to the Russian Government.[49]

Weizmann's labours could not bear immediate fruit. In the absence of an official British statement, his crusade for a British Palestine lacked the conviction it might otherwise have had. London however was in a pre-dicament, since it was in no position at that time to make its views public. The idea of a British Palestine had to remain a secret; however sympathetic to Zionist aspirations it might have been, no declaration could be issued before sounding out the co-signatories to the Asia Minor Agreement. How cautious the Foreign Office was on this point is evident from Graham's advice. When asking Weizmann to urge Russian Jews to elicit a statement in favour of Zionism from their Government, he specifically warned him that the possibility of a British protectorate of Palestine should not be raised.[50] But Weizmann disregarded this advice and, it seems, dispatched his letter to Tschlenow through private, not official channels.[51] Its text gave the impression that Britain would not accept responsibility for Palestine unless Jews themselves desired it, imply-ing an altruism too excessive to be credible. The phrase 'England was not yearning to annex Palestine' reflected perhaps the view held at the Foreign

Office (a notion strengthened in Weizmann after his meeting with Graham on 24 April), but not by Lloyd George and the War Cabinet. Of this difference Weizmann was completely unaware. In the Foreign Office view a pro-Zionist declaration could bear only a tripartite character. This was how Cecil calculated his move, fully in line with that adopted by O'Beirne, Crewe, and Grey in March 1916. Cecil's dilemma was embarrassing. 'Little time ago I suggested to Buchanan a declaration to satisfy Jewish national aspirations, and he discouraged the idea. I am not myself convinced', Cecil wrote to Ormsby-Gore, 'that he is right, but it is very difficult to go against his advice in such a matter at such a time, so I think it is doubtful whether the Government would or would not give such a letter as is described.'[52]

Regard for the Conjoint Foreign Committee was another factor which did not allow greater freedom of action. So sensitive was the Committee that on 27 April Graham had to reassure Wolf that the Government would not enter into any arrangement with the Zionists without prior consultation with 'all sections' of Jewish opinion in Britain, a promise reiterated by Cecil on 8 May. Notwithstanding these assurances, on 16 May Claude Montefiore called on Milner to suggest that it would be 'very unwise' for the Government to follow such 'unreliable guides' as Weizmann and Sokolow. Milner noted that Montefiore was 'tremendously anti-Zionist'; none the less Montefiore impressed him as 'an able, temperate and most honest man', and he finally agreed with his visitor that the Russian Jews were 'very revolutionary . . . anti-annexation and anti-British', on whom any message from the British Government, 'even about Palestine', was unlikely to have an effect.[53]

Persuasively as Montefiore may have argued, he, like his Committee, suffered from one serious disability: they had no alternative policy to offer. Wolf endeavoured to show that Russian Jews were, by and large, moderate and supported the war party, but when questioned more closely by Reginald Leeper of the Intelligence Bureau about possible ways and means of making Jews friendlier to England, he was unable to make any positive contribution. Leeper asked bluntly: 'Suppose the British Government were to authorise an official statement expressing their readiness to establish a Jewish State in Palestine, do you think this would make the Jews more friendly to England?' Wolf replied that in his opinion such a statement would not alter the situation substantially.

> The Zionists would, no doubt, be very enthusiastic, but their
> political influence *qua* Zionists was inconsiderable. They were a
> minority among the Russian Jews, the great bulk of [whom] . . .

were more concerned in establishing their National Autonomy in Russia itself than in founding a State in Palestine. Moreover, the Extreme Left among the Jewish politicians were irreconcilably opposed to the Zionists . . . Hence an official statement by the British Government might have an effect quite contrary to what was intended.

Moreover, he argued, 'the Jewish Socialists, who have far more political influence . . . than the Zionists, would regard it as an interference against themselves and would resent it accordingly'.[54]

Graham, forewarned by Sykes, was not deceived by Wolf's bias, the more so as there was nothing in the enclosed memorandum of Vinaver to support his contention that Zionist influence was ineffectual. 'Dr. Weizmann is always positive that the vast majority of Jews in Russia are Zionists,' was Graham's reaction. Weizmann's star was now in the ascendant and Graham respected and trusted him. Sokolow too, both in Paris and in Rome, was acquitting himself admirably, and the suggestion that he should attend the Zionist Conference in Petrograd commended itself to Cecil and Hardinge. Information that the provincial press in Russia was under Zionist influence tended further to undermine Wolf's contention.[55]

It was however not before the end of May, on the arrival of the dispatch (of 23 April) from Henry Brown, the Vice-Consul at Nikolaev, that a breakthrough was made. Interested primarily in trade, and disclaiming any religious prejudice, Brown, more than other British diplomats, was in a position to probe the undercurrents of Jewish opinion in Russia. He realised that it was the alliance with the odious Tsarist regime that had dissipated much of the earlier Jewish sympathy for England, to the point of engendering a positive dislike; a sentiment subsequently accentuated by a swing towards Germany. That this inclination persisted despite the fall of Tsardom could, in his opinion, be attributed largely to commercial considerations. The British capitalist and tradesman was feared, whereas the German was not. Brown concluded:[56]

The Jew is heart and soul for a separate peace, though with his customary caution, he works warily . . . It is not convenient for him to show his hand yet, nor is it desirable that his views should be known, as a large section of his community is interested in the Zionist movement. Russia is hardly able to preserve her own territories, France and Italy have their hands full with their own business, and the United States is too far off [from Palestine but] Great Britain is already there and fast smashing up the Turkish power, and therefore it is to Great Britain they must look for the realisation of their hopes. The stigma of concluding a separate peace must be on the Russian, not on the Jew, as he—the Jew—will then secure Palestine, and at the same time preserve for himself the rich Russian fields.

Much more complex motives lay behind the Jewish desire for peace. The Jews were the first casualty of the war and they had nothing to gain from its continuation. But Brown's assessment, however cynically it was put, that Palestine was the key to entice them into the British orbit proved correct. Nor was this thesis any longer disputed at the Foreign Office, especially when it was corroborated by other evidence; that submitted by M. Alchevsky was illuminating. Alchevsky was a Siberian-born Jew formerly in the employ of the Jewish Colonisation Association of the Baron de Hirsch Fund in the Argentine, and subsequently associated with Sir Murdoch Macdonald's Land Company in Egypt. Not a Zionist, he was anxious to see Jewish colonisation in Palestine developed under the British flag. He thought that pacifism and anti-British sentiment among Russian Jews were not incurable. A high-powered delegation, representing all shades of opinion of British Jewry and headed by a personality of the standing of Lord Reading or Lord Swaythling, might make a considerable appeal, but the most effective weapon in countering the 'no annexation' cry was Palestine. The British overestimated the influence of the extremists and overlooked that of the Jews, seven million strong, whose power was 'enormous owing to the fact that practically all could read and write, which the Russian workman and peasant cannot'.[57]

Encouraged by this information, Ormsby-Gore hoped that if the Russian Jews were won over, they might well buttress the efforts of the British Labour Delegation, then in Petrograd, to counter 'the German-inspired misrepresentations of Britain as a self-seeking Imperialistic Power'. Owing to their superior education and control of the provincial press, they were well qualified to create a favourable climate of opinion. 'The emancipated Jewish intelligentsia is an organised section of the Russian body politic which must be taken into account politically, and it might be worthwhile to get British and American Jewry into closer touch with it.' He wrote to Graham:

I really believe our Petrograd people underestimate the power of the Jews in Russia. It may be small in Petrograd but in Odessa and the south it is really something to reckon with. The Jewish provincial press is a great force and the Germans realise it and will capture the machine unless we do something to counteract their efforts.

Graham replied:

> There is no doubt that the way to get at the Jewish proletariat, which is after all the most important factor in the community in Russia at the present moment, is through Zionism, and as we are now committed to that policy we may as well get as much benefit out of it as we can. As you know, over two million Jews in Southern Russia have recently committed themselves to the Zionist policy.

Graham also briefed Gore about his conversation with Weizmann, and informed him that as Sokolow was unexpectedly delayed in Paris, Boris Goldberg, a reliable Russian Jew, was sent to Petrograd with a message to the Zionist Conference to show 'the sympathy and support which the movement received from His Majesty's Government in general and from Mr. Lloyd George, Mr. Balfour and Lord Robert Cecil in particular'. He added:[58]

> Dr. Weizmann is strongly of the opinion, and we all agree with him, that the best medium for working upon the Russian Jewish community is through Russian Jews and not by sending British or American Jews. To send such emissaries as Lord Reading and still more Lord Swaythling, at the present moment, would surely be worse than useless, and the effect of such a mission on the non-Jewish revolutionary elements must be considered.

The influence of Weizmann and his Russian-born colleagues domiciled in England seems to have outweighed that of British Jews, but Graham's statement calls for closer scrutiny. Briefed by Sykes before the latter's departure for the East, he was under the impression that London was 'committed' to the Zionist policy. This was erroneous, since on 18 July (the day when Lord Rothschild forwarded to Balfour a draft formula for a declaration), he himself told Wingate that Lloyd George and Balfour had given assurances of support 'in general terms' to the Zionist Organisation, and on 21 September, he told Clayton:[59]

> Our general attitude is one of sympathy without commitment to definite pledges. Mr. Lloyd George, Mr. Balfour and Lord Robert Cecil are in strong sympathy with Zionist ideas and aspirations, and a draft letter to Lord Rothschild has been under the consideration of the War Cabinet . . . But the whole question has been hung up, mainly owing to a memorandum by Mr. E. Montagu . . . I am afraid, therefore, that I cannot say more than 'general sympathy without commitments'.

Graham was also mistaken in assuming that Boris Goldberg had left for Russia; it was not until early in July[60] that he left London. Perhaps the fact that the British Government was not yet in a position to endorse a public message of sympathy with Zionist aspirations delayed Goldberg's departure. Whatever the reason, it is clear that the Zionist Conference in Petrograd had to rely solely on Weizmann's and Sokolow's assurances.

Weizmann made every effort to bring his Russian colleagues into line. It was of the utmost importance, he insisted in his cable of 4 June to Petrograd, for all leading Zionist Federations to co-ordinate their efforts. Those in England, South Africa, Canada and the United States supported unanimously the plan of an 'integral Jewish Palestine under British trust with all necessary guarantees [for] national development [into a Jewish] Commonwealth'. He invited the Conference to follow suit and lay the plan before the Russian Government. 'We are for internationalisation Holy Places and decidedly opposed international or plural control or condominium rest of Palestine. . . . [I am] authorised [to] state that in interview with Secretary of State for Foreign Affairs, I received assurances of encouragement and support our plans.'[61]

This telegram was despatched through Military Intelligence[62] and there is no evidence to show that the Foreign Office was aware of its contents. It is most unlikely that it would have approved a formula pointing so bluntly to a British trusteeship of Palestine, and Robert Cecil (to whom Weizmann referred as 'Secretary of State for Foreign Affairs') would have been surprised to learn that he had given Weizmann his unreserved 'assurances of encouragement and support'.[63]

Sokolow's message to the Petrograd Conference, cabled from Paris on the same day, was much more flexible. Elated by his success at the Quai d'Orsay, he asked Rosoff:[64]

Try to obtain from Russian Government such approval as received from other Entente Powers . . . I am united . . . with Weizmann . . . in all our work. We . . . consider British protection as the ideal solution. Practically this will be the case . . . particularly after *fait accompli*, but formally . . . Entente protection is still current in diplomatic quarters. In Italy I worked [for] British protection. In America too this will be the tendency [but] to accentuate it . . . here would be detrimental. We have to consider the Amour Propre and the [French] ambition. The work outside Great Britain and English speaking countries . . . must be in a more general form and purely Zionistic . . .

We must also win sympathy of other Powers because any

antagonist is dangerous. Moreover, we have to consider also possibility other combinations, whether we would like them or not. I
hope you will act accordingly . . . Underline in your resolution
our irrevocable national historic rights. Emphasize our gratitude
and devotion to Great Britain . . . but render also affectionate
homage to other great Powers . . . which recognised in their
declarations . . . the justice of our cause.

Despite his professed agreement with Weizmann on the ultimate
objective of British-oriented Zionism, there was in Sokolow's message a
conspicuous divergence regarding tactics. Faced with French sensitivity,
and with the fortunes of war still in the balance, he realised that a too
outspoken advocacy of British protection could be self-defeating.

At the receiving end, Tschlenow had even more cogent reasons for
treading warily. Unlike Sokolow, who had severed relations with the
Berlin Executive, Tschlenow took an active part in shaping its policies
and felt bound to abide by its decisions; that adopted in December 1914,
that there must be no negotiations with any power at war with Turkey,
was still valid. So was the principle of neutrality. Zionism was an international movement which aimed to solve an international problem and it
was not in its interest to subordinate itself to one particular power or bloc
of powers. The German Zionist leaders untiringly reiterated this tenet. So
did Tschlenow. However welcome the news about the progress made in
London and Paris, a one-sided association with the Entente was bound to
jeopardise the security of Palestinian Jews.

In his presidential address to the All-Zionist Conference on 6 June,
Tschlenow paid tribute to Britain's understanding of the Jewish question
but, to keep the balance, he pointed also to the debt owed to Turkey for
offering asylum to Jewish refugees from Spain in the sixteenth century.
The ill-treatment of Palestinian Jews was all the more painful since the
charges of disloyalty levelled against them were not true. The Zionist
movement was not linked to any particular power but aspired to international recognition and the creation of a home secured by public law.
This principle had been laid down in the Basle Programme and remained
valid.[65]

The conference proved a success. It was attended by 550 delegates,
thirty of whom, in uniform, represented Jewish soldiers from various
fronts, given leave by the military authorities. It won the recognition of
the Provisional Government, and messages of congratulation were
received from the Minister for Foreign Affairs, M. Tereshchenko, M.
Chkheidze, President of the Council of Workers' and Soldiers' Deputies,

the Mayor of Petrograd, as well as from five hundred cultural and political organisations from all over the country. The Conference did not pretend to speak on behalf of all sections of the Russian Jewish community. This was left to a special congress about to be convened, but it considered it to be within its rights to take a stand on the question of Palestine. Its resolutions may be summarised as follows:

(a) The link between the Jewish people and their historic homeland in Palestine had never been severed.

(b) The achievements of Jewish colonists testified to their ability to reclaim a barren land and create in Palestine a centre of civilisation; a focal point for Jewry at large.

(c) Jewish national aspirations were in complete harmony with the principle of self-determination; their right to Palestine, based on historical connection, was both incontestable and imprescriptible.

The Conference hoped that these claims would earn universal recognition, and that a representative of the Jewish people would be admitted to the future peace conference. Satisfaction was expressed that Zionist aspirations were meeting with growing understanding in various countries of Europe and America, and that England in particular, which traditionally sympathised with the Jewish people, showed a 'benevolent attitude'. The reference to England evoked enthusiastic applause.[66]

The Foreign Office was gratified. 'The reference to England,' Graham noted, 'was worked in by Dr. Weizmann, and it is certain that our best card in dealing with the Russo-Jewish proletariat is Zionism.'[67] By contrast, the English Zionists were dissatisfied. The Petrograd resolutions ignored their programme completely. 'This verbiage was not what was wanted.'[68] Weizmann had some harsh words to say to Tschlenow when he arrived in London in October 1917, but Tschlenow was on solid ground when arguing that it was impolitic to give the British *carte blanche* before having any written guarantee of support from them.[69] Following the publication of the Balfour Declaration, Weizmann at last had his way, but during the interim period he had to rest content with his Russian colleagues remaining friendly to England but uncommitted.

Charles Webster also regretted that 'the aspirations of the Russian Zionists were more international in character than those of the London Bureau',[70] but the Foreign Office was not perturbed. Despite Russia's implicit dissociation from the Asia Minor Agreement, the proviso of international administration of Palestine was still valid, and the resolutions of the Petrograd conference fitted well into this pattern; it was rather the formula of a British protectorate that could have been embarrassing. On this issue the Foreign Office remained conservative. Sir George Clerk rejected Ormsby-Gore's suggestion that Alchevsky would call on him: 'his views,' Clerk noted, 'advocating the placing of Palestine under British Protection, may be unimpeachable, but I fear that at this stage, they are impractical.' Alchevsky's subsequent memorandum elicited no response.[71] Even more indicative was the reaction to a section in Weizmann's speech of 20 May in which he expressed the hope that as a result of the war 'Palestine will be protected by such a mighty and just Power as Great Britain. Under the wing of this Power, Jews will be able . . . to carry out the Zionist scheme.' The text of this speech was forwarded to the Foreign Office on 23 May, but it was not until 20 August that Clerk read it, when he noted: 'I cannot believe that such a publication at the present moment will fail to rouse direct opposition in France and Italy, to say nothing of Russia and other states,' To which Balfour added: 'I fear the phrase "protected by G. Britain" is fatal—it goes far beyond the Rothschild message.'[72]

However, what was said could not be unsaid and Balfour held Weizmann in too high esteem to censure him for his indiscretion. Since Weizmann's return from Spain, where he had astutely headed off the mischievous Morgenthau mission, he was *persona gratissima* with Balfour and an asset to British policy. It was in Spain a month earlier that Weizmann had hit upon the idea of sending Felix Frankfurter and Lewin Epstein (who accompanied Morgenthau) to Russia. A week later he cabled from Paris: 'Baron Edmond de Rothschild . . . attaches the *greatest possible* value to [Sokolow's] *speediest* departure to Russia. Baron Edmond told me to-day that he has heard that Kerensky expects support from the Jews. I am, therefore, very anxious that American Jews should also go. Frankfurter, Lewin Epstein, Loewenthal . . . are eminently suitable.' The Foreign Office agreed that such a visit might be of 'real value' to the Allied cause but to their consternation, Washington, after the failure of the Root mission, was reluctant to sponsor any more missions to Russia.[73]

As it turned out, Sokolow was needed in London, and Boris Goldberg could not leave before the beginning of July. In the end Goldberg did not go to Russia but to Copenhagen where, on neutral soil, the rump Zionist Executive (*Das Aktions Komitee*) was due to meet on 29 July.[74] It was in this forum that the most crucial decisions were taking place. The principal *dramatis personae* were Professor Otto Warburg, Dr Arthur Hantke, representing the German, and Dr Tschlenow, the Russian Zionists. Goldberg's intention was to secure the latter's approval of the policy initiated in London, euphemistically termed 'the demands'.[75] Although there was nothing specific in these 'demands' pointing to any preference in respect of the future ruler of Palestine, the inference drawn was that it would be British. Goldberg took pains not to mention the Executive by name, thereby obliquely questioning its authority, but when Tschlenow made his consent conditional on the approval of that body, it became evident that to give official sanction to Sokolow's and Weizmann's activities, Warburg's and Hantke's approval was necessary.

When Hantke took the floor it became evident that Goldberg's mission was not going to have a smooth passage. Though unable to point to any diplomatic achievement comparable to that of the London Bureau, he freely criticised their 'demands'. They were too moderate and approached the British orbit too closely. Nor did they offer any guarantee that the Jews would have a decisive voice in the shaping of Palestine's future. Weizmann's statements aroused vain hopes and bore no relation to the factual achievements. 'All in all,' he complained, 'Weizmann and Sokolow have acted too independently and consulted neither the Executive nor the Committee in the Hague.'

The divergence was resolved when Tschlenow declared that in principle he accepted the 'demands' on the understanding that, to correct the balance, parallel assurances must be elicited from the Central Powers as well. This would comply with the Basle Programme, which aimed to solve the Jewish problem openly and with the support of all Powers concerned. The Russian Zionists were anxious that the right of the Jewish people to a national home in Palestine should be recognised at the future peace conference and that unrestricted colonisation should be internationally guaranteed 'irrespective of the Arab majority'. If Palestine remained under Turkish sovereignty, they wanted one power or a group of powers to be appointed as Trustees of the Jewish National Home. The Russian Government could be relied on, to give its support. Prince Lwow, when Prime Minister, his Foreign Minister Miliukow, and other Ministers were ready to issue a declaration of sympathy similar to that given to Sokolow by the French and Italian Governments; if he had not rushed to accept it, this was because he hoped to obtain a better formula, expressed in more concrete terms. He felt justified in temporising because he had received positive assurances that when the question of Palestine was discussed at the forthcoming Inter-Allied War Aims Conference in Petrograd, Zionist representatives would be consulted. The Provisional Government under Kerensky was no less favourably disposed to the Zionist cause than its predecessor, and the strongly worded protest of the Entente Powers, lodged at Tereshchenko's suggestion, against the Turkish policy of evacuation was encouraging.

Throughout their deliberations, the participants reaffirmed their desire to canvass maximum support in all possible quarters. British-oriented Zionism was tacitly allowed to plough its own furrow, but the movement as a whole had to steer clear of any involvement in power politics, let alone of subordination to one of the warring camps. The international character of official Zionism thus remained essentially unaltered.

The failure of Goldberg's mission drove Weizmann and Sokolow to a state of near despair. All direct appeals to Tschlenow were of no avail. 'For the last six months,' Tschlenow replied to Sokolow, 'you have been demanding from us a public statement in favour of your conception . . . You will surely agree with us that before making such a statement we must have clear and positive promises [from the British Government] . . . So far we have not got them . . . In Russia we have been given much more definite pledges.' Was it at all certain, Tschlenow went on, that Britain was going to persevere in the Palestine campaign, and what would happen if she failed to defeat the Turks? The risks were too grave not to be taken into account.[76]

Far from being seduced by the London Bureau school of thought, Tschlenow tried to persuade Brandeis that the Executive's policy was the only sensible one to follow. The principle of active neutrality decided upon early in the war and faithfully pursued had been unanimously endorsed at the Executive meeting in Copenhagen. It was still right and expedient. In the future too they intended to look for friends everywhere; they would not determine the future of Palestine—their wishes were not decisive, and a one-sided orientation could do great harm. They would apply their entire forces in one direction only when the situation had become clearer. Meanwhile Brandeis's friends in Washington could do good work in connection with the forthcoming peace conference.[77]

There was little need to tell Brandeis of the importance of enlisting American support. This Brandeis endeavoured to do to the best of his ability. The crucial dilemma was—in which direction to channel America's goodwill: in that advocated by Tschlenow or that urged by Weizmann? Until the United States entered the war Brandeis scrupulously followed the directives of the Zionist Executive in Berlin. This was in keeping with American neutrality and was dictated by the overriding necessity to do nothing that could give the Turks ammunition against the Palestinian Jews. But after America entered the war Brandeis could give his Anglophile proclivities freer rein. At heart he agreed with Weizmann that for the Zionists England was the best choice, but his mind was not entirely at ease since America was not at war with Turkey and Britain was strongly suspected of nourishing the annexationist and imperialistic designs so unpopular with President Wilson. Brandeis's initial reserve about Weizmann's pressing invitation to work in favour of a 'Jewish Palestine under a British Protectorate'[78] is therefore understandable. It was not until Brandeis met Balfour that Weizmann's protestations of Britain's disinterestedness could be substantiated. Neither Balfour nor Lord Eustace Percy nor Sir Eric Drummond, who accompanied the Secretary of State, shared Lloyd George's annexationist inclinations. When they told Brandeis that it was preferable to place the country under an Entente or even better an American protectorate they were sincere. Balfour's idealism, broad humanity, and understanding of the Jewish problem projected an entirely different image of Britain from that suggested by the secret treaties, and finally convinced Brandeis of the correctness of Weizmann's judgement.

As for Balfour, the prime concern of his mission to the United States was to prepare the ground for full co-operation, to stimulate interest and goodwill. He had also to offset the unfavourable impression that the Asia Minor Agreement had made on Wilson. Brandeis's position in the President's council might well have facilitated the building of new bridges of friendship between the two countries. As Mrs Dugdale put it, Brandeis was 'a great figure in the world of law and politics, to whom President Wilson himself was readily accessible, a man who could meet a British Secretary of State on equal terms'. It was therefore important for Balfour to meet Brandeis, Palestinian policy being one of the subjects on which Balfour intended to explore American feeling. His meeting with Brandeis was more than rewarding. Brandeis, as Balfour remarked later to Lord Eustace Percy, was 'the most remarkable man he had met in the United States'.[79]

In addition to the memorandum prepared by Justice Felix Frankfurter some seventeen years later,[80] we are fortunate to have contemporary records of the Balfour–Brandeis discussions; one of them is an account of the meeting between Eric Drummond and Brandeis, the other a brief summary of a subsequent meeting between Balfour and Brandeis. Drummond noted:[81]

Mr. Balfour,

I met Mr. Brandeis, who is the leader of the Zionist movement in the United States and who . . . has great personal influence with the President, this morning. He was going to see the President with regard to the question of Palestine immediately, and wished to have a talk with me on the subject before doing so.

I found that what he aimed at was equal rights and opportunities for Jews in Palestine combined with the maintenance of the autonomy which the present Jewish local institutions enjoy there. He expressed a strong preference for a British protectorate over the country, as he had been most favourably impressed by our treatment of Egypt.

Replying unofficially, Drummond stated that a British protectorate would be possible only if all the Allies approved of it, and added that in order to avoid friction it might even be necessary to create an international protectorate. Brandeis did not seem to support this solution with any enthusiasm; Drummond replied that should jealousies between European Powers prevent Great Britain from becoming the protecting Power, perhaps the United States would be willing to assume that role. Brandeis was by no means averse to the idea, but he still preferred the British alternative. He pointed out that as the majority of American citizens were still opposed to the war and were reluctant to undertake any responsibilities overseas, it would be inopportune to ventilate such a proposal. He thought, however, that in the course of the war the position might change and he promised to keep the matter in mind. Sir Eric concluded:

> From what he said it was fairly clear that the Zionists ultimately aim at a Jewish National State, but are convinced that the immediate step to be secured is the recognition of equal opportunity for Jews in Palestine; they do not intend now to put forward any proposal which goes beyond this.
>
> I told him that as long as the demand was confined to such a general proposition I did not see how the Allied Governments could do otherwise than welcome it, but I warned him that if mention was made of a Jewish State the position might be entirely changed.

This note, dated 24 April, did not reach the Foreign Office until 13 June, when Drummond was already back in London. A draft of the note was prepared to brief Sir Reginald Wingate but by then Drummond considered certain aspects of his conversation with Brandeis out-dated and objected to its despatch:

> I should be inclined *not* to send this to [Cairo]. Mr. Brandeis had a later interview with Mr. Balfour [on 10 May?], when I believe he took up a much more definite attitude than he did in my conversation with him. He advocated 'a national home for Jews in Palestine' under a British protectorate, and I understand received promises of Mr. Balfour's personal support for the Zionist Movement.[82]

This summary does not necessarily suggest that Balfour accepted the idea of a British protectorate in Palestine; in fact he did not, but he was certainly less reserved than his Private Secretary about the ultimate objective of the Zionist movement which was a Jewish State. Balfour was none the less wary of making any public pronouncement on this subject, although he was pressed to do so by Brandeis during their official meeting on 10 May. Brandeis recorded that Balfour outlined the complexities of the situation and pointed out that any public declaration at that moment 'would be hemmed in in view of the sensibilities of the other powers, whereas, if we [Zionists] exercised patience and allowed events to take their natural course, we would obtain much more.'[83] Though unsuccessful in eliciting a declaration from Balfour, Brandeis could be satisfied with the assurances he had received in private. According to Frankfurter, Balfour's long talk with Brandeis was summed up in his quiet but emphatic remark: 'I am a Zionist'. On 14 May Brandeis let Weizmann know that his talks with Balfour, Eustace Percy, and Eric Drummond on Palestine were 'very encouraging', and three days later he telegraphed Rothschild that he had had a satisfactory talk with President Wilson and Balfour.[84] At Military Intelligence Webster observed: 'The way was thus prepared for the acceptance by the Government of the United States of the policy eventually determined upon by Great Britain.'[85]

We shall see later how important it was to obtain President Wilson's *imprimatur* to a British presence in Palestine and the rôle that the Zionists played in this respect. An identical service to that rendered by Brandeis was expected from the Russian Zionists as well. For reasons already mentioned, they had other considerations to bear in mind; but had a comparable rapport to that of Balfour-Brandeis been established with the Russian Zionist leaders, would it have had a bearing on their attitude to Britain? What impact would a declaration of the kind proposed by Cecil have had on Russian Jewry, or even private assurance of sympathy, as advised by Sykes? Judging from the general disposition of Russian Jews and the enthusiastic response to the Balfour Declaration, it can be assumed that a gesture of good will sometime in spring or summer of 1917 would not have fallen on barren ground.

12   Sir Mark Sykes in the East

It will be recalled that before Sykes's departure for the East it had been arranged that Weizmann would follow and that, as soon as Jerusalem was liberated, Weizmann would set in motion a propaganda campaign in favour of 'a Jewish Palestine under British protection'. Weizmann's trip, however, did not materialise. The setbacks that the British Army encountered on the Gaza front made his mission less urgent, but it was principally the revelation of the Anglo-French Agreement that deterred him. Mindful of Scott's warning against going on a fool's errand, he finally decided that it was better for him to stay in London.[1]

However, had Weizmann gone to Egypt he would not have wasted his time. There the Fashoda spirit died hard and Weizmann could not have found a more receptive audience than among the British officers to whom the Sykes-Picot Agreement was just as unwelcome. It was indeed his insistence on a British Palestine that a year later made him so popular both with Wingate and Clayton when he arrived in Egypt at the head of the Zionist Commission. The usefulness of Zionism in countering French claims to Palestine was pointed out by Hogarth as early as July 1917;[2] an idea that he must have appropriated from Sykes during the latter's stay in Cairo, but late in the spring of that year, with the stalemate on the Gaza front, it seemed less urgent. The reasons that Sykes so emphatically pressed Weizmann to come to Cairo were quite different from those earlier ones. On 28 April he cabled Graham:[3]

> Aaron Aaronsohn asks me to inform you that Tel-Aviv has been sacked. 10,000 Palestine Jews are now without home or food. Whole of Yishuv is threatened with destruction. Jemal has publicly stated [that] Armenian policy will now be applied to Jews . . . Aaron Aaronsohn advises, and I agree [that] in present crisis Weizmann's presence here essential.

Ten days later additional reasons emerged.[4]

> I propose to use Weizmann easing Judeo-Arab situation by promoting good feeling and co-operation; assisting in organization of

local Zionists and improving such of our intelligence service as depends on Jewish information and making plans for political action [in case of] our advance. It is the opinion of Aaronsohn that W[eizmann] should come . . . However, if W. sees fit to appoint Aaronsohn to act in his place . . . the latter would be ready to do so, but . . . should receive from W. and his friends . . . detailed instructions.

Since meeting Sykes in London, Aaronsohn had gone from strength to strength. When he arrived in Cairo towards the end of 1916, he had still to go a long way to convince the British authorities of his good faith, but ultimately he was admitted to their inner circle[5] and soon proved his worth. The Arab Intelligence system was 'extremely bad', and in spite of all efforts to improve it, very little news could be elicited about enemy movements. Even when some information did filter through, it was too stale to be of any use.[6] By contrast not only did Aaronsohn gather a great deal of information, but by re-establishing contact with his group in Zichron-Yaakov, he was able to furnish first-hand reports on Turkish troop movements, morale, and conditions behind the enemy lines. Moreover, with his well-trained mind, he was able to give useful advice to the British on other matters, including military questions, so much so that it was humorously commented among the General Staff that 'Aaronsohn is running the G.H.Q.' A co-author of the *Palestine Handbook*,[7] an indispensable military guide, he was also invited to write for the *Arab Bulletin*.[8]

Aaronsohn considered himself a representative of his people. He made no secret of his convictions and did his best to win support for them among the British. The most notable converts to the Zionist cause were William Ormsby-Gore,[9] Philip Graves,[10] Major Wyndham Deedes,[11] and Colonel Richard Meinertzhagen.[12] But uppermost in Aaronsohn's mind was a swift invasion of Palestine to crush the Turk and deliver the Yishuv from likely disaster. The sluggish pace of the British advance exasperated him. He was convinced that, if properly handled, a lightning victory on the Palestinian front was possible. His plan consisted of: (a) withdrawal of the ill-starred Salonica Expedition; (b) a surprise landing in Haifa-Acre bay; (c) capture of the Mount Carmel ridges and the Valley of Esdraelon, followed by (d) a lightning assault on Jerusalem. The Turks, he was informed, had just completed the fortification of Jerusalem's southern and western approaches and, drawing on rich historical precedent, he pointed out that the city had in most cases been captured from the north. He submitted this scheme to Deedes on 2 April and on the next day to General Clayton. 'Palestine is a ripe fruit. A good shake-up and it will fall in your hands.' The General was interested and complimented Aaronsohn on his 'sound logic and thorough . . . knowledge'. Clayton discussed the project thereafter with General Murray, O.C. Egypt, but a decision could be taken only in London.[13]

Aaronsohn's exposition did not fall on sterile ground. Wingate twice took up the subject of a landing in Alexandretta, or preferably in Palestine, in his correspondence with the Foreign Office and the Chief of the Imperial General Staff.[14] However, London remained unresponsive; Sykes later told Aaronsohn that since the Gallipoli débâcle the British were wary of initiating any further landings.[15] So great were the psychological effects of Gallipoli and the setbacks at Gaza, that in the summer of 1917 General Allenby estimated that to capture Jerusalem at least twenty British divisions (500,000 men) would be required to counter eighteen Turkish divisions, supplemented by two German. However, during Allenby's offensive in the autumn of that year, it became apparent that only 20,000 Turkish rifles opposed 100,000 British; that Turkish transport had completely broken down (the Turks were not even in a position to get their guns away during their retreat); and that the morale of their troops was much lower than was originally thought. The British had greatly overrated their opponent's strength[16] and the analogy between Gallipoli and conditions at the Alexandretta-Gaza seaboard was erroneous. Palestine was not perhaps a 'ripe plum' as Aaronsohn's rhetoric suggested, but his estimate that a surprise landing combining land and naval operations could have given the British an easier victory was essentially correct.

No Englishman admired Aaronsohn more than Sir Mark Sykes, who thought that Weizmann would do well to appoint him as his representative in Cairo. An official Zionist blessing would have enhanced Aaronsohn's status in the eyes of the British authorities there and raised his standing among his fellow Jews, especially in Palestine, where his group was practically ostracised. The Palestinian Jews followed the leadership of the Berlin Zionist Executive and, fearing to invite Turkish reprisals, steered clear of the spy-ring. However, the Zionist leaders in London knew nothing about Aaronsohn's Intelligence network and it was not before 18 July, following Sykes's return to London, that Sokolow and Weizmann suggested that a committee should be formed in Egypt 'to further the Zionist cause . . . and give all possible assistance to Entente interests in Palestine . . . to receive and distribute relief funds' for the Jewish population in Palestine, with Aaronsohn acting as secretary. He was reported to be 'entirely trustworthy', and the military authorities in Egypt were asked to permit him to forward remittances to Palestine.[17]

Sykes's second reason for insisting on Weizmann's trip to Egypt concerned Arab-Jewish relations. He had just concluded his discussions with the Syrian notables in Cairo and was on the point of going to Jedda to see King Hussein and his son Emir Feisal. At this juncture an Arab-Zionist dialogue could have been useful, but a whole year elapsed before it materialised. In the meantime, in the absence of contact, and with the Turks taking full advantage of the Balfour Declaration to rouse the Syrians against the British, Arab-Jewish relations suffered a further setback.

Sykes had three meetings with the Syrian representatives. Picot conducted separate discussions. They resulted in the Syrians agreeing to Franco-British tutelage of an Arab State or Confederation of States in areas 'A' and 'B'; to military protection and the employment of French and British financial and political advisers in their respective spheres of interest. No objection was raised to 'a permanent military occupation' of Bagdad by Britain, and to a similar status for France in the Syrian littoral. With regard to Palestine the delegates agreed that it presented 'too many international problems for a new and weak state such as the Arab must be to assume responsibility for . . . but that in the event of Jews being recognised as a Millet or "Nation" in Palestine . . . actual [non-Jewish] population must have equal recognition.'[18] Considering the Syrian nationalists' propensity to extremism, this was a successful outcome. The Syrians recognised the special position of Palestine and were prepared to accept a status of equality for the native Arabic-speaking population there, should the Jews be accorded special privileges for immigration and colonisation. Sykes's line of argument is spelled out in a note written more than a year later:[19]

> Palestine and Syria must be separate. It is inconceivable that an
> infant Syrian State should be able to cope with Palestinian problems.
> Palestine is . . . of international interest to the followers of three
> great international religions and must be treated as such. . . . In
> talking both to the King of the Hedjaz, to Emir Feysal, and to
> Syrian intellectuals I have always found the following argument
> effective: 'You have in view the ultimate emancipation and freedom
> of Syria from all tutelage and protection . . . but can you expect
> that the world will let you manage your own affairs without inter-
> ference, if the Government of Syria is responsible for Jerusalem,
> Bethlehem . . . and the Jewish colonies? If you have Palestine as a
> part of Syria, the various elements interested in Palestine will
> undoubtedly control your own affairs.'

Sykes's advice to the Syrians not to antagonise the Jews bore fruit, but his objective was much wider. As Aaronsohn was quick to detect, he cherished the idea of an Arab-Jewish-Armenian alliance as a 'buffer' to Egypt,[20] a concept which was, in due course, to crystallise into a major item of his policy. With Russian and American hostility to territorial annexation, he hoped that at the future peace conference this would give the British the best justification for their presence.

> With regard to Russia [he wrote to Sir Percy Cox], I am most anxious, as I feel sure that the extremists in power are determined that no one shall benefit territorially from the war . . . Our only weapon with these people is the theory of racial individuality and the argument that we cannot abandon conquered races to incurable oppressors like Turks and Germans . . . Our administration . . . should have a nominal autonomy under departmental advisers, nominated by the [British] Resident; these advisers to have fixity of tenure and executive authority. This combined with military occupation gets us all we want. . . .
> The idea of Arab nationalism may be absurd, but our [Peace] Congress case will be good if we can say we are helping to develop a race on nationalist lines under our protection.[21]

Sykes left Egypt for Jedda on 1 May to acquaint King Hussein with the terms of the Asia Minor Agreement and to reassure him about French aims in the Syrian interior. He was to reaffirm also the Allies' determination to support Arab aspirations, but to make it clear that the British would retain such military and political predominance in Bagdad and adjacent districts as their strategic and commercial interests would require. Hussein was also to be told that extension of his dominion beyond Hedjaz was dependent upon its acceptance by the native peoples concerned. On his way Sykes called on Feisal at Wejh. Feisal's misgivings were set at rest by Sykes's explanation of the nature of the Anglo-French Agreement and its relation to the Arab Confederation. The interview with Hussein on 5 May went off equally well. Hussein was anxious lest French annexation of Syria would expose him to the charge of having led the Syrian Moslems into rebellion against the Turk only 'to hand them over to a Christian Power', but Sykes reassured him.[22]

There is no indication in Sykes's cables whether the question of Palestine was also discussed, but the cryptic reference that he had reached 'the same point' with Feisal and Hussein as he had with the Syrian delegates in Cairo, and his note of 2 August 1918 already quoted suggest that he did.

The second meeting with Hussein took place on 24 May with Picot also present. The King admitted that the Arabs depended on Allied help and professed his readiness to co-operate with them for the realisation of Arab aspirations, but there was disagreement about the powers to be accorded to European advisers. The King rejected the idea of giving them executive authority, while Sykes urged its essential importance, as otherwise Arab rule would be 'helpless and corrupt', whereas 'under European administration it would prosper'. The differences were subsequently patched up, and on the following day, reaffirming his confidence in Britain, Hussein stated that he would be content if the French pursued the same policy towards Arab aspirations in the Syrian littoral as the British did in Bagdad. With this Picot was satisfied. Before the meeting broke up Feisal gave Sykes a separate message from his father restating his position that he was ready to co-operate 'to the fullest extent' both with France about Syria and with England about Mesopotamia, but asked to be helped vis-à-vis Idrisi and Ibn Saud. 'We beg that Great Britain will endeavour to induce them to recognise the King's position as the leader of the Arab movement.'[23]

A manifesto signed by Feisal, as Commander of the Arab Forces, and King Hussein was thereafter issued to the Arabs in Syria promising to deliver them from Turkish tyranny. It acknowledged the British support of the Arab revolt and thanked the French Government for joining England in recognising Arab independence. 'Our duty', the manifesto stated, 'compels us to offer the necessary guarantees for the . . . rights of these two Great Powers' and 'when the war is over, their men and money will help us to reform our country which has been ruined by those [Turkish] tyrants.'[24]

Two months later Hussein told Lawrence that he had trapped Picot into admitting that France would be satisfied with a parallel position in Syria to that which Great Britain desired in Iraq.[25] However, as events showed, it was not Picot who had been trapped. The British had no intention of abandoning Mesopotamia,[26] which Hussein hoped would be only temporarily occupied, and the French therefore saw no reason to curb their own ambitions in Syria. This was the origin of the conflict between the Sharifians and the French, after the war, with its grim outcome for Feisal's Government in Damascus in July 1920. However, in May 1917, when Hussein met Sykes in Jedda, he seemed to be concerned more with his own position in Arabia proper than with Syria's 'independence'.

With his self-styled coronation in October 1916 making little impact on his rivals in Arabia, he expected Britain to establish his position for him. But this was precisely what the British could not do. Their obligation, undertaken during the negotiations before the Hedjaz revolt, was, as Wingate said, 'to "keep the ring" . . . within which Arab autonomy shall have free play', but Britain did not guarantee Hussein's pre-eminence, whereas he considered that the manner in which these negotiations were conducted implied their approval of that position. Clayton also was of the opinion that the mere fact that all negotiations were conducted with Hussein (there being no other prominent leader with whom the Arab question could be discussed), did not imply that the British regarded him as 'the future ruler of all Arab races . . . Great Britain has never pledged herself to anything of this sort and has always treated the Sherif as a "spokesman" or "champion" of the Arab race.' But Hussein 'perverted [British] assurances into a support of himself as supreme ruler.'[27] Such an interpretation was inadmissible, and was bound to provoke the fears of other Arab chiefs and injure British relations with them. The India Office claimed that even the status of *primus inter pares*, the utmost to which Hussein could be entitled, had first to be voluntarily recognised by his fellow Arab rulers. Those, however, considered themselves as good as Hussein, and any move by the British to promote his status was bound to be counter-productive. It would have made Ibn Saud suspicious of British *bona fides*; nor would Mustapha al-Idrisi have tolerated Hussein's aggrandisement. The suggestion had to be finally written off as 'inopportune' and 'inadvisable'.[28]

With his ambitions frustrated, and condemned by the Moslem world for siding with the infidel against Turkey, Hussein had to vindicate his revolt, and perhaps calm his own conscience as a Moslem, by stepping up his claims elsewhere. Hence his statement to Lieutenant-Colonel C. E. Wilson, the British representative at Jedda, that 'the McMahon agreement . . . gave me Syria and Mesopotamia'; hence his statement to Lawrence that the Hedjaz and Syria 'are like the palm and fingers of one hand . . . They are Arab countries [which] deserved independence and it is my duty to see they get it.' To Wingate such an interpretation of McMahon's letter of 24 October 1915 was completely 'unjustifiable'; he found it incredible that King Hussein could nourish such illusions. 'We must eventually take steps', he advised London, 'to correct any erroneous opinion he may have or profess to have . . . in regard to the future of the Syrian littoral and Palestine.'[29] At the Foreign Office, Clerk predicted with resignation: 'more future trouble', whereas Graham agreed with Wingate that sooner or later the British 'must enlighten the King as to the true facts of the situation . . . Possibly he is really . . . aware of them and is bluffing.'[30]

By contrast, Clayton, more familiar with the Arab mind, was spared the shock of disillusionment. 'Sykes', he confided to Storrs, 'seems very pleased with the result of his work but your knowledge of these people will enable you to appreciate their attitude in such matters and prevent your putting too much faith in any satisfactory assurances which they may give as the result of an interview with a strong personality like Sykes. We must expect them to go back a good deal on their statements when Sykes's personal influence is removed.' A subsequent meeting with Fuad Khetib confirmed Clayton's earlier impression that Hussein had either failed to understand the tenor of the Jedda conversations or that he was 'determined not to understand it and put his own interpretation' on them. Clayton refused to attach great importance to the affair and thought that events would be too strong for Hussein and eventually impel him either 'to fall into line, or fall out'.[31]

The King, however, was not inclined to toe the line, nor, for want of alternative rebels against Turkey, was it expedient for the British to drop him. As a result, Hussein felt free to take full advantage of British hesitations and Sykes's negligence to draft his own record of the conversations in Jedda. For this omission Sykes had to pay the penalty when a year later, to his surprise, Hussein feigned ignorance of the Anglo-French Agreement and pretended to have learned of it first from Djemal Pasha's Damascus speech in December 1917 which received wide publicity. Sykes was all the more astonished as the King had been given a comprehensive 'outline and details' of the Agreement not only by himself and Picot, but later also by Colonel Bremond and Commander Hogarth who went to Jedda specially for this purpose.[32]

Whatever his subsequent disappointment, during the summer of 1917 Sykes was completely satisfied with the results of his mission. Nothing could disturb his facile optimism, and even if some question marks still lingered in his mind, they were pushed into the background by a much graver issue. On his return to London,[33] he found that the Foreign Office 'had been carefully destroying everything [he] had done in the past two years', pushing ideas of separate peace negotiations with Turkey. 'Luckily' he commented, 'Zionism held good and the plots to bring Morgenthau over and negotiate a separate peace with Turkey . . . were foiled.'[34] But though Morgenthau's mission had been successfully headed off by Weizmann, the idea of a separate peace with Turkey was by no means dead. It was supported not only by 'Parker, Tyrrel, Mallet and Co.,' to whom Sykes referred in rather uncomplimentary terms, but by such a serious-minded statesman as Lord Robert Cecil, and it found a staunch advocate in no less a personality than Lord Milner. Sykes did his utmost to counter this dangerous drift. It preoccupied him as late as December 1917. But before going into this matter, we must first turn to the abortive Morgenthau mission.

13 A Separate Peace with Turkey or an Arab-Zionist-Armenian Entente?

Contrary to what is generally assumed,[1] the idea of detaching Turkey from the Central Powers did not originate with Morgenthau; it was essentially a State Department move to which President Wilson gave his unqualified *imprimatur*. American-Turkish relations were cordial, and on 2 April 1917, when war with Germany was already in the air, Nessimy Bey, the Turkish Foreign Minister, hastened to reassure Abram Elkus, the American Ambassador in Constantinople, that Turkey's attitude to the United States remained friendly, and he saw no reason for it to change. Though forced to sever diplomatic relations with Washington, the Porte managed, much to Elkus's satisfaction, to resist the Wilhelmstrasse's pressure to declare war on the United States. Turkey's good-will was matched by that of America, President Wilson firmly believed that all the evil stemmed from German militarism; that the peoples of Austria-Hungary, Bulgaria and Turkey desired to assert their independence;[2] the corollary being that should some equitable proposition be made to them they might opt out of the war, leaving Berlin isolated. Germany's rulers would in that case be more likely to come to their senses and, in this way, a 'bloodless victory' could be achieved.

Balfour, at the time in the United States, agreed that, should Turkey and Austria be willing to break away from Germany, 'certain concessions [by the Allies] should be made to them.'[3] About ten days later State Secretary Lansing informed Balfour about conversations he had had with Henry Morgenthau, the former United States Ambassador at Constantinople, as well as with the former Consul-General in the Balkans from whom he gathered that conditions in Turkey were deteriorating, that the Germans were detested, and that the Turkish authorities were ready to consider terms for a separate peace. Balfour was also told that Morgenthau was willing to go unofficially to Switzerland to pursue the matter. Balfour saw no harm in making the attempt, 'while if matters took a favourable form, results might be of enormous advantage'.[4] This was fully in line with the British Government's policy. The Prime Minister was known to have been 'for long in favour of some scheme of this kind' and a War Cabinet decision was not required.[5] In fact, there was nothing unusual in the American initiative. Secret *pourparlers* through various go-betweens to bring about a separate peace with Turkey dated back to the early stages of the war.[6] The idea had the support of the Chief of the Imperial General Staff;[7] the main stumbling block was Russia's claim to Constantinople. Nevertheless, the possibility of some arrangement with Turkey was kept in sight. 'should circumstances become more favourable'.[8] Such circumstances presented themselves following the March Revolution, when Russia renounced any annexationist claim. The original purpose of the Eastern Campaign was 'to knock the props from under Germany' in the hope of shortening the war, and as late as October 1917, Lloyd George told the War Cabinet that it was necessary first to deal the Turks 'a heavy military blow and then offer them terms designed to buy them out'.[9] But if diplomacy alone could be utilised to extract favourable peace terms from Turkey, so much the better. This was why the British Government at first welcomed America's initiative. London's suggestion that Egypt would be more suitable for taking soundings (since there were so many enemy agents in Switzerland) had the added advantage that relief to Palestine Jews could provide ideal camouflage.[10] The real object of the mission however was to get in touch with Talaat Pasha and other Turkish Ministers and secure their consent to an Allied submarine assault on the *Goeben* and *Breslau*, the German warships which dominated Constantinople. Their destruction was to be a signal for the Turks to revolt against Germany and conclude a separate peace. No matter how fantastic the scheme seemed to be, Lord Hardinge thought it unwise to discourage it; he suggested that Fitzmaurice should meet Morgenthau in Gibraltar. However, following Spring-Rice's warning the Foreign Office had second thoughts. On 9 June Spring-Rice cabled:[11]

> Morgenthau is undoubtedly closely connected with Germans in the United States and has some influence in the White House as he organised financial side of Presidential campaign. Very great care should be taken in dealing through him. He wished to have commission as special Ambassador and he is anxious to play a part. He is closely connected with many influential people in Turkey, especially the Jews and Dunmais, whose influence was powerful in Young Turk Party and like most Jews wishes to save Turkish Empire. His sympathies are probably more German than British but he is opposed to German Militarist régime . . . Food and trade . . . is an important factor in United States policy and opening of Dardanelles to Russian trade . . . is greatly desired.

Morgenthau's idea of 'Syrian autonomy under a Christian Government', a pattern which presumably was to apply to Palestine, as well as the news that President Wilson was determined on 'expulsion of Turks from Europe', not necessarily from the Asiatic provinces, came as a real bombshell in Whitehall. Graham's reaction was unequivocal: 'It is evident that a policy of expelling the Turks from Europe at the probable price of leaving them in control of or with suzerainty over Syria, Palestine and Mesopotamia is not one for our support', to which Lord Hardinge added: 'There is an element of danger in such negotiations since we may find ourselves in conflict with President Wilson, and this would be to play Germany's game.'[12]

Ormsby-Gore assessed the position in its geo-political context. For Britain to let the Turco-Teutonic combine survive in such a unique strategic area was unthinkable, and at this juncture it was vital not to lose sight of two great world forces: Islam and Jewry. A solution that would leave the Arabs and the Zionists in Turkey would sooner or later involve the British Empire in another struggle. 'If our declared war aims mean anything, surely Armenia . . . Syria and Palestine . . . have the same claim to liberation as Belgium.' Idealistic motives apart, the overriding concern for Ormsby-Gore was to secure 'such lines of defence for the British Empire as may prevent the German hegemony or penetration of South-Western Asia'. He concluded:[13]

> The separation of Syria and Palestine from the control of a Power dominated or controlled by Germany is the only security that can assure our position in Bagdad and along the Red Sea. . . . It is the only security that will ensure an Ententophil solution of the Palestine question and which will prevent Zionism being thrown into the arms of the King of Prussia. The Germans are at this moment making a bid to capture Zionism.

Ormsby-Gore's memorandum was written four days after Weizmann and Malcolm had called on him. Weizmann had been forewarned of Morgenthau's trip by Brandeis and Malcolm had learned about other peace feelers put out by Aubrey Herbert, M.P., Marmaduke Pickhall and Samuel Block, leaders of a Turcophile society in England. They protested against what they called 'a gross betrayal of their cause'. Morgenthau was described as 'pro-German', acting 'on behalf of an international ring of Jewish financiers . . . violently hostile, both to Great Britain and Zionism'. Weizmann was all the more perturbed since the German Government, he learned, had approached the Berlin Zionists, through Lepsius, with a view to coming to terms with them.[14] He called twice thereafter at the Foreign Office where his representations were couched in even stronger language. He was followed by Malcolm and subsequently by Wickham Steed, the editor of *The Times*. Graham was now convinced that Morgenthau's mission could no longer serve any useful purpose and Cecil requested Spring-Rice to secure its postponement though without causing offence to the President or American opinion.[15]

Zionist-Armenian remonstrances were all the more welcome as they gave the British an ideal excuse for making known their displeasure with the American move without offending them. The wheels were however already in motion. Spring-Rice's repeated attempts to influence the State Department were unsuccessful. Lansing remained adamant. Morgenthau was to go as the President's representative to enquire into Jewish affairs but without authority to negotiate peace terms. Any such initiative had to come first from Turkish Ministers, on which Morgenthau had to report; and, apparently to mollify the British Zionists, Polk, Counsellor in the State Department, reassured Spring-Rice that the mission's standing would be enhanced by the presence of Felix Frankfurter, who was 'a real Jew and a Zionist and not a reformed Jew like Morgenthau'. Spring-Rice's arguments carried little conviction since, apart from Balfour's earlier consent, Ribot also warmly approved of the mission, insisting that 'no stone should be left unturned to influence Turkey'. The French Government deputed M. Weyl, of the Tobacco Monopoly Company, to confer with Morgenthau and Lansing suggested that Weizmann too should meet the mission.[16] On 19 June the State Department authorised the following statement, to be published. It appeared in the *New York Times* the following day:

> In an effort to ameliorate the conditions of the Jewish communities, the President has sent abroad former Ambassador Henry Morgenthau and Professor Felix Frankfurter of the Harvard Law School, now serving as assistant to Secretary of War, Baker, Mr. Morgenthau and Frankfurter will proceed to Egypt and from there conduct an investigation to ascertain the means of relieving the situation among the Jews in Palestine.

To buttress its argument, that relief was not merely a cloak for some insidious purpose, the State Department appended an additional item which appeared in the *New York Times* of 21 June:[17]

> Jacob Schiff, Felix M. Warburg, Louis Marschall and thirty other members of the Joint Distribution Committee . . . voted yesterday

to give the Morgenthau Commission 'unlimited funds' for the relief of the Jews in Palestine . . . $800,000 had already been sent to the relief of the Jews in Palestine and an attempt would be made to send millions should the avenue be opened. Morgenthau and his associates should have entire discretion on the disbursement of the relief funds.

On 26 June Colville de Rune Barclay, the Chargé d'Affaires at the British Embassy in Washington, confirmed that Morgenthau would act as 'a special representative of President Wilson'. However, he was not authorised to treat with the Turkish Government, but merely had to pass on communications. Whether Morgenthau understood correctly his terms of reference is, as his later conduct proved, doubtful. But the most intriguing aspect of his mission is the association with the Zionists. Even more puzzling was the insistence on Weizmann meeting Morgenthau at Gibraltar. 'I hope you will leave nothing undone', Lansing cabled Walter Page, the American Ambassador in London, 'to secure Mr. Balfour's consent, as it is considered most important that Mr. Morgenthau see Mr. Weizmann.'[18]

Why this should be so is a matter for speculation. Had Morgenthau seen his task confined solely to disbursement of relief money he would hardly have required Weizmann's assistance. He was well thought of by the Palestinian Jews and his effective intercessions with the Porte on their behalf, when Ambassador in Constantinople, were appreciated. A mission of goodwill at a time of stress would have certainly been welcomed in Palestine without requiring Weizmann's approval. But Morgenthau apparently nourished more ambitious ideas than philanthropy or service as President Wilson's postman. If 'Syrian autonomy under a Christian Government' was the scheme he was pregnant with, it was quite legitimate to assume that a similar pattern for Palestine applied, namely, Jewish autonomy under the trusteeship of the Great Powers within the framework of Ottoman sovereignty. This was the official Zionist aim proclaimed ever since the first Zionist Congress in Basle in 1897, about which Morgenthau had learned from his friend Richard Lichtheim, the head of the Zionist Agency in Constantinople. Morgenthau however was completely in the dark about the London Bureau school of thought, and must have erroneously projected on Weizmann the official Zionist policy. Moreover, he may have been aware of the correspondence between Abram Elkus, his successor in Constantinople, and Jacob Schiff in New York. It related to concessions for Jewish immigration and colonisation in Palestine to be granted by Turkey as a *quid pro quo* for assistance given by

Jewish financial circles in America to the Ottoman Treasury. Both Talaat and his Minister of Finance, Djavid Bey, showed themselves favourably disposed to this idea,[19] and now Morgenthau might have wished to finalise these preliminary negotiations and strike a bargain. The reference to 'millions' of dollars decided upon by the Joint Distribution Committee, which far exceeded the relief requirements of the Palestine Jews, might have had something to do with this project. Lord Robert Cecil indeed suspected that Morgenthau was eager to obtain some large concessions of land in Palestine, while Oliphant was clear that Morgenthau was 'out to play a part *qua* Jew' and that his views and actions were determined by this wish.[20]

If Morgenthau's intention was indeed to play a political game of this nature, his insistence on meeting Weizmann becomes intelligible. He was, of course, quite unaware that he was thereby inviting his own defeat. Colonel House, a much more experienced diplomat, warned him against an encounter with a leading British Zionist while on his way to Egypt and advised him to arrange a meeting on the way back.[21] Counsellor Polk was also sceptical about the mission,[22] but Morgenthau seems to have been infected by Lansing's optimism and ignored House's advice.

Weizmann was willing to go to Gibraltar and was particularly delighted with the news that Felix Frankfurter was accompanying Morgenthau, 'Frankfurter is a first-rate man in whom all Jews have confidence,' he told Graham. This suited the British well. Originally, Balfour intended that Sir Lewis Mallet should meet Morgenthau, but as the object of the American mission became public, he feared that if anyone of Mallet's standing became involved, it would appear that the British were joining 'an international deputation to beg the Turks to make a separate peace'. To minimise the adverse effects of such publicity, it was thought more prudent to despatch Weizmann. There is however no truth in the suggestion that by sending Weizmann Balfour intended to obstruct Morgenthau and sidetrack President Wilson. On 27 June he cabled Spring-Rice that Morgenthau would be given all facilities by the British High Commissioner in Egypt, through whom he would communicate 'any peace offers which the Turks were disposed to make'.[23] But Weizmann did better than expected; Morgenthau was no match for Weizmann. As the latter recalled humorously: 'It was no job to persuade Mr. Morgenthau to drop the project. He simply persuaded himself.'[24]

The discussions took place on 4 and 5 July, with Colonel Weyl representing the French, and Weizmann the British Government. According to Morgenthau's information, Turkey's position was precarious; her finances were exhausted, and relations with the Germans strained; Talaat and Enver at each other's throats. Enver was pro-German, corrupt, and interested in continuation of the war, whilst Talaat was a genuine patriot, popular among the masses, honest and poor. To an imaginative mind such a state of affairs might have suggested that the time was ripe for a palace revolution with Talaat overthrowing Enver and paving the way for a separate peace. But if this was what Morgenthau hoped for he was not equipped for seeing the job through. His unfounded self-confidence gave way to resignation, followed by complete capitulation, leaving Weizmann free to deliver the final blow. Morgenthau was told that 'on no account should the Zionist Organisation be compromised by his negotiations . . . identified or mixed up even with the faintest attempts to secure a separate peace'. Morgenthau thereupon indicated that he under-stood the Zionists' position.[25]

Weizmann's victory was complete. By carrying the British view that no peace with Turkey would be satisfactory unless Armenia, Mesopo-tamia, Syria and Palestine were detached from the Ottoman Empire, he destroyed any prospects of useful discussions between Morgenthau and the Turkish ministers. With Frankfurter also under Weizmann's spell, Morgenthau found himself completely isolated.[26] Had he limited his discussions to matters of relief[27] Weizmann would have been hard put to it to dissuade him from going to Palestine. But by sailing into unchartered waters of high policy (on which he had absolutely no authority to speak) Morgenthau invited his own defeat. No less serious was his decision to change his prescribed route. Much annoyed, the State Department reminded him that he had been instructed to deal solely with matters relating to the Jews in Palestine, and he was requested to proceed, together with Frankfurter, to Cairo. This he could not do, as in the meantime he had left for Paris, sending Frankfurter home to report to the President. Wilson impressed on Morgenthau the desirability of not discussing his mission since its purpose had been 'thoroughly misunderstood'.[28] Spring-Rice gained the impression that the President wished to keep his emissary out of the country without offending him.[29] The mission ended as a complete fiasco,[30] and was allowed to die a natural death.

Weizmann reaped the full benefit of Morgenthau's ineptitude since the factors making for a separate peace with Turkey were far weightier than might have been presumed. The French Government, Weizmann learned from Colonel Weyl, was prepared to meet the Turks on much more favourable terms than the British. This information was confirmed by Ribot's telegram to President Wilson, the contents of which were conveyed to Weizmann by Frankfurter. With their fearfully heavy losses on the Western front, and unable to spare more troops for the Eastern campaign, the French preferred the *status quo ante* in Western Asia to the prospect of Britain emerging as the dominant Power there. This was brought home to Weizmann in Paris when Professor Basch said: 'We shall not . . . fight for England's absurd ideas of conquest of Mesopotamia and Palestine.' Given Basch's status as a leading journalist and influential follower of M. Caillaux, Weizmann could not take such views lightly. Caillaux's star was in the ascendant in French politics and he strongly favoured an understanding with Germany, 'the true friend of France', and with Turkey, at England's expense. The Foreign Office had, therefore, good reason to be pleased with Weizmann's efforts. 'Dr. Weizmann is a shrewd observer and confirmed all we hear of French war-weariness,' Graham noted. '[He] has been eminently successful in dissuading Mr. Morgenthau from proceeding either to Egypt or Switzerland.' Balfour too was pleased. Rumours that the British were flirting with the idea of peace with Turkey, such as were bound to proliferate if Morgenthau arrived in Egypt, would have fed suspicions among the Egyptian and Arab population that the war was not going well for the Allies, while his scheme of Syrian autonomy within the framework of Ottoman sovereignty would have made the Arab Decentralisation Party turn to America and away from England and France.[31]

The end of Morgenthau's mission did not mean that the Foreign Office dismissed the idea of peace with Turkey altogether, although, if concluded, it had to be on British, not on French or American terms. On 7 July, only two days after Weizmann's success in Gibraltar, Sir Horace Rumbold, the British Minister in Berne, noted that a number of leading Turkish politicians[32] had arrived in Zurich with the object of making a peace proposal. Cecil lost no time in suggesting that any Turkish advances should be given a sympathetic hearing. Lord Milner was also interested, whilst Balfour made no objections. A fortnight later Rumbold learned that Talaat wished to instigate a military uprising in order to get rid of Enver, and in return for England's support was ready to concede certain constitutional changes in Syria, Mesopotamia, and Armenia. The Turks in Zurich, acting on Talaat's behalf, also decided that the pro-German policy should be superseded by an Anglo-Turkish understanding, provided there was 'no complete partition of Turkey'.[33]

Lord Hardinge was elated. Whatever lay behind this conspiracy, anything concrete that came out of it could only be to Britain's advantage. Cecil thought that 'it would be madness to let slip such a chance'; Mallet, a stalwart Turcophile, considered it 'essential' to meet Turkish overtures, whilst Clerk, though sceptical of Talaat's chance of success, concerned about the deteriorating conditions in Russia, and the military impasse, insisted that the British should do everything in their power to detach Turkey; a peace of exhaustion would leave Berlin free to carry out the *Mittel-Europa* scheme which, for the Allies, would be tantamount to having lost the war.[34]

This trend of policy now gaining ground at the Foreign Office disturbed Sykes. Returning from Paris, where he had met Weizmann, and enjoying the Prime Minister's support, he delivered one of his most scathing attacks on what he termed 'the Foreign Office pro-Turk gang'. Their ideas were ill-advised and risky. The C.U.P. leaders were 'masters in the old art of chicane . . . bounded by no moral scruple', their only motive for negotiating peace was their desire to improve their bargaining position after the war. A soft peace with Turkey would leave Germany as the dominant power in the East. 'Our main object should be to smash the Bagdad Railway' and all that it meant. He feared that Turkey might liberalise her policy towards her subject peoples, granting autonomy to the Arabs, and special colonising facilities to the Jews. If in addition the French financiers fell under German influence, and Pan-Islamism became a pawn in Turco-German hands, Britain would eventually be at their mercy and her position in India and Egypt exposed to perpetual harassment. To forestall such an eventuality, it was essential that the friendship between England and France should be given a permanent foundation and that their respective imperialist leanings be transformed into patronage of the oppressed peoples. Under their wing an Arab-Jewish-Armenian alliance could form a barrier against Turco-German influence. The Zionist eyes were fixed on Britain, the Armenians were ready to accept French assistance, and the Arabs, though apprehensive of 'British imperialism and French finance . . . would prefer British and even French help to Turkish or German dominion'. It was at this juncture that Sykes asked Clayton to expedite the arrival in London of the representatives of the King of the Hedjaz and the Syrians in Cairo with a view to forming an Arab-Zionist-Armenian Committee; the Zionists were to be represented by Weizmann and the Armenians by James Malcolm in London and Nubar Pasha in Paris.[35]

Persuasive as Sykes's arguments may have been, the Foreign Office had to bear in mind other considerations. Early in September Ismail Muchtar Bey, the Secretary of the Ottoman Senate, confided to a British agent in Geneva that the Turks would have liked to go over to the Allies; they were willing to open the Straits to the Allied fleets to sink the German

warships anchored in the Bosphorus, but the indispensable prerequisite
was that the Allies guaranteed Turkish independence. A separate message
from Rahmi, Vali of Smyrna, known for his integrity, sounded even
more promising. Cecil became impatient.

> I am not satisfied that we are doing everything possible to detach
> individuals of importance in Turkey . . . Has Sir H. Rumbold been
> informed that we are ready to offer any terms consistent with our
> obligations to Arabs and Armenians to detach Turkey? . . . I
> suppose we should struggle for terms for the Jews also . . . After
> our victories at Beersheba and Gaza we could afford to be more
> active.

Clerk, who in the meantime had drawn closer to Sykes's point of view,
replied that any soundings for peace might be regarded as a sign of weakness and tend to stiffen Turkish terms. Balfour also thought that for the
British to take the initiative was still too premature, only to provoke Lord
Milner to question the Foreign Minister's judgement. The object of the
military campaign in the East, Milner maintained, was not necessarily 'to
occupy . . . many more square miles of Turkish territory, but so hammer
the Turks that they may get thoroughly sick of the War and want to
come out of it'. However, mere hammering was not enough. The British
must open a door of escape for the Turks and make the prospects of peace
attractive to them. If they were told that dismemberment of the Ottoman Empire was no more than a paper division, and that the Allies were
prepared to forgo the spoils, then Talaat and his party would find it
easier to emancipate themselves from Germany. However, if the British
were fastidious, or lacked adequate channels of communication, perhaps their American friends would be able to suggest a more suitable
approach.[36]

Milner's suggestion conjured up a vision of the defunct Morgenthau
mission being resuscitated. This put Sykes in a quandary. He was senior
enough in rank, and his standing as an expert in Turkish affairs high
enough, to pit his will against Mallet, Tyrrel, or even Cecil, but to cross
swords with a leading member of the War Cabinet was beyond his reach.
It was therefore most fortunate for him that Hankey gave him an opening
by inviting him to air his views on Turkish peace terms. Sykes accepted
the challenge with alacrity. He pointed out that Talaat was fully capable
of killing Enver, allowing someone to make a sham peace, and then
declaring war again by engineering another revolution. Turkish un-
reliability was not the only factor governing Sykes's thinking. Britain,
ointly with France, had certain moral responsibilities:

We are pledged to Zionism, Armenian liberation and Arabian independence. Zionism is the key to the lock. I am sanguine that we can demonstrate to the world that these three elements are prepared to take common action and stand by one another. If once the Turks see the Zionists are prepared to back the Entente and the two oppressed races, they will come to us to negotiate.

To bring this about the British should declare openly that their avowed policy was that Zionism, Armenian and Arab freedom were the Allies' only desiderata; that promotion of an alliance and common action between these three peoples was an immediate objective; and that whilst military operations would be pressed vigorously, the Turks should be told that the Allies harboured no sinister designs against Turkey proper.[37] This amounted to the complete elimination of Turkish influence over her Asiatic provinces (from the Taurus passes southwards), and its super-session by an Arab-Zionist-Armenian Entente under an Anglo-French ægis. It was to serve as an antidote to a soft peace with Turkey and form the nucleus of a new order in the Middle East. Sykes had formulated this concept three or four months earlier. He realised that the Asia Minor Agreement was becoming anachronistic. When originally drawn up, it had provided in selected areas for a certain degree of autonomy for the peoples concerned, but left an avenue open to annexation. By 1917 annexation had become a dirty word, frowned on by the Socialists in Russia and by the United States. If Britain and France were not to be compromised, their policy should be based on the principle of national self-determination. The Agreement should therefore be modified: areas 'A' and 'B' assimilated with the 'blue' and 'red' zones respectively and administered in consonance with the ascertained wishes of the peoples concerned. The Allies would be then on much firmer ground at the future peace conference. With regard to Palestine, because of the Zionists' dislike of any form of internationalisation or condominium, the best solution would be 'to get Great Britain appointed trustee of the Powers'. International administration could be limited to the Holy Places in Jerusalem and Bethlehem, with France granted some position as a patron or protector of the various Catholic institutions elsewhere in the country. In the Arabs, the Zionists, and Armenians Great Britain and France had assets which could be useful at the peace conference. It was therefore their 'duty to get these peoples righted . . . on lines compatible with [their own] economic and political interests'. Otherwise the only beneficiaries would be Turkey and Germany. Sykes wound up:[38]

I want to see a permanent Anglo-French Entente allied to the Jews,

Arabs and Armenians which will render Pan-Islamism innocuous and protect India and Africa from the Turco-German combine.

Sykes's flexible and empirical mind could accommodate the interests of all parties concerned, but his extreme optimism blinded him to the pitfalls. His scheme presupposed a durable alliance with France, which at least in the Middle East proved an illusion. The forces which ranged the two Powers on different sides were too potent to be offset by Sykes's personal harmonious relationship with Picot, or even by the Foreign Office's scrupulous adherence to the terms of the Agreement. In Paris Picot was accused of having given away 'everything' to England, while Sykes was criticised by Curzon and those of like mind for being too indulgent to France.[39] Ribot might publicly deny the German Chancellor's charges of French ambitions to occupy Syria,[40] but in fact France, like Italy, remained annexationist-minded. The Asia Minor Agreement, though originally meant to be provisional, became for France sacred text. This alienated the British establishment in Cairo still further. To them the Agreement—their *bête noire*—was ill-conceived and the sooner it was disowned the better. While both Wingate and Hogarth relentlessly harped on the need for its revision, Clayton preferred to rely on his own ingenuity to render it obsolete. Their argument was that Russia's renunciation of her claim and America's proclaimed principles undermined its validity, and that the justification of British claims outweighed by far those of France. Britain was carrying the main burden of the military campaign in the East, whereas France's contribution was negligible; France was unpopular in the Orient, whereas British protection was desired by 'the majority of the Muslim and Christian Arabs', and by the Zionists.[41]

Sykes's hope that, in return for help to make France more acceptable to the Moslem population in Syria, Paris would agree to the British exclusive control of Palestine, proved equally ill-founded. But the greatest miscalculation concerned the Arabs. The expectation that Pan-Arabism would form an antidote to the Turco-German inspired Pan-Islam, turned out to be false. As a strong believer in the virtues of nationalism, Sykes projected on to the Arabs the image of the nineteenth-century liberation movements in the Balkans. This was doubly an error, for, unlike the Balkan nationalities who were predominantly Christian, and looked to European Powers for help in their struggle against the Ottoman Empire, the Arabs did not regard Turkish rule as alien. Although aware of their separate linguistic and cultural identity, they had no serious desire to cut themselves off from the Ottoman Empire, the embodiment of Islam, legitimised by time and acceptance, their loyalty to which overrode any other. The Arabs considered themselves primarily as Muslim subjects of a Muslim Empire.[42] Their quarrel with the C.U.P. leaders was a domestic issue. It concerned the manner in which the Empire should be governed, but its basic statehood or corporate identity was never questioned. The pre-war Arab national movement was essentially reformist in character. The name of the Decentralisation Party denoted its purpose: administrative rather than political. Muhammad Rashid Rida, one of its founding fathers, unrelentingly stressed the Arabs' loyalty to the Ottoman State and accused the European imperialists of fomenting Arab separatism. The *Fatat* and the *Ahd* secret societies which preached the doctrine that the Arabs must break away, by violence if necessary, from Turkey, did not elicit a response among their fellow-countrymen.[43] The Arab revolt, on which Sykes and his friends pinned so much hope, never materialised. Throughout the war Moslem solidarity proved stronger than British-sponsored Arab nationalism. Hussein stood condemned by the bulk of his co-religionists for assisting the infidel against a Moslem Power. The assumption that Mecca could supplant Constantinople as the nerve-centre of the Arab world proved wrong, and by March 1918 a meeting of senior British officers in the East, chaired by General Wingate,[44] conceded that politically the Arab movement was a failure. There was little sympathy for the Sharifians in the Moslem world. In Arabia proper, the Imam, Idrisi, and Ibn Saud rejected Hussein as their temporal overlord; so did the inhabitants of Syria and Mesopotamia. Egyptian opinion disdained him,[45] and in India the Moslems regarded him as 'a rebel . . . and a poor substitute for H.M. the Sultan of Turkey'.[46]

Sykes was much influenced (as other British officers were) by Dr Faris Nimr, the editor of *Mokattam*, and Said Pasha Shucair, a Moslem notable, when he met them in Cairo in July 1915. Both pro-British, they thought that in the foreseeable future Syria would not be able to exist as an independent state 'even for a day', and that therefore some form of European control was indispensable. Realistic as this assessment was, the authentic voice of Syrian intellectual nationalists was that of Rashid Rida, whom Sykes quite mistakenly thought had no personal following. Rida was a theologian and a publicist, subsequently a politician of note, who had made his mark on Pan-Arab and Pan-Islamic thought early in the war. He impressed Sykes as an 'uncompromising, fanatical Moslem', whose first loyalty was to Constantinople. Turkey symbolised for him Mohammedan independence, but should she suffer a military defeat, he thought it would be necessary to set up instead 'an absolutely independent' Arab-Moslem state stretching from the northern borders of Syria and Mesopotamia down to Arabia. He refused to entertain the idea of control by European Powers or the appointment of European advisers exercising authority. 'The Arabs could easily manage their own affairs.'[47]

Rida's views were coloured by his positive dislike of the European way of life and hostility to Christianity. The fact that Hussein made himself dependent on a non-Muslim Power, made Rida a bitter opponent of the Hashimite family; their revolt against Turkey was 'the worst disaster that has befallen Islam in this age'. England was 'the enemy of Islam; "The British Government",' he wrote, ' "has taken upon itself to destroy the religion of Islam . . . after destroying its temporal rule".'[48]

Not all Britons disregarded these feelings. In 1915 the de Bunsen committee was fully aware of them, as well as of the risks involved should Turkey be dismembered. A devolutionary scheme allowing a gradual development from autonomy to independence under nominal Ottoman suzerainty, was in their opinion more in harmony with the aspirations of the non-Turkish nationalities.[49] The prospect of a general Arab uprising proved however too alluring, and the spectre of Germany gaining the upper hand in the Middle East too alarming for the findings of the Committee to prevail. But the price had to be paid. The likelihood of the Ottoman Empire's collapse gave rise to a great deal of agitation throughout the Islamic world and, with General Murray's troops knocking, albeit unsuccessfully, at the gates of Gaza, the Syrian colony in Cairo was deeply disturbed. Consequently, the Arab Decentralisation Party took a more radical position, preaching 'complete independence of all Arab territories, including Syria'. Despite Picot's assurances that no annexation was contemplated and that autonomy and independence was the eventual aim of the Entente, the Arabs and Syrians remained sceptical. President Wilson's declaration on America's war aims had an electrifying effect on the Syrian and Arab nationalists, and Wingate had good reason to fear that, should Morgenthau's devolutionary scheme for Syria leak out in Egypt, the Turcophile Arab Decentralisation Party would turn to America for support against the West European allies. For the latter's difficulties Wingate blamed the French, depicting them as the stumbling-block, once removed, would enable the British to get on with the Arabs perfectly well. But Hogarth was nearer the truth when conceding five months later that the Arab and Syrian nationalists wanted neither the French nor the British as their protectors.[50]

For Arab nationalism was essentially Moslem,[51] and as such it was also anti-European and anti-Christian.[52] Here lay the root of the difficulty of marrying Western imperialism, even in its enlightened form, with Arab nationalism. It explains why an Arab-Zionist-Armenian entente was difficult to implement. The Syrian and Palestinian Arabs might have had their own reasons for disliking the Zionists, but it was the latter's association with a European Power which prejudiced in advance any chance of an understanding. Their objectives were diametrically opposed: the Zionists considered British protection indispensable to their security and development, whereas the Arabs hoped to dispense with it.

To General Clayton, Sykes's scheme of an Arab-Zionist-Armenian entente looked unreal. Arab-Syrian particularism was rife, and with the intense factional in-fighting, there was hardly any starting-point from which to build a wider combination. Disunity among the Arabs was not at all disadvantageous, since, as he told Wingate in January 1916, it was 'our main safeguard against the establishment of a united [Arab] Kingdom which might be a threat to British interests'.[53] But by the summer of 1917 disagreement among the Arabs was no longer an asset, since it prevented him from working out a coherent policy. Ignorant of Whitehall's relations with the Zionists, Clayton feared additional complications. On 20 August he wrote to Sykes:[54]

> Lack of any knowledge of the policy, of any, decided upon as regards the Jewish question makes it increasingly difficult to deal with Aaronsohn and other Jews who are becoming restive and impatient. If no definite line has yet been settled we can quite well keep them in play—but we ought to know. Indeed, I am not sure that it is not as well to refrain from any definite pronouncement just at present. It will not help matters if the Arabs—already somewhat distracted between pro-Sherifians and those who fear Meccan domination, as also between pro-French and anti-French— are given yet another bone of contention in the shape of Zionism in Palestine as against the interests of the Moslems resident there. The more politics can be kept in the background, the more likely are the Arabs to concentrate on the expulsion of the Turks from Syria, which, if successful, will do more than anything to promote Arab unity and national feeling.

Lawrence too seemed worried at that time about London's Zionist policy. On 12 August when Aaronsohn met him, he felt he was listening to a scientific-minded Prussian anti-Semite speaking English: 'If the Jews will favour the Arabs they shall be spared, otherwise they shall have their throats cut.'[55] A year later both Clayton and Lawrence had come to realise that Zionism was a profitable card for the British to play. Linked with the Sharifian movement, it could constitute one of the twin pillars on which the British position in the region could rest. But in 1917 they still feared that its introduction would undermine their tenuous relationship with the Arabs. However, it was not Clayton's advice that delayed the publication of the British declaration of sympathy with Zionism but the controversy among the Jews themselves.

14 The Conjoint Foreign Committee and the Zionists

In July 1915 negotiations between the Conjoint Foreign Committee and the Zionists reached a deadlock. It was not until August of the following year that a new round of discussions began when James de Rothschild, at his father's instigation (Edmund de Rothschild in Paris) invited both Weizmann and Wolf to a private meeting at his home. Nothing positive was achieved, however; the disputants merely restated their positions. Wolf hoped that the question of Jewish nationality and of 'special rights' in Palestine would be kept in abeyance, but to Weizmann this was not possible, since Jewish nationalism was fundamental to Zionist philosophy. Characteristically, he refused to theorise and contented himself with probing Wolf's reaction to the possibility of the Zionists establishing independent relations with the British Government. At first equivocal, Wolf finally decided that there were 'vital and irreconcilable differences of principle and method'. These, he told James de Rothschild, transpired from the recently published essays entitled Zionism and the Jewish Future,[1] from which he concluded that the Zionists did not merely propose to establish a Jewish nationality in Palestine but claimed that 'all the Jews [formed] . . . a separate and dispossessed nationality, for which it is necessary to find an organic political centre'. Statements to this effect, particularly when penned by such leading spokesmen as Weizmann and Gaster, could justify the theory of total Jewish alienation and play directly into the hands of anti-Semites, with the result that the situation in Russia and Rumania 'would become the common lot of Jewry throughout the world'.[2]

Wolf's fear was caused by his misreading of the term 'nationality' mistaking conformity for civic loyalty. In popular usage the term denotes membership of a nation, that is a people bound together by ethnic, religious, or linguistic ties, as distinguished from a somewhat narrower term, citizenship, used to denote the status of those nationals with full political privileges. Only in the latter case does nationality imply a duty of allegiance to a State and the right to enjoy its protection. The Zionists thought in categories accepted in Central and Eastern Europe, where the term *Nationalität*, though etymologically akin to the English word 'nationality', was semantically different and bore a distinct ethnic connotation[3] but Wolf and his friends followed the English usage, applicable strictly in a legal-political sense. Sokolow, who endeavoured to dispel Wolf's misconception, took pains to explain that for the Zionists nationality was an ethnographical and cultural concept, not one of citizenship. Hence the apprehension that Zionist ideology could invalidate the Jewish claim to political rights in a non-Jewish country was groundless. 'Alien', as used by Weizmann was meant in a spiritual sense and referred to an individual who differed from his neighbours in mentality and characteristics, which had nothing to do with citizenship and cast no reflection on a man's loyalty or patriotism, as the example of the Welsh and the Scots in Britain showed. Only those Jews living in Palestine would constitute a nation, or a nationality, in a political sense, and it was therefore erroneous to assure that the national centre in Palestine would claim political allegiance from Jews living elsewhere. The *raison d'être* of the Palestinian centre was to create a favourable milieu for uninhibited self-expression, and to deepen Jewish national consciousness in the Diaspora. 'The Jewish people need not bread alone and not political rights alone.'[4]

Wolf finally admitted that his fears about 'special rights' were exaggerated. He was also satisfied with Sokolow's assurances that the notion of a privileged Jewish class was 'utterly foreign' to Zionist principles, and had no place in their programme; they stood for equality of political rights and of economic opportunities for 'all classes, creeds, races and nationalities in Palestine'. However, with regard to the question of Jewish nationality, Wolf was not reassured. He realised that the 'cultural policy' was not as innocuous as he had originally imagined; it was merely a euphemism for national indoctrination. The idea of Pan-Hebraic nationalism was bound to alienate the Jews from their environment and give rise to dangerous misunderstandings. He had no objection to the development of Jewish nationalism in Palestine, but in other countries it was 'an empty word which can do no good'. Otherwise, he was satisfied to find in Sokolow's memorandum 'an appreciable approximation' to his own views and a possible basis for negotiation and eventual agreement.[5]

If this was what he hoped for, his lecture given in Edinburgh in March 1917 was not calculated to promote this end. He reiterated the thesis that the Jews had always been a religious community; the passage of two thousand years had made them a European people; their prayers for the restoration of Jerusalem had merely a symbolic meaning. The Great Sanhedrin of 1807 had given their verdict on Jewish identity, and the idea of a secular nationalism was 'a new and utterly revolutionary departure in Jewish life . . . not essentially bound up with Judaism . . . substitution of the national for the religious bond has operated destructively against all religious observance.' Moreover, with the prevailing tendency in Western Europe towards ethnic and cultural homogeneity, for the Jews to assert a distinct nationality was inexpedient and risky; the Zionists were confusing eschatology with politics.

Wolf's lecture, entitled 'The Jewish National Movement', was published in April 1917 in the *Edinburgh Review* and subsequently issued as a pamphlet. It coincided with the appearance of two other pamphlets, one by Sir Philip Magnus, M.P., *Jewish Action and Jewish Ideals*, a reprint of an article in the *Jewish Chronicle* of 13 November 1891, and one by Claude G. Montefiore, *Nation or Religious Community*, a reprint of the Presidential address to the Jewish Historical Society of England on 3 December 1899. Time had not changed the beliefs of the writers, or diluted their aversion to nationalism, which for the Jews, in Magnus's words, was 'a step backward, a reversal of the law of historical development'.

The appearance of several pamphlets in rapid succession, and their selective distribution was taken by the Zionists as a calculated move to discredit their ideology. A reply was given by Leon Simon, a student of Ahad Ha'am, a rising publicist and scholar. Judaism, he maintained, needed not a diffusion but a concentration of its resources. Without a centre, without its own milieu where it could flourish, disintegration, both cultural and physical, was inevitable. The notion that Judaism was merely a universal religion, without historical and national associations, was a chimera. In this respect the rulings of the Great Sanhedrin were of dubious validity since they had been dictated by local political exigencies, regardless of the position of the Jewish masses in Eastern Europe. Nationality was a state of mind, not necessarily identical with the status of citizenship. The problem of dual political allegiance was therefore illusory. Zionism was not merely a reaction to anti-Semitism. It stood for the unity of the Jewish people as an ethnic group, with a home in Palestine as its centre.[6]

Two years earlier, Harry Sacher had also claimed that it was the anti-national Jew rather than the Gentile who usually raised the question whether Zionism and patriotism were compatible. Typical of British thought was what Lord Acton had written sixty years earlier: The combination of different nations enriched civilised life; the coexistence of several nations under the same state was 'a test as well as best security of freedom.'[7] It was in keeping with this concept that Herbert Samuel, in his already cited memorandum, reached the conclusion he did; and on the other side of the Atlantic, in June 1915, Brandeis advised his country-men:[8]

> Let no American imagine that Zionism is inconsistent with patriotism. Multiple loyalties are objectionable only if they are inconsistent . . . Every Irish-American who contributed towards advancing Home Rule was a better man and a better American . . . Every American Jew who aids in advancing the Jewish settlement in Palestine, though he feels that neither he nor his descendants will ever live there, will likewise be a better man and a better American for doing so.

The anti-Zionists missed this point and failed to realise, that unlike France or Germany, in English-speaking countries the concept of diversity, not uniformity, held the field. But the most peculiar aspect of the controversy was its unreality. Since the Zionists were not seeking to establish a Jewish state immediately, questions of political allegiance did not arise. The only political allegiance was to be to the government in Palestine which was envisaged as British. The Foreign Office was at a loss to follow the dispute as Oliphant's minute shows: 'When Jews fall out, it is none too easy for Christians to decide whether the Zionists or anti-Zionists are in the wrong.'[9]

Though the Zionists and the anti-Zionists were poles apart in the realm of ideology, a working compromise between them was not beyond reach. Careful comparison between Wolf's 'formula' and the Zionist pro-gramme[10] shows that on practical matters the differences were only of emphasis and degree. While Wolf referred to 'reasonable facilities for immigration and colonisation', the Zionists demanded 'liberty of immigration to Jews of all countries'. Wolf suggested that the Jewish population in Palestine should be secured in the enjoyment of civil and religious liberty, equal political rights with the rest of the population, as well as 'municipal privileges in towns and colonies', whereas the Zionists claimed the right 'to enjoy full national, political and civic rights [and] . . . internal autonomy'. Late in October 1917, when the British Government was consulting all shades of Jewish opinion on the draft declaration, the out-standing elements in Montefiore's proposal were: 'free and unimpeded Jewish immigration into Palestine . . . unrestricted Jewish colonisation . . . such municipal and local autonomy for the Jews . . . as circumstances may demand'.[11] This was an exact echo of the Zionist practical school of thought which dominated during the pre-war period and officially was still valid for the Berlin Zionist Executive.

True, the London Zionist Programme of November 1916 demanded that Palestine be recognised as 'the Jewish National Home' and that the Suzerain Government should grant a Charter to a Jewish Company for Colonisation and Development, but Wolf's 'formula', by his own admission, was not necessarily a programme and, given an opportunity for joint discussion, it could still be modified. It emphasised 'the historic interest' of Palestine for the Jews all over the world and, save for the principle of Jewish nationhood, he was convinced, it was only a variation of the Basle Programme which referred to 'a home . . . secured by public law'.[12] Only two questions remained controversial: that of the Chartered Company, and nationality. Following Sokolow's explanation, Wolf waived his objections to the first item and with regard to the second, he made an important step forward when declaring to Balfour, at the end of January 1917, that the Conjoint Committee would have no objection if the Jewish community in Palestine developed into 'a local Jewish nation and a Jewish State', provided it 'did not claim the allegiance of the Jews of Western Europe', or demand a privileged status *vis-à-vis* the non-Jewish population. Apart from these reservations, he assured Balfour, the Conjoint Committee left 'a perfectly free hand to the Zionists, and [was] even disposed, within certain limits, to co-operate with them in promoting their schemes'.[13] This was in fact, if Wolf was to be believed, what the Committee meant when publishing their letter to *The Times* of 24 May. He told Jacques Bigart, secretary of the Alliance Israélite:[14]

> If you will read our Statement carefully, you will find that it concedes almost everything of any practical importance to the Zionists. It favours a Jewish settlement; it favours self-government for such a settlement; it even engages not to oppose a national status for such a settlement; so long as the nationality is a local one, and is agreeable to the Sovereign Power. The only objection . . . relates to safeguarding the position of Jews in other countries. What we say, in effect, is: 'Do what you please in Palestine, and we will not obstruct you; we may even support you; but do not interfere with us; do not jeopardise our position as loyal nationals of the country in which we live.'

Wolf was unaware that the Zionists had adopted an identical position. Whatever their concept of Jewish identity, they were sensible enough to restrict its application to Palestine. The London Bureau Programme of November 1916 ('The Demands') stated unequivocally that only 'the Jewish population in Palestine (present and future) to be officially recognised by the Suzerain Government as possessing national status.'[15] In a letter to Brandeis, Sokolow explained the motives of Zionist policy:[16]

To spare a collision with the Assimilationists we do not attempt to meddle with the national or religious conception of Jews in other countries [than Palestine] whether they consider themselves as a nation, race or religion. We content ourselves with recognising the Jews in Palestine, present and future, as a nationality . . . leaving all theoretical discussions with regard to Diaspora to time and the free will of the individual. . . . We may or may not defend Jewish nationalism in the Diaspora . . . but we are concerned with its development only in Palestine.

At the meeting with Sykes at Gaster's home on 7 February 1917,[17] Gaster made it clear that a Jewish nationality in Palestine would not interfere with the loyalty of Jews outside Palestine. Weizmann thought it essential that 'the Jews who went to Palestine would constitute [there] a Jewish nation'. Herbert Samuel pointed out that 'if it was intended to create in Palestine a Jewish nation *eo nomine*, care must be taken to explain the sense in which the term was used'. To which Sacher replied that only a state involved political obligations. A nation was a spiritual entity and implied no civic duties. He elaborated this point in a memorandum written a few months later:[18]

A Jewish National Home in Palestine would exact *political* obligation only from such Jews as were citizens of Palestine. Other Jews would owe it no *political* obligation. It would, however, be a centre of spiritual influence, an exemplar of the genuinely Jewish life . . . But that *spiritual* tie would be purely voluntary, a matter for free acceptance or rejection by the individual Jew.

This principle fitted admirably with the Conjoint Committee's expectations. However, if no rapprochement with the Zionists was forthcoming, it was not because areas for agreement were lacking but because neither party was aware of their existence. The irony of the episode was that, though both parties genuinely recognised the need for some display of unity, neither was prepared to compromise. In fact, there was much more common ground for a working arrangement than the Zionists and the Conjoint Committee realised, but with channels of communications blocked, and relations charged with suspicion and antipathy, this could not surface.

That an understanding was possible was demonstrated during the peace conference in Paris when mutual distrust evaporated. In their 'Statement of Policy on the Palestine Question', the Joint Foreign Committee on behalf of the Anglo-Jewish community urged:

that the political, economic and moral organisation of the country be such as to facilitate the increase and self-government of the Jewish population with a view to its eventual predominance in the government of the State in accordance with the principles of democracy.

Unlike the Zionists, the Committee refrained from using the term 'autonomous Commonwealth' although this was clearly the implication of their text. They emphasised that Jews all over the world did not constitute a separate political nationality, or owe the future Government of Palestine their political allegiance. With this exception, there was little difference between the Committee's statement and that of the Zionists.[19]

This was in the spring of 1919. Two years earlier the controversy had been at its peak. At the root of the trouble was absence of a dialogue. The fault was not entirely that of the Conjoint Committee. In a speech at a meeting of the Board of Deputies at the end of October 1916, David Alexander expressed the desire to reach some understanding with the Zionists.[20] Sokolow welcomed the proposal, but despite assurances of mutual goodwill the correspondence soon lapsed into an exchange of formalities. What happened was that the Zionists, moving to a higher plane of diplomacy following their crucial meeting with Sykes, found it more congenial to cultivate their relations with the British Government on their own. Puzzled and irritated by the delay, Wolf pressed for a resumption of joint conferences, only to elicit from Sokolow the formula of the Basle programme as a pre-condition for further negotiations. In the Committee's eyes this meant total capitulation, and was duly rejected.[21] Negotiations never got off the ground.

The publication of Wolf's article in the *Edinburgh Review* raised the temperature further, but it was the news that the Zionist programme had been approved in principle by both the British and French Governments that brought the crisis to the boil. This information was reported to Wolf by Bigart, following Sokolow's meeting with the Alliance's representatives in Paris. Wolf now feared that should the nationalist doctrine, as espoused by Weizmann and Gaster, be officially adopted, the position of emancipated Jews as citizens of their native countries would be in great danger.[22] Alarmed at the prospect of being presented with a *fait accompli*, he told the Zionists bluntly that the Conjoint Committee must now resume full liberty of action and reserve for themselves the right to publish the correspondence that had passed between them.[23] At the same time he sought to find out from the Foreign Office whether Bigart's report was correct, since

a great injustice would be done to the Anglo-Jewish community, and very serious mischief might result, if an agreement on the Palestine question were concluded without our participation, more especially as the gentlemen with whom His Majesty's Government have so far been in negotiation, are all foreign Jews, having no quality [sic] to speak for the native Jews of the United Kingdom.

He reminded the Foreign Office that the Committee's right to speak on the Palestine question had been raised as early as 1 October 1916, in their letter to Viscount Grey, then Foreign Secretary.[24]

The Zionists were not perturbed. There was nothing improper in the correspondence that could cast doubt on their bona fides, but in Sokolow's absence Joseph Cowen advised Wolf against publication as it would be prejudicial to common Jewish interests. Cowen's advice followed closely on James de Rothschild's protest to Wolf; the correspondence was strictly private, and he had agreed to act as intermediary on the understanding that none of it would reach the press.[25] The Foreign Office too warned Wolf to refrain from polemics in public, while the Palestine question was under consideration, but Wolf, strongly suspecting that Rothschild, or still worse, Weizmann was behind the warning, was in no mood to listen to advice. He assured the Foreign Office that the Committee did not contemplate public polemics, but, as their negotiations with the Zionists had reached deadlock, publication of the correspondence was necessary. 'This, however, is an internal communal matter, in which ... the Foreign Office would not desire to interfere.'[26] On this Lord Drogheda minuted:

> This shows how warily we must walk in encouraging Zionism. We are not committed definitely to Zionism yet ... certainly not to the full realization of Zionist aspirations—and ... we can safely reply that the Conjoint Foreign Committee can rest assured that their views have not been lost sight of and that no new policy in regard to the future of Palestine will be adopted by His Majesty's Government without every opportunity being given to all sections of the British Jewish Community to express their views on this question.

This minute was written on the very day Cecil received Weizmann and reinforced his doubt whether Weizmann's views mirrored those of the Anglo-Jewish community as a whole. Two days later Graham informed Wolf that no agreement on the Palestine question had been reached and that the Government was 'sincerely anxious to act in all matters affecting the Jewish community not only in its best interests but with due regard to the wishes and opinions of all its sections, and they will not depart from these guiding principles.' However, Wolf was still uneasy until he met Cecil who, repeating Graham's statement, emphasised that the Government would 'never make arrangements without taking into account, if not consulting, the whole of Jewish opinion'. At the same time he cautioned Wolf against entering into any public controversy as this would be both embarrassing to the Government and harmful to the Jewish community.[27]

Notwithstanding these assurances, Montefiore sought a separate interview with Lord Milner. He was heartened to hear that the attitude towards the Zionists was still undetermined, and though the Prime Minister was sympathetic, the Palestine question had lost some of its urgency due to the setbacks on the Gaza front. Milner thought that Montefiore was exaggerating the dangers of Zionism. It was ridiculous to suppose, he said, that an autonomous Jewish community in Palestine under a British Protectorate would in any way jeopardise the civil rights of Jews in countries such as the United States, Great Britain or France. As for Russia, if the liberal régime survived, 'a Jewish Commonwealth in Palestine would not upset the emancipation'. Should the reactionary régime return to power, however, 'the Jews would have a bad time, even if no single Jew were in Palestine at all. So *mutatis mutandis* as regards Roumania.' The causes of anti-Semitism did not relate to the status of the Jewish community in Palestine. 'He clearly thought', Montefiore recorded, 'that, in our dislike of Zionism, we greatly exaggerated its importance and dangers.'[28]

Despite these firm promises, on 17 May, the day after Montefiore's interview with Milner, the Conjoint Committee, flouting all advice, embarked on a path calculated to bring a showdown with the Zionists.

In view of . . . the rupture of the negotiations with the Zionists; the energy with which [they] were prosecuting their plans, the favour with which these plans were regarded in official quarters, and Mr. Sokolow's mission to the French and Italian Governments—the Presidents decided to submit to the Conjoint Foreign Committee a definite Statement of Policy on the Palestine Question, with the recommendation that it should be published at an early date.

By twelve votes, with two abstentions, the hastily convened meeting endorsed the statement to be issued to the press.[29]

Dr Hertz, the Chief Rabbi, who was present by invitation but without a vote, dissented from the proposed action and walked out. Fearing a schism within the community, he implored Wolf on the following day not to publish the statement; it was foolish to attach so much importance to Weizmann's and Gaster's essays. But Wolf would not yield; publication was 'inevitable'. Learning from Hertz what was afoot, Leopold Greenberg also tried to avert the impending storm; the quarrel must not be made public or brought to the advice of the Foreign Office. But Wolf had made up his mind; the Committee could no longer remain silent as their constituents were becoming impatient and demanding information.[30]

To forestall an explosion the Zionist members of the Board of Deputies, at a meeting on 20 May, introduced a conciliatory motion: British Jews hoped that 'the historical claims of the Jewish people on their ancient homeland will be recognized and that Palestine will be made a Jewish centre'. The text avoided the controversial issue of nationalism, and in fact contained all the elements which, by their own admission, were acceptable to the anti-Zionists. None the less, after a spirited debate, the resolution was defeated by thirty-three votes to twenty-one. The Zionist members were not discouraged and introduced a second motion:

> Now that the establishment of a Jewish Home in Palestine is a matter of practical politics this Board recommends that the Conjoint Foreign Committee enter into negotiations with the Zionist Authorities with a view to formulating a joint policy to be presented to the British Government; and that in the event of a mutual policy being agreed upon a manifesto be immediately issued to that effect.

This formula too had to be withdrawn.[31] Whether Weizmann's address made on the same morning to a Zionist Conference in London, helped to stiffen the anti-Zionist stand is a matter for conjecture. Weizmann declared that a Jewish Commonwealth was the Zionists' final ideal. 'I am entitled to state that His Majesty's Government is ready to support our plans.' He rebuked the 'small minority' which disputed the very existence of the Jews as a nation and held it responsible for the disunity within the Jewish ranks. 'But', he added:[32]

> if it comes to a plebiscite . . . there can be no doubt on which side the majority of Jews will be found . . . We do not want to give the world the spectacle of a war of brothers . . . But we warn those who will force an open breach that they will find us prepared . . . We say to all our opponents, 'Hands off the Zionist Movement'.

The warning remained unheeded. The decision had been taken three days earlier and there was no going back. In defiance of his own promise, Wolf authorised the publication of the 'Statement' in *The Times* (24 May) before showing it to Cecil. The next day he was embarrassed to receive a note from Graham saying that Lord Robert wished to see a copy of the

Statement before it was made public. Apologetically, Wolf admitted that the publication had been 'a little hurried', but there was no getting over the fact that he had violated his pledge. In an attempt to mollify the Foreign Office he pointed out that the 'Statement' had been drawn up in 'most conciliatory terms', and that it could well serve as 'a starting point for fresh negotiations, and as the basis for a compromise'.[33] This ignored the fact that the Zionist motion, submitted and rejected at the meeting of the Board of Deputies on 20 May, could offer a compromise. Nor could the Committee complain at being presented with a *fait accompli* by the Zionists, since no pledge had been given by either side to abstain from negotiations with the British Government or its Allies. On the contrary, at the first joint meeting on 14 April 1915[34] it was agreed that 'nothing that took place at the Conferences should be held to bind either side', as Wolf himself reminded a meeting of the Anglo-Jewish Association on 3 June 1917, when he was criticised by Rabbi Gaster for negotiating (early in 1916) with the Foreign Office behind the Zionists' backs.[35] By bringing the question into the open, the Committee no doubt hoped to force the issue their way. But if their purpose was to make the Zionists more pliable —the term 'compromise' being used as a synonym for bringing them into line—the method chosen was self-defeating.

The Zionists were furious. Lord Rothschild declared in a letter to *The Times* (27 May):

> We Zionists cannot see how the establishment of an autonomous Jewish State under the ægis and protection of one of the Allied Powers can be considered for a moment to be in any way subversive to the position or loyalty of the very large part of the Jewish people who have identified themselves thoroughly with the citizenship of the countries in which they live.

The Chartered Company, he went on, was merely a directing agency for immigration and colonisation; the Zionists had 'no wish for privileges at the expense of other nationalities'. Weizmann also stated in the same issue that it was 'a cardinal and immutable principle of Zionism to see that all races and sects in Palestine should enjoy full justice and liberty'; the Chartered Company would not be administered to the detriment of others.

If the Conjoint Committee hoped to find in *The Times* a favourable platform they were mistaken. Wickham Steed, the editor, was friendly to the Zionists[36] and his leader (29 May) left no doubt where his sympathies lay. He dismissed the contentions of assimilationists as fallacious and degrading. 'Only an imaginary nervousness suggests that the realization of territorial Zionism . . . would cause Christendom to round on the Jews and say, "Now you have a land of your own, go to it".' The Zionist movement had fired millions of poverty-stricken Jews in the ghettoes with a new ideal. 'It tended to make [them] proud of their race and to claim recognition, as Jews.'

Montefiore and Alexander, realising that they had miscalculated, tried to backtrack. Through an intermediary, they informed Zionists that they were still willing to negotiate, provided both parties dropped their respective pre-conditions and the *status quo ante* was restored. But the position could not be reversed; now it was the Zionists whose attitude hardened. Weizmann, at any rate, was in no mood to compromise. He thought it useless to join hands with those whose attitude to Palestine did not go beyond philanthropy. If the Zionist Organisation in the course of negotiations were compelled to shelve even one iota of its programme, it would lose its identity and sense of direction. A renewed suggestion that agreement on a common constructive policy was still possible, elicited no response. Nor did the call of the Anglo-Jewish Association for a *modus vivendi* find a sympathetic ear. The Manifesto in *The Times* embittered the Zionists to such a degree that cordial relations were no longer possible and on 11 June Wolf's suggestion for a resumption of joint conferences was finally rejected.[37]

Emotions apart, the Zionists had reason to assume that they could dispense with their opponents' co-operation. The Foreign Office was moving towards a more definite commitment, and there was a noticeable change of opinion among the Anglo-Jewish community as well. That Lord Rothschild and the Chief Rabbi[38] had identified themselves openly with their cause was a great gain. A movement to draw orthodox Jewry nearer to Zionism was gathering momentum and a special conference of Rabbis was to be convened. Also mooted was the idea of a general Jewish Congress in Britain. None of this materialised, but the Zionists had reason to feel that the balance of opinion had begun to tilt definitely in their favour. The London Lodge of the B'nai Brith, a non-Zionist body, took the lead in a movement to unseat the Conjoint Committee[39] and on 23 June a mass meeting of the Jewish National Union expressed its conviction that the recognition of the principle of Jewish nationality was 'essential for the solution of the Jewish problem'. It pledged its support for the creation of a 'permanent Home for the Jewish people in the Holy Land'. The Union consisted of thirty-six associations and institutions with an aggregate membership of over ten thousand. Its President was Rabbi Gaster.[40]

The Executive Committee of the Jewish Congress in South Africa (the representative body of that community) protested strongly against the Manifesto in *The Times* and affirmed their conviction that 'only by the re-establishment of an autonomous national centre in Palestine can the future of Jewry be secured, that such a solution can in no way injure the position or status of Jewish citizens in countries' of their domicile.[41] On 4 June the Council of the United Jewish Societies of the Anglo-Jewish Association expressed its 'profound disapproval' . . . and dissatisfaction at the conduct of the Conjoint Committee and asked its representative on the Committee to resign. Wolf could not draw much comfort from the Alliance Israélite either. In vain he implored his friends in Paris to issue a parallel statement in the press, especially as British Jewry had so persistently adhered to and indeed advocated the principles enunciated by the Great Sanhedrin. Bigart, whilst assuring him that no change in the Alliance's traditional attitude to Zionism had taken place, regretted that he could not follow suit.[42]

But the greatest shock that the assimilationists suffered was the resolution passed at a meeting of the Board of Deputies on 17 June, by a majority of 56 votes to 51, expressing 'profound disapproval [of] the views of the Conjoint Committee as promulgated in the communication published in *The Times*'. The assault was led by the B'nai Brith members of the Board, but the Zionists too could congratulate themselves on their successful lobbying. The resolution added that the Committee had lost the confidence of the Board and called upon its representatives to resign.[43] The latter were accused of taking undue liberty in matters of high policy without consulting the constituent bodies of the Committee. The balance of power within the Board of Deputies had now changed.

Wolf had to put the best face on it that he could when explaining the vote of censure to the Foreign Office the following day: the confrontation had shown that the warring parties were 'more evenly balanced' than had been generally supposed but, considering that the foreign element in the community outnumbered the native-born, and the poor outnumbered the well-to-do, the division showed that 'not only are the English-born and well-to-do classes on the side of the Conjoint Committee, but that a large portion of the foreign and poor elements are also on that side'. He concluded: 'My own impression is that eventually very considerable constitutional changes will be made, but these will not be to the advantage of the Zionists.' His arguments carried little conviction. Harold Nicolson minuted: 'Evidently Mr. Wolf is now in decline,' and Graham was clear: 'This is a very different opinion to that held by the Zionists . . . I believe this note signifies the dissolution of the Conjoint Foreign Committee.'[44]

Graham was right. Not only was the Conjoint Committee dissolved; the leadership of Anglo-Jewry was radically changed. Sir Stuart Samuel, M.P., Herbert Samuel's brother, accepted the office of President of the Board of Deputies, Lord Rothschild became one of the two Vice-Presidents, and Nathan Laski, the recognised head of the Manchester Jewish community and a foremost opponent of the anti-Zionists, was elected treasurer. There was more than a change of leadership; the spirit that henceforth animated the Board marked a definite break with the past. With the *ancien régime* coming to an end, the Foreign Office was no longer bound by a previous commitment and could move freely towards a closer association with the Zionists.

The episode became a *cause célèbre* in Anglo-Jewish history, a monument to mutual misunderstanding. The Zionists never forgave the Conjoint leaders for advertising their opposition in *The Times*. Yet it would be wrong to condemn outright these otherwise respected figures in the Anglo-Jewish community. Their action was panicky and ill-judged, not malevolent. That they could have committed such a blunder was a sad commentary on their state of mind. The danger they wanted to ward off was but a product of their own imagination.

On the other hand, the Zionists were guilty of indiscretions which tended to magnify their opponents' suspicions. Sensible enough to restrict the application of the concept of Jewish nationality to Palestine, they blundered in not making those most concerned aware of their thinking. A timely gesture might well have averted the crisis. This omission was compounded by presentation of the Basle Programme as a pre-condition for the resumption of negotiations. For the Conjoint Committee this plank was a non-starter, and thus the chance of any meeting of minds, let alone of a closer understanding of each other's point of view, was wrecked in advance. With their diplomatic status in the spring of 1917 elevated, the Zionists chose to go it alone in their dealings with the British Government. But since the agreement between the Committee and the Foreign Office was still in force, such tactics could not lead them far. It is indeed doubtful whether the British Government would have ventured to issue a declaration of sympathy with Zionism before consulting all sections of the Anglo-Jewish community. In the circumstances, the Committee could have done the Zionists no greater service than by acting as they did and thereby bringing upon themselves their own defeat, although it was only a narrow majority at the Board of Deputies that gave victory to the Zionists.

The Committee's downfall was not accidental. Their concept could not withstand the test of the times. The Jewish problem was too complex to be solved by emancipation alone; it was an illusion to expect anti-Semitism to abate once emancipation became general. Prejudice cannot be legislated out of existence, and the formula of an Englishman, Frenchman, or German of Jewish persuasion did not meet the case. But it was primarily the aftermath of Jewish emancipation in Russia in the spring of 1917 that confounded the theory of Wolf and his friends. It took only a few months for their cloudless optimism to give way to mounting concern about the recurrence of anti-Semitism.[45] By contrast, the Zionists were spared much of the shock. As realists, they anticipated that some disorders might take place at the end of the war and their policy was shaped accordingly. As early as April 1917, when the Jewish world was still dazzled by the newly-won liberties of their co-religionists in Russia, Lord Rothschild was far-sighted enough to write to Weizmann:[46]

Apart from the first and foremost great national aims and sentiments of our people which are strikingly and consistently being urged now in every country, there is to my mind a very much greater need for establishing *the real Jewish nation again in Palestine*. We must think of the future; the bulk, quite 40%, of the Russian nation is illiterate and uneducated and have been urged on for centuries against the Jews. Our people are the educated class in Russia, therefore now that they have equal rights they will forge *ahead and outside the rest of the Russian Peoples in all walks of life and thus raise up a new form of hatred and envy*. Therefore, we ought by urging on our government here to adopt the *Zionist cause* as their own to enable us to reduce the number of Jews remaining in Russia as much as possible and so lessen the chances of future trouble. The national aspirations must, of course, take first place but I feel sure we shall do wrong if we do not keep the possibility of *future Russian trouble* well to the front in the Zionist programme.

The spectacular rise of Zionism in Russia gave the lie to the Conjoint Committee's forecast that liberalisation would deal a death blow to Jewish nationalism. To equate conditions in Russia with those in Western Europe a hundred years earlier was misleading, for unlike the French Revolution of 1789, the Russian Revolution of March 1917 granted liberties not only to the individual but also to national minorities. This spared the Russian Jew the dilemma which confronted the Great Sanhedrin, and left them free to determine their identity.[47]

The notion that Jewish nationalism was incompatible with patriotism and prejudicial to civic status was an even greater fallacy, as the course of events after the Balfour Declaration showed. Not only did the civic status of the Jews in the West remain unaffected, but on 28 June 1918 the Foreign Office reassured Wolf that the British Government 'have the closest sympathy with the emancipation of the Jews in Eastern and South Eastern Europe and are anxious to do everything in their power to secure a just and permanent settlement of the Jewish question throughout the regions concerned'.[48]

At the root of the assimilationists' failure lay the application of the doctrine enunciated by the Great Sanhedrin to the British scene; and the Anglo-Jewish establishment, in insisting that adjustment of their identity was a pre-condition to their political and cultural integration, displayed an inept understanding of the British mind and of the British political and social make-up. Ironically, it was Gentile society in England that proved itself more appreciative of the unique character of the Jewish people rather than the assimilated Jew. To many of the Gentiles Jewish opposition to Zionism was incomprehensible. The Times (29 May) was not the only daily to expose the absurdity of the fear of dual loyalties. The Manchester Guardian (19 October 1917) wrote:

> Those Jews, who think that the establishment of a Jewish State would impair the rights of Jews in other countries . . . have a very imperfect knowledge of the foundations of political liberty and of religious tolerance in England . . . Whatever may be said about the establishment of a Jewish State . . . it is undoubtedly a British and Allied interest and should be recognized by Jews, who desire the welfare of their adopted countries.

And on the following day the Liverpool Post reassured the sceptics that Jewish nationhood, accepted by the majority of Christendom and Jewry 'will not deprive individual Jews . . . of equal citizenship . . . but will add once more a Jewish collective entity from which in the past humanity has reaped some of its richest fruits.'

Professor R. W. Seton-Watson was full of admiration for the race which had defied assimilation 'so stubbornly and so successfully; the modern tendency of individual Jews to repudiate what is one of their chief glories suggests an almost comic resolve to fight against the course of nature.'[49] Blanche Dugdale saw in assimilation 'a kind of escapism',[50] while Viscount Bryce considered Israel's persistence as a nation 'a unique phenomenon'. He was confident that the existence of a national home in Palestine would not expose the Jews to any suspicion of disloyalty by their Gentile neighbours.[51] Sir Mark Sykes asserted that 'no British Jew will be less British because he can look at the cradle of his race with pride',[52] and

Neville Chamberlain, addressing himself to non-Zionist Jews, dismissed as 'groundless' their fears that the establishment of a new Jewish state would provoke some suspicion of their loyalty to their own country. Quite the contrary; 'the existence of this new Jewish State would only add to the dignity and influence of Jews in other countries'.[53] 'I am an immense believer in separate nationalities,' Balfour was reported to have stated.[54] Zionist ideology appealed to him both as a philosopher and a student of history; while that of the assimilated Jews was totally incomprehensible. 'Why can I afford to be a Zionist and not they?' he wondered.[55] Nor could Colonel Patterson, the Irish Commander of the Judeans, understand why any Jew should be an anti-Zionist, since the Zionist ideal in no way interfered with the rights and privileges of other Jews.[56] In 1922, in a veiled reference to certain individuals who still felt uneasy about Zionism, Sir John Simon said: 'A man like myself, whose father was a Welshman, whose mother was an Englishwoman, and who married an Irish wife, am not very likely to fail in practical sympathy with the national aspirations of any race.'[57] Far better equipped to appreciate the peculiarities of Jewish nationalism was Lloyd George. He explained his Welsh patriotism by saying: 'National feeling has nothing to do with geography; it is a state of mind.'[58]

During the war nationalism and the course of small nationalities became respectable, and the assimilated Jew who refused to move with the times found himself, paradoxically, in conflict with his own Government's policy. So angry was Sykes with Lucien Wolf that, lumping him together with Jacob Schiff, he labelled the anti-Zionists collectively as 'pro-Turks, who have become pro-Germans, and . . . are definitely fixed in that camp'.[59] Since Zionism constituted an essential part of his Middle Eastern policy, it followed that those who opposed it were playing the enemy's game.

Nor did Wolf's personality make his case more attractive. In diplomatic skill he was no match for the Zionist leaders. In 1914–16, when he was still regarded by the Foreign Office as representing Anglo-Jewry, Weizmann unobtrusively but persistently cultivated relations with influential members of British society. His unerring intuition and his ability to convey his message were inestimable assets, and stood him in good stead when the new Government was formed in December 1916. Lloyd George considered him a friend and could meet him as an equal. Balfour also took Weizmann into his confidence.[60] But infectious as Weizmann's idealism was, the Zionists won their case not on the merits of their ideology—of which Sokolow was the foremost exponent—but because, unlike their opponents, they had something tangible to offer Britain.

With the French declaration to Sokolow on 4 June, and the dissolution of the Conjoint Foreign Committee on 17 June, the Balfour Declaration was well on its way. The idea of a declaration was, of course, not novel. It had been considered by the Foreign Office in March 1916, and again in April of the following year. To none of these moves were the Zionists a party. Nor were they aware of the agreement between the Conjoint Committee and the Foreign Office obliging the latter to consult all sections of Anglo-Jewish opinion before making public any statement on Palestine. It was not until early April 1917, shortly before Sykes's departure for the East, that Weizmann suggested that a suitable declaration be made as soon as Palestine came under British occupation. The setbacks at the Gaza front rendered this impracticable, but by May some Zionists were becoming impatient. In the United States Brandeis sounded out Balfour,[1] and in London, Gaster complained that 'the fact that we have nothing in black and white is not satisfactory'.[2] It took Weizmann, however, another month to reach the conclusion that a declaration by the British Government could no longer be postponed. For some time he was concerned with the theme hammered home by the German press (ranging from the Conservative *Reichsbote* to the liberal *Frankfurter Zeitung*), which urged Berlin to show a more accommodating attitude to the Zionist movement, but it was not before receiving information from Zionist sources that he became seriously alarmed. On 12 June he called on Graham and told him that a prominent Zionist leader[3] had been asked by the German envoy in Copenhagen whether the Zionists could act as intermediaries between the Central and Allied Powers during the peace negotiations; in his opinion, the international character of the Zionist Organisation made it eminently suitable for such a rôle. The Zionist leader professed himself ready to consult his friends in the neutral countries, provided the German Government gave a binding promise in writing that it would negotiate on the basis of the principle of 'no annexations and no indemnities', and gave a solemn pledge to support the Zionist claim to Palestine. He was then summoned to Dr Zimmermann, the German Foreign Minister, for an

244

interview, the sequel of which was not known, but in Weizmann's opinion it indicated 'a serious attempt by the German Government for peace settlement'.

Not all the information reaching Weizmann was accurate. There is no evidence to confirm the report that the German Government was eager to employ the Zionists as peace intermediaries. The relevant records, both in the German Foreign Ministry files and German-Zionist correspondence, are silent on this issue. True, Zimmermann was sympathetic towards the Zionists but when Weizmann approached Graham, Zimmermann was on the point of resigning, and his successor, Richard von Kühlmann, evinced no serious interest; the articles in the German press reflected the views of some sections of German public opinion but were not, as Weizmann and Whitehall erroneously supposed, officially inspired by the Wilhelm-strasse. There is however no reason to question Weizmann's sincerity. For Zionism to fall under German influence would have been a serious blow to his efforts to anchor the movement firmly to Britain, particularly at a time when it was emerging as a leading force in the Jewish world. A congress in Southern Russia, representing two million Jews, adopted the Zionist programme by 333 votes to 36. In the United States, Canada, and South Africa the movement was spreading; in Italy developments were encouraging, and 'even in France Mr. Sokolow had achieved a very notable success and had had an extremely favourable reception both in the Jewish and the French official world'. The only opponents consisted of a 'small oligarchy of Jewish cosmopolitan financiers . . . and of a small fraction of Jewish Socialists'. To counter German moves, Weizmann insisted, it was essential for the British Government to give public expression to its sympathy and support.[4]

Weizmann was preaching to the converted. Propaganda in Russia was badly needed and the British were handicapped in getting their message through. As early as January 1916 Lockhart complained that it was almost impossible for a foreigner to conduct propaganda without giving offence. Nor did the March Revolution improve the position. The Russian had an ingrained dislike of outside interference and the paternalistic attitude shown by the British press was bitterly resented.[5] It was not without some justification that a member of Parliament noted that 'all the German gold . . . has not done as much harm in Russia to the cause of the Allies as the insulting series of articles in The Times'.[6] Lloyd George's message to Lvov enjoining the Russian people to strengthen their resolve in prosecuting the war[7] failed to achieve the desired effect. Exhortation in this sense was interpreted as 'traps laid by the capitalists . . . to further the wicked aims of those plundering imperialists: Britain, France and Italy'.[8] With the notable exception of Bruce Lockhart the British Consuls were ill-equipped to counter German propaganda. Nor did the delegation of the British Labour Party succeed in damping down the 'no annexation' cry; they later admitted that their mission to Russia was a failure.[9] Harold Nicolson was despondent: 'England is very unpopular, and nothing we could do would be of any use. Russian opinion regarded us with all the hatred of the debtor to the creditor, and anything against us was readily believed ... Any propaganda on our part would only irritate them more, as they were determined to dislike us.'[10]

This helps to explain why the Zionists were *personae gratae* at the Foreign Office. In return for meeting their wishes, they could produce in Russia and elsewhere an army of voluntary propagandists, all the more effective since they had the obvious advantage of being citizens of their respective countries. Russian Jews disliked the war. It was not of their choosing and they had nothing to gain from its continuation. Both for political and economic reasons they were inclined more towards Germany than to England, but recognition of their rights in Palestine, as Vice-Consul Brown attested,[11] might make all the difference. Not only would it immunise them against German-inspired pacifist propaganda but their influence in the press and public life could be brought to bear. The military campaign in Palestine would be presented as an act of liberation and Britain's presence there linked to the principle of self-determination. Moreover, having a close interest in the success of Allied arms, they would be all the more eager to support the moderate element in the Provisional Government against the extremists and, considering the precarious balance of power within the coalition, this was not without significance.

Graham wasted no time. The day after Weizmann's visit he advised Lord Hardinge as follows:

> It would appear that in view of the sympathy towards the Zionist movement which has already been expressed by the Prime Minister, Mr. Balfour, Lord R. Cecil, and other statesmen, we are committed to support it, although until Zionist policy has been more clearly defined our support must be of a general character. We ought, therefore, to secure all the political advantage we can out of our connection with Zionism, and there is no doubt that this advantage will be considerable, especially in Russia, where the only means of reaching the Jewish proletariat is through Zionism, to which the vast majority of Jews in that country adhere.

He suggested that if the forthcoming meeting of the Board of Deputies (on 17 June) should decide in the Zionists' favour, the Prime Minister or the Foreign Secretary should issue an appropriate message of sympathy. Balfour was taken aback. 'How can H.M.G. announce their intention of "protecting" Palestine without consulting our Allies? And how can we discuss dismembering the Turkish Empire before the Turks are beaten? Personally I still prefer . . . U.S.A. in the protectorate, should we succeed in securing it.'

Graham was not discouraged; he had not intended raising the question of 'protection' at all; in view of French susceptibilities this was inopportune. The Zionists themselves were fully aware of the delicate situation and all they desired was a formal repetition, preferably in writing, of the verbal assurances they had already received from various members of the British Government. This, Graham insisted, 'is essential . . . if we are to secure Zionist political support which is so important to us in Russia at the present moment'. A formula modelled on Cambon's letter of 4 June which Sokolow had just brought back from Paris, would, he thought, satisfy the Zionists. Sokolow intended to go to Russia and, if armed by parallel British assurances, his task would be greatly eased.[12]

With the Conjoint Committee out of the picture, and the French Government willing to promote Zionist aspirations, two major obstacles against the British coming down publicly in the Zionists' favour were thus removed, and Balfour's earlier misgivings were overcome. On 19 June, when Lord Rothschild and Weizmann met the Foreign Secretary, they were able to show on whose side the majority of British Jews were, and asked him for a declaration of support, Balfour agreed and suggested that a draft proposal be submitted. Cecil remarked: 'I wanted to do this several weeks ago but was deterred by the advice of Sir G. Buchanan.'[13]

A month elapsed before Rothschild was able to forward a text to Balfour. The Zionists, perhaps underestimating the strength of their position, were remarkably modest in their claims. The man who restrained them was Ahad Ha'am. It was characteristic of this prudent, self-critical, but also over-cautious thinker, to advise Weizmann early in the war 'to be "modest" in . . . demands and content . . . with the claim of unrestricted immigration and cultural work in Palestine in the hope that in due course [the Jews] will attain a status of autonomy under the banner of Great Britain. We have to steer clear from excessive political phraseology.'[14] Weizmann, though Ahad Ha'am's disciple, was more ambitious. He made no secret of his ultimate goal, and on 23 January 1915 he told the Political Committee that the arrangement made for Palestine should be such as to enable the Zionists to work there 'freely so that it should lead ultimately to a Jewish Commonwealth'.[15] But the Committee followed more moderate counsels. Its members, chiefly adherents of the 'practical', as opposed to the 'political' school of thought, shied away from any references to the idea of Jewish statehood. A 'state' was equated with government, and they did not feel sufficiently mature for such a task. Nor were the conditions in Palestine ripe enough. 'We do not ask for a Jewish but for a pro-Jewish administration, not for a Jewish but for a pro-Jewish policy.'[16] Their 1916 programme spoke of 'a separate [Jewish] national unit or nationality' to be recognised by the Suzerain Government and of 'proportionate representation on any local legislative or executive bodies . . . which may be appointed by the Suzerain'.[17] However, by the end of November the Committee took a further step, asking that Palestine should be recognised as the Jewish National Home; the Jewish community there given autonomy; the Suzerain Government should grant a Charter to a Jewish Company for the Colonisation and Development of Palestine, the Company to have power to take over any concessions for works of a public character, the right of pre-emption of Crown or other lands (not held in private or religious ownership), and such other powers and privileges as were common to Charters or Statutes of similar colonising bodies.[18] The Company was to give the Zionists power in the economic sphere and compensate for the political sovereignty they were unable and unwilling to demand.

The idea of a Charter (used also by Herzl during his negotiations with the Sultan), was essentially English and as such comprehensible to the British mind. This was not the case with regard to the term 'Jewish National Home', unknown in the British political vocabulary. 'We have heard before of States and Commonwealths, of dominions and colonies, but never of national homes' was a typical comment of a Gentile Zionist.[19] The word 'home' carried a wealth of sentimental associations but had no political content. It was vague and subject to various interpretations ranging from 'a Jewish state' to a 'cultural centre'. From the Zionist point of view its choice was not a fortunate one. In later years Weizmann and his friends had a running battle with successive British Governments to retain some of its original meaning, and it was with genuine regret that he confessed in his autobiography that the November 1916 programme was the work of 'a group of amateur state builders . . . None of us had had any experience in government and colonization . . . We were journalists, scientists, lawyers, merchants, philosophers. We were one or two generations removed . . . from the ghetto.'[20]

The term 'National Home' originated in the *Heimstätte* of the Basle Programme, to which in November 1916 Sokolow prefixed the word 'national'. When the Basle Programme was drafted in 1897, the choice before the Programme Committee was between *Jüdisches Gemeinwesen* (Jewish Commonwealth) and *Heimstätte* (homestead). Herzl favoured *Gemeinwesen* but Nordau thought *Heimstätte* would be less offensive to the Turks and, at his suggestion, the First Zionist Congress adopted it.[21] Following the 1908 Young Turk Revolution the Zionists were forced to modify their phraseology still further, to the point of denying that they had ever contemplated a Jewish state. But calculations which were imperative *vis-à-vis* the Turks seemed quite unnecessary in Britain in 1917. Moreover, there is reason to believe that the phrase 'Jewish Commonwealth' would have alarmed the anti-Zionists less than 'National Home'. From what has been quoted already it could be inferred that they would not have objected to a British declaration in favour of unrestricted Jewish immigration and colonisation in Palestine, even though this might have led eventually to the emergence of a Jewish state. In other words, there were better prospects of a *modus vivendi* between Zionists and anti-Zionists on the basis of Herzl's terminology than that of Ahad Ha'am and Sokolow.

On doctrinal grounds, the importance of the word 'national' is self-evident; but there must have been more practical reasons for the Zionists to insist on its use. In the age of nationalism the principle that a nation had the right to a state of its own was universally accepted in the Western world. Moreover, international law recognises nations alone as entities possessing the right to self-determination, the corollary being that, since states were created on the basis of nationality, recognition of Jewish nationality entitled them to a state. This was the logic behind Sokolow's attempt to get from France recognition of Jewish nationality, a principle which he followed in England as well. Recognition of a Jewish nationality was to legitimise the Jewish right to Palestine and ease the transition from the status of autonomy to a state. But if this was the line of thinking that determined Zionist tactics, it was only partially right. The principle of identity between state and nation was applicable to a people inhabiting a certain stretch of territory; in these circumstances the administration was to conform to the wishes of the people concerned. The Jewish case was different. Only a small fraction of their people lived in Palestine, and recognition of Jewish nationality, even if extended to those living outside it, did not necessarily confer upon them the title to Palestine. What made their claim sound was their unbroken historical connection with the country. The fact that they possessed no alternative state of their own elsewhere gave the principle of 'historical connection' a unique character, recognised later by the League of Nations and quoted in the Preamble to the Palestine Mandate. It was on the basis of this principle that the

Zionists defended their case in subsequent years, not on the fact that they constituted, or claimed to constitute, a nation. In 1917, 'nationality' was a risky instrument. 'Historical connection' was a sounder card to play. No section of Jewish opinion contested it. A formula asking for such political and economic conditions in Palestine as to make the eventual establishment of a Jewish State possible, might have proved less divisive than 'National Home'. It is uncertain whether the British Government would have been prepared to endorse the term 'Jewish state' or 'Jewish Commonwealth' in the text of the declaration, but the balance of evidence suggests a positive answer. Grey took Samuel by surprise when expressing his desire to see a Jewish State in Palestine. Lloyd George expressed himself in similar vein. The O'Beirne-Crewe formula approved by Grey was more far-reaching in its wording than the Zionists would have ventured to suggest at that time or in the following year. Balfour too thought in terms of Jewish statehood. Sykes's terminology was more modest, but he was reported to have said that he expected the Jewish community in Palestine to grow to a million and a half in thirty years and agreed that 'so powerful a community could be self-governing'. His only reservation was that Jewish settlement should not dispossess the Arab population.[22]

Perhaps most indicative of the British attitude to Zionist aspirations was the reaction to Weizmann's speech of 20 May 1917, mentioned already, in which he said that the creation of a Jewish Commonwealth was the Zionists' 'final ideal'; the way to this goal lay through a series of intermediate stages, one of which was that Palestine would be

> protected by such a mighty and just Power as Great Britain. Under the wing of this Power Jews will be able to develop and set up the administrative machinery which, while not interfering with the legitimate interests of the non-Jewish population, would enable [them] to carry out [their] scheme. I am entitled to state that His Majesty's Government is ready to support our plans.

Asked by Lord Onslow whether there was any official sanction for Weizmann's statement, John Buchan, Director of the Department of information, replied:[23]

> Your question . . . is not a very easy one to answer: I think that we can agree to Dr. Weizmann's definition if it is taken in the proper sense, but there has never been any public pronouncement.
> I imagine that the British Government has no objection to a Jewish Palestine as such—at any rate to the establishment in Palestine of a very large Jewish Colony. But I do not think that any opinion

has ever been expressed as to the precise form of Government under which Palestine should exist: it is not desirable to announce publicly that it should be either a sovereign Jewish State, or a British protectorate . . .

Least of all do we wish it to be a second Monte Carlo or an international banking centre.

In May, when Weizmann made his speech, Balfour was in the United States and was completely unaware of it, but three months later when it was brought to his attention (in connection with a request of the Zionists in Egypt for permission to publish it), he reacted sharply: 'I fear the phrase "protected by G. Britain" is fatal—it goes far beyond the Roth-schild message.' It was not 'Jewish Commonwealth' that dismayed Balfour so much as the reference to a British protectorate.[24]

The Foreign Office position can be deduced from Harold Nicolson's minute, dated 5 July 1917: 'Our present attitude towards the Palestine question is based on a compromise between the desirability of encouraging Jewish national aspirations and the necessity of avoiding the creation of suspicion in the French Colonial party.'[25] Nicolson did not specify what he meant by 'Jewish national aspirations' but he was fully *au courant* with Weizmann's definition; twenty-nine years later, when the State of Israel was proclaimed, he did not conceal his pleasure 'at this realisation of the hopes of Zionism'.[26] There is nothing to support the suggestion that when the formula for a declaration was first considered 'at the Foreign Office end the key-words seemed to have been "asylum" or "refuge" '.[27] In fact, all the evidence points the other way. For the Foreign Office the chief difficulty was the question of 'protection', not the formulation of Zionist objectives.

Moreover, one must bear in mind that during the First World War terminology with regard to nascent nationalities was not clearly defined. Thus, 'Arab State or Confederation of States' was loosely used, although it was a matter of common knowledge that the Arabs, if left to themselves, would have been in no position to sustain such an entity without the support or protection of a foreign power. 'Arab state' meant Arab autonomy, and 'Jewish Commonwealth' meant Jewish autonomy. Much to the surprise of the Programme Committee of the First Zionist Congress, Herzl stated:[28]

People did not understand . . . the title of the pamphlet [*Der Juden-staat*]. I did not propose *einen jüdischen Staat* (a Jewish State), but I proposed to give the territory the name *Judenstaat* (Jews' State). Had I wanted a State like all other states of the world, I would have labelled it as '*ein jüdischer Staat*', but I did not dream of making it like any other State. I was thinking of a Jewish territory, well protected [by the Powers], well organised, and run by a modern [Jewish] Company . . . Such a territory I would call *Judenstaat* . . . All the protests against this non-existent idea are mere clap-trap. We want a Jewish *Gemeinwesen* with all securities for freedom.

To give their blessing to such an interpretation of 'Jewish state' or 'Commonwealth' was not difficult for the British Government, especially since a declaration did not necessarily bind its authors to implement it but merely to facilitate its attainment. Had the Jewish community spoken with one voice the British Government might have been prepared to endorse a more far-reaching formula than that of 2 November 1917.

Not all the Zionists felt happy about the tactics adopted by the London Bureau. In Manchester, Harry Sacher, a leading member of the British Palestine Committee, was convinced that the British needed the Zionists and that greater concessions could be obtained by showing that the Jews were 'a *power*'. He had serious misgivings about the London Bureau staking everything on the British. Zionism was an international movement and as such had to keep its options open. Moreover, given the pragmatic frame of mind of the British, it was too risky for the Zionists to tie their hands unilaterally. He felt uneasy about Weizmann placing so much faith in Sykes, whose interest, he suspected, lay 'primarily in Arabs, not in Jews'. It was the Arab question that disquieted Sacher most. On 14 June he confessed to a friend: 'At the back of my mind there is firmly fixed the recognition that even if all our political schemings turn out in the way we desire, *the Arabs will* remain our most tremendous problem . . . It is going to be extraordinarily difficult and it will give us unhappy years.'[29] It was this issue that prompted Sacher to adopt a radical position.

Weizmann had no hand in drafting the formula, but before leaving for Gibraltar at the end of June, he agreed that Sacher should outline one.[30] It read as follows:

The British Government declares that one of its essential war aims is the reconstitution of Palestine as a Jewish State and as the National Home of the Jewish People.

It declares that . . . [there] must be an Integral Palestine . . . that there should be set up in the Peace Conference . . . a protectorate by a Power or Powers; [with] the object . . . [of] facilitating . . . the reconstitution of Palestine as a Jewish State and as the National Home . . .

The British Government further declares that it recognises the Zionist Organisation as the representative and spokesman of the Jewish People . . . a Chartered Company to be constituted and endowed with all requisite political and economic powers for a fulfilment of this task.

By comparison, Sokolow's draft was moderate. Under its terms the British Government accepted 'the principle of recognising Palestine as the National Home of the Jewish People' to be taken under its protection at the conclusion of peace; with internal autonomy and the right to free immigration, the details to be elaborated at a later date with the representatives of the Zionist Organisation.[31]

Sacher was thoroughly dissatisfied. 'I am persuaded' he wrote to Sokolow, 'that this matter is of the first importance and that my original idea of asking for as much as possible is the right one. I think my own draft erred in not going far enough . . . The various drafts you have sent me are thoroughly mistaken in conception.'[32] Sokolow was not impressed. 'If we want too much we shall get nothing; on the other hand, if we get some sympathetic declaration, I hope we will gradually get more and more.'[33] Sokolow carried the majority of the Political Committee[34] with him and could speak with authority. He was in an even stronger position since he enjoyed the support of Ahad Ha'am, who considered Sacher's draft unsuitable. The declaration was to express merely 'a *general* agreement' of principle, and there was no prospect, in Ahad Ha'am's opinion, that the British Government would undertake any binding obligation at that time. From what Sokolow reported about the Foreign Office position, he thought it expedient to produce a short and general draft, dropping all conditions or, still better, to leave the initiative to the British to propose their own draft.[35]

Sacher would not give ground and forwarded a draft from his friend Herbert Sidebotham. It was like his own except for the important passage that 'by a Jewish State is meant a state composed not only of Jews, but one whose dominant national character . . . shall be as Jewish as the dominant national character of England is English'; Sacher insisted that the Committee should use the phrase 'the reconstitution *of* Palestine'—'of' as distinct from 'in'. 'Reconstitution *of* Palestine' was a kind of insurance policy against Arab domination. 'We must control the *State* machinery in Palestine; if we don't the Arabs will. Give the Arabs all the guarantees they like for cultural autonomy; but the State must be Jewish. Also the Chartered Company must be *political* as well as an economic institution.'[36]

Sacher wanted the suzerain power to provide an umbrella for the gradual Jewish take-over, though with due respect for the civic rights of the native population. The Jews were to have a predominant say in the running of the country even during the transitional period. 'We shall endeavour . . . from the first to secure as the administrative head of all Palestine a Jew sympathetic to the national cause, and to staff the Palestine Civil Service as largely as possible with competent Jews, principally from England.'

Sokolow did not disagree with Sacher's objectives but differed regarding method and timing. He admitted that it was desirable to obtain the 'strongest possible declaration', though not at the start; the Sacher-Sidebotham drafts bound the British too closely for them to underwrite it as the 'first declaration'. Sacher was finally told that the draft proposed by the Political Committee was the maximum that the Zionists could expect from the Government at that stage.[37]

It is possible, though there is no supporting evidence from British sources, that Sokolow was advised to go slow. If so, he might have considered that stage by stage diplomacy would yield better results than maximal demands. As transpires from his statements,[38] he intended first to elicit from the British 'a general approval of Zionism', and only afterwards to present more concrete demands to be followed by specific negotiations on the extent of autonomy, the nature of the Charter Company, and provisional administration, once the Turks were driven out of Palestine. Sound as this strategy seemed to be, events made it inapplicable. Montagu's opposition during the ensuing months disheartened Lord Rothschild so much that he thought it inadvisable for the Zionists to press for further concessions; otherwise, he feared, the British would 'finally decide *not* to make any declaration at all'.[39] It was not until early in 1919, at the peace conference in Paris, that the Zionists presented their programme for a Jewish Commonwealth. But by then much of their bargaining power had been dissipated. Germany was beaten, Russia was out of the picture, and Arab opposition loomed darkly in the background. The favourable conditions prevailing during the summer of 1917 never recurred.

The Zionist draft was presented by Lord Rothschild to Balfour on 18 July.[40] It contained two principles: recognition of Palestine as the National Home of the Jewish people, and recognition of the Zionist Organisation.[41] Sacher considered it 'inadequate' and 'defective in form'. Two or three weeks later he helped to persuade the British Labour Party to include in its manifesto a recommendation that Palestine should be liberated from the Turk and become 'a free state under international guarantee, to which

... the Jewish people ... may return and may work out their own salvation'. Later in its proposed terms of peace, the Labour Party included the phrase *Jewish Palestine*. 'This', wrote Sacher, 'is the biggest score of a diplomatic kind we have made during the war, and without arrogance, it isn't Chaim and Sok[olow]... who have won it but our group' in Manchester.[42]

At the Foreign Office the formula submitted by Rothschild was received without comment and only minor verbal alterations were made before it was passed on to the War Cabinet. Early in August, pending the War Cabinet's approval, the following draft reply was ready:[43]

Foreign Office
August 1917

Dear Lord Rothschild,

In reply to your letter of July 18th, I am glad to be in a position to inform you that His Majesty's Government accept the principle that Palestine should be reconstituted as the national home of the Jewish people.

His Majesty's Government will use their best endeavours to secure the achievement of this object and will be ready to consider any suggestions on the subject which the Zionist Organisation may desire to lay before them.

(Initialled) A.J.B.

The favourable tone was dictated partly by the fear of Russian withdrawal from the war, which prompted the Allies, meeting in Paris 25–6 July, to decide that 'every sacrifice' should be made to retain Russia in the Alliance, and among the means discussed, propaganda figured high on the agenda.[44] A psychological offensive was needed in the United States also. Having entered the war reluctantly, the American people suspected that their Government had been dragged into it by the Allies. In the eastern cities, where the Jewish population was concentrated, the attitude to the war bordered on indifference. Congress vacillated and the subscriptions to the War Loan were slow in forthcoming.[45] To England this boded ill since the country seemed to be on the verge of a 'financial disaster ... of incalculable gravity', the consequences of which could be 'worse than a defeat in the field'.[46] Wilson, in sympathy with the Allies, wanted to support their cause more energetically, but was handicapped by the strong opposition to his administration from 'all' the leaders of big business and finance. Among the financial magnates, the Jews 'alone ... were inclined to support him.' They were of great help during his election campaign,

for which they were rewarded by appointments to high office.[47] Influential in domestic politics as they were, in foreign affairs the American
Jews, like their co-religionists in Russia, opposed annexations. Nor were
they enthusiastic about the prospect of Britain becoming the sole mistress
of Palestine. Morgenthau was no exception. Thanks to Weizmann's
skill, his mission was dead, but not his idea. As late as September, Tschlenow told his friends in London that the Russian Zionists considered
Morgenthau's initiative 'extraordinarily important'[48] while in New York
the Jewish Committee hoped that after the war Palestine would be
neutralised and internationalised.[49]

Given this interest in winning the good-will of world Jewry, approval
of the draft declaration seemed a foregone conclusion, so much so that
Philip Kerr, Lloyd George's secretary, thought it superfluous for the
Prime Minister to send a special message to a Jewish Congress which was
about to convene in Salonica on 2 September. Harold Nicolson agreed
that 'the Rothschild message should suffice for all purposes' and Graham
too was confident that the War Cabinet's approval would be only a
formality; the actual drafting would thereafter be left to the Foreign
Office. 'If the idea of giving a declaration is approved in principle,' he
noted on 1 August, '*we will draft one for submission*. Possibly the opportunity of the Prime Minister's forthcoming speech on Saturday [4
August] might be taken for some declaration in the sense desired. I know
this would be particularly gratifying to the Zionists.'[50] However, it took
Balfour more than three months to send his reply to Rothschild, and then
in a drastically amended form, on which the Foreign Office was hardly
consulted.

The initial reason for the delay, it appears, was that the Foreign Office
neglected to forward to the War Cabinet the required number of copies
and forgot to ask its Secretary to put the matter on the waiting list.[51] Two
weeks were thus lost. But, once formalities had been complied with, the
question received immediate attention. Ormsby-Gore was the first to
comment. He suggested the following amendment:

> His Majesty's Government will use their best endeavours to facilitate
> the achievement of this object by the Jewish people and will be
> ready etc.

Ormsby-Gore substituted 'facilitate' for 'secure' and inserted the phrase
'by the Jewish people', explaining that:

> The great thing to guard against is the appearance of a Christian
> power 'forcing' the realization of Zionist aims. Such forcing would

arouse a conflict with the Arab population of Palestine at once, and would upset a certain powerful section of non-Zionist Jews. The work of 'practical Zionism' must be carried out by the Jews themselves and not by Great Britain.[52]

A few days later Lord Milner suggested an alternative draft:

His Majesty's Government accepts the principle that every opportunity should be afforded for the establishment of a home for the Jewish people in Palestine, and will use its best endeavours to facilitate the achievement of this object, and will be ready to consider any suggestions on the subject which the Zionist Organizations may desire to lay before them.

'He thinks', Ormsby-Gore noted, 'the word "reconstituted" is much too strong, and also the word "secure".'[53] But Milner introduced some additional alterations. With an eye on the anti-Zionist Jews in Britain, he omitted the word 'national' and substituted the indefinite article for the definite one. Moreover, he inserted the phrase '*in* Palestine', which in later years gave rise to a bitter controversy on the scope of the Jewish enterprise. The only evidence about Milner's reasoning is a note from Montefiore written after his interview with Milner on 16 May 1917:[54]

His own views appeared to be between our formula and the full Zionist scheme. He seemed to favour the establishment of a Jewish community in Palestine, or parts of Palestine, under a British Protectorate. Within its own borders such a community would be autonomous, but it would not be an independent State, would have no foreign relations, and in its dealings with other nationalities in Palestine it would be subject to the control of the British authority, which would, of course, insist on fair treatment for Christians and Mahommedans, *even within the Jewish zone.*

Time did not change Milner's views. On 27 June 1923 he told the House of Lords:

I think we have only to go on . . . with the policy of establishing not a Jewish Government of Palestine but a Jewish Home there, which will receive as many Jews as the country can reasonably support while at the same time taking care . . . that the interests of the Arab population do not suffer . . . There are about 700,000 people in Palestine, and there is room for several millions . . . You cannot have either an Arab Government in Palestine or a Jewish Government in Palestine, but you must have in that country some neutral Power

which will keep the balance between the different races . . . To hold
the balance even between these various interests . . . some Mandatory
Power will always be required.

However in August 1917, when Milner's amended draft was circulated, none of the Ministers concerned seemed to have read into it all the
implications that came to the surface later. Milner himself did not dispute
Balfour's interpretation of the Jewish National Home,[55] though it
differed greatly from his own. But since, on all counts, no early establishment of a Jewish state was envisaged, it was not Milner's or Balfour's
phraseology that seemed to matter. Most of the War Cabinet's time was
taken up by consideration of the criticism made by Edwin Montagu, the
newly-appointed Secretary of State for India, who questioned the very
rationale of the Government's policy.

16   The Struggle for the Declaration

Balfour's draft reply to Rothschild filled Montagu with horror. His state of mind can be gauged from the title he chose for his memorandum, *The Antisemitism of the Present Government*, the first in his crusade to suppress the proposed declaration. Zionism, he insisted, was 'a mischievous political creed' which no patriotic citizen in Britain could support. It was a confession of unfitness for civic liberties, a self-imposed exclusion from public life. Since the emancipation of Jews in Russia it had become an obsolete doctrine, and it was inconceivable that the British Government would recognise it. The Jews were not a nation. A national home would turn them into aliens and expose them to expulsion, while Palestine would become 'the world's Ghetto'. In Great Britain too, the impetus to deprive them of their citizenship would be enormously increased. The editors of the *Morning Post* and like-minded Englishmen supported Zionism because they wanted 'to get rid of us' but the Government's policy, though not deliberately anti-semitic, was nonetheless 'anti-semitic in result and will prove a rallying ground for anti-semites in every country in the world'. Whitehall had become the instrument of an organisation which was largely run by 'men of enemy descent or birth'.

> I would willingly disfranchise every Zionist. I would be almost tempted to proscribe the Zionist Organization as illegal and against the national interest. But I would ask of a British Government sufficient tolerance to refuse to endorse a conclusion which makes aliens and foreigners by implication, if not at once by law, of all their Jewish fellow-citizens.

For identical reasons Montagu objected to the formation of the Jewish Regiment since it would 'force a nationality upon people who have nothing in common'.[1]

Montagu's fear that recognition of Zionism would cause his fellow-Jews to lose their liberties was misplaced. Such a practice was totally alien to English law.[2] Deeply disturbed, he pushed his arguments to their extreme conclusion, but his assault was not left unchallenged. The reply came from Ronald MacNeill, M.P., who subsequently (in 1922–4) served as Under-Secretary of State for Foreign Affairs. The tone of his memorandum is authoritative; presumably it was intended to brief Cabinet Ministers. MacNeill unequivocally dismissed Montagu's views as unrepresentative and erroneous. 'The constitution of the Jewish State in Palestine would impose no obligation on an Englishman or Frenchman of Jewish blood to change his allegiance, his home, or his status.' While their position would remain unaffected, the status of the Jewish population in Palestine and the neighbouring countries would be elevated. The national home would also provide an asylum for those individuals wishing to escape poverty and persecution. For even should the Russian Revolution put an end to intolerance, Russia was not the only country where the lot of the Jew was unhappy; Palestine, under improved conditions, would be able to support a population of some five to six millions. Lastly, it would satisfy Jewish national sentiment. 'Nationality' and 'race consciousness', the writer went on, were in high degree characteristic of the Jewish people. Montagu's antipathy blinded him to this fact and led him to his paradoxical identification of Zionism with anti-Semitism, whereas historically, one was the antithesis of the other. The spirit of nationality among the Jews had been an active force for centuries; Palestine had never ceased to attract them. Heretofore, owing to adverse political conditions, their aspirations could not be realised. However,

> the settlement that must follow the present War may, for the first time, provide such an opportunity. The Allies have proclaimed that the settlement must be based on the principle of nationality. It would be a strange and glaring anomaly, if while professing to observe that principle, we were to deny or ignore the claims of nationality in the case of the people who have throughout history clung to them more tenaciously than any other . . .
> . . . The future of Palestine is one of the problems that must be solved . . . and the proposal to make that country the domain of a reconstituted Jewish state, the 'National home of the Jewish people,' has attractions both from an historical and a political point of view.[3]

The Zionists had powerful supporters in official circles but their opponents, though defeated in the Board of Deputies, had not given up. An official announcement about the formation of the Jewish Regiment in the *London Gazette* (23 August 1917) prompted an influential deputation of British Jews to call on Lord Derby to protest against the Regiment's title. They argued that some 40,000 Jews had served in the British forces, and that it was unfair to them to stake the whole reputation of English

Jews as fighters on the performance of this regiment. So perplexed was Lord Derby that, during a War Cabinet meeting held on 3 September, he proposed to abandon the title 'The Jewish Regiment' and to give the unit a number, leaving its particular characters open. He proposed to form four battalions, composed mainly of conscripted foreign Jews, to which a number of English Jews would be attached as instructors. Since it had not always proved possible to maintain the original character even of Irish and Scottish regiments, the War Cabinet accepted Lord Derby's recommendation, though without prejudice to reconsideration of the question should circumstances change. However, with regard to the projected declaration, the principal issue that concerned the War Cabinet, no ground was to be given. When Montagu was allowed to restate his views he found himself completely isolated. Against him it was argued that the existence of a Jewish state or autonomous community in Palestine would not weaken but rather strengthen the position of Jews; that the majority of them sympathised with Zionism, and that only a small, albeit influential, section of British Jews were opposed to it. Cecil, deputising for Balfour, insisted that it would be most advantageous to the Allies to enlist Zionist good will. They had a strong and enthusiastic organisation, particularly in the United States, and 'to do nothing was to risk a direct breach with them'. He was then asked to inform the American Government of the British Government's intention to make a declaration of sympathy with the Zionist movement, but before doing so to ascertain the views of President Wilson.[4]

The brief was not a fortunate one since it was unlikely that Wilson would show his hand before knowing what the British intention was. 'We are being pressed for a declaration of sympathy with the Zionist movement,' Colonel House told the President on 4 September. 'There are many dangers lurking in it, and . . . I would be chary about going too definitely into that question.'[5] And on 11 September he told Eric Drummond that he had brought Cecil's enquiry to the President's attention but, in the latter's opinion, the time was 'not opportune for any definite statement further perhaps than one of sympathy provided it can be made without conveying any real commitment. Things are in such a state of flux . . . that he does not consider it advisable to go further.'[6]

This dilatory and non-committal language was not what was expected. The Foreign Office was impatient. On 9 September Weizmann told Clerk that the forthcoming Jewish New Year (on 17 September) would provide a splendid opportunity for the British Government to publish the declaration. 'It would be of enormous value, as Jews all over the world congregate on that day in great masses in the synagogues and I know what effect the announcement would have on the minds and hearts of my sorely tried people.'[7] Weizmann's advice however was not relayed to Washington, as had been intended, since House's telegram of 11 September reached the Foreign Office first.

In the meantime Montagu, far from accepting defeat, made a new move. He told Cecil that the Zionists were not in a majority; the contest at the Board of Deputies on 17 June showed that the opposing parties were more or less evenly balanced, and it was misleading to consider the ratio in purely numerical terms. He made use of Wilson's discouraging message and insisted that a British declaration would be 'a cruel blow' to many English Jews. However, if unavoidable, the following formula would be less objectionable:[8]

> His Majesty's Government accepts the principle that every opportunity should be afforded for the establishment in Palestine for [sic] those Jews who cannot or will not remain in the lands in which they live at present, will use its best endeavours to facilitate the achievement of this object, and will be ready to consider any suggestions on the subject which any Jewish or Zionist organisations may desire to lay before it.

This formula was similar to that used by the Jewish Territorial Organisation. It had been drawn up to suit entirely different conditions in order to find a refuge for persecuted Jews in a territory other than Palestine. It was most unlikely that the Zionists would have considered it. Nor was it accepted by the British.

Graham was nonplussed. 'A draft letter to Lord Rothschild has been under consideration by the War Cabinet,' he told Clayton, 'but the whole question has been hung up, mainly owing to a memorandum by Mr. E. Montagu, who represents a certain section of rich Jews and who seems to fear that he and his like will be expelled from England and asked to cultivate farms in Palestine. The division of opinion on the subject in the Jewish ranks has complicated matters, and President Wilson has also given the opinion that we ought not to move fast.'[9]

The situation however was by no means desperate. On 21 September Ormsby-Gore assured the Foreign Office that only a preliminary discussion at the War Cabinet had taken place and with the Prime Minister's return from Wales the subject was likely to be raised again. Weizmann was going to suggest that a declaration be published at the forthcoming Inter-Allied Zionist Conference in London; Tschlenow was on his way from Russia, and Aaronsohn from Egypt; it would also be easy to get some American Zionist over.[10] Two days earlier Balfour had promised

Weizmann to see the Prime Minister on his return, and discuss the question of the declaration. 'I think', Weizmann confided to Scott, 'that if the facts are made clear to the P.M. he would *act* at once and if we both could have a quarter of an hour talk with him it would probably settle the matter.'[11] However, owing to Lloyd George's indisposition the meeting could not take place before the end of the month, but despite the delay there was no reason for the Zionists to be anxious. On 21 September, Balfour reassured Lord Rothschild; Montagu was '*not* a member of the Cabinet *only* of the *Government* . . . his views are quite mistaken'. Balfour asked Rothschild to urge Brandeis, as well as other American Zionist leaders, to bring pressure to bear upon President Wilson to break the deadlock.[12] This Weizmann had already done, sending on 19 September the text of the draft declaration to Brandeis, which had been submitted on 18 July by Rothschild to Balfour. After seven days Brandeis replied:[13]

> From talks I have had with the President and from expressions of opinion, given to closest advisers, I feel I can answer you that he is in entire sympathy with declaration quoted in yours of the 19th, as approved by Foreign Office and Prime Minister. I, of course, heartily agree.

Wilson's interest in Zionism was long-standing. He had made known his position on several occasions; that disclosed during Balfour's visit to the United States is, perhaps, the most revealing. 'I was received', Brandeis noted,[14]

> by President Wilson, with whom I discussed, not for the first time, the . . . Jewish question . . . and received assurances that our Administration felt keenly interested in the Zionist aims. The President felt that the formula of the Basle Program admirably suits the situation, and I was assured that he would, at the right time, give utterance to his opinions in support of our idea, and that, moreover, he would use his influence as circumstances permitted, with other governments to help carry out our plans.

It was apparently at this juncture that Wilson explained that 'whilst he was determined to aid the Zionist cause, he would not add to the possible friction between allied powers by previous action; nor would he countenance the proposals launched in England for an American suzerainty over Palestine and Armenia.'[15] This statement helps to solve the mystery behind Brandeis's cable to Weizmann of 24 September 'to get French [and] Italians to inquire what attitude of President is on declaration referred in yours of 19th.'[16] It also explains Wilson's cool response to Cecil's overture, and, conversely, his favourable response to Brandeis. Cecil's approach to House might have given the impression that either the British were resorting to a stratagem to improve their diplomatic position *vis-à-vis* France and Italy, or that they were attempting to commit the United States to a protectorate over Palestine. If these were the fears lingering in the minds of House and Wilson, Brandeis should have had no difficulty in dispelling them. Armed with the draft which Weizmann had sent him, he was able to show that in fact it made no reference to any protectorate, British or American, and that there was no inconsistency between the text of the declaration and the Basle programme.

On 19 September Weizmann also asked what views were held in Washington with regard to American military participation in the Palestine campaign; Brandeis replied: 'Some delay in decision is inevitable.'[17] This could have meant much or nothing, but as it turned out, in this respect Brandeis was not successful. America was not at war with Turkey nor did she declare war.

The Zionist leaders had additional reason for pressing the British Government to speed up the declaration. Propaganda for a German-Jewish Palestine was disquieting. Official and semi-official German newspapers were hammering home the theme that the Central Powers should insist at the forthcoming peace negotiations that the Jewish settlement in Palestine should be placed under German protection. At the Foreign Office too, Graham was becoming increasingly impatient. He warned Lord Hardinge of the disadvantages in delay. 'It cannot be doubted that Zionist propaganda among the Russian Jews was extremely useful to us,' and it was imperative that Sokolow should go to Russia to state the British case and arouse enthusiasm for the expulsion of the Turks from Palestine. But how could he go before a firm assurance to the Zionists had been given? Zionist propaganda in America was also very desirable. An officially inspired campaign was being conducted in the German press, and Zionist sympathies would be divided should Germany succeed in inducing Turkey to make some tangible concessions. The French Government had already given the Zionists a 'somewhat vague letter of sympathy'. Why could not the British Government go as far as the French? 'Apart from the merits of the question itself, our political interests seem to lie in encouraging Zionism.'[18]

Lord Hardinge agreed. '*Pace* Mr. Morgenthau, I think we might and ought to go as far as the French.' But Balfour did not feel free to act: 'Yes. But as the question was (in my absence) decided by the Cabinet against the Zionists I cannot do anything till the decision is reversed.'

Balfour somewhat overstated the case, as no definite decision had been taken by the War Cabinet, but Graham did not leave the matter to chance and submitted a memorandum on the French position as a gentle hint to Balfour to re-think the matter.[19]

In contrast, Lloyd George was brisk and decisive. He too was under the impression that the Germans might steal a march on the Allies by capturing the Zionist movement. The outcome of the war was still very much in doubt, he thought that the British ought to mobilise 'every opinion and force throughout the world which would weaken the enemy and improve the Allied chances.'[20] A conversation with Weizmann of two or three minutes (on 28 September?) sufficed for Lloyd George to instruct his secretary to put down 'Palestine' on the agenda of the next War Cabinet meeting.[21]

Notwithstanding assurances from Balfour and the Prime Minister, on 3 October, the day before the War Cabinet was to meet, Rothschild and Weizmann asked that their case should be considered in the light of British imperial interests and the principles for which the Entente stood. The declaration 'would enable us ... to counteract the demoralizing influence which the enemy press is endeavouring to exercise', and to 'make the necessary preparations for the constructive work ... as soon as Palestine is liberated.'[22] The offer bore the character of a *quid pro quo*. This was how Lloyd George understood it: 'The Zionist leaders gave us a definite promise that, if the Allies committed themselves to giving facilities for the establishment of a National Home for the Jews in Palestine, they would do their best to rally to the Allied cause Jewish sentiment and support throughout the world ... Such were the chief considerations which, in 1917, impelled the British Government towards making a contract with Jewry.'[23]

Had the drafting of the declaration been left to Graham, it would (as is evident from the minutes already quoted) have followed the principles set out in Cambon's letter of 4 June, but the job was left to other hands. The matter rested with Lord Milner. As Leopold Amery recorded, Milner was satisfied with neither his own nor Balfour's draft. Half an hour before the War Cabinet was to meet (on 4 October), he confided his difficulties to Amery and asked him whether he could draft 'something which could go a reasonable distance to meeting the objectors, both Jewish and pro-Arab, without impairing the substance of the proposed declaration'. Amery sat down and quickly produced the following:[24]

His Majesty's Government view with favour the establishment in Palestine of a National Home for the Jewish race, and will use their best endeavours to facilitate the achievement of this object, it being clearly understood that nothing shall be done which may prejudice the civil and religious rights of the existing non-Jewish communities in Palestine or the rights and political status enjoyed by Jews in any other country who are contented with their existing nationality.

Since Amery reintroduced the word 'National', omitted in Milner's draft, he had to make a specific proviso in order to still the fears of some Jewish objectors. But why was it so important to make the proviso with regard to 'the civil and religious rights of the existing non-Jewish communities in Palestine'? And who were the 'pro-Arab' elements whose objections Milner found it necessary to meet? Pro-Arabism, in the sense which required a dilution of commitment to the Zionists, was not yet born. British Arab protagonists were known to be, in most cases, also vigorous advocates of the Zionist policy. Nor did Clayton's warning to Sykes on 20 August, already quoted, make any impression. His letter remained private and no copy of it is to be found among the official files. More influential was that of Gertrude Bell, Assistant Political Officer in Bagdad. Her reports were popular with the India Office; and a copy of one on Syria was forwarded to the Foreign Office. She wrote:[25]

Two considerations rule out the conception of an independent Jewish Palestine from practical politics. The first is that the province . . . is not Jewish, and that neither Mohammedan nor Arab would accept Jewish authority; the second that the capital, Jerusalem, is equally sacred to three faiths, Jewish, Christian and Moslem, and should never, if it can be avoided, be put under the exclusive control of any one local faction.

Miss Bell was apparently under the impression that the British Government was about to give its blessing to the establishment of a Jewish state as soon as Palestine was liberated. This was obviously not the case, and though her report seemed to have commended itself to the Foreign Office in general, the revelant paragraph on Palestine elicited no comment. For Montagu, however, it was a real find. 'Is it conceivable . . . that there is room in Palestine for a large extension of the population? If this does not occur, what part of the existing population is it proposed to dispossess?' Zionism, he asserted, was impractical. Weizmann's scientific contribution to the Allied cause was great, but on this question 'he is near to being a religious fanatic'. His enthusiasm for Zionism had led him to disregard practical potentialities, and to take into account the susceptibilities of those who differed from him 'among those of his own religion or of those of other religions whom his activities, if successful, would dispossess'.[26]

Montagu's memorandum appeared in print on 9 October 1917, five days after the 4 October War Cabinet meeting. But it is possible that the Bell report was in his hands some time earlier and that, in an effort to win Milner's support, he showed it to him shortly before the meeting. If this conjecture is correct, Milner's haste in redrafting the proposed declaration is comprehensible, as are the provisos inserted by Amery. The first was to safeguard the rights of the native Moslem and Christian communities and protect them against possible dispossession; the word 'in' was the operative word intended to ensure against the imposition of Jewish domination on other inhabitants of Palestine. The purpose of the second proviso was to dispel the misconception that Jews *qua* Jews, irrespective of their convictions and place of domicile, 'belonged to Palestine' and owed allegiance to the National Home. The provisos, however, as Amery recorded, 'gave away nothing that was not self-evident', and were not meant to impair the substance of the proposed declaration. They had to serve the 'immediate purpose' of stilling opposition and thus to make the birth of the declaration possible. The 'scope and authority of the National Home in Palestine' was to be decided by future developments.[27]

It was hoped that the War Cabinet meeting of 4 October would be decisive. The Prime Minister was in the chair. Balfour opened by disclosing that the German Government was endeavouring to capture the sympathy of the Zionist movement, a prospect which the British could hardly tolerate since the Zionists commanded the support of the majority of Jews in Russia and America and possibly in other countries as well. It was opposed by a number of wealthy Jews in England for fear of dual loyalties, but Balfour thought there was 'nothing inconsistent between the establishment of a Jewish national focus in Palestine and the complete assimilation and absorption of Jews into the nationality of other countries', and even when Zionist aspirations were realised and a Jewish citizenship established in Palestine, the nationality of other Jews in their respective countries would remain unaffected. Balfour then read what was described as a 'very sympathetic declaration' by the French Government and stated that he knew that President Wilson was 'extremely favourable to the Movement'. Milner thereupon presented the draft which had been amended by Amery, but neither this nor Balfour's statement had any effect on Montagu. No matter what safeguards were inserted, the term 'national home for the Jewish people', he maintained, would have a prejudicial effect on the status of British Jews and of their co-religionists in other countries. Nor would it be possible for him to negotiate with the peoples of India were the British Government to announce that his national home was somewhere in Turkish territory.

Curzon followed Montagu. He had found during his pre-war visit that Palestine was for the most part 'barren and desolate . . . a less propitious seat for the future Jewish race could not be imagined.' He asked how it was proposed to get rid of the existing majority of Moslem inhabitants and introduce Jews in their place. For Curzon, Zionism was 'sentimental idealism, which would never be realised'. His assertion that there could be no settlement of Jews unless the native Moslems were dispossessed fortifies the suspicion that he too may have seen the Bell report. However, despite Montagu's and Curzon's arguments, the Cabinet was not deflected from its course. But before taking a final decision it was thought appropriate to invite the views of some representative Zionists, as well as some Anglo-Jewish leaders who held opposing opinions. Attention was drawn to the contradiction between the messages of House and Brandeis, and it was decided to consult President Wilson afresh.[28]

Montagu persisted. Shortly after the meeting he wrote to Lloyd George:

> Did I believe as you in a Jewish Nation . . . [and] that great idealism overcomes practical difficulties, I might have been less opposed to your view. But it is a matter of deep regret to me that you should find yourself in opposition to Rufus [Lord Reading] and myself . . . you are being . . . misled by a foreigner, a dreamer, an idealist, who . . . sweeps aside all practical difficulties.

He feared that official endorsement of Zionism would have an adverse effect on his mission to India. 'The population of India has pinned its faith on me, I . . . alone can save them.' He wondered whether to resign in protest against the proposed declaration, a move which in India would be interpreted as a victory for the illiberal elements in British politics; on the other hand, to remain in the Government would be tantamount to a voluntary death warrant to his own status and that of his fellow-Jews; submission to anti-Semitism.[29]

Montagu was fully aware of the depth of pro-Turkish sentiment in India and, as late as December 1919, he pleaded against the dismemberment of the Ottoman Empire.[30] His consternation, on the eve of his departure, is therefore understandable. A British invasion of Palestine, coupled with a Zionist declaration, would point clearly to the disappearance of Moslem sovereignty over Jerusalem, and might put the success of his mission in the balance. It was indicative of his predisposition that in the same letter to Lloyd George he insisted that Palestine was not British and that 'it can never be part of the British Empire'.

This was hardly in line with Lloyd George's policy. Receiving no reply, Montagu circulated yet another memorandum, his last before sailing for India, in which he reproduced Miss Bell's remarks on Palestine, as well as the statement made by Rabbi Adler in 1878, as the most authentic definition of Jewish identity.[31] The memorandum made no impression. Nor did various pamphlets which Lord Swaythling (Montagu's brother) forwarded to the members of the War Cabinet, carry much conviction. Ormsby-Gore dismissed them as 'out of date, being reprints of views given before the rise of the Zionist movement'.[32]

From mid-October things began to move faster. At Balfour's request, Wilson was shown the latest draft declaration, with which he agreed. However, he asked that it should make no mention of his approval, since he had arranged that this should be made public after an approach from American Jews.[33] Independently on 9 October Weizmann sent the formula to Brandeis, urging that it was 'essential to have not only President's approval of text but his positive recommendation without delay', and that support from American Zionists and even from prominent non-Zionists was also desirable and urgent. Ten days later Brandeis was able to break to Weizmann the good news that the President had sent the desired message to London, but was of the opinion that a public declaration of his own would be 'injudicious'.[34] Major Webster, studying the correspondence, concluded that the main reason for Wilson's qualified attitude was that the United States was not at war with Turkey; 'of the personal sympathy of the President with the Zionist aims, there could, however, be no doubt, and his attitude was one factor in determining the decision of the British Cabinet.' Webster paid tribute to Brandeis's skill in eliciting from the President his blessing on the British move.[35]

When, at the request of the War Cabinet, representatives of British Jewry submitted their comments on the draft declaration,[36] it became evident that the only bone of contention between the Zionists and the non-Zionists was the term 'national home'; on practical matters there was a remarkable consensus. Montefiore must have made a strong impression when asserting that neither he nor his friends desired to impede colonisation and immigration into Palestine:

on the contrary, we desire to obtain free facilities for them. We are in favour of local autonomy . . . we are in favour of the Jews, when their numbers permit it, ultimately obtaining the power which any

large majority may justly claim . . . there can be no objection to
Jews who *want* to form themselves into a nationality in that country,
but it must be effected without any prejudice to the character and
position of the Jews as nationals of other countries.

He regretted the phrase 'a national home' and suggested an alternative
formula. It was a formidable threat since it contained sufficient substance
to beat the Zionists on their own ground. It read:

His Majesty's Government is anxious that free and unimpeded
Jewish immigration into Palestine should be established. It views
with favour unrestricted Jewish colonisation in that country. It will
do its best to facilitate such immigration and colonisation. It will also
seek to secure such municipal and local autonomy for the Jews as
may be possible and as the circumstances of the case may demand;
it being clearly understood &c.

However, Montefiore added, if the Government believed that their
own formula could serve Britain better, he was prepared to abandon his
position.

Leonard Cohen, Chairman of the Jewish Board of Guardians, followed
broadly Montefiore's line, though less persuasively. Sir Philip Magnus,
M.P. objected to the use of 'national home' and thought that 'a centre of
Jewish culture' was more appropriate. The response of Sir Stuart Samuel,
the newly-elected Chairman of the Board of Deputies, could be described
as middle-of-the-road, although in official circles it was taken to be
mildly pro-Zionist. His brother, Herbert Samuel, approved of the British
policy reiterating his concept that, should Palestine fall under German
influence, Egypt would be exposed to constant danger. 'The best safeguard would be the establishment of a large Jewish population, preferably
under British protection.' The declaration would win for the British the
lasting gratitude of Jews throughout the world, but he deemed it more
prudent to withhold its publication until after the Turks were driven out
of Palestine. The Chief Rabbi, Dr Joseph Hertz, said that the declaration
would mark 'an epoch in Jewish history'; millions of Jews would regard
it as the realisation of their 'undying hope of restoration'. The reference to
the civil and religious rights of the existing non-Jewish communities in
Palestine was in complete harmony with the basic principle of the
Mosaic code.[37] Lord Rothschild's reaction was more qualified. The second
proviso was a slur on Zionism, as it presupposed that the national home
might jeopardise the political status of Jews in their countries of domicile.
Otherwise he welcomed the British move. Weizmann felt confident that

the declaration would provide 'a powerful impetus towards the regeneration . . . of an ancient country and an ancient people', and would mark 'a notable step forward on the path of human progress'. He suggested that 'Jewish people' be substituted for the 'Jewish race' and 're-establishment' for 'establishment'; 'by the small alteration the historical connection . . . would be indicated and the whole matter put in its true light'. Sokolow too was not completely happy about the wording. He would have preferred a declaration along the lines worked out by himself and his friends, presented on 18 July by Lord Rothschild. However, he realised that the two provisos were necessary to satisfy all sections of British Jewry. He supported the amendments proposed by Weizmann and hoped that the declaration would be hailed with gratitude and enthusiasm.

The Zionists gave their consent with mixed feelings. Weizmann recalled: 'We . . . examined and re-examined the formula, comparing the old text with the new. We saw the differences only too clearly, but we did not dare to occasion further delay by pressing for the original formula.' He went on:[38]

> It is one of the 'ifs' of history whether we should have been intransigent, and stood by our guns. Should we then have obtained a better statement? Or would the Government have become wearied of these internal Jewish divisions, and dropped the whole matter? . . . Our judgement was to accept, to press for ratification. For we knew that the assimilationists would use every delay for their own purposes.

Rothschild was of the same opinion: 'I fear', he wrote Sokolow on 13 October, 'that the Government will finally decide *not* to make any declaration at all, for I hear our enemies have been very active.'[39]

Perhaps the Zionists overrated the strength of their opponents; they were certainly mistaken in regarding all of them as 'enemies'. Montefiore was ready to assist them. Nor did he object to the revival of the Jewish nationality in Palestine. It was the fear, albeit illusory, that the 'national home' would have adverse implications for the civic status of Jews outside Palestine that provoked opposition. With this exception, Montefiore's formula was not without merit. For, in contrast to the vagueness of 'national home', which under the Mandate gave rise to conflicting interpretations, Montefiore's draft contained practical elements which could have provided a safer road towards the creation of a Jewish majority in Palestine and ultimately to the Jewish Commonwealth. Had the Zionists managed to sort out their differences with the Anglo-Jewish Establishment, Montagu's opposition would have carried little weight and the insertion of the provisos made unnecessary.

There was an additional reason why the London Zionists could afford no further procrastination for, without tangible proof of a British commitment, they had little chance of winning their friends abroad over to their policy. In vain Weizmann pleaded with Tschlenow that under the Berlin leadership Zionism would be subordinated to German interests, that under Ottoman sovereignty colonisation work in Palestine was doomed, and that neutrality led nowhere. Tschlenow remained unconvinced. Zionism was an international movement and the policy decided upon by the Executive early in the war, to rally support in all possible quarters, was valid. However impressive Weizmann's and Sokolow's achievements were, the nature of British promises was not clear. Were the Zionists conceded rights 'in Palestine, or . . . to Palestine?' Were the 'Demands' as well as the Chartered Company taken into account? Did the Arab question have any bearing on the British attitude and how was it proposed to redress the imbalance between the Jewish minority and an Arab majority? And lastly, did the British regard Palestine important enough to risk '*heavy* sacrifices' to rout the Turks? Tschlenow made his position clear. From Bergen, in Norway (where he was awaiting conveyance to England in a British cruiser) he told Sokolow and Weizmann that unless they were given a 'definite and concrete declaration' by London, the Russian Zionists would not be able to follow suit; statements made by the French and Italian Governments, however valuable, were hardly binding promises. In Russia, he had achieved more. At the Foreign Ministry he was assured that at the future peace conference the Russian Government would insist on recognition of the Jewish character of Palestine; protection by the Allied Powers of a Jewish autonomous community; alternatively, should Palestine remain under Ottoman sovereignty, supervision by the European Powers. These, Tschlenow said were 'clear and definite promises', which he hoped would be elicited from Whitehall as well.[40]

Tschlenow's journey was delayed; he did not arrive in London until the end of October. Without waiting for him Weizmann on 10 October contacted the Russian Zionists directly. The news, received later, that the British would support Zionist aspirations changed their mood completely. Nor did they raise any objections to the provisos with regard to the non-Jewish population in Palestine and the civic status of Jews outside it. On 6 November before the Balfour Declaration was released for publication, Rosoff wired: 'if it should be necessary to obtain the support of the Russian Ministry, Dr. Weizmann need only wire to secure such support.'[41]

Unlike Tschlenow, Aaronsohn hardly needed to be persuaded of the merits of a pro-British orientation. He arrived in London on 1 October and during the crucial month rendered valuable assistance. Both the War

Office and the Foreign Office had a high opinion of his contribution to Military Intelligence and his presence weighed heavily in the Zionists' favour. Sykes did not flatter him unduly when acknowledging his share in Allenby's victory, for it was Aaronsohn's idea of outflanking Gaza and capturing Beersheba by surprise that was the key to success. General Murray paid dearly for disregarding the advice, but Allenby was so captivated by the Beersheba scheme[42] that he soon made it the cornerstone of his strategy.

The move, though brilliant, did not escape criticism. 'No General Staff and no General would have been justified in basing a plan of campaign upon chances of this nature,' was General Robertson's verdict. 'Had they done so, and had the campaign failed, they would have been justly condemned.'[43] Allenby's decision was not taken frivolously. It was based on comprehensive intelligence data provided by the Aaronsohn group pointing clearly to the fact that the Beersheba sector was the weakest link in the Turkish defences and one where a British onslaught was least expected.[44] Perhaps the most crucial information was that the wells in that region had been left untouched. The General Staff later noted that 'only the fluke of finding water . . . near Beersheba made it possible'.[45]

Allenby won a resounding victory but the Aaronsohn group was less fortunate. A terrible retribution awaited them when their ring was uncovered by the Turkish authorities at the end of September. Eighteen months later Ormsby-Gore, paying tribute to the Aaronsohn family, wrote:[46]

> They were . . . the most valuable nucleus of our intelligence service in Palestine during the War. Aaronsohn's sister, was caught by the Turks and tortured to death and the British Government owes a very deep debt of gratitude to the Aaronsohn family for all they did for us in the war . . . Nothing we can do for [them] . . . will repay the work they have done and what they have suffered for us.

General Macdonogh confirmed that Allenby's victory would not have been possible without the information supplied by the Aaronsohn group. In Brigadier Gribbon's opinion it saved thirty thousand British lives in the Palestine campaign. Clayton considered the group's service 'invaluable', while Allenby singled out Aaronsohn as the staff officer chiefly 'responsible for the formation of Field Intelligence organisation behind the Turkish lines'.[47]

Aaronsohn did not learn about the tragedy which had befallen his family at Zichron-Yaakov before 1 December, when on a mission in the United States; but an ominous note was sounded by Wingate who had great sympathy for Aaronsohn's cause, and who had facilitated his trip to London.[48] On 20 October Wingate cabled:

> Military Authorities learn that [Alexander] Aaronsohn[49] recommends that his brother Samuel should be allowed to come to Egypt to give a message of encouragement to his people in Palestine. This message will appear to local eyes to have the authority of H.M.G. and it is therefore desirable that you should inform me how much Samuel is authorized to say. There is no objection to his coming to Egypt and if he does so, please telegraph to me what instructions are given to him.[50]

Harold Nicolson suggested: 'Allow Mr. Aaronsohn to go and authorize him to say that H.M.G. have viewed with the deepest sympathy the sufferings of the Jewish people in Turkey and that they trust that the present war will see the final emancipation of the Jewish race.' Neither Clerk nor Graham made any objection but, as the Zionist question was likely to come up before the War Cabinet the following day, they thought that instructions to Wingate could be postponed until after that date. If the declaration was approved, Graham added, 'we can then, at last, make full use of Jewish propaganda'. As nothing emerged from the War Cabinet during the next two days, Nicolson renewed the pressure. Graham assured him that the Zionist question was bound to come up the following day (25 October), 'it must certainly be settled this week, so we can still hold up'.[51]

There seemed, in fact, no reason for further delay. Exhaustive evidence collated by the War Cabinet Secretariat left no room for doubt where the Jewish world stood.[52] In England too the Zionists were emerging as a dominant force. About three hundred synagogues and societies passed unanimous resolutions in favour of 'the reconstruction of Palestine as the National Home of the Jewish people'. These 'remarkable results', Graham noted, destroyed the myth that British Jews were predominantly anti-Zionist. Now, 'outside a small, influential clique, Jewish feeling appears almost unanimously favourable to the Zionist idea'.[53] He became less optimistic, however, when he learned that Curzon was preparing a memorandum requesting the War Cabinet to postpone their final decision. Deeply concerned, Graham presented one of his most forceful statements. On 24 October, the day before the Cabinet was to meet, he wrote to Balfour:[54]

> I understand that consideration by the War Cabinet of the assurance to be given by His Majesty's Government to the Zionists is again

being postponed. I beg respectfully to submit that this further delay will have a deplorable result and may jeopardize the whole Jewish situation. At the present moment uncertainty as regards the attitude of His Majesty's Government on this question is growing into suspicion, and not only are we losing the very valuable co-operation of the Zionist forces in Russia and America, but we may bring them into antagonism with us and throw the Zionists into the arms of the Germans who would only be too ready to welcome this opportunity ... The German Press has already taken up the question of Zionism and the danger to Germany of allowing the Zionists to depend on the support of the Allies. We might at any moment be confronted by a German move on the Zionist question and it must be remembered that Zionism was originally if not a German at any rate an Austrian idea.

Graham reminded Balfour that the French had already given an assurance of sympathy to the Zionists 'in rather more definite terms' than the British were proposing. The Italian Government and the Vatican had also expressed support. President Wilson was sympathetic and was prepared to make a declaration 'at the proper moment'. He went on:

Information from every quarter shows the very important role which the Jews are now playing in the Russian political situation. At the present moment the Jews are certainly against the Allies and for the Germans, but almost every Jew in Russia is a Zionist and if they can be made to realise that the success of Zionist aspirations depends on the support of the Allies and the expulsion of the Turks from Palestine we shall enlist a most powerful element in our favour.

Mr. Tschlenoff, the Chief of the Russian Zionists, is now on his way to England and is likely to arrive shortly. Special facilities for his journey from Bergen have been granted to him. It is most desirable that the assurance from His Majesty's Government should be given before his arrival.

The moment this assurance is granted the Zionist Jews are prepared to start an active pro-Ally propaganda throughout the world. Dr. Weizmann, who is a most able and energetic propagandist, is prepared to proceed himself to Russia and to take charge of the campaign. Propaganda in America is also most necessary. I earnestly trust that unless there is very good reason to the contrary the assurance from His Majesty's Government should be given at once.

It has been contended that the feeling of the British Jews is against Zionism but I would call attention to the fact that within the last week 300 representative Jewish bodies have forwarded unanimous resolutions in favour of the movement.

Graham's sense of urgency is understandable. On 8 October disquieting information had reached the Foreign Office from the Legation at Berne suggesting that a meeting had taken place in Berlin between Richard von Kühlmann, the German Foreign Minister, Djemal Pasha, and a leading Zionist, and that certain promises with regard to Palestine had been made with the intention of obtaining Jewish support in raising a new war loan. Count Bernstorff was also stated to have had discussions with the Jews in Constantinople, whilst the German Minister at Berne had had a long interview with a prominent Swiss Jew on the same question. From these and other items the British Legation inferred that the German Government were making 'an attempt to counteract the effect of the British effort to liberate Palestine'.[55]

The news that the Germans had begun to consider Zionism as a 'war asset' was disturbing. Sykes suspected that the Germans, hitherto wary of offending their ally, were taking advantage of Turkey's progressive dependence to exploit the Jews 'for their own war ends'.[56] Official German files discount such a possibility. Kühlmann was not noted for friendship to the Zionists and there was no substance in the report that he had taken part in the meeting with Djemal Pasha. It is true that on 28 August, at the suggestion of Dr Göppert, head of the Political Department at the German Foreign Ministry, two Zionist leaders met the Ottoman Commander, but the meeting ended inconclusively. It was also correct that Romberg, the German Minister at Berne, had received a deputation of Swiss Jews and that Count Bernstorff had given the distinct impression of favouring the Zionists, but whatever *pourparlers* might have been taking place, for Kühlmann Turkey's sensitivity remained the overriding concern. Whitehall, however, had no reason to question the accuracy of the report received from Berne; it fitted neatly into the pattern of the new policy reportedly taking shape in Berlin and Constantinople. According to a reliable agent, the Turks were contemplating the grant to Syria and Mesopotamia of limited autonomy and establishing a *modus vivendi* with the Sharif of Mecca.[57] This led Toynbee to the conclusion that the Porte intended to modify its attitude to the non-Turkish nationalities; the leaders of the Committee of Union and Progress were 'Real-Politiker and not doctrinaire', an impression strengthened by the news of the Kaiser's impending visit to Constantinople to inaugurate a new era in Turkish domestic policy.[58] A liberalised Turkey—and the removal of Djemal Pasha from his post made such a possibility credible—would deprive the British of their trump card as champions of oppressed nationalities in the Near East and expose their military offensive to criticism. A Turco-German accommodation with the Jews would have created a very awkward situation for London and weakened its bargaining position at the future peace conference.

The British press was clamouring for action. The *Manchester Guardian* (19 October) argued that if the Turks continued to rule Palestine after the war, the British position in Egypt would be precarious. Syria should be given to France and Palestine to 'a Jewish State dependent on this country'. The *Methodist Times*, the *Globe*, the *Weekly Dispatch*, the *Irish Times*, the *Liverpool Courier* and the *Liverpool Post* (of 20 October) expressed themselves in similar vein. But the strongest editorial came from *The Times* (26 October), pointing to the need to rally Jewish influence to counteract 'the insidious German propaganda in Russia'.

This point was pressed by Balfour at the War Cabinet meeting on the 25th.[59] Lloyd George, who had also received Graham's memorandum, recalled nineteen years later that it was 'vital' for the British to win the sympathies of the Jewish community.[60] In the circumstances Curzon could hardly afford to be dilatory. He was known for his industry and rapidity in the despatch of business and his memorandum was completed within two days. Far from seeking to sabotage the declaration, his chief objective was to clarify the nature of the British commitment. He feared that the Government was raising expectations among Zionists that it would never be able to fulfil. Palestine, a poor land, without mineral wealth, could maintain only a small population; half a million native Mohammedans would not be content 'either to be expropriated for Jewish immigrants, or to act merely as hewers of wood and drawers of water'. A Jewish State, particularly with its capital in Jerusalem, was 'a dream . . . incapable of realisation'. However, if the National Home was meant to be only a 'spiritual centre' or 'a reservoir of Jewish culture', there was no reason why everyone should not be a Zionist; he would gladly support such a policy, especially as it was recommended by considerations of the highest expediency, and as a check to German designs. But in his judgement it was a policy 'very widely removed from the romantic and idealistic aspirations of many of the Zionist leaders', which would not provide 'either a national, a material, or even a spiritual home for any more than a very small section of the Jewish people'.[61]

It now fell to Sir Mark Sykes, as the foremost expert on the Middle East, to demolish Curzon's arguments and show that Zionism was not a utopian ideal. This he did easily since Curzon's thesis, however closely reasoned, was based on faulty information. Palestine's resources—and here Sykes was able to draw on massive evidence—were universally under-estimated. Having known the country since 1886, he was of the opinion that, given security, adequate means of communication, and modernisation, the population could be doubled within seven years without dispossessing anyone. Colonisation in Palestine had never failed, certainly not the Zionist colonisation. Though hampered by the Ottoman Government, they had caused the desert to bloom, and their colonies were self-supporting and prosperous. Sykes predicted that within forty years, with political restrictions abolished, the population would be quadrupled, or even quintupled. The devastation wrought by the war made colonisation all the more imperative. 'If the Zionists do not go there . . . some one will, nature abhors vacuum.'[62]

With the anti-Zionists' arguments defeated, Balfour was now able to wind up the debate in the War Cabinet which had lasted for two months. The meeting which ended it took place on Wednesday 31 October. According to the official minutes,

The Secretary of State for Foreign Affairs stated that he gathered that everyone was now agreed that, from a purely diplomatic and political point of view, it was desirable that some declaration favourable to the aspirations of the Jewish nationalists should now be made. The vast majority of Jews in Russia and America, as, indeed, all over the world, now appeared to be favourable to Zionism. If we could make a declaration favourable to such an ideal, we should be able to carry on extremely useful propaganda both in Russia and America. He gathered that the main arguments still put forward against Zionism were twofold:—
   (a) That Palestine was inadequate to form a home for either the Jewish or any other people.
   (b) The difficulty felt with regard to the future position of Jews in Western countries.
   With regard to the first, he understood that there were considerable differences of opinion among experts regarding the possibility of the settlement of any large population in Palestine, but he was informed that, if Palestine were scientifically developed, a very much larger population could be sustained than had existed during the period of Turkish misrule. As to the meaning of the words 'national home', to which the Zionists attach so much importance, he understood it to mean some form of British, American or other protectorate, under which full facilities would be given to the Jews to work out their own salvation and to build up,

by means of education, agriculture, and industry, a real centre of national culture and focus of national life. It did not necessarily involve the early establishment of an independent Jewish State, which was a matter for gradual development in accordance with the ordinary laws of political evolution.

With regard to the second point, he felt that, so far from Zionism hindering the process of assimilation in Western countries, the truer parallel was to be found in the position of an Englishman who leaves his country to establish a permanent home in the United States, whereas, in the present position of Jewry, the assimilation was often felt to be incomplete, and any danger of a double allegiance or non-national outlook would be eliminated.

Curzon was next to speak. He admitted the force of arguments in favour of a declaration and agreed that the majority of Jews held Zionist rather than anti-Zionist opinions. He dissociated himself from Montagu, but none the less was unable to share the optimistic views regarding the future of Palestine. He feared that the British were raising 'false expectations which could never be realised', but finally admitted that some expression of sympathy would be a 'valuable adjunct' to British propaganda. None of the Ministers contested Balfour's interpretation of the meaning of the term 'National Home', and he was authorised to take a suitable opportunity to make the following declaration:[63]

His Majesty's Government views with favour the establishment in Palestine of a national home for the Jewish people, and will use its best endeavours to facilitate the achievement of this object, it being clearly understood that nothing shall be done which may prejudice the civil and religious rights of existing non-Jewish communities in Palestine, or the rights and political status enjoyed by Jews in any other country.

Amery had reason to be pleased that only 'two minor alterations, viz. the substitution of Jewish "people" for Jewish "race", and the abbreviation of the last line to "Jews in any other country" ' were requested by the Zionist leaders.[64] The alternative formulas proposed by the non-Zionist leaders were ignored. It was now left to Graham to put the final touches to the letter to be sent to Lord Rothschild by Balfour—a modest reward for his persistent labours. The preamble read:[65]

Dear Lord Rothschild, 2 November, 1917

I have much pleasure in conveying to you, on behalf of His Majesty's Government, the following declaration of sympathy with

Jewish Zionist aspirations which has been submitted to, and approved by, the Cabinet.

The letter ended:

> I should be grateful if you would bring this declaration to the knowledge of the Zionist Federation, and secure that it is given the necessary publicity.

Denied a greater share in drafting, Graham had at least the satisfaction of taking charge of the propaganda machinery. The ink on Balfour's signature was hardly dry when he called a meeting (on 2 November) to discuss the best methods of obtaining full political benefits from the declaration. Weizmann, Sokolow, Aaronsohn, and Sykes were present. Elated by their victory, the Zionists were just waiting for the opportunity to win their people to the Allied cause. Russia was the chosen priority and a special mission, headed by Sokolow, Tschlenow, and Jabotinsky, was to go there; Jabotinsky, Graham noted, was 'just the type of man required'. Aaron Aaronsohn was to go to America, his brother Samuel was expected in Egypt, while Weizmann, after paying a short visit to Paris to concert activities with Baron Edmond de Rothschild, was to remain in London to superintend the organisation.[66]

'It is a pity that so much time has been lost. With skilful management of the Jews in Russia the situation may still be restored by the spring,' Lord Hardinge commented. Balfour too was impressed by the results of the meeting and suggested that Graham's report be circulated to the Cabinet. But it was the telegram from General Barter, assistant military attaché in Petrograd, that drove home the awareness of how much the British Government had been overtaken by events. Concerned by rumours about the desire of the Bolshevik party (which had just captured power in Petrograd) to conclude a separate peace with Germany, Barter enquired, on 26 November:

> Would it be possible for Allies to make some sort of conditional promise that in the event of a successful termination of War, Palestine would be given to the Jews? Such an announcement would immediately have a powerful effect in this country where Jewish influence is great and where craving for promised land and distinct nationality is greater even than in England.

Owing to the breakdown of communications, the news about Balfour's letter to Rothschild did not reach Russia until 29 November, but by the following day Graham already knew how enthusiastically it had been received. 'It is a misfortune', he noted, 'that our declaration was so long delayed.' To which Hardinge added: 'I wish we could make a definite statement as suggested last autumn.'[67] Belated as the declaration was, London was still to reap some notable advantages from it. But before inquiring into them, we must first recapitulate the motives which led to the declaration and examine its meaning.

17   Motives and Effects

The Balfour Declaration, Sir Charles Webster said, was 'the greatest act of diplomatic statesmanship of the First World War'.[1] There was no precedent for what the Zionists were asking. Unlike other small nationalities in physical possession of territories, whose demand for independence fitted well within the doctrine of self-determination, the Jewish inhabitants of Palestine constituted only a minority of the population; the Zionists had therefore to go back nearly two thousand years to establish a claim to the country. The people for whom they strove were dispersed all over the world, with no central organisation and no consensus with regard to their identity, let alone what kind of 'home' they wanted in Palestine; a national one, a religious one, or merely a refuge for persecuted individuals. That the Zionists emerged in 1917 as the leading force within Jewry testified to their organisational skill and the appeal made by their programme, thus making it easier for the British Government to come down in their favour; for, unlike the Anglo-Jewish establishment, the Zionists showed that they could carry the majority of their people with them. The approach of the former to the Palestine question was parochial, and conditioned by unproven fears that their civic status would be undermined, whereas the Zionists aimed at identifying their own interests with those of Britain. Considering how marginal was their influence in Whitehall at the beginning of the war, this was no mean feat.

But the greatest challenge that confronted the Zionists was on the diplomatic plane. Palestine was an international problem and the British could not make a decision before consulting their Allies. Had the French objected, as they did in March 1916, there would have been no Balfour Declaration. It was largely as a result of Sokolow's efforts that Jules Cambon gave him such an unequivocal declaration; the statements made by the Italian Government and the Vatican were also helpful. Brandeis was instrumental in winning Wilson's approval of the proposed formula, while Tschlenow could show that as a result of his efforts, the support he received from both the Lwow and the Kerensky Government went much further than that given to his friends in London, Paris, and Rome. It would not be too far-fetched to say that the Zionists in Germany also had some influence on the publication of the Balfour Declaration. Though primarily concerned with safeguarding the Yishuv by maintaining good relations with the German Government, they inadvertently created an atmosphere of competition among the Powers, thus indirectly accelerating the decision-making process in London. The Zionists gained much in prestige by having Lord Rothschild as their representative. Weizmann told him that he was certain that when its history comes to be written, it will be rightly said that 'the name of the greatest house in Jewry was associated with the granting of the Magna Carta of Jewish liberties'.[2] But it is in fact Weizmann himself who emerged as the central figure in the struggle. He had no hand in drafting the Declaration; the formula proposed by Sacher, his intimate friend, was rejected, but it was Weizmann who was largely responsible for bringing British statesmen, public men, and officials to look favourably on Zionism. Of unbounded energy, singleness of purpose and determination, he possessed great driving power and personal magnetism. His enthusiasm was infectious, but his success sprang from his lucidity of exposition and his ability to put his message across. He was particularly adept in reading the British mind.[3] He found a ready ear because he was able to show that he could influence Jewish opinion and that Zionism was advantageous to Britain. Webster bore witness to the excellence of his techniques. Drawing on his personal experience, Sir Charles wrote:[4]

Dr. Weizmann's work was largely done in intimate interviews . . . He once told me that 2,000 interviews had gone to the making of the Balfour Declaration. With unerring skill he adapted his arguments to the special circumstances of each statesman. To the British and Americans he could use biblical language and awake a deep emotional undertone; to other nationalities he more often talked in terms of interest. Mr. Lloyd George was told that Palestine was a little mountainous country not unlike Wales; with Lord Balfour the philosophical background of Zionism could be surveyed; for Lord Cecil the problem was placed in the setting of a new world organization; while to Lord Milner the extension of imperial power could be vividly portrayed. To me who dealt with these matters as a junior officer of the General Staff, he brought from many sources all the evidence that could be obtained of the importance of a Jewish National Home to the strategical position of the British Empire, but he always indicated by a hundred shades and inflexions of the voice that he believed that I could also appreciate better than my superiors other more subtle and recondite arguments. This skilful presentation of facts would, however, have been useless, unless he had convinced all with whom he came into contact of the probity of his conduct and the reality of his trust in the will and strength of Britain . . . By the time the Peace Conference had begun, his cause had become so much a part of British policy that it was only a question of how it could be best translated into practice with the consent and goodwill of the Arabs and the French.

Imbued with a strong sense of mission, Weizmann refused to consider himself a diplomat in the usual sense of that word. In 1919 he told an audience that if he had achieved anything it was because he was not a diplomat: 'I went to Balfour as a man of the people, as one who is far from diplomacy. I spoke to him with feeling and sincerity, and that is why he understood me.' Four years later, at a meeting in New York, he attributed his success to eighty generations of Jews who stood behind him: 'The forces accumulated during thousands of years spoke through me.'[5]

Balfour was not the only Briton who was sensitive to the 'voice of Jewish history'. How powerful was its impact was demonstrated by Ronald MacNeill in his masterly memorandum, already quoted. Commenting on Montagu's charges in the latter's 'Antisemitism of the Present Government', MacNeill pointed out that the spirit of nationality had been an active force among the Jews for centuries before it made itself felt among European nations. During the Middle Ages it had produced numerous pseudo-Messiahs, and after lying dormant, revived once again during the nineteenth century. This reawakened self-consciousness stimulated their craving for Palestine, which had never ceased to attract them and now became the goal of practical aspirations. It would be a 'glaring anomaly', MacNeill concluded, if the Allies, after having proclaimed that the post-war settlement must be based on the principle of nationality, were to deny or ignore the claims of the people who had throughout history clung to their nationality more tenaciously than any other.[6]

Balfour was a self-confessed Zionist but, as his niece and biographer attested, the share attributed to him in the Declaration that bears his name was exgagerated.[7] He had no hand in its drafting, and the records show how irresolute and cautious he was. He preferred to act in unison with his colleagues, even to be pressed by the Foreign Office rather than to lead it, and it was not before 31 October 1917, after being prodded by Graham, that he threw all his weight into the scales at the crucial Cabinet meeting. The lead in shaping Middle East policy was given by Lloyd George, and his responsibility for the Declaration was greater. In day-to-day matters the Prime Minister's authority was delegated to the War Cabinet Secretariat. Sykes considered Zionism an essential ingredient of the New Middle East Order, and in his October 1917 memorandum demolished Curzon's argument that Palestine was unsuitable for colonisation, and that the influx of Jews was bound to displace the native inhabitants. Ormsby-Gore and Amery assisted Milner in amending the original draft of the declaration; the former was well-informed and analytical, the latter detached and able to judge the merits of the issue against the background of British war aims. But the unacknowledged hero is Sir Ronald Graham. Seconded by Robert Cecil, Lord Hardinge, and Harold Nicolson, he pressed unremittingly for an early statement. Had its drafting been left to him, it would have emerged in better shape than it did. It would, however, be true to say that the Balfour Declaration was the result of a collective effort (other personalities, both Jewish and British were mentioned in the course of our narrative) rather than the work of a single individual.

Sykes's meeting with the Zionist leaders at Gaster's home on 7 February 1917 and his encouragement to Sokolow in Paris and Rome have misled many historians into thinking that the dominant motive behind the Balfour Declaration was the wish to extricate Britain from the Asia Minor Agreement and so avoid the establishment of an international régime in Palestine. This theory is as old as the Balfour Declaration itself.

Yet, had this been the case, Cambon's statement of 4 June should have stampeded the British into outdoing their competitors by an even stronger commitment. The fact remains that they did not. Nor did Graham, in any of his notes, or Balfour during Cabinet meetings, urge the necessity of countering the Quai d'Orsay. Sykes himself realised, while in Paris, that it was premature for the British to press for a revision of the Agreement, and believed that no prominence should be given to Zionist desiderata before French ambitions in Syria were satisfied.

While the war lasted, a more effective means was found to limit Allied French and Italian influence in Palestine. On 13 November 1917 Sykes suggested that Jerusalem should be kept under martial law 'to avoid Franco-Italian complications', and two weeks later Allenby was instructed to reject any idea of a joint administration of the occupied territories whilst operations were still in progress, though the impression had to be avoided that the British were contemplating the annexation of Palestine. The idea originated with Wingate, who was anxious to prevent an international régime, even as a provisional arrangement, and therefore suggested that Palestine should be held on a purely military basis. But in order to allay French and Italian susceptibilities, a few of their officers should serve under Allenby's command, provided that this in no way jeopardised the future British political position.[8] It was not until the peace conference at San Remo in the spring of 1920 that full use was made of Zionism to undo the 1916 Agreement and ensure sole British trusteeship of Palestine; when the Balfour Declaration was discussed this consideration was hardly taken into account. Its publication in 1917 has to be seen within the context of the global British-German confrontation. Geographically, Palestine occupied a position of great strategic importance, and it was a major British interest that it should not remain or fall into unfriendly hands. How important it was not to allow the Turks to retain possession of Palestine was emphasised again and again, as the records already quoted show. German influence could be tolerated still less. In March 1916, the mere possibility that Jews might opt for a German protectorate of Palestine, as argued by Edgar Suarès, sufficed for Grey to approve unequivocally a far-reaching formula proposed by O'Beirne and Crewe. And in 1917 it was only after reports reached London that Germany intended to capture the Zionist movement that Balfour invited Rothschild and Weizmann to submit a draft formula. It was feared that a Turco-German declaration would rally Jewish opinion throughout the world behind the Central Powers and strengthen their diplomatic position; in a broader sense a reformed Turkey would have deprived the Allies of their role as protectors of the oppressed nationalities and of plausible justification for the dismemberment of the Ottoman Empire. Hankey's warning that a peace conference might descend upon the warring Powers suddenly, and that the Germans might take the initiative in presenting their terms,[9] had a bearing on the War Cabinet's calculations. Aware that large sections of Jewry shared Morgenthau's idea of Jewish autonomy in Palestine under Ottoman sovereignty, it was important to the British Government to win them over. The Balfour Declaration was meant to torpedo the supposed German-Turkish move and to undermine their negotiating position at the peace conference.

It is true that articles in the German press, considered to be judicious leaks, misled both Weizmann and Graham into thinking that they heralded a major political move, and that the report from the British Legation in Berne was erroneous. None the less, it would be wrong to suggest that the British had miscalculated badly, for, declaration or no declaration, Germany, in control of millions of Jews in Eastern Europe, held important cards which she could use most effectively when the future of Palestine was discussed. Britain had therefore a compelling need to preempt any move by the Central Powers. The report of the Legation at

Berne acted merely as a catalyst. Moreover, there was every reason to suppose that Germany, committed by treaty to safeguard the integrity of the Ottoman Empire, would do everything in her power to recover her ally's lost provinces. Early in November 1917, information reaching the Legation at Berne indicated that Turkey had been promised aid to drive the British out of Palestine and Mesopotamia, and that Belgium would not be evacuated unless Jerusalem was restored to the Sultan. As late as May 1918, rumours were circulating that Germany intended to set up in Palestine an autonomous German-Jewish State under Turkish suzerainty.[10] It was not until a year after the Declaration that German armies were defeated and the Turks were driven back beyond the Taurus; in 1917 the position was still critical and the outcome of the war hung in the balance. The best that the British could manage was to strike a blow against the Turks and follow up any local successes with negotiations. These, however, would not promise much, since if Germany were left in possession of a great deal of Allied territory, Britain would have to barter away any territories that she might have conquered. With Russia having suffered more than seven million casualties, and France having lost nearly two million dead, Britain's claim to spoils of war would have rested on shaky moral ground.[11] Nor did Allenby's conquest of Jerusalem change the overall military situation, since with the conflict on the Eastern and Western fronts unresolved, it was feared that Britain might have to give up her territorial gains.[12] In these circumstances an additional weapon had to be employed. As Sykes pointed out:[13]

What we may not be able to get by force of arms we may well get ... by negotiation if the national elements are on our side at the Conference.

This was why Britain had to play the nationalist card. It was also the *raison d'être* of the compact with Zionism. A British-oriented Jewish National Home, it was thought, could be a major asset, and conversely an obstacle to German ambitions in that vital region. That the Allies would eventually triumph and be able to impose their own peace terms could not at that time be taken for granted.

For Britain, acquisition of Palestine was an irreducible strategic requirement. But even if the Central Powers were decisively defeated, a claim based on military conquest alone would have been inadmissible. It would have violated the principle of non-acquisition of territories by war enunciated by President Wilson and the Provisional Russian Government, and alienated world opinion. With annexations condemned, the only course open to the Western Allies was to link their war aims with the principle of self-determination. Two weeks before the Balfour Declaration was approved by the War Cabinet, Sykes wrote to Cecil:[14]

> As regards purely British interests it is, I think, desirable . . . without in any way showing any desire to annex Palestine or to establish a Protectorate over it, to so order our policy, that when the time comes to choose a Mandatory power for its control, by the consensus of opinion and the desire of the inhabitants, we shall be the most likely candidate.

Zionist wishes played directly into British hands, freeing them of any annexationist taint. Weizmann was rendering a singular service when he urged his friends in Russia and America to impress upon their Governments that England's sole desire in protecting Palestine was 'to give the Jews the possibility of getting on their feet and living independently'. Twenty-five years later Sir Charles Webster confirmed that it had been realised that a declaration on the national home would ease acceptance by other powers of Britain's position in Palestine, an assumption that was proved correct by events.[15]

Short-term motives were no less compelling. As pointed out already, the majority of Jews in Russia supported the Provisional Government. The *Bund* and those associated with the Mensheviks affirmed their loyalty, the middle classes identified themselves fully with the Constitutional Democratic Party, while the Union of Jewish Soldiers pledged themselves to fulfil their patriotic duty. Jews *qua* Jews felt instinctively that their real interests lay in a stable régime and the maintenance of liberty. This was important because in both London and Paris it was thought that continued Russian participation in the war was essential, and this depended on the stability of the Provisional Government, a state of affairs not easy to reach, considering the weakness of the coalition and the challenge it was meeting from the Soviets. Kerensky's future hinged on the measure of support he was likely to obtain from the moderate elements: the Cadets, the Social Revolutionaries, and the Mensheviks,[16] among whom the Jews played a significant rôle.

On 12 May, a meeting at which Curzon presided and in which Cecil, Hardinge, Hankey, and Amery participated, decided that it was imperative to strengthen the hands of the moderates and frustrate the extremists who were advocating a separate peace with the Central Powers. For this purpose it was suggested that a Labour delegation should visit Russia and persuade the Social Revolutionary and Menshevik leaders to moderate their 'no annexations' cry. Among the territories concerned was Palestine, the acquisition of which was regarded by Curzon and his colleagues as a *sine qua non.*[17] The delegation proved unsuccessful. The Russians both in Government and opposition resented foreign interference and used the opportunity to voice their displeasure at the unnecessary prolongation of the war; the most vociferous critics were Jewish extremists. At the heart of the difficulty was the inability of the British to harmonise their war aims with those of Russia. The moderate Socialists denied the right to acquire territory by military conquest, not would they admit that the ill-treatment of peoples by the Turks could confer such a right. The intellectuals failed to understand why the Western Allies refused to make sacrifices comparable to those made by Russia, who had renounced her claim to Constantinople and the Straits. Statements made in Paris and London were received with a mixture of indifference and distrust.[18]

It was here that the Zionists could be used. They alone could present the British claim to Palestine in a more favourable light and refute the accusations that Britain was an expansionist power. Zionism, in the eyes of the Provisional Government, conformed to the principle of national self-determination and was recognised as legitimate; it could therefore provide a respectable reason for a British presence in Palestine. Moreover, from the spring of 1917, London realised that the best method of countering pacifist propaganda among Jews was Zionism. Though loyally fulfilling their duty, Russian Jews had little enthusiasm for the war. However, if brought to the realisation that their aspirations in Palestine were inextricably bound up with an Allied triumph, it would make all the difference. Yet, for reasons already explained, during the spring and summer of 1917, the British were prevented from taking any action to win them over. Graham's impatience is understandable. By October, when Russia had ceased military operations, the spectre of a Russo-German rapprochement assumed nightmarish proportions. The Germans would be able to purchase the foodstuffs and raw materials essential to their war machine. If Whitehall needed any assurance, General Barter's telegram confirmed it. On 26 November (before news of the Balfour Declaration reached Russia) he advised London that one way to frustrate Bolshevik peace overtures to Germany was a 'conditional promise that in the event of a successful termination of war, Palestine would be given to the Jews'; another was an appeal from the British Labour and French Socialist Parties to the Russian people.[19] However, it was already too late.

Propaganda was badly needed in America as well. Her military potential was slow in unfolding and her people were apathetic, whilst Britain's financial dependence was growing at an alarming rate. Jewish magnates were known to be fervent supporters of the President, and though not necessarily accepting Zionist doctrine, were eager—the foremost example was Jacob Schiff—to assist colonisation in Palestine. Account was also taken of Jewish influence in finance and the press. That leaders of American Jewry took pains to urge their co-religionists in Russia to work against the idea of a separate peace between their country and Germany[20] was encouraging, but the fact that a wide section of American Jewry favoured the development of an autonomous Jewish settlement in Palestine under Ottoman sovereignty was disconcerting. The Balfour Declaration was meant to convert them to the idea of a British, alternatively an American trusteeship, and obtain President Wilson's endorsement.

It would be too cynical to suggest that Britain acted solely from selfish motives. Asked bluntly by Colonel Meinertzhagen whether the Declaration bearing his name was a reward for wartime services, Balfour replied emphatically that both he and the Prime Minister had been influenced 'by the desire to give the Jews their rightful place in the world; a great nation without a home is not right'.[21] Aloof and imperturbable, Balfour felt passionately on two things; one was the need to maintain friendship with the United States, the second was Zionism.[22] Schooled in Jewish history and civilisation, he regarded the destruction of Judea by the Romans as 'one of the great wrongs' and 'a national tragedy' for the Jews, which the Allied Powers were attempting to redress.[23] In a speech in the House of Lords on 21 June 1922 he denied that the Declaration sprang from purely materialistic considerations. It attempted to offer at least a partial solution to a problem to which there was no parallel in human history. It was a reminder to Jews scattered in every land that Christendom was 'not oblivious to their faith . . . of the service they have rendered to the great religions of the world'. Sir Mark Sykes, speaking as a Christian, attested that in helping Zionism he felt that he was doing something to make 'a great amend'.[24] Cecil regarded it as 'one of the noblest movements' of the day, a venture in practical idealism. A Jewish Palestine was 'the first constructive effort in the new settlement of the world after the War'.[25] Both Lord Harlech (formerly Ormsby-Gore) and Leopold Amery pointed to the idealistic motives behind the Declaration;[26] Sir Charles Webster suggested that negotiations with the Zionists would never have come to fruition had not Lloyd George been a man exceptionally well versed in the Bible, and his Foreign Minister found a cause that held a strong emotional appeal for him; 'others who played a part in the negotiations were also genuinely moved by the prospect of re-creating a Jewish National Home in Palestine'.[27]

Undoubtedly there was a strong undercurrent of sympathy towards Zionism, which was reflected in the press.[28] It was consistent with the encouragement to small and oppressed nationalities. But, as the official

records show, sentiment did not determine state policy. The Declaration
would hardly have been made unless it had been the considered judgement
of the Foreign Office and the War Cabinet that it was clearly in the British
interest to do so. There was a combination of motives rather than one
which led to the final decision, but what dominated was the desire for
security.

We must now examine to what extent the Declaration lived up to the
expectations of its sponsors, and what benefits were derived from it by
Britain and the Zionist movement. If the primary objective was to swing
Jewish opinion towards Britain, this was achieved beyond all expectations.
Messages from Jewish communities in various parts of the world poured
into London expressing gratitude and appreciation. Whether in Greece,
Italy, or South America, in the Entente or neutral countries, the Declaration aroused a wave of mystic elation which enhanced Britain's prestige.
A characteristic eulogy came from the Jewish Correspondence Bureau in
The Hague (10 November), asserting that Britain had secured for herself
a place of honour in Jewish history; they would never forget that it was
the first Great Power to recognise their claim to Palestine. Even Mow-
showitz, Wolf's representative, had to admit that Balfour's letter made
'an extraordinary impression' on Jews in the neutral countries. The press
in general expressed warm sympathy and followed with great interest the
progress of British troops in Palestine. Sykes was pleased that no one
would now be able to accuse Britain of 'crusading'. That Salonica Jewry,
formerly regarded as 'the brain and nerve centre' of the Young Turk
movement, applauded London so warmly, was a good omen: 'If Salonica
is prepared to drop the C.U.P. we may expect a different political situation
in the Near East.' Two weeks later he summed up:[29]

> It is important to note that wherever there are Jews there are
> Zionists, in theory at least, and that, no matter what views these
> may have held about the war up till now, henceforth the goal of
> their ambitions rests in Entente hands.

In England the Zionists were in a state of near euphoria. They embarked
on a massive campaign to popularise the idea of a British Palestine and
gave maximum publicity to the Declaration. They felt that nothing comparable in historical significance had occurred since the proclamation of
Cyrus the Great in 538 B.C. Israel Sieff referred to it as 'the political
charter of the Jewish Nation', 'the first *post bellum* act of reconstruction
in the new world ... We Jews know what England's pledge means.'
Lord Rothschild assured Balfour of the gratitude of ten million of his

co-religionists.[30] This was certainly true of those in Russia, where the Declaration had an almost volcanic effect.

Because of a breakdown in communications, the news reached Russia after a delay of three weeks. In spite of the general disorder there it spread quickly and was greeted with great joy. Thanksgiving services in the synagogues and public meetings were held all over the country. Zionist papers published special editions and the press in general commented very favourably. So great was the enthusiasm that it was thought unnecessary to send Jabotinsky on a special mission to Russia. 'A new era' had opened, Rosoff cabled Tschlenow. But the latter, then in London, was more cautious. To him neutrality was almost an article of faith; nor would he depart from his principle that Zionism should be internationally-oriented. Overt pro-British demonstrations might jeopardise the Palestinian Jews. He realised that the British needed the Zionists and they should therefore have sanctioned a less ambiguous formula. It was not until the conquest of Jerusalem that he accepted Weizmann's and Sokolow's policy.[31] In Russia, however, the Declaration was taken as synonymous with a promise that Palestine would be handed over to the Jews. On 29 November, at a demonstration in Odessa, a crowd estimated at about 150,000 marched in procession to the British Consulate cheering and singing the British and Jewish national anthems. Senator Oscar Gruzenberg made an impassioned speech and thanked the British Government and people. On the following day a deputation of rabbis waited on the Consul, while youth organisations vowed to do everything in their power to build a Jewish state in Palestine. Similar public demonstrations took place in Petrograd, Moscow, Kiev, Nicolaiev, and elsewhere. Some discordant voices were heard from Jewish socialists warning against enticement by 'the imperialist interests of the British bourgeoisie', but these were drowned in the general chorus of jubilation and excitement.[32]

To Whitehall this was good news. 'In Russia and the United States of America, the spontaneous response is even greater than I could have expected', Sykes told Picot. 'Splendid results are recorded in Odessa, Kiev and Petrograd.' Graham regretted that the Declaration had not been issued four months earlier. 'Not my fault', Balfour commented laconically, while Hardinge noted that 'it might possibly have made all the difference'.[33]

Ironically, the Bolsheviks' seizure of power practically coincided with the date of the Declaration. But what concerned the British Government, during the following months, was not their political theory, distasteful as it was to the West, but the possibility that they might conclude a separate peace. It was feared that such a move, besides its direct military implications, would nullify the economic blockade of Germany. Moreover, it was assumed that the Russians would be unable to embark upon reconstruction of their country without foreign assistance, and that therefore they would fall under German influence for some time. The only comfort that London and Paris could draw from this otherwise dismal situation, was that on 7/20 November 1917 the Ukraine proclaimed itself an independent Republic and an ally of the Powers who were at war with Germany. When the Bolsheviks, however, declared war on the Rada, the government set up in the Ukraine, Whitehall had to decide whether to continue support of the Ukrainians and other dissident national minorities. On Balfour's advice, it was decided not to interfere in Russia's internal affairs and so avoid an open breach with Petrograd, a policy to which the French subscribed. On the other hand, the South was the granary of the country rich in raw materials. It was therefore equally important to obtain the good will of the Ukrainians and the Federation of the Provinces in South-Eastern Russia in order to deny their resources to Germany. The British Consul-General in Odessa was instructed to make every effort to prevent supplies from reaching the Central Powers. The Jews, quoted as supporters of Ukrainian national aspirations, were also expected to render some help in this direction.[34] They had fifty deputies in the Central Rada, a Minister dealing with Jewish affairs,[35] and were prominent in trade.

In London, the Zionists lost little time. On 1 December Sokolow urged Nahum Syrkin to prevail upon the Rada, of which he was a member, to congratulate the British Government on their recent Declaration. He was also asked to improve the Allied image in the press, and counteract anti-British propaganda. 'You are aware, no doubt, of the . . . support which is being offered to us by the British Government. Our cause is practically bound up with the victory of Great Britain and her Allies.'[36] A few weeks later Vinnichenko, the Ukrainian Foreign Minister, expressed his appreciation of the Declaration and promised his support at the future peace conference. The spokesmen for the Polish and Russian Socialists also greeted this 'great act' with acclaim.[37] To encourage pro-Entente sentiment, Weizmann suggested that Jabotinsky should after all be sent to the Ukraine, an idea that General Macdonogh seems to have favoured. What disturbed Weizmann most was the information that the Germans intended to establish agencies in Southern Russia to purchase foodstuffs, oil, and other raw materials, and on 21 December a strongly worded telegram, signed by Tschlenow, Sokolow, and himself was dispatched to the Zionists in Petrograd, Kiev and Rostov, emphasising the harm this would do to the Allies and the Palestine cause. 'Considering the great influence that our people have in these branches [of trade] we appeal to you to use all your influence and energy' at whatever cost to prevent the Germans from carrying out this scheme.[38] Brandeis was also urged to exert pressure on Russian Jews from the American end.[39]

The situation, however, changed quickly. Red troops invaded Ukrainian territory, and by the first half of January 1918 had occupied Mariopol, Odessa and Nikolaiev; another detachment was marching from Kharkov on Kiev. Foreign help was sought, and the Central Rada entered into 'negotiations' with the delegates of the Central Powers to the Brest-Litovsk Conference. The price to be paid was an obligation on the Ukraine to furnish a million tons of supplies. In protest the Bolshevik delegation left the Conference and their troops occupied Kiev, forcing its Government to flee. The Germans, however, were quick to retaliate. On 1 March 1918 they captured Kiev and reinstated the Rada. Henceforth the Rada and its successor under Hetman Skoropadsky were subservient to the Government of the Reich,[40] and in these circumstances it was futile to expect the Jews to go against their Government's policy. Moreover, they had their own reasons for welcoming the Germans. With internal security deteriorating, the German troops proved their only protectors. When they retreated at the end of 1918, the country was thrown into a state of utter chaos, and the Jews became the principal victims.[41]

In Russia proper Zionist activities were not affected by the change of régime. In May 1918 a successful 'Palestine week' was held in Petrograd, in which almost the whole Jewish population and some non-Jews took part. Special editions of newspapers in both Russian and Yiddish appeared, and the collection of funds exceeded expectations. A Zionist conference, at which sixty delegates attended, met in Moscow on 5–8 May and applauded the Balfour Declaration as the first step to international recognition of a Jewish Palestine. In the elections to the all-Russian Jewish congress the Zionists emerged as the leading party; in the Ukraine they outstripped the four opposing parties combined (Bund, Folkspartei, Fareinikte, and Poale Zion). With a total membership of 300,000 in some 1,200 branches, they virtually dominated Russian Jewry.[42] Weizmann had therefore good reason to believe that, if convinced that a Jewish Palestine under British ægis was feasible, Russian Jews would help to make Russia a 'barrier against German Berlin-to-Bokhara dreams'; in 1918 he believed that Germany, not the Bolsheviks, posed the main threat to the British Empire and to the Middle East in general.[43] It was in line with this concept that early in July he suggested that a number of Palestinian Jews should be sent to Russia on a propaganda mission, to spread the idea that replacement of Turkish sovereignty in Palestine by British trusteeship at the end of the war was in the Jewish national interest. Their second task was to accelerate the formation of a Jewish detachment for the Palestinian front. The proposal was supported by General Macdonogh[44] but nothing came of it. In the latter part of the year Russian Jews were cut off from the rest of the world; nor could they join the Jewish delegation to the Peace Conference in Paris, early in 1919. Webster summed up:[45]

> The total effect of this [London Zionist Bureau] propaganda in Russia has been considerable, though perhaps hardly as much as had been hoped. The revolution occupied most of the attention of the Russian Jews, and the consolidation of their newly won liberties was their main object. The general feeling amongst them was far from friendly to Great Britain. The efforts of the Zionists have undoubtedly done a great deal to counteract this feeling and aroused an enthusiasm for, and a belief in, the ideals of Great Britain, at a time when the Russian masses of all parties were exceedingly hostile . . .
>
> The political conditions of Russia have prevented Russian Jewry from playing that part in Zionism which under different circumstances they would undoubtedly have done.

Following Russia's withdrawal from the war, German ambitions in the East acquired new vigour. The Turks expected that Jerusalem would soon be recaptured. Convinced that the break-up of Russia had sealed the outcome of the war, they saw their dream of a great Moslem Empire near to realisation. An intercepted cable from Constantinople to the Turkish Legation in Berne indicated that after crushing Italy, Germany intended to send a large army to the Eastern front to inflict another defeat like that of Kut-el-Amara upon the British. This promise had been confirmed by the Kaiser during his recent visit to Constantinople.[46] Those Turks favouring a separate peace hinted that they were ready to decentralise the Empire, putting it on a federal basis; the Asiatic provinces would enjoy 'real' autonomy under Ottoman suzerainty. On 29 January 1918, Muktar Bey and Hakkim Bey came from Constantinople to Geneva with an offer to an intermediary of the British Legation to grant freedom of passage through the Straits, and to solve the question of nationalities on the basis of principles enunciated by President Wilson; Syria and Palestine would present 'no difficulty'.[47]

The French were reported to be favourably disposed, but the British rejected the proposal. 'I trust', Graham noted, 'that whatever semblance of Turkish sovereignty might possibly be left at Bagdad, no crescent and star will ever again fly over Jerusalem', an opinion shared by Balfour. Toynbee was opposed to Ottoman rule in any territories in Western Asia, and pointed out that in future bargaining it would be useful to play the Arab,

Armenian, and Zionist cards for all their worth. This sounded like an echo of Sykes's concept, to which Curzon also subscribed. In contrast to his former reservations about a pro-Zionist declaration, he noted: 'We have pledged ourselves, if successful, to secure Palestine as a national home for the Jewish people, are we to contemplate leaving the Turkish flag over Jerusalem?' Whatever the future of Palestine, it should never be allowed to be Turkish. It would destroy 'the remotest chance of fulfilment' of Jewish aspirations. Nor would the Armenians, the Syrians, or the Arabs have a fair chance, should the Turk remain as the overlord in Asia Minor.[48]

In the delicate balance that existed between the warring Powers, each gain counted. Rumbold was delighted to learn about the enthusiasm with which the Declaration had been received by the German and Austrian Zionists. Their official organ, the *Jüdische Rundschau* (16 November) hailed it as an event of 'historic importance', and as the first official acknowledgment of Zionism by a great Power. Although the article advised against complete reliance on the Entente, the fact that every Jew in the Empires of the Central Powers was aware that Lord Rothschild and Jacob Schiff had declared their support for the national home in Palestine, and that it was the Anglo-Saxon Powers which were the most likely to make Zionism a reality, could not fail to make a lasting impression. This was confirmed by a War Office Intelligence informant, said to be acquainted with Zionist affairs.[49]

In Rumania, the Declaration had an electrifying effect. A Jewish-Rumanian leader who had arrived in Switzerland testified that people hitherto indifferent, and even hostile to Zionism, particularly among the upper class, had declared their willingness to settle in Palestine at the end of the war, to invest capital in the country and 'promote the political, economic and cultural development of the Jewish State'. The occupation of Jerusalem by British troops was warmly applauded. Sykes hoped that the Declaration would have a positive effect on Ottoman Jewry as well,[50] but Talaat could not let the British retain the initiative. In an interview with Julius Becker, a correspondent of the *Vossische Zeitung* (published 31 December 1917) he dismissed the Balfour Declaration as '*une blague*' and promised to cancel the restrictions on Jewish immigration to Palestine. He referred to Turkey's traditional tolerance of her Jewish citizens; it was the only country in which anti-Semitism was unknown. He demonstrated his sincerity by speaking on 5 January at a conference of leading German Jews in Berlin, called by Emmanuel Carasso, deputy to the Ottoman Parliament and his *alter ego* in Jewish affairs. Eighteen days later, when returning from Brest-Litovsk, he approved the formation of a Chartered Company to take care of Jewish colonisation in Palestine on an autonomous basis. The scheme put Whitehall on the defensive, but Toynbee, who studied the reports closely, was confident that Britain still held an 'incalculable advantage' over her enemies. 'The cards seem to be in our hands, and it ought to be easy for us to dispose of the Carasso scheme by counter-propaganda—though we cannot afford to leave it unanswered.'[51]

It was the task of Albert Hyamson to provide the answer. Hyamson was a Zionist and a civil servant who in December 1917 was put in charge of a Jewish branch of the Foreign Office information department under Colonel Buchan. In close collaboration with the London Bureau, he could freely use the Jewish Correspondence Bureau in The Hague and the Bureaux in Copenhagen and Berne to feed the press in neutral countries, in the Central Powers, and in Eastern Europe with news items and articles favourable to the Entente and to Zionism. He subsequently established contact with every Jewish newspaper in the world. It was only when his branch was transferred to the Ministry of Information under Lord Beaverbrook that trouble began. Lacking Buchan's understanding, Beaverbrook fell under the spell of Sir Charles Henry and Lionel de Rothschild, the leaders of the League of British Jews (an organisation of strongly anti-Zionist complexion), with the result that Hyamson's work was hampered by lack of funds and administrative difficulties. The Foreign Office found it incomprehensible since the Jewish branch was 'the most effective weapon' the British possessed; Balfour later told Beaverbrook that Britain was 'definitely committed' to the policy which had won the public support of her Allies and which should be promoted by propaganda. Beaverbrook, however, stuck to his guns, and Hyamson and his staff had to resign. In Sykes's absence, Ormsby-Gore wrote:

> I am not suggesting that we can do anything by propaganda amongst the wealthy assimilated non-Zionist Jews, but amongst the middle and proletarian class of Jewish intelligentsia whose ranks contain so many of the journalists, teachers, political wire pullers etc. of the world. It is the existence of this type of Jew all over the world that makes pro-British propaganda amongst Jews so important. We have now a unique opportunity of influencing their political objective and it seems nothing short of a tragedy that Lord Beaverbrook should lightly throw away so important an instrument.

That Ormsby-Gore should have felt so strongly is not surprising. More than half the Jews of the world were under German, Austro-Hungarian, and Turkish control. 'These Jews will in the future lean either toward England or toward Germany and their influence is not to be despised . . . we should leave no stone unturned to encourage those elements which wish to guide it aright and in accordance with our ideas and our interests.'[52]

The Central Powers did not remain silent. On 5 January 1918 von dem Bussche-Haddenhausen, Under-Secretary of State at the Auswärtiges Amt, made a declaration complementary to that of Talaat. This was followed by promises that the civic rights of Jews in East European countries would be safeguarded at the future peace conference. Talaat maintained the momentum and invited a delegation of Jewish organisations (*Vereinigung Jüdischer Organisationen Deutschlands*) to come to Constantinople to negotiate on immigration, land purchase in Palestine, and autonomy. This indicated, as Colonel Wade, the British military attaché at the Legation in Copenhagen, observed, that the Turks had begun to appreciate the significance which the Jewish Palestine movement might also have for them.[53] The effect of these moves was felt not only in London but also in Jerusalem. They prompted Clayton to advise General Money, Chief of the Military Administration, to give a more liberal interpretation to the 'Laws and Usages of War' (Manual of Military Law), since too strict observance of the regulations incompatible with Zionist policy might throw the Zionist movement into the arms of America, or even Germany. This would deal 'the death blow . . . to pro-British Zionism, and at the same time to any hope of securing Zionist influence at the Peace Conference in favour of a British Palestine.'[54]

The Palestinian Jews, by and large, were 'strongly pro-British'. They received the British Army as liberators and the youth volunteered enthusiastically for the Jewish Battalions.[55] So impressed was Percy Cox, the Civil Commissioner in Bagdad, that he recommended that Weizmann, or his representative, should visit Bagdad in order to influence the Jewish community to favour the British presence. Cox was troubled by the incompatibility between annexation and the principle of self-determination and hoped that if the Iraqui Jews were encouraged they would carry with them the rural population which was 'quite inarticulate'.[56]

For their part, the Turks at the end of August 1918 sent Chief Rabbi Nahum to the Netherlands and Sweden to persuade his co-religionists throughout the world to back Turkey and the integrity of the Empire. Nahum was known to be a close friend of Morgenthau, and always advocated closer links with the United States. The idea was said to have originated with Carasso, but Zionists in neutral countries were forewarned by the London Bureau and Nahum's mission failed. The Porte, however, did not lose hope and, as late as December, by then no longer masters of their Asiatic provinces, they contemplated an invitation to the United States to give them protection, in the hope that President Wilson would oppose the partition of the Ottoman Empire.[57] Whatever the President's reaction would have been, American Jewry by then was firmly committed to a British trusteeship for Palestine.

In the United States the effect of the Balfour Declaration was not immediate. British sincerity was not at first taken for granted, while the realists argued that the bearskin had been divided before being caught. But after the capture of Jerusalem all former doubts vanished. With the exception of Reform rabbis, the Bund, and individuals like Morgenthau, who considered Zionism utopian, the Jews were enthusiastic. M. Jusserand, the French Ambassador in Washington, noted:

> L'entrée des Anglais à Jérusalem a causé dans les milieux israelites une joie intense. On sait que la ville de New York contient, à elle seule, plus de Juifs qu'il n'y en avait en Palestine aux temps bibliques. Beaucoup se sont pris à espérer que, eux aussi, allaient pouvoir, après tant de siècles, se former en nation, ce qui est l'idéal extrême du sionisme.

Their conversion to the cause of the Entente seemed to be complete. Even the *American Jewish Chronicle*, formerly under the influence of the Berlin Zionist Executive, now followed London's lead. Most elated were the Zionists. At a convention in Baltimore on 16–17 December, and at mass meetings at San Francisco and other cities, the Declaration was eulogised as consonant with the principles of democracy and justice for small nationalities.[58]

Gentiles too seemed to be affected by it. The Reverend Dr O. A. Glazebrook, formerly American Consul in Jerusalem, declared at a thanksgiving celebration held in New York that it was the duty of every Jew to see that England and the Allies won the war.[59] Spring-Rice was entirely out of touch with the situation when he told Balfour that good and cordial relations with the large Jewish population in the United States could not be promoted by a friendly attitude to the Zionist movement. 'You could not conciliate all the Irish by making Carson a Viscount . . . The great mass of the Jews appear to be bitterly opposed to the Zionist leaders.'[60] Nor did his statement a week later, that the Zionists were a 'small minority', and that 'too intimate relations with them would alienate the opposing faction' win credibility at the Foreign Office, as Graham's and Cecil's reactions show, though in the same cable he qualified his verdict by admitting that the Zionists were 'the most able and intelligent, and amongst them are our best friends like Rabbi Wise'.[61]

For London, the overriding objective was to get President Wilson's approval of British policy in Palestine, and this was exactly what Weizmann tried to do. His letter to Brandeis of 14 January 1918, shows how eager he was to reconcile British, American, and Jewish interests:

It must be abundantly clear that there is a complete coincidence of American-British-Judean interests as against Prusso-Turkish interests. This is why we insisted so much on a powerful representation of America on our Commission. It is clear that Great Britain can retain Palestine and make it into a British Palestine only under two fundamental conditions: 1) when the Jews of the world will demand it 2) when the powerful democracies of England and America also partly of France and Italy will help towards it . . . the Jewish Palestine must become a war aim for America exactly in the same way as Alsace Lorraine or an independent Poland.

It took Brandeis three months to reply that 'international situation definitely renders American membership on [the Zionist] Commission impossible'.[62] America was not at war with Turkey and Wilson disapproved of participation in any Zionist political activities in Palestine that might be construed as aiming at Turkey's dismemberment. In the end, only an observer, Walter Meyer, was attached to the Commission. It was from him that Ormsby-Gore learned about the current trend of American policy. It indicated a strong opposition, particularly in military circles, to a British trusteeship. Nor was there any prospect that America would undertake the responsibility herself.[63]

The difficulty could have been resolved had the United States Government declared war against Turkey. This was what both Weizmann and Sokolow attempted to bring about, and this was one of their main reasons for sending Aaronsohn to America. On his arrival, Aaronsohn soon assessed the strength of the Turcophile forces, but, he assured Weizmann, 'on our part we shall bring all influence to bear to promote declaration of war against Turkey'.[64] How important the issue was to the Allies could be gauged from a decision by the Allied Naval Council to persuade America to declare war against Turkey.[65] Dr Ami, representing Lord Reading, the newly-appointed Ambassador to Washington, told the Zionist Convention in Pittsburgh, held on 23–27 June 1918, that Britain was taking Palestine not for herself but for the Jewish people. 'It is the policy of England to do everything reasonably within her power to put the Jews back in the home of their ancestors.' This was an echo of Ormsby-Gore speaking to a Jewish conference in Jaffa on 17 June, that England and her Allies were not bent on acquisition of territory; 'they are fighting for an ideal'.[66] Yet despite his protestations Washington would not abandon its neutrality *vis-à-vis* Turkey.

This was why Wilson's declaration to Rabbi Stephen Wise on 31 August 1918, repeating almost verbatim Balfour's letter to Rothschild, was taken both by the Zionists and by the British as a minor victory.[67] The New York correspondent of the *Daily Telegraph* said that, next to the recognition of the Czechoslovaks, the President's action was construed in America as 'by far the most important thrust at the morale of the Central Powers'. But it was only towards the end of the war that things began to move faster. Theodore Roosevelt, announcing the peace programme of the Republican party, included in it the liberation of Armenians and Syrians from Turkish rule, as well as making Palestine into a Jewish state.[68] A number of Senators and Representatives expressed themselves in a similar vein.[69] On 17 December 1918 the American Jewish Congress, meeting in Philadelphia, passed by an overwhelming majority a resolution affirming its desire for the establishment of a Jewish Commonwealth under the trusteeship of Great Britain.[70] That millions of Americans should have invited Britain to assume responsibility for Palestine sounded incredible to Balfour, when Wise informed him of the resolution.[71] But the biggest gain was President Wilson's change of heart during the Peace Conference. With the Ottoman Empire in ruins, he could afford to abandon his previous standpoint. He showed his hand when meeting Weizmann on 14 January 1919. There was hardly any need to persuade him that Britain should take over responsibility for Palestine; he welcomed it. He agreed also with Weizmann that French claims should be rejected. He showed great sympathy for Weizmann's programme and spent more time with him than originally intended. Elated, Weizmann gave a full account of his interview to Mallet, on which Balfour minuted: 'The Prime Minister should see this.' Toynbee, who was present in Mallet's office, observed: 'If the President's mood is that described by Dr Weizmann, the present moment is very favourable for securing his sympathy for the British case in the Middle East.'[72] Weizmann met Colonel House and Professor Westermann, a member of the American delegation, and thereafter issued a statement to the press that the President promised 'his entire support for "a Jewish Palestine full and unhampered" '. He also promised that the Jewish claim to national rights would have the most ample opportunity of being heard and considered by the Peace Conference.[73] A month later Wilson met Lloyd George and gave his approval to the Balfour Declaration.[74]

Wilson's stand was consistent with the line adopted by his staff. William Yale suggested that Palestine should be separated from Syria and be constituted as a National Home for the Jewish people under the mandate of Britain acting as custodian for the League of Nations.[75] This was practically identical with what the American Intelligence section recommended.[76]

On 2 March 1919, at the White House, Wilson received a deputation of the American Jewish Congress, consisting of Stephen Wise, Judge Julian Mack, Louis Marshall, and Bernard Richards, its Secretary. He was confident that the Allied nations, with the fullest concurrence of the American Government, were agreed that in Palestine 'shall be laid the foundations of a Jewish Commonwealth'. This phrase caused a stir among some of the State Department officials, who were concerned by its adverse effect on the Arabs in Palestine. An enquiry showed that Wilson's statement was authentic and the White House was therefore advised to issue an official denial, but the President's answer was so ambiguous that it was decided that it was safer not to make any denial.[77] Wilson did not change his mind; some time during the summer, meeting Wise, he assured him: 'Have no fear, Palestine will be yours.'[78] However, with isolationism gaining ground, American influence on the peace settlement gradually diminished.

America eventually withdrew from Paris, and, with Italy and other Powers playing only a secondary rôle, Britain came face to face with France. In June 1917, when Cambon gave his assurance to Sokolow, he assumed that the Zionist enterprise would be carried out under joint Franco-British auspices; this not being the case, antagonism was bound to develop. That the Balfour Declaration evoked little or no response in France was not a promising sign. On 27 December 1917, speaking in the French Chamber on the occasion of the fall of Jerusalem, Pichon pointedly remarked that the government which was to replace that of the Turk 'n'est pas le régime special de la France ou de l'Angleterre; ce sera un régime international'.[79] Le Temps (11 December) hoped for the best—that England would not pursue selfish objectives since too many international interests were involved in the Holy Land, one of which was the aspirations of the Jews which should be respected. More typical of the French press was La Libre Parole (3, 7 December) which stated bluntly that 'France will not give up Palestine'. Picot was bitterly disappointed at not being invited to share in the administration of the conquered territories in accordance with the 1916 Agreement. Suspecting that this was the thin end of the wedge, he found compensation in playing off the Palestinian Arabs against the Zionists and the British. As Chief Political Officer, Meinertzhagen was forced to the conclusion that one of the factors contributing to unrest in the country was French propaganda.[80]

The French Government tried to play down the Balfour Declaration, interpreting it as 'a promise to protect and somewhat extend the existing Zionist colonies'. It resisted also any suggestion that the northern borders of Palestine should extend as far as the river Litani and Mount Hermon. In these circumstances, Forbes Adam believed that the only effective way was to approach Clemenceau directly, to explain to him frankly the Zionist case and appeal to him to bring about a settlement on the basis of nationality to which both the British and the French subscribed; a suggestion on which Curzon commented: 'Neither can it be worthwhile for the French to set against themselves the Zionists of the whole world.'[81]

It was not until the meeting of the Supreme Council at San Remo on 24 April 1920 that Curzon, then Foreign Minister, was able to make full use of Zionism in support of the British claim. Berthelot, his opposite number, denied that the Balfour Declaration had been accepted by the Allies; the French Government 'had never taken official cognisance' of it; it had long been 'a dead letter'. Curzon thereupon pointed to Pichon's letter to Sokolow of 9 February 1918: 'I am happy to affirm that the understanding between the French and British Governments on this question is complete.' When Berthelot insisted, not without some justification, that the Declaration had never been regarded as a 'basis for the future administration of Palestine', Curzon was on safe ground when he replied that 'the Jews themselves were really the best judges of what they wanted'.[82]

That Curzon should have mentioned the Jews alone, keeping silent about the wishes of the Arab population regarding future administration, although Berthelot tried to make the most of it in his arguments, is significant. In December 1918 the Imperial War Cabinet had decided that it was desirable that the trusteeship of Palestine should fall on the United States or Britain, and that as far as possible the choice should be 'in accordance with the expressed desires (a) of the Arab population, (b) of the Zionist community in Palestine'.[83] This was based on the belief expressed by Curzon during a meeting of the Eastern Committee on 5 December 1918 that 'from all the evidence we have so far, the Arabs and the Zionists in Palestine want us'.[84] This was obviously not the case. The Syrians and the Palestinians regarded the Hedjaz revolt, and the British share in it, with suspicion and dislike. Given the choice, they would have preferred to remain under Turkish domination rather than fall under 'the Christian yoke'.[85] Ormsby-Gore, when visiting Palestine in the spring of 1918, noted that if the country was ever to be properly developed, and still more, if it was ever to be British, it was only the Zionists who could bring this about.

Mark's blessed Arabs are a poor show in this country—they may be better on the other side of the Jordan . . . We are getting reports that the Arabs in territory occupied by us are beginning to forget what they suffered under the Turks (political memories are short) and think we should do more for them. Gratitude in the East is largely limited by what you get out of people in hard cash![86]

He was all the more disappointed since, when working on the Arab Bureau in Cairo, he was still under the firm impression that England was the only European nation that carried 'real prestige' among the native Moslems.[87]

In the first flush of victory over the Turks, the Allies still cherished the illusion that their protection of the liberated nationalities accorded with the wishes of the indigenous population. This belief lay behind the joint Anglo-French declaration of 7 November 1918.[88] But this optimistic view soon foundered against the rock of reality. In his memorandum of 1 January 1919 to the Supreme Council at the Peace Conference, Emir Feisal asserted that Syria was 'sufficiently advanced politically to manage her own affairs'. He welcomed foreign technical advice but not at the expense of 'the freedom we have just won for ourselves by force of arms'.[89] He was authorised by the Council of Syria and its religious chiefs to demand no less than 'complete independence',[90] a desire that was re-affirmed by the General Syrian Congress in Damascus on 2 July 1919, which included delegates from Mesopotamia and Palestine as well. It coincided with the investigation made by the American Commission under H. C. King and C. R. Crane, which found that there existed among the Arab population a strong desire for complete independence for a United Syria, including Palestine, but that if supervision was necessary, that of the United States was preferred.[91] The work of the Commission was of questionable merit and its report was not published, yet there was no getting over the fact that the aspirations of the Allies and of the indigenous population diverged. The British were particularly embar-rassed, since even their protégé, King Hussein, rejected the mandatory principle thus precluding any agreement with the Arabs.[92] To a devout Moslem in charge of the Holy Places, the idea of accepting the protection of a Christian state was repugnant. Nor could Hussein risk being accused by his fellow Arabs of handing over their countries to a European Power. Hence his insistence that what in fact was promised to him by McMahon was Arab 'independence'. The conflict of principle between the British and the Arabs was absolute. Whatever the long-term repercussions in the

Middle East, it was obvious that the British case for protecting Palestine could not rest on the wishes of the local population.

With regard to the Jews the position was quite different and, given that acquisition of territory by war was not admissible, it was on them alone that the British had to rely. On 16 August 1918, Ormsby-Gore told the Zionist Political Committee that Whitehall was not in a position to expound the idea of a British Palestine, but that the Zionists could. He urged them to approach all the powers concerned at the future peace conference.[93] This they did. The termination of hostilities coincided with the first anniversary of the Balfour Declaration, and telegrams poured into London from all parts of the world; those from territories formerly occupied by German and Austrian troops merited particular attention. All of them welcomed the idea of a British trusteeship.[94] In a memorandum dated 3 February 1919 to the Supreme Council at the Peace Conference the Zionists were specific:[95]

> We ask that Great Britain shall act as Mandatory of the League of Nations for Palestine. The selection of Great Britain as Mandatory is argued on the ground that this is the wish of the Jews of the world, and the League of Nations in selecting a Mandatory will follow, as far as possible, the popular wish of the people concerned.

Zionism thus helped to legitimise Britain's position in Palestine, which otherwise would have been based solely on military conquest. Judging retrospectively, Professor Webster thought that the partnership between Britain and the Zionists had accomplished its main purpose.[96] Britain had acquired a friendly base in Palestine and a massive popularity among Jews everywhere.

It is true that the Declaration added to Britain's difficulties with the Arabs,[97] but there is no firm evidence to suggest that its position in Palestine, and in the Middle East in general, would have been more secure had it not been committed to Zionism. On this point it is useful to quote Clayton's statement to Weizmann on 7 November 1922, when he noted that, following Egyptian independence, granted that year, the strategic importance of Palestine had correspondingly increased. Its administration, however, was strongly bound up with the Zionist policy because only a thriving and prosperous Palestine could provide an effective base from which to protect the Suez Canal. Weizmann thereupon remarked that some Englishmen might suggest keeping Palestine, but dropping the Zionist policy. To which Sir Gilbert replied that 'although such an attitude may afford a temporary relief and may quieten the Arabs for a short time, it will certainly not settle the question as the Arabs don't want the British in Palestine, and after having their way with the Jews, they would attack the British position, as the Moslems are doing in Mesopotamia, Egypt and India.'[98] Ormsby-Gore, judging retrospectively, thought that those British *Realpolitiker* who supported the Zionist policy in 1917 were right in desiring to have in the midst of the 'uncertain Arab world ... a well-to-do, educated, modern [Jewish] community, ultimately bound to be dependent on the British Empire'.[99]

Britain used Zionism to confirm her position in a vital strategic area, but the Zionists too derived enormous benefits. Their claim to be recognised as a nation[100] was granted. The Balfour Declaration specifically referred to the 'Jewish people' and, following its incorporation into the Mandate and approval by the United States, the 'Jewish people' became an entity recognised by international law. Recognition of Zionism was in line with the principle of self-determination and with the struggle of small nationalities for freedom and independence.[101] It was, as Ormsby-Gore put it, 'a Jewish "risorgimento" '.[102] The contention that Judaism was merely a religion was dismissed by the Foreign Office as 'palpably false'.[103]

Zionism became a factor in world politics[104] and it was therefore a British interest that it should gain predominance in Jewry. This did not mean that the British had any intention of interfering, let alone foisting upon individuals convictions other than those they held. Events showed that emancipation of the Jews as a people was not incompatible with their emancipation as individuals. It was ironic that the leaders of the Conjoint Foreign Committee asked Balfour to issue a supplementary declaration for Jews in Eastern Europe, since that of November 1917 touched only on 'one aspect' of the Jewish problem. The committee was reassured that, as had already been publicly stated, the British Government had 'the closest sympathy with the emancipation of the Jews in Eastern and South-Eastern Europe and are anxious to do everything in their power to secure a just and permanent settlement of the Jewish question throughout the regions concerned'.[105]

Contrary to the gloomy prognostications of some, Jewry emerged in the aftermath of the Balfour Declaration more united than before. Rifts among those nationally minded were almost completely healed. The Jewish Territorial Organisation declared its readiness to co-operate with the Zionists, and Leopold Greenberg ended his feud with Weizmann.[106] Non-Zionists also came to terms with the Declaration, though not necessarily with the national concept. The Conjoint Committee in the memorandum already quoted, had to admit that the Declaration had evoked 'feelings of gratitude from Jews all over the world', and their

Statement of Policy, approved by the Board of Deputies of British Jews and the Council of the Anglo-Jewish Association, demanded from the Peace Conference:[107]

> that the political, economic and moral organisation of the country [i.e. Palestine] be such as to facilitate the increase and self-government of the Jewish population with a view to its eventual predominance in the government of the State, in accordance with the principles of democracy.

Save for the term 'autonomous Commonwealth', this formula was almost a repetition of that used by the Zionists.

Montagu kept silent; he must have been embarrassed by Cox's suggestion that Weizmann should visit Bagdad in order to bring the Jewish community there nearer to Britain. The League of British Jews did some harm to Hyamson's branch at the Ministry of Information, only to make Balfour reaffirm his commitment and Lloyd George reassure the Foreign Minister that Sir Charles Henry had misinterpreted the statement made to him and his fellow anti-Zionists. 'I have always been a strong supporter of your policy on the question of Zionism, and nothing that was said by Henry, Swaythling, or Philip Magnus in the least affected my opinion.'[108] In the end, the League fell into line. On 18 December 1918, its Executive Committee told Lloyd George that it had decided to support the British policy as outlined in the Declaration of 2 November 1917; it found itself in 'general agreement' with the Zionist proposals to the Peace Conference and was satisfied with assurances from the Zionists that no claim would be made that Jews constituted one political nationality all over the world. They objected to the use of the term 'Jewish Commonwealth', since this implied 'a State limited to one religious community'; otherwise they were prepared to co-operate with the Zionist Federation and place their services at the disposal of the British Government.[109]

The Orthodox, the *Agudas Isroel*, formerly bitter opponents of the Zionists, also changed their attitude and declared their readiness to co-operate with them. From Zurich, where hundreds of delegates from various countries met on 18–25 February 1919, they called upon the Peace Conference to recognise Palestine as the country of people of Israel, whose religious duty it was to rebuild the land and establish there a broadly based settlement in amicable understanding with the non-Jewish population.[110] Symptomatic of the change was the admission of Chief Rabbi Nahum, in the early twenties, that the Balfour Declaration had become the basis for the settlement of the Jewish question: 'the Jews of Turkey . . . do not fail to co-operate with all their might with the rest of the Jews in the intellectual, economic and commercial restoration of Palestine'.[111]

After November 1917, Jewry was never the same again. In spite of the slow evolution of their diplomacy early in the war, the Zionists had won a tremendous victory. Henceforth, they became the central and most dynamic force within Jewry. Weizmann and Sokolow rocketed to fame; the former took over the command of the Zionist movement, the headquarters of which were subsequently transferred from Berlin to London. But the greatest gain was the recognition of the collective Jewish right to Palestine. The Balfour Declaration did not create the National Home; such a 'home' existed in embryo before the war under the Turkish régime. The Declaration only gave it a legal foundation, subsequently endorsed by the League of Nations and the United States of America. At the end of March 1919 the German delegation to the Peace Conference also fully supported the Zionist programme.[112] So did Emir Feisal in his Agreement with Weizmann of 3 January 1919.[113] The only exception was the Syrian and Palestine Arab nationalists. This boded ill for the future.

18   The Meaning of the Declaration

Few pledges or statements of British Middle Eastern policy were so thoroughly examined at all administrative levels as the Balfour Declaration. It was 'not issued in haste, or lightheartedly . . . still less was it issued in ignorance of the facts of the case'.[1] It was made as 'a deliberate act of the British Cabinet, as part of their general foreign policy and their war aims'.[2] As Lloyd George told the House of Commons on 17 November 1930, it was a 'truly national [policy] in the sense that it represented the views of the three parties in the State'. It had acquired international status since the principal Allies, Russia, France, Italy and the United States, had given it their prior approval. Thereafter the French Government on 14 February 1918, and the Italian on 9 May 1918, publicly endorsed it; as did the United States Congress in a joint resolution of 30 June 1922, approved by the President three months later.[3]

The validity of its international status was demonstrated by the Principal Allied Powers at the San Remo Conference in April 1920 and in the Treaty of Sèvres on 20 August 1920 (Article 95). Turkey's failure to ratify the Treaty did not affect the Declaration, since, as Balfour stated, whatever might happen to the Treaty of Sèvres, those parts of it dealing with mandates would remain unaffected. The Balfour Declaration was thereafter incorporated into the Mandate of Palestine which was approved by the Council of the League of Nations on 24 July 1922; the Mandatory Power was made responsible for its implementation.[4]

Amery regarded it as a 'charter to Zionism—one of the most momentous declarations that have ever been made in recent history', while Smuts referred to it as 'the foundation of a great policy of international justice. The greatest, most ancient historic wrong has at last been undone.'[5] It was, he told Ramsay MacDonald, the Prime Minister, in October 1930, 'a definite promise to the Jewish world'.[6] Lloyd George went so far as to state that the Balfour Declaration was 'a contract with Jewry'. What he meant by the term 'contract' is not clear; it could hardly have been used in the strictly legal sense. Most likely it was used in a moral sense. This was not necessarily less binding, for Lloyd George specifically pointed out that the Zionist leaders had given the British 'a definite promise . . . to rally to the Allied cause Jewish sentiment and support throughout the world', concluding that the Zionists 'kept their word in the letter and the spirit', and that the only question that remained was whether the British meant (in the later thirties) to honour theirs.[7] Professor Temperley, who had earlier aired the view that the purpose of the Declaration was to enter into 'a definite contract between the British Government and Jewry', explained that in spirit it was 'a pledge that in return for services to be rendered by Jewry, the British Government would "use their best endeavours" to secure the execution of a certain definite policy in Palestine'.[8] That the Declaration was regarded by the British Government in this light, is fully borne out by official documents now open to inspection.

On 9 November, the day it was released for publication, Balfour assured Lord Rothschild that the Zionist policy had been 'deliberately adopted, after full consideration and discussion by the Cabinet', and would not be abandoned; Rothschild had heard that certain Jewish M.Ps, headed by his cousin Lionel, intended to petition the Government to rescind the message that had been sent to him. About nine months later, Balfour reminded Lord Beaverbrook, whose view was influenced by the anti-Zionist League of British Jews, that Britain was 'definitely committed to a declared policy' which ought to be advocated by propaganda.[9] Commitment to Zionism (as well as to Armenian liberation and Arabian independence) militated against recurrent proposals for a separate peace with Turkey. Not only did Sykes argue this, but even Curzon. 'Almost in the same week that we have pledged ourselves, if successful, to secure Palestine as a national home for the Jewish people,' he wrote on 16 November 1917, 'are we to contemplate leaving the Turkish flag over Jerusalem?' A month later he pointed out that Jewish aspirations would not have a chance of realisation if the Turks were allowed to reoccupy Palestine. Curzon, regarded Zionism unwaveringly as a mistake, but accepted it as Cabinet policy.[10] More conscious by far of the moral obligation was Graham. To him any modification was both unethical and inconsistent with British interests. 'We are committed and must support it wholeheartedly if we wish to reap the full political results.'[11] In November 1918, Sykes considered it essential to make it clear to Palestinian Arabs that while their interests would be safeguarded, the Balfour Declaration was 'a settled part of [British] policy . . . concurred in by the Entente as a whole'.[12] An almost identical attitude was taken by Winston Churchill, Colonial Secretary, when visiting Palestine in March 1921.[13]

In 1922, when the Balfour Declaration came under attack, Ormsby-Gore stated in the Commons (4 July) that it would be 'absolutely dishonourable' to go back on it. Neville Chamberlain was emphatic that Britain was 'definitely pledged' and that he would oppose any proposal to renounce it, as did Sir John Simon, M.P.[14] Sir John Shuckburgh, head of the Middle East Department of the Colonial Office, recalled that the Declaration was made at a time when the cause of the Allies was in extreme peril, and to throw the Zionists overboard when the peril was over would be shameful.[15] D. G. Hogarth, in his Introduction to Philip Graves's book *Palestine, The Land of Three Faiths*, wrote that the Balfour Declaration was as binding an engagement as Great Britain had ever been committed to, and that she should do her best to fulfil it within the narrower limits of interpretation of the 1922 White Paper which the Zionists had officially accepted. This was consistent with the official standpoint. On 27 June 1923, the Duke of Devonshire, then Colonial Secretary, declared in the House of Lords that the Balfour Declaration was the basis on which Britain accepted the administration of Palestine from the principal Allied Powers. 'It is not possible for us to say that we wish to reserve certain portions of the Mandate and dispense with others.' It would be tantamount to admitting the impossibility of carrying out the obligations termed as 'trust'.[16] When subsequently the Government considered changing its policy, as became evident from the 1939 White Paper, Winston Churchill attacked the decision as 'alien to the spirit of the Balfour Declaration' and a violation of the pledge made to world Jewry and the Zionist Federation.[17] That this was an undertaking to the Jewish people, and not only to the Jewish population of Palestine, had been confirmed earlier by Prime Minister MacDonald in his letter of 13 February 1931 to Dr Weizmann.[18]

To what then had the British Government pledged itself? The Declaration was an ambiguous document; the British, it seems, undertook to use their best endeavours to facilitate the achievement of something which remained undefined. The key phrase—'a home for the Jewish people'—was vague and susceptible to many interpretations. There was no precedent for its use. Textual interpretation alone therefore would not be helpful. The purpose of this chapter is not to enter into legalistic polemics over its meaning but to show how the Declaration was understood by the contemporary press, by men in public life, and particularly by those who had a hand in shaping it.

Its recipients, the Zionists in Britain, felt confident that their aspirations had found 'solid ground . . . the period which begins now is Fulfilment'.[19] Isaac Halevi Herzog, the Rabbi of Belfast, saw in the Declaration 'an epoch making event . . . the preparatory stage leading towards Redemption and

Restoration of Israel'.[20] The Jewish community in Petrograd congratulated the British Government on its intention to establish 'a Jewish Government in Palestine'. The Provisional Executive Committee for General Zionist Affairs in the United States took Balfour's letter to Rothschild to mean a promise to establish a Jewish state, while Felix Frankfurter, at the annual convention of American Zionists held at Pittsburgh on 23–27 June 1918, discussed, in the presence of a representative of the British Embassy, 'the political and legal foundations of the Jewish State'.[21]

This reading was typical of Jews and non-Jews alike. What the British press expected during 1917 can be gauged from the following sample. *Common Sense* (10 March) wrote that the British Government should regard it as its 'duty to obtain a Hebraic Palestine, as one of the terms of peace'. The military correspondent of the *Daily Chronicle* (30 March) advocated the revival of 'the Jewish Palestine', while the leading article in the same issue discussed the prospect of building 'a Zionist state . . . under British protection'. The *Weekly Dispatch* (1 April 1917) called for 'the restoration by Britain . . . of the Jewish polity'. The *New Europe* (12, 19, 26 April) referred again and again to 'a Jewish Palestine' and 'a Jewish State', a term which was used also by the *Liverpool Courier* (24 April), the *Spectator* (5 May), and the *Glasgow Herald* (29 May). *The Times Literary Supplement* (16 August) noted that 'Palestine may slowly grow . . . and develop into an autonomous [Jewish] protected State . . . forming part of the Empire'. The *Methodist Times*, the *Globe*, the *Daily News* and other papers which appeared in October 1917 pointed out that it would be in the closest interests of Britain if Palestine was re-constituted as 'a Jewish country', and 'a Jewish State', while the *Manchester Guardian* (19 October), in a long article about Middle East policy, thought it would be wise 'to give Syria to France, and Palestine to a Jewish State dependent on this country'. Following the publication of the Balfour Declaration the press referred to the possible realisation of Zionist aspirations in terms of Jewish statehood.[22]

In the United States also the press used the term Jewish National Home interchangeably with 'Jewish State', 'Jewish republic', and 'Jewish commonwealth'.[23] Theodore Roosevelt suggested that one of the Allies' conditions for peace should be that Palestine be made into a Jewish state, a proposal that he reiterated at a Republican party meeting in New York. The Rev. Dr O. A. Glazebrook, formerly American Consul in Jerusalem, at a thanksgiving celebration at Carnegie Hall on 26 December 1917, welcomed the prospect of a 'Zionist state', and Senator Charles McNary, like many other American politicians and public men, was confident that the Jewish people would settle in the old-new home 'to make Palestine a veritable state'.[24] During the Peace Conference President Wilson declared that his Government and the American people agreed that in Palestine 'shall be laid the foundation of a Jewish Commonwealth'. He offered Dr Weizmann his 'entire support . . . full and unhampered'.[25] The Intelligence Section of the American Delegation to the Peace Conference recommended that 'there be established a separate state in Palestine', and that 'it will be the policy of the League of Nations to recognize Palestine as a Jewish state, as soon as it is a Jewish state in fact'.[26]

In February 1919, M. Tardieu, the French representative on the Council of Ten, issued an official statement that France would not oppose the placing of Palestine under British trusteeship and the formation of a Jewish State.[27] The French attitude gradually changed, but at the meeting of the Supreme Council at San Remo on 24 April 1920 M. Berthelot, when questioning Curzon on British intentions with regard to Zionism, still referred to 'the new projected State'.[28] The best definition of how the French understood the Zionist aspirations was given in *Le Matin* (27 February 1919): 'The minimum programme consists in assuring the Jewish community in Palestine of special rights . . . The maximum is the constitution of a true Jewish state in Palestine. The aim, in either case is the same.'

M. Politis, the Greek Foreign Minister, told the editor of the Salonica Jewish organ *Pro-Israel* that 'the establishment of a Jewish State meets in Greece with full and sincere sympathy . . . A Jewish Palestine would become an ally of Greece', terminology that was used by the Greek chargé d'affaires in Stockholm, and by M. Cofina, a Jewish deputy for Salonica to the Greek Chamber.[29] In Switzerland, noted historians like Professors Tobler, Forel-Yvorne, and Rogaz welcomed the idea of the establishment of a Jewish state; the last named referring to it as 'a sacred right' of the Jews.[30] In Germany, official circles and the press in general took the Balfour Declaration to mean a British sponsored state for the Jewish people.

British statesmen encouraged this belief. On 2 December 1917, at a thanksgiving meeting at the London Opera House, Lord Robert Cecil assured his audience that his Government's intention was that 'Arabian countries should be for the Arabs, Armenia for the Armenians, and Judea for the Jews'. Neville Chamberlain, in an address at Birmingham on 13 October 1918, spoke of 'the new Jewish State'. The Marquess of Crewe, in a message sent on the first anniversary of the Balfour Declaration, expressed himself in a similar vein.[31] And on the second anniversary, General Smuts was confident that Britain 'would redeem her pledge . . . and a great Jewish state would ultimately rise'. Herbert Samuel, in a speech on 2 November 1919, pointed out the difficulties involved in the 'immediate establishment of a complete and purely Jewish State in Palestine', but in the same breath recommended that 'with minimum of delay the country may become a purely self-governing Commonwealth under the auspices of an established Jewish majority'.[32] Samuel was at that time adviser to the Government on matters of Palestinian administration. More colourful was Winston Churchill's statement: 'there should be created in our own lifetime by the banks of the Jordan a Jewish state under the protection of the British Crown which might comprise three or four millions of Jews.'[33]

Captain Hopkin Morris, M.P., had therefore good reason to argue in 1930 that 'the Zionists were led to believe that they were to have established in Palestine a Jewish State', a contention that was reiterated by Philip Noel-Baker M.P., nine years later.[34] In his recently published *Memoirs*, Lord Sieff pleads guilty to having thought at the time that the Balfour Declaration 'had ushered in an independent Jewish State under the camouflage of a Jewish national home'.[35] 'What else could a "National Home" mean?' Hogarth wrote in his Introduction to Graves's book: 'What would differentiate sufficiently the status of Jews in Palestine after the War except predominance? If we explained in 1917 as we have done since (but not before 1922), that the Balfour Declaration implied no intention on our part so to favour Jews that they should become the dominant element in the population, how many Zionists would have rallied to our side?'

As has been noted earlier in these pages, British official documents, as well as other evidence, confirm Hogarth's opinion. The O'Beirne-Crewe formula of March 1916 conjured up the prospect of eventual Jewish self-government. From the beginning of the war Grey sympathised with the idea of a Jewish state. Sir Mark Sykes, asked in March 1917 about the size of the Jewish community that Palestine would support, replied: 'in thirty years, one million and a half', and he agreed that 'so powerful a community could be self-governing'. Five weeks later he told Monsignor Pacelli that the main object of Zionism was to evolve 'a self-supporting Jewish community'. John Buchan thought that the British Government had no objection to 'a Jewish Palestine', or at any rate to the establishment of 'a very large Jewish Colony', though it was not desirable to announce publicly that 'it should be either a sovereign Jewish State or a British protectorate'. Ronald MacNeill advocated the reconstitution of the Jewish state which would give refuge to four or five million Jews; he used the term 'Jewish state' synonymously with 'the National Home'. Late in November, General Barter proposed making 'some sort of conditional promise that in the event of a successful termination of War, Palestine would be given to the Jews'. The Foreign Office made no objection to any of these statements. It is worth recalling that Curzon's opposition to a pro-Zionist declaration was based on the belief that the Government intended to found a Jewish state, an idea that he considered impracticable. It is however Balfour's statement, at the crucial War Cabinet meeting on 31 October 1917, that should be taken as the most authoritative interpretation of the meaning of the words 'national home'. It was

> some form of British, American or other protectorate, under which full facilities would be given to the Jews to work out their own salvation and to build by means of education, agriculture and industry a real centre of national culture and focus of national life. It did not necessarily involve the early establishment of an independent Jewish State, which was a matter for gradual development in accordance with the ordinary laws of political evolution.[36]

These words, as Lloyd George recalled,

> were not challenged at the time by any member present, and there could be no doubt as to what the Cabinet then had in their minds. It was not their idea that a Jewish State should be set up immediately by the Peace Treaty without reference to the wishes of the majority of the inhabitants. On the other hand, it was contemplated that when the time arrived for according representative institutions to Palestine, if the Jews had meanwhile responded to the opportunity afforded them by the idea of a National Home and had become a definite majority of the inhabitants, then Palestine would thus become a Jewish Commonwealth.[37]

There was certainly no doubt what was in Balfour's and Lloyd George's minds at that time. A few weeks after the Declaration the latter told Colonel House that the British desire was for 'Palestine to be given to the Zionists under British or . . . under American control'.[38]

A 'Jewish State' or 'Commonwealth' was however a matter of the distant future; the immediate commitment of the British was limited to the terms of Balfour's letter. Thus when Walter Page, the United States Ambassador in London, enquired of Cecil on 20 December (Balfour was at that time indisposed) what the intentions of the British Government were with regard to the future administration of Palestine, Cecil explained that the policy was 'to allow Palestine to become the national home of the Jews, by which he understood that full facilities would be given for their immigration there and for their establishment in the country; that no detailed plans as to the government of Palestine had, so far, yet been elaborated, but that under the Franco-British Treaty it had been provided that it should be internationalised.' Cecil added that there was much to be said in favour of 'placing Palestine under the protection of the United States of America'.[39] This was inconsistent with Page's own report, according to which he had been told by Cecil that the British Government pledged itself to place the Jews in Palestine 'on the same footing as other nationalities. No discrimination shall be made against them'. The State Department was under the impression that Balfour's letter pointed to the creation of a Jewish state in Palestine and Page's report was received with astonishment.[40] However, if Cecil indeed told Page what the latter reported, it was apparently because, by taking a leaf from Brandeis' book, he hoped to make British policy more acceptable to the State Department. According to Sir Eric Drummond, who met Brandeis in April 1917, the American Zionists aimed ultimately at 'a Jewish National State' but were convinced that the immediate step should be to secure 'the recognition of equal opportunity for Jews in Palestine'.[41]

Four days after the Cecil-Page meeting, the Foreign Office advised Sir George Buchanan that the statement he had suggested could not at present be issued since 'it would be dangerous to attempt to define limits of Jewish state'.[42] The difficulty that prevented the British from clarifying their position emerges from Balfour's reply to a Parliamentary question on 14 November whether approval of a national home for Jews entailed 'a state with independence or autonomous rule under [British] French or Allied protection'. Balfour said that it was not possible at that stage to forecast the future constitution of Palestine. A similar question was put a year later by Major C. L. Caccia, Secretary to the British Section of the Supreme War Council, to which Ormsby-Gore replied that none of the Allied undertakings affected the sovereignty of Palestine, and that no undertakings had been made with regard to 'the formation either now or hereafter of a Jewish State'.[43] This was correct in so far as it referred to the texts of the respective Allied declarations; but not to their intentions. In 1937, representing the British Government at a meeting of the League of Nations Permanent Mandates Commission, Ormsby-Gore affirmed that the partition scheme 'transformed the Balfour Declaration from a declaration regarding the beginning of a policy into a policy of which they could see the end, namely the establishment of an independent sovereign Jewish State. That, certainly, was the conception in Lord Balfour's mind.'[44] In 1918, however, it was still premature to speak in such blunt terms. Five days after writing to Caccia, Ormsby-Gore told the Jewish Maccabean Society in London that the main task lay not 'in creating immediately an autonomous State . . . for which the country was not ready politically . . . but in the work of reconstruction under a benevolent Power, who will act as trustee . . . and will assist the Jewish colonists to create in Palestine new traditions and healthy economic conditions.'[45]

In 1917 it was not in the British interest to limit the scope of the Declaration, still less to give it an ambiguous character. The draft submitted by Rothschild on 18 July was readily endorsed by Balfour and the Foreign Office; Graham and Hardinge were prepared to go at least as far as Cambon's statement made to Sokolow on 4 June. The two provisos that Amery subsequently inserted were meant to overcome opposition and make the birth of the declaration possible, not to weaken it. The vagueness of the Balfour Declaration was not the result of deliberate British policy but was of the Jews' own making; and, since the Zionists alone were responsible for the introduction of the term 'national home', it may be useful to examine how they understood it.

Appearing before the Palestine Royal Commission in 1937, Weizmann explained that the word 'national' meant being 'able to live like a nation', and 'home' stood 'in contradiction to living on sufferance'.[46] In 1916 he wrote that 'Palestine will be the home of the Jewish people, not because it will contain all the Jews in the world, but because it will be the only place in the world where the Jews are masters of their own destiny', their 'national centre'.[47] Weizmann never concealed that his ultimate objective was a Jewish state. The Political Committee, however, followed more moderate counsels. Sokolow dismissed Sacher and Sidebotham's draft proposals as too binding upon the British Government. Even so, he did not disagree with their objectives; he differed only with regard to the method and timing. His intention was first to elicit from the British 'a general approval of Zionism', and only afterwards to present more concrete demands on the scope of Jewish autonomy and Palestine's future administration.[48]

For the Zionists the Declaration was not a definitive document. It was only a skeleton of principles on which flesh had to be grafted. They soon realised—and this was particularly true of Tschlenow—that the formula was not satisfactory. The concept of the 'national home' was not sufficiently intelligible and had to be replaced by a more meaningful item. On 12 December Tschlenow, Sokolow, and Weizmann cabled to Rosoff in Petrograd that ' "demands" will be revised and your remarks [in] letter 10 [December] taken into consideration'.[49] It was planned to dispatch a Commission to Palestine in order to lay the foundations of a provisional administration, and advise the military authorities with regard to the native Jewish population. A few months later a draft constitution was elaborated according to which Palestine should be reconstituted as a Jewish Commonwealth.[50]

The Zionist Political Committee were greatly encouraged by what they heard from Ormsby-Gore during their meeting on 16 August 1918, soon after his return from Palestine. He was convinced that the creation of a 'Zionist Palestine' would be in the interest of the country, the Near East, and the British Empire. However, so long as the Jews were in a minority, an attempt to force the pace in the direction of a Jewish State would be self-defeating. During the transitional period practical work should take precedence over politics and the Palestinian Jews would have to be given the widest autonomy in all spheres of life.[51]

With these tactics the Zionists essentially agreed but, as the Peace Conference approached, they wanted to give the term 'national home' a more dynamic character and dispel some of its ambiguity. On 19 November 1918 they submitted a draft proposal stating that:

> The establishment of a National Home for the Jewish People . . . is understood to mean, that the country of Palestine should be placed under such political, economic and moral conditions as will favour the increase of the Jewish population, so that in accordance with the principle of democracy it may ultimately develop into a Jewish Commonwealth, it being clearly understood etc. [here followed the terms of the two provisos inserted into the text of the Balfour Declaration].

The American Jewish Congress, which met in Philadelphia on 17 December 1918 adopted a similar resolution, as did congresses in Palestine, Austria-Hungary, Poland, the Ukraine, South Africa and in other parts of the world, representing millions of Jews. The Zionist Organisation used this formula, with minor verbal alterations, as a draft proposal for submission to the Peace Conference.[52] Even Ahad Ha'am the moderate philosopher, urged that Great Britain in its capacity of Trustee 'shall place the country under such conditions . . . as will lead up to the . . . development of the Jewish Commonwealth on national lines; it being clearly understood', etc.[53]

On 4 December 1918 Weizmann told Balfour that the 'national home' policy presupposed free immigration and large-scale colonisation, so that within a generation four to five million Jews would settle in Palestine and thus make it 'a Jewish country'. Balfour wondered whether such a policy would be consistent with the declaration named after him, especially with regard to the non-Jewish communities in Palestine. Weizmann replied in the affirmative, pointing to the positive experience in England, where the freedom of various non-English groups and individuals was not abused by the majority of the population. Similarly, 'in a Jewish Commonwealth there would be many non-Jewish citizens, who would enjoy all the rights and privileges of citizenship, but the preponderant influence would be Jewish. There is room in Palestine for a great Jewish community without encroaching upon the rights of the Arabs.' Balfour agreed that the Arab problem could not be regarded as a serious obstacle, but objected to the interview being made public.[54]

Although cautious in public, Balfour's attitude in private remained consistent. A year earlier he had told Paul Cambon 'that it would be an interesting experiment to reconstitute a Jewish kingdom'.[55] Asked bluntly by Colonel Meinertzhagen whether his declaration was 'a charter for ultimate Jewish sovereignty in Palestine', or an attempt 'to graft a Jewish population on to an Arab Palestine?' Balfour replied, choosing his words carefully: 'My personal hope is that the Jews will make good in Palestine and eventually found a Jewish State. It is up to them now; we have given them their great opportunity.'[56] In September 1918, when writing a preface to Sokolow's *History of Zionism*, he intended to insert the phrase 'the eventual Jewish State', but, forewarned by A. E. Zimmern on the adverse repercussions this might have among the Arabs, he decided to omit it, noting: 'Personally, this is what I should like to see. But it may prove impossible, and in any case it is not likely to become more possible if it is prematurely discussed.'[57] Three months later, in talking to Stephen Wise, he defined the phrase 'national home' 'not as a home of the limited number of Jews now in Palestine, but as the future home of millions of your people who may ultimately wish to make their permanent home' there. On 15 February 1919, in an interview with Weizmann, he referred to the 'national home' as the 'Jewish Commonwealth'.[58]

On strategic grounds, the General Staff seemed also to have favoured the idea of 'a buffer Jewish State' in Palestine, provided that it could be created without disturbing Mohammedan sentiment.[59] Feisal's agreement with Weizmann on 3 January 1919 was encouraging, but the unexpected antagonism of the Palestinian Arabic-speaking population had an inhibiting effect. Influenced by General Clayton's reports, Ormsby-Gore now strongly objected to the use of the phrases 'Jewish Commonwealth', 'Jewish state', and 'Jewish Palestine' in public pronouncements, since it tended to substantiate Arab suspicion that they were to be turned over to Jewish domination.[60] On 21 March 1919 a meeting was held at which Sir Louis Mallet, Commander Hogarth, Major James Rothschild, Major Waley, Miss Bell, Colonel Lawrence, Mr Baker, Mr Vansittart, and Mr

Forbes Adam were present. With Balfour's prior approval the phrase 'Jewish Commonwealth' was deleted from the Zionist proposal and replaced by 'the Jewish National Home' (para 5), and the subsequent item (Ia) read: 'It [the Mandatory Power] shall aim at ultimate creation in Palestine of an autonomous Commonwealth.' The Committee subsequently proposed to substitute the words 'self-governing Commonwealth' for 'autonomous Commonwealth'.[61]

The omission of the word 'Jewish' did not necessarily preclude the development of the 'national home' into a 'Jewish Commonwealth'. This could be inferred from item II, para 5, of the Committee's draft, which read: 'it shall be the duty of the Mandatory Power inter alia to promote (a) Jewish immigration and settlement on the land . . . (b) to establish a Council or councils representing Jewish opinion both in Palestine and in the world generally . . .' Ormsby-Gore was confident that, should there be a large Jewish immigration, 'Jews will eventually predominate in the Government of the Palestine State', but to say so publicly so long as they were in a minority was unwise.[62] A few months later he said that should there be 'a completely independent Jewish State in Palestine tomorrow, he would be delighted, but until the Jews were a majority in Palestine he did not see how this was practicable'.[63] And in answer to some Zionist extremists he wrote: 'to declare a Jewish State in Palestine at present, or even in the near future, would not make a Jewish state in fact; it would be merely a rule of Jewish oligarchy in a country that is at present less Jewish than Pinsk, Vilna, and the East side of New York.'[64]

At the Foreign Office eventual Jewish majority in the country was taken almost for granted. In answer to a query from Colonel Meinertzhagen, Chief Political Officer in Syria and Palestine, about the clauses 13, 14 and 15 in the draft mandate, Forbes Adam explained that their primary object was 'to provide for the possession and control of the Christian and Mohammedan Holy Places in such a way as to ensure that it should not be injuriously modified by a Jewish Government if and when the future Palestinian Government takes this form, and after the termination of the British mandate.' The minute was repeated verbatim by Sir Eyre Crowe in a dispatch to Curzon for Meinertzhagen's consumption.[65]

More illuminating as to the understanding at the Foreign Office of the term 'national home' is Forbes Adam's memorandum, dated 30 December 1919:

The British Government by their support of Zionism have . . .
accepted the natural implications which Zionists give to the
declaration of a National Home, i.e., an attempt to make Palestine

a state in its natural geographical and historic frontiers and by gradual immigration and special economic facilities to turn this state into a Jewish state. Only time and experience can show how far the Zionist aspiration is realisable; while it is not expected that Palestine will ever be able to give a home to all the Zionists in the world, it is thought that eventually some three (3) million instead of the present 60,000 Jews may be able to settle, and that hope and self-respect may be given to a large part of Eastern Jewry who can never actually go to live in Palestine.

Behind British policy, therefore, is the recognition of the principle of Jewish nationality, which is the essence of Zionism and the intention to lay in the Turkish Peace Settlement the foundation for the reconstruction of a Jewish Palestine, as of an Armenia for the Armenians.

Neither Vansittart nor Curzon, who minuted this memorandum, disagreed with this definition.[66]

Hogarth, who took a gloomy view of Palestine's future, thought that the British would have reason to be thankful 'if and when the Jewish people is sufficently numerous and established to take Palestine over'.[67] This was the outcome that both Lloyd George and Balfour expected, though for other reasons. In July 1919, they told Colonel Meinertzhagen that they envisaged 'a Jewish sovereign State emerging from the Jewish National Home promised under the terms of the Balfour Declaration'. Balfour explained that all development must be based on the principle that Zionists were 'the Most-favoured Nation in Palestine'. In a meeting on 22 July 1921, at which Churchill, Maurice Hankey, Edward Russell, Chaim Weizmann and Meinertzhagen were also present, both Lloyd George and Balfour said that 'by the Declaration they always meant an eventual Jewish State'.[68]

The first official interpretation was given in the June 1922 White Paper,[69] for which Churchill as Colonial Secretary was responsible. The relevant passage reads:

When it is asked what is meant by the development of the Jewish National Home in Palestine, it may be answered that it is not the imposition of a Jewish nationality upon the inhabitants of Palestine as a whole, but the further development of the existing Jewish community, with the assistance of Jews in other parts of the world, in order that it may become a centre in which the Jewish people as a whole may take, on grounds of religion and race, an interest and a pride.

This definition does not sit well with Churchill's earlier statement in the *Illustrated Sunday Herald*, already quoted, and has often been understood to preclude the establishment of a Jewish state. The Palestine Royal Commission, however, concluded that though the phraseology was intended to conciliate Arab opinion, there was 'nothing in it to prohibit the ultimate establishment of a Jewish State'. Churchill himself testified that 'no such prohibition was intended . . . One reason why no public allusion to a State was made in 1922', the Report goes on, 'was the same reason why no such allusion had been made in 1917. The National Home was still no more than an experiment.'[70]

In 1923, when the Duke of Devonshire denied—as did subsequently successive British Governments—that it had been the original intention to facilitate the growth of the 'national home' into a state,[71] he was introducing an interpretation to suit altered political circumstances. This was not the case with the Palestine Royal Commission, whose version can therefore be given greater credence:[72]

> the words 'the establishment in Palestine of a National Home' were the outcome of a compromise between those Ministers who contemplated the ultimate establishment of a Jewish State and those who did not. It is obvious in any case that His Majesty's Government could not commit itself to the establishment of a Jewish State. It could only undertake to facilitate the growth of a Home. It would depend mainly on the zeal and enterprise of the Jews whether the Home would grow big enough to become a State . . .
>
> His Majesty's Government evidently realised that a Jewish State might in the course of time be established but it was not in a position to say that this would happen, still less to bring it about of its own motion. The Zionist leaders, for their part, recognised that an ultimate Jewish State was not precluded by the terms of the Declaration, and so it was understood elsewhere.

The word 'facilitate', however, had more than a passive connotation; it meant to give active aid. On 8 March 1922 Sir A. Geddes, the British Ambassador in Washington, assured the American Zionist delegation that his Government 'would not recede from the pledge, and that it would aid the Jewish people to rebuild Palestine',[73] a statement that was fully in keeping with the text of the Mandate, endorsed by the Council of the League of Nations a few months later. Article II reads:[74]

> The Mandatory shall be responsible for placing the country under such political, administrative and economic conditions as will secure

the establishment of the Jewish national home, as laid down in the preamble.

The word 'secure', introduced originally in the Zionist formula of 18 July 1917 and amended by Milner to 'facilitate',[75] reappeared; this, taken together with the word 'shall' (repeated in other articles as well), underlined the positive obligation of the Mandatory to create such conditions as to make the realisation of Zionist aspirations possible. During the thirties, when enthusiasm to meet this obligation waned, the qualifying clauses were interpreted in such a way as to whittle down the scope of the national home. Examination of the relevant records shows that this was inconsistent with the original intention.

Amery testified that the various provisos which he drafted 'gave away nothing that was not self-evident . . . it served its immediate purpose' of overcoming opposition and easing the birth of the declaration without impairing its substance. The substitution of the indefinite for the definite article was meant to prevent the impression that Palestine was considered as the only home of the Jews,[76] and thereby to assuage the fear of the anti-Zionists that their status would be undermined. But as soon as this proved unfounded, the definite article reappeared in pronouncements made by British statesmen[77] and in official records; article II of the Mandate, already quoted, referred specifically to the establishment of 'the' Jewish national home.

The introduction of the qualifying 'in' seemed to be necessary since recognition of Palestine as the National Home of the Jewish people would have suggested the imposition of Jewish nationality on the existing non-Jewish inhabitants, which was not what the Zionists themselves desired. The implication was that physically the national home extended only as far as the Jewish settlement in Palestine, but this did not mean that there was an intention of debarring the Jews from settling in any part of the country provided it did not involve displacement of the native population or violation of their civil or religious rights. In June 1919, in an interview with Balfour, and in the presence of Lord Eustace Percy and Felix Frankfurter, Justice Brandeis stated that in the Balfour Declaration the British had committed themselves to an undertaking that 'Palestine should be the Jewish homeland and not merely that there be a Jewish homeland in Palestine'; that 'there must be economic elbow room for a Jewish Palestine . . . that meant adequate boundaries, not merely a small garden within Palestine'; and that in order to ensure a sound economic life, 'the future Jewish Palestine must have control of the land and the natural resources'. Balfour agreed with Brandeis.[78]

Naturally the Arabic-speaking population in Palestine was to remain undisturbed, and in some places Jews and Arabs were to live in mixed communities, but none the less the word 'in' was not meant in a limiting geographical sense; it was used merely as a preposition; the area of the national home covered 'the whole of historic Palestine'. This was the conclusion of the Palestine Royal Commission, confirmed nine years later by Amery.[79] One of the witnesses who appeared before the Commission was Jabotinsky. He pointed out that in several articles of the Mandate (especially articles 4, 18, and 23), where the word 'in' was used, it applied to the whole and not to part of the country. Furthermore, in the Preamble itself the expression 'in Palestine' was used not only in connection with the establishment of the National Home but also with regard to the safeguarding of the civil and religious rights of the non-Jewish communities, and it was inconceivable that the latter obligation applied only to a part of Palestine. The Basle programme also referred to 'einer . . . gesicherten Heimstätte in Pälestina', though there was hardly any doubt what the Zionists wanted.[80] This is probably why the Zionists at that time failed to notice the loophole. The limitation was understood to be political rather than geographical, which suited the Zionists admirably since all they aspired to was control of their own affairs, not of others. They had no desire to dominate the Arabs even when the Jewish population in Palestine emerged as a majority.

Was there any inherent conflict between the promise to facilitate the growth of the national home and the first clause of the Declaration, and was it inconsistent with the principle of self-determination? In 1931 Prime Minister Ramsay MacDonald advanced the theory that the Declaration involved the British Government in 'a double undertaking . . . to the Jewish people on the one hand, and to the non-Jewish population of Palestine on the other'.[81] This was so, but it did not necessarily mean that these undertakings were of equal weight, or that they were mutually exclusive. The safeguarding clauses did not have the same status as the operative parts of the Declaration. The text does not treat the Jews and non-Jews on an equal footing. The distinction is clear; the former were referred to in connection with their 'Zionist aspirations' and their 'national home', the latter as 'the existing non-Jewish communities', entitled to enjoy 'civil and religious' rights, not political. Assurances to the Jews were positive and conveyed to them directly, those to the non-Jews by implication only. No promises were made to the Palestinian Arabic-speaking population. The relevant clause circumscribed, but could not bar, the implementation of Zionist aspirations. Moreover, while the rights of the native non-Jewish communities stemmed from residence in the country, Jewish rights were independent of it, and it was only the Jews who were recognised as a national entity. Arab national aspirations were recognised and encouraged outside Palestine.

The Declaration was made to the Jewish people as a whole.[82] Hence, as Ernst Frankenstein, the jurist, put it, the beneficiary of the National Home was not the Jewish population of Palestine but the newly-recognised entity, the Jewish people, and therefore, in spite of not being in actual possession of the country and not inhabiting it, every Jew in the world had the right though not the obligation to turn towards his National Home. 'Every Jew [was] a potential inhabitant of Palestine.'[83] The issue therefore was not one between the actual Jewish population in Palestine and the whole Arab race, as was asserted in the late thirties and forties, but between Arab native residents and the Jewish people. This assumption is borne out also by the Hogarth message to King Hussein, which referred to 'the Jewish opinion of the world', as compared to 'the freedom of the existing population'.[84] The British Government was alive to the fact that the Jews were outnumbered in Palestine by the Arabic speaking population, but arithmetic could not serve as the primary guide, since the right of the Jews outside Palestine had to be taken into account. This was why the principle of self-determination could not be applied. The following statements are illuminative. On 19 February 1919 Balfour wrote to Lloyd George:[85]

> The weak point of our position of course is that in the case of Palestine we deliberately and rightly decline to accept the principle of self-determination. If the present inhabitants were consulted they would unquestionably give an anti-Jewish verdict. Our justification for our policy is that we regard Palestine as being absolutely exceptional; that we consider the question of the Jews outside Palestine as one of world importance, and that we conceive the Jews to have an historic claim to a home in their ancient land; provided that home can be given them without either dispossessing or oppressing the present inhabitants.

Balfour nourished no ill-feeling towards the Arabs. On 17 November 1919, in a speech in Parliament, he referred to Arab troops in most flattering terms and expressed the hope that the world would see a renaissance of Arab civilisation. But with regard to Palestine he was convinced that the Jewish claim was superior: 'Zionism, be it right or wrong, good or bad, is rooted in age-long traditions, in present needs, in future hopes, of far profounder import than the desires and prejudices of the 700,000 Arabs who now inhabit that ancient land.'[86] On 30 July 1919 he told Colonel Meinertzhagen that the Zionists were 'the Most-favoured Nation in Palestine', and agreed that the principle of self-determination could not be applied indiscriminately to the whole world. Palestine was 'a case in point and a most exceptional one'. To those who argued that its fate should be decided by a plebiscite, he would reply that then the Jews of the world must be consulted.[87] Three weeks earlier he had told Brandeis that Palestine presented 'a unique situation . . . which inevitably excluded numerical self-determination . . . We are dealing not with the wishes of an existing community but are consciously seeking to reconstitute a new community and definitely building for a numerical majority in the future.'[88] This was in line with the exposition of Arnold Toynbee and Louis Namier. In their joint memorandum of 19 December 1917 they wrote:[89]

> The objection raised against the Jews being given exclusive political rights in Palestine on a basis that would be undemocratic with regard to the local Christian and Mohammedan population is certainly the most important point which the anti-Zionists have hitherto raised, but the difficulty is imaginary. Palestine might be held in trust by Great Britain or America until there was a sufficient population in the country fit to govern it on European lines. Then no undemocratic restrictions of the kind indicated in the memorandum would be required any longer.

A year later Toynbee made a further point. Explaining why in this case the principle of self-determination was not applicable, he stated that, as in Armenia, there would in Palestine be a mixed population, the Jewish colonists being one element of that population 'which for special reasons, will be entitled to a position more than mathematically proportionate to its numbers at the start'. For this and other reasons, 'the desires of the inhabitants, or of the several sections of them, will have to some extent, to take the second place'.[90] Conversely, when the Supreme Council of the Peace Conference discussed in its meeting at San Remo on 22 April 1920 the frontiers of Greater Armenia, an analogy was made with Palestine. It was pointed out that the Zionists' case was not based on numerical superiority of Jews inhabiting Palestine, and that this principle could serve as a guide for Greater Armenia as well.[91]

The general expectation, as all the evidence adduced above shows, was that the Palestinian Jews would be gradually transformed from a minority into a majority. Had this not been the case there would have been hardly any need to incorporate the proviso in question. A conversation between

M. Berthelot, the French Foreign Minister, and Curzon, at the Supreme Council in San Remo, is illuminating. Berthelot questioned whether the administration of the 'new projected [Jewish] State' would be different from other states, implying that its constitution would be undemocratic. Curzon replied that it was of 'the highest importance to safeguard the rights of minorities, first the rights of the Arabs and then of the Christian communities'. Reference to the Arabs and Christians as 'minorities', though at that time they constituted a definite majority, reflected the certitude that the Jews would emerge eventually as a majority, thus making the establishment of their state possible.[92] This was also how the Intelligence Section of the American Delegation to the Peace Conference understood the problem:

> It is right that Palestine should become a Jewish state if the Jews being given the full opportunity, make it such . . . At present however, the Jews form barely a sixth of the total population of 700,000 . . . England as mandatory, can be relied on to give the Jews the privileged position they should have without sacrificing the rights of the non-Jews.[93]

In a speech in the House of Commons on 17 November 1930 Lloyd George confirmed that the Balfour Declaration conferred upon the Jews 'special rights and interests in that country'.

The reaction to Moslem and Arab protests gives additional indication of the British reading of the proviso in question in relation to the operative part of the Declaration. On 7 November 1917 the Islamic Society in Great Britain recalled the pledge that the British Government had made to keep inviolate the places of Moslem worship, including those in Palestine, and protested against the claims of the Zionists. Harold Nicolson minuted: 'we expressly reserved the rights of non-Jewish communities in our declaration, and I fail to see how they could expect more', a comment with which Drogheda, Clerk, Graham, and Oliphant agreed; Sykes, aware of the Society's Turcophile proclivities, dismissed them as a 'crew of seditionists and C.U.P. agents' of whom no notice should be taken. Five months later, when the Society protested anew against the establishment of a Jewish state in a Moslem country, he assured them that steps had been taken by General Allenby to safeguard the civil and religious interests of the inhabitants of the occupied territories irrespective of creed.[94] On 15 February 1918 he told the Syrian leaders in Cairo that the British Government intended to guarantee the inviolability of the Holy Places, to offer an opportunity to Zionist colonisation, and to secure the existing population against expropriation, exploitation, or subjection.[95]

A more comprehensive interpretation was given in the Hogarth Message. It asserted the Entente Powers' determination that in Palestine 'no people shall be subjected to another, nor would the Moslem Holy Places, particularly the Mosque of Omar, be subordinated to any non-Moslem authority.' Thereafter followed the core of the document:

> That since the Jewish opinion of the world is in favour of a return of Jews to Palestine and inasmuch as this opinion must remain a constant factor, and further as His Majesty's Government view with favour the realisation of this aspiration, His Majesty's Government are determined that in as far as is compatible with the freedom of the existing population both economic and political, no obstacle should be put in the way of the realisation of this ideal.

Hussein was advised that the Arab cause would benefit politically from the support of world Jewry, and that since the Zionist leaders were determined to carry out their objectives by friendship and co-operation with the Arabs, their offer should not be thrown aside lightly.[96]

During the thirties protagonists of the Arab case saw in the Hogarth Message a 'fundamental departure from the text of the Balfour Declaration', since the latter guaranteed only 'civil and religious rights', while the Hogarth Message specified 'both economic and political freedom of the existing population'.[97] This contention is not tenable. Legally, the Hogarth Message could not overrule an earlier commitment of greater weight, and politically, as the text shows, it was not intended to emasculate the Declaration. On the contrary, it emphasises that the interest of world Jewry in the return of their people to Palestine 'must remain a constant factor', and that, as the British Government viewed this aspiration with favour, 'no obstacle should be put in the way of [its] realization'. Zionism was legitimate and Hussein was urged to come to terms with it, which he did. As for the word 'political' to which Antonius attaches such great importance, this, as its interpretation in the relevant clauses of the Mandate shows, was a reference not to sovereignty, but in all likelihood to self-government. Official records show that the primary objective of the Message was to blunt the edge of Turkish propaganda and reassure the Arab leaders that their co-religionists in Palestine would not be dominated, let alone evicted, by the Jews, that their Holy Places would not be desecrated, and that the Zionists were in no way inimical to their cause.

It is now possible to establish that the Hogarth Message was drafted by Sykes and amended by Hardinge. In the present context, this is important, since neither used the word 'political' in any other document when referring to the rights of the non-Jewish population. On 12 December 1917 Picot was assured by Sykes that the relevant clause in the Declaration amply safeguarded local Arab interests in Palestine and at the end of January 1918 Military administration was advised:

> to keep Zionism on right lines, that is, to avoid the danger of its being construed as either dangerous to the existing population or likely to prejudice the safety of the Christian and Muslim holy places, yet at the same time to give it full facilities in way of reconstruction of existing colonies and institutions.
>
> As regards the existing population it should be our policy to act with complete impartiality and foster co-operation.

Hardinge found this policy unexceptionable.[98]

More revealing is the discussion that took place between the British and French delegations at the San Remo Conference. Berthelot pressed for recognition of 'the political rights of the non-Jewish communities', but Curzon answered evasively that 'in English all ordinary rights were included in "civil rights" '. Thereupon Alexandre Millerand, the French Premier, remarked that by 'political rights' he understood 'the right to vote and to take part in elections', which left Curzon silent.[99] As the British Foreign Minister was certainly aware of the distinction between 'political' and 'civil', it is likely that the same reason that made the authors of the Balfour Declaration refrain from using the word 'political' applied to Curzon as well, since its inclusion might have precluded the transformation of the 'national home' into a Jewish state.

This did not necessarily mean that Palestinian Arabs were to be denied political rights indefinitely. On 22 June 1921, when asked to define British responsibilities at a meeting of the Imperial Cabinet, Churchill replied: 'to do our best to make an honest effort to give the Jews a chance to make a National Home there for themselves'; adding that 'if, in the course of many years they become a majority in the country, they naturally would take it over ... *pro rata* with the Arab. We made an equal pledge that we would not turn the Arab off his land or invade his political and social rights.'[100] The connection between Arab 'political' rights and the Jewish majority is significant, as only then could Arab political rights be recognised. The Arab minority would then be represented in a Jewish government in proportion to its numerical strength.

Had the native Arab population remained quiescent Palestine might well have developed along the lines envisaged by Churchill, but their attitude was consistently negative. Britain was accused of a breach of the promise given by McMahon to Hussein in return for the Arab rôle in the overthrow of the Turk; of issuing the Balfour Declaration without their knowledge, let alone consent; and, by the same token, of violating their right to self-determination. They maintained that Britain had no right to turn Palestine over to a third party.[101]

The British Government, however, did not admit any breach of faith or broken promises. Palestine was not covered by the McMahon-Hussein understanding; al-Faruqi and Hussein themselves excluded it from their desiderata, since, unlike the Syrian interior, it was not a purely Arab territory. With the general uprising failing to materialise, it was the Arabs who remained on the debit side. Their military contribution to Allenby's campaign was marginal, and by June 1918, Wingate concluded that such successes as the Arabs had achieved 'must be attributed almost entirely to the unsparing efforts of the British and Allied officers attached to the Sheriffian forces'. How hazardous was the position of these officers was attested by Lieutenant-Colonel W. F. Stirling: 'We realized that if Allenby's push failed, we should have little or no chance of escaping . . . The Arabs would be sure to turn against us.'[102] Lawrence complained that the Syrian-Palestinians would rather see the Judean Hills stained with the blood of the London Territorials than take sides in the fight for their own freedom.[103]

Lloyd George recalled that during the deliberations on the Balfour Declaration the British Government wished to consult the Palestine Arabs but this was not possible because they were fighting against the Allied forces.[104] From a strictly legal point of view this was hardly necessary since Turkish, not Arab, sovereignty was involved; Palestine did not constitute a separate administrative unit and its Arabic-speaking population was not a recognised entity. According both to Ormsby-Gore and Yale, in Palestine, as in Syria, there was a 'kaleidoscope of races and creeds'; national history, tradition and sentiment were practically absent.[105] Moreover, the Palestinian Arabs had not the status of hosts whose approval of the Jewish National Home had to be solicited; the Jews had an unalienable right to Palestine independently of Arab wishes. In 1921, when the merits and demerits of the Zionist policy were discussed in the British Cabinet, it was pointed out that 'the Arabs had no prescriptive right to a country which they had failed to develop to the best advantage'. About three years earlier, when discussing the future of the Arabah in the Negev, Toynbee used a similar argument, asserting that the Zionists had 'as much right to this no-man's land as the Arabs, or more'. Colonel G. S. Symes, Sir Reginald Wingate's secretary, also thought that as the native non-Jewish inhabitants in Palestine had 'never shown any great effort to develop their own country, their right could not be given the same consideration as those of the others.'[106]

The Balfour Declaration did not give Palestine away to the Jews; it was a *de jure* recognition of a situation that existed *de facto*. Nor was it a hostile gesture to the Arabs. The British Government acted on the assumption that the two Semitic races would be able to co-habit harmoniously and that the Arab cause in general would benefit from Jewish co-operation. Yet, the overriding consideration was that the Jews had a stronger claim, and that Palestine was a *sui generis*.

Original sponsors of the policy had no regrets. Cecil was of the opinion that no Arab state had any ground for complaint since recognition of a Jewish national home was 'part of the terms on which the Arab State was brought into existence, subject of course, to the rights of individual Arabs being fully protected.'[107] Milner, proclaiming himself a strong supporter of the pro-Arab policy and a believer in Arab independence, was convinced that the Arabs were making a 'fatal mistake' in claiming Palestine as part of the Arab Federation.

> Palestine can never be regarded as a country on the same footing as the other Arab countries. You cannot ignore all history and tradition in the matter. You cannot ignore the fact that this is the cradle of two of the great religions of the world. It is a sacred land to the Arabs, but it is also a sacred land to the Jew and the Christian, and the future of Palestine cannot possibly be left to be determined by the temporary impressions and feelings of the Arab majority in the country of the present day.[108]

In a letter to the Prime Minister, Neville Chamberlain, Ormsby-Gore struck a similar note: 'Palestine is a unique country—not just an old bit of the Arab world as Nuri Pasha continues to claim. It is of universal significance in history.'[109] And Balfour pointed out that it was the British who had established an independent Arab sovereignty in the Hedjaz.

> I hope that they will remember that it is we who desire in Mesopotamia to prepare the way for the future of a self-governing, autonomous Arab State, and I hope that, remembering all that, they will not grudge that small notch—for it is no more than that geographically, whatever it may be historically—that small notch in

what is now Arab territories being given to the people who for all these hundreds of years have been separated from it.[110]

The advice remained unheeded and subsequently Arab-Zionist relations entered a darker and less controllable phase. This problem, however, lies outside the scope of the present volume.

Notes

Chapter 1   Palestine—a Strategic Bulwark of Egypt?

1 Colonel Churchill, *Mount Lebanon* . . . (London 1853), 1, pp. v–x, cited in Nahum Sokolow, *The History of Zionism* (London 1919), 1, p. 156.
2 Lucien Wolf, *Notes on the Diplomatic History of the Jewish Question* (London 1919), pp. 119–20, Churchill to Sir Moses Montefiore, 11 June 1841.
3 I. Friedman, 'Lord Palmerston and the Protection of Jews in Palestine 1839–1851', *Jewish Social Studies* (January 1968), pp. 31, 33, 35.
4 *British Documents on the Origins of the War, 1898–1914*, ed. G. P. Gooch and H. W. V. Temperley (London 1934), 5, *The Near East*, pp. 189–95 (hereafter *B.D.*); Cmd 3006; Lord Cromer, *Modern Egypt* (New York 1908), vol. 2, pp. 267–9.
5 Public Record Office, London, CAB 38/11/9 (1906). For brevity's sake the prefix PRO before the relevant Cabinet Papers (CAB), War Office (W.O.) and Foreign Office files (F.O.) is omitted.
6 Inspector-General of the Forces. In 1912 appointed Chief of the Imperial General Staff and from 5 August 1914 to 18 December 1915 (by then Field-Marshal), Commander-in-Chief of Expeditionary Force in France.
7 CAB 38/12/42, meeting of the C.I.D. 6 July 1906; *ibid.*, 'A Turco-German invasion of Egypt'. Note by Sir John French, 16 July 1906.
8 See p. 4.
9 CAB 38/12/44, 'Remarks on Sir John French Memorandum', 23 July 1906; however, French's arguments found a ready ear in Lord Esher (CAB 38/12/45, 'Memorandum by . . .' 24 July 1906). In 1910 Esher succeeded Lord Morley as chairman of the Sub-Committee of Imperial Defence.
10 CAB 38/12/54, Note dated 16 October 1906.
11 *Convention between Great Britain, Germany, Austria-Hungary, Spain, France, Italy, the Netherlands, Russia and Turkey respecting Free Navigation of the Suez Maritime Canal, signed at Constantinople, October 29, 1888.* HMSO [Cmd 5623], Commercial, No. 2 (1889). Suez Canal (text in French). Article I of the Convention reads: 'The Suez Canal shall always be free and open to every vessel of commerce or of war in time of war or in time of peace, without restriction of flag'; and Article IV says that 'no act of hostility shall be committed in the Canal or its ports of access, or within a radius of three maritime miles from these ports'.

12 W.O. 106/41, Lord Lansdowne to the Secretary of War, 8 March 1902; also Sanderson (F.O.) to W.O., 18 March 1902, *ibid.*

13 *Declaration between the United Kingdom and France respecting Egypt and Morocco.* Signed at London, 8 April 1904. HMSO. 1905 [Cd 2384]. Treaty Series, no. 6, 1905. The relevant passage reads: 'His Britannic Majesty's Government declare that they adhere to the stipulations of the Treaty of the 29th October, 1888 and that they agree to their being put in force. The free passage of the Canal being thus guaranteed.'

14 CAB 38/20/15, 'The Attack on Egypt by Turkey', Paper prepared by the General Staff, 9 May 1912. Secret; W.O. 106/41, Sanderson (F.O.) to W.O., 18 March 1902.

15 W.O. 106/41, File C 3(2), Memorandum, dated 29 March 1904.

16 W.O. 106/41, File C 3(14), 'Coercion of Turkey by Military Operations in Syria-Haifa', 1906, Secret.

17 W.O. 106/42, Files: C 3(14b), C 3(26), C 3(35), 'Scheme of an attack on Haifa', 1906.

18 W.O. 106/43 (1), File C 3(29), 'Plan of Military General Operations in Syria and Palestine', Sub-Committee of Imperial Defence, 1909.

19 CAB 16/12, other members of the Sub-Committee were E. Grey, R. B. Haldane, Lord Esher, W. G. Nicholson, J. D. P. French, J. S. Ewart, and L. I. Ottley.

20 W.O. 106/42, File C 3(35b), Notes by Major-General R. St G. Gordon, 6 June 1910, and 9 May 1911 (*ibid.*, File C 3(35c)); Memorandum by J. R. Chancellor, Secretary of Colonial Defence Committee, 20 January 1911. Secret, 123 B, Printed, *ibid.* (a copy also in CAB 38/17/7); remarks of Brigadier-General Wilson, D.M.O., 9 May 1911 on the Memorandum of Secretary of C.D.C.

21 CAB 38/20/15, 'The Attack on Egypt by Turkey', Paper prepared by the General Staff, 9 May 1912. Secret, 149 B.

22 B.D., 10, pt i, p. 481, Grey to Buchanan, 4 July 1913.

23 Prince Lichnowsky, *Heading for the Abyss. Reminiscences* (London 1928), p. 322, Lichnowsky to Bethmann-Hollweg, 4 July 1913.

24 B.D., 9, pt ii, no. 336; also Raymond Poincaré, *Au Service de la France* (Paris 1926) 'ni intention d'agir, ni desseins, ni aspirations politiques d'aucune sorte' (vol. 2, p. 412); in English translation *The Memoirs of Raymond Poincaré* (London 1926), vol. 1, p. 336.

25 In the text the date is 1913. This is obviously a misprint.

26 Poincaré, *Au Service . . .*, 2, pp. 411–12; Poincaré, *Memoirs . . .*, 1, pp. 336–8.

27 B.D., 9, pt ii, p. 444, Grey to Goschen, 24 January 1913, dis. no. 32; *Die Grosse Politik der Europäischen Kabinette* (Berlin 1922–7), Bd 34, 1, p. 236, Lichnowsky to A.A., 22 January 1913; see also Lichnowsky, *op. cit.*, p. 318, Lichnowsky to Jagow, 2 June 1913.

28 See e.g. Lichnowsky to Jagow, 26 June 1913, in Lichnowsky, *op. cit.*, p. 322.

29 *Ibid.*, p. 323, Lichnowsky to Bethmann-Hollweg, 4 July 1913; cf. above note 23.

30 With heavy investments in Turkey, the French had their own interest in

keeping the Ottoman Empire alive. On 17 August 1914 Paléologue, the French Ambassador in St Petersburg, reminded Sazonow, the Russian Foreign Minister, that the preservation of the 'territorial integrity and political independence of Turkey remains one of the guiding principles of French diplomacy'. (Poincaré, *Au Service*, 5, p. 115; see also *ibid.*, 6, pp. 92–5).

31 Sokolow, *History of Zionism*, 2, App. lxxxv, pp. 391–2. Colonel Conder, in conjunction with Kitchener, carried out in 1913–14 an extensive survey of Palestine sponsored by the Palestine Exploration Fund, which was a camouflage for British Intelligence Service. The survey was begun in the 1870s.

32 These quotations are taken from documents cited in Leonard Stein: *The Balfour Declaration* (London 1961), pp. 24–33.

33 Robert G. Weisbord, 'Israel Zangwill's Jewish Territorial Organization and the East African Zion', *Jewish Social Studies* (April 1968), pp. 89–108.

34 *Ibid.*, App. p. 106; also *Jewish Chronicle*, 2 August 1968, p. 8.

35 Sokolow, *History of Zionism*, 1, xxix–xxx.

36 Weisbord, *loc. cit.*, Churchill to Zangwill, 1 January, 13 July 1906, App. pp. 105–6, 109, also p. 95.

37 *Jewish Chronicle*, 18 December 1964 (cited by the late Randolph Churchill). I am grateful to C.S.T. Publications for permission to publish this letter.

38 See p. 1.

Chapter 2   The Samuel Proposal and British Policy in Turkey-in-Asia

1 Viscount Samuel Memoirs (London 1945), p. 139; Stein, *op. cit.*, pp. 103, 106. On Gaster see pp. 30, 119–20.

2 *Samuel Papers* (copies at St Antony's College, Oxford). Note dated 9 November 1914; extracts in Samuel, *Memoirs*, pp. 140–2.

3 Stein, *op. cit.*, p. 140. On Scott see *ibid.*, chap. 7 and Lloyd George, pp. 140–4. Among the *Lloyd George Papers* at the Beaverbrook Library (G 33/1/16) there is a letter from Leopold Greenberg (on whom see p. 181) to Lloyd George, dated 16 February 1906, describing the activities of Dr Theodor Herzl and the aims of the Zionist movement.

4 Chaim Weizmann, *Trial and Error* (London 1949; New York 1966), p. 194.

5 CAB 37/123/43, January 1915. A copy also in *Samuel Papers* and selected sections quoted in Stein, *op. cit.*, pp. 109–10. The memorandum was circulated to the Cabinet (F.O. 800/100, Sir E. Grey's Private Papers, Samuel to Grey, 22 January 1915).

6 *Samuel Papers*, Note, dated 9 November 1914; *Memoirs*, p. 141.

7 From 18 December 1914 to 9 January 1915, and again from 8 November to 25 November 1915.

8 F.O. 371/2480/2506, Cheetham to Grey, 7 January 1915, tel. no. 10; also pp. 97–8.

9 *Trial and Error*, p. 189.

10 Stein, *op. cit.*, p. 139.

11 This may have accounted for Weizmann's uncertainty about Samuel's

reaction as well as Ahad Ha'am's influence. In November 1914 Ahad Ha'am wrote to Weizmann: 'I think that we should be moderate in our claims and content ourselves with the right of colonization and cultural activity. Let us hope that eventually, with the implementation of these two objectives, we shall achieve in Palestine an autonomous life under the aegis of England.' Asher Ginsburg, *Ig'rot Ahad Ha'am* (*Letters of* . . . in Hebrew). Jerusalem 1924, vol. 5, p. 204. On Ahad Ha'am see pp. 31-2.

12 Stein, *op. cit.*, pp. 126-7.

13 Weizmann, *Trial and Error*, pp. 191, 224-5.

14 Samuel, *Memoirs*, p. 143. Lord Reading to Samuel, 5 February 1915.

15 See pp. 16, 141, 169-73.

16 Samuel, *Memoirs*, pp. 143-4.

17 *Samuel Papers*. Note dated 7 February 1915 (omitted in *Memoirs*).

18 See p. 115.

19 Yechiel Tschlenow, a Russian Zionist leader, on whom see pp. 35-6, 198-9.

20 *Samuel Papers*, Note dated 14 February 1915.

21 Samuel, *Memoirs*, pp. 144-5.

22 F.O. 371/2448/6905, Wolf to F.O., 2 March 1915, encl. 'Memorandum on an interview with Mr Herbert Samuel on 28 February, 1915'. Cited also in Stein, *op. cit.*, pp. 107-8, from the papers of the Conjoint Foreign Committee. On Wolf see *ibid.*, pp. 173-5 and pp. 34-5 of present work.

23 CAB 37/126/I, a copy also in *Samuel Papers* and reproduced in full in John Bowle, *Viscount Samuel. A Biography* (London 1957), pp. 172-7.

24 On Weizmann's 'synthetic' Zionism see *Trial and Error*, pp. 138, 140, 156-7.

25 *Ibid.*, pp. 224-5.

26 In his March memorandum the wording remained practically identical with that of January, but he rearranged the text to underline the desirability of a British protectorate.

27 The writer was unable to trace any reference to this effect in the Cabinet Papers.

28 See e.g. E. Kedourie, *England and the Middle East* (London 1956), p. 31; also Stein, *op. cit.*, pp. 240-1. For the writer's conclusion on this matter see below, pp. 15-21, 101, 109, 112, 117, 169-74.

29 It began on 19 February 1915. For the diplomatic background see W. W. Gottlieb, *Studies in Secret Diplomacy during the First World War* (London 1957), pp. 77-108, 115-31; R. Rhodes James, *Gallipoli* (London 1965).

30 E. A. Adamov, *Die Europäischen Mächte und die Türkei wärend des Weltkrieges. Die Aufteilung der Asiatischen Türkei* (Dresden 1932), no. 13, p. 13, Benckendorff to Sazonow, 18 February/3 March 1915.

31 'neither we nor the French liked that thing': Viscount Grey, *Twenty-Five Years* (London 1925), 2, p. 182; Sazonow's letter of 19 February/4 March 1915 is reproduced in Adamov, *op. cit.*, no. 16, pp. 16-17 and in *Documents on British Foreign Policy, 1919-1939*, ed. E. L. Woodward and R. Butler, First Series, 4 (HMSO 1952), pp. 635-6, cited hereafter as *D.B.F.P.* On the French position see Poincaré, *Au Service*, vol. 6, pp. 92-5. On the importance of

Constantinople and its environs to Russia see Gottlieb, *op. cit.*, pp. 63–71, 90–2.

32 *D.B.F.P.*, 4, p. 636. On Russia's contribution to the war see Winston S. Churchill, *The World Crisis 1915* (London 1923), pp. 407–8.

33 CAB 42/2/5, Meeting 10 March 1915, 'Russia and Constantinople'. On Germany's overtures to Russia for a separate peace see Gottlieb, *op. cit.*, p. 104; Fritz Fischer, *Griff nach der Weltmacht* (Düsseldorf 1961), pp. 223–35, 278–88; and to France, pp. 274–8.

34 *D.B.F.P.*, 4, p. 637.

35 Earl of Oxford and Asquith, *Memories and Reflections* (London 1928), vol. 2, p. 69. Asquith's assertion is not entirely correct, as Lord Haldane supported them also.

36 Balfour joined the coalition Government on 27 May 1915 as First Lord of the Admiralty, but it seems that he had participated in the meetings of the War Council earlier.

37 CAB 42/2/5, War Council. Meeting 10 March 1915, on which see also above, n. 33. For a short reference to this meeting, see Asquith, *op. cit.*, vol. 2, p. 64; and Grey, *op. cit.*, 2, p. 180.

38 CAB 42/2/10, 'Alexandretta and Mesopotamia', Memorandum by Lord Kitchener, 16 March 1915. Secret, G.12.

39 CAB 42/2/11, 'Alexandretta and Mesopotamia', Memorandum by the Admiralty, 17 March 1915. Secret. G.13; and CAB 42/2/13, 'Alexandretta. Its Importance as a future Base', Remarks by Admiral Jackson, 15 March 1915, Secret, G.15.

40 CAB 42/2/8, 'The Future Settlement of Eastern Turkey in Asia and Arabia'. Notes by A. Hirtzel, 14 March 1915. Secret, G.16.

41 CAB 42/2/8, Note by General Sir Edmund Barrow on the Defence of Mesopotamia, 16 March 1915.

42 On which see pp. 19–21.

43 CAB 42/2/14.

44 Grey, *op. cit.*, 2, p. 230.

45 As note 43.

46 *Asquith Papers*, vol. 27, pp. 93–9, Bodleian Library, MSS Dept, Oxford, Private letter. Cited by kind permission of Mr Mark Bonham-Carter. On Fisher, see also below, n. 57.

47 As late as 10 April 1916, at a dinner given to a group of French parliamentarians on an official visit to London he stated that the purpose of the Allies was to pave the way for an international system which will secure 'the principle of equal rights for all civilized States'; it was not their intention to destroy their enemies. That Asquith turned his fire against 'the military domination of Prussia' and made no mention of Turkey, either directly or by implication, was not accidental. (*What Britain is Fighting For . . .* A speech by the Rt Hon. Asquith on 10 April 1916). Off-print published by the *Daily Chronicle* (London 1916). For a contrary view on this matter see Stein, *op. cit.*, p. 103.

48 CAB 27/1, 30 June 1915, C.I.D. Secret, 220 B; also in CAB 42/3/12. In

addition to its Chairman, the Committee was composed of Mr G. R. Clerk representing the Foreign Office, Sir T. W. Holderness of the India Office, Admiral Sir H. B. Jackson of the Admiralty, Major-General C. E. Calwell, of the War Office, Sir H. Llewellyn Smith of the Board of Trade, and Lieutenant-Colonel Sir Mark Sykes. Lieutenant-Colonel M. P. A. Hankey, Secretary of the Committee of Imperial Defence also participated.

49 Though shorn of Constantinople and the Straits, which were to go to Russia, and the Persian Gulf, to be allotted to England.

50 See pp. 16–17.

51 'We proclaimed at the outset that our quarrel was with the German-led Government at Constantinople, not with the Turkish people.' Cf. this statement of the Committee with our interpretation of Asquith's Guildhall speech, see pp. 8, 18–19.

52 See Map V, attached to the Report. The northern border of the *vilayet* of Palestine (no. 5) ran from Acre to Tadmor (Palmyra) eastwards, covering the whole territory, well into the Syrian desert. The southern border extended from Gaza to Aqaba.

53 This was the only extract published (Cmd 5974 (1939)), Annexe J, p. 51; Stein, *op. cit.*, pp. 246–7.

54 See pp. 13, 16–17.

55 Stein, *op. cit.*, p. 133; also p. 114, n. 43.

56 From 3 February 1907 to 26 April 1913, served as Ambassador in Washington. Lord Bryce wrote to Samuel on 8 March: 'I very much agree with your memorandum in principle ... and I am extremely glad you have put the matter before the Cabinet.' (Samuel, *Memoirs*, p. 744.) Cf. pp. 124–5.

57 Fisher wrote to Samuel on 29 April: 'I read your excellent paper with conviction as to the inclusion in the English sphere of Palestine, and ... I am giving it all my support.' *Samuel Papers*, reproduced in full in Bowle, *op. cit.*, p. 178.

58 Stein, *op. cit.*, p. 57.

59 Dated 12 March 1915. Drummond served successively as Private Secretary to Asquith (1 March 1912 to 15 June 1915), to Grey (15 June 1915 to 11 December 1916), and thereafter to Balfour; when the latter became Foreign Secretary, Drummond accompanied him on a special mission to the United States in May–June 1917 (see pp. 200–1).

60 CAB 37/126/1, March 1915.

61 The relevant entries are reproduced in full in Samuel, *Memoirs*, pp. 142, 143; Weizmann, *Trial and Error*, p. 193; Bowle, *op. cit.*, pp. 171, 178, and in Stein, *op. cit.*, pp. 111, 112.

62 On Montagu see Stein, *op. cit.*, pp. 496–501; S. D. Waley, *Edwin Montagu* (London 1964).

63 Weizmann, *Trial and Error*, p. 194.

64 See J. A. Spender and Cecil Asquith, *Life of Herbert Henry Asquith, Lord Oxford and Asquith* (London 1932), vol. 1, p. 202: 2, pp. 13, 254; Waley, *op. cit.*, *passim*.

65 *Asquith Papers*, 27, pp. 38–41. E. S. Montagu to Asquith, 16 March 1915. Cited by kind permission of Mrs Judith Gendel, formerly Montagu. Asquith's entry in his diary was made on 13 March, and the preceding one on 28 January 1915. However, considering his close relationship with Montagu, it is natural to assume that he was familiar with Montagu's views before receiving his letter of 16 March.

Chapter 3 The Zionists and the Assimilationists

1 See chapter 15.
2 Isaiah Berlin, 'The Origins of Israel', *The Middle East in Transition*, ed. Walter Laqueur (London 1958), p. 205. See also Yehezkel Kaufman, *Gola V'Nehar* (Tel Aviv 1929), I, pp. 169, 208; Hans Kohn, *The Idea of Nationalism* (New York 1946), pp. 27–60; Salo W. Baron, *A Social and Religious History of the Jews* (New York 1952), I, p. 31.
3 Diogène Tama, *Collection des Actes du Grand Sanhédrin* (Paris 1807), pp. 65–73, 83, 90–1, 191; Diogène Tama, *Collection dex procès-verbaux et décisions du Grand-Sanhédrin* (Paris 1807), pp. 47–9; J. Graetz, *Geschichte der Juden*, II, chapter 6; Simon M. Dubnow, *Die neuste Geschichte des jüdischen Volkes, 1789–1914* (Berlin 1920–3), I, pp. 125–53; Sokolow, *op. cit.*, I, pp. 82–5; R. Anchel, *Napoléon et les Juifs* (Paris 1928), pp. 128–225.
4 Cf. Jacob Katz, *Exclusiveness and Tolerance, Studies in Jewish-Gentile Relations* (Oxford 1961; New York 1962), p. 188.
5 Frederick Hertz, *Nationality in History and Politics* (London 1957), p. 163.
6 Even more impressive than his much-quoted speech in the House of Commons is Macaulay's essay published in the *Edinburgh Review*, January 1831.
7 For references in nineteenth-century English literature to that idea see Sokolow, *op. cit.*, I, pp. 1–63, 91–145, 161–6, 206–12. It is worth recalling that Cromwell's invitation to Menasseh ben Israel was given in the belief that the settlement of Jews in England would bring their restoration to Zion nearer. On British nationalism see Hans Kohn, 'The Genesis and Character of English Nationalism', *Journal of the History of Ideas*, I, 1940; Ernest Barker, *The Character of England* (Oxford 1947).
8 The full story has been told in James Picciotto, *Sketches of Anglo-Jewish History* (London 1875), pp. 381–401; Albert M. Hyamson, *A History of the Jews in England* (London 1928), pp. 260–72, 290–3; Cecil Roth, *A History of Jews in England* (Oxford 1964), pp. 241–66. The Parliamentary debates on the subject are reproduced in Moses Margoliouth, *The History of the Jews in Great Britain* (London 1851), 2, pp. 257–95: 3, pp. 1–75, and in Charles Egan, *The Status of Jews in England* (London 1848), pp. 50–149.
9 I. Friedman, 'Lord Palmerston and the Protection of Jews in Palestine', p. 40.
10 See pp. 228–9, 239.
11 *Nineteenth Century*, July 1878. Rabbi Adler officiated in 1891–1911. On Chief Rabbi Herschell's (1802–42) interest in the project of Jewish settlement in

Palestine see Friedman, 'Lord Palmerston', etc., p. 30. Chief Rabbi Hertz (1913-46), was an avowed pro-Zionist.

12 The full text of the address is reproduced in Margoliouth, *op. cit.*, 2, pp. 263-4.

13 See pp. 269, 270.

14 In *Zionism and the Jewish Future*, ed. Harry Sacher (London 1916), pp. 87-98.

15 Published in 1862. Translated from German by M. Waxman (New York 1945); see Isaiah Berlin, *The Life and Opinions of Moses Hess* (Cambridge 1959); Edmund Silberner, *Moses Hess* (Leiden 1966).

16 *Mivhar Kitveihem* (Selected Writings, Tel Aviv 1943). See particularly Alkalai's 'The Third Redemption' (1843) and Kalischer's 'In Seeking Zion' (1862) transl. in Arthur Hertzberg, *The Zionist Idea. A Historical Analysis and Reader* (New York 1959), pp. 125-7, 111-14.

17 Theodor Herzl, *The Jewish State* (New York 1946), p. 76.

18 *Ibid.*, pp. 79-81; *The Complete Diaries of Theodor Herzl*, ed. Raphael Patai, transl. by H. Zohn (New York, London 1960), 2, pp. 655-60.

19 Notably Peretz Smolenskin, Moshe Leib Lilienblum and Eliezer Ben-Yehuda. Selected writings are reproduced in Hertzberg, *op. cit.*, pp. 142-77; also Charles Freundlich, *Peretz Smolenskin: His Life and Thought* (New York 1966).

20 Typical of the prevalent mood of the Jewish intelligentsia was the confession of a group of students made in a synagogue of Kiev, cited in Ben Halpern, *The Idea of the Jewish State* (Harvard 1961), p. 62.

21 On whom see Leon Simon, *Ahad Ha'am. A Biography* (London 1960).

22 On which see Caesar Seligmann, *Geschichte der jüdischen Reformbewegung* (Frankfurt 1922); David Philipson, *The Reform Movement in Judaism* (London 1931); Plant W. Gunter, *The Rise of Reform Judaism* (New York 1963).

23 'Slavery in Freedom' (1891), in *Nationalism and the Jewish Ethic: Basic Writings of Ahad Ha'am*, ed. Hans Kohn (New York 1962), pp. 54, 64-5.

24 'Judaism and the Gospels' (1910), *ibid.*, p. 319.

25 'A Spiritual Centre' (1907), in *Ten Essays on Zionism and Judaism*, transl. Leon Simon (London 1922), pp. 123-4.

26 Leon Simon, *op. cit.*, pp. 217-20. The only exception during the pre-war period was his response to Montefiore's work *The Synoptic Gospels*.

27 From 1878 a joint body of the Board of Deputies of British Jews and the Anglo-Jewish Association. It was dissolved in June 1917 (see pp. 239-40) and reconstituted in February 1918 under the name of the Joint Foreign Committee. The Board of Deputies was founded in 1760. It was composed of elected representatives of synagogues and other Jewish institutions. On its origins see Picciotto, *op. cit.*, pp. 113-31. The Anglo-Jewish Association was a membership organisation founded in 1871 as a counterpart to the Alliance Israélite Universelle of Paris.

28 *Trial and Error*, pp. 52-4, 86, 139-41, 156, 209, 215-16, 231-2, 262; Israel M. Sieff, 'The Manchester Period', in *Chaim Weizmann, A Biography by Several Hands*, ed. M. W. Weisgal and J. Carmichael (London 1962), p. 102; *The Letters and Papers of Chaim Weizmann*, Series A, 1, ed. Leonard Stein (Oxford 1968), pp. 112-15, 123-5, 132, 194-6, 227-30, 256.

29 *Trial and Error*, pp. 46-8, 183-4.

30 *Ibid.*, p. 70; *The Letters . . . of Chaim Weizmann*, pp. 79-80, 88, 91.

31 Richard Crossman, *A Nation Reborn* (London 1960), p. 19.

32 *Trial and Error*, p. 144.

33 CAB 21/58, Gore to Hankey, 19 April 1918. A statement in a similar vein was made by the late Professor Sir Charles Webster to the author on 15 June 1960.

34 *Trial and Error*, pp. 41-2.

35 Letter to *The Times*, 28 May 1917.

36 Isaiah Berlin, 'The Biographical Facts', in *Chaim Weizmann. A Biography by Several Hands*, p. 25.

37 Dorothy Thompson, 'The Mark of the Chosen' in *Chaim Weizmann*, ed. Meyer Weisgal (New York 1944), p. 23.

38 *Trial and Error*, pp. 199, 202.

39 Ahad Ha'am to Weizmann, 22 November 1914. *Ig'roth Ahad Ha'am* (Tel Aviv 1924), 5, p. 204.

40 Weizmann to Harry Sacher and Leon Simon, 28 November 1914, cited in Stein, *op. cit.*, p. 177.

41 On Wolf see pp. 49-52, 62. Forh is credentials authorising him to speak on the Committee's behalf, see letter to the Foreign Office signed by David Alexander, Claude Montefiore and Leopold de Rothschild, encl. in Wolf to Tyrrell, 12 January 1915 (F.O. 371/2475/4800).

42 *Observer*, 28 June 1896, cited in Josef Fraenkel, *Lucien Wolf and Theodor Herzl* (London 1960), p. 12.

43 Cited *ibid.*, pp. 7, 17. On Wolf's association with Herzl see also *Diaries*, 1, p. 411.

44 Cited *ibid.*, pp. 21, 24.

45 On whom see Stein, *op. cit.*, pp. 76-7, 175-6.

46 F.O. 371/2817/42608, Alexander and Montefiore to Grey, 1 October 1916.

47 Confirmed by the Eleventh Congress in 1913. For statements made by the Zionist leaders see Stein, *op. cit.*, pp. 64-5. Wolf relied heavily on Sacher's article in the *Sociological Review*. In its issue of January 1912 Sacher wrote: 'The Zionist Congress held at Basel in August last [i.e. 1911] changed the governing body of the movement . . . On its political side the movement has become very modest in its demands . . . for the present it is content with freedom to settle, to plant colonies, to found schools to revive a Hebrew culture. Its ambition is to create not a *Juden-Staat* but a home for the Jewish spirit.'

48 F.O. 371/2817/243400, memorandum by Lucien Wolf dated 20 November 1916, p. 13, encl. in Wolf to Oliphant, 1 December 1916.

49 Cited in Stein, *op. cit.*, pp. 177-8.

50 At the Fifth Zionist Congress in December 1901 Dr Martin Buber and Dr Weizmann (on behalf of the Democratic Faction) proposed the following motion: 'Congress explains that by the word "culture" it implies the national education of Jews.' (*die Erziehung des jüdischen Volkes in nationalen Sinne*) 'It regards this as an important part of the Zionist programme and declares it to

be obligatory on every Zionist.' (*V Zion. Congress Prot.*, p. 389. For Weizmann's speech *ibid.*, pp. 392–3).

51 *Gemeinwesen.* Tschlenow spoke in German. However, before arriving in London, at a meeting of the Zionist Executive in Copenhagen in December 1914, he used the term 'the Jewish National Centre in Palestine' (*Yechiel Tschlenow, Memoirs, Letters, Speeches*, ed. S. Eisenstadt (Tel Aviv 1937), p. 46.

52 F.O. 371/2488/51705, 'Report on a Conference with the Delegates of the Zionist Organisation', also a copy of a letter to the Zionists dated 27 April 1915. Communicated to the Foreign Office by Lucien Wolf on 28th inst. No corresponding report made by the Zionists came to light.

53 C.F.C./1915 170ff., Sokolow to Wolf, 11 May 1915; a draft copy dated 3/5/15 is found in Central Zionist Archives, file A 100/27.

54 CZA, A 18/22, Wolf to Sokolow, 11 June 1915.

Chapter 4   The Jews and the War

1 On which see Stein, *op. cit.*, pp. 118, 139–41, 153–5.

2 F.O. 800/95, Sir E. Grey Private Papers, Cecil's minute dated 18 August 1915 to Russell (Grey's diplomatic secretary).

3 In 1906 Cecil wrote to the Zionist Federation: 'The central idea underlying the Zionist movement seems to me worthy of support. Apart from all other considerations, it appears to me that the restoration of the Jewish nation offers satisfactory solution' (cited in Sokolow, *op. cit.*, 1, p. 299).

4 Stein, *op. cit.*, pp. 186–7, where Weizmann's version of the interview is recorded.

5 The text of the order is reproduced in Salo W. Baron, *The Russian Jew under Tsars and Soviets* (London, New York 1964), pp. 189–90; see also *The Jews in Eastern War Zone* (New York 1916); *Denkschrift der Poale-Zion: Die Juden im Kriege* (Haag 1917); Jonas Kreppel, *Juden und Judentum von Heute* (Zürich 1925), pp. 72–91; Simon Dubnow, *Die neuste Geschichte des jüdischen Volkes* (Berlin 1929), 10, pp. 510–13; Fischer, *Griff nach der Weltmacht*, pp. 163–4.

6 F.P. 371/2445/155, Wolf to Oliphant (F.O.) 2 July 1915; F.O. 371/2446/155, same to same, 15 September 1915; *Annual Report of the Board of Deputies of British Jews. Foreign Affairs Committee for 1915* (encl. in same to same, 12 November 1915, *ibid.*).

7 *Jewish Chronicle*, 22 October 1915, p. 12. Interview with Boris Goldberg.

8 Baron, *op. cit.*, p. 191.

9 F.O. 371/2454/105582, Buchanan to Grey, 7, 13 September 1915, dis. nos. 132, 136.

10 F.O. 371/2455/105582, same to same, 1, 15 October and 13, 25 November 1915, dis. nos. 1, 157, 177, 183, enclosing reports submitted by Vice-Consul Lindley.

11 F.O. 371/2454/105582, 'Memorandum regarding . . . Public Opinion in Moscow', encl. 2 in no. 1 to Buchanan to Grey, 12 August 1915, dis. no. 113, Confidential. Lockhart had a thorough command of the Russian language and

was in close touch with various sections of public opinion (*ibid.*, Bayley to Buchanan, 9 August 1915). His reports were much appreciated at the Foreign Office.

12 Weizmann, *Trial and Error*, p. 196; see also pp. 209–12.

13 F.O. 371/22553/18272, Pitts (Vice-Consul) to Baldwin (Minister), Braila, 25 January 1915, encl. in Baldwin to F.O., 28 January 1915, dis. no. 7.

14 F.O. 371/1970/36711, R.S. [Ronald Storrs], 'Note on public opinion in Egypt', 1 September 1914, encl. in Cheetham to Crowe, 1 September 1914. Private.

15 F.O. 371/2445/145, 'Memorandum from the Jewish Conjoint Foreign Committee', 3 June 1915. For a dossier of documents exonerating the Jews from charges made against them by Russian military authorities on espionage, see *ibid.*, Leopold de Rothschild to F.O., 1 September 1915; also speeches in the Duma, *ibid.*, no. 114766 and F.O. 371/2454/105582, Wolf to Oliphant, 17 August 1915 and enclosure. For the position of Jews under German occupation see Baron, *op. cit.*, pp. 192–5.

16 F.O. 371/2448/16905, Gottheil to Spring-Rice, 16 March 1915, encl. in Spring-Rice to Grey, 27 March 1915, dis. no. 117. On Gottheil see also Stein, *op. cit.*, pp. 197, 199.

17 F.O. 371/2835/18095, Gottheil to Wolf, 11 March 1916, encl. in Wolf to Montgomery, 29 March 1916. The alleged emissary was Isaac Strauss, sent not by the Zionist Bureau in Berlin but by the Information Department of the German Navy.

18 F.O. 371/2448/16905, Spring-Rice to Grey, 27 March 1915, dis. no. 117.

19 F.O. 371/2744/4039, Borden to Perley, Ottawa, 31 December 1915, Confidential, encl. in Butler to Drummond, 1 February, 1916.

20 *Ibid.*, Butler to Drummond, 1 February 1916; *ibid.*, Perley (Ottawa) to Bonar Law (London), 28 January 1916.

21 F.O. 371/2579/178994, communication by Sir Gilbert Parker, 22 October 1915.

22 F.O. 371/2448/16905, no. 43239, minute of Lord Eustace Percy, dated 14 April 1915. Before the war Percy served on the staff of the British Embassy in Washington. In 1914 he was transferred to the Foreign Office. In May–June 1917 accompanied Balfour on a special mission to the United States.

23 See minutes on Wolf to Oliphant, 6 January 1916, F.O. 371/2744/4039. There is a biography by Harold Nicolson, *Sir Arthur Nicolson. First Lord Carnock* (London 1930).

24 CAB 37/143/39, 'Memorandum, Sir George Buchanan's Audience with the Emperor on February 3, 1916'. Confidential. Circulated to the Cabinet on 1 March 1916.

25 F.O. 371/2454/105582, encl. 2 in no. 1, in Buchanan to Grey, 12 August 1915, dis. no. 113, Confidential.

26 CAB 37/123/58, Report . . . by Gilbert Parker, January 1915, Confidential; F.O. 371/2559/35166, Prof. James Reeves to D. C. Boulger (London) 13 March 1915; CAB 37/124/59, 'American Opinion', Report of Kenneth Durant, 29 January 1915; CAB 37/124/59, 'American Opinion', Rep. of Lancelot

Smith, 13 January 1915; F.O. 371/2501/182727, Spring-Rice (Washington) to Grey, 21 November 1915; CAB 42/8/9, L. C. Christie to Robert L. Borden (Prime Minister of Canada), 27 January 1916; CAB 37/140/30, Spring-Rice to Grey, 13 January 1916, Confidential; CAB 37/141/35, same to same, 29 January 1916, Confidential. The first section of this despatch, though without specifying the date, is reproduced in Sir Cecil Spring-Rice, *The Letters and Friendships of* . . . ed. Stephen Gwynn (London 1930), vol. 2, pp. 309–10. On resentment in the U.S.A. against British interference with American-German trade see also F.O. 800/105, Bryce to Grey, 24 January, 4, 5 February 1916; same to Drummond, 8, 9, 15 February 1916.

27 F.O. 371/2559/3516, Spring-Rice to Primrose (F.O.), 1 April 1915; F.O. 371/2835/18095, same to Cecil, 29 January 1916. There is a biography by Cyrus Adler, *Jacob Schiff, His Life and Letters*, 2 vols (London 1929); on orientation of American Jewry see also Stein, *op. cit.*, chapter 12, and my forthcoming book, *Germany and Zionism: 1897–1918*.

28 Cyrus Adler and Aaron M. Margalith, *With Firmness in the Right. American Diplomatic Action Affecting Jews, 1840–1945* (New York 1946), pp. 263–92.

29 F.O. 371/2448/16905, Spring-Rice to Grey, 27 March 1915, dis. no. 117.

30 By this he meant apparently the recognition of Jewish national rights in Palestine.

31 F.O. 371/2579/187779, Kallen to Zimmern, encl. in Zimmern to Percy, 22 November 1915, private letter. Horace M. Kallen makes no mention of this episode in his book *Zionism and World Politics* (London 1921).

32 'I agree that the best thing to do would be to send out some English Jew to America to see what could be done to win the Jewish press. I doubt if Lucien Wolf is the man for that, and I should be inclined to use his offer of service, in the first place to find out whether he can suggest anyone else.' (*Ibid.*, E. P[ercy] to Cecil, note dated 5 December.) See also Cecil's note to Sir Gilbert Parker of 14 December 1915, to this effect (*ibid.*).

33 F.O. 371/2480/3055. This file (January–September 1915) contains an extensive correspondence with the American and French Embassies on which the following section is based. Between December 1914 and July 1915, the total sum transferred to Palestine amounted to £100,000 in gold. Thereafter remittance of funds in bullion or cash was prohibited. (Harvey, Governor of Bank of England to Bradbury, Treasury Chambers, 7 September 1915; and F.O. to McMahon, 17 September 1915, *ibid.*) The import of oil, however, was prohibited lest the Turks requisition it for military purposes. (W.O. to F.O., 5 May and Admiralty to F.O., 6 May 1915, *ibid.*); on the efforts of the U.S. Government see Frank E. Manuel, *The Realities of American-Palestine Relations* (Washington 1949), pp. 134–46.

34 F.O. 383/91/251. The total number of refugees was estimated at 11,000.

35 There is a biography on Jabotinsky by Joseph B. Schechtman, *Rebel and Statesman*, 2 vols (New York 1956); esp. chaps 1, 3, 4, 12.

36 Vladimir Jabotinsky, *The Story of the Jewish Legion* (New York 1945), pp. 43–5, cited in Schechtman, 1, p. 207.

37 F.O. 371/2835/18095, Hamilton to Jabotinsky, London, 17 November 1915 (a copy); also Patterson to Jabotinsky, Gallipoli, 10 November 1915; C.O. 8th Corps to G.H.Q., M.E.F., 4 October 1915. Note (a copy); also Colonel A. Cavendish, A.A.G., G.H.Q. to G.O.C., 8th Corps, 5 November 1915 (*ibid.*).

38 The author of *With the Zionists in Gallipoli* (London 1916).

39 F.O. 371/2835/18095, Patterson to Jabotinsky, Cape Helles, 10 November 1915.

40 Jabotinsky, *op. cit.*, pp. 52, 62.

41 F.O. 371/2835/18095, Amery (W.O.) to Cecil (F.O.) 11 January 1916. Amery thought that Herbert Samuel might become honorary Colonel-in-Chief of the Unit.

42 *Ibid.*, minute of H. G. Locock. From June 1915 to September 1917 private secretary to Lord Robert Cecil; Creedy (W.O.) to Locock (F.O.), 17 January 1916. Private letter.

43 *Ibid.*, Patterson to Robert Cecil, 19 January 1916.

44 *Ibid.*, undated minute on Locock's note of 19 January 1916; also Locock to Patterson, 24 January 1916.

45 'There is undeniable truth in what he says about the only possible method of propaganda . . . [General] Maxwell appears to have already realised this and what is now suggested is only an extension of a principle that has already been admitted.' (Gowers to Montgomery, 26 January 1916. Private letter, *ibid.*)

46 *Ibid.*, Jabotinsky to Masterman, 26 January 1916; encl. 'Memorandum on Jewish Eastern Legion'.

47 *Ibid.*, same to same, 31 January 1916; Cecil to Amery, 4 February 1916; same to Jabotinsky, 10 February 1916.

48 F.O. 371/2816/39700, Amery to Cecil, 26 February 1916. Private letter.

49 *Ibid.*, annotation on the minute sheet dated 6 March 1916.

50 See pp. 53–4.

51 F.O. 371/2816/39700, Cecil to Amery, March 1916.

52 The newly-appointed Superintending Under-Secretary for Prisoners and Aliens Department at the Foreign Office. This Department was abolished on 26 October 1916 and superseded by a new one called the Prisoners of War Department, with Lord Newton as its Controller till August 1919. The propaganda headquarters remained at Wellington House, headed by E. A. Gowers.

53 F.O. 371/2816/39700, Masterman to Lord Newton, 27 March 1916. Private letter.

54 F.O. 371/2835/18095, no. 98116, minutes of N[ewton] dated 27 May 1916, and of Lord Hardinge.

55 *Ibid.*, Wolf to Montgomery, 5 April and 22 May 1916.

56 See pp. 260–1.

57 Herbert Samuel and Israel Zangwill, not members of the Zionist Federation, also supported the idea.

Chapter 5 Jewish Palestine—A Propaganda Card

1 F.O. 371/2835/18095, Summary of Basch's letters, Paris, Chambre des Députes (undated), encl. in Wolf to Cecil, 18 February 1916, cf. Stein, *op. cit.*, pp. 218–19.

2 F.O. 371/2579/187779, Bigart (Paris) to Wolf, 10 December 1915, encl. in Wolf to Cecil, 16 December 1915.

3 *Ibid.*, Wolf to Cecil, 16 December 1915, and enclosed memorandum; cf. Stein, *op. cit.*, pp. 220–1.

4 *Ibid.*, private note, dated 16 December 1915.

5 F.O. 371/2835/18095, Spring-Rice to Cecil (cable, no number), 2 February 1916; same to same 29 January 1916, private letter received 11 February 1916.

6 *Ibid.*, minutes of Cecil dated 11 February 1916 and of Percy, 16th instant.

7 Spring-Rice, *op. cit.*, 2, p. 422, 4 January 1918.

8 See Stein, *op. cit.*, pp. 34–41 and my forthcoming *Germany and Zionism*.

9 CAB 23/13, no. 135A and no. 140A, Cabinet meetings of 9 and 16 May 1917.

10 F.O. 371/2835/18095, Wolf to Cecil, 18 February 1916; Cecil to Wolf, 24 February 1916, Private.

11 F.O. 371/2817/42608, Wolf to Oliphant, 3 March 1916 and enclosed memorandum; also Oliphant's minute on a conversation with Wolf at the Foreign Office on 2 March 1916. Cf. Stein, *op. cit.*, p. 222.

12 *Ibid.*, minutes dated 6 and 7 March. Harold Nicolson was the son of Sir Arthur Nicolson (on whom see p. 41). Since October 1914 served as Third Secretary at the Foreign Office. Lancelot Oliphant was an Assistant Clerk at the Foreign Office. On O'Beirne see p. 46.

13 *Ibid.*, Wolf to Oliphant, 6 March 1916; Oliphant to Wolf, 9 instant; Cecil's minute dated 17 March 1916.

14 His grandfather, Felix Suarès, a well-known Italian-Jewish banker, settled in Egypt in the mid-nineteenth century and later, together with Sir Ernest Cassel of London, established the National Bank of Egypt and the *Credit Foncier Égyptien*. Edgar was a non-Zionist (letter of Mr Jacques Maleh to the author, 4 January 1966).

15 F.O. 371/2671/35433, McMahon to Grey, 11 February 1916, dis. no. 30 and enclosed report dated 27 January 1916.

16 *Ibid.*, minute dated 23 February 1916.

17 *Ibid.*, minute of H. O'B[eirne], dated 28 February 1916.

18 Report no. 3. General Records of the Department of State. Record Group 59. State Decimal File 1910–29. File 763. 72/13450. National Archives, Washington, 1951. Microfilm copy at St Antony's College, Oxford.

19 See my forthcoming *Germany and Zionism*. Fitzmaurice later showed some friendly interest in Zionism; Stein, *op. cit.*, p. 34, n. 121.

20 Gooch and Temperley, *B.D.*, 10, Pt ii, no. 1, Lowther (Constantinople) to Grey, 22 August 1910; also Stein, *op. cit.*, pp. 38–41.

21 F.O. 383/222/599, p. no. 209164. From May 1912 till February 1914 Kidston served on the Staff of the British Embassy in Constantinople. On 14 March

1916 transferred to the Foreign Office. Kidston later modified his views and during the Balfour Declaration period became a pro-Zionist.

22 pp. 134–5. During the war Professor Seton-Watson served on the British Propaganda Bureau for East European countries. Dönmeh (Turkish for 'Apostates') is a name of a Judeo-Moslem sect founded by those adherents of Shabbetai Tzevi who followed his example in adopting in 1666 the Islamic faith. Though ostensibly Moslem, the sect maintains many Jewish practices in secret, believes in Shabbetai Tzevi as the Messiah, and in certain antinomian doctrines. Some of the Dönmeh, notably Djavid Bey, took a leading part in the Young Turk Revolution of 1908.

23 F.O. 371/2671/35433, minute dated 28 February 1916.

24 See p. 59.

25 As note 23, Grey's minute dated 29 February; Nicolson's and Crewe's minutes dated 3 March 1916.

26 James Pope-Hennessy, *Lord Crewe, 1858–1945* (London 1955), p. 146. I am grateful to Mr Leonard Stein for drawing my attention to this point. (Letter to the author, 15 May 1968.)

27 Stein, *op. cit.*, pp. 111–12, 185.

28 F.O. 371/2671/35433, minute dated 3 March 1916; F.O. 371/2579/188244, Cecil to Sir John Simon, 22 December 1915.

29 F.O. 371/2817/42608, O'Beirne's note to Sir Arthur Nicolson, dated 7 March. For Wolf's note see p. 52.

30 *Ibid.*, minutes dated 8, 11 March 1916; also F.O. 800/96, Sir E. Grey's Private Papers, F.O. (Drummond) to Bertie tel. no. 633, and to Buchanan, tel. no. 574, 11 March 1916; cf. Stein, *op. cit.*, pp. 223–4 citing Adamov.

31 However, the relevant section, found in F.O. 800/176, Private Papers of Sir Francis Bertie, reads:

> Sir Edward is however of opinion that by holding out the prospect of allowing the Jews in the course of time when their Colonists have become powerful enough in Palestine to compete against the Arab population to take into their own hands the arrangement of the internal affairs of the country, excluding Jerusalem and the Holy Places, the attraction of the scheme to the majority of the Jews might be largely increased.

32 See p. 61.

33 See pp. 13–14.

34 See pp. 81–96, 117.

35 See pp. 22, 53, 56–7.

36 F.O. 800/96, Drummond to Crewe, 11 March 1916.

37 F.O. 371/28171/42608, Buchanan to Grey, 14, 15 March 1916, tel. nos 361, 371.

38 Central Zionist Archives, Jerusalem, hereafter CZA, L 6/64/I, Tschlenow's statement at a meeting of the Zionist Executive in Copenhagen on 30 July 1917. The date on which the interview with Gulkievich took place is not given, but presumably early in 1916. On Tschlenow see above, pp. 13, 35–6.

39 CZA, L 6/88, cited in a circular letter dated 29 April 1915.

40 Professor of Natural Science in Edinburgh and Glasgow Universities. Member of the Russia Society.

41 F.O. 371/2456/148237, Simpson (Edinburgh) to Grey, 1 October 1915. Private letter.

42 F.O. 800/176, Private Papers of Sir Francis Bertie, Bertie to Grey, 13 March 1916, Private and Confidential.

43 *The Diary of Lord Bertie of Thame* (London 1924), 2, pp. 145, 153, 170.

44 'Fancy the Christian Holy Places in the custody of the Jews ... What would the Pope, and Italy, and Catholic France, with her hatred of Jews, say to the scheme? A portion of Uganda was offered to the Zionists by Chamberlain some years ago, but it was not good enough for them. Edmond de Rothschild had spent a good deal of money on establishment of Jews in Palestine: it is his hobby: he does not wish to go thither himself, for he has become French, he says, but there are thousands of his brethren who for material and sentimental reasons long to leave the countries where they are now, and to go to the Promised Land again.' (*Ibid.*, 1, pp. 105-6); also see pp. 147, 156-7.

45 F.O. 371/2817/42608, Bertie to Grey, 22 March 1916, tel. no. 343; also same to same, 22 March 1916, dis. no. 121 and encl. President of the Council, Ministry for Foreign Affairs to British Ambassador in Paris, 21 March 1916 (copy). Briand took office on 30 October 1915, and acted also as Foreign Minister.

46 Nor does Edy Kaufman in his dissertation 'La France et la Palestine, 1908-1918' (University of Paris May 1970) enlighten us on this question. It is worth while however to cite here a letter, dated 12 April 1916, in which Briand assured Basch that in none of the talks between France, England and Russia on the disposition of conquered Turkish territories in Asia Minor and on the Arab question, did France and Britain 'forget the defence, the extension and freedom of the Jewish colonies in Palestine' (reproduced *ibid.*, p. 456). This statement supports our argument. That Briand was sympathetic to Jewish colonisation of Palestine was attested also by M. Aberson, a Russian Zionist resident in France, to the Zionist Bureau in Berlin [CZA, 3/811, Aberson (Geneva) to Jacobson (Berlin), 8 April 1916].

I am grateful to Dr Kaufman for permitting me to quote Briand's letter as well as other documents from the French Ministry for Foreign Affairs reproduced in his dissertation.

47 *Ibid.*, minute dated 23 March 1916; seen also by Arthur Nicolson, Oliphant and Grey.

48 *Ibid.*, p. no. 130062, Oliphant's minute dated 27 June 1916.

49 F.O. 800/96, 'The Position of Great Britain with regard to her Allies', memorandum by Grey, dated 18 February 1916.

50 F.O. 371/2817/42608, Memorandum by Sokolow, dated 12 April 1916 and minutes by Henry Cumberbatch dated 3, 13 April. From 1908 to 1914 Cumberbatch served as Consul-General in Beirut. From January 1915 employed in the Foreign Office.

51 An engineer in the Fairfield Works, London.

52 F.O. 371/2817/42608, Coster to F.O. Petition (with eighteen signatures) dated 12 July 1916; de Bunsen to Coster, 12 July 1916 (drafted by Harold Nicolson).

53 *Ibid.*, minutes dated 21, 29 June 1916. Thus on 4 July Wolf received two conflicting messages: a written one, along the lines suggested by Lord Hardinge, and a verbal one, as advised by Grey.

54 *Ibid.*, no. 140352, extracts from Wolf's diary on his visit in Paris (copy); encl. in Wolf to Oliphant, 18 July 1916. Cf. also Stein, *op. cit.*, pp. 230-1.

55 CAB 37/148/15, Spring-Rice to Grey, 4 May 1916, and CAB 37/151/43; same to Montgomery, 7 July 1916, Confidential (original in F.O. 395/6/34397); CAB 37/154/22, same to Grey, 25 August 1916, Confidential; F.O. 371/2793/39522, same to same, 18 April 1916; CAB 42/22/4, 'Our Financial Position in America'. Note by R. McKenna, Chancellor of the Exchequer, CAB 42/19/2, Personal Memorandum by H. P. A. Hankey, prepared for the Prime Minister, 2 September 1916. See Pt iii, and Pt iv; F.O. 395/6/34597, Spring-Rice to Montgomery, 7 July 1916, Confidential; copy in CAB 37/151/43.

56 See p. 51.

57 Kallen, *op. cit.*, pp. 135-6, 156, 166; also Jacob de Haas, *Louis D. Brandeis* (New York 1929), p. 79; cf. figures cited in Stein (pp. 188-9) from other sources.

58 CZA L 6/64/I, report by Goldberg at the meeting of the Zionist Executive in Copenhagen, 29 July 1917. Goldberg was a Russian Zionist leader. During the war served as roving ambassador between London, Copenhagen, and Russia. In February-March 1916 was on a special mission to the United States. On Goldberg see also Stein, *op. cit.*, pp. 538-9.

59 See pp. 130-2.

Chapter 6   The McMahon-Hussein Correspondence and the Question of Palestine*

1 Hansard, 1 March 1923, col. 232, statement by Duke of Devonshire, the Colonial Secretary.

2 F.O. 371/14495, Pol. Eastern General (1930), minute by W. J. Childs, dated 16 July 1930; minute by G. W. Rendel, dated 21 July 1930.

3 The McMahon-Hussein Correspondence was published first in George Antonius, *The Arab Awakening* (London 1938). App. A. pp. 413-27 and in British White Paper, Cmd 5957 (1939). Now freely available at the Public Record Office, London in F.O. 371/2486/34982, Turkey (War), Pol. 1915 and F.O. 371/2767/938, Turkey (War), 1916; set out conveniently in print in the last volume, p. no. 69301, encl. in I.O. to F.O. 11 April 1916.

4 CAB 37/155/33, Grey to Rodd, 21 September 1916.

5 F.O. 371/2486/34982, Grey to McMahon, 14 April 1915, tel. no. 173, Confidential; McMahon to F.O., 30 June 1915, tel. no. 306; F.O. 371/2774/42233, p. no. 140075 (draft announcement); also *The Times*, 28 July 1916.

6 This term used in Grey's Note to Cambon of 16 May 1916 (*Documents on*

* This is an amplified version of an article published in the *Journal of Contemporary History* (April 1970), pp. 83-122.

British Foreign Policy, 1919–1939) referred thereafter as *D.B.F.P.*, ed. E. L. Woodward and R. Butler (HMSO 1952), 1st series, 4, p. 247, para. 10) was later, at Cambon's suggestion (*ibid.*, p. 249) modified to a less obtrusive one: 'uphold' (*soutenir*). However, this verbal alteration did not imply any diminution in Great Britain and France's status.

7 CAB 42/6/10, Evidence of Lt-Col. Sir Mark Sykes on the Arab Question before the War Committee, 16 December 1915, G.46 Secret.

8 See Hussein's letters to McMahon, dated 14 July, 5 November 1915.

9 McMahon to Hussein, 17 December 1915. In Antonius the date of this letter is erroneously printed 13 December.

10 F.O. 882/2, 'Note on the Arab Question' by Cdr Hogarth, dated 16 April 1916.

11 D. G. Hogarth, 'Wahabism and British Interests', *Journal of the British Institute of International Affairs*, vol. 4 (1925), p. 72. Cf. p. 95.

12 F.O. 371/2486/34982, McMahon to Grey, 26 October 1915, dis. no. 131. Secret; same to F.O., 5 November 1915, tel. no. 674; same to Grey, 14 May 1915, tel. no. 1881, Confidential; also same to same, 18 October.

13 *Clayton Papers*, Clayton to Jacob (Aden), 11 March 1916; same to Beach, 17 April 1916. Private letter. I am very grateful to Mr S. W. Clayton and to Lady Clayton for permitting me to study these Papers.

14 Ronald Storrs, *Orientations* (London 1939), pp. 160–1.

15 F.O. 371/2786/34982. Verbal message of Muhammad Ibn Arif, on Sharif Hussein's behalf, to Storrs, Alexandria, 18 August, 1915 and R[onald] S[torrs's] Note dated 19 inst. Secret; encl. in McMahon to F.O., 26 August 1915, dis. no. 94, Secret. In this dispatch Hussein's letter of 14 July is enclosed. Storrs noted a striking resemblance between the terms proposed by the Sharif and the views frequently expressed by Sheikh Rashid Rida (on whom see pp. 98–9, 223–4), especially with regard to the frontiers, which tended also to confirm the suspicion that the Sheikh was in communication with Jedda.

16 McMahon to Hussein, letter dated 30 August 1915.

17 'Exactly how much territory should be included in this State it is not possible to define at this stage.' (Grey to McMahon, 14 April 1915, as above, note 5.)

18 As above, note 4.

19 On whom, see Antonius, *op. cit.*, pp. 168–9; Kedourie, *op. cit.*, pp. 36–8, 39–40, and an illuminating article by the same author: 'Cairo and Khartoum on the Arab Question 1915–18', *The Historical Journal*, vol. 7, no. 2, (1964) pp. 280–97.

20 F.O. 371/2486/34982, 'Memorandum on the Young Arab Party', dated 11 October 1915, encl. in no. 1, and 'Statement of Muhammad Sharif el-Faruqi', 12 inst., encl. no. 2 in McMahon to Grey, 12 October 1915, dis. no. 121, Confidential. Al-Faruqi told a similar story to the British military authorities in Gallipoli. He claimed to be a descendant of the Prophet and was anxious to go and see Sharif Hussein of Mecca. Sir Ian Hamilton was however warned to be 'exceedingly careful' not to commit the British Government in any negotiations with deserters or emissaries from the Ottoman army without prior authorisation from the War and Foreign Offices. (F.O. 371/2480/128226,

Hamilton to W.O. 25 August 1915, encl. in W.O. to F.O. 8 September 1915; F.O. to W.O., 15 September.)

21 Antonius, *op. cit.*, p. 153, 157–8. Cf. Storrs's observation above, note 15.

22 *Auswärtiges Amt Akten, Türkei* no. 177: *Der Libanon* (Syrien), Bd 12, Prüffer to Djemal Pasha. Memorandum dated 5 December 1915 (in French), encl. in Prüffer to Metternich (Ambassador in Constantinople), 10 December 1915; Bd 13, Loytved-Hardegg to A.A., Damascus, 6 May 1916.

23 Djemal Pasha, *Memories of a Turkish Statesman, 1915–1919* (London 1922), pp. 213, 167.

24 F.O. 371/2486/34982, 'Memorandum on the Young Arab Party' by Lt-Col. G. F. Clayton, Confidential, encl. in McMahon to Grey, 12 October 1915, dis. no. 121.

25 Storrs, *Orientations*, p. 155.

26 About which Balfour complained at a meeting of the War Committee on 20 November 1915, see CAB 42/5/17; see p. 204.

27 F.O. 371/2486/34982, Maxwell to Kitchener, 12 October 1915, tel. no. 2012, encl. in W.O. to F.O. 15 October 1915; see also same to same 16 inst., encl. in W.O. to F.O. 18 inst.

28 *Ibid.*, Kitchener to Maxwell, 13 October 1915, encl. in W.O. to F.O., 15 inst.

29 *Ibid.*, McMahon to F.O., 18 October 1915, tel. no. 623; same to Grey, 18 October 1915, Personal; same to F.O., 20 October 1915, tel. no. 626; same to same, inst., tel. no. 627.

30 *Ibid.*, Grey to McMahon, 20 October 1915, tel. no. 796; McMahon to Grey, 26 October 1915, dis. no. 131. Secret (enclosed also Hussein's letter dated 24 inst.); same to F.O., 26 October, tel. no. 644.

31 'As you rightly say, it is very much to the High Commissioner's credit that he boldly took the responsibility on himself of replying to the Sherif without further reference, and I greatly hope that the latter will not stick out about the frontiers.' (Wingate to Clayton, 1 November 1915, Private, *Wingate Papers*, Box 135/5). I am grateful to Mr Richard Hill, formerly at the School of Oriental Studies, Durham University and to Mr I. J. C. Foster, Keeper of Oriental Books, for permitting me to consult these Papers.

32 F.O. 371/2486/34982, India Office to F.O. 4 November 1915; also same to same, 22 October 1915.

33 F.O. 371/2486/34982, 'Negotiations with the Grand Sherif'. Memorandum by Secretary of State for India, dated 8 November 1915, signed A[usten] C[hamberlain]. Hayil was situated east of Najd, subsequently conquered by Ibn Saud.

34 F.O. 800/58, Private Papers of Sir E. Grey, Crewe to Bertie (Paris), 17 December 1915, Private; a copy in CAB 42/6/11.

35 F.O. 371/2486/34982, undated minute on p. no. 181834 of 30 November 1915.

36 *Ibid.*, McMahon to F.O., 30 November 1915, tel. no. 887.

37 'In your desire to hasten the movement we see . . . grounds for apprehension . . . First . . . is the fear of the blame of the Moslems of the opposite party . . .

that we have revolted against Islam and ruined its forces.' (Hussein's letter to McMahon, dated 5 November 1915).

38 McMahon's letter to Hussein, dated 17 December 1915 (in Antonius's mistakenly given as 13 December), Antonius's transcription (or translation) of this section (see p. 424) is faulty and distorts the meaning of McMahon's intention. This transpires also from McMahon's dispatch (no. 16 dated 24 Jan. 1916) to Grey that 'everything will depend . . . on the extent and success of Arab cooperation during the war', as well as on the nature of the conditions under which both the British and the Arabs might find themselves at the conclusion of the war.

39 Hussein to McMahon, letter dated 1 January 1916. Again, Antonius's translation 'noted its contents' (p. 424) is at variance with the British one.

40 Antonius glosses over this aspect of the Correspondence (see p. 173) and highlights merely 'Great Britain's pledge'. He admits, however, that the obligations with regard to military performance 'had been debated orally with the Sharif's messenger' (p. 176).

41 F.O. 371/2486/24982, McMahon to F.O., 30 November 1915, tel. no. 736; 'The object was to persuade the French representative of the necessity of offering to the Arabs and Syrians, in the Syrian area to be allotted to the French, some measure of independence conditional on their assisting the Allies, thus putting a check to the Turkish and German aims.' (Parker (W.O.) to Clerk (F.O.) 29 November 1915, 'Note on the Arab movement.' (*ibid.*).)

42 On October 18, 1919 Lloyd George told M. Clemenceau that one of the conditions on which the whole agreement was based was that 'the Arabs should fulfil their part'. Lloyd George went on to impress upon the French Prime Minister that the Arabs did fulfil this condition (see *D.B.F.P.* First Series, iv, no. 334, p. 483). However, as this statement was motivated by Lloyd George's desire to undermine the French claims to the interior of Syria, it could not be accepted as an impartial assessment, particularly when compared to his own testimony; on which see p. 79 of present work.

43 F.O. 882/2, 'Note on the Arab Question' by Cdr Hogarth, 16 April 1916, secret; also F.O. 371/2768/938, encl. in McMahon to Grey, 19 April 1916, dis. no. 83.

44 F.O. 371/2768/938, Hussein to Morghani, 28 December 1915, encl. in McMahon to F.O., 7 February 1916, dis. no. 26. McMahon commented that the Sharif made it clear that the question of the boundaries was broached only as 'a basis of negotiations' and that there was no indication that once the boundaries of the Arab Kingdom were laid down, he would not be prepared to accept 'considerable modifications'.

45 *Ibid.*, McMahon to F.O., 24 January 1916, dis. no. 16.

46 *Clayton Papers*, Clayton to Hall (London), 2 February 1916; to Jacob (Aden), 11 March 1916.

47 F.O. 882/14, Hogarth to Hall, 3 May 1916, 'Anglo-Franco-Russian Agreement'. Hogarth however erred in assuming that the Sharif did not recede from the claims which he put forward the previous autumn for 'the inclusion

of the whole of Syria and Palestine, up to latitude 37°N in the area of Arab Independence'. For Hogarth's mistake see my reply to Professor Toynbee's comments, *Journal of Contemporary History* (October 1970), pp. 194-7.

48 F.O. 371/2767/938, Hussein to McMahon, 18 February 1916 (unsigned), encl. in McMahon to Grey, 29 February, dis. no. 42. This letter was not published by Antonius.

49 McMahon wrote 'We take note of your remarks concerning the vilayets of Bagdad, and will take the question into careful consideration when enemy has been defeated . . . As regards the northern parts [i.e. Syria and Palestine] we note with satisfaction your desire to avoid anything which might possibly injure the alliance of Great Britain and France . . . Moreover, when the victory has been won the friendship of Great Britain and France will become yet more firm and enduring . . .'

50 F.O. 371/3384/747, Wingate to Balfour, 21 September 1918, dis. no. 219 and enclosed notes.

51 F.O. 882/22, Abdullah to Allenby, Cairo, 28 April 1920 (translated from Arabic). McMahon wrote to Hussein on 10 March 1916: 'I am pleased to inform you that His Majesty's Government have approved of meeting your requests [re gold, food, arms, etc.] and that which you ask to be sent with all haste is being dispatched . . .' (F.O. 371/2768/938, encl. in McMahon to Grey, 13 March 1916, dis. no. 54). Abdullah however quoted this section thus: 'His Majesty's Government have approved all [sic] your claims (demands)' [sic].

52 F.O. 371/2773/42233, Walton to Secretary of Government of India, 29 May 1916, encl. in I.O. to F.O., 27 June 1916.

53 *Ibid.*, *The Sherif of Mecca and the Arab Movement*, Memorandum prepared by the General Staff, dated 1 July, 1916; a copy in CAB 42/16/1 and in *Clayton Papers*.

54 F.O. 371/2768/938, Hussein to McMahon, 18 February 1916. (Received early in March.) Printed p. no. 69301 (heretofore unpublished).

55 *Ibid.*, note to the Sharif dated 10 March 1916; enclosed also in McMahon to Grey, 13 March 1916, dis. no. 54; I.O. to F.O., 24 March 1916. Aziz Ali Bey al-Masri, founder of the *al'-Ahd* society subsequently Chief of the Hedjaz Staff; Antonius, *op. cit.*, pp. 118-20, 122-3; 159-61, 212; *D.P.F.P.*, *op. cit.*, 10, pt ii, pp. 832-8; Storrs, *Orientations*, pp. 183-202.

56 *Ibid.*, Sykes to D.M.I., encl. in Buchanan to F.O., 13 March 1916, tel. no. 355.

57 *Ibid.*, Rep. of General Lake (Basra), 30 March 1916, encl. in I.O. to F.O., 31 inst.; F.O. (on Grey's instruction) to McMahon, 5 April 1916, tel. no. 363; McMahon to F.O., 18 April 1916, tel. no. 272, where Hussein's letter of 29 March is quoted. A translated copy of this letter is enclosed in McMahon to Grey, 16 April 1916, dis. no. 79, Secret.

58 As note 48.

59 F.O. 370/2768/938, Clayton to Sykes, encl. in McMahon to F.O., 20 April 1916, tel. no. 278.

60 F.O. 882/2, 'Note on The Arab Question' by Hogarth, 16 April 1916; also F.O. 371/2768/938 encl. in McMahon to Grey, 19 April 1916, dis. no. 83,

Secret. The Arab Bureau in Cairo was established on 17 February 1916. On its administration and staff see F.O. 371/2771/18845. Six months later Ormsby-Gore commented: 'For the present . . . and probably for many generations an idea of an Arabian Empire under a single head is necessarily illusory. Practical politics and economics forbid . . . its realisation; but it would be idle to deny the existence of this conception . . .' (F.O. 882/14, 'Arabia', note by O.-Gore, October 1916.)

61 F.O. 371/2768/938, McMahon to F.O., 30 April 1916, tel. no. 312.

62 Much indicative of the attitude held at that time in Cairo and Khartoum is the Wingate-Clayton correspondence. On 15 November 1915 Wingate wrote to Clayton: 'If the embryonic Arab state comes to nothing, all our promises vanish and we are absolved from them . . . if the Arab State becomes a reality, we have quite sufficient safeguards to control it.' (Cited in Kedourie, 'Cairo and Khartoum on the Arab Question', p. 285.) And on 22 May 1916 Clayton wrote to Wingate: 'Luckily we have been very careful indeed to commit ourselves to nothing whatsoever.' (*Ibid.*, p. 288.) The impression of William Yale, the American Intelligence Officer in Cairo, was that the British were 'exceedingly careful not to promise the Sharif too much'. (*Yale Papers*, Rep. No. 2, dated 5 November 1917, p. 10.)

63 As note 61.

64 F.O. 371/2768/938, Minute dated 3 May 1916, on p. no. 80305. An observation to similar effect was minuted by Grey and O'Beirne see F.O. 371/2767/938, p. no. 51288.

65 As note 48.

66 F.O. 371/2773/42233, cited in McMahon to F.O., 3 July 1916, tel. no. 532; same to same, 11 June 1916, tel. no. 443; F.O. 371/2775/42233, Wingate to C.I.G.S., 24 October 1916, tel. no. 527, encl. in W.O. to Lord Hardinge (F.O.) 27 October. A report produced for the War Council (CAB 42/23/3) revealed that the Arabs were incapable of defending Rabeqh. As the Foreign Office Clerk minuted: 'The Sherif is hopeless . . . if we can, we should try to save him in spite of himself, for the consequences of his collapse may be most serious for us.' (F.O. 371/2776/42233, p. no. 251855, dated 13 December 1916.)

67 F.O. 371/2773/42233, McMahon to F.O., 9 July 1916, tel. no. 554.

68 *Ibid.*, Viceroy of India to I.O., 6 July 1916, encl. in I.O. to F.O. 7 inst.; same to same, 8 July 1916; F.O. 371/2774/42233, same to same 13, 14, 15 July; CAB 42/15/15 W.O. meeting 30 June 1916.

69 F.O. 371/2775/42233, McMahon to F.O., 13 September 1916, tel. no. 778; same to same, 27 October 1916, tel. no. 939, quoting Hussein's telegram.

70 F.O. 371/2776/42233, Grey to Bertie, 22 November 1916, dis. no. 779.

71 F.O. 371/2773/42233, 'The Sherif of Mecca and the Arab Movement'. Memorandum prepared by the General Staff dated 1 July 1916; CAB 42/16/1; CAB 42/15/5.

72 CAB 37/161/9, meeting of the War Council, 9 December 1916 (a copy in CAB 23/1, no. 1 (11)); also CAB 42/24/8 and CAB 42/24/13 W.C. meetings

on 16 and 20 November 1916; Cab 42/20/8, General Robertson's memorandum dated 20 September 1916.

73 F.O. 371/2775/42233, W.O. to Grey, 5 October 1916; F.O. 371/2776/42233, W.O. to F.O., 9 November 1916. Secret.

74 F.O. 371/2781/201201, Appreciation by Sir Mark Sykes of the 'Arabian Report', no. xi (New Series), 27 September 1916. Secret.

75 F.O. 371/2775/42233, 'Situation in Syria'. Memorandum by Sir Mark Sykes, 14 October 1916; CAB 42/21/3.

76 Clayton Papers, Private letter, dated 15 December 1917.

77 T. E. Lawrence's military contribution has been grossly exaggerated in literature. Commenting on the Seven Pillars of Wisdom, General Sir Harry G. Chauvel, formerly Commander of the Australian Division in the Egyptian Expeditionary Force, wrote: 'Lt. Colonel Joyce has been kept in the background. He was in charge of the Hedjaz Mission, while Lawrence was only the liaison officer between Feisal and General Allenby. Joyce was the organiser of the only fighting force of any real value in the whole of the Arab Army, and I always thought that he had more to do with the success of the Hedjaz operation than any other British officer.' (Chauvel to the Director of the Australian War Memorial in Canberra, Melbourne, 1 January 1936, Allenby Papers, copy at St Antony's College, Oxford.) I should like to thank Miss Elizabeth Monroe, Senior Fellow of the College, for allowing me to consult and quote from these Papers; cf. also Hubert Young, The Independent Arab (London 1933), pp. 145, 198. As for the total expenditure on subsidy of the Arab Revolt see below, note 91. For the numbers and use of the Northern Arab Army see Kedourie, England and the Middle East, pp. 117–18.

78 Philip Graves, Palestine, the Land of Three Faiths (London 1923), pp. 40, 112–13. Before 1914 Graves was The Times's correspondent in Constantinople, later Staff Officer in Eastern theatres of war; from 1916 a member of the Arab Bureau in Cairo and subsequently on the Arab section of the General Headquarters of the Expeditionary Force in Palestine.

79 C. S. Jarvis, Three Deserts (London 1936), p. 302.

80 Lloyd George, The Truth about the Peace Treaties (London 1938), vol. 2, pp. 1026–7, 1140, 1119. Cf. also statement made by Winston Churchill (Hansard, 23 May 1939, Col. 2174).

81 F.O. 371/3391/4019, Clayton to F.O., 15 June, 15 September 1918; Hansard, 19 June 1936, col. 1379, statement by James de Rothschild, M.P.

82 Palestine Royal Commission Report (HMSO), July 1937, Cmd 5479, p. 22.

83 Antonius, op. cit., App. D, pp. 433–4; Kedourie, England and the Middle East, pp. 113–15.

84 Kedourie, England and the Middle East, pp. 119–22.

85 E. Kedourie, 'The Capture of Damascus, October 1918', Middle Eastern Studies, vol. 1 (October 1964), no. 1, p. 76.

86 Palestine Royal Commission. Minutes of Evidence . . . Colonial no. 134 (London 1937), p. 292.

87 F.O. 371/2776/42233, Wingate (Khartoum) to F.O., 22 November 1916, tel.

no. 29. Private and Personal; F.O. 371/2781/193557, 'Arabian Report', no. xix, 29 November 1916.

88 Djemal Pasha, *op. cit.*, pp. 167, 213. Also p. 71 of present work.

89 F.O. 371/3384/747, Wingate to Balfour, 21 September 1918, dis. no. 219.

90 Charles K. Webster, 'British Policy in the Near East', in *The Near East*, Lectures on the Harris Foundation (Chicago 1942), ed. Ph. W. Ireland, p. 156. Professor Webster served during the First World War in the Military Intelligence, under General Macdonogh.

91 Storrs, *op. cit.*, pp. 160–1. Storrs estimated that the total cost of the Arab Revolt to the British taxpayer amounted to the sum of £11,000,000 in gold (*ibid.*, p. 160, n. 1). This tallies with official records (F.O. 371/3048/22841).

92 Though it did not 'shatter' the solidarity of Islam nor did it endanger materially the Khalifat as Clayton claimed in his Note dated 28 September 1916 in *Clayton Papers*.

93 *The Letters of T. E. Lawrence*, ed. David Garnet (London 1938), p. 576.

94 See e.g. Antonius, *op. cit.*, pp. 176–82.

95 *Statement of British Policy in Palestine*, 3 June 1922, Cmd 1700, p. 20.

96 The statements are conveniently reproduced in The Jewish Agency for Palestine, *Documents Relating to the McMahon Letters* (London 1939), pp. 14–19; *Documents Relating to the Palestine Problem* (London 1945), pp. 22–7.

97 The Committee's report is published in Cmd 5974 (1939), see pp. 10, 24, 46.

98 See pp. 69–70, 84.

99 Letter to McMahon dated 9 September 1915.

100 See p. 69.

101 F.O. 371/2486/34982, 'Memorandum on the Young Arab Party', by Lt-Col. G. F. Clayton, 11 October 1915, Secret, encl. no. 1 in McMahon to Grey, 12 inst., dis. no. 121, Confidential, cited also above, notes 20, 24.

102 *Ibid.*, dated 16 October 1915, encl. in W.O. to F.O., 18 October.

103 This was also the impression of Aubrey Herbert, M.P. who met at that time Clayton, Cheetham and the High Commissioner (undated Note by Aubrey Herbert, received at the F.O. on 5 November 1915, p. no. 164659, *ibid.*).

104 *Ibid.*, McMahon to F.O., tel. no. 623; Grey to McMahon, 2 November 1915, tel. no. 860.

105 *Ibid.*, Sykes to D.M.O., tel. no. 19, encl. in McMahon to F.O., 20 November 1915; also in F.O. 371/2767/938, encl. in Nicolson's 'Memorandum on Arab Question', dated 2 February 1916; CAB 37/142/6. Al-Faruqi's statement to Sykes was appended to Nicolson's memorandum as an indication that the Arab leaders' claim was confined to the Syrian hinterland.

106 Lloyd George, *The Truth . . .*, 2, p. 1032.

107 F.O. 371/2486/34982, McMahon to Grey, 18 October 1915, Personal.

108 The translation of this note of the Sharif to McMahon differs from that of Antonius.

109 *Ibid.*, McMahon to F.O., 18 October 1915, tel. no. 623, cited also above, p. 83, note 104.

110 As early as 1907, Consul Blech estimated the number of Jews 'in the whole of

Palestine ... at 100,000 out of total population of 400,000–450,000'. (F.O. 371/356 no. 40321 (no. 62), Blech to Sir N. O'Conor, 16 November 1907, reproduced in *British Consulate in Jerusalem, 1838–1914*. Documents edited by A. M. Hyamson (London 1941), 2, p. 570. German sources, both Consular and Zionist, confirm this pre-war figure. A. Ruppin's estimate of 85,000 in his *The Jews in the Modern World* (London 1934), pp. 55, 389, is slightly underestimated.

111 *Palestine, the Land of Three Faiths*, pp. 53–4. On Graves see above note 78.

112 F.O. 371/7797 (1922), E 2821/65, McMahon to Shuckburgh, 12 March 1922, encl. in Shuckburgh to Forbes-Adam, 13 March.

113 F.O. 371/2486/34982, McMahon to Grey, 26 October 1915, dis. no. 131.

114 See p. 21.

115 F.O. 371/2486/34982, F.O. (Grey) to McMahon, 20 October 1915, tel. no. 796.

116 On Suarès's scheme and the response it evoked see pp. 52–9.

117 F.O. 371/2486/34982, the copy is enclosed in McMahon to F.O., 26 August 1915, dis. no. 94, Secret.

118 See pp. 53, 60–1.

119 Letter to *The Times*, 12 July 1922.

120 P.R.O., 30/57.

121 See p. 72.

122 CAB 42/6/9.

123 CAB 42/2/5, meeting of the War Council, 10 March 1915.

124 CAB 42/2/10, Memorandum by Lord Kitchener, 16 March 1915, Secret G.12.

125 CAB 24/9, G.T. 372; a copy in *Sykes Papers* confidential reel, microfilmed copy at St Antony's College, Oxford. Cf. pp. 141–2.

126 CAB 27/36, E.C. 2201, the memorandum is not signed and undated, but presumably November 1918; a copy in CAB 24/68, G.T. 6185 and in F.O. 371/3384/747.

127 CAB 24/72/I, G.T. 6506, 'Memorandum respecting the Settlement of Turkey and the Arabian Peninsula', Secret. On the Hogarth message see pp. 91, 328–9.

128 See pp. 85–6.

129 See pp. 82–4.

130 Letters to the author, 27 October, 3, 14 November 1969.

131 Professor Toynbee's arguments are identical to those advanced by the Arab Delegation to London in 1922.

132 See pp. 84–7.

133 F.O. 882/14, 'Palestine Political' Memorandum by W. O[rmsby-] G[ore], dated 12 January 1917, p. 267.

134 F.O. 371/14495 (1930), 'Memorandum on the Exclusion of Palestine from the Area assigned for Arab Independence by McMahon-Hussein Correspondence of 1915–16', Confidential, dated 24 October 1930.

135 F.O. 371/6237 (1921), 'Summary of Historical Documents from ... 1914 to the outbreak of Revolt of the Sherif of Mecca in June 1916', Secret, dated 29 November 1916, no. 10812. Printed in January 1921. Found in the Arab Bureau file 28 E(4) under the title *Hedjaz Rising Narrative*. In vol. 1, pp. 110–12

there is a summary setting out what was and what was not agreed with Hussein; reproduced also in Child's memorandum, pp. 51-2. Childs pinpointed, quite correctly, that by substituting the word 'line', which was not used by McMahon, for 'districts'—the author of the *Hedjaz Rising Narrative* committed a serious error. One of the reasons that it was printed and resubmitted in 1921 was to draw the attention to the mistranslated passage in McMahon's letter of 24 October 1915, which corrupted its meaning (see minute sheet).

The original form of the 'Summary of Historical Documents' is found in F.O. 882/5, pp. 121-326. Its author was Ormsby-Gore but the paternity of the mistake goes to D. G. Hogarth (F.O. 882/2, 'Note on the Arab Question', dated 16 April 1916) cited also pp. 74-5. Hogarth's note was reproduced verbatim, without mentioning its author, in Ormsby-Gore's 'Summary'; in an App. of a memorandum of the General Staff, 1 July 1916 (on which see above note 53); and enclosed in McMahon to Grey, 19 April 1916 (F.O. 371/2668/938). For a fuller discussion about Hogarth's mistake see my reply to Professor Toynbee's comments, *Journal of Contemporary History* (October 1970), pp. 194-7.

136 See pp. 81, 91-2; H. G. Hogarth's 'Introduction' to Graves, *The Land of Three Faiths*, p. 5 and Graves, *ibid.*, p. 54; my reply to Toynbee, *loc. cit.*

137 Childs, however, errs in putting Sir Mark Sykes in the same category as the Arab Bureau's author of the *Hedjaz Rising Narrative* who influenced Toynbee. Quite the contrary, Sykes's telegram of 20 November 1915 (see p. 83) indicates clearly that he well understood al-Faruqi's outline of the boundaries of the Arab State. So does his cable on the following day. It implied Sykes's recognition of the traditional French standing in the Syrian littoral and Palestine, qualified only by the British claim to Haifa and its environs, to be obtained from the French in the form of a concession. Moreover, the task of the British, Sykes added, would be 'to get Arabs to concede as much as possible to the French', in return for the latter's concession to Arab desideratum in the Syrian hinterland.

Again, Childs is pushing his argument too far by suggesting that the Arab Bureau had some ulterior motives in misinterpreting McMahon's letter of 24 October 1915. As shown in my reply to Professor Toynbee's comments (*loc. cit.*) this was due to a genuine mistake.

138 CAB 27/24. Messrs Philip Knightley and Colin Simpson in their recent book *The Secret Lives of Lawrence of Arabia* (London 1969) took Curzon's statement as well as that of the Arab Bureau as most 'conclusive' evidence that 'Britain *did* knowingly, first promise Palestine to the Arabs as part of an independent Arab area' and thereafter published the Balfour Declaration (p. 106). This is, of course, quite erroneous.

Dr Fayez Sayegh made a similar mistake when consulting a copy of Toynbee's memorandum 'The British Commitments to King Hussein', found among the *Westermann Papers*, now at the Hoover Institution at Stanford University, California. Dr Sayegh's findings were published in an article in the

Lebanese magazine *Hiwar* (summarised in a leading article in *The Times*, 17 April 1964, p. 15). Significantly, Toynbee's conclusion made no impression on the late Professor W. L. Westermann, who served as an adviser on Turkish affairs to the American delegation to the Peace Conference in Paris. Nor did they make any impact on William Yale (see p. 92).

139 Hansard, 19 July 1920, col. 147.

140 F.O. 371/5066, E. 14959/9/44, 'Memorandum on Palestine Negotiations with the Hedjaz', by H[ubert] W. Y[oung], dated 29 November 1920. Its circulation was authorised by Curzon, the Foreign Minister.

141 E.g. Hansard, 11 July 1922, cols 1032–4, statement by Winston Churchill, Colonial Secretary; also Cmd 1700, 3 June 1922, p. 20.

142 Lloyd George, *The Truth* . . ., 2, pp. 1142–9.

143 Letter to *The Times*, 23 July 1937; see also pp. 85–6; Philip Graves, *op. cit.*, p. 54. In October 1916 Hussein proclaimed himself 'King of the Arab countries' but the Allied Governments recognised him as the 'King of the Hedjaz' only.

144 F.O. 371/2486/34982, McMahon to F.O., 7 November 1915, tel. no. 677.

145 See pp. 82–4.

146 *Wingate Papers*, Box 135/5, Wingate to Clayton, 1 November 1915, Private.

147 Letter dated 5 November 1915.

148 CAB 24/10/447, G.7,447, Secret, Ormsby-Gore's memorandum on Zionism, dated 14 April 1917.

149 *Yale Papers*, Rep-s, nos 3 and 5 dated 12, 26 November 1917; Lloyd George, *The Truth*, 2, p. 1142.

150 Antonius, *op. cit.*, p. 269.

151 For the full text see Cmd 5964 (1939); Cmd 5974 (1939), pp. 48ff.; also Stein, *op. cit.*, pp. 632–3.

152 Quoted in Jewish Agency for Palestine, *Documents Relating to the McMahon Letters* (London 1939), p. 6, and *Documents Relating to the Palestine Problem* (London, J.A.P. 1945), pp. 16–17; briefly mentioned by Antonius, *op. cit.*, p. 269. Antonius had reason to believe that the article was written by King Hussein.

153 Letter to *The Times*, 21 February 1939, reproduced in *Documents Relating to the McMahon Letters*, pp. 18–19 and in *Documents Relating to the Palestine Problem*, p. 25.

154 *Clayton Papers*, Clayton to Sykes, 4 February 1918; same to same, 4 April 1918; same to Miss Bell, 17 June 1918, private letters.

155 *Allenby Papers*. 'Meeting of Sir Edmund Allenby and the Emir Feisal . . . in Damascus on 3 October 1918.' Copy of a record written by General Sir H. G. Chauvel (on whom see p. 355, note 77); identical copy in Chauvel's 'Comments on the Seven Pillars of Wisdom', pp. 11–14, dated 31 October 1935; cf. Hubert Young, *The Independent Arab*, pp. 255–7.

156 David Hunter Miller, *My Diary at the Conference of Paris* (New York 1924), 4, p. 226; also Lloyd George, *The Truth*, 2, p. 1042.

157 For the text see Jewish Agency for Palestine: *Memorandum submitted to the Palestine Royal Commission* (London 1936), pp. 296–8; Antonius, *op. cit.*, pp.

437-9 and for a discussion Stein, *op. cit.*, pp. 641-3. The original text of the Agreement did not survive. A carbon copy is found at the Central Zionist Archives, Jerusalem, Yad Weizmann, Rehovoth and in F.O. 608/98, Peace Congress, 1919, Pol. no. 159, File 375/2/2; 'Feisal altered the "Jewish State" of Weizmann's draft to "Palestinian State", throughout.' Minute of Arnold J. Toynbee, dated 18 January 1919 (*ibid.*, no. 227, File 375/2/1).

158 *Yale Papers*, Rep. dated 27 October 1919. The full text relating to Palestine reads: 'to set up a separate political unit under the Mandate of Great Britain, under whose guidance the Zionists will ... be allowed to carry out their projects to make of it a National Home for the Jewish people'. Rustum Haidar, a member of the Arab Delegation told Yale that, with certain modifications with regard to Syria, Feisal would be 'ready to accept his solution'. Sir Henry McMahon said that Yale's proposals were in accordance with the agreements he made with King Hussein and urged Yale to see Lord Allenby. Yale's scheme is reproduced also in full in David Garnett, ed., *The Letters of T. E. Lawrence*, p. 286 but the version on Palestine is given in an abridged form. William Yale, formerly a U.S. Intelligence Officer in Cairo served, during the Peace Conference, as a member of the American Commission.

159 H. W. V. Temperley, *The History of the Peace Conference* (London 1920-4), 6, p. 175.

160 F.O. 882/22, Allenby (High Commissioner to Egypt) to Feisal, 12 May 1920.

161 *Ibid.*, Hussein to Allenby, 25 May 1970.

162 *Ibid.*, message from Prime Minister to King Hussein, dated 16 June 1920, urgent (a copy); Allenby to F.O. 3 July 1920, tel. no. 5172/977, and Hussein to Allenby, 2 July 1920.

163 *Ibid.*, El Khatib to Allenby, 27 July 1920; Hussein to Batten (Jedda), 29 August 1920; Batten to Arab Bureau, 14 September 1920. For the Sharifians' misinterpretation of the meaning of McMahon's letter dated 10 March 1916, see pp. 75.

164 *Ibid.*, 'Conversation with ... El Khatib', note by (signature undecipherable), Acting Director, Arab Bureau, 28 August 1920.

165 F.O. 882/23, Allenby to F.O. 9 June [1920], tel. no. 558. The Foreign Office instructed Allenby to tell Feisal that Samuel's appointment had been decided upon on account of his high reputation and administrative experience and because 'his authority with the Zionists, coupled with his well known sympathy with the Arabs, will enable him to hold the scale even and exercise a pacifying and moderating influence ... We believe that the Emir and the Arabs will find him a sincere friend.' (F.O. to Allenby, 16 June 1920, tel. no. 534; Allenby (Cairo) to Feisal (Damascus) 16 June 1920.)

166 F.O. 371/6237, E 986/4/91, *Report on Conversation* ... 20 January 1921. Present: R. C. Lindsay, Major H. W. Young, Col Cornwallis, Emir Feisal, Brig.-Gen. Haddad Pasha, Rustum Haidar, see also F.O. 371/6238, E 2133/4/91, F.O. to Herbert Samuel (Jerusalem) 22 February 1921 referring to Lindsay-Feisal conversation; Winston Churchill's statement, Hansard, 11 July 1922, cols 1032-4.

167 Above, p. 89, note 134.

168 As note 166, minute dated 21 January 1921. The reference to the Zionists is referred to on p. 310.

169 See pp. 74–5; Article XI of the Asia Minor Agreement (May 1916) stated pointedly that 'the negotiations with the Arabs as to the boundaries of the Arab State or Confederation of States shall continue'. Major Young in his memorandum (see above note 140), pointed to the fact that 'no actual agreement was ever arrived at . . . although . . . certain definite undertakings were given . . . by Sir H. McMahon in his letter of 25 [sic] October 1915'. Mr Harmsworth, the Under-Secretary of State for Foreign Affairs, in a speech in the House of Commons on 24 October 1921, stated categorically that 'no formal Treaty was concluded between His Majesty's Government and the King of the Hedjaz in 1915 . . . These undertakings were embodied in a long and inconclusive correspondence; and on certain points no specific agreement was reached.' (Col. 461).

170 See D. G. Hogarth, 'Wahabism and British Interests', p. 73.

171 'Memorandum on British Commitments to King Husein' on which see p. 88 note 126.

Chapter 7   The Sykes-Picot Agreement, the Arab Question, and Zionism

1 *Clayton Papers*, 'A . . . summary of views held by prominent and representative Syrians, both in Egypt and Syria . . .' (unsigned and undated) also F.O. 371/2480/2506 encl. in McMahon to Grey, 15 February 1915, dis. no. 23.

2 *Clayton Papers*, comment, dated 4 March 1915, on Doughty Wylie's memorandum.

3 F.O. 371/2480/2506, Cheetham to Grey, 5 January 1915, dis. no. 4, encl. Clayton's note of 3 January; same to same, 7 January, tel. no. 10 (copies in *Clayton Papers*); cf. p. 11.

4 *Ibid.*, McMahon to Grey, 15 February 1915, dis. no. 23, and enclosures.

5 See pp. 223–4.

6 F.O. 882/2, memorandum dated 12 February 1915 and supplement.

7 F.O. 882/14, 'attitude towards British occupation', Intelligence report, dated 17 September 1914, signed Aris El Gamal (a Christian who advocated British occupation).

8 F.O. 882/13, 'Pan-Islam', note dated 6 September 1914; F.O. 882/16, Arab Bureau to Miss Bell (Basra), 8 July 1916.

9 *Clayton Papers*, memorandum by 'Syrians in Cairo' (anonymous) April 1915.

10 F.O. 882/18, Intelligence Section, G.H.Q., E.E.F. (unsigned copy) to Buckley, 28 March 1916. No copy of this report was sent to the Foreign Office.

11 F.O. 371/2480/2506, minutes dated 16 January and 15 February 1915, on pp. nos 5189, 23865.

12 For the full text see F.O. 371/2480/1940, Bertie to Grey, 30 December, 1914,

dis. no. 538. For French interests see W. W. Gottlieb, *Studies in Secret Diplomacy during the First World War* (London 1957), pp. 80–1; Jukka Nevakivi, *Britain, France and the Arab Middle East, 1914–1920* (London 1969); William I. Shorrock, 'The Origin of the French Mandate in Syria and Lebanon . . . 1901–1914', *International Journal of Middle East Studies*, 1 (July 1970), no. 2, pp. 133–53.

13 Gottlieb, *op. cit.*, p. 81.

14 F.O. 371/2480/2506, Grey to McMahon, 17 February 1915, tel. no. 91. The French Ambassador in Petrograd confirmed that the term 'Syria' comprised Palestine and the Holy Places, though with regard to the latter special arrangements might be made. The Russians, however, rejected the French claim to Palestine. (F.O. 800/88, Private Papers of Sir E. Grey, Buchanan to Grey, 18 March 1915, tel. no. 320.)

15 F.O. 882/2, Clayton to Tyrrel, 18 December 1915; same to Sykes, 13 December 1915; also *Clayton Papers*.

16 F.O. 371/2486/34982, McMahon to Grey, 26 October 1915, dis. no. 131, Secret.

17 *Ibid.*, minutes dated 19, 27 October, 5 November 1915 on pp. 152901, 158561, 164659.

18 *Ibid.*, Grey to McMahon, 20 October 1915, tel. no. 796; same to same, 6 November 1915, tel. no. 860; 'Negotiations with the Grand Sheriff', memorandum by Secretary of State for India, 8 November 1915.

19 *Ibid.*, Grey to Bertie, 10 November 1915, dis. no. 878; Grey's minute on p. no. 158561; also *D.B.F.P.*, i, iv, p. 481.

20 Other members were Sir G. Clerk and E. Weakley (Foreign Office), Major-General C. E. Calwell and Lt-Col. A. C. Parker (War Office), Sir T. Holderness and Sir A. Hirtzel (India Office).

21 F.O. 371/2486/34982 Foreign Office note dated 27 November 1915; A. Nicolson's minute of the same date; Parker (War Office) to Clerk (Foreign Office). Note on the Arab movement dated 29 November; F.O. 882/2; Parker to Clayton, 18, 23 November 1915; Parker to Calwell, 22 November 1915.

22 F.O. 371/2490/108253. Sykes (Cairo) to Calwell, 14 July 1915, Secret, encl. in W.O. to F.O., 6 August 1915; also F.O. 882/13. On (A) and (D) courses see pp. 19–21.

23 F.O. 882/2, Note by Lt-Col. Jacob, 14 March 1915; F.O. 882/13, 'Note on British Policy in the Near East' by Wingate, 26 August 1915; F.O. 371/2491/148549, Sykes to W.O., 23 October 1915, tel. no. 16, encl. in W.O. to F.O., 25 October; Clerk's minute 27 October.

24 F.O. 371/2490/108253, Sykes to Calwell, 14 July 1915, encl. in W.O. to F.O., 6 August 1915; F.O. 371/24982, Sykes to D.M.O. (W.O.) 15, 19, 20, 21, 28 November, 2 December 1915, encls in McMahon's tels to F.O. On al-Faruqi's statement see pp. 83–4; on Dr Nimir see p. 223.

25 CAB 42/6/9 and 42/6/10, evidence of Lt-Col. Sykes on the Arab Question before the War Committee, 16 December 1915, G46 Secret.

26 See pp. 19–21.

27 F.O. 800/58, Private Papers of Sir E. Grey, Crewe to Bertie, 17 December 1915; CAB 42/6/11.

28 F.O. 371/2486/34982, 'The Arab Question', memorandum dated 21 December 1915; F.O. to McMahon, 27 December, tel. no. 262; F.O. 882/2 Parker to Clayton, 21 December 1915; also as below note 32.

29 Sir Arthur Nicolson employed two sets of arguments: (a) that if the Turks were allowed to carry out 'wholesale massacres of Christians', all French property in Syria would be destroyed, and (b) that should conditions in the East deteriorate, the British might have to transfer some of their forces in France to Egypt. The first argument was furnished by Sykes (originally aired by Dr Faris Nimir, a Syrian notable in Cairo), and the second by Col. Parker.

30 See p. 5.

31 See pp. 15–16, 101.

32 F.O. 371/4180/2117, Note prepared by the British Delegation to the Peace Conference (undated), encl. in Mallet to Curzon, 26 May 1919, dis. no. 809.

33 F.O. 371/2767/938, 'Arab Question', memorandum initialled G[eorges] P[icot] and M[ark] S[ykes]. Secret series. 5 January 1916, War Dept. What follows is based on this memorandum.

34 Covering roughly the Arabian Peninsula and the Ottoman provinces of Basra, Bagdad, Jerusalem, Damascus, Aleppo, Mosul, Adana and Diarbekir. It is worth recalling that the provinces of Basra, Bagdad, Adana, Diarbekir and Jerusalem were subsequently excluded from Arab claims. That Sykes should have inflated them so much suggests that either he was not conversant with the details of the McMahon-Hussein Correspondence, or that he had deliberately put Arab desiderata at the highest in order to counter French claims.

35 For the provisions of the Sykes-Picot Agreement see D.B.F.P. i, iv, pp. 241–51; Lloyd George, The Truth, 2, pp. 1023–4, and for a discussion: Kedourie, op. cit., chapter 2, and Stein, op. cit., pp. 260–6.

36 See pp. 20–1.

37 R. de Gontaut-Biron, Comment la France s'est installée en Syrie (Paris 1923), p. 34; also p. 147 of present work.

38 Lloyd George, The Truth, 2, pp. 1023, 1025, 1115. Curzon's comment cited by Lloyd George was made on 5 December 1918 at a meeting of the Eastern Committee (CAB 27/24, p. 7).

39 W. K. Hancock, Smuts. The Sanguine Years, 1870–1919 (Cambridge 1962), 1, p. 499.

40 F.O. 371/2767/938, 'Memorandum on the Arab Question' dated 2 February 1916; copy in CAB 37/142/6.

41 Bertie, Diary, 2, p. 317.

42 F.O. 882/2, Sykes (London) to Clayton (Cairo), 28 December 1915.

43 Fully reproduced in Kaufman, 'La France et la Palestine' (dissertation), pp. 352–4.

44 F.O. 608/107 p. no. 2256. Peace Conference, 'French claims in Syria', memorandum by Sir A. Hirtzel, 14 February 1919. This memorandum was

written in response to the charges made by the Arab delegation. Hirtzel asked that Feisal should be reminded that France's contribution to the Arab revolt was made at Verdun, and that had the French failed there, Feisal's fate would have been entirely different.

45 Antonius, *op. cit.*, p. 248.

46 Lloyd George, *The Truth*, 2, p. 756.

47 *D.B.F.P.*, i, iv, p. 245. Grey to Cambon, 16 May 1916.

48 *Ibid.*, p. 251; also comments in Stein, *op. cit.*, pp. 614–15, note 13.

49 F.O. 371/2767/938, Note by Sir A. Hirtzel, dated 10 January 1916, encl. in Holderness to Nicolson, 13 January; Macdonogh to Nicolson, 6 January 1916. War Dept. Secret Series.

50 *Ibid.*, 'Memorandum on the Proposed Agreement with the French', by Captain W. R. Hall, encl. in Hall (Admiralty) to Nicolson (F.O.), 12 January 1916, War Dept. Secret Series. The First Sea Lord, Admiral Jackson, approved of this memorandum, but there is no indication whether Balfour, at that time First Lord of the Admiralty, consulted it.

51 See p. 338 note 57.

52 F.O. 800/106, Curzon to Grey, 3, 20 February 1916; Grey to Curzon, 22 February 1916.

53 F.O. 371/2767/938, 'Arab Question', note dated 4 February 1916; also CAB 37/142/10. Briand apparently thought that Picot had yielded too much to Sykes, and proposed that a substantial slice of the 'Brown area' should be incorporated into the French 'Blue area'. However, warned by Paul Cambon that Kitchener might prevail upon the British Government to change its mind altogether, the French Government endorsed the Agreement without further delay (8 February). Kitchener was known to be irritated at the French insistence on the Salonika expedition. (Kaufman, pp. 355–6; Grey, *op. cit.*, 2, p. 231; Lloyd George, *The War Memoirs* (London 1936), 1, p. 314; A. Pingaud, 'Partage de l'Asia Mineure pendant la grande guerre (1914–1917)'; Étude de diplomatie secrète', *Revue d'Histoire de la Guerre Mondiale*, April 1939, p. 103.)

54 'The French Ambassador pressed me earnestly to sign a note of agreement about Asia Minor. I again referred to the point of its being conditional upon action taken by the Arabs. M. Cambon said that it was well understood that it was dependent upon an agreement with the Sherif of Mecca and this provisional character was already in writing.' (F.O. 371/2768/938, Grey to Bertie, 11 May 1916, tel. no. 350; also F.O. 882/16; cf. Grey's account to Rodd on 21 September 1916 in CAB 37/155/33.)

55 On which see *D.B.F.P.* i, iv, pp. 635–8; and on Grey's attitude, pp. 15–16, 18 of present work.

56 Reproduced in full in Stein, *op. cit.*, pp. 233–4.

57 F.O. 371/2767/938, Sykes's memorandum on an interview with M. Picot, dated 16 January 1916. On this occasion Picot suggested that Britain should accord French-Syrian railways running rights to Haifa in return for British running rights to Alexandretta. Moreover France would support Britain in her negotiations with Russia for a settlement of the Turco-Persian frontier in

return for British support for France in her negotiations with Italy and Russia regarding the northern and western boundaries of Syria. Another point provided that in the event of Britain desiring at some future date to evacuate Cyprus, France should be given the first offer. The French Government feared, apparently, that the British might hand the island over to Greece and the latter pass it on to Italy.

58 See p. 115.

59 On 11 April 1916 Sykes wrote to Clayton: 'I am now on excellent terms with Picot . . . [although] French attitude in regard to Arabs, at present, not sufficiently conciliatory.' (F.O. 371/2768/938, p. no. 68931 dispatched by Foreign Office to McMahon, 14 April 1916, tel no. 287.)

60 F.O. 371/2767/938, Buchanan to Foreign Office, 12, 17 March 1916, tel. nos. 351, 370, 382, Secret.

61 See pp. 56-9.

62 The idea of settling Indians in Mesopotamia originated with Lord Kitchener. CAB 42/2/10, 'Alexandretta and Mesopotamia', dated 16 March 1915.

63 F.O. 371/2767/938, Buchanan to F.O., 14 March 1916, Private and Secret (on Sykes's behalf).

64 *Ibid.*, minutes dated 15 March 1916.

65 *Ibid.*, Nicolson to Buchanan, 16 March 1916; Sykes to F.O., in Buchanan to Nicolson, 18 March 1916. As to the solution suggested on 14 March, see p. 114.

66 *Ibid.*, Sykes to F.O., in Buchanan to F.O., 16 and 18 March 1916, tel. no. 377, Urgent, Private and Secret; O. Beirne's minute, dated 17 March 1915, p. no. 51288; F.O. 371/2768/938, Sykes to D.M.I., encl. in Buchanan to F.O., 1 April 1916.

67 *Ibid.* Clayton to Sykes, encl. in McMahon to F.O., 20 April 1916, tel. no. 278; McMahon to F.O., 22 April 1916, tel. no. 284.

68 F.O. 371/2486/34982, McMahon to F.O., 10 December 1915, tel. no. 761; F.O. 882/12. Clayton to Wingate, 28 January 1916; F.O. 882/2, same to Parker, 10 December 1915.

69 F.O. 371/2768/938, F.O. to McMahon, 27 April 1916, tel. no. 339. For its full text see F.O. 371/2767/938, p. no. 23579 and an attached map; cf. also F.O. 371/2768/938, Grey to Cambon, 16 May 1916, reproduced in *D.B.F.P.*, i, iv, pp. 245-7.

70 F.O. 882/14, Hogarth to Hall, 3 May 1916, 'Anglo-Franco-Russian Agreement.'

71 See p. 358 note 135.

72 F.O. 371/2768/938, McMahon to F.O., 4 May 1916, tel. no. 329; F.O. 882/16, Deedes (Cairo) to D.M.I. (London), 3 May 1916; F.O. 371/2774/42233, 'Note on the Arab Question', 5 July 1916 (unsigned). A copy in the *Clayton Papers*, signed G.F.C.[layton].

73 F.O. 371/2768/938, Grey's minute on p. 84855 and F.O. (Grey) to McMahon, 6 May 1916, tel. no. 371.

74 'The proposals as regards British and French desiderata must in addition

depend upon the general arrangements, which may be reached in regard to the Ottoman Empire in Asia at the conclusion of peace.' (F.O. 371/2767/938, Grey to Buchanan, 23 February 1916, tel. no. 36; also F.O. 882/16.) Grey, as his initials show, took note of Weakley's advice not to make a public declaration before the Turks had been driven out of their Asiatic provinces. However, in principle, Weakley thought that the Arab leaders should be made aware of British policy and what assistance London was prepared to give to ensure the success of the Arab movement. (F.O. 371/2767/938, Weakley's observation, dated 17 March 1915.)

75 F.O. 371/2768/938, p. no. 80305, minutes dated 3 May 1916.

76 F.O. 371/2767/938, Buchanan to F.O., 17 March 1916, tel. no. 382.

77 Lloyd George, *The Truth*, 2, p. 1023.

78 See p. 208.

Chapter 8 The Breakthrough

1 See pp. 114-16.

2 Excerpts from *Gaster's Diary* in Stein, *op. cit.*, pp. 278-9, note 27 and pp. 285-9, notes 2-13. For Napoleon's interest see F. Kobler, 'Napoleon and the Restoration of the Jews to Palestine: Discovery of an Historic Document', *New Judea*, xvi, no. 12, xvii, nos. 1-2, 3, 5.

3 *Yoman Aaron Aaronsohn* [Diary of Aaron Aaronsohn] (Hebrew) (Tel-Aviv 1970), p. 251, entry 27, April 1917, referred to hereafter as *Aaronsohn's Diary*. The author consulted the *Diary* before its publication, for which he wishes to thank Mr Yoram Ephrati, Curator of the Aaronsohn Archives, Zichron Yaakov, Israel.

4 The above is based on Aaronsohn's letter, dated Copenhagen, 9 October 1916, to Justice Julian Mack in New York ('the Confessions'), reproduced in full in *Aaronsohn's Diary*, pp. 101-13. *Yishuv* is a Hebrew word which stands for the Jewish settlement in Palestine.

5 F.O. 371/2783/221220, W.O. to F.O., reports of 'an inhabitant of Athlit', dated 3, 9, 16, 23 and 30 November 1916; *ibid.*, W.O. observations on reports dated 3 and 23 November.

6 Sir Charles Webster, *The Founder of the Jewish National Home* (Rehovoth [1955]), pp. 21-2; reprinted in *The Art and Practice of Diplomacy* of the same author (London 1961), p. 119.

7 On Sykes's arrival in Cairo Aaronsohn noted in his *Diary*: 'We immediately broached intimate subjects. He told me that since he was talking with a Jewish patriot, he would entrust me with very secret matters, some of which were not even known to the Foreign Office', p. 251, entry, 27 April 1917. Later Sykes told Captain Bentwich 'how deeply impressed he was by Aaronsohn, who inspired him with the vision of a Jewish Renaissance in Palestine'. (Norman and Helen Bentwich, *Mandate Memories: 1918-1948* (London and New York 1965), p. 13.)

8 See pp. 127, 140, 204.

9 As expounded in his *Dar-Ul-Islam* (published 1904); summarised in Kedourie, *op. cit.*, pp. 70–2.

10 *Aaronsohn's Diary*, entry 30 October 1916, pp. 120–1.

11 F.O. 882/25, *Arab Bulletin*, 4 December 1916, no. 33, pp. 504–7, 'Syria, Economic and Political Conditions'. Reference is made to Aaronsohn's biography and his 'strongly Zionist sympathies', but his name is not mentioned.

12 F.O. 371/3043/1142, 'The Italians and the Franco-British Agreement', memorandum by Sir M. Sykes, dated 22 November 1916; and D[rogheda]'s memorandum 'Italy and the Partition of the Turkish Empire', dated 15 January 1917. On negotiations with the Italians before the Conference held at St Jean de Maurienne on 19 April 1917 see F.O. 371/3043/1142; and after the Conference F.O. 371/3044/1142. For a discussion from the Italian point of view see M. Toscano, *Gli Accordi di San Giovanni di Moriana* (Milan 1936) and F. E. Manuel, 'The Palestine Question in Italian Diplomacy, 1917–20', *Journal of Modern History* (Chicago 1955).

13 Stein, *op. cit.*, pp. 362–8. James Malcolm's story of the part he played in bringing about an Anglo-Zionist entente must be taken with a grain of salt (*ibid.*, p. 364 n. 13). However, it is instructive to note Malcolm's letter to Nubar Pasha, dated 22 June 1917, where he wrote: 'Until recently Jewish influence on the whole was on the side of Germany. But as you know, during the last few months, thanks very largely to us, Armenians, it has been thrown on the side of the Allies.' (F.O. 371/3057/104218.)

14 Sokolow, *History of Zionism*, 'A Tribute to Sir Mark Sykes', 2, pp. xviii–xix; Shane Leslie, *Mark Sykes. His Life and Letters* (London 1923), p. 269.

15 F.O. 371/2774/42233, 'The Problem of the Near East' by Sir M. Sykes, 20 June 1916; CAB 42/6/9 and CAB 42/6/10. Meeting of the War Council, 16 December 1915. Sykes's antipathy to French financiers was aired as early as 18 March 1914, in a speech in the House of Commons (Hansard, vol. lix, cols. 2169–70). He considered international finance in Turkey one of the 'root causes' of European conflicts, and labelled it 'organized corruption' responsible for oppression of the native peoples, rendering reforms 'nugatory, in order that individual fortunes might be built up'. Mark Sykes, *Future of the Middle East* (London 1918), p. 5.

16 *Sledmere Papers*, no. 27, Sykes to Lord Hardinge, 15 October 1916.

17 F.O. 800/105, Bryce to Grey, 6 April 1916.

18 See pp. 38, 61.

19 Kenneth O. Morgan, 'Lloyd George's Premiership: a study in "Prime Ministerial Government"', *Historical Journal*, xii, 1, 1970.

20 Samuel, *Memoirs*, p. 143, Lord Reading to Samuel, 5 February 1915; cf. pp. 9–16, of present work.

21 Trevor Wilson, ed., *The Political Diaries of C. P. Scott, 1911–1928* (London 1970), entry 27, November 1914, p. 113.

22 Lloyd George, *The Truth . . .*, 2, p. 1116; *idem, War Memoirs*, 2, p. 1084, cf. p. 18 of present work.

23 Webster, *The Founder of the National Home*, p. 29; idem, *The Art and Practice of Diplomacy*, p. 125.

24 'My father had a positive hero-worship for the Welsh Wizard [and] I think it is a reasonable deduction that Lloyd George had considerable admiration for my father from the extraordinary amount of authority which he allowed him in the Middle and Near Eastern negotiations . . . My mother's memory was in agreement with these deductions.' (Christopher Sykes to the author, letter dated 6 December 1967); see also Christopher Sykes, 'Memories of my father . . .', *Explorations*, ed. M. Mindlin and Ch. Bermant (London 1967), p. 147.

25 Sokolow, *History of Zionism*, 2, pp. xxiv–v.

26 Lloyd George, *The Truth . . .*, 2, p. 1026.

27 Preface to *Chaim Weizmann*, ed. Paul Goodman (London 1945), p. 11; also see pp. 44–6.

28 L. S. Amery, *My Political Life* (London 1953), 2, pp. 115–16. The unhappy experience during the Mandate years did not cloud Amery's vision of Arab-Jewish cooperation and he fervently hoped that the young nation of Israel might 'eventually be accepted by its neighbours as one of themselves' (*ibid.*, p. 116).

29 Captain Gore 'collected information about the economic and agricultural conditions and possibilities of Southern Palestine which has been much appreciated by the Military Authorities'. (Report of the Arab Bureau, 31 January 1917, *Wingate Papers*, Box 145/1.)

30 F.O. 882/14, pp. 285–303; a copy in F.O. 800/210, Balfour Private Papers.

31 CAB 21/15, memorandum by W. O. G[ore], 1 April 1915; Gore to Hankey, 4 April; Hankey to Gore, to Robertson, 10 April; cf. F.O. 882/14, 'Present Economic and Political Conditions in Palestine' [1917], by Aaronsohn.

32 Stein, *op. cit.*, p. 314 (citing Milner's letter to Samuel). For Milner's attitude to Zionism see *ibid.*, pp. 310–18.

33 Tom Jones, *Lloyd George* (O.U.P. 1951), p. 48. On Scott see Stein, *op. cit.*, chapter 7 and *passim*; David Ayerst, 'Towards a national home', *Manchester Guardian*, 2 November 1967.

34 *The Political Diaries of C. P. Scott*, ed. Wilson, pp. 113, 225.

35 *The Public Papers of Woodrow Wilson*, ed. Ray Stannard Baker and William E. Dodd (New York 1926), pp. 407–14.

36 Cited in Stein, *op. cit.*, p. 365; *The Political Diaries of C. P. Scott*, p. 258.

37 Stein, *op. cit.*, pp. 301–4, 316–17, also 135, 301–4; Herbert Sidebotham, *Great Britain and Palestine* (London 1937), pp. 22–3, 32–52; Harry Sacher, 'Dr. Weizmann—The Manchester Period', *Chaim Weizmann*, ed. Meyer Weisgal (New York 1944), pp. 187–93.

38 No memorandum 'handed in person to Sir Ronald Graham' could be found among the Foreign Office files, as claimed by Sidebotham (*op. cit.*, p. 33). On Graham's reference to a conversation with Sidebotham sometime in March 1917 see p. 148. On Graham see p. 138.

39 Marginal annotation on Drogheda's memorandum, on which see p. 367 note 12.

40 *Aaronsohn's Diary*, p. 251, entry 27 April 1917. No account of Sykes's relations with the Zionists during January–April 1917, could be traced in the Foreign Office records.

41 Samuel Landman, 'Balfour Declaration—Secret Facts Revealed', *World Jewry*, vol. 2, nos 42–3, 11 February, 1 March 1935; 'From October 1916 to March 1917 the F.O. was against [Zionism] and the War Cabinet had to keep certain steps from their knowledge . . . The spirit of Sykes-Picot dominated the F.O. . . . Graham, Lord Hardinge and a few others were not yet pro-Zionists . . .' (letter to the author, 21 April 1966). Mr Landman served as Secretary-General to the World Zionist Organisation in 1917–22.

42 Beaverbrook Library, *Lloyd George Papers*, F 45/2/4; cited in Stein, *op. cit.*, pp. 370–1 without source.

43 CZA, A 18/41/8, *Sokolow Papers*, Tschlenow to Sokolow, 18/31 March 1916.

44 Landman's letter (above, note 41) and subsequent interview with the author.

45 *Weizmann Archives* (hereafter *W.A.*), Weizmann to Sieff, 3 February 1917.

46 Jon Kimche, *The Unromantics* (London 1968), p. 26, Sieff to Weizmann 4 February [1917]. The year 1916 given in Kimche is wrong (see my review of *The Unromantics* in the *Jewish Chronicle*, 1 March 1969).

47 CZA L6/90/1, 'Memorandum on the Conference . . .', a copy in *W.A.* and in *Samuel Papers* (at St Antony's College, Oxford); Stein, cf. *op. cit.*, pp. 370–4.

48 In 1905 there were 40,000 Jewish inhabitants in Jerusalem out of a total of 60,000. The remainder consisted of 7,000 Moslems and 13,000 Christians (*Encyclopaedia Britannica*, 11th ed., 1910–11). In 1913 there were 48,400 Jews, 10,050 Moslems, and 16,750 Christians, making a total of 75,200 (*Calendar of Palestine for the Years 5673–74* [Hebrew, 1912, 1913/14].

49 CZA, Z 4/728, notes on meetings of 8, 9, 10 February 1917; copy in *W.A.*; Ministère des Affaires Etrangères (hereafter MAE), Archives Politiques, Guerre, 1914–1918, Question Juive, III, Picot to Ribot, 5 May 1917. For this and other documents from the archives of the French Foreign Ministry shown to me, I should like to thank Dr Edy Kaufman. Cf. Stein, *op. cit.*, pp. 374–6.

50 F.O. 371/3043/1142, Bertie to F.O., 5, 8 March 1917, tel. nos 599, 193.

51 *Sledmere Papers*, no. 32.

52 From this two-way traffic of correspondence the Military Intelligence gleaned their knowledge both on 'the growth of the Zionist movement . . . and its connection with British policy in Palestine'. F.O. 371/471/1051, *Notes on Zionism*, pt i, dated February 1918, encl. in W.O. to F.O., 20 May 1919. Hereafter Military Intelligence Rep. (Webster). The author of the *Notes* was Major Charles K. Webster. His task was to assess the importance of Zionism to British interests (statement to the author, May 1960).

53 CAB 21/13, 'Plan of Operation in Syria', memorandum by General Robertson, C.I.G.S., 22 February 1917, very secret; *W.A.*, 'Interview with Sir Mark Sykes', memorandum by H. Sidebotham, 9 March 1917.

54 See pp. 43–7; Jabotinsky, *The Story* . . ., pp. 71–3, 78–9; Schechtman, *op. cit.*, I, pp. 223–6; Stein, *op. cit.*, pp. 487–9, 493–6; Weizmann, *Trial and Error*, p. 216; Vera Weizmann, *The Impossible Takes Longer* (London 1967), pp. 53, 58–60.

55 Jabotinsky, *The Story* . . ., pp. 78–86; Lt-Col. J. Henry Patterson, *With the Judeans in the Palestine Campaign* (London 1922), p. 15.

56 CAB 24/9, G.T. 353, 'Proposed Corps for Service in Egypt and Palestine', letter from Jabotinsky and Trumpeldor to the Prime Minister, 24 January 1917. Joseph Trumpeldor served as an officer in the Russian Army during the war with Japan in 1905. In 1912 he settled in Palestine but early in the war left for Egypt, where he organised the Zion Mule Corps to which he was appointed Captain and served in Gallipoli till the evacuation. He remained on duty till May 1916 when the Corps was disbanded. He was described by Brigadier-General R. C. Boyle as 'a plucky, steadfast and enthusiastic soldier'. (See App. I, encl. in Trumpeldor to Sykes, 15 February 1917, *Sledmere Papers*, no. 34.) He was killed in 1920 when defending the isolated settlement of Tel-Hai in Upper Galilee against Syrian marauders.

57 Schechtman, *op. cit.*, p. 236. Sykes to Jabotinsky, 14 February 1917.

58 See p. 169.

59 F.O. 371/3101/65760, Jabotinsky to Sykes, 25 March 1917; Eric Drummond's Note (on Sykes's behalf), 28 March 1917; minutes by Clerk and Hardinge, 30 March 1917.

60 'As a matter of fact, Mr. Samuel and Mr. Montagu, I believe, do not agree'; Grey's minute of 4 July 1916 (F.O. 371/2817/42608).

61 Fully reproduced from *Montagu Papers* in Christopher Sykes, *Two Studies in Virtue* (London 1953), pp. 212–14; cf. above, pp. 22–4.

62 F.O. 800/210, Balfour's Private Papers, Memorandum by Lucian Wolf, 31 January 1917, encl. in Wolf to Drummond, 7 February 1917, strictly confidential.

63 F.O. 371/3101/65760, Amery to Balfour, 23 March 1917; F.O. 800/204, same to same, 29 March 1917, encl. Jabotinsky to Amery 25 March (copy). The author was unable to trace among the War Cabinet records the statement which Amery attributed to Balfour. The records however are in most cases summaries of decisions, not a *procès-verbal*, and it is unlikely that a casual statement like that made by Balfour would have been recorded.

64 Minutes by Drummond (F.O. 800/204), and Balfour (F.O. 371/3101/65760), 30(?) March 1917; F.O. (Graham) to W.O., 7 April 1917.

65 Jabotinsky, *The Story* . . ., pp. 82–4; Schechtman, *op. cit.*, pp. 237–8.

66 Beaverbrook Library, F 14/4/34, D[erby] to P.M., 9 April 1917.

67 CAB 24/10/447, 'Zionism and the suggested Jewish Battalions for Egyptian Expeditionary Force'; memorandum by Ormsby-Gore, 14 April 1917, secret.

68 F.O. 371/3101/65760, W.O. to F.O., 16 April 1917; F.O. to W.O., 24 April; Jabotinsky to F.O., 20 April 1917.

69 In his memoirs Amery justifiably took credit for the part he played not only

in the Balfour Declaration, but also in the genesis of the Israel Army (*My Political Life*, 2, p. 118).

70 Stein, *op. cit.*, pp. 380-3. On Balfour's interest in Zionism see *ibid.*, chapter 9 and *passim*; Blanche Dugdale, *Arthur James Balfour*, 2, chapter xi (particularly p. 217).

71 CAB 24/9, G.T. 372, 'Notes on a Conference held at 10 Downing St., on 3 April 1917'; copy in *Sledmere Papers*. On Sykes's mission to the East see chapter 12 of present work.

72 Weizmann to Scott, 20 March 1917, cited in Stein, *op. cit.*, pp. 378-9; *The Political Diaries of C. P. Scott*, p. 271.

73 CZA, Z 4/728; Stein, *op. cit.*, p. 384.

74 F.O. 371/3045/2087, Wingate to F.O., 12 March 1917, tel. no. 257; F.O. (Graham) to Wingate, 14 March 1917, tel. no. 260; F.O. (Sykes) to Wingate, 2 April 1917, tel. no. 338.

75 F.O. 882/16, pp. 53-6, 'The Status and Functions of the Chief Political Officer and French Commissioner'; *Wingate Papers*, Box 145/2, encl. in Robertson (W.O.) to Murray (Cairo), 21 February 1917, secret.

76 Below, pp. 148-9.

77 *Wingate Papers*, Box 145/5, private letter, 19 April 1917; for Bertie's dispatches see pp. 59-60, 147, 156-7.

Chapter 9   Achievements in Paris and Rome

1 Adamov, *op. cit.*, no. 282. 'Instructions . . .' Paris, 2 April 1917, pp. 232-6; the original document in MAE, Archives Politiques, Guerre 1914-1918, Syrie Palestine, x, pp. 137-42, 2 April 1917, reproduced in Kaufman's dissertation, app. V.

2 CZA, A 18/26, *Sokolow Papers*, Sokolow to [Weizmann], Rome, 12 May 1917.

3 MAE, Archives Politiques, Guerre 1914-1918, Question Juive, Picot to Ribot, 5 May 1917.

4 *Ibid.*, note by Jules Cambon, 11 March 1917.

5 See my forthcoming *Germany and Zionism*.

6 As note 4.

7 Stein, *op. cit.*, p. 399.

8 *The Impossible Takes Longer*, p. 69.

9 F.O. 371/3045/2087, Sykes to Graham, cited in Bertie to F.O., 6 April 1917, tel. no. 324.

10 *Ibid.*; CAB 21/96.

11 *Sledmere Papers*, Sykes to Graham, 15 April 1917.

12 F.O. 371/3045/2087, Sykes to Graham, cited in Bertie to F.O., 6 April, 1917, tel. no. 324.

13 *Ibid.*, Oliphant's minute, 8 April; Bertie to Graham, 12 April 1917.

14 F.O., 371/3052/78324, Sykes (Rome) to Graham, 15 April 1917, dis. no. 2, encl. in Graham's minute of 21 April. Circulation of this letter was restricted

to the War Cabinet, Balfour and Hankey ('no-one else should see it'); Rodd (Rome) to Graham, 15 April 1917, tel. (no number), from Sykes no. 8 (*ibid.*).

15 *Sledmere Papers*, no. 41; Stein, *op. cit.*, p. 401.

16 F.O. 371/3045/2087, p. no. 73658, minute dated 13 April 1917.

17 F.O. 371/3052/78324, p. no. 78324, minute dated 17 April; note to Lord Hardinge, 21 April 1917.

18 *Sledmere Papers*, no. 44, Graham to Sykes, 19 April 1917, Private.

19 F.O. 371/3052/78324, minutes by Hardinge and Cecil, 21 April 1917.

20 See pp. 181-2, 190.

21 CZA, Z 3/400, Report on Sokolow's mission to Paris, April 1917, p. 27 (copy in *W.A.*); F.O. 371/3045/2087, Sykes to Graham, cited in Bertie to F.O., 9 April 1917. For the original version in French see below, p. 373, note 56; cf. Stein, *op. cit.*, p. 400.

22 CZA, Z 3/400, Report on Sokolow's mission to Paris, April 1917, p. 31.

23 *Sledmere Papers*, Sykes to Graham, 8, 9 April 1917; Stein, *op. cit.*, pp. 401-2; Sokolow, *History of Zionism*, 2, p. xxx.

24 F.O. 371/3045/2087, Sykes for Graham, cited in Bertie to F.O., 9 April 1917.

25 F.O. 371/3043/1142, memorandum by E[ric] D[rummond], 17 January 1917, encl. in Drogheda's memorandum of 15 January.

26 See pp. 123, 156.

27 F.O. 371/3052/78324, Sykes (Rome) to Graham, 15 April 1917, dis. no. 3.

28 *Ibid.*, Sykes to Graham, cited in Rodd to F.O., 15 April 1917, tel. (no. ?). At the Foreign Office Oliphant commented: 'I have little faith in M. Picot, who always appears to me to be a very tough person. He and M. Berthelot together may give us endless trouble.' Cecil added: 'Picot's outburst about Constantinople was very pernicious.' (Minutes, dated 17 April.)

29 F.O. 371/3055/88107, Cecil (F.O.) to Vaughan (Madrid), 28 April 1917, tel. no. 63, confidential, reporting on conversation with the Spanish Ambassador.

30 CZA, A 18/26, Report, dated 4 May 1917, on an interview with the Pope; Stein, *op. cit.*, p. 406-8. Sykes, *Two Studies in Virtue*, p. 200-2.

31 *Sledmere Papers*, no. 49, de Salis to Drummond (for Sykes), 11 May 1917.

32 See Luke 21:20-7; Matthew 24:2, 9, 16, 30, 34; Mark 13:2, 14, 20, 26.

33 'La Dispersione d'Israello del Mondo Moderno', *La Civilta Cattolica*, 10, 1 May 1897, pp. 257-8.

34 *The Complete Diaries of Theodor Herzl*, ed. Raphael Patai (New York, London 1960), i, pp. 332, 352-4; ii, pp. 587-92; iv, pp. 1593-5, 1601-5. On the Vatican's reaction to the First Zionist Congress see Josef Fraenkel, 'The Zionist Debut', *Jewish Chronicle*, 23 August 1957.

35 Stein, *op. cit.*, p. 409.

36 Cited in Tullia Zevi's 'Rome and Jerusalem', *Jewish Chronicle*, 24 November 1967, p. 7.

37 *La Civilta Cattolica* (Rome 1922), 3, pp. 116-31.

38 Cited in Pinchas E. Lapid, *The Last Three Popes and the Jews* (London 1967), p. 282.

39 F.O. 371/2445/155, Wolf to Oliphant (F.O.), 16 July 1915; and a copy of Leopold Rothschild's note to Lord Lansdowne (undated and unsigned); F.O. 371/2835/18095; Wolf to Drummond, 17 April 1916. On the Lugano Pact see F.O. 371/2741/37661, encl. in J. H. Retinger to Bonham Carter, 25 May 1916; also E. Drummond's note dated 3 June 1916; cf. Stein, *op. cit.*, pp. 410–13.

40 As note 30. In his *Trial and Error* Dr Weizmann commented: 'Although the Vatican had never formulated any claims in Palestine, it had a recognised interest in the Holy Places. But then practically all Palestine could be regarded as a Holy Place. There was Galilee … the Jordan Valley … Jerusalem and Bethlehem and Nazareth. On such principles, very little of Palestine was left.' (p. 240.)

41 F.O. 371/3053/84173, Rodd (Rome) to Balfour, 10 May 1917, dis. no. 128.

42 Stein, *op. cit.*, pp. 414–15.

43 'Military Intelligence Rep.' (Webster), *op. cit.*, p. 7.

44 Bertie, *op. cit.*, 2, pp. 122–3, entry, 20 April 1917; F.O. 800/176, Bertie to Hardinge, 22 April 1917.

45 Vera Weizmann, *op. cit.*, p. 70–1. The date given there, 25 April, is obviously a misprint, as on that day Weizmann met Cecil.

46 F.O. 371/3053/84173, memorandum dated 25 April 1917.

47 CZA Z 4/1586, Weizmann's note, 25 April 1917; cited partly also in *Trial and Error*, pp. 241–2; and in Stein, *op. cit.*, pp. 391–2. No copy of Weizmann's note could be traced among the Foreign Office files, which he claimed to have forwarded there.

48 Introduction to M. de V. Loder, *The Truth about Mesopotamia, Palestine and Syria* (London 1923); above, p. 92 note 3.

49 Edgar Dugdale, *The Balfour Declaration* (London 1940), p. 29.

50 *Manchester Guardian*, 10 December 1917.

51 Cited in Stein, *op. cit.*, p. 565.

52 Lloyd George, *The Truth*, 2, p. 1149.

53 *Trial and Error*, pp. 241, 265.

54 F.O. 371/3052/78324, F.O. to Wingate (for Sykes), 28 April 1917, tel. no. 440.

55 F.O. 371/3053/84173, Graham to Admiralty, 2 May 1917 (Admiralty's approval for temporary release was granted on 11 May); F.O. to Wingate, 4 May 1917, tel. no. 461; Sykes to Graham, cited in Wingate to F.O., 8 May 1917, tel. no. 498; undated minutes by Cecil; also Hansard, 9 May 1917, col. 1043.

56 See p. 150. The original text reads as follows: 'Après résultats favorables negotiations Londres et Paris étais reçu avec bienveillance au Ministère ici Ai pleine confiance victoire assurera réalisation nos aspirations Sionistes pales-tiniennes. Sokolow.' (F.O. 371/3053/84173, encl. in Malcolm to Graham, 24 April 1917.)

57 Vera Weizmann, *op. cit.*, p. 70.

58 F.O. 371/3053/84173, cited in F.O. to Rodd (Rome), 1 May 1917, tel. no. 782; Sokolow to Weizmann, cited in Rodd to F.O., 7 May 1917, tel. no. 305; Weizmann to Sokolow, in F.O. to Rodd, 14 May 1917, tel. no. 881; **Sokolow**

to Weizmann, in Rodd to F.O., 16 May 1917, tel. no. 431. Sokolow was allowed to use British Embassy cipher facilities (see F.O. 371/3045/2087, Rodd to F.O., 24 April, tel. no. 358, and F.O. reply of 25 April, tel. no. 744).

59 F.O. 371/3053/84173, Paul Cambon to F.O., 23 May 1917; MAE, Question Juive, III, Jules Cambon to Paul Cambon, 22 May 1917.

60 F.O. 371/3053/84173, French Embassy to F.O., 25 May 1917; Sokolow to Rosoff, 4 June 1917, encl. in Weizmann to Graham, 11 June 1917.

61 Reproduced in Stein, *op. cit.*, pp. 416–17.

62 See p. 275.

63 *Sokolow Papers*, Sokolow to Ribot, 1 December 1930. Quoted by kind permission of the late Dr Florian Sokolow and Dr Celina Sokolow.

Chapter 10   British War Aims Reassessed

1 F.O. 800/176, Private Papers of Lord Bertie, Graham to Bertie, 16 April 1917; cf. pp. 147–50.

2 F.O. 371/3053/84173, pp. nos 104024, 105772, minutes dated 23, 25 May.

3 CAB 21/77; CAB 23/40; see pp. 173–4.

4 See pp. 18–21.

5 CAB 24/4, G. 182. 'German and Turkish Territories captured in the War', memorandum by Curzon, 5 December 1917.

6 CAB 37/139/56, 'Germany's Position in the World', Lecture published in *Hamburger Fremdenblatt*, 3 December 1915. Circulated to the Cabinet.

7 *Preussische Jahrbücher* (May 1916), p. 283, cited in Sir Arthur Hirtzel's memorandum, 25 May 1916. CAB 42/16/1; *Schwäbische Merkur*, 17 May 1916, reproduced in App. I, *ibid.*

8 See Fischer, *Griff nach der Weltmacht*, pp. 138–9, 146–52; Egmont Zechlin, 'Friedensbestrebungen und Revolutionierungsversuche', *Aus Politik und Zeitgeschichte*, Beilage zur Wochenzeitung *Das Parlament*, 21 June 1961; Henry C. Meyer, *Mitteleuropa in German Thought and Action 1815–1945* (The Hague 1955).

9 CAB 42/16/1, 'The War with Turkey', memorandum by Sir Arthur Hirtzel, 25 May 1916, Secret; F.O. 371/2774/42233, 'The Problem of the Near East', by Sir Mark Sykes, 20 June 1916.

10 CAB 37/160/11, 'Note by Sir Mark Sykes on the Political Situation in the Middle East', 22 November 1916.

11 CAB 42/1/12, Meeting of the War Council, 8 January 1915; CAB 42/5/6, Memorandum on the conduct of the war by Lt-General Sir W. R. Robertson, 5 November 1915, G.33; CAB 42/2/1, Note by M. P. A. Hankey, 1 March 1915, G.10; CAB 42/4/2, 'Military Situation . . .' appreciation by the General Staff, 2 October 1915; CAB 42/7/5, memorandum by Balfour, 29 December 1915; CAB 42/7/6 and CAB 42/5/3, meeting of the War Committee, 5 November 1915; CAB 42/6/14, Paper by General A. J. Murray, 16 December 1915; *ibid.*, 'Conclusions of the War Council on Future Military Policy', 28 December 1915; CAB 42/17/5, 'The Assistance that Diplomacy might render

to Naval and Military Operations', Note by W. R. Robertson, 12 February 1916, Secret; CAB 42/7/6.

12 CAB 42/19/2, 'Personal Memorandum by Hankey prepared for the Prime Minister' [Asquith]. Lloyd George received a copy on 8 December 1916; CAB 42/22/15, 'General Review . . .' by General J. R. Robertson, October 1916.

13 CAB 23/1/8, no. 4, and CAB 23/1, no. 25, Notes by C.I.G.S., 14, 29 December 1916; meetings of the War Cabinet, 15 December 1916; 2 January 1917. Under Lloyd George's premiership the term 'War Cabinet' superseded 'War Council'.

14 CAB 28/2, I.C. (13), I.C. (13d), Anglo-French Conference, 28 December 1916.

15 F.O. 371/3045/2087, F.O. to Bertie, 1 January 1917 and enclosed memorandum of de Fleuriau (French chargé d'affaires) of the same date; Balfour to the French Embassy, 5 February 1917; Wingate (Cairo) to F.O. 28 February 1917, tel. no. 211; extract from record of conversation between Balfour and Marquis Imperiali, 14 March 1917; also Prince Borghese to F.O., memorandum of the same date; F.O. to French Embassy, 31 March 1917; W.O. to F.O., 28 March 1917; F.O. (Graham) to Wingate, 14 March 1917, tel. no. 260; CAB 23/2/100 (11), CAB 23/2/116 (3), War Cabinet meetings, 21 March, 4 April 1917.

16 D.B.F.P., First Series, iv, p. 485. Another argument was that 'the inhabitants of Palestine, whether Arab or Zionist, appeared to favour a British mandate'. (Ibid.).

17 The Times, 18 January 1917, p. 9.

18 F.O. 395/139/15729, Lloyd George to Buchan, 1 February 1917; Buchan to Montgomery, 25 March 1917.

19 Ibid.

20 Vladimir Jabotinsky, Turkey and the War (London 1917), pp. 142–3, 209–10, 261, 263. On Jabotinsky's connections with The Round Table see Stein, op. cit., p. 321, note 43. Among other publications appearing in 1917, it is worth mentioning: Alexander Aaronsohn, With the Turks in Palestine; R. W. Seton-Watson, The Rise of Nationality in the Balkans; Arnold J. Toynbee, Turkey: A Past and a Future; and by the same author, The Murderous Tyranny of the Turks.

21 The Political Diaries of C. P. Scott, pp. 267–8.

22 CAB 23/43, Procès-verbal of the first and second meeting of the Imperial War Cabinet, 20, 22 March 1917.

23 CAB 23/2/109; CAB 23/2/111.

24 CAB 23/13, 'Plan of Operation in Syria', memorandum by C.I.G.S., 22 February 1917. Cf. Sykes's statement at the meeting of the War Cabinet on 15 December 1916, CAB 23/1/8, no. 4.

25 On the battles in Gaza see George MacMunn and Cyril Falls, Military Operations in Egypt and Palestine (London 1928), i, pp. 279–320, 326–49.

26 CAB 23/2, no. 126, War Cabinet meeting, 25 April 1917.

27 CAB 23/2/124.

28 CAB 24/10, G.T. 448, 'Notes on Possible Terms of Peace', by L. S. Amery, 11 April 1917.

29 CAB 21/77, meetings on 17, 19, 23 April 1917; 'Report ... on Terms of Peace', 28 April 1917.

30 CAB 23/2, no. 126, War Cabinet meeting, 25 April 1917. According to the official record Lloyd George proposed to the Conference that when peace was made, and the territories of the Ottoman Empire distributed between France, Britain, Italy, and Russia, 'the interests of those Powers would be taken afresh into equitable consideration'. (CAB 28/2, I.C.19, Anglo-French-Italian Conference, 19 April 1917.)

31 CAB 23/40, Imperial War Cabinet meeting, 1 May 1917.

32 Fischer, *Griff nach der Weltmacht*, p. 577; see pp. 165–6.

33 Arnold J. Toynbee, *Turkey: A Past and a Future* (New York 1917), pp. 66–72, 83. Reproduced also verbatim in an anonymous article on the future of Turkey, published in the June 1917 issue of *The Round Table*. Professor Toynbee told the author that he did contribute several articles to *The Round Table* during the First World War, and that he thinks the one in June 1917 was probably by him. (Letters to the author dated 9 and 11 August 1967.)

34 CAB 24/10/447, G.T. 447, Secret. Memorandum on Zionism, by Ormsby-Gore, 14 April 1917; *idem*, 'Jewish Colonies in Palestine', in *Arab Bulletin*, no. 39, 19 January 1917, citing also Albert Hyamson's article in the October 1916 issue of the *Quarterly Review*.

35 See p. 127.

36 Arnold J. Toynbee, *Acquaintances* (Oxford 1967), pp. 152–3.

Chapter 11 A Missed Opportunity

1 F.O. 371/3015/171081, Annual Report of the Conjoint Foreign Committee, encl. in Wolf to F.O., 31 August 1917. On the *Bund* (*Der Algemeiner Yidiche Arbeterbund in Russland und Polin* [The General Jewish Workers' Organisation in Russia and Poland] see Stein, *op. cit.*, pp. 67–8; Bernard J. Johnpoll's *The Politics of Futility: The General Jewish Workers' Bund of Poland, 1917–43* (Oxford 1968); Leonard Schapiro, 'The Role of the Jews in the Russian Revolutionary Movement', *The Slavonic and East European Review*, xl, no. 94 (December 1961), pp. 148–67.

2 Military Intelligence Report, *op. cit.*, p. 5.

3 CZA, L 6/64/I, Tschlenow's statement at the meeting of the Zionist Executive on 29–31 July 1917 in Copenhagen; Sokolow, *op. cit.*, 2, p. 28. However, according to the official report submitted to the 1913 Zionist Congress, the number of *shekel* payers in Russia was slightly under 36,000.

4 Arie Zenziper, *Ten Years of Zionist Persecution in Soviet Russia* (Hebrew), Tel Aviv 1930, p. 20.

5 Abraham Heller, *Die Lage der Juden in Russland von der Märzrevolution 1917 bis zur Gegenwart* (Breslau 1935), pp. 23–4, Table I.

6 Military Intelligence Report, *op. cit.*, p. 5.

7 Yechiel Tschlenow, *His Life, Activities, Memoirs, Letters and Speeches* (Hebrew), Tel Aviv 1939, pp. 365–7.

8 CAB 24/4, G.164, Secret, Note by M. P. A. Hankey, 17 October 1917; cf. Sokolow, *op. cit.*, 2, pp. 38–42.

9 F.O. 371/2996/811, Lockhart's memorandum, 23 March 1917, encl. in Buchanan to Balfour, 26 March, dis. no. 75; Knox's report, cited in Buchanan to F.O., 9 April 1917, tel. no. 496.

10 CAB 24/3, G.150, Secret. 'Report on the visit of the Labour Delegation to Russia, April–May 1917.' The delegation consisted of James O'Grady, Will Thorne, and Stephen Sanders; F.O. 271/2996/811, Report by Vice-Consul Brown, encl. in Buchanan to F.O., 10 May 1917, tel. no. 658.

11 F.O. 371/2454/105582, Lockhart's memorandum (section 'Discontent with England'), encl. in Buchanan to Grey, 12 August 1915, dis. no. 113; F.O. 371/2745/5724, Lockhart's report, 22 January 1916, encl. 2 in no. 1, in same to same, 28 January 1916, dis. no. 19; Lloyd George, *War Memoirs*, 1, pp. 273, 932, 961–2; CAB 24/143, 'Eastern Reports' (hereafter E.R.), no. xi, citing Buchanan's telegram to the F.O., 9 April 1917, no. 494; E.R. no. xv, citing same to same, tel. no. 644, 8 May 1917; E.R. no. xvi, tel. no. 682, 12 May 1917.

12 Stein, *op. cit.*, pp. 323–4, 430.

13 F.O. 371/2996/811, Wolf to Oliphant, 14 April 1917; *The Times*, 28 March 1917, p. 6.

14 F.O. 395/108/56108, Dr Gavronsky to Buchan, 9 June 1917, Confidential; Intelligence minute, 14 June 1917.

15 F.O. 371/2884/72706, p. no. 110241; cf. Hansard, cols. 2090–1, 22 May 1917; Picton Bagge (Odessa) to F.O., 31 May 1917, tel. no. 53, and enclosed translation of the articles of the *Odessa Novosti*, 30 May. On 12 May 1917 the King of Rumania assured a Jewish deputation that Jews who had fought for the country would be given political rights, and a week later Prime Minister Bratianu declared in Parliament that equality of rights would be granted to Jewish subjects in Rumania. (*Ibid.*, Barclay (Jassy) to F.O., 12, 22 May 1917, tel. nos. 255, 274.)

16 CAB 24/143, Appreciation of E.R., nos xi, xvi, 12 April, 17 May 1917.

17 F.O. 371/3101/65760, Jabotinsky to F.O., 20 April, 8 May 1917; minutes by Nicolson and Intelligence Dept.

18 Stein, *op. cit.*, pp. 23–34; a profile by David Kessler, *J.C.*, 25 November 1966.

19 F.O. 371/2480/3055, Greenberg to Primrose, 20 April 1915.

20 Archives of the Board of Deputies of British Jews, Conjoint Foreign Committee, Correspondence.

21 F.O. 371/3052/78324, 'Russian Jews and the Revolution', memorandum by L. J. Greenberg, encl. in Greenberg to Mr B. (?), 16 April 1917, Private.

22 *Ibid.*, Cecil's note to Lord Hardinge, 19 April 1917; F.O. 371/3053/84173, G. Hamilton to F.O., 24 April 1917; draft by H. G. N[icolson], 24 April 1917; dispatched to Petrograd, tel. no. 791, Paris, tel. no. 1065, and Cairo, tel. no. 422; Buchanan to F.O., 27 April 1917, tel. no. 590.

23 F.O. 371/3053/84173, cited in Wingate to F.O., 28 April 1917, Private and Confidential.

24 A splinter group which broke away from the Zionist movement in 1905 following the rejection of the Uganda scheme by the Seventh Zionist Congress in Basle. The I.T.O. hoped to find an alternative territory to Palestine for Jewish immigration and settlement. Its leader was Israel Zangwill. See D. I. Marmor, 'The Diplomatic Negotiations of the Jewish Territorial Association and the Reasons for their Failure' (Hebrew), *Zion* (Jerusalem, September 1945–April 1946, and July 1946); also p. 335, note 33.

25 F.O. 371/3052/78324, cited in Wingate to F.O., 24 April 1917, tel. no. 9; F.O. 371/3053/84173, cited in Wingate to F.O., 8 May 1917, tel. no. 498; also pp. 203–4.

26 See Graham's minute on Sykes's telegram of 28 April 1917 (see above note 23); also, p. 190.

27 *Aaronsohn's Diary*, entries 26 March, 22 May 1917, pp. 228, 278–9.

28 F.O. 371/3101/65760, Jabotinsky to F.O., 6 May 1917; Kerr to Graham, 5 May 1917.

29 *Ibid.*, P.S. to Kerr's letter. This was obviously an overstatement. On Weizmann's controversy over the question of the Legion see Stein, *op. cit.*, pp. 493–6.

30 F.O. 371/3101/65760, Graham to W.O., 7 May 1917; same to same, 24 April 1917.

31 On 8 August 1917. Russian subjects in England were given the choice between returning to Russia for military service and service in the country of residence. See Kerensky's circular distributed by the Russian Embassy in London to Russian citizens of military age in Britain, F.O. 395/108/56108, p. no. 158191. The problem was discussed between the British and Russian Governments as early as 1916. F.O. 371/2819/122263.

32 See, pp. 260–2.

33 By 1917 it was estimated that there were about 6,000,000 killed, captured or permanently disabled. Lloyd George, *War Memoirs*, 1, p. 934; also p. 939.

34 Churchill, *The World Crisis*, p. 25; Grey, *op. cit.*, 2, p. 177.

35 CAB 23/13, no. 135A. W.C. meeting, 9 May 1917; CAB 23/2/134, 8 May; CAB 23/13, no. 200 (a), W.C. meeting, 30 July 1917; CAB 23/13, no. 135A; on Smuts's attitude cf. the versions in Lloyd George, *War Memoirs*, 2, p. 1087 and Hancock, *op. cit.*, pp. 432–5.

36 CAB 23/13, no. 210 (a); copy in W.O. 106/718, Secret.

37 CAB 24/13, G.T. 703, 'Policy in view of Russian Developments', 12 May 1917, Secret.

38 F.O. 371/3010/74424, cited in Buchanan to F.O., 10 April 1917, tel. no. 501.

39 CAB 24/143; appreciation of E.R. no. xv, 10 May 1917, Secret.

40 *Sledmere Papers*, no. 47, Ormsby-Gore to Sykes, 8 May 1917, private and confidential.

41 *Aaronsohn's Diary*, entries 23, 27 April 1917, pp. 246–8, 252–3.

42 F.O. 371/3055/87895, Wingate to Balfour, 26 June 1917, dis. no. 136 and

enclosures; F.O. to Buchanan and to Bayley (N.Y.), 19 July 1917, tel. no. 1528, 1081. Poale Zion was the Zionist Labour Party, founded in 1905 in Russia.

43 CAB 24/143, E.R. no. xviii, citing Cecil to Buchanan, 21 May 1917, tel. no. 1029. 'British Note to the Russian Government.'

44 I. Friedman, 'German Intervention on behalf of the *Yishuv*, 1917, *Jewish Social Studies* (January 1971), pp. 35–6.

45 CAB 24/143, E.R. no. xviii, citing Buchanan to F.O., 27 May 1917, tel. no. 779.

46 F.O. 371/3012/93027, Intelligence Weekly Report, V, 21 May 1917, signed R.A.Z.

47 F.O. 395/108/82072, encl. in U.S. Embassy in London to F.O., 10 June 1917; also *Papers Relating to the Foreign Relations of the United States: 1917* (1926), Supplement 2, *The World War*, 1 (1932), pp. 71–3. For Wilson's earlier statements see Albert Shaw (ed.), *The Messages and Papers of Woodrow Wilson* (New York 1924), 1, pp. 234–47, 348–56.

48 F.O. 395/108/82072, F.O., 9 June 1917 (dispatched 11 June).

49 Stein, *op. cit.*, pp. 422–7, 435; see p. 158 of present work.

50 Military Intelligence Report (Webster), *op. cit.*, p. 5.

51 Letter from Weizmann Archives (Rehovoth) to the author, 25 January 1968.

52 F.O. 800/198, Lord Robert Cecil, Private Papers, Cecil to Ormsby-Gore, 15 May 1917.

53 F.O. 371/3092/4637, Graham to Wolf, 2 April 1917; Cecil's memorandum, 8 May 1917, below, pp. 234–5; F.O. 800/198, Cecil to Milner, 17 May 1917; Milner to Cecil, 17 May, and encl. Montefiore to Milner, 16 May 1917.

54 F.O. 371/3012/102649, encl. in Wolf to Oliphant, 21 May 1917; C.F.C. (1917), Memorandum by Wolf, 21 May 1917. No copy of this memorandum has so far come to light among the Foreign Office files, though it appears Leeper acknowledged its receipt.

55 F.O. 371/2996/811, p. no. 94865, minute by Graham, Cecil and Hardinge, 11 May 1917; CAB 24/143, Appreciation of E.R. no. xvi, 17 May 1917 by Ormsby-Gore.

56 F.O. 371/2996/811, Brown (Nikolaev) to Bagge (Odessa), 23 April 1917, encl. 4 in no. 1, in Buchanan to F.O., 6 May 1917, dis. no. 109, received at the F.O., 26 May 1917.

57 F.O. 371/3012/95062, Ormsby-Gore to Milner, 25 May 1917, Confidential. The figure given by Alchevsky is inaccurate. The 1897 census showed 5,215,800 Jews in Tsarist Russia (Solomon Schwarz, *The Jews in Soviet Union*, Syracuse 1951, p. 11); by 1914 the figure had risen to approximately 6,000,000.

58 CAB 24/143, Appreciation of E.R. no. xviii, 31 May 1917 by Ormsby-Gore, Secret; F.O. 371/3012/95062, Ormsby-Gore to Graham, 30 May 1917; Graham to Ormsby-Gore, 9 June 1917. Harold Nicolson was also of the opinion that 'it would be of little use to send *British* Jews. American or other Jews might be a different matter'. (*Ibid.*, minute dated 6 June.) Goldberg was recommended to Graham by Weizmann (F.O. 371/3053/84173, Weizmann

to Graham, 22 May 1917; F.O. to D.I.D., 24 May, and F.O. to Weizmann, 28 May).

59 F.O. 371/3055/87895, Graham to Wingate, 18 July 1917, Private; *Wingate Papers*, Box 146, Graham (F.O.) to Clayton (Cairo), 21 September 1917, Private and Confidential.

60 Stein, *op. cit.*, p. 438.

61 Reproduced in full, *ibid.*, p. 436.

62 Cited in full in Report of Military Intelligence (Webster), *op. cit.*, p. 5.

63 On Weizmann's interview with Cecil on 25 April, see pp. 157–8.

64 F.O. 371/3053/84173, Sokolow to Rosoff, 4 June 1917, Strictly confidential, encl. in Weizmann to Graham, 11 June 1917.

65 Tschlenow, *op. cit.*, pp. 369–73.

66 F.O. 371/3053/84173, Rosoff to Weizmann, 20 June 1917, tel. from Petrograd; cf. Sokolow, *op. cit.*, 2, pp. 39–42.

67 *Ibid.*, minute by Graham, read also by Hardinge and Balfour.

68 Stein, *op. cit.*, p. 438.

69 See, pp. 272, 292.

70 Military Intelligence Report, *op. cit.*, p. 5.

71 F.O. 371/3053/84173, Ormsby-Gore to Graham, 11 July 1917; Clerk's minute, 17 July; Alchevsky's memorandum, 18 August 1917.

72 F.O. 371/3053/84173, p. no. 162458, minute 20 August 1917. On Weizmann's speech see *ibid.*, encl. in Weizmann to Graham, 23 May 1917, and on Rothschild's formula, Stein, *op. cit.*, p. 470.

73 F.O. 371/3053/84173, Weizmann (Madrid) to Graham, 9 July 1917; F.O. 371/3057/104218, Weizmann (Paris) to Graham, 16 July 1917; Clerk (F.O.) to Spring-Rice, 21 July 1917, tel. no. 2865; Spring-Rice to F.O., 22, 23 July 1917, tel. nos. 2102, 2111. On Root mission see George F. Kennan, *Soviet-American Relations, 1917–20* (London 1956), pp. 19–23, 26, 42, 48, 50, 59.

74 The following section is based on the minutes of this meeting: CZA, L 6/64/I, unless otherwise quoted.

75 For the draft of these 'demands' (shown to Sir Mark Sykes and acted upon by Sokolow in Paris and Rome) see Stein, *op. cit.*, p. 369.

76 Letter to Sokolow, 24 September 1917, cited in Stein, *op. cit.*, pp. 440–1.

77 CZA, L 6/12/X, Tschlenow to Brandeis, 9 September 1917.

78 Stein, *op. cit.*, pp. 423–6. Weizmann assured Brandeis that the Zionist Organisation trusted 'implicitly to British rule . . . They see in British protectorate the only possibility for a normal development of a Jewish Commonwealth in Palestine . . . Great Britain would not agree to a simple annexation of Palestine [but] it would certainly protect and support a Jewish Palestine.' (*Ibid.*, pp. 422–3.)

79 Blanche E. C. Dugdale, *Arthur James Balfour* (London 1936), 2, pp. 186–212, 230–1; Lloyd George, *War Memoirs*, 1, pp. 997–9. Balfour arrived in America 21 April, and left for Canada 23 May.

80 Reproduced in Stein, *op. cit.*, p. 426 from the *Dugdale Papers*.

81 F.O. 371/3053/84173, note 24, April 1917.

82 *Ibid.*, marginalium, 18 June 1917, on the draft to Wingate. This was prepared by Harold Nicolson but not sent.

83 *W.A.*, Brandeis to James de Rothschild, 16 December 1917 (draft). It is not clear whether the letter was in fact sent to Rothschild. For Balfour's views see pp. 138–41, 197, 200–2, 243, 251, 255, 278–9, 284, 290, 310, 319, 325–6, 331–2.

84 Stein, *op. cit.*, pp. 426–8.

85 Military Intelligence Report, *op. cit.*, p. 3.

Chapter 12 Sir Mark Sykes in the East

1 See pp. 142, 157, 159–60; Stein, *op. cit.*, pp. 390–3.

2 F.O. 371/3054/865526, 'Note on the Anglo-Franco-Russian Agreement', by D. G. Hogarth, 10 July 1917, encl. in D.I.D. to F.O., 13 July 1917, Secret.

3 F.O. 371/3055/87895, tel. no. 474.

4 F.O. 371/3053/84173, cited in Wingate to F.O., 8 May 1917, tel. no. 498.

5 *Nili*, ed. Livneh, pp. 193–4; Stein, *op. cit.*, pp. 293–4; Bentwich, *Mandate Memories*, p. 12.

6 F.O. 882/6, p. 214 (illegible) to Robertson, 19 March 1917; CAB 23/4, no. 296, War Cabinet meeting, 12 December 1917.

7 *Nili*, ed. Livneh, pp. 195–9; *Aaronsohn's Diary*, pp. 154–241. Among Aaronsohn's contributions should be mentioned *Personalities of South Syria*: I. *South Palestine*, II. *Transjordan*, III. *North Palestine* (F.O. 371/3051/66398).

8 See *e.g.* no. 48 (21 April 1917), *Syria, Palestine—Present Economic Conditions*, pp. 180–7; no. 64 (7 October 1917), *Palestine: The Jewish Colonies*, pp. 388–92. The *Bulletin* was the organ of the Arab Bureau in Cairo. It was printed but very limited in circulation and regarded as strictly confidential.

9 Stein, *op. cit.*, p. 295 note 39; 'I am a great admirer of Aaronsohn's abilities.' (Ormsby-Gore to Sykes, 8 May 1917, *Sledmere Papers*, no. 47.)

10 In 1908–14 *The Times*'s correspondent in Constantinople. During the war on General Staff Intelligence in Egypt. Served also as Assistant Political Officer to Sir Mark Sykes. On 18 March 1917 Graves wrote to Sykes: 'I have seen a great deal of *Aaronsohn*. He is good stuff with lots of knowledge and grit, and reconciles me much to Zionism.' (*Sledmere Papers*, no. 38.)

11 In 1913–14 served as Captain of the Imperial Ottoman Gendarmerie; in 1915 served in the Gallipoli Campaign; and in 1917 transferred to the Intelligence Dept. G.H.Q., E.E.F.

12 In 1917 Chief Field Intelligence Officer on General Allenby's staff. In his *Middle East Diary* Meinertzhagen wrote: 'My best agent . . . was . . . Aaron Aaronsohn, a man who feared nothing and had an immense intellect.' (London 1959), p. 211, also p. 5; Stein, *op. cit.*, p. 294, note 37.

13 *Aaronsohn's Diary*, pp. 232–3, 235, 265, entries 3, 6 April, 9 May 1917.

14 *Wingate Papers*, Box 145/5, Wingate to Graham, 28 April 1917, Private and Personal; Box 145/7, Wingate to Robertson, 12 June 1917.

15 *Aaronsohn's Diary*, p. 268, entry 11 May 1917.

16 CAB 23/4, no. 296, War Cabinet meeting, 12 December 1917.

17 F.O. 371/3055/87895, Graham to Wingate, 18 July 1917, tel. no. 735. H.M.S. *Managem*, patrolling regularly between Alexandria and Athlit, south of Haifa, was used for this purpose and up to September 1917, when his group was uncovered by the Turks, Aaronsohn was able to transfer at least two thousand pounds in gold. (*Nili*, ed. Livneh, p. 178.)

18 F.O. 371/3053/84173, Sykes to F.O., 30 April 1917, tel. no. 80; Yale, *op. cit.*, rep. no. 3, 12 November 1917. The names of the Syrian representatives were not mentioned in Sykes's cable. Among those tipped for this purpose were Rafik Bey El-Azm (alternatively his brother, Hakki), Muktar Bey El-Sulh, and Hassan Bey Hamada (*Wingate Papers*, Box. 145/3, Clayton to Symes, 22 March 1917). On the Syrian colony in Cairo see Lord Cromer, *Modern Egypt* (London 1908), pp. 214-19.

19 F.O. 371/3381/146, Sykes's note, 2 August 1918.

20 *Aaronsohn's Diary*, p. 253, entry 28 April 1917.

21 *Sledmere Papers*, no. 36, Sykes (Aden) to Cox (Bagdad), 23 May 1917.

22 F.O. 371/3054/86526, Graham (F.O.) to Wingate, 28 April 1917, tel. no. 442; Wingate to F.O., same date tel. no. 472; same to same, 7 May 1917, tel. no. 496, citing Sykes's cable from Jedda of 6 May, which tallies with Clayton's statement to Ronald Storrs on 7 May. Clayton wrote: 'He [Hussein] has also been told of the general tenor of our arrangements with the French which I think has relieved his mind, as he was obviously under the impression that their intentions were for annexation on a very considerable scale.' (*Clayton Papers*.)

23 F.O. 371/3054/86526, Sykes (Aden) to F.O., 24 May 1917; F.O. 882/16, Note by Capt. George Lloyd, June 1917; Note by Fuad el-Khatib, taken down by Lt-Col. Newcombe, June 1917.

24 *Wingate Papers*, Box 145/6, Manifesto (translated), dated 28 May 1917.

25 F.O. 371/3054/86526, Note by Lawrence, 29 July 1917, encl. in Wingate to Balfour, 16 August 1917, dis. no. 179.

26 Clayton was obviously displeased at the French position in Syria being made dependent on the British in Mesopotamia (*Wingate Papers*, Box 145/6, Clayton to Symes, 27 May 1917). The British considered that their claims to Bagdad far outweighed those of the French to Syria (*Ibid.*, Note by Lt-Col. Newcombe, 20 May 1917).

27 F.O. 371/3380/68, 'A Note on Arab Policy', by Wingate, 23 December 1917, encl. in Wingate to Balfour 25 December, dis. no. 315; *Wingate Papers*, Box 145/4, Memorandum by Clayton, 3 April 1917; *Clayton Papers*, Clayton to Storrs ('My dear Ronee'), 7 May 1917. The Entente Powers refused to recognise Hussein as 'King of the Arab Nation', a title which he claimed but addressed him merely as the 'King of the Hedjaz' (F.O. 371/2782/217652).

28 F.O. 371/3054/86526, I.O. (Shuckburgh) to F.O., 12, 15 June 1917; Oliphant's minute on a conversation with Col. Jacob, p. no. 108249; Cox to I.O., 2 June 1917, Wingate to F.O., 12 July 1917, tel. no. 730.

29 *Ibid.*, Wingate to Balfour, 16 August 1917, dis. no. 179 and enclosures. In

fairness, however, it should be noted that Hussein made no mention of Palestine. He singled out only the Lebanon and Syria.

30 *Ibid.*, minutes, 11, and 15 September 1917.

31 *Clayton Papers*, Clayton to Storrs, 7 May 1917; Clayton to Sykes, 30 July 1917.

32 F.O. 371/3381/146, p. no. 123868, Sykes minute (undated, end (?) of June 1918). On Djemal Pasha's speech see W.O. 106/1420, pp. 196–8, and on Hogarth's mission see pp. 91, 328 of present work.

33 Sykes returned to his office in mid-July. If the date 14 June given by Mr Stein, (*op. cit.*, p. 355) is correct, Sykes must have paid only a flying visit, returning thereafter, to Paris where he stayed till mid-July.

34 *Sledmere Papers*, no. 69, Sykes to Clayton, 22 July 1917; a copy in *Clayton Papers*.

Chapter 13   A Separate Peace with Turkey or an Arab-Zionist-Armenian Entente?

1 Weizmann, *Trial and Error*, pp. 246–51; Frank E. Manuel, *The Realities of American, Palestine Relations* (Washington 1949), pp. 155–8; William A. Yale, 'Ambassador Henry Morgenthau's Special Mission of 1917', *World Politics* (April 1949), pp. 308–20; Stein, *op. cit.*, pp. 352–8.

2 *F.R.U.S.*, 1917, Suppl. 1, p. 206, Elkus to Lansing, 2 April 1917; Suppl. 2, p. 18, same to same, 5 April 1917; *ibid.*, pp. 96–100. The President's Flag Day Address, 14 June 1917. On efforts to separate Austria see Victor S. Mamatey, *The United States and East Central Europe, 1914–1918* (Princeton 1957), pp. 56–7, 88–90 and *passim*.

3 *The Intimate Papers of Colonel House*, ed. Charles Seymour (London 1928), 3, p. 58.

4 F.O. 371/3057/104218, Balfour to F.O., 24 May 1917, tel. no. 1445. On Lansing's conversation with Morgenthau see Yale, *loc. cit.*, pp. 309–10.

5 *Ibid.*, minutes by Hardinge and Cecil.

6 A list of various attempts is conveniently summarised in Lord Drogheda's memorandum, dated 20 November 1917 (*ibid.*, p. n. 222199).

7 CAB 42/17/5, Memorandum, 12 February 1916.

8 CAB 42/7/6, War Cabinet decision adopted 22 February 1916.

9 CAB 23/13, no. 247b, meeting held 11 October 1917.

10 F.O. 371/3057/104018, F.O. (Cecil) to Barclay (Washington), 26 May 1917, tel. no. 1917; also same to same, 30, 31 May 1917, tel. no. 1518.

11 *Ibid.*, F.O. to Spring-Rice, 1 June 1917, tel. no. 2012; Spring-Rice to F.O., 9 June 1917, tel. no. 1591. On Dönmeh see p. 347 note 22.

12 *Ibid.*, same to same, 9, 12 June 1917, tel. no. 1591, 1660; minutes by Graham and Hardinge, 14 June 1917, p. no. 117850.

13 CAB 24/143, Appreciation of E.R. no. xx, by Ormsby-Gore, 14 June 1917; also of no. xviii, dated 31 May 1917.

14 *Sledmere Papers*, no. 55, note by Ormsby-Gore, 12 June 1917, Secret and confidential; Weizmann, *Trial and Error*, p. 246. Johannes Lepsius was a German

pastor and a distinguished historian. During the war interceded with the German Government on behalf of the Armenians. No evidence has come to light to support Weizmann's contention that he acted as intermediary between the German Government and the Zionists.

15 F.O. 371/3057/104218, p. nos. 114918, 11707. Graham's minutes, 9, 13 June; Cecil to Spring-Rice, 14 June 1917, tel. no. 2252.

16 *Ibid.*, Spring-Rice to F.O., 12, 14 June 1917, tel. no. 1660.

17 Minutes of the meeting of the Joint Distribution Committee tally with the *New York Times* communiqué. They read *inter alia*: 'The Joint Distribution Committee, in deciding to give Mr. Morgenthau unlimited authority to act on behalf of the War Relief Committee here ... [is] determined to place at his disposal as large sum as may be required and which will be expended at his discretion ... It is believed that Mr. Morgenthau and Prof. Frankfurter will be enabled from Egypt, to open negotiations with the Turkish Government which will result in securing permission to forward food and other supplies to the Jews of Jaffa, Jerusalem and elsewhere. It is hoped that he will be able to re-establish the Jews expelled from Jaffa, and elsewhere in their homes ... President Wilson, Secretary of State Lansing, and other officials of the United States Government, from the beginning of the War, have evinced unusual interest in the problem of relieving the Jews in the war zones, and the mission gives further recognition of this fact.' I am grateful to Dr Yehuda Bauer for sending me a copy of this document from the archives of the Joint Distribution Committee by permission of the Secretary.

18 F.O. 371/3055/87895, Barclay to Balfour, 26 June 1917, tel. no. 344; *F.R.U.S.* 1917, Suppl. 2, vol. 1, p. 109, Lansing to Page, 25 June 1917; p. 127, Willard (Madrid) to Lansing, 13 July 1917; pp. 130–1, Morgenthau to Lansing, 17 July 1917; p. 139, Polk to Morgenthau, 20 July 1917.

19 CZA, Z 3/62, Lichtheim to Zion. Exec. (Berlin), 21 December 1916.

20 F.O. 371/3057/104218, Cecil's minute and cable to Spring-Rice, 17 June 1917, tel. no. 2308; Oliphant's minute, 12 June 1917, p. no. 117007; F.O. to Wingate, 22 June 1917, tel. no. 631.

21 Yale, *loc. cit.*, p. 312, House to Morgenthau, 13 June 1917, citing from Col. E. M. House's unpublished letters.

22 F.O. 371/3055/87895, Barclay to Balfour, 26 June 1917, tel. no. 344.

23 F.O. 371/3057/104218, p. no. 121910, Graham's minute, 20(?) June 1917; Balfour to Spring-Rice, 27 June 1917, tel. no. 2468, Secret; F.O. to Wingate, 22 June 1917, tel. no. 631.

24 Weizmann, *Trial and Error*, p. 250, where the episode is vividly described (pp. 246–51); Vera Weizmann, *op. cit.*, pp. 73–5.

25 F.O. 371/3057/104218, Weizmann (Gibraltar) to Graham, 6 July 1917; copy in CZA and *W.A.*

26 *Ibid.*, also *F.R.U.S.*, 1917, Suppl. 2, vol. 1, p. 122; Felix Frankfurter, *Reminiscences* (London 1960), p. 149, also pp. 178–9, 187.

27 According to Weizmann, Morgenthau brought with him four hundred thousand dollars in gold for that purpose (*Trial and Error*, p. 248).

28 *F.R.U.S.*, 1917, Suppl. 2, vol. 1, p. 129, Polk to Morgenthau, 14 July 1917; F.O. 371/3057/104218, Spring-Rice to F.O., 18 July 1917, tel. no. 2061.

29 F.O. 371/3057/104218, Spring-Rice to F.O., 22 July 1917, Personal.

30 Yale, *loc. cit.*, p. 320, citing House's unpublished Diary.

31 F.O. 371/3057/104218, Weizmann (Gibraltar) to Graham, 6 July 1917; Graham's minute to Hardinge, 23 July 1917, p. no. 146484 (circulated to the War Cabinet) and minute p. no. 138184, 13 July 1917; Wingate to F.O., 1 July 1917, tel. no. 692.

32 Among those mentioned were Rifaat Effendi, President of the Ottoman Senate, Muchtar Effendi, Senate's Secretary, Hadji Adil Bey, President of the Chamber of Deputies, and Fethi Bey, Turkish Minister at Sofia. They were later joined by Fuad Selim Bey, Turkish Minister at Berne, and his military attaché.

33 F.O. 371/3057/104218, Rumbold (Berne) to F.O., 6, 22 July 1917, tel. no. 551; minutes by Cecil and Balfour; F.O. to Rumbold, 11 July 1917, tel. no. 669; Report by Binns (Berne), 22 July 1917; memorandum by Aubrey Herbert, 22 July, encl. in Rumbold to Drummond, 23 July 1917.

34 *Ibid.*, minutes by Hardinge and Cecil, 8(?) July; memorandum by Mallet, 13 July 1917; Note by Clerk, 31 July 1917 (printed) but written before Sykes memorandum of 29 July.

35 F.O. 371/3057/104218, Memorandum by Sykes, 29 July 1917 (originally written as a letter to Cecil, *Sledmere Papers*, no. 71); F.O. 371/3044/1173, Memorandum by Sykes, 18 July 1917; *Sledmere Papers*, no. 70, Sykes to Clayton, 22 July 1917 (a copy in *Clayton Papers*).

36 F.O. 371/3057/104218, Graham's note, 1 August 1917; Rumbold to F.O., 7 September 1917, tel. no. 800; Granville (Athens) to F.O., 3 November 1917, tel. no. 1990; minutes by Cecil, Clerk, and Balfour; Memorandum by Milner, 12 November 1917.

37 *Ibid.*, Sykes to Hankey, 14 November 1917.

38 F.O. 371/3059/159558, 'Memorandum on the Asia Minor Agreement', by Sykes, 14 August 1917, Secret.

39 *Sledmere Papers*, no. 69, Sykes to Drummond, 20 July 1917.

40 F.O. 371/3059/143893, Wingate to F.O., 8 August 1917, tel. no. 832, citing the Paris paper *El-Mokattam* of 4 August.

41 F.O. 371/3056/93808, Wingate to F.O., 3 July 1917, tel. no. 696; F.O. 371/3054/86526, 'Note on the Anglo-Franco-Russian Agreement', by D. C. Hogarth, 10 July, encl. in D.I.D. to F.O., 13 July 1917.

42 Bernard Lewis, *The Middle East and the West* (London 1963), pp. 72–3, 87; Z. N. Zeine, *Arab-Turkish Relations and the Emergence of Arab Nationalism* (Beirut 1958), p. 99 and *passim*.

43 Albert Hourani, *Arabic Thought in the Liberal Age 1798–1939* (Oxford 1967), chapter ix, also pp. 282–5, 299, 302–3, 344; also *Wingate Papers*, Box 101/17/2.

44 Among those present were Major-General Sir Percy Cox, Brigadier-General Gilbert F. Clayton, Colonel C. E. Wilson, Lt-Colonel Symes, Lt-Colonel Jacob, Commander D. G. Hogarth, and Major Cornwallis.

45 F.O. 371/3407/70822, Meeting held at the Residency in Cairo, 23 March 1918.

46 F.O. 371/3409/114901, Memorandum of A. Majid (Deputy Spdt of Police C.I.D.), encl. in I.O. to F.O., 28 June 1918; *Wingate Papers*, Box 145/7, 'Notes on an Interview between Zafar Ali Khan and Director of Criminal Intelligence', 12 June 1917, Secret.

47 F.O. 371/2490/108255, Sykes (Cairo) to Calwell (D.M.I.), 14 July 1915, Secret, encl. in W.O. to F.O., 6 August 1915; see also pp. 98–9 of present work.

48 Hourani, *op. cit.*, pp. 235–6, 243, 304.

49 CAB 42/3/12, Report of the Committee on Asiatic Turkey, 30 June 1915, pp. 12, 22, 23.

50 *Wingate Papers*, Box 145/5, pt 2, Wingate to Hardinge, 17 April 1917; F.O. 371/3057/104218, Wingate to F.O., 1 July 1917, tel. no. 692; *Yale Papers*, rep. no. 3, 12 November 1917; F.O. 371/3054/86526, Hogarth to Ormsby-Gore, 26 October 1917, encl. in Gore to Graham, 27 November 1917.

51 For the relations between Islam and Arab nationalism see S. G. Haim, 'Islam and the Theory of Arab Nationalism', *Welt des Islams*, 4 (1955), pp. 124–49.

52 Lewis, *op. cit.*, pp. 103–6, 114, 115–16, 135–6 and *passim*. The xenophobia of the Moslems in Syria was detected by the British Consul in Damascus as early as 1910 (F.O. 424/225, Devey to Lowther, 3 September 1910, tel. no. 40, encl. in Lowther to Grey, 27 September 1910, dis. no. 687) and confirmed by his German opposite number (*Auswärtiges Amt Akten, der Weltkrieg* no. 11G, Bd. 4, Loytved-Hardegg to A.A., 26 November 1914; Bd 6, Loytved-Hardegg to Wangenheim (Constantinople), 21 December 1914). The Germans however, claiming to be the 'true' protectors of Islam, enjoyed a definite advantage over the British and French.

53 F.O. 882/12, Clayton to Wingate, 28 January 1916.

54 *Clayton Papers*, Clayton to Sykes, 20 August 1917.

55 *Aaronsohn's Diary*, pp. 328–9.

Chapter 14 The Conjoint Foreign Committee and the Zionists

1 Ed. Harry Sacher (London 1916). In his essay 'Zionism and the Jewish Problem', Weizmann wrote: 'The efforts of the emancipated Jew to assimilate himself to his surroundings ... deceive nobody but himself. The record of the emancipated Jews in his loyalty to his country ... is unimpeachable. Nonetheless, he is felt by the outside world to be still something different, still an alien ... and the position of the emancipated Jew, though he does not realize it himself, is even more tragic than that of his oppressed brother [in Eastern Europe] ... It is this central problem—the homelessness of the Jewish people—that Zionism attacks.' (pp. 6–7.)

2 F.O. 371/2817/426081, Memorandum by Wolf, 17 August 1916, Weizmann's rejoinder, 3 September 1916, Wolf to James de Rothschild, 31 August 1916 (copies), encl. in Wolf to Oliphant, 1 December 1916.

3 The nearest German equivalent to 'nationality' is the term *Staatsangehörigkeit*, i.e. state-belonging.

4 As note 2. Memorandum by Sokolow, 11 October 1916.

5 *Ibid.*, 'Note on the Zionist Memorandum' by Wolf, 20 November 1916.

6 Leon Simon, *The Case of the Anti-Zionists. A Reply* (London 1917).

7 Harry Sacher, *Zionism and the State*. Zionist Pamphlets, no. 5 (London 1915).

8 Louis D. Brandeis, *The Jewish Problem: How to Solve It* (New York 1934, new ed.), pp. 21–2; reprinted in Zionism, ed. P. Goodman and A. Lewis, *op. cit.*, pp. 107–8; Jacob de Haas, *Louis D. Brandeis* (New York 1929), pp. 184–5; *Brandeis on Zionism* (Washington 1942), pp. 28–9.

9 F.O. 371/2817/426081, p. no. 243496, minute, 1 December 1916.

10 CZA, A 100/27, 'Draft of Programme for a Jewish Resettlement of Palestine', 25 November 1916. For Wolf's 'formula' see p. 49.

11 See pp. 269–70.

12 F.O. 371/2817/426081, Wolf to Rothschild, 31 August 1916, encl. in Wolf to Oliphant, 1 December 1916.

13 See pp. 137–8.

14 C.F.C./1917, p. 505, Wolf to Bigart, 5 June 1917.

15 As note 10.

16 *W.A.*, Sokolow to Brandeis, 7 April 1917.

17 On which see pp. 130–2.

18 CZA, Z 4/120, 'Introductory Note to the Memorandum' (undated, presumably June or July 1917).

19 F.O. 608/98, Peace Conference 1919, file 375/2/1 (a copy in F.O. 371/4217/66287, and in Joint Foreign Committee, *The Peace Conference, Paris, 1919*, pp. 112–13). For the text of the Zionist statement to the peace conference see 'Reports of the Executive to the XII Zionist Congress', 1, pp. 74–83; F.O. 371/4170/1051, Simon to Graham, 21 February 1919.

20 *Jewish Chronicle*, 27 October 1916.

21 C.F.C./1917, pp. 283–4, Sokolow to Wolf, 31 October 1916; p. 448, Wolf to Sokolow, 8 March 1917; p. 450, Sokolow to Wolf, 15 March 1917; pp. 451–3, Wolf to Sokolow, 26 March 1917.

22 C.F.C./1917, p. 505, Wolf to Bigart (Paris), 5 June 1917.

23 *Ibid.*, p. 459, Wolf to Sokolow, 26 April 1917.

24 F.O. 371/3092/4637, Wolf to Oliphant, 21 April 1917, Confidential, encls. Report of Alliance Israélite, April 1917, and a copy of C.F.C. to Grey, 1 October 1916. The original letter to Grey is found in F.O. 371/2817/42608. There is no documentary indication however that Grey recognised the Committee as the sole spokesman on the Palestine question. (A copy of Wolf's letter to Oliphant is also in C.F.C./1917, pp. 462–3.)

25 C.F.C./1917, pp. 460–1, Cowen to Wolf, 4 May 1917; p. 470, Rothschild to Wolf, 30 April 1917.

26 *Ibid.*, pp. 465–8, Wolf's memorandum on a telephone conversation with Oliphant, 1 May 1917; Oliphant's minute on this conversation, 30 April

1917. (F.O. 371/3042/4637, p. no. 88484); F.O. 371/3092/4637, Wolf to Oliphant, 2 May 1917 (a copy in C.F.C./1917, p. 471).

27 F.O. 371/3092/4637, minute by Drogheda, 25 April 1917, p. no. 83962; Graham to Wolf, 27 April 1917 (C.F.C./1917, p. 463); Cecil's memorandum, 8 May 1917; C.F.C./1917, pp. 472-3, Wolf to Montefiore, 8 May 1917. Wolf reported amongst others: 'No doubt Government is making full enquiries and examining the plans of the Zionists but that need not disturb us so long as no agreement is concluded—and none will be concluded—without previous consultations with us.'

28 C.F.C./1917, pp. 474-8, Interview with Lord Milner, 16 May 1917; cf. p. 190.

29 Ibid., pp. 479, 489-90, 'Statement of Policy'. Of the total of twenty-one members, seven were absent.

30 Ibid., Hertz to Montefiore, 30 May 1917 (pp. 549-51); Wolf to Montefiore, 1 June 1917 (pp. 553-8, where Hertz-Wolf correspondence is quoted), pp. 542-7, Wolf's memorandum on a conversation with Greenberg, 22 May 1917.

31 Ibid., pp. 531a-2, Wolf to Oliphant, 22 May 1917. The date inserted on the original text forwarded to the Foreign Office was mistyped 30 April 1917. No corresponding documents from the Zionist sources to confirm the facts given in Wolf's letter have come to light.

32 Cited in Sokolow, op. cit., 2, p. 56.

33 F.O. 371/3053/84173, Wolf to Oliphant, 18 May 1917. (A copy in C.F.C./1917, pp. 530-1.) Graham to Wolf, 24 May 1917; Wolf to Graham, 25 May 1917. The letter of the Conjoint Foreign Committee to The Times is reproduced fully in Sokolow, op. cit., 2, pp. 58-61; F.O. Handbooks, no. 162, Zionism, pp. 39-42; Sykes, Two Studies in Virtue, op. cit., App. A, pp. 231-40 and selected excerpts in Stein, op. cit., pp. 454-5. Paul Goodman's assertion that Wolf was the author of the letter to The Times (The Jewish National Home, p. 221) is credible if we compare it with the arguments advanced in his correspondence with the Zionists.

34 See pp. 35-7.

35 C.F.C./1917, pp. 525-9, Memorandum . . . by Lucien Wolf, 6 June 1917.

36 Stein, op. cit., pp. 323-6; Jabotinsky, The Story . . ., p. 80.

37 W.A., Harry Lewis to Weizmann, 30 May 1917; Weizmann to Lewis, 1 June 1917; Lewis to Weizmann, 3 June 1917; C.F.C./1917, pp. 511-12, Wolf to Cowen, 4 June 1917; p. 513, Cowen to Wolf, 11 June 1917.

38 See Hertz's letter to The Times, 25 May 1917.

39 W.A., unsigned note, 23 May 1917; Weizmann to Goodman, 7 June 1917; Goodman to Weizmann, 8 June; Goodman, The Jewish National Home, pp. 23, 102; Gaster Papers, Dywien to Gaster, 5, 8 June 1917; Gaster to Weizmann, 11, 20 June 1917.

40 F.O. 371/3053/84173, J.N.U. to F.O., 24 June 1917. The Organisation was, in fact, known as the National Union for Jewish Rights.

41 C.F.C./1917, p. 502, tel. from Johannesburg, 1 June 1917. The text was

endorsed by a mass meeting on 3 June (F.O. 371/3055/87895, encl. in Buxton to C.O., 9 June, encl. in C.O. to F.O., 24 June).

42 C.F.C./1917, pp. 500, 501, C.U.J.F.S. to C.F.C., 4 June 1917; p. 505, Wolf to Bigart, 5 June 1917 (also p. 503, 23 May 1917); p. 510, Bigart to Wolf, 21 June 1917.

43 Goodman, *The National Home*, p. 23; Stein, *op. cit.*, p. 458; *W.A.*, Sieff to Weizmann, 11 June 1917.

44 F.O. 371/3053/84173, Wolf to Oliphant, 18 June 1917; minutes by Nicolson and Graham, p. no. 121745.

45 F.O. 371/3012/102649, Wolf to Oliphant, 31 July 1917, encl. Blank's report, 7 July 1917 (a copy in C.F.C./1917, pp. 713–30). Dr Rubin Blank was a leading personality in the Jewish community in Petrograd and active in Russian politics. On 10 August he informed Wolf that extreme reactionaries, as well as extreme Left revolutionaries, blamed the Jews for the war. They accused them of sabotaging the making of peace with Germany for the sole purpose of ruining Russia. Voluminous literature in this vein was found at the headquarters of the Bolshevik Party (F.O. 371/3015/154307, Wolf to Oliphant, 13 August 1917; copy in C.F.C./1917, pp. 710–11).

46 *W.A.*, Rothschild to Weizmann, 19 April 1917; Weizmann, 'Zionism and the Jewish Problem', *Zionism and the Jewish Future*, pp. 8–9.

47 A manifesto issued by the representatives of all Jewish parties in Russia stated that not only had the Russian Jews acquired equality of rights as individuals and citizens but, as soon as they determined their identity at the forthcoming Congress, their 'national rights' as a people would be confirmed as well. The text of this manifesto is reproduced in German translation in *Die Judenfrage der Gegenwart Documentensammlung*, ed. Leon Chasanowitsch and Leo Motzkin (Stockholm 1919, pp. 35). The elections to the Congress took place in the autumn of 1917, but because of the disturbed state of the country and the rise of the Bolsheviks to power, the Congress never met.

48 F.O. 371/3386/856, Graham to Wolf, 28 June 1918 (drafted by Harold Nicolson).

49 Cited in Brandeis's address, on which see p. 230 note 8.

50 Blanche Dugdale, 'The Balfour Declaration', Goodman, *The National Home*, p. 4.

51 Sokolow, *History of Zionism*, 1, pp. xxxv–xxxvi, letter to Sokolow, 30 January 1918.

52 *Manchester Guardian*, 10 December 1917.

53 *Jewish Chronicle*, 18 October 1918.

54 Cited in *Zionism*, ed. P. Goodman and A. Lewis, p. 154.

55 Blanche Dugdale, *Arthur James Balfour*, 2, p. 216, 226.

56 Lt-Col. J. Henry Patterson, *With the Judeans in the Palestine Campaign* (London 1922), pp. 19–21.

57 CZA, Z 4/4066, Speech at Bradford, 9 November 1922.

58 Richard Lloyd George, *Lloyd George* (London 1960), p. 17.

59 F.O. 371/3057/104218, Memorandum by Sykes, 29 July 1917.

60 Foreword by Earl Lloyd George to *Chaim Weizmann*, ed. Paul Goodman, p. 9; *ibid.*, Harry Sacher, 'Dr. Weizmann the Statesman', p. 52; *ibid.*, Edgar Dugdale, 'Man and Statesman', pp. 26–7.

Chapter 15 In Search of a Formula

1 See pp. 52–9, 142, 202.

2 *W.A.*, Gaster to Weizmann, 7 May 1917.

3 This may have been Dr Victor Jacobson, head of the Zionist Agency in Constantinople before the war, and subsequently a member of the Zionist Executive in Berlin.

4 F.O. 371/3058/123458, Graham's note to Lord Hardinge, 13 June 1917, confidential. On Germany's policy see my forthcoming *Germany and Zionism*.

5 F.O. 371/2745/5724, Lockhart to Buchanan, 22 January 1916, encl. in Buchanan to Grey, 28 January, dis. no. 19, confidential; F.O. 371/2996/811, Buchanan to F.O., 1 April 1917, dis. no. 79, encl. Report of F. Lindley; F.O. 395/108/56108, Sir George Riddel to Balfour, 8 March 1917. Private.

6 Hansard, 26 July 1917, col. 1518.

7 The text is given in *The Times*, 23 March 1917.

8 F.O. 371/2996/811, Report of Vice-Consul Brown (Nicolaev), 22 May 1917, encl. in Buchanan to Cecil, 7 June 1917, dis. no. 128.

9 CAB 24/3, G 150, Secret, 'Report on the visit of the Labour Delegation to Russia', April–May 1917; CAB 24/143, Appreciation of E.R. no. xiv, by Ormsby-Gore, 3 May 1917. The mission of Arthur Henderson, a Labour member of the War Cabinet, turned into an even greater fiasco. His *volte face*, following his visit to Russia, seriously compromised the British Government. CAB 23/13, no. 201 (a), W.C. meeting, 1 August 1917; Lloyd George, *War Memoirs*, 2, pp. 1116–40.

10 F.O. 371/2996/811, p. no. 124895, minute, 21 June 1917.

11 Above, pp. 191–2.

12 F.O. 371/3058/123458, Graham's note, 13 June 1917; minute by Balfour (undated).

13 F.O. 371/3058/123458, p. no. 123458, Balfour and Cecil's minutes (undated); *W.A.*, Rothschild to Weizmann, 17 June 1917; Weizmann to Sacher, 20 June; Weizmann to Scott, 20 June; *Trial and Error*, pp. 255–6.

14 *Ig'rot Ahad Ha'am*, 5, p. 204, Ahad Ha'am to Weizmann, 22 November 1914.

15 *Chaim Weizmann*, ed. Goodman, p. 21.

16 S. Tolkowsky, 'Zionism as a Practical Object', *Zionism*, ed. P. Goodman and F. Lewis, p. 243.

17 *Reports of the Executive of Zionist Organisation to the XIIth Zionist Congress*, Political Report (1921), App. I.

18 CZA, A 100/27, Draft of Programme for a Jewish Resettlement of Palestine, 25 November 1916.

19 Wyndham Deedes, *Palestine—A National Home for the Jews* (London 1937), p. 2.

20 *Trial and Error*, p. 235.

21 Nahum Sokolow, 'How the Basle Programme was made', *The Zionist Review* (October 1917), 1, no. 6. Sokolow was a member of the drafting committee.

22 *W.A.*, Herbert Sidebotham's interview with Sykes, 9 March 1917.

23 F.O. 395/139/15725, Buchan to Lord Onslow, F.O., 8 June 1917. Confidential.

24 F.O. 371/3053/84173, Wingate to F.O. (from Clayton to Graham), tel. no. 870, Balfour's minute, 20 August 1917.

25 F.O. 371/3055/87895, p. no. 132608.

26 Harold Nicolson, *Diaries and Letters, 1945–1962*, ed. by Nigel Nicolson (London, Collins 1968), pp. 139–40.

27 Stein, *op. cit.*, p. 468. Mr Stein seems also to attach too great importance to Sykes's memorandum of 22(?) September (*ibid.*, pp. 511–12). There is no copy of this memorandum among the Foreign Office files or War Cabinet papers. It probably remained private and had no bearing on the War Cabinet's deliberations. However, if the memorandum was meant primarily for Zionist consumption (*ibid.*, pp. 522–3), Sokolow's unwillingness to consider the Sacher-Sidebotham formula is understandable. But it is worth noting that Sykes's views did not necessarily reflect those held by the Foreign Office and by Balfour.

28 As note 21.

29 *W.A.*, Sacher to Leon Simon, 13 April, 9, 13 May, 14 June, 2 July 1917.

30 *Ibid.*, Sacher to Weizmann, 22 June, Sacher to Simon, 2 July 1917.

31 Copies of the drafts in the Weizmann Archives, encl. in Sokolow to Simon, 5 July 1917 and in CZA, A 111/29.

32 CZA, Z 4/120, Sacher to Sokolow, 9 July 1917.

33 Dated 10 July, cited in Stein, *op. cit.*, p. 466.

34 Its members were J. Cowen, J. Ettinger, Simon Marks, I. M. Sieff, Leon Simon, S. Tolkowsky and Ahad Ha'am.

35 *Ig'rot*, 5, pp. 303–4, Ahad Ha'am to Sokolow, 11 July 1917. 'S' stands for Sacher.

36 CZA, Z 4/120, Sacher to Sokolow, 11 July 1917; 'Introductory Note to the Memorandum', Private and confidential (undated).

37 *W.A.*, Sokolow to L. Simon, 13 July 1917; CZA, Z 4/117, Sokolow to Rothschild, 29 August 1917; *ibid.*, Z 4/120, Sokolow to Sacher, 13 July 1917.

38 CZA, Z 4/117, undated copy. The addressee is not specified but the contents suggest that it was Lady Rothschild; L 4/63, Minutes of the meeting of the London Zionist Political Committee, 28 August 1917.

39 *Ibid.*, Z 4/117, Rothschild to Sokolow, 13 October 1917.

40 Stein, *op. cit.*, pp. 468–71.

41 CZA, Z 4/117, Sokolow to Rothschild, 18 July 1917.

42 CZA, Z 4/120; Sacher to Sokolow, 14 July 1917; *W.A.*, Sacher to L. Simon, 11 August 1917. The text of the Labour manifesto is reproduced in *British Labour Policy on Palestine: A collection of documents . . . 1917–38*, ed. S.

Levenberg and J. Pedro (London 1938), p. 9; also S. Levenberg, 'Zionism in British Politics', *The Jewish National Home*, ed. Goodman, pp. 112–13.

43 F.O. 371/3083/143082, copy in CAB 24/24, G.T. 1803, Secret; CAB 21/58.

44 CAB 23/13, no. 200 (a), War Cabinet meeting, 31 July 1917; CAB 24/21, G.T. 1531, Secret.

45 CAB 24/24, G.T. no. 1802, 'The American Attitude to War', Memorandum by John Buchan, 8 August 1917; F.O. 800/208, C.X. (secret note) for Balfour, 13 April 1917; F.O. 800/209, Memorandum by Sir William Wiseman on Anglo-American Relations, August 1917, Confidential; Lloyd George, *War Memoirs*, I, p. 1017; British Museum, Dept. of MSS. Balfour Papers, no. 49738, Spring-Rice to Cecil, 9, 14 June 1917.

46 F.O. 800/209, Balfour to House, in Wiseman to Bayley (N.Y.), 28 June 1917; F.O. (Balfour ?) to Spring-Rice, 29 June 1917.

47 *Ibid.*, Spring-Rice to Balfour, 28 December 1917.

48 CZA, A 18/41/2/8, Tschlenow to Weizmann and Sokolow, Bergen, 11/24 September 1917.

49 *Le Giornale D'Italia* (Rome), 16 June 1917, encl. in Wingate to Graham, 23 July 1917; F.O. 371/3083/143082.

50 F.O. 371/3053/84173, Kerr (Downing Street) to F.O., 21 August 1917; Nicolson's minute, 22 August; F.O. 371/3083/143082, p. no. 143082, minute by Graham.

51 CAB 21/58, Nicolson to Longhurst, 17 August 1917; Longhurst to Nicolson, 20 August.

52 CAB 21/58, Note, 18 August 1917.

53 *Ibid.*, Ormsby-Gore to Hankey, 23 August 1917.

54 C.F.C./1917, p. 475.

55 See pp. 278–9.

Chapter 16   The Struggle for the Declaration

1 CAB 24/24, G.T. 1868, 'The Antisemitism of the Present Government', Memorandum by Montagu, 23 August 1917. For attacks by the *Morning Post* on Montagu see Stein, *op. cit.*, p. 498.

2 See J. Mervyn Jones, *British Nationality Law* (Oxford 1956), pp. 9–38, 75–86, 154–73.

3 F.O. 371/3083/143082, 'Note on the Secretary of State for India's Paper on Anti-Semitism of the Government', by R. McN (copy, undated, but presumably end of August 1917).

4 CAB 23/4, no. 227 (1), 227 (2), Secret.

5 Reproduced in Manuel, *op. cit.*, pp. 167–8.

6 F.O. 371/3083/143082; CAB 24/26, G.T. 2015; Stein, *op. cit.*, p. 505.

7 F.O. 371/3083/143082.

8 CAB 24/27, G.T. 2191, Montagu to Cecil, 14 September 1917. The original is among the Cecil Papers at the British Museum, MSS Dept.

9 *Wingate Papers*, Box 149, Graham to Clayton, 21 September 1917.

10 F.O. 371/3083/143082, Oliphant to Hankey, 20 September 1917; Ormsby-Gore to Oliphant, 21 September (a copy in CAB 21/58).

11 *W.A.*, Weizmann to Scott, 20 September 1917.

12 *Ibid.*, Rothschild to Weizmann, 21 September 1917; partly quoted in *Trial and Error*, p. 258.

13 CAB 24/27, G.T. 2158, despatched on 26 September 1917 (received 27 September); Stein, *op. cit.*, pp. 506–7; Weizmann, *Trial and Error*, pp. 257–8.

14 *W.A.*, Brandeis to James de Rothschild, 16 December 1917. Mr Stein overlooked this document. Had he consulted it, he would have modified his views on Wilson (pp. 505–7, 529–30). On Wilson's attitude to Zionism see also Stephen Wise, *Challenging Years* (London 1951), pp. 16, 113–14, 119–21; Stephen S. Wise and Jacob De Haas, *The Great Betrayal* (New York 1930), p. 35; Jacob De Haas, *Louis Brandeis*, pp. 79, 81, 87, 89; Kallen, *Zionism*, p. 166.

15 De Haas, *Louis D. Brandeis*, p. 88.

16 *W.A.*

17 CAB 24/27, G.T. 2158, cable, dated 26 September 1917. (Not found among Zionist sources.) The idea of urging the Americans to participate in the Palestinian campaign was suggested first by Lloyd George and Balfour to Weizmann. (*W.A.*, Weizmann to Scott, 30 July 1917.)

18 F.O. 371/3083/143082, Rothschild to Balfour, 22 September 1917; Graham to Hardinge, 'Zionist Aspirations', note, 24 September 1917.

19 *Ibid.*, minute by Hardinge and Balfour, 26 September 1917.

20 Lloyd George, *The Truth*, 2, pp. 1118–21.

21 Stein, *op. cit.*, p. 513.

22 F.O. 371/3083/143082, Rothschild and Weizmann to Balfour, 3 October, 1917; Stein, *op. cit.*, pp. 514–15.

23 Lloyd George, *The Truth*, 2, pp. 1139, 1122.

24 Amery, *op. cit.*, 2, pp. 116–17.

25 F.O. 371/3059/162432, 'The Turkish Provinces in Asia' (no. 4), Syria. Memorandum by Gertrude Bell, Bagdad, 23 June 1917, encl. in Hirzel (I.O.) to Graham, 30 August 1917.

26 CAB 24/28, G.T. 2263, 'Zionism', memorandum by Montagu, 9 October 1917. (A copy in CAB 21/58.)

27 Amery, *op. cit.*, 2, pp. 116–17.

28 CAB 23/4, no. 245 (18), W.C. meeting, 4 October 1917.

29 Beaverbrook Library, Lloyd George Papers, F 39/3/30, Montagu to Lloyd George, 4 October 1917.

30 F.O. 371/4239/151671, 'The Turkish Peace', Secret. Memorandum, 18 December 1919; also *idem*, memorandum, 1 January 1920.

31 CAB 24/28, G.T. 2263, Secret, 'Zionism', Memorandum, 9 October 1917.

32 CAB 21/58, Swaythling to Storr, 10 October 1917; Ormsby-Gore's minute, 13 October 1917.

33 F.O. 371/3083/143083, Balfour to Wiseman (New York), for House, 6 October 1917, tel. no. 21; Wiseman to Drummond (London), 16 October 1917, tel. no. 27. Circulated to the War Cabinet.

34 Weizmann, *Trial and Error*, p. 260; CZA, Z 4/1593, Brandeis to Weizmann, 19 October 1917.

35 Military Intelligence Report, *op. cit.*, p. 4.

36 The list of names to whom the draft declaration had been submitted was approved by the Prime Minister. Montagu selected four non-Zionists and Weizmann four Zionists. The name of Herbert Samuel was added at Rothschild's suggestion. What follows is based on letters submitted to the Secretary of the War Cabinet. The originals are to be found in CAB 21/58 and printed in CAB 24/4, G. 164, Secret. App. I to a Note on 'The Zionist Movement' by M. P. A. Hankey, 17 October 1917.

37 'And if a stranger sojourn with thee in your land, ye shall not vex him. But the stranger that dwelleth with you shall be unto you as one born among you, and thou shalt love him as thyself.' (Leviticus, 19:33–4.)

38 Weizmann, *Trial and Error*, pp. 260–1.

39 CZA, Z 4/117, Rothschild to Sokolow, 13 October 1917.

40 *W.A.*, Weizmann to Tschlenow, 4 September 1917; CZA, A 18/41/2/8, Tschlenow to Sokolow and Weizmann, Bergen, 11/24 September 1917.

41 All the telegrams are quoted in Military Intelligence Report (Webster), *op. cit.*, pp. 5–6. The one dated 26 October from Rosoff to Weizmann is in F.O. 371/3054/84173.

42 *Aaronsohn's Diary*, Interview with Allenby, p. 315, entry 17 July 1917; meeting with Sykes, p. 356, entry 16 November 1917.

43 P.R.O., W.O. 106/727, Robertson (C.I.G.S.) to Secretary of War, Memorandum, 14 December 1917, Secret (copy in CAB 24/35). On the importance of water in military calculations in this sector see W.O. 158/611, 'Notes on the Palestine Operations', Memorandum by Philip W. Chetwode, Lt-General, C.E.F., 21 June 1917.

44 *Nili*, ed. Livneh, pp. 325–6, where documentary material is reproduced. For the military operation see A. P. Wavell, *The Palestine Campaign* (London 1928), pp. 115–38.

45 Allenby Papers (St Antony's College, Oxford), Allenby to Wavell, 27 March 1939.

46 F.O. 371/4167/801, Ormsby-Gore to Lord Harmsworth, 22 March 1919, Secret. In fact, Sara Aaronsohn committed suicide after being tortured. On 7 October 1917 Weizmann sent the following message of encouragement to the Aaronsohn group: 'Your heroic sufferings are greatest incentive [in] our difficult work ... to secure a Jewish Palestine under British auspices ... *Chazak Ve'ematz* until Eretz Israel is liberated.' *W.A.*, Aaronsohn to his brother Alexander (in Cairo), London, 7 October 1917. The letter did not reach its destination before Palestine was liberated by the British Army. I am grateful for this information to Mr Yoram Ephrati, the Curator of the Aaronsohn Archives, Zichron-Yaakov, Israel.

47 *Nili*, ed. Livneh, pp. 327–8, where the above is cited. Allenby's letter dated 14 July 1919 in his own hand is reproduced in facsimile (*ibid.*, pp. 328–9).

48 *Ibid.*, pp. 209, 337. Wingate's purpose was to get greater co-ordination

between Aaronsohn and the Zionists in London. Herbert, an officer at the British Residency in Cairo, noted: 'Now [the High Commissioner] would be glad to see if not a reconciliation but a *modus vivendi* between Aaronsohn and Weizmann. H.E. might be very frank and say that of course he had for some time past had his hands tied officially because he was uncertain as to the extent of support which H.M.G. intended to give to Zionism . . . Now he gathered that H.M.G. had given their approval to the Zionist cause and if that was so it was his duty to see that no split or division of opinion [among Jews] should occur.' (*Wingate Papers*, Box 146, Note by Herbert, 20 August 1917.)

On the same day Wingate wrote to Balfour: 'An additional reason for not alienating [Aaronsohn] . . . is that the military authorities attach importance to retaining the use of the organization which he has created in Palestine. He is in a position to destroy this organisation, and there is little doubt that, in his present frame of mind, he will be tempted to do so, unless some concession is made to his views. How far his differences with the Zionists in England are due to questions of principle and how far to wounded susceptibilities, I am not able to say.' (F.O. 371/3053/84173, Wingate to Balfour, 20 August 1917, dis. no. 182, Confidential; copy in *Wingate Papers*.)

49 The author of *With the Turks in Palestine* (London 1917). Aaron's brother, who replaced him in Military Intelligence in Egypt whilst the former was in England and the United States.

50 F.O. 371/3055/87895, Wingate to F.O., 20 October 1917, tel. no. 1108.

51 *Ibid.*, p. no. 201862, minutes dated 22, 24 October 1917.

52 CAB 24/4, G. 164, 'The Zionist Movement', Note by the Secretary, 17 October 1917, Secret, App. III.

53 F.O. 371/3054/84173, Weizmann to F.O., 23 October 1917 and enclosed list. Owing to a slip of the pen 'November' appears instead of October; Graham's minute to Hardinge, 24 October 1917.

54 F.O. 371/3054/84173, Graham to Balfour, 24 October 1917.

55 F.O. 371/3053/84173, Heron Goodhart (Chargé d'Affaires) to Balfour. Berne, 2 October 1917, dis. no. 647, Confidential. The despatch was seen also by Balfour and Lord Hardinge.

56 CAB 24/143, Appreciation of E.R. no. xxxvii by Sykes, 11 October 1917. Earlier, on receipt of an article written by Dr C. A. von Bratter which appeared in the *Vossische Zeitung* (1 August 1917) under the title, 'The Fight for Palestine', Graham minuted: 'An interesting article—it foreshadows Germany encouraging Zionism in a Palestine remaining Turkish.' (Forwarded by Townley to Balfour, The Hague, 3 August 1917, dis. no. 181, 371/3053/ 84173.)

57 F.O. 371/3060/169829, Rumbold to F.O., 29 August 1917, tel. no. 747.

58 F.O. 371/3060/175608, 'Pan-Turanian Movement', Memorandum by A. J. Toynbee, 7 September 1917, Secret; F.O. 371/3055/87895, Wingate to Allenby, 17 October 1917, Private (copy); CAB 24/143, E.R. Rep. no. xl, Rumbold to F.O., 25 October 1917, tel. no. 988 (copy).

59 CAB 23/4, no. 257 (12), W.C. meeting, 25 October 1917.

60 Hansard, 19 June 1936, col. 1343. Graham's memorandum is among the Lloyd George Papers at the Beaverbrook Library.

61 CAB 24/30, G.T. 2406, Memorandum by Curzon, 26 October 1917. Reproduced with minor omissions in Lloyd George, *The Truth*, 2, pp. 1123–32.

62 F.O. 371/3083/143082, Memorandum by Sykes, encl. in Drummond's note, 30 October 1917 to Balfour advising the Foreign Secretary that Sykes was anxious for his memorandum to remain anonymous.

63 CAB 23/4, no. 261 (12). Selected extracts in Lloyd George, *The Truth*, 2, pp. 1136–8 and in Stein, *op. cit.*, pp. 546–7.

64 Amery, 2, p. 117.

65 F.O. 371/3083/143082, where the first draft and the copy of the letter sent to Rothschild is found. On Lord Hardinge's suggestion, however, the last paragraph from 'and secure' till 'publicity' was omitted: 'The publication will depend upon Lord Rothschild to whom the declaration of the Govt. will be made in a reply to his original letter' of 18 July. (*Ibid.*, minute, 1 November 1917.) In January 1924 Lord Rothschild presented the original copy to the British Museum (MSS Dept, MS. no. 41178, folios 1 and 3, facsimile in Stein).

66 F.O. 371/3083/143082, Graham's note to Hardinge, 3 November 1917.

67 *Ibid.*, minutes by Hardinge and Balfour, 3 November 1917; F.O. 371/3054/ 84173, Barter to C.I.G.S., 26 November 1917, tel. no. 1389, Secret; minutes, 30 November 1917. 'Autumn' was apparently a slip for spring, 1917 when Cecil proposed that a declaration be made by the Allied Powers.

Chapter 17   Motives and Effects

1 Webster, *The Founder of the National Home*, pp. 14–15.

2 CZA, Z 4/117, Weizmann to Rothschild, 2 November 1917.

3 Norman Angell, 'Weizmann's Approach to the British Mind', pp. 77–84; Shalom Asch, 'He Shall Stand Before Kings', pp. 124–8, *Chaim Weizmann*, ed. Meyer Weisgal (New York 1944); Meinertzhagen, *Middle East Diary*, pp. 67, 204; Graves, *The Land of Three Faiths*, p. 42; Samuel, *Memoirs*, pp. 147–8.

4 Charles Kingsley Webster, *The Art and Practice of Diplomacy* (London 1961), pp. 5–6; interview with the author, 15 June 1960.

5 *Chaim Weizmann*, ed. Weisgal, p. 145.

6 F.O. 371/3083/143082, 'Note on the Secretary of State for India's Paper on Anti-Semitism of the Government', by R[onald] Mc[Neill] [undated copy, presumably end of August 1917]; see pp. 259–60 of present work.

7 Blanche E. C. Dugdale, 'The Balfour Declaration: Its origins', *The Jewish National Home*, ed. Paul Goodman (London 1943), p. 5.

8 *Wingate Papers*, Box 145/7, Clayton to Wingate, 12 October 1917, private; F.O. 371/3055/87895, Chief London to Chief Egypt force, 26 November; F.O. to Wingate, 26 November, tel. no. 1129; F.O. 371/3061/214354, Sykes note, 13 November; Cambon to Balfour, 21 November; Balfour to Cambon, 23 November; Bertie to F.O., 15, 30 December, tel. nos 1482, 1556; F.O. to Wingate, (?) January 1918, tel. no. (?).

9 CAB 24/15: G.T. 938, 'Arrangements for the Eventual Peace Conference', Note by the Secretary of the War Cabinet, 5 June 1917; F.O. 371/3083/143082, Bertie to F.O., 22 July 1917, private and confidential, 'Germany may at any moment make peace proposals for which Entente Powers ought to be prepared'.

10 F.O. 371/3058/139616, Rumbold to F.O., 7 November 1917, tel. no. 1053; F.O. 371/3381/207, same to same, 16, 31 January 1918, tel. nos 58, 136; F.O. 371/3393/6554, same to same, 6 February 1918, dis. no. 97; F.O. 371/3381/207, 'The Present State of Mind in Turkey', memorandum by A. J. Toynbee, 25 May 1918.

11 CAB 23/12, no. 200b, 31 May 1917; CAB 23/40, 1 May 1917. Statements by the Prime Minister.

12 CAB 24/37, G.T. 3145, G.T. 3191, memoranda by Robertson, 29 December 1917, 3 January 1918.

13 F.O. 371/3059/159558, 'Memorandum on the Asia Minor Agreement', by Sir Mark Sykes, 14 August 1917.

14 Cited in Leslie, op. cit., p. 274, Sykes to Cecil, 13 October 1917.

15 Webster, 'British Policy in the Near East', The Near East, ed. Ireland, p. 160.

16 CAB 24/4, G 152, 'British Mission to Russia . . .', report by Arthur Henderson, 16 July 1917.

17 CAB 24/13, G.T. 703, 'Policy in view of Russian Developments', memorandum by Curzon, 12 May 1917.

18 CAB 24/3; G 150, 'Report on the visit of the Labour Delegation to Russia, April-May 1917'; F.O. 371/3315/17365, 'Bolshevik Revolt and Commencement of Negotiations for an Armistice', memorandum by Brig.-General A. Knox, Petrograd, 4 December 1917; see pp. 179–81, 188 of present work.

19 F.O. 371/3054/84173, Barter (Petrograd) to C.I.G.S., 26 November 1917, tel. no. 1389; cf. p. 280.

20 F.R.U.S., 1917, Supplement II, vol. 1, p. 25, Marshall, Morgenthau, Schiff, Strauss, Rosenwald to Baron Gunzburg (Petrograd), 16 April 1917; F.O. 371/2996/811, Spring-Rice to F.O., 17 April 1917, tel. no. 1017; Spring-Rice, op. cit., 2, p. 388.

21 Meinertzhagen, op. cit., pp. 9, 24, 139.

22 Harold Nicolson, 'Marginal Comment', Spectator, 3 January 1947.

23 Dugdale, Balfour, 2, pp. 116, 216; Jewish Chronicle, 26 July 1918 (speech to American Zionist Unit).

24 Manchester Guardian, 10 December 1917.

25 Ibid.; Jewish Chronicle, 1 November 1918.

26 Lords, 21 July 1937, vol. 326, col. 2237; Commons, 22 May 1939, vol. 347, cols 2013–16.

27 Webster, 'British Policy . . .', The Near East, ed. Ireland, p. 158.

28 See e.g. Manchester Guardian (1 October); Liverpool Post (20 October).

29 F.O. 371/3054/84173; F.O. 395/144, Appreciation of E.R. nos. xliv, xlvi, 30 November, 14 December 1917.

30 F.O. 371/3054/84173, Weizmann and Sokolow to Balfour, 19 November

1917; CZA, Z 4/261, speech by I. Sieff, 30 December 1917; F.O. 371/3083/143082; Rothschild to Balfour, 4 November 1917.

31 CZA, Z 4/929, Rosoff(?) to Weizmann(?), 9 December 1917; F.O. 371/3054/84173, Rosoff to Tschlenow, 29 November 1917; Tschlenow, *op. cit.*, pp. 48–51. Tschlenow died in London in February 1918.

32 F.O. 371/3054/84173, Bagge to F.O., 30 November 1917, tel. no. 156, urgent; F.O. 371/3386/856, same to same, 30 November, 10 December, dis. nos. 60, 62; Buchanan to Balfour, 13, 15 December, dis. nos. 281, 286 and encs.; CZA, Z 4/305/1, Central Zionist Committee in Petrograd to Weizmann, 16 November, 18 November 1917; *Daily Telegraph*, 6 December; *Jewish Chronicle*, 28 December 1917, 25 January 1918.

33 F.O. 371/3054/84173, Sykes to Picot, 12 December 1917, tel. no. 1181; minutes by Graham, Hardinge, and Balfour, p. 233438.

34 CAB 23/4, W.C. no. 304 (10); W.C. no. 295, App. G.T. 2932, Note by Balfour, 9 December 1917; W.C. 308, App. Memorandum by Milner and Cecil (accepted by Clemenceau and Pichon), 23 December 1917; F.O. 371/3017/216696, Rodd to F.O., 26 November 1917, tel. no. 972; F.O. 371/3018/224839, Buchanan to F.O., 7, 18 December 1917, tel. nos 1963, 2054, note by Drogheda, 18 December 1917; F.O. 371/3019/229217, Buchanan to F.O., 19 December, tel. no. 2076; F.O. to Bagge (Odessa), 26 December 1917, tel. no. 164.

35 Heller, *op. cit.*, pp. 29–30; CAB 23/4, W.C. 304 (10).

36 F.O. 371/3054/84173, Sokolow to Syrkin, 1 December 1917.

37 *Jewish Chronicle*, 25 January 1918.

38 F.O. 371/3020/241481, W.O., note, 21 December 1917; F.O. 371/3019/229217, Echiel, Nahum, Chaim to Syrkin, Rosoff, Rabinowicz, and Mintz, 21 December; Weizmann to Graham, 23 December; Graham to Buchanan, 27 December, tel. no. 2546; same to Bagge, 28 December 1917, tel. no. 171.

39 Stein, *op. cit.*, p. 573. Stein's argument that this was one of the main motives behind the Balfour Declaration is not borne out by the sequence of events. The idea that Russian Jews might be instrumental in frustrating German purchases was advanced in the latter part of December 1917, i.e. about seven weeks after the Declaration had been published. Nor was it meant to impress the extreme left-wing Jewish elements. 'We could hope for nothing from Trotski, who was a Jew of the international type', reads the minute of the War Cabinet meeting on 21 December 1917 (CAB 23/4, W.C. 304 (10)). Regarded as 'fanatics' and 'pro-German agents' (see e.g. Knox's memorandum, above note 18), London had no illusions about Trotski and his friends. Hence, Stein's conclusion that the British Government committed 'a two-fold miscalculation' (p. 570) has no foundation. One should also treat with circumspection Stein's criticism of Lloyd George, who testified that it was believed that the Declaration would help to secure for the Entente the aid of Jewish financial interests in the United States (pp. 575–6). As shown in our narrative, neither Gentile nor Jewish American financiers were over-enthusiastic to raise the war loan for the Allies (above, pp. 225–6), but it was assumed

that recognition of Jewish rights to Palestine might have made all the difference to the latter. There was of course a wider spectrum of motives which led to the final decision about the Declaration than those mentioned by Lloyd George and Stein. (See also my article, 'The Declaration—Myths and Motives', *Jewish Chronicle, Balfour Declaration Supplement*, 3 November 1967.)

40 W. E. D. Allen, *The Ukraine* (Cambridge 1940), pp. 282–90; Fischer, *op. cit.*, 708–25.

41 Heller, *op. cit.*, pp. 30–40. On the anti-Jewish pogroms in 1919–21 see *ibid.*, pp. 40–5; Allen, *op. cit.*, pp. 313–14; W. H. Chamberlain, *The Russian Revolution, 1917–21* (New York 1935), 2, pp. 223–31; and source material: *The Pogroms in the Ukraine . . . 1917–20, Historical survey with documents and photos* (Paris 1927), published by the Comité des Délégations Juives (in French and English).

42 F.O. 371/3388/1495, Boris Goldberg (Petrograd) to Zionist Bureau (London), 27 May 1918; *Zionist Review*, July, September, November 1918; *Jewish Chronicle*, 22 March 1918; Zenziper, *op. cit.*, p. 39. The all-Russian Jewish Congress, however, was not allowed to meet.

43 F.O. 371/3346/173211, note by E. Drummond, 14 October 1918.

44 F.O. 371/3409/116970, Clayton to F.O., 2, 12 July, 31 August, tel. nos. 269, 5, 131; D.M.I. to F.O., 13 July; F.O. to Clayton, 22 August 1918, tel. no. 173.

45 Military Intelligence Report, *op. cit.*, pp. 6, 12.

46 W.O. 106/1420, Memorandum on Pan-Turanism (copy, not signed), 12 December 1917; F.O. 371/3062/228671, Rumbold to F.O., 29 November 1917, tel. no. 1167, see p. 287 of present work.

47 CAB 25/1/27, Annexe (A), 'Notes on an Interview with Dr. Parodi', 18 December 1917; F.O. 371/3388/1396, Rumbold to F.O., 31 January, 16 February 1918, tel. nos. 139, 234.

48 F.O. 371/3388/1396, p. no. 30340, minutes by Graham and Balfour, 17 February 1918; CAB 24/39, G.T. 3359, 'Memorandum on the Turkish Attitude towards Peace', by Toynbee(?), 16 January 1918; CAB 24/32, G.T. 2648, 'Peace Negotiations with Turkey', 16 November 1917; CAB 24/4, G. 182, 'German and Turkish Territories Captured in the War', 5 December 1917, memoranda by Curzon; see pp. 164–5, 219, 221 of present work.

49 F.O. 371/3054/84173, Rumbold to Balfour, 8 December 1917, dis. no. 886; F.O. 395/144, E.R. xlvi, 13 December 1917, App. I.

50 W.O. 106/1420, Political, 'Attitude of the Rumanian Jews in regard to the Future of Palestine', 11 January 1918; F.O. 371/3060/175608, p. no. 220908, minute by Sykes, 24 November 1917.

51 F.O. 371/3388/1495, Paget (Copenhagen) to Balfour, 4 February 1918, dis. no. 24, and enclosures; CAB 24/42, G.T. 3635, 'Memorandum on the Attitude of Enemy Governments towards Zionism', Intelligence Bureau Dept. of Information, 13 February 1918.

52 F.O. 371/3383/747, Sokolow to Sykes, 5, 12 July and enclosed memorandum; Hyamson to Sykes, 25 July; Balfour to Beaverbrook, 16 August 1918; F.O. 371/3409/116565, Hyamson to Nicolson, 12 September; Ormsby-Gore to

Nicolson, 13 September 1918; CZA, Z 4/177, 11 (1918). The Jewish branch was eventually re-established at Lord Northcliffe's department.

53 F.O. 371/3400/37581, Weekly Report on Turkey, 12 March 1918, Intelligence Bureau; F.O. 371/3388/1495, Wade (Copenhagen), report, 11 July 1918.

54 *Clayton Papers*, Memorandum, 19 May 1918.

55 *Ibid.* Clayton to F.O., 18 November 1918, tel. no. 19018; CZA, Z 4/242, Sieff to Ochberg, 3 June 1918; F.O. 371/3409/110098, Weizmann (Jerusalem) to Sokolow, 19 June 1918.

56 F.O. 371/3387/993, 'Future of Mesopotamia', Memorandum by P. Z. Cox, 22 April 1918, encl. in Montagu to Governor of India, 9 August 1918.

57 F.O. 371/3411/154108, D.M.I. to F.O., 7 September; Hardinge to D.M.I., 17 September 1918; F.O. 371/3418/194681, Webb (Constantinople) to F.O., 5 December 1918, tel. no. 110.

58 *W.A.*, De Haas to Weizmann, 13, 19 December 1917; F.O. 371/3390/3026, Jusserand to Pichon, 14 December 1917, encl. in Gort to Sykes, 31 December 1917; F.O. 371/3386/856, Consul-General (San Francisco) to Balfour, 8 February 1918, dis. no. 19.

59 *The Times*, 27 December 1917; *Jewish Chronicle*, 28 December 1918.

60 Spring-Rice, *op. cit.*, 2, p. 421, to Balfour, 21 December 1917.

61 F.O. 371/3054/84173, Spring-Rice to F.O., 28 December 1917, tel. no. 4029, and minutes by Graham and Cecil.

62 F.O. 371/3394/11053, Weizmann to Brandeis, 14 January 1918; Brandeis to Weizmann, 8 April 1918.

63 CAB 21/56, Ormsby-Gore to Crewe, 31 October 1918.

64 See p. 264. F.O. 371/3381/207, Sokolow to Brandeis, 4 January 1918; CZA, Z 4/1074, Aaronsohn (New York) to Weizmann, 24 December 1917.

65 CAB 24/51, G.T. 4505, 'Relations of the U.S. with the Ottoman Empire . . .' (forwarded to the U.S. Government, 11 May 1918); G.T. 4554, Allied Naval Council to Supreme War Council, 15 May 1918.

66 *Jewish Chronicle*, 26 July, 16 August 1918; F.O. 371/3388/1495, British Embassy (Washington) to Balfour, 30 July 1918, dis. nos. 668, 671.

67 F.O. 371/3395/11053, encl. in Barclay to Balfour, 6 September 1918, dis. no. 766; minutes by Sykes, Cecil, and Toynbee; Stephen Wise, *Challenging Years* (London 1961), pp. 120–1, where Wilson's declaration is published.

68 *Jewish Chronicle*, 13 September, 8 November 1918.

69 *The American War Congress and Zionism* (New York 1919), pp. 38–9, 60, and *passim*.

70 F.O. 371/3386/856, Wise to De Haas, 13 December; Barclay to F.O., 18 December 1918, tel. no. 5584.

71 Stephen Wise, 'The Balfour Declaration. Its significance in the United States', Goodman, *The Jewish National Home*, p. 45; Wise, *op. cit.*, p. 122.

72 F.O. 608/98, f.375/2/1, Memorandum by Louis Mallet, 14 January 1919, *most confidential*; minutes by Balfour and Toynbee, 17 January.

73 *The Times*, 16, 18 January 1919; *Jewish Chronicle*, 17 January 1919.

74 *Jewish Chronicle*, 21 February 1919.

75 *Yale Reports*, 'Records of the American Commission to Negotiate Peace', Record Group 256, case 887N.00/26 (microfilm at St Antony's College, Oxford).

76 Esco Foundation, *Palestine, A Study of Jewish, Arab and British Policies* (Yale 1947), I, pp. 245–50.

77 As note 75, Westerman to Bullitt, 11 April 1919; note by the Secretary to the Commissioners, (?) April 1919, no. 230; Wilson to (?), 13 April; Lansing to Bliss, 18 April 1918; Wilson's statement to the A.J.C. leaders was published in *New York Times*, 3 March 1919, and in the Egyptian press on the following day.

78 Wise, *op. cit.*, p. 123.

79 *Journal Officiel*, 27 December 1917, second sitting.

80 *Yale*, report no. XVII, 4 March 1918; *D.B.F.P.*, i, iv, Meinertzhagen to Curzon, 26 September, 10 November 1919, pp. 426, 528.

81 *D.B.F.P.*, i, iv, Memorandum by Forbes Adam, 30 December 1919, pp. 607–10.

82 *D.B.F.P.*, i, viii (London 1958), pp. 159–68. The translation of Pichon's letter is by Curzon. For the full text see Sokolow, 2, p. 128; and that of Imperiali of 9 May 1918, *ibid.*, p. 129.

83 CAB 24/72/1 and 2, G.T. 6509.

84 CAB 27/24; Lloyd George, *The Truth . . .*, 2, p. 1142.

85 See p. 80.

86 CAB 21/58, Ormsby-Gore (Tel-Aviv—Jaffa) to Hankey, 19 April 1918; cf. Meinertzhagen, *op. cit.*, pp. 6–7.

87 F.O. 882/14, 'The Politics of Jerusalem', Ormsby-Gore (Cairo), 29 December 1916.

88 For the full text see Cmd 5974, p. 51.

89 Miller, *My Diary at the Conference of Paris*, 4, pp. 297–9.

90 F.O. 371/4153/275, encl. in Clayton to Balfour, 24 February 1919.

91 *F.R.U.S.*, Paris Peace Conference, 1919, xii, pp. 780–1, 787–9.

92 F.O. 371/5066, E 14959/9/44, 'Memorandum on Possible Negotiations with the Hedjaz', by H[ubert] Y[oung], 29 November 1920.

93 F.O. 371/3395/11053, Report by Ormsby-Gore, 27 August 1918, Annexe 2, p. 13.

94 F.O. 371/3386/856; F.O. 371/3414/181911, Lord Kilmarnock (Copenhagen) to F.O., 6 November 1918, tel. no. 3284; F.O. 608/98, f.375/2/1, Weizmann to Balfour, 24 January 1918.

95 Miller, *My Diary at the Conference of Paris*, 5, pp. 15–29.

96 Webster, *The Founder of the National Home*, p. 35.

97 This question lies outside the scope of the present volume. The author hopes to deal with it at a later stage.

98 CZA, Z 4/16112, 'Notes on Conversation between Sir Gilbert Clayton and Dr. Ch. Weizmann on the Policy and Situation in Palestine', 7 November 1922 (a copy in *W.A.*).

99 F.O. 371/21862, Political Eastern (1938), E 559/1/31, Ormsby-Gore to Neville Chamberlain, 9 January 1938.

100 'Where there is a human mass claiming recognition as a nation, there the case for such a recognition is complete.' (Rothschild and Weizmann to Balfour, 3 October 1917, F.O. 371/3083/143082.)

101 Speeches by Cecil, Sykes, Ormsby-Gore and others at the London Opera House, 2 December 1917 (*Jewish Chronicle*, 7 December 1917); press references collated in Sokolow, *op. cit.*, 2, p. 144; see pp. 325–7 of present work.

102 F.O. 371/3395/11053, 'The Zionist Movement', by Ormsby-Gore, April 1917 (a slip for 1918).

103 F.O. 371/3388/1495, p. no. 178317, minute by Kidston, 27 October 1918.

104 F.O. 395/144, Appreciation of E.R., no. xlv by M. S[ykes], 7 December 1917. A similar conclusion was reached also by Major Endres in the *Münchener Neusten Nachrichten* (cited in *Palestine*, 2, pp. 233–4 and *The Times* of 25 November 1917), and Dr Manfred Georg in the *Deutsche Montags-Zeitung* (26 November, cited also in *Palestine*, 2, p. 199).

105 F.O. 371/3386/856, Montefiore and Stuart Samuel to Balfour, 18 June 1918, encl. in Wolf to Oliphant; Graham to Wolf, 28 June 1918.

106 F.O. 371/3054/84173, Israel Zangwill to F.O., 18 November 1917; *W.A.*, Greenberg to Weizmann, 2 November 1917.

107 F.O. 371/4217/66287, Wolf to Dutasta, 14 April, encl. in Balfour to Curzon, 20 April 1919.

108 See pp. 297, 310. The Beaverbrook Library, *Lloyd George Papers*, F3/3/30, Lloyd George to Balfour, 27 August 1918.

109 F.O. 371/3386/856, Lionel de Rothschild, Lord Swaythling, Philip Magnus, Marcus Samuel to Lloyd George, encl. in Cohen to Balfour, 18 December 1918.

110 F.O. 371/4170/1051, Rumbold to Curzon, 7 March 1919, dis. no. 138.

111 Haim Nahum, 'Jews', *Modern Turkey*, ed. E. G. Mears (New York 1924), p. 97.

112 *Deutsche Allgemeine Zeitung*, 1 April 1919, morning ed.

113 See p. 92.

Chapter 18 The Meaning of the Declaration

1 Hansard, 22 May 1939, cols 2013–16, statement by Leopold Amery.

2 Ormsby-Gore, 'Great Britain, Palestine and the Jews', *The Nineteenth Century* (October 1920), p. 622.

3 Sokolow, *History of Zionism*, 2, pp. 127–9; *Congressional Record*, 30 June 1922.

4 *Official Journal of League of Nations* (June 1922), p. 546; August 1922, Minutes of the 19th Session. On 24 July 1923 Turkey ratified the Treaty of Lausanne and renounced her former Asiatic provinces; the future of Palestine had been settled earlier by the Powers concerned at the Conference in San Remo. For the text of the Mandate see Cmd 1785.

5 *Jewish Chronicle*, 25 October, 1 November 1918.

6 Hansard, 13 February 1931, cols 751–7.

7 Lloyd George, *The Truth* ..., 2, pp. 1122, 1139; *Palestine Royal Commission Report* (Cmd 5479), p. 23. Mr Stein was good enough to tell the author that the Declaration could in no way be construed as 'a contract in the proper sense of that term. A true contract must be an agreement between two parties enforceable by either and capable of interpretation by a judicial tribunal' ... [The Declaration] 'was not framed or vetted by lawyers'. He added subsequently: 'I certainly agree that, though the Declaration was, as I still think, a political document and not framed as a legal document would have been, it was morally binding, and was so regarded by British statesmen both at the time of the Declaration and afterwards. This does not, however, imply that it was in any proper sense a contract. It would be possible to point to many other political declarations by the British or other governments which it would be right to regard as morally binding, notwithstanding that they were not legal documents and had no contractual character' (letters to the author, 6, 12 May 1971); cf. Stein, *op. cit.*, p. 553.

8 Temperley, *History of the Peace Conference*, 6, pp. 173–4.

9 F.O. 371/3083/143082, Rothschild to Balfour, 8 November; Balfour to Rothschild, 9 November 1917; F.O. 371/3383/747, Balfour to Beaverbrook, 16 August 1918; pp. 297 of present work.

10 See p. 221. CAB 24/32, G.T. 2648, 'Peace Negotiations with Turkey', by Curzon, 16 November 1917; CAB 24/4, G.182, 'German and Turkish Territories Captured in the War', by Curzon, December 1917; F.O. 371/6237, E 986/4/91, Curzon's minute, 21 January 1921.

11 F.O. 371/3055/87895, p. 240635, 21 December 1917; also F.O. 371/4179/2117, p. 47756, 30 March 1919.

12 F.O. 371/3386/856, Report by Sir Mark Sykes (Jerusalem), 15 November 1918, encl. in Clayton to Balfour, 5 December 1918.

13 Paul L. Hanna, *British Policy in Palestine* (Washington 1942), pp. 79–80.

14 CZA, Z 4/4066, Chamberlain to A. Cohen, Birmingham, 7 November 1922; *ibid.*, speech by Simon at Bradford, 9 November 1922.

15 P.R.O., C.O. 733/35, 'The Zionist Policy, memorandum by Shuckburgh, 21 December 1922.

16 Cf. Cmd 1989 (1923), 4 October 1923.

17 Cmd 6019; Hansard, 23 May 1939.

18 Hansard, 13 February 1931, cols 751–7.

19 Sokolow, *History of Zionism*, 2, pp. 124–7.

20 *Jewish Chronicle*, 12 April 1918. In 1915 Rabbi Herzog became the Chief Rabbi of All Ireland, in 1936 of Palestine, and in 1948 of the State of Israel.

21 F.O. 371/3386/856, Central Committee of the Zionist Organisation in Russia to Buchanan, 30 November/13 December 1917; *W.A.*, Provisional Committee to Weizmann(?), November 1917; F.O. 371/3388/1495, British Embassy (Washington) to Balfour, 30 July 1918, dis. no. 668.

22 Sokolow, *History of Zionism*, 2, 74–9, 85–97; *Zionist Review* (December 1917), where quotations from the press are reproduced; Stein, *op. cit.*, pp. 562–3.

23 American Emergency Committee for Zionist Affairs, *The Balfour Declaration and American Interests in Palestine* (New York 1941), pp. 8–10.

24 *Jewish Chronicle*, 13 September, 8 November 1918; The Zionist Organisation of America, *The American War Congress and Zionism* (New York 1919), p. 60. The booklet contains statements by 61 Senators from 43 States, and 239 Representatives from 44 States and 3 territories supporting the Balfour Declaration and the Zionist aspirations, made between June and December 1918.

25 *Jewish Chronicle*, 17 January 1919; *The Times*, 18 January 1919; Lloyd George, *The Truth* . . ., 2, p. 1140.

26 D. H. Miller, *My Diary at the Conference at Paris*, 4, pp. 263–4.

27 Weizmann, *Trial and Error*, p. 306; *Jewish Chronicle*, 7 March 1919.

28 *D.B.F.P.*, First Series, viii, p. 161.

29 *The Near East*, 21 December 1917, cutting in W.O. 106/1420; *Jewish Chronicle*, 1, 22 March 1918, cf. statement made by King Alexander of Greece, *ibid.*, 22 February 1918.

30 *Ibid.*, 1 March 1918.

31 *Ibid.*, 7 December 1917, 18 October 1918; *Zionist Review*, November 1918, p. 107.

32 *Jewish Chronicle*, 21 November 1919; *Zionist Bulletin*, 5 November, 10 December 1919.

33 *Illustrated Sunday Herald*, 8 February 1920.

34 Hansard, 17 November 1930, col. 155; 22 May 1939.

35 Israel Sieff, *Memoirs* (London 1971), p. 97.

36 See pp. 9, 58, 61, 250–1, 260, 278–81; *W.A.*, 'Interview between Sidebotham and Sir Mark Sykes', 9 March 1917.

37 Lloyd George, *The Truth* . . ., 2, pp. 113–19; *Palestine Royal Commission Report*, Cmd 5479, p. 24.

38 *The Intimate Papers of Colonel House*, ed. Charles Seymour (London 1928), 3, p. 240.

39 F.O. 371/3061/21435, Balfour to Spring-Rice, 27 December 1917, confidential.

40 *F.R.U.S.*, 1917, Suppl. 2, i, p. 473, Lansing to Page, 15 December; Selig Adler, 'The Palestine Question in the Wilson Era', *Jewish Social Studies* (October 1948), p. 310.

41 See pp. 200–2.

42 W.O. 106/1420, F.O. to Buchanan, 24 December 1917, tel. no. 2525 (a copy). The author has been unable to find the original document in the F.O. files.

43 CAB 21/58, Caccia to Ormsby-Gore, 20 October, Ormsby-Gore to Caccia, 22 October 1918.

44 Stein, *op. cit.*, p. 555, citing Minutes of 32nd Session of the P.M.C., p. 180.

45 *Jewish Chronicle*, 1 November 1918.

46 *Palestine Royal Commission, Minutes of Evidence Heard at Public Session*, Colonial no. 134 (London 1937), p. 18.

47 Weizmann, 'Introduction' in Sacher, *Zionism and the Jewish Problem*, p. 8; cf. C. R. Ashbee, *A Palestine Notebook 1918–23* (London 1923), p. 109.

48 See pp. 235, 247–54.

49 *W.A.*, (?) to Rosoff, 12 December 1917.

50 CZA, Z 4/120, Sacher to Simon, 24 November 1917; Z 4/241, 'Heads of Scheme for Provisional Government of Palestine', April 1918.

51 F.O. 371/3395/11053, annex 2, meeting of the London Zionist Political Committee, 16 August 1918. Lord Robert Cecil thought that Ormsby-Gore's views were 'sound and valuable' and recommended them for consideration by the Middle East Department (minute sheet no. 152266).

52 F.O. 371/3385/747, 'Proposals . . .', encl. in Weizmann to Crowe, 9 December 1918; F.O. 608/98, f.375/2/1, 'Resolutions . . .', encl. in Weizmann to Balfour, 24 January 1918; F.O. 371/4170/1051, 'Proposals . . .', encl. in Simon Graham, 3 February 1918. Cf. 'Proposal' submitted by the C.F.C. to the Peace Conference, pp. 232–3 of present work.

53 'Proposals for the Peace Conference', reproduced in facsimile in Gelber, *op. cit.*, facing p. 232; L. Simon, *Ahad Ha'am, A Biography*, pp. 262–3.

54 F.O. 371/3385/747, 'Note on the Interview with Mr. Balfour, December 4 1918 . . . in the Foreign Office', encl. in Weizmann to Crowe, 9 December 1918; marginal annotations by Balfour; Balfour to Weizmann, 18 December 1918.

55 *The Diary of Lord Bertie*, 2, p. 233, 30 December 1917.

56 Meinertzhagen, *Middle East Diary*, p. 9, 7 February 1918.

57 F.O. 800/210, Balfour's Private Papers, Zimmern to Balfour, 16 September, Balfour to Zimmern, 19 September 1918. On Zimmern see Arnold Toynbee, *Acquaintances* (Oxford 1967), pp. 49–61.

58 Stephen Wise, 'The Balfour Declaration . . .', *The Jewish National Home*, ed. Goodman, p. 45; Wise, *Challenging Years*, p. 122; CZA, Z 4/1933/II, 'Memorandum on Balfour's interview with Weizmann', 15 February 1919.

59 F.O. 371/3385/747, 'The Strategic Importance of Syria to the British Empire', G.S., W.O., 9 December 1918.

60 F.O. 608/98, f.375/2/1, 'Zionist Proposals . . .', note by Ormsby-Gore, 22 January 1919; minutes by Sir Louis Mallet and Lord Hardinge.

61 F.O. 608/99, f.375/2/7. The amended proposal was used thereafter almost verbatim in the draft Treaty of Peace between Turkey and the Allied Governments (F.O. 371/4231/100141, encl. in Balfour to Curzon, 5 July 1919, chapter 5—Palestine) and served as prototype for the related clauses of the Mandate.

62 F.O. 608/98, f.375/2/1, note 12 February 1919.

63 *Jewish Chronicle*, 28 November 1919.

64 Ormsby-Gore, 'Great Britain, Palestine and Jews', *The Nineteenth Century and After*, October 1920, pp. 623–4.

65 F.O. 608/98, f.375/2/1, Crewe to Curzon, 24 October 1919.

66 F.O. 371/4215/50535, 'France and the Northern Frontier of Palestine', by E. G. Forbes Adam, 30 December 1919.

67 F.O. 882/17, Memorandum by Hogarth, 18 December 1918.

68 Meinertzhagen, *op. cit.*, pp. 205, 190, 24–5, 104.

69 Cmd 1700, pp. 17–21; also Cmd 3530, App. V.

70 Cmd 5479, pp. 32–3.

71 'every provision has been made to prevent it [i.e. a National Home] from becoming in any sense a Jewish State or a State under Jewish domination.' (*Lords*, 27 June 1923, col. 676.)

72 Cmd 5479 p. 24.

73 *Jewish Chronicle*, 10 March 1922.

74 Cmd 1785 (24 July 1922).

75 See pp. 256–7.

76 Amery, *op. cit.*, 2, pp. 116–17; pp. 265–6 of present work.

77 *Zionist Bulletin*, 28, 30 April 1920, British Labour leaders to Lloyd George (San Remo); Memorandum to the British Government by Neville Chamberlain, Samuel Hoare and others.

78 *D.B.F.P.*, First Series, iv, pp. 1276–8, memorandum by Frankfurter, 24 June 1919.

79 Cmd 5479 (July 1937), p. 38; Statement of Leopold Amery before the Anglo-American Committee of Inquiry (30 January 1946), p. 112.

80 Vladimir Jabotinsky, *Evidence submitted to the Palestine Royal Commission* (London 1937).

81 As note 6.

82 As notes 17, 18.

83 Ernst Frankenstein, *Palestine in the Light of International Law* (London 1946), p. 35.

84 Cmd 5964 (1939).

85 F.O. 371/4179/2117, Balfour to the Prime Minister, 19 February 1919 (copy of an extract).

86 *D.B.F.P.*, First Series, iv, Memorandum by Balfour, 11 August 1919, p. 345.

87 Meinertzhagen, *op. cit.*, p. 25.

88 As note 78.

89 F.O. 371/3054/84173, Reference to despatch from Sir H. Rumbold, 19 December 1917, by A. J. T[oynbee] and L. B. N[amier]. Like Toynbee, Namier was working at that time for the Intelligence Bureau of the Information Department of the Foreign Office.

90 CAB 24/72/1 and 2, Memorandum by Toynbee, 21 November 1918, cited in full in my discussion with Professor Toynbee, *Journal of Contemporary History* (October 1970), p. 194.

91 *D.B.F.P.*, First Series, viii (London 1958), p. 110.

92 *Ibid.*, p. 161.

93 Miller, *My Diary at the Conference at Paris*, 4, pp. 263–4.

94 F.O. 371/3054/84173, The Islamic Society to Home Secretary, 7 November 1917, minutes by Nicolson and others, 14–17 November; F.O. 371/3406/61085, same to Balfour, 5 April 1918; Wellesley to Islamic Society, 24 April; Nicolson to Ispahani, 25 May 1918.

95 F.O. 371/3398/27647, Sykes to the Syrian Committee in Cairo, 15 February 1918.

96 F.O. 371/3054/86526, draft telegram to Wingate, no. 24, 4 January 1918, signed by Sykes, amended by Hardinge and Graham; printed in Cmd 5964 (1939).

97 Antonius, *op. cit.*, p. 268.

98 F.O. 371/3054/86526, Sykes to Picot, 12 December 1917, tel. no. 1181; F.O. 371/3395/11053, 'Suggested Policy of Provisional Administration', memorandum by Sykes, 19 January 1918, and minute by Hardinge; F.O. 371/3388/2070, Sykes to Clayton, 24 January 1918, tel. no. 113.

99 *D.B.F.P.*, First Series, viii, pp. 168–70.

100 Lloyd George, *The Truth . . .*, 2, p. 1193.

101 Antonius, *op. cit.*, pp. 243–75; Henry Cattan, *Palestine: The Arabs and Israel* (London 1969), pp. 12–16, 21–2; Seminar of Arab Jurists, *The Palestine Question* (The Institute for Palestine Studies, Beirut 1968), pp. 68–73.

102 F.O. 371/3393/7659, Wingate to F.O., 16 June 1918, dis. no. 121, see enclosure; Lt-Col. W. F. Stirling, *Safety Last* (London 1953), p. 90; see chapter 6 of present work.

103 F.O. 882/14, *Arab Bulletin, Supplementary Papers, No. 1*, 1 February 1918, 'Syrian Cross Currents', by T. E. Lawrence, p. 4; see pp. 78–9 of present work.

104 Lloyd George, *The Truth . . .*, 2, pp. 1026–7, 1140, 1119; cf. Hansard, 23 May 1939, Churchill's statement, col. 2174.

105 F.O. 882/14, Arab Bureau, 'Palestine-Political', memorandum by W. O. G[ore], 12 January 1917; Yale Reports, 'Records of the American Commission to negotiate Peace', Record Group 256, case 867 N/00/26, October 1919.

106 CAB 23/26, no. 70 (21), Cabinet meeting, 18 August 1921; F.O. 371/3398/27647, p. no. 190447, minute by A. J. T[oynbee], 2 December 1918; Yale Report no. 3, 13 November 1917.

107 R. Cecil, 'Foreword', J. de V. Loder, *The Truth about Mesopotamia, Palestine and Syria* (London 1923).

108 Hansard, Lords, 27 June 1923, cols 669–70.

109 F.O. 371/21862 Political Eastern (1938), E559/1/31, Ormsby-Gore to Neville Chamberlain.

110 Balfour, *Opinions and Arguments* (London 1927), speech at the Albert Hall, 12 July 1920.

Bibliography

Unpublished sources

PUBLIC RECORD OFFICE, LONDON: CABINET PAPERS

Papers of the Committee of Imperial Defence 1906–1914

CAB 38/11/9	CAB 38/12/45	CAB 38/16/12
CAB 38/11/19	CAB 38/12/46	CAB 38/17/7
CAB 38/12/42	CAB 38/12/54	CAB 38/20/15
CAB 38/12/44	CAB 38/13/7	

Papers of the War Council 1914–1916

CAB 37/121/117	CAB 37/139/40	CAB 37/148/15
CAB 37/122	CAB 37/139/56	CAB 37/150/28
CAB 37/123/43	CAB 37/139/63	CAB 37/151/43
CAB 37/123/58	CAB 37/139/69	CAB 37/154/22
CAB 37/124/59	CAB 37/140/30	CAB 37/155/33
CAB 37/126/1	CAB 37/141/35	CAB 37/160/8
CAB 37/127/36	CAB 37/142/5	CAB 37/160/11
CAB 37/133/21	CAB 37/142/6	CAB 37/161/9
CAB 37/138/17	CAB 37/142/10	
CAB 37/139/24	CAB 37/143/39	

Papers of the War Council 1915–1916

CAB 42/1/12	CAB 42/2/13	CAB 42/5/6
CAB 42/2/1	CAB 42/2/14	CAB 42/5/17
CAB 42/2/3	CAB 42/3/12	CAB 42/6/9
CAB 42/2/5	CAB 42/4/2	CAB 42/6/10
CAB 42/2/8	CAB 42/4/3	CAB 42/6/11
CAB 42/2/9	CAB 42/4/13	CAB 42/6/14
CAB 42/2/10	CAB 42/4/14	CAB 42/7/5
CAB 42/2/11	CAB 42/4/15	CAB 42/7/6
CAB 42/2/12	CAB 42/5/3	CAB 42/8/9

CAB 42/11/9   CAB 42/19/2   CAB 42/23/6
CAB 42/15/5   CAB 42/20/8   CAB 42/23/9
CAB 42/16/1   CAB 42/21/1   CAB 42/24/8
CAB 42/16/2   CAB 42/21/13   CAB 42/24/13
CAB 42/16/5   CAB 42/22/4   CAB 42/25/6
CAB 42/17/5   CAB 42/22/14
CAB 42/17/6   CAB 42/22/15

War Cabinet Papers 1917-1918

CAB 4/6/1   CAB 21/96
CAB 16/12   CAB 25/1/27 (Annexe [A])
CAB 21/13   CAB 27/1   CID 220B
CAB 21/15   CAB 27/24
CAB 21/56   CAB 27/36   E.C. 2201
CAB 21/58   CAB 28/2   I.C. (13) (13d) (19)
CAB 21/77

CAB 23/1, (25), (48), (60)   CAB 23/4/282 (4)
CAB 23/1/8 (4)   CAB 23/4/295, App. G.T. 2932
CAB 23/1/48   CAB 23/4/296
CAB 23/1/50 (7)   CAB 23/4/302 (11)
CAB 23/2/109 (3)   CAB 23/4/304 (10)
CAB 23/2/109 (4)   CAB 23/4/306
CAB 23/2/100 (11)   CAB 23/4/308 (8)
CAB 23/2/111 (1)   CAB 23/26/70 (21)
CAB 23/2/116 (13)   CAB 23/13/115 A
CAB 23/2/124 (3)   CAB 23/13/135 A
CAB 23/2/126 (11)   CAB 23/13/191 A
CAB 23/2/134 (6)   CAB 23/13/200 A & B
CAB 23/3/163 (2)   CAB 23/13/201 A
CAB 23/4/227 (1)   CAB 23/12/210 A
CAB 23/4/227 (2)   CAB 23/13/247 A & B
CAB 23/4/245 (18)   CAB 23/13/273 A
CAB 23/4/257 (12)   CAB 23/13/308
CAB 23/4/261 (12)   CAB 23/13/351
CAB 23/4/277 (2)   CAB 23/13/358 A
CAB 23/4/277 (6)   CAB 23/13/360

CAB 24/3 G. 101   CAB 24/4 G. 157
CAB 24/3 G. 102   CAB 24/4 G. 162
CAB 24/3 G. 103   CAB 24/4 G. 164
CAB 24/3 G. 137   CAB 24/4 G. 182
CAB 24/3 G. 150   CAB 24/3 G. 199
CAB 24/4 G. 152

CAB 24/9 G.T. 353
CAB 24/9 G.T. 372
CAB 24/10 G.T. 447
CAB 24/10 G.T. 448
CAB 24/13 G.T. 703
CAB 24/14 G.T. 811
CAB 24/15 G.T. 938
CAB 24/21 G.T. 1531
CAB 24/24 G.T. 1802
CAB 24/24 G.T. 1803
CAB 24/24 G.T. 1868
CAB 24/24 G.T. 2015
CAB 24/26 G.T. 2016
CAB 24/27 G.T. 2158
CAB 24/27 G.T. 2191
CAB 24/28 G.T. 2263
CAB 24/35 G.T. 2977
CAB 24/35 G.T. 2991
CAB 24/36 G.T. 3040
CAB 24/37 G.T. 3112

CAB 24/37 G.T. 3145
CAB 24/37 G.T. 3164
CAB 24/37 G.T. 3167
CAB 24/37 G.T. 3180
CAB 24/37 G.T. 3191
CAB 24/39 G.T. 3359
CAB 24/42 G.T. 3635
CAB 24/42 G.T. 3648
CAB 24/46 G.T. 3031
CAB 24/51 G.T. 4505
CAB 24/51 G.T. 4554
CAB 24/66 G.T. 5955
CAB 24/67 G.T. 6015
CAB 24/68 G.T. 6185
CAB 24/72/1 & 2 G.T. 6506
CAB 24/72 G.T. 6508
CAB 24/72/1 & 2 G.T. 6509
CAB 24/72 G.T. 6514
CAB 24/75 G.T. 6839

Imperial War Cabinet Papers

CAB 23/40   CAB 23/43

War Cabinet Eastern Reports

CAB 24/143   January–July 1917
CAB 24/144   July 1917–March 1918
CAB 24/145   March 1918–September 1919

FOREIGN OFFICE FILES (P.R.O.)

Turkey (War) Political 1914

F.O. 371/2139/2139
F.O. 371/2140/5867
F.O. 371/2147/79829
F.O. 371/2147/80137

F.O. 371/2147/81633
F.O. 371/2147/81635
F.O. 371/2147/680137

Turkey (War) Political 1915

F.O. 371/2475/4800
F.O. 371/2480/1495

F.O. 371/2480/1940
F.O. 371/2480/1941

F.O. 371/2480/1942
F.O. 371/2480/2506
F.O. 371/2480/3055
F.O. 371/2486/34982

F.O. 371/2488/51705
F.O. 371/2490/108253
F.O. 371/2490/128226
F.O. 371/2491/148549

Turkey (War) Political 1916

F.O. 371/2767/938
F.O. 371/2768/938
F.O. 371/2773/42233
F.O. 371/2774/42233
F.O. 371/2775/42233

F.O. 371/2776/42233
F.O. 371/2781/201201
F.O. 371/2783/221220
F.O. 371/2783/254662
F.O. 371/2786/34982

Turkey (War) Political 1917

F.O. 371/3042/4637
F.O. 371/3043/1142
F.O. 371/3044/1142
F.O. 371/3044/1173
F.O. 371/3045/2087
F.O. 371/3045/72449
F.O. 371/3051/66398
F.O. 371/3051/66398
F.O. 371/3052/78324
F.O. 371/3053/84173
F.O. 371/3054/84173
F.O. 371/3054/86526
F.O. 371/3054/87288
F.O. 371/3055/87895
F.O. 371/3055/88107

F.O. 371/3056/93808
F.O. 371/3056/94642
F.O. 371/3057/103481
F.O. 371/3057/104218
F.O. 371/3058/120602
F.O. 371/3058/123458
F.O. 371/3058/139616
F.O. 371/3058/140092
F.O. 371/3059/143893
F.O. 371/3059/149651
F.O. 371/3059/159558
F.O. 371/3059/162432
F.O. 371/3060/175608
F.O. 371/3061/214354
F.O. 371/3062/228671

Turkey (War) Political 1918

F.O. 371/3380/68
F.O. 371/3380/146
F.O. 371/3381/146
F.O. 371/3381/207
F.O. 371/3383/675
F.O. 371/3383/747
F.O. 371/3384/747
F.O. 371/3385/747
F.O. 371/3386/856
F.O. 371/3387/993
F.O. 371/3388/1495
F.O. 371/3388/1396

F.O. 371/3388/2070
F.O. 371/3390/3026
F.O. 371/3391/4019
F.O. 371/3392/6554
F.O. 371/3393/6554
F.O. 371/3393/7659
F.O. 371/3394/11053
F.O. 371/3395/11053
F.O. 371/3396/13513
F.O. 371/3398/27647
F.O. 371/3400/37581
F.O. 371/3403/52131

F.O. 371/3406/61085
F.O. 371/3407/70822
F.O. 371/3409/110098
F.O. 371/3409/114901
F.O. 371/3409/116565

F.O. 371/3409/116970
F.O. 371/3411/154108
F.O. 371/3411/155461
F.O. 371/3414/181911
F.O. 371/3418/194681

Turkey Political 1919–20

F.O. 371/4153/275
F.O. 371/4167/801
F.O. 371/4170/1051
F.O. 371/4171/1051
F.O. 371/4178/2117
F.O. 371/4179/2117
F.O. 371/4180/2117

F.O. 371/4184/2117
F.O. 371/4215/50535
F.O. 371/4216/66287
F.O. 371/4217/66287
F.O. 371/4231/100141
F.O. 371/4239/151671

Arab Bureau Papers 1916–1920

F.O. 882/2
F.O. 882/3
F.O. 882/5
F.O. 882/6
F.O. 882/7
F.O. 882/12

F.O. 882/13
F.O. 882/14
F.O. 882/15
F.O. 882/16
F.O. 882/18
F.O. 882/19

F.O. 882/23
F.O. 882/25 (contains
the issues of the *Arab
Bulletin* and the *Arab
Bulletin Supplement*)

Turkey (War) Prisoners 1915

F.O. 383/91/251

Turkey (War) Prisoners 1916

F.O. 383/222/599

Peace Conference, Paris 1919

F.O. 608/98 files: 375/1/10, 375/2/1, 375/2/2
F.O. 608/99 files: 375/2/5, 375/2/7
F.O. 608/107 file: 384/1/7

Eastern Political, General

F.O. 371/5066 (1920), f. E 14959/9/44
F.O. 371/5067 (1920), f. E 16103/9/44
F.O. 371/6237 (1921), f. E 155/4/91
F.O. 371/6237 (1921), f. E 986/4/91

F.O. 371/6238 (1921), f. E 2133/4/91
F.O. 371/7797 (1922), f. E 2821/2821/65
F.O. 371/14495 (1930), f. E 6491/427/65
F.O. 371/21862 (1938), f. E 559/1/31
F.O. 371/23224 (1939), f. E 136716/31

Egypt (War) Political 1914

F.O. 371/1970/36711

Egypt (War) Political 1916

F.O. 371/2671/35433   F.O. 371/2671/179533

Balkans (War) Political 1915

F.O. 371/2253/18272

Balkans (War) Political 1917

F.O. 371/2884/72706

The War, Political 1917

F.O. 371/3083/143082

Russia (War) Political 1915

F.O. 371/2445/155   F.O. 371/2454/105582
F.O. 371/2446/155   F.O. 371/2455/105582
F.O. 371/2448/6905   F.O. 371/2456/148237
F.O. 371/2448/16905

Russia (War) Political 1916

F.O. 371/2741/3661   F.O. 371/2746/12434
F.O. 371/2744/4039   F.O. 371/2747/37661
F.O. 371/2745/5724

Russia (War) Political 1917

F.O. 371/2996/811   F.O. 371/3012/95062
F.O. 371/3010/74424   F.O. 371/3012/102649
F.O. 371/3010/86523   F.O. 371/3012/103717
F.O. 371/3012/93027   F.O. 371/3013/132296

F.O. 371/3014/146478
F.O. 371/3015/154307
F.O. 371/3015/158842
F.O. 371/3015/165304
F.O. 371/3015/171081
F.O. 371/3016/208373

F.O. 371/3017/216696
F.O. 371/3018/224839
F.O. 371/3019/229217
F.O. 371/3020/241481
F.O. 371/3315/17365

Russia, News, Political 1917

F.O. 395/108/56108
F.O. 395/108/82072

F.O. 395/109/96621

United States (War) News 1916

F.O. 395/6/34597

F.O. 395/7/34597

United States (War) Political 1916

F.O. 371/2793/39522

Miscellaneous, News (General) Political 1915

F.O. 371/2525/18357
F.O. 371/2559/35166
F.O. 371/2579/178994

F.O. 371/2579/187779
F.O. 371/2579/188244

Miscellaneous, News (General) Political 1917

F.O. 395/139/15725
F.O. 395/139/15729

F.O. 395/44/47254
F.O. 395/152/207617

Miscellaneous (War) General, Political 1916

F.O. 371/2816/39700
F.O. 371/2817/426081

F.O. 371/2819/122263
F.O. 371/2835/18095

Miscellaneous (War) General, Political 1917

F.O. 371/3092/4637

F.O. 371/3101/65760

Private Papers of Sir Edward Grey (1916)

F.O. 800/58
F.O. 800/88

F.O. 800/95
F.O. 800/96

F.O. 800/105
F.O. 800/106

Private Papers of Lord Kitchener (1915–16)

P.R.O. 30/57

Private Papers of Sir Francis Bertie (1916)

F.O. 800/176

Private Papers of A. J. Balfour (1917–20)

F.O. 800/204	F.O. 800/208	F.O. 800/210
F.O. 800/205	F.O. 800/209	

Private Papers of Lord Robert Cecil (1917)

F.O. 800/198

War Office Files (P.R.O.) 1906–1914

W.O. 106/41, files C 3(2); C 3(14)
W.O. 106/42, files C 3(13c); C 3/14(b); C 3(26); C 3(35b); C 3(36c)
W.O. 106/43, f. C 3/29

War Office Papers (P.R.O.) 1917–18

W.O. 106/727	W.O. 106/1420	W.O. 158/611
W.O. 106/1417		

Colonial Office Files (P.R.O.)

C.O. 733/35

The British Museum, Dept of MSS

Private Papers of:
A. J. Balfour nos. 41178, 49738
Lord Robert Cecil no. 51093
C. P. Scott, vol. 5093

Beaverbrook Library, London. Private Papers of David Lloyd George

F 3/3/30	F 39/3/30	F 45/2/4
F 14/4/34		

The Sudan Archive, School of Oriental Studies, University of Durham, Durham

Sir Reginald Wingate Papers, 1915–1919, Boxes 135–51
Sir Gilbert Clayton Papers, 1914–1919

St Antony's College, Oxford

The Sledmere Papers, 1914–1919 (in microfilm)
The William Yale Papers 1917–1919 (in microfilm)
The Herbert Samuel Papers 1914–1925 (xeroxed)
The Edmund Allenby Papers 1918 (xeroxed)

The Bodleian Library, MSS Dept, Oxford

The Herbert Asquith Papers, vol. 27 (1915–16)

Auswärtiges Amt Akten, Bonn (microfilm at P.R.O., London)

Der Libanon (Syrien) no. 177, Bd 12
Der Weltkrieg, no. 11G *Bände* 4, 6

The Central Zionist Archives, Jerusalem, Israel

Z 3/62	Z 4/261	Z 4/1933/II
Z 3/400	Z 4/305/I	Z 4/16112
Z 4/117	Z 4/728	L 6/12/X
Z 4/120	Z 4/929	L 6/63
Z 4/170	Z 4/1074	L 6/64/I
Z 4/177/II	Z 4/1586	L 6/88
Z 4/241	Z 4/1591	L 6/90/I
Z 4/242	Z 4/4066	

Herbert Bentwich Papers

A 100/27

Akiva Ettinger Papers

A III/29

Harry Sacher Papers

Z 4/120

Israel Sieff Papers 1917–1919

Z 4/242; Z 4/261

Nahum Sokolow Papers 1915–1918

A 18/41/2/5	A 18/22	A 18/25
A 18/41/2/8	A 18/24	A 18/26

The Weizmann Archives, Rehovoth, Israel

Weizmann Papers January 1917–January 1918 (the files are not numbered)
Harry Sacher Papers June–August 1917

Records of the Conjoint Foreign Committee, Anglo-Jewish Association, London

C.F.C./1915; C.F.C./1916; C.F.C./1917

Archives of the Board of Deputies of British Jews

London, 1916–1918 (the files are not numbered)

Published sources

(a) OFFICIAL PUBLICATIONS AND COLLECTIONS OF OFFICIAL DOCU-
MENTS

British Documents on the Origins of the War, 1898–1914, ed. by G. P. Gooch and
    H. W. V. Temperley, vol. 5, *The Near East* (London, HMSO 1934)
Documents on British Foreign Policy, 1919–1939, ed. E. L. Woodward and R. Butler,
    First Series, vol. 4 (London, HMSO 1952)
Documents on British Foreign Policy, ed. R. Butler and J. P. I. Bury, First Series, vol.
    8, 1920 (London, HMSO 1958)
British Consulate in Jerusalem, 1838–1914, Documents ed. by A. M. Hyamson
    (London Jewish Historical Society 1941), 2 vols
*Convention between Great Britain, Germany, Austria-Hungary, Spain, France, Italy,
    the Netherlands, Russia and Turkey respecting Free Navigation of the Suez Maritime
    Canal, signed at Constantinople, October 29, 1888.* HMSO [Cmd 5623], Commer-
    cial, no. 2 (1889)
Declaration between the United Kingdom and France respecting Egypt and Morocco.
    Signed at London, 8 April 1904. HMSO 1905 [Cmd 2384], Treaty Series, no. 6,
    1905
Great Britain, Foreign Office, *Syria and Palestine*, Peace Handbook, no. 60 (London,
    HMSO 1920)
    —*Zionism*, Peace Handbook, no. 162 (London 1920)

Statement of British Policy in Palestine, 3 June 1922 (Churchill White Paper), Cmd 1700

Palestine Royal Commission Report Cmd 5479 (July 1937), Peel Report (London, HMSO 1937)

Palestine Royal Commission. Minutes of Evidence . . . Colonial, no. 134 (London 1937)

Correspondence between Sir Henry McMahon and the Sherif Hussein of Mecca, July 1915–March 1916, Cmd 5957 (Miscellaneous no. 3), London 1939

Report of a Committee set up to Consider Certain Correspondence between Sir Henry McMahon and the Sherif of Mecca in 1915 and 1916. Cmd 5974 (London 1939)

Palestine Settlement of Policy, Cmd 6019, The White Paper of May 1939 (London 1939)

Great Britain. *Parliamentary Debates, House of Commons*, Fifth Series, vols 138–393

Great Britain. *Parliamentary Debates, House of Lords*, Fifth Series, vols 34–128

Papers relating to the Foreign Relations of the United States, 1917 (1926), Supplement 2, *The World War*, vol. 1 (1932)

—*Paris Peace Conference 1919*, vol. xii

United States, *Congressional Record*, 30 June 1922

Adler, Cyrus and Margalith, Aaron M., *With Firmness in the Right. American Diplomatic Action Affecting Jews, 1840–1945* (New York, The American Jewish Committee 1946)

Adamov, E. A., *Die Europäischen Mächte und die Türkei während des Weltkrieges. Die Aufteilung der Asiatischen Türkei nach den Geheimdokumenten deschen. Ministeriums für Auswärtige Angelegenheiten* (Dresden 1932)

Die grosse Politik der europäischen Kabinette (Berlin 1922–7), Bd 34

League of Nations, *Official Journal*, August 1922, *Minutes of the 19th Session of the Council*

—Permanent Mandates Commission, Minutes of the Seventh Session held at Geneva from October 19th to October 30th 1925. C648 M.237.1925 VI, C.P.M. 328

(b) OFFICIAL ZIONIST PUBLICATIONS AND OF OTHER JEWISH ORGANISATIONS

Zionist Organisation, *Reports of the Executive of the Zionist Organisation to the XIIth Zionist Congress*, Political Report (London 1921)

Jewish Agency for Palestine, *Memorandum submitted to the Palestine Royal Commission* (London, J.A.P. 1936)

—*Documents Relating to the Balfour Declaration and the Palestine Mandate* (London, J.A.P. 1939)

—*Documents Relating to the McMahon Letters* (London, J.A.P. 1939)

—*Documents Relating to the Palestine Problem* (London, J.A.P. 1945)

American Emergency Committee for Zionist Affairs, *The Balfour Declaration and American Interests in Palestine* (New York 1941)

The Zionist Organisation of America, *The American War Congress and Zionism* (New York, Z.O.A. 1919)

Annual Report of the Board of Deputies of British Jews. Foreign Affairs Committee for 1915 (London 1915)

Conjoint Foreign Committee, Annual Report 1916 (London 1916)
—1917 (London 1917)

Joint Foreign Committee, *The Peace Conference, Paris, 1919* (London 1919)

American Jewish Committee, *The Jews in the Eastern War Zone* (New York 1916)

Denkschrift der Poale Zion: Die Juden um Kriege (The Hague 1917)

Die Judenfrage der Gegenwart, Documentensammlung, ed. Leon Chasanowitsch and Leo Motzkin (Stockholm 1919)

(c) LETTERS, DIARIES, MEMOIRS, CONTEMPORARY STATEMENTS, ETC.

AARONSOHN, AARON, *Yoman* [Diary of . . .] *Aaron Aaronsohn, 1916–1919* (Tel-Aviv, Karni 1970)

AARONSOHN, ALEXANDER, *With the Turks in Palestine* (New York, Houghton Mifflin 1916)

AHAD HA'AM, *Nationalism and the Jewish Ethic: Basic Writings of Ahad Ha'am*, ed. Hans Kohn (New York, Schocken Books 1962)

   Ten Essays on Zionism and Judaism, transl. Leon Simon (London, George Routledge & Sons 1922)

   Ig'rot Ahad Ha'am [Letters of Ahad Ha'am] (Tel-Aviv, Beit Ahad Ha'am 1924)

AMERY, LEOPOLD S., *My Political Life* (London, Hutchinson 1953), 3 vols

   Preface to *Chaim Weizmann*, ed. Paul Goodman (London, Gollancz 1945)

ASHBEE, C. R., *A Palestine Notebook, 1918–23* (London, Garden City, N.Y., Doubleday 1923)

ASQUITH, H. H. (Earl of Oxford and Asquith), *Memories and Reflections, 1852–1927* (London, Cassel 1923), 2 vols

   What Britain is Fighting For . . ., off-print published by *Daily Chronicle* (London 1916)

BALFOUR, A. J., *Opinions and Arguments* (London, Hodder & Stoughton 1927)

BENTWICH, NORMAN and HELEN, *Mandate Memories: 1918–1948* (London, Hogarth Press, New York, Schocken Books 1965)

BERTIE, FRANCIS, *The Diary of Lord Bertie of Thame* (London, Hodder & Stoughton 1924), 2 vols

BRANDEIS, LOUIS D., *The Jewish Problem: How to Solve It* (Cleveland, Ohio, J. Saslaw 1934)

   Brandeis on Zionism. A Collection of Addresses and Statements (Washington, Z.O.A. 1942)

CECIL, ROBERT, 'Foreword' to J. de V. Loder, *The Truth about Mesopotamia, Palestine and Syria* (London, Allen & Unwin 1923)

CHURCHILL, COL. CHARLES, *Mount Lebanon . . .* (London, Saunders & Otley 1853), vol. I

CHURCHILL, WINSTON S., *The World Crisis 1915* (London, Thornton Butterworth 1923)

CROMER, EVELYN, LORD, *Modern Egypt* (London, McMillan 1908), 2 vols

DJEMAL, AHMED PASHA, *Memories of a Turkish Statesman, 1915–1919* (London, Hutchinson 1922)

FRANKFURTER, FELIX, *Reminiscences* (London, Secker & Warburg 1960)

GARNETT, DAVID, *The Letters of T. E. Lawrence* (London, Doubleday Doran 1938)

GRAVES, PHILIP, *Palestine, the Land of Three Faiths* (London, Jonathan Cape 1923)

GREY, VISCOUNT, *Twenty-Five Years* (London, Hodder & Stoughton 1925)

HELLER, ABRAHAM, *Die Lage der Juden in Russland von der Märzrevolution 1917 bis zur Gegenwart* (Breslau, M. H. Marcus 1935)

HERTZBERG, ARTHUR, *The Zionist Idea. A Historical Analysis and Reader* (New York, Doubleday and Herzl Press 1959)

HERZL, THEODOR, *The Jewish State* (New York, American Zionist Emergency Council 1946)
    The Complete Diaries of Theodor Herzl, ed. Raphael Patai (New York, London, Herzl Press, Thomas Yoseloff 1960), 5 vols

HOUSE, EDWARD M., *The Intimate Papers of Colonel House*, ed. Charles Seymour (London, Ernest Benn 1928), 3 vols

JABOTINSKY, VLADIMIR, *Turkey and the War* (London, Fischer Unwin 1917)
    The Story of the Jewish Legion (New York, Bernard Ackerman 1945)
    Evidence submitted to the Palestine Royal Commission (London, New Zionist Publications no. 3, 1937)

JARVIS, C. S., *Three Deserts* (London, John Murray 1936)

KALISCHER, ZVI HIRSCH and ALKALAI, YEHUDA, *Mivhar Kitveihem* [selected writings] (Tel-Aviv, Mitzpe 1943)

KALLEN, HORACE, *Zionism and World Politics* (London, Heinemann 1921)

LAWRENCE, T. E., *Seven Pillars of Wisdom* (London, Jonathan Cape 1935)

LICHNOWSKY, KARL, PRINCE, *Heading for the Abyss. Reminiscences* (London, Constable 1928)

LEVENBERG, S. and PEDRO, J., *British Labour Policy on Palestine, A collection of documents, speeches and articles, 1917–1938* (London, Palestine Labour Studies Group, no. 12, 1938)

LLOYD GEORGE, D., *The War Memoirs* (London, Odhams Press 1936), 2 vols
    The Truth about the Peace Treaties (London, Gollancz 1938), 2 vols

LUNCZ, ABRAHAM MOSES, *Luah Eretz-Israel, 5673–4* [*Calendar of Palestine for the Years 5673–4 (1912, 1913–14)*] (Jerusalem, Author's Publishing House 1914)

MEINERTZHAGEN, COL RICHARD, *Middle East Diary, 1917–1956* (London, Cresset Press 1959)

MILLER, DAVID HUNTER, *My Diary at the Conference of Paris* (New York, Appeal Printing Co. 1924), vol. 4

MORGENTHAU, HENRY, *All in a Life-Time* (London, Heinemann 1923)

NICOLSON, HAROLD, *Diaries and Letters, 1945–1962*, ed. Nigel Nicolson (London, Collins 1968)

ORMSBY-GORE, WILLIAM, 'Great Britain, Palestine and the Jews', *The Nineteenth Century and After* (October 1920)

PATTERSON, LT-COL. HENRY J., *With the Judeans in the Palestine Campaign* (London, Hutchinson 1922)

PATTERSON, LT–COL. HENRY J., *cont.*
   With the Zionists in Gallipoli (London, Hutchinson 1916)
POINCARÉ, RAYMOND, *Au Service de la France* (Paris, Plon 1926). Also in English
   translation, *The Memoirs of Raymond Poincaré* (London 1926)
SACHER, HARRY, *Zionism and the State*. Zionist Pamphlets, no. 5 (London 1915)
   ed., *Zionism and the Jewish Future* (London, John Murray 1916)
SAMUEL, HERBERT, VISCOUNT, *Memoirs* (London, Cresset Press 1945)
SCOTT, C. P., *The Political Diaries of C. P. Scott, 1911–1928*, ed. Trevor Wilson
   (London, Collins 1970)
SIDEBOTHAM, HERBERT, *Great Britain and Palestine* (London, Macmillan 1937)
SIEFF, ISRAEL, *Memoirs* (London, Weidenfeld & Nicolson 1971)
SIMON, LEON, *The Case of the Anti-Zionists. A Reply* (London 1917)
SPRING-RICE, SIR CECIL, *The Letters and Friendships of . . .*, ed. Stephen Gwynn
   (London, Constable 1930), 2 vols
STIRLING, LT-COL. W. F., *Safety Last* (London, Hollis & Carter 1953)
STORRS, RONALD, *Orientations* (London, Readers' Union 1939)
TAMA, DIOGENÉ, *Collection des Actes du Grand Sanhédrin* (Paris 1807)
   Collection des procès-verbaux et décisions du Grand Sanhédrin (Paris 1807)
TOLKOWSKY, S., 'Zionism as a Practical Object', *Zionism*, ed. P. Goodman and
   F. Lewis (London, Fisher Unwin 1916)
TOYNBEE, ARNOLD J., *Turkey: A Past and a Future* (New York, G. H. Doran
   1917)
   Acquaintances (Oxford University Press 1967)
TSCHLENOW, YECHIEL, *Pirkey Hayav U'Peulato, Zichronot, Ketavim, Neumim,
   V'Michtavim* [His Life, Activities, Memoirs, Letters and Speeches] ed. S. Eisen-
   stadt (Tel-Aviv, Eretz-Israel Press 1937)
WEIZMANN, CHAIM, *Trial and Error* (London, Hamish Hamilton 1949; New
   York, Schocken Books 1966)
   'Zionism and the Jewish Problem', *Zionism and the Jewish Future*, ed. Harry
   Sacher (London 1916)
   The Letters and Papers of Chaim Weizmann, ed. Leonard Stein (Oxford Uni-
   versity Press 1968). Series A, vol. I
WEIZMANN, VERA, *The Impossible Takes Longer* (New York, Harper 1967)
WILSON, WOODROW, *The Public Papers of Woodrow Wilson*, ed. Ray Stannard
   Baker and William E. Dodd (New York, Harper & Brothers 1925–7)
   The Messages and Papers of Woodrow Wilson, ed. Albert Shaw (New York,
   G. H. Doran 1924), I
WISE, STEPHEN, *Challenging Years* (London, East and West Library 1961)
WISE, STEPHEN and DE HAAS, JACOB, *The Great Betrayal* (New York, Bren-
   tano's 1930)
WOLF, LUCIEN, *Notes on the Diplomatic History of the Jewish Question* (London,
   Spottiswoode, Ballantyne 1919)
YOUNG, HUBERT, *The Independent Arab* (London, John Murray 1933)
ZEN ZIPER, ARIE, *Esser Shnot Redifot Haziyonim B'Russia ha Sovietit* [Ten Years of
   Zionist Persecution in Soviet Russia] (Tel-Aviv, Achdut Press 1930)

(d) STUDIES

ADLER, CYRUS, *Jacob Schiff, His Life and Letters*, 2 vols (London, Heinemann 1929)

ALLEN, W. E. D., *The Ukraine* (Cambridge University Press 1940)

ANCHEL, ROBERT, *Napoléon et les Juifs* (Paris, Les Presses Universitaires de France 1928)

ANTONIUS, GEORGE, *The Arab Awakening* (London, Hamish Hamilton 1938)

ASQUITH, SPENDER J. A. and CECIL, *Life of Herbert Henry Asquith, Lord Oxford and Asquith* (London, Hutchinson 1932)

BARKER, ERNEST, *The Character of England* (Oxford University Press 1947)

BARON, SALO W., *A Social and Religious History of the Jews* (Columbia University Press 1952)

The Russian Jew under Tsars and Soviets (London, New York, Macmillan 1964)

BERLIN, ISAIAH, *The Life and Opinions of Moses Hess* (Cambridge University Press 1959)

BOWLE, JOHN, *Viscount Samuel. A Biography* (London, Victor Gollancz 1957)

CATTAN, HENRY, *Palestine: The Arabs and Israel* (London, Longmans, Green 1969)

CROSSMAN, RICHARD, *A Nation Reborn* (London, Hamish Hamilton 1960)

DE HAAS, JACOB, *Louis D. Brandeis* (New York, Bloch Publishing Co. 1929)

DUBNOW, SIMON, *Die neuste Geschichte des jüdischen Volkes*, 1789–1914 (Berlin, Alexander Eliasberg 1920), 3 vols

DUGDALE, BLANCHE, *Arthur James Balfour* (London, Hutchinson 1936), 2 vols

EGAN, CHARLES, *The Status of Jews in England* (London, R. Hastings 1848).

ESCO FOUNDATION, *Palestine. A Study of Jewish, Arab, and British Policies* (Yale University Press 1947), 2 vols

FISCHER, FRITZ, *Griff nach der Weltmacht* (Düsseldorf, Droste 1961)

FRANKENSTEIN, ERNST, *Palestine in the Light of International Law* (London, Narod Press 1946)

FREUNDLICH, CHARLES, *Peretz Smolenskin: His Life and Thought* (New York, Bloch Publishing Co. 1966)

GELBER, N. M., *Hazharat Balfour V'Toldotea* [History of the Balfour Declaration] (Jerusalem, Z.O. 1939)

GEORGE, LLOYD RICHARD, *Lloyd George* (London, Muller 1960)

GONTAUNT-BIRON, R. DE, *Comment la France s'est installée en Syrie* (Paris, Plon 1923)

GOTTLIEB, W. W., *Studies in Secret Diplomacy during the First World War* (London, Allen & Unwin 1957)

GUNTER, PLANT W., *The Rise of Reform Judaism* (New York, World Union of Progressive Judaism 1963)

HALPERN, BEN, *The Idea of the Jewish State* (Harvard University Press 1961)

HANCOCK, SIR WILLIAM K., *Smuts. The Sanguine Years*, 1870–1919 (Cambridge University Press 1962), 2 vols

HANNA, PAUL L., *British Policy in Palestine* (Washington, D.C., American Council on Public Affairs 1942)

HERTZ, FREDERICK, *Nationality in History and Politics* (London, Routledge & Kegan Paul 1957)

HOURANI, ALBERT, *Arabic Thought in the Liberal Age 1798–1939* (Oxford University Press 1967)

HYAMSON, ALBERT M., *A History of the Jews in England* (London, Methuen 1928)

INSTITUTE OF PALESTINE STUDIES, *The Palestine Question. Seminar of Arab Jurists* (Beirut, I.P.S. 1968)

JAMES, MERVYN J., *British Nationality Law* (Oxford University Press 1956)

JAMES, R. RHODES, *Gallipoli* (London, Macmillan 1965)

JOHNPOLL, BERNARD J., *The Politics of Futility: The General Jewish Workers' Bund of Poland, 1917–43* (Oxford University Press 1968)

JONES, TOM, *Lloyd George* (Oxford University Press 1951)

KATKOV, GEORGE, *Russia 1917. The February Revolution* (London, Longmans 1967)

KATZ, JACOB, *Exclusiveness and Tolerance, Studies in Jewish-Gentile Relations* (Oxford University Press 1961)

KAUFMAN, EDY, 'La France et la Palestine, 1908–1918' (doctoral dissertation, Sorbonne 1970)

KAUFMAN, YEHEZKEL, *Gola V'Nehar* [Diaspora and an Alien Land] (Tel-Aviv 1929)

KEDOURIE, ELIE, *England and the Middle East* (London, Bowes & Bowes 1956)

KENNAN, GEORGE F., *Soviet-American Relations, 1917–20* (London, Faber & Faber 1956)

KOHN, HANS, *The Idea of Nationalism* (New York, Macmillan 1946)

KREPPEL, JONAS, *Juden und Judentum von Heute* (Zürich, Amalthea Verlag 1925)

LAPID, PINCHAS E., *The Last Three Popes and the Jews* (London, Souvenir Press 1967)

LESLIE, SHANE, *Mark Sykes. His Life and Letters* (London, Cassel 1923)

LEWIS, BERNARD, *The Middle East and the West* (London, Weidenfeld & Nicolson 1963)

MACMUNN, GEORGE and FALLS, CYRIL, *Military Operations in Egypt and Palestine* (London, HMSO 1928–30)

MAMATEY, VICTOR S., *The United States and East Central Europe, 1914–1918* (Princeton University Press 1957)

MANUEL, FRANK E., *The Realities of American-Palestine Relations* (Washington, Public Affairs Press 1949)

MARGOLIUTH, MOSES, *The History of the Jews in Great Britain* (London, R. Bentley 1851)

MEYER, HENRY C., *Mitteleuropa in German Thought and Action 1815–1945* (The Hague, Martinus Nijhoff 1955)

NEVAKIVI, JUKKA, *Britain, France and the Arab Middle East, 1914–1920* (London, Athlone Press 1969)

NICOLSON, HAROLD, *Sir Arthur Nicolson. First Lord Carnock* (London, Constable 1930)

PHILIPSON, DAVID, *The Reform Movement in Judaism* (London, Macmillan 1931)

PICCIOTTO, JAMES, *Sketches of Anglo-Jewish History* (London, Trübner 1875)

POPE-HENNESSY, JAMES, *Lord Crewe, 1858–1945* (London, Constable 1955)

ROTH, CECIL, *A History of the Jews in England* (O.U.P. 1964)

SCHECHTMAN, JOSEPH B., *Rebel and Statesman* (New York, Thomas Yoseloff 1956), 2 vols

SCHWARZ, SOLOMON, *The Jews in the Soviet Union* (Syracuse University Press 1951)

SELIGMANN, CAESAR, *Geschichte der jüdischen Reformbewegung* (Frankfurt, Kaufmann Verlag 1922)

SILBERNER, EDMUND, *Moses Hess* (Leiden, E. J. Brill 1966)

SIMON, LEON, *Ahad Ha'am. A Biography* (London, East and West Library 1960)

SOKOLOW, NAHUM, *A History of Zionism* (London, Longmans 1919), 2 vols

STEIN, LEONARD, *The Balfour Declaration* (London, Vallentine, Mitchell 1961)

SYKES, CHRISTOPHER, *Two Studies in Virtue* (London, Collins 1953)

TEMPERLEY, H. W. V., *The History of the Peace Conference* (London, Hodder & Stoughton 1920–24), 6 vols

TOSCANO, MARIO, *Gli Accordi di San Giovanni di Moriana* (Milan 1936)

WALEY, S. D., *Edwin Montague* (London, Asia Publishing House 1964)

WAVELL, ARCHIBALD P., *The Palestine Campaign* (London, Constable 1928)

ZEINE, Z. N., *Arab-Turkish Relations and the Emergence of Arab Nationalism* (Beirut, Khayat's 1958)

(e) ARTICLES AND PAMPHLETS

ADLER, SELIG, 'The Palestine Question in the Wilson Era', *Jewish Social Studies* (October 1948)

BERLIN, ISAIAH, 'The Origins of Israel', *The Middle East in Transition*, ed. Walter Laqueur (London, Routledge & Kegan Paul 1958)

'The Biographical Facts', *Chaim Weizmann. A Biography by Several Hands*, ed. M. W. Weisgal and J. Carmichael (London, Weidenfeld & Nicolson 1962)

CECIL, ROBERT, 'Foreword' to *The Jewish National Home*, ed. Paul Goodman (London, J. Dent 1943)

DEEDES, WYNDHAM, *Palestine—A National Home for the Jews* (London 1936)

DUGDALE, BLANCHE, 'The Balfour Declaration', *The Jewish National Home*, ed. Goodman, *op. cit.*

DUGDALE, EDGAR, *The Balfour Declaration* (London, J.A.P. 1940)

'Man and Statesman', *Chaim Weizmann*, ed. Paul Goodman (London, Gollancz 1945)

FRAENKEL, JOSEF, *Lucien Wolf and Theodor Herzl* (London, Jewish Historical Society of England 1960)

FRIEDMAN, ISAIAH, 'The Declaration—Myths and Motives', *Jewish Chronicle*, Balfour Declaration Supplement, 3 November 1967

'Lord Palmerston and the Protection of Jews in Palestine, 1839–1851', *Jewish Social Studies* (January 1968)

'The McMahon Correspondence and the Question of Palestine', *Journal of Contemporary History* (April 1970)

'The McMahon-Hussein Correspondence, Reply to Arnold Toynbee', *Journal of Contemporary History* (October 1970)

'German Intervention on behalf of the Yishuv, 1917', *Jewish Social Studies* (January 1971)

GEORGE, D. LLOYD, Foreword to *Chaim Weizmann*, ed. Paul Goodman, *op. cit.*

GILLON, D. Z., 'The Antecedents of the Balfour Declaration', *Middle Eastern Studies* (May 1969)

HAIM, SYLVIA, 'Islam and the Theory of Arab Nationalism', *Welt des Islams*, 4 (1955)

HOGARTH, DAVID G., 'Wahabism and British Interests', *Journal of the British Institute of International Affairs*, 4 (1925)

KEDOURIE, ELIE, 'Cairo and Khartoum on the Arab Question 1915–18', *The Historical Journal*, vii, 2 (1964)

'The Capture of Damascus, October 1918', *Middle Eastern Studies* (October 1964)

'Sir Mark Sykes and Palestine, 1915–1916', *Middle Eastern Studies* (October 1970)

KIMCHE, JON, *The Unromantics* (London, Weidenfeld & Nicolson 1968)

KOBLER, F., 'Napoleon and the Restoration of the Jews to Palestine: Discovery of an Historic Document', *New Judea*, vol. xvi, no. 12, vol. xvii, nos 1–2, 3, 5

KOHN, HANS, 'The Genesis and Character of English Nationalism', *Journal of the History of Ideas*, 1 (1940)

LANDMAN, SAMUEL, 'Balfour Declaration—Secret Facts Revealed', *World Jewry*, ii, nos 42–3 (11 February, 1 March 1935)

MANUEL, FRANK E., 'The Palestine Question in Italian Diplomacy, 1917–20', *Journal of Modern History* (Chicago 1955)

MARMOR, D. I., 'The Diplomatic Negotiations of the Jewish Territorial Associations and the Reasons for their Failure' (Hebrew), *Zion* (Jerusalem, September 1945–April 1946, and July 1946)

MORGAN, KENNETH O., 'Lloyd George's Premiership: A Study in "Prime Ministerial Government" ', *The Historical Journal*, xii, 1, 1970

NAHUM, HAIM, 'Jews', *Modern Turkey*, ed Mears, E. G. (New York, Macmillan 1924)

PINGAUD, A., 'Partage de l'Asia Mineure pendant la Grande Guerre (1914–1917); Étude de diplomatie secrète', *Revue d'Histoire de la Guerre Mondiale* (April 1939)

SACHER, HARRY, 'Dr. Weizmann—the Manchester Period', *Chaim Weizmann*, ed. Meyer Weisgal (New York, Dial Press 1944)

'Dr. Weizmann the Statesman', *Chaim Weizmann*, ed. Paul Goodman, *op. cit.*

SCHAPIRO, LEONARD C., 'The Role of the Jews in the Russian Revolutionary Movement', *Slavonic and East European Review* (December 1961)

SHORROCK, WILLIAM I., 'The Origin of the French Mandate in Syria and Lebanon . . . 1901–1914', *International Journal of Middle East Studies* (July 1970)

SIEFF, ISRAEL M., 'The Manchester Period', *Chaim Weizmann: A Biography by Several Hands*, ed. M. W. Weisgal and J. Carmichael (London, Weidenfeld & Nicolson 1962)

SOKOLOW, NAHUM, 'How the Basle Programme was made', *The Zionist Review*, 1, no. 6 (October 1917)

SYKES, CHRISTOPHER, 'Memories of my father . . .', *Explorations*, ed. M. Mindlin and Ch. Bermant (London, Barrie & Rockliff 1967)

THOMPSON, DOROTHY, 'The Mark of the Chosen', *Chaim Weizmann*, ed. Meyer Weisgal, *op. cit.*

VERETÉ, MAYIR, 'The Balfour Declaration and Its Makers', *Middle Eastern Studies* (January 1970)

WEBSTER, CHARLES K., 'British Policy in the Near East', *The Near East*, ed. Ireland, P. W. (Chicago University Press 1942)
'The Founder of the Jewish National Home', *The Art and Practice of Diplomacy* (London, Chatto & Windus 1961)

WEISBORD, ROBERT G., 'Israel Zangwill's Jewish Territorial Organisation and the East African Zion', *Jewish Social Studies* (April 1968)

YALE, WILLIAM A., 'Ambassador Henry Morgenthau's Special Mission of 1917', *World Politics* (April 1949)

ZECHLIN, EGMONT, 'Friedensbestrebungen und Revolutionierungsversiche', *Aus Politik und Zeitgeschichte*, Beilage zur Wochenzeitung *Das Parlament*, 21 June 1961

(f) NEWSPAPERS AND PERIODICALS

Das Parlament, 21 June 1961 (weekly)
Jewish Chronicle, 1917–20 (weekly)
La Civilta Cattolica (Rome), X, 1897, III, 1922 (quarterly)
Liverpool Post, 1917–1919 (daily)
Manchester Guardian, 1916–19 (daily)
Palestine, 1917–20 (monthly)
Preussische Jahrbücher, May 1916 (quarterly)
Quarterly Review, October 1916
Round Table, 1917–18 (quarterly)
Sociological Review, January 1912 (quarterly)
Spectator, 3 January 1947 (weekly)
The Times, 1916–1919 (daily)
Zionist Bulletin, 1917–19 (weekly)
Zionist Review, 1917–19 (weekly)

Index